The Conduct of Hostilities in Internationa
Law, Volume II

First published 2012 by Ashgate Publishing

2 Park Square, Milton Park, Abingdon, Oxfordshire OX14 4RN
711 Third Avenue, New York, NY 10017

Routledge is an imprint of the Taylor & Francis Group, an informa business

First issued in paperback 2018

British Library Cataloguing in Publication Data
The conduct of hostilities in international humanitarian
  law.
  Volume II. – (The library of essays in international
  humanitarian law ; v. 2)
  1. Humanitarian law. 2. War (International law)
  3. Combatants and noncombatants (International law)
  4. War–Protection of civilians.
  I. Series II. Schmitt, Michael N. III. Heintschel von
  Heinegg, Wolff.
  341.6'7–dc23

Library of Congress Control Number: 2011946160

ISBN 978-0-7546-2936-8 (hbk)
ISBN 978-1-138-37863-6 (pbk)

Contents

PART III OBJECTS

PART IV TACTICS

Acknowledgements

The editors and publishers wish to thank the following for permission to use copyright material.

Cambridge University Press for the essays: Ian Brownlie (1965), 'Some Legal Aspects of the Use of Nuclear Weapons', *International and Comparative Law Quarterly*, **14**, pp. 437–51. Copyright © 1965 British Institute of International and Comparative Law; Knut Dörmann (2003), 'The Legal Situation of "Unlawful/Unprivileged Combatants"', *International Review of the Red Cross*, **85**, pp. 45–73. Copyright © 2003 International Committee of the Red Cross; Geraldine Van Bueren (1994), 'The International Legal Protection of Children in Armed Conflicts', *International and Comparative Law Quarterly*, **43**, pp. 809–26. Copyright © 1994 British Institute of International and Comparative Law.

Chatham House, Royal Institute of International Affairs for the essays: Richard R. Baxter (1951), 'So-Called "Unprivileged Belligerency": Spies, Guerrillas, and Saboteurs', *British Year Book of International Law*, **28**, pp. 323–45; G.I.A.D. Draper (1971), 'The Status of Combatants and the Question of Guerilla Warfare', *British Year Book of International Law*, **45**, pp. 173–218. Copyright © 1971 G.I.A.D. Draper.

Copyright Clearance Center for the essays: Yoram Dinstein (2002), 'Unlawful Combatancy', *Israel Yearbook on Human Rights*, **32**, pp. 247–70. Copyright © 2002 Israel Yearbook on Human Rights; Michael N. Schmitt (2004–05), 'Humanitarian Law and Direct Participation in Hostilities by Private Contractors or Civilian Employees', *Chicago Journal of International Law*, **5**, pp. 511–46. Copyright © 2005 Chicago Journal of International Law; Judith Gardam and Hilary Charlesworth (2000), 'Protection of Women in Armed Conflict', *Human Rights Quarterly*, **22**, pp. 148–66. Copyright © 2000 Johns Hopkins University Press; William Gerald Downey, Jr (1950), 'Captured Enemy Property: Booty of War and Seized Enemy Property', *American Journal of International Law*, **44**, pp. 488–504. Copyright ©

International Society for Military Law and the Law of War for the essay: Dieter Fleck (1974), 'Ruses of War and Prohibition of Perfidy', *Military Law and the Law of War Review*, **13**, pp. 269–304.

Manitoba Law Journal for the essay: L.C. Green (1978–79), 'The Status of Mercenaries in International Law', *Manitoba Law Journal*, **9**, pp. 201–46.

MIT Press Journals for the essay: R.R. Baxter (1977), 'Conventional Weapons Under Legal Prohibition', *International Security*, **1**, pp. 42–61.

Naval War College for the essay: Christopher Greenwood (1998), 'The Law of Weaponry at the Start of the New Millennium', *International Law Studies*, **71**, pp. 185–231.

Series Preface

Over half a century ago, Sir Hersch Lauterpacht, then Whewell Professor of International Law at the University of Cambridge, observed that 'if international law is the vanishing point of law, the law of war is at the vanishing point of international law'. He was wrong. While it is true that the law of war, or international humanitarian law as it has become known, is particularly vulnerable to the vagaries of political, social and economic influences, it has nevertheless proven itself a robust normative regime that positively shapes man's most destructive undertaking – warfare. No other body of law can be credited with saving more lives or alleviating as much suffering.

These six volumes comprise a collection of particularly significant works on humanitarian law. They are intended for use by scholars, practitioners and students who seek to better understand the topics addressed herein, together with their lineage. Just as importantly, they allow users to begin to separate the wheat from the chaff. The proliferation of publications in the field, in part a sad reflection of the fact that armed conflict remains so horribly pervasive, as well as the digitization that facilitates access to journals that would not otherwise be readily available, often results in information overload. A Ministry of Defence legal adviser looking for background material to address a situation involving belligerent occupation will, for instance, uncover scores of articles. The student writing a dissertation on the law of targeting or a scholar penning an article on detention will find him- or herself buried in material. Unfortunately, some of what they unearth will prove misguided, out of context or simply wrong. This collection will not break down these obstacles in their entirety. But it does afford a useful starting-point by offering topically arranged humanitarian law journal essays that have been thoroughly vetted by many of the top experts in the field.

In this regard, a few words on the process used to choose the essays are helpful. It began with the selection of those subjects that we believed comprised the *sine qua non* of international humanitarian law – development, principles, scope, application, conduct of hostilities, detention, occupation, and implementation and enforcement. We then contacted over 60 recognized humanitarian law experts, both academics and seasoned legal advisers. They were provided the topics and asked in a very open-ended fashion to identify pieces they considered 'classics', believed to be 'essential' in a compilation of this nature, have found to be especially influential, used regularly in their work or deserved greater attention on the basis of their quality and insights. The experts were asked to pay particular attention to those essays that may have been 'forgotten' over time, but merited 'rediscovery'. Many of them responded in depth. We also benefited from the work of a five-member team from Emory Law School's International Humanitarian Law Clinic which conducted an exhaustive literature review to locate essays relied on regularly by writers – the 'usual suspects', if you will. Finally, as editors we took the liberty of adding a few pieces to the pool *sua sponte*.

Armed with a daunting inventory of candidates for inclusion, we began the difficult task of whittling it down. Many essays proved to be consensus choices among the experts; often the Emory team had also identified them. These provided the skeleton for the project. We then fleshed out the collection based on two key factors: quality assessments by the experts and topic coverage. The latter criterion proved particularly central to the process, for our objective was to produce a collection that not only contained thoughtful and influential works, but also addressed most key humanitarian law topics.

Beyond esteem factors and topical relevance, some essays were selected on account of their temporal significance, that is, having been written at key junctures in the development of international humanitarian law. As an example, the collection includes pieces written in the immediate aftermath of the First and Second World Wars and the attacks of 11 September 2001. Others were published soon after adoption of the 1949 Geneva Conventions or the 1977 Additional Protocols. We hope they both afford insight into the perspectives at play as humanitarian law was evolving and provide a context for understanding the genesis of contemporary norms.

In the end, we were unable to include many insightful and influential works. Exclusion was frequently a mere matter of being cursed with too many good choices on a particular topic. Although no reader is likely to be entirely satisfied with the essays included, or comfortable with the omission of others, we hope the rigorous selection process has resulted in a collection that is both useful and enlightening.

This project would not have been possible without the help of many supporters. We are, of course, deeply indebted to the many international experts who took time from their busy schedules to offer recommendations and comments over the course of the three-year effort. Although we cannot possibly name them all, particular appreciation is due to Ken Anderson, Yutaka Arai, Louise Arimatsu, Laurie Blank, Gabriella Blum, Bill Boothby, Ove Bring, Claude Bruderlein, Knut Dörmann, Alison Duxbury, William Fenrick, Dieter Fleck, Steven Haines, Agnieszka Jachec-Neale, Dick Jackson, Marie Jacobsson, Claus Kress, William Lietzau, Noam Lubell, Lindsay Moir, John Murphy, Sean Murphy, Mary Ellen O'Connell, Bruce Oswald, Hays Parks, Stephen Pomper, Jean-Francois Queguiner, Noelle Quenivet, Adam Roberts, A.P.V. Rogers, Peter Rowe, Joseph Rutigliano, Robert Sloane, Dale Stephens, Ken Watkin and Sean Watts.

We are equally indebted to the brilliant group of young scholars at Emory Law School, whom we dubbed our 'IHL Detectives' – Flora Manship, Carmel Mushin, Jeannine Privat, Nandini Rao and, in particular, Benjamin Farley. Their ability to identify and locate 'lost treasures' of humanitarian law was awe-inspiring. All have since graduated, and we wish them the very best in their professional careers.

Three people deserve special mention and gratitude. Laurie Blank, Director of the Emory's International Humanitarian Law Clinic, ably and tirelessly supervised her team. Beyond supervision, she also devoted an enormous amount of her own time to the substance and administration of the project. At European University Viadrina, Kaya Kowalski took on the task of collating materials and later working with us as we made the final selections for the collection. She was unflappable in the face of our long and sometimes contentious deliberations and always exceptionally good-natured and professional. Finally, we thank our editor at Ashgate, Valerie Saunders, who showed the patience of Job throughout.

We hope this collection proves valuable in the years to come. For our part, it was a fascinating endeavour.

MICHAEL N. SCHMITT
Newport, Rhode Island, USA

and

WOLFF HEINTSCHEL VON HEINEGG
Frankfurt (Oder), Germany

Introduction

Weapons

Part I of this volume deals with the subject of weaponry, a topic which straddles international humanitarian law and arms control. The lineage of attempts to limit weaponry is long. Even before the era of modern codification, international law prohibited or restricted such weapons as poison, pikes and crossbows. But the nineteenth century marked the birth of an era of continuous codification of weapons norms. For instance, the 1868 St Petersburg Declaration renounced the use of certain explosive projectiles, while the Hague Conventions and Declarations of 1899 addressed various 'means of warfare', including weapons launched from balloons, asphyxiating gas, expanding bullets and those of a nature to cause superfluous injuries. As noted in Volume I, the 1907 Hague Peace Conference limited the use, *inter alia*, of automatic submarine contact mines. Later treaties, or attempts to craft them, dealt with such issues as submarines, gas, bacteriological toxins, weapons with non-detectable fragments, incendiaries, anti-personnel mines, blinding lasers and environmental modification.

Efforts to limit or prohibit the use of weapons have not been without controversy. For instance, the United States did not become party to the 1925 Gas Protocol until 1975, and then only with a reservation as to reprisal. And it took 19 years for the United States to become party to the Incendiary Weapons Protocol, with both a reservation and understanding. More recently, certain key states have declined to become party to the 1997 Ottawa Anti-Personnel Mines Convention and the 2008 Convention on Cluster Munitions. Perhaps the defining instance of contentiousness over weaponry was the International Court of Justice's decision to issue an advisory opinion regarding the legality of nuclear weapons in 1996. Many states, including all nuclear powers (which embraces all permanent members of the Security Council), vehemently opposed the proceedings and the Court's findings.

Much of the disagreement results from an inherent tension between those who believe that weapons are adequately dealt with by general international humanitarian law principles and rules and others who advocate specific weapons regimes. The former point to the principle of distinction and its prohibition on indiscriminate use, including use which violates the rule of proportionality, as well as the requirement to take precautions in attack by using a feasible means or method of warfare likely to minimize civilian harm without forfeiting military advantage. By these norms, it is unlawful to use a weapon if another weapon would suffice but cause less collateral damage, or when the expected harm to civilians is excessive relative to the anticipated military advantage to be achieved through its use. This faction points out that prohibitions or restrictions on specific weapons deprive commanders of options that, in certain circumstances, might reduce civilian harm.

Those taking the opposite position suggest that the general norms are too vague and malleable to effectively preclude the use of weapons that pose particular risks to civilians or civilian property. For instance, it is often difficult to determine with certainty whether this or that weapon is better placed to limit collateral damage; such inquiries are always contextual. Directly prohibiting or restricting the use of a weapon deprives states and their military forces of any opportunity to creatively justify the use of the weapons in question.

At their core, weapons debates reflect the tension between military necessity and humanitarian considerations that undergirds all international humanitarian law. On the one hand, weapons make possible the achievement of military aims. On the other, they cause collateral damage. It is unsurprising, therefore, that attempts to prohibit or restrict particular weapons are often met with disfavour on the part of militaries and states likely to go to war, but with support from groups dedicated to humanitarian purposes and states unlikely to engage in armed conflict. Ultimately, though, the shared goal must be to achieve the right balance between the military and humanitarian imperatives. The first three essays in Volume II exemplify this tension.

In 'The Law of Weaponry' (Chapter 1), Christopher Greenwood, presently a judge on the International Court of Justice, characterizes the law of weaponry as 'one of the oldest and best established areas of the law of war' but one that is 'also widely regarded as one of the least effective' (p. 3). Greenwood asserts that because the law of weaponry has not kept pace with the development of means and methods of warfare, 'much of the law and the legal literature in this field has a distinctly anachronistic feel' (ibid.), amusingly citing a leading textbook that points out that 'cannons must not be loaded with chain shot, crossbar shot, red-hot balls, and the like' (pp. 3–4). That said, he acknowledges some success, such as the bans on use of chemical or biological weapons.

As Greenwood notes, 'the law of armed conflict is ... based upon the assumption that States engaged in an armed conflict will necessarily inflict death and injury upon persons and damage to property, and seeks to limit these effects by preventing the infliction of suffering and damage which is unnecessary because it serves no useful military purpose' (p. 7). Accordingly, '[t]he principal objective of the law of weaponry is the protection of these values' (ibid.). Of course, other objectives also underlie this body of law – disarmament, in particular.

The development of weaponry law has not always been linear or logical. For instance, Greenwood observes that:

> Deep-seated taboos found in many societies regarding certain types of injury or means of inflicting harm have meant that certain types of weapons (those employing or causing fire, for example) have been treated as particularly horrific, without any serious attempt being made to compare their effects with those produced by other weapons. (p. 9)

Moreover, those seeking limitations can be self-interested. The classic example is that discussed in Volume I – attempts to limit the use of submarines – which was partly motivated by Great Britain's desire to maintain naval supremacy.

Several key foundational principles underlie the law of weaponry. Foremost among these is the principle of unnecessary suffering, first set forth in the 1868 St Petersburg Declaration. It prohibits methods or means of warfare that cause unnecessary suffering and have no military purpose to combatants. Determining where this threshold lies 'requires a balancing of the military advantage which may result from the use of a weapon with the degree of injury and suffering which it is likely to cause' (p. 13). Unfortunately, '[t]his balancing act is

... easier to state in the abstract than it is to apply, since one is not comparing like with like and there is considerable uncertainty regarding the factors to be placed on each side of the scales' (ibid.). The principle further requires a comparison with other weapons in determining whether the injuries and suffering in question are 'necessary'. This assessment may prove difficult to accomplish, for one must also consider such factors as availability, logistics and force protection. Greenwood concludes that the principle has only 'limited effects', observing that there is not 'a single example of a weapon which has entered into service during the twentieth century and which is generally agreed to fall foul of this principle' (p. 16).

Also fundamental in the law of weaponry is the principle of discrimination which prohibits the use of indiscriminate weapons and the indiscriminate use of discriminate weapons. The prohibitions on directly attacking civilians, the rule of proportionality and the requirement to take precautions in attack also reside in the principle. The 1990–91 Gulf War demonstrated that these rules were 'workable' (p. 20).

Although international humanitarian law clearly dominates issues of weapons legality and the lawful use of weapons, Greenwood notes that it 'does not operate in isolation and the rest of international law cannot be disregarded in determining whether the use of a particular weapon is lawful' (p. 34). He cites three bodies of law as potentially relevant, all discussed in the International Court of Justice's Nuclear Weapons Advisory Opinion. The first is human rights, particularly the prohibition on arbitrary deprivation of life. Greenwood adopts the Court's position that, while the right to life applies in armed conflict, it is subject to the *lex specialis* of humanitarian law. The second is international environmental law; the Court concluded that no prohibition on the use of nuclear weapons could be derived from it. Finally, the *jus ad bellum* was deemed applicable to the use of weaponry, in particular the self-defence criteria of necessity and proportionality.

> The logic of the Charter and customary law provisions on self-defense means that the modern *jus ad bellum* cannot be regarded as literally a 'law on going to war,' the importance of which fades into the background once the fighting has started and the *jus in bello* comes into operation. (p. 36)

Ultimately, Greenwood concludes that '[w]ith the law of weaponry, as with most of the law of armed conflict, the most important humanitarian gain would come not from the adoption of new law but the effective implementation of the law we have. That should be the priority for the next century' (p. 40).

Richard Baxter, Professor of Law at Harvard University at the time, addresses the issue of weapons other than weapons of mass destruction in 'Conventional Weapons Under Legal Prohibitions' (Chapter 2). The essay was written as the international community was deciding to convene the UN conference that ultimately led to adoption of the 1980 Convention on Conventional Weapons and its accompanying protocols. It is valuable not only for its discussion of the core principles of weapons law, but also for its rich account of the ensuing negotiations. What becomes immediately apparent is that when assessing bans or restrictions on weaponry, states look closely to their own national interests, especially as to how their forces will be affected on the battlefield.

Baxter traces the modern lineage of the law governing weapons to the 1868 St Petersburg Declaration. Two principles expressed in that instrument continue to infuse international humanitarian law, including weapons law. First, 'the only legitimate object which States should endeavour to accomplish during war is to weaken the military force of the enemy', a provision that serves as the basis for the principle of distinction. Second, 'it is sufficient to disable the greatest possible number of men'; 'this object would be exceeded by the employment of arms which uselessly aggravate the sufferings of disabled men, or render their death inevitable'. This provision is the original source of the principle of unnecessary suffering. In 1996 the International Court of Justice recognized distinction and unnecessary suffering as 'cardinal principles' of international humanitarian law in its *Nuclear Weapons* Advisory Opinion. Together with the weapons provisions of the Hague conferences, mentioned above, and the 1925 Gas Protocol, they formed the core of the weapons-specific law throughout the Second World War. In this regard, Baxter notes that:

> What law existed was either pitched on a very high level of abstraction (as was true of the prohibition on weapons causing unnecessary suffering) or was directed to specific weapons or projectiles of marginal utility (for example 'dum-dum' bullets) in comparison with the enormous technological developments that had taken place in the art of warfare. (p. 54)

The conflict in Vietnam drew attention to the issue of weapons in the 1960s and 1970s, for by then it seemed that '[t]he law was … an ineffective instrument for establishing some control over weapons, even if good-faith effort were made to apply it' (p. 56). Discussion on weapons at the 1974–77 Diplomatic Conference on the Reaffirmation and Development of International Humanitarian Law Applicable in Armed Conflicts 'turned out to be in large measure one between "haves" and "have-nots"' (p. 60), with the latter seeking to limit the weaponry of the former. While efforts to address specific weapons generally failed, the Diplomatic Conference adopted a resolution recommending a further conference on conventional weapons. The conference began the following year, the Conventional Weapons Convention and its accompanying Protocols being adopted in 1980.

Writing before the conference concluded, Baxter interestingly comments on the likelihood of particular weapons being addressed in the envisioned convention. He was doubtful about the prospects for incendiary weapons provisions because a number of key states saw them as having real battlefield utility; the conference did produce a protocol on such weapons, but the United States did not become a party for nearly two decades. For the same reason, he was equally pessimistic about the likelihood of restrictions on small-calibre projectiles and fragmentation and blast weapons (including cluster bomb units). While no agreement could be reached on these systems, a separate convention on cluster munitions was adopted three decades later. Baxter was correctly optimistic that agreement could be reached on regulating, but not prohibiting, the use of anti-personnel landmines and booby traps.

Ian Brownlie, who would become the Chichele Professor of Law at Oxford, deals with the sensitive topic of nuclear weapons in 'Some Legal Aspects of the Use of Nuclear Weapons' (Chapter 3). This essay was written in 1965, at the height of the Cold War and over two decades before the International Court of Justice addressed the subject. Brownlie acknowledges that the weapons are in a special category, but nevertheless insists:

Taliban fighters combatant status was their lack of a uniform or other distinguishing garb. Missing in the public debate at the time was the fact that the forces were not dressed as civilians, but rather had adopted the attire of the Northern Alliance forces with whom they were fighting; Parks labels this clothing 'non-standard uniforms'.

Despite misunderstanding to the contrary, the Third Geneva Convention does not require military personnel to wear uniforms; equally, it is not a war crime to fail to wear one. Instead, Article 4A of the treaty imposes a condition on 'militias and members of other volunteer corps, including those of organized resistance movements' to have 'a fixed distinctive sign recognizable at a distance'. The legal issue is whether this requirement is implicit as regards members of the regular armed forces. Parks concludes that:

> Wearing a partial uniform, or even civilian clothing, is illegal only if it involves perfidy ... Military personnel wearing non-standard uniform or civilian clothing are entitled to prisoner of war status if captured. Those captured wearing civilian clothing may be at risk of denial of prisoner of war status and trial as spies. (pp. 178–79)

The question then becomes: what is a non-traditional uniform? Parks points to the principle of distinction as informing the answer since a uniform is one of the ways of effectuating the protection civilians enjoy under international humanitarian law. He notes that '[m]ilitary wear of uniforms during conventional combat operations in international armed conflict reflects the general customary practice of nations' (p. 181), with certain specified exceptions. His examination of historical state practice and the Third Geneva Convention's negotiation records lead him to find that uniforms, uniforms worn with some civilian clothing and civilian clothing to which a distinctive emblem has been attached are 'uniforms' as a matter of law and thus the individuals attired in them are entitled to prisoner-of-war status. Civilian clothing with arms and other accoutrements, such as body armour, meets the requirement that fighting forces be distinguishable from the civilian population, but is not a uniform proper and may subject the individual to denial of prisoner-of-war status. However, it will shield that person from charges of spying if caught away from the civilian population because he or she is engaged in clearly military duties. Wear of purely civilian clothing is lawful for intelligence-gathering and is only an international humanitarian law violation if perfidy occurs. This last position is generally supported by Additional Protocol I's (to which the United States is not party) controversial relaxation of the requirement for combatants to distinguish themselves from the civilian population.

Parks concludes that '[t]he law of war requires military units and personnel to distinguish themselves from the civilian population in international armed conflict' (p. 209). While the Third Geneva Convention delineates the standards combatants are expected to satisfy, 'military personnel may distinguish themselves from the civilian population in other ways, such as physical separation' (ibid.). The law does not prohibit the wearing of non-standard uniforms or civilian clothing 'so long as military personnel distinguish themselves from the civilian population, and provided there is legitimate military necessity for wearing something other than standard uniform' (p. 208). He cautions, however, that it is a practice that 'should be exercised only in extreme cases determined by competent authority' (ibid.).

The distinction between combatants and civilians is further examined in Yoram Dinstein's 'Unlawful Combatancy' (Chapter 7). Dinstein, former President of Tel Aviv University, draws a strict divide between non-combatants (civilians) and combatants. He distinguishes lawful from unlawful combatants, the latter consisting of civilians who take up arms without legal authority (as in the case of resistance fighters meeting the four conditions or members of a *levée en masse*). Unlawful combatants are not entitled to prisoner-of-war status since a *conditio sine qua non* of said status is that the combatancy be lawful. Moreover, since only civilians enjoy protection from attack, unlawful combatants may be lawfully targeted. This position is somewhat controversial, with others maintaining that civilians who participate in the conflict retain their status as such, but lose protection from attack for such time as they so participate.

Like Baxter and Draper, Dinstein examines the question of whether unlawful combatants may be prosecuted for the mere fact of their participation. He rejects the *Quirin* decision that 'they are subject to trial and punishment by military tribunals for acts which render their belligerency unlawful', arguing instead that they may only be prosecuted for those individual acts which constitute crimes under international or domestic criminal law. In other words, while the fact of unlawful belligerency does not render the unlawful combatant subject to prosecution as such, acts which provide the basis for characterization may. For instance, when soldier A kills enemy soldier B, he or she has committed murder under domestic law, but the *jus in bello* provides soldier A with a 'legal shield, protecting him from trial and punishment, by conferring upon him the status of a prisoner of war' (p. 230). But if the same act is committed by an unlawful combatant, no shield is available and the individual may be tried in accordance with the domestic law of a state enjoying jurisdiction over the matter.

Dinstein then turns to the matter of prisoner-of-war status, finding the Hague Regulations and Third Geneva Convention conditions regarding 'other militia' applicable to the armed forces. He cites the 1968 Privy Council case of *Mohamed Ali* as support. Beyond the express requirements in the Third Geneva Convention, three others attach: organization, belonging to a party and lack of duty of allegiance to the detaining power. Dinstein takes the position that the wearing of a fixed distinctive emblem is both a collective and a individual responsibility. The organization must adopt, for instance, a uniform. Once it does, the failure of a member of the group to wear it at the critical time will deprive that person of entitlement to prisoner-of-war status. As to carrying arms openly and observance of the *jus in bello*, he believes that 'the correct approach is that their fulfillment should be monitored primarily on an individual basis and only secondarily on a group basis' (p. 242). Thus, 'John Doe has to answer for his actual behavior. However, if no opportunity for individual verification presents itself … it is possible to establish how the group behaves in general and extrapolate from the collectivity to the individual' (pp. 242–43). But when a group fails to meet the conditions, no member of the group may qualify as a lawful combatant, despite any individual compliance.

Finally, Dinstein comments on Additional Protocol I's controversial Article 44, which dispenses with the requirement to distinguish oneself when circumstances make doing so problematic and narrows the requirement to carry arms openly to those times when the individual is visible to the enemy during deployment to an engagement and the engagement itself. It provides that when individuals fail to comply with these relaxed requirements, they are deprived of prisoner-of-war status, but nevertheless are to 'be given protections equivalent in all respects to those accorded to prisoners of war' (p. 244). Dinstein joins the widespread criticism of Article 44, noting that civilians will suffer thereby because regular forces are likely to treat civilians more harshly if they believe that their opponents are allowed to pose as civilians without losing their prisoner-of-war status. He concludes: 'for contracting Parties to the Protocol, the general distinction between lawful and unlawful combatants becomes nominal in value' (p. 246).

Knut Dörmann, Legal Adviser for the ICRC, adopts a different perspective. In 'The Legal Status of "Unlawful/Unprivileged Combatants"' (Chapter 8) he explores whether a category of 'unlawful combatants' who benefit from neither the Third nor Fourth Geneva Conventions exists. The possible existence of a 'gap' between the conventions has generated intense debate, particularly in terms of the detention of individuals involved in transnational terrorism and those who engage in hostilities but do not meet the conditions for prisoner-of-war status. Dörmann takes the position that the conventions are seamless: individuals are either combatants or civilians.

The conditions for combatant status are those set forth in the Third Geneva Convention, as supplemented by Additional Protocol I provisions on the subject for states party. As noted, the latter are controversial. All other individuals are civilians, who enjoy no right to participate in hostilities except for the unique case of the *levée en masse*. Civilians who do participate may be targeted, although there is disagreement over the precise nature of the participation that qualifies them to be lawfully targeted.

The focus of the essay is, however, on the issue of the status and treatment of civilians who, having taken a direct part in hostilities, are captured or detained. The terms 'unlawful combatant' and 'unlawful/unprivileged belligerent' have been used to refer to such individuals, but do not appear in treaty law. They include civilians who take up arms or engage in other acts of direct participation and members of militia and other volunteer corps (including resistance movements) that do not meet the conditions of the Third Geneva Convention. In that they do not benefit from that convention, the question is whether they enjoy protection under the Fourth.

Article 4 of the Fourth Geneva Convention applies to 'persons ... who, at a given moment and in any manner whatsoever, find themselves, in case of a conflict or occupation, in the hands of a Party to the conflict or Occupying Power of which they are not nationals'. It expressly does not apply to those protected by the Third Convention. Therefore, Dörmann concludes that civilians who participate in hostilities and those members of militia or volunteer groups who do not meet the requirements of the Third Convention are necessarily covered by the Fourth, with the exception of individuals encompassed in a nationality exception. He points to the fact that in limiting certain protections vis-à-vis spies, saboteurs and others suspected of engaging in activities threatening security, the Fourth Convention refers to them as 'protected persons', thereby confirming the general premise that persons who directly participate in hostilities are covered by the convention. Similarly, Article 45(3) of Additional Protocol I affords protection to '[a]ny person who takes part in hostilities, who is not entitled to prisoner-of-war status and who does not benefit from more favourable treatment in accordance with the Fourth Convention'. Dörmann contends that there would be no need for the Fourth Convention reference if there were not at least some individuals who benefit from the convention despite their participation in hostilities. In support of his position, he offers a careful review of the *travaux préparatoires*, legal literature on the subject and case law.

Substantively, the protections set forth in the Fourth Geneva Convention are at their peak when an 'unlawful combatant' is in enemy hands in occupied territory. They are relaxed to an extent when the individual is held in enemy territory and at their weakest while he is on the battlefield. Dörmann emphasizes that Article 75 of Additional Protocol I represents the minimum protections to which such individuals are entitled. It is noteworthy in this respect that in 2011 the United States acknowledged Article 75 guarantees as reflecting customary law.

Michael Schmitt, co-editor of these volumes, deals with the issue of direct participation in 'Humanitarian Law and Direct Participation in Hostilities by Private Contractors or Civilian Employees' (Chapter 9). This essay was written for an early meeting of the group of experts convened by the ICRC between 2003 and 2008 to consider direct participation in hostilities by civilians. The subject came to the fore as tens of thousands of contractors and government civilian employees flooded into Afghanistan and Iraq. They ranged from private security contractors who engaged in actual fighting to workers in mess halls. At one point, there were more private security contractors in Iraq than the combat forces of any Coalition contingent except for the Americans. The essay briefly surveys the consequences of direct participation, but focuses on the issue of when they attach.

The threshold question is the legal status of these individuals. Schmitt characterizes them as civilians, for they are not formally part of the armed forces, are not a paramilitary or law enforcement force incorporated into the armed forces and cannot qualify as militia or volunteer forces because they are not part of a state's armed forces and, in any event, do not meet the Third Geneva Convention requirements. Certain of the individuals may qualify as '[p]ersons who accompany the armed forces' and thereby be entitled to prisoner-of-war status, but they remain civilians.

Their civilian status raises the question: when do they become 'unlawful combatants' – in other words, direct participants in the hostilities? Schmitt suggests that:

> Direct participation ... seemingly requires 'but for' causation (in other words, the consequences would not have occurred but for the act), causal proximity (albeit not direct causation) to the foreseeable consequences of the act, and a mens rea of intent. In other words, the civilian must have engaged in an action that he or she knew would harm (or otherwise disadvantage) the enemy in a relatively direct and immediate way. The participation must have been part of the process by which a particular use of force was rendered possible, either through preparation or execution. (p. 303)

He concludes: 'the best tack when analyzing a particular act is assessing the criticality of the act to the direct application of violence against the enemy' (p. 304).

Of course, there will be many grey-area cases. Schmitt argues that they should be interpreted liberally in favour of finding that the act amounts to direct participation. He justifies the approach by suggesting that 'the liberal approach provides an incentive for civilians to remain as distant from the conflict as possible because they can therefore avoid being directly targeted and are less susceptible to being charged criminally for their acts of participation' (p. 305).

Schmitt also addresses the vexing temporal issue – that is, the meaning of the phrase 'for such time' in the norm. It is one that has direct application on the battlefield, for outside this period a civilian who has previously directly participated enjoys immunity from attack. A strict interpretation of the standard results in a 'revolving door' of targetability, leading Schmitt to query, 'Can it possibly be that those who directly participate in hostilities regain their civilian immunity whenever they successfully return from an operation even though they fully intend to subsequently recommence hostile action?' (p. 305). The ICRC has taken the position in the *Interpretive Guidance on the Notion of Direct Participation in Hostilities* that they can, that the 'revolving door' is not a malfunction of international humanitarian law. Schmitt charges that this approach 'flies in the face of logic grounded in the realities of armed conflict' (p. 306). For him, '[t]he sole practical interpretation of direct participation's temporal aspect is one in which a civilian who participates in hostilities remains a valid military objective until unambiguously opting out through extended nonparticipation or an affirmative act of withdrawal' (ibid.).

Leslie Green, then Professor at the University of Alberta, considers an important subset of fighters in 'The Status of Mercenaries in International Law' (Chapter 10). This essay was written in light of the mercenary experience in several African conflicts and in the immediate aftermath of Additional Protocol I's denial of combatant status to such individuals and adoption of the Organization of African Unity's Mercenary Convention in 1977. However, the 1989 International Convention against the Recruitment, Use, Financing and Training of Mercenaries had not yet been adopted.

Like most of Leslie Green's works, this essay is rich in historical background. Drawing on the works of Bynkershoek, Ayala, Vitoria, Grotius, Suarez, Belli, Pufendorf, Wolff and Vattel, he notes that learned commentators have long struggled with the use of foreign troops and others who harbour no particular loyalty to the belligerent for which they are fighting. Ayala, for instance, took the position that 'sovereigns should be urged to employ as soldiers in war natives rather than foreigners, for the latter serve for pay rather than duty' (p. 317).[1] In contrast, Vattel was rather taken by the notion, praising the fact that Swiss mercenaries 'have never quit service at the first payment overdue' (p. 322).[2] By the nineteenth century, most writers appear to have adopted the position that:

> ... the use and enlistment of foreign volunteers was legitimate, and there was a tendency to accept that the provision of such personnel under an agreement made between a non-belligerent sovereign and a country at war, or about to enter war, was not incompatible with neutrality. (p. 326)

Green also examines historical national views on using external forces. The English, in light of their traditional opposition to a standing army, relied heavily on forces recruited from abroad. France, by contrast, depended more heavily on its own forces, largely because general conscription gave it a ready supply of troops. The United States, especially opposed to the notion of foreign soldiers (perhaps because of the extensive use of them by the British), went

---

[1]   Citing Balthazar Ayala, *De Jure et Officiis Bellicis et Disciplina Militari*, trans. J.P. Bate, Washington, DC: Carnegie Institute, 1912, p. 188.

[2]   Citing E. de Vattel, *Le Droit des Gens, on Principe de la Loi Naturelle*, Washington, DC: Carnegie Institute, 1916, pp. 239–40).

so far as to forbid its nationals from fighting for states with which the United States was at peace.

In that both classical writers and state practice were split over the legality of mercenaries, it is difficult to draw firm conclusions as to the traditional state of the law. By the turn of the twentieth century, however, international law on the subject began to crystallize. For instance, the 1907 Hague Conventions V and XIII on neutrality placed limitations on activities in neutral territory, such as recruitment. But it was not until the national liberation movements of the 1960s that international attention was directly drawn to the matter, in great part because of the involvement of mercenaries in the Congo. In that case, the UN Security Council condemned the use of mercenaries, although less out of opposition to mercenarism than concern that they were destabilizing the situation.

The Angolan civil war marked a further turning-point in attitudes towards the use of mercenaries, with the General Assembly passing a resolution declaring that 'the practice of using mercenaries against movements for national liberation and independence constitutes a crime [and]... the mercenaries are criminals'. States began to take action through domestic legislation and the Diplomatic Conference that led to the Additional Protocols took up the issue. The results were modest. Additional Protocol II makes no mention of mercenaries, although it is in such conflicts that they are most likely to participate. Additional Protocol I provided a definition of mercenaries and denied them, at least for states party to the instrument, the right to combatant and prisoner-of-war status. It did not criminalize serving as a mercenary. Accordingly, mercenaries are essentially 'unlawful combatants'.

Certain categories of individuals are especially vulnerable to suffering during armed conflicts. In 'The International Legal Protection of Children in Armed Conflicts' (Chapter 11), Geraldine Van Bueren, Professor at the University of London, deals with the tragic situation of children caught up in war. She notes, for instance, that between 1984 and 1994, 'internal armed conflicts have led to 1.5 million child deaths, 4 million children disabled as a result of war wounds and 5 million children living in refugee camps' (p. 364). Sadly, the situation of children in conflict remains dire.

Prior to the 1949 Fourth Geneva Convention, international humanitarian law accorded children little specific protection. The 1907 Hague Regulations only protected 'family honour and rights' during occupation. The ICRC, working with the International Union for Child Warfare, did produce a draft Convention on the Protection of Children in Emergency and Armed Conflict, but unfortunately the war intervened.

Although the Fourth Geneva Convention contains 17 articles on children, Van Bueren highlights the lack of a minimum age for participation in the hostilities or any specific protection for children during a non-international armed conflict. She praises the additional protection the Additional Protocols afford children, including the setting of a minimum age of participation, but notes that key states are not party to the instrument. The protocols set the minimum age of recruitment at 15 and impose a requirement to take all feasible measures to ensure that younger children do not participate in hostilities, a standard later confirmed by the 1989 Convention on the Rights of the Child. Interestingly, Additional Protocol I uses the term 'direct' as modifying 'part'; Protocol II did not and therefore arguably sets a lower threshold for participation. After Van Bueren's essay was published, the Rome Statute of the International Criminal Court adopted this standard. In 2000 an Optional Protocol to the

Convention of the Rights of the Child raised the age of compulsory recruitment to 18 for parties thereto.

As to child civilians, Van Bueren makes the important point that all protections for civilians set forth in international humanitarian law include children. In certain cases, children are afforded particular protection, although this requires a difficult calculation of interests. For instance, in the Fourth Geneva Convention 'States balanced the damage to a child through family separation against the risks of injury in a conflict zone and believed that less harm would come to children through evacuation' (p. 375). Accordingly, the Convention encourages the belligerents to conclude local agreements facilitating such evacuation.

Although adoption of humanitarian law to enhance standards for the protection of children is a positive step, Van Bueren concludes that it is more important to create mechanisms and practices that enhance the likelihood of *de facto* protection. In particular, she argues that 'the proposed draft Protocol additional to the Convention on the Rights of the Child will represent a squandered opportunity if its sole purpose is the raising of minimum ages' (p. 380). That is exactly what it did.

In 'Protection of Women in Armed Conflict' (Chapter 12), Judith Gardam of the University of Adelaide and Hilary Charlesworth of Australian National University address another especially vulnerable category of persons in armed conflict. They note, 'the focus on violence – in particular on sexual violence – tends to obscure other important aspects of women's experience of armed conflict that ... have been largely ignored' (pp. 381–82). Their essay considers the full range of international humanitarian law protections women enjoy.

Gardam and Charlesworth claim that 'it is clear that [the law's] provisions operate in a discriminatory fashion in relation to women' (p. 385). They point to the fact that although there are 43 provisions in the 1949 Geneva Conventions and Additional Protocols, 'they all deal with women in their relationships with others, not as individuals in their own right' (p. 392). For instance, 19 of them are aimed at the protection of children. Moreover, although there are numerous provisions dealing with the 'honour' of women, honour is 'constituted solely on the basis of certain sexual attributes, the characterizing features of which are what is seen as important to men, namely the chastity and modesty of women' (p. 392). The offences regarding women also employ the language of protection rather than of prohibition and are not grave breaches. Gardam and Charlesworth conclude that international humanitarian law provisions regarding women are 'presented as less important than others' (ibid.). For them, humanitarian law is 'inherently discriminatory' (p. 398).

They argue that the 'boundaries of IHL' (p. 393) – referring to distinctions between humanitarian law, human rights and refugee law – contribute to the problem. As an example, they single out the principle of proportionality. In their view, the principle does not require the consideration of the long-term effects of attacks, such as starvation, disease and the dislocation of the population. Many international humanitarian law experts would dispute this sweeping statement. But the point Gardam and Charlesworth are making is that women are particularly affected by post-attack conditions that may extend beyond the end of the conflict. Similarly, humanitarian law rules relating to humanitarian assistance, which are especially important with regard to women, only apply during an armed conflict (including periods of occupation), not thereafter.

As to the way ahead, Gardam and Charlesworth raise the possibility of 'a reinterpretation of the existing provisions of IHL to take account of gender perspectives and changing interpretations of the rules' (p. 396). They highlight the work of the International Criminal Tribunals for the Former Yugoslavia and Rwanda and their relevance to the 'place of rape in the system of grave breaches' (p. 397). They also raise the possibility of enhanced dissemination of those rules that relate to women, as well as greater attention to issues of 'reconstruction and peacebuilding initiatives after the cessation of hostilities' (p. 398). For them, the ICRC bears particular responsibility in addressing such matters.

Objects

Part III of this volume deals with aspects of armed conflict that are of contemporary importance. Captured property, a topic that has not attracted great attention on the international scene, is of great significance to fielded forces and their legal advisers, particularly in cases involving forces operating in enemy territory and those which arm themselves, at least in part, with enemy equipment. Protection of the environment was addressed in Additional Protocol I and the Environmental Modification Convention, following widespread environmental damage during the Vietnam War, but it was not until the Gulf War of 1990–91, with release of oil in the Persian Gulf and the setting of oil wells ablaze, that the international community took notice again and militaries began to adjust their operations accordingly.

In 'Captured Enemy Property' (Chapter 13), written not long after the conclusion of the Second World War, William Downey, then Chief of International Law for the US Army, defines captured enemy property as 'any property which is useful in war or is taken or seized on the ground of military necessity for the purpose of depriving the enemy of its use or of turning it to the captor's advantage' (p. 403). Only enemy personal property, as distinct from real property, can be taken or seized, although enemy real property may be used when necessary. Enemy personal property includes enemy public property (owned by the state) and enemy private property (owned by corporations, individuals and other non-governmental entities).

Booty is a subset of captured enemy property. Booty 'is limited to movable articles on the battlefield and in besieged towns. Private property which may be taken as booty is restricted to arms, munitions, pieces of equipment, horses, military papers, and the like. Public enemy property which may be seized as war booty is limited to movables on the battlefield, and these need not be for military operations or necessity' (p. 404).[3] Captured enemy property is a broader concept as it encompasses that personal property which an occupation force seizes or requisitions.

Enemy public property captured on the battlefield (booty) becomes the property of the capturing power. Downey cites a number of cases from the Second World War in which Allied soldiers were convicted for seizing funds in possession of German forces. Title to property vests upon capture and is good even as to the original owner. For instance, if enemy forces lawfully seize booty and that booty is subsequently captured by another force, the latter enjoys good title over the property. A number of classes of property are exempt from such seizure.

---

[3]   Citing Daniel H. Lew, 'Manchurian Booty and International Law', *American Journal of International Law*, **40**, (1946), pp. 584–89, at p. 586.).

These include medical material and transports, except in the case of necessity, works of art and science, and historical monuments. Enemy private property cannot be captured unless it is used for military purposes.

Property seized or requisitioned during an occupation is subject to more extensive regulation. Article 53 of the 1907 Hague Regulations provides that '[a]n army of occupation can only take possession of cash, funds, and realizable securities which are strictly the property of the State, depots of arms, means of transport, stores and supplies, and generally, all movable property belonging to the State which may be used for military operations'. Enemy private property may not be seized unless it is employed for military purposes, but it may be requisitioned. To the extent possible, it must be paid for in cash; when doing so is not feasible, a receipt may be given, with payment made as soon as feasible. Downey points out that '[t]he ultimate disposition of captured enemy property is not a question for international but for domestic law' (p. 414).

The continuing relevance of Downey's analysis is apparent from the provisions on the seizure of property found in the ICRC's *Customary International Humanitarian Law* study. Rule 49 provides that '[t]he parties to the conflict may seize military equipment belonging to an adverse party as war booty', although the commentary to the rule expands the class of seizable items slightly beyond military equipment. Rule 51 addresses occupied territory. It accepts as lawful the confiscation of movable public property of use for military purposes. Private property may not be confiscated, but may, in certain cases, be requisitioned.

The topic of the environmental impact of warfare is dealt with by Michael Schmitt in 'Green War' (Chapter 14), which was written as the subject was beginning to draw serious academic and policy interest after the Iraqi actions during the 1990–91 Gulf War. During this war, Iraqi forces damaged or destroyed some 598 oil wellheads; 508 were set ablaze and 82 were damaged in a way that caused oil to be released into the Persian Gulf.

The exact parameters of the environmental provisions of international humanitarian law remain unsettled. Customary *jus in bello*, as recognized in Article 6(b) of the Charter of the International Military Tribunal, prohibits the 'wanton destruction of cities' towns or villages, or devastation not justified by military necessity'. This is obviously a highly subjective standard. For instance, in that the smoke from the Iraqi oil-well fires created obscurants that complicated Coalition air strikes, were the actions militarily necessary and to what extent did the actual Iraqi objectives in setting them ablaze affect application of the norm? Customary law also contains the principle of proportionality. But to what extent is harm to the environment factored into the proportionality calculation and does it extend to long-term harm that may not immediately occur? Should an anthropocentric approach, focusing on the harm caused to humans by environmental damage, be taken or an intrinsic value one, which treats the environment as of value in itself? And to what extent is harm to the environment relative to cultures and across time? Such conundrums are by no means limited to environmental matters, but they are certainly complicated by them.

As with customary law, most treaty law applicable during armed conflict is non-environment-specific. Article 23(g) of the 1907 Hague Regulations merely prohibits the destruction of the enemy's property unless 'imperatively demanded by the necessities of war', while the principle of proportionality codified in Additional Protocol I makes no mention of the environment. Similarly, Additional Protocol I's provisions on objects containing dangerous forces, specifically dams, dykes and nuclear electrical generating stations, is certain to have positive environmental benefits, but is not based on a desire to protect the environment. Numerous other general treaty provisions can also apply to protect the environment.

But for the first time, Additional Protocol I sets forth two provisions expressly for the environment. Article 35(3) provides that '[i]t is prohibited to employ methods or means of warfare which are intended, or may be expected, to cause widespread, long-term and severe damage to the natural environment'. Article 55(1) prohibits 'the use of methods or means of warfare which are intended or may be expected to cause [widespread, long-term and severe] damage to the natural environment and thereby to prejudice the health or survival of the population', as well as reprisals against the natural environment. Note the distinction. The former is an absolute prohibition on damage that meets the three conditions. By contrast, the latter requires that the harm caused must affect the population. Combined, the two provisions satisfy members of both the anthropocentric and intrinsic value camps. Note also that the level of requisite harm is set at an exceptionally high level. Even so, certain states, including the United States, object to the articles on the basis that harm to the environment is more appropriately addressed through application of general norms, especially proportionality.

The Environmental Modification Convention, negotiated contemporaneously with Additional Protocol I, takes a different approach. It is classic 'Hague Law' in that it prohibits particular methods and means of warfare, rather than extending protections to specified individuals and objects. In operative part, it bars parties from 'engag[ing] in military or any other hostile use of environmental modification techniques having widespread, long-lasting or severe effects as the means of destruction, damage or injury' to any other state. Examples would include causing earthquakes or tsunamis. The resulting level of harm in the prohibition is lower than that of Additional Protocol I in that it is non-cumulative – any of the three forms of harm qualify (although the difficulty of interpreting the terms remains). The provision also adopts the intrinsic value approach in the sense that human impact is not a precondition to applicability.

Schmitt concludes that '[t]he existing environmental law of war neither adequately echoes community values nor serves to foster its aspirations' (p. 515). It is unwieldy in application because most of the applicable law is not environment-specific. Moreover, there are interpretive obstacles, such as the absence of a definitive definition of the terms 'widespread', 'long-term' and 'severe'. Finally, the law lacks internal coherence in that '[e]ach facet was developed in response to very different problems, in varying contexts and at different times' (ibid.) and adopts approaches – anthropocentric and intrinsic value – that are not necessarily harmonious.

Tactics

Perfidy and ruses have become pervasive practices on the battlefield, particularly in Afghanistan and Iraq. Insurgents have discovered that perfidious acts often effectively counter the technological advantages Coalition forces enjoy. This is especially true with regard to the use of suicide bombers disguised as civilians, often women.

Part IV addresses this issue, which has burst onto the contemporary asymmetrical battlefield, with the final essay of the volume, 'Ruses of War and Prohibition of Perfidy' (Chapter 15), by

Dieter Fleck of the German Ministry of Defence. Written before the Diplomatic Conference that led to adoption of the Additional Protocols, it is especially relevant to the customary nature of the prohibition.

Article 37 of Additional Protocol I provides that:

> It is prohibited to kill, injure or capture an adversary by resort to perfidy. Acts inviting the confidence of an adversary to lead him to believe that he is entitled to, or is obliged to accord, protection under the rules of international law applicable in armed conflict, with intent to betray that confidence, shall constitute perfidy.

The article cites the examples of feigning intent to negotiate under a flag of truce or of surrender; incapacitation by wounds or sickness; civilian, non-combatant status; and protected status by the use of signs, emblems or uniforms of the UN or of neutral or other states not parties to the conflict. Certain states take the position that the reference to capture is not customary.

Ruses, as distinct from perfidy, are lawful. They include, *inter alia*:

> [s]urprise and ambush, the passing of false intelligence, the use or imitation of enemy signals, passwords, codes, signs, voices and orders, the removal of landmarks and signposts, bogus troop movement and strength, pretended inactivity, the use of dummy vehicles and positions, the camouflaging of uniforms and vehicles with nets and foliage, the use of cover, the employment of every conceivable decoy, the use of spies, the removal of unit badges from uniforms and escape in civilian clothes.

Fleck defines ruses as 'all acts of war aimed at inducing the enemy to compromise his position or to expose himself to danger' (p. 536). This definition comports with that in Additional Protocol I, Article 37(2): 'acts which are intended to mislead an adversary or to induce him to act recklessly but which infringe no rule of international law applicable in armed conflict and which are not perfidious because they do not invite the confidence of an adversary with respect to protection under that law'.

The prohibition of perfidy is an interesting rule of international humanitarian law in that it derives not only from concern about protected persons and objects, but also the 'belligerents' sense of honour and the idea that a certain basis of mutual confidence must be preserved even on the battlefield' (p. 536). It has a long lineage. Grotius took the position that 'words, gestures, and signals commonly used in a specific sense are illicit means of deceiving the enemy because "they are based on tacit agreement between the parties"' (p. 538). The 1863 Lieber Code prohibited deception through misuse of such items as enemy flags, uniforms or national emblems and flags of truce. Later, Article 23(f) of the 1907 Hague Regulations prohibited killing or wounding 'treacherously' as well as 'improper use of as flag of truce, of the national flag or of the military insignia and uniform of the enemy, as well as the distinctive badges of the Geneva Convention' (p. 565, n. 48) The First Geneva Convention of 1949 also affords protection against the misuse of the distinctive emblem.

A somewhat controversial issue is the wearing of enemy uniforms. Fleck notes that during the Second World War 'the use of enemy uniforms was regarded as forbidden in all circumstances' (p. 544). However, following the post-war *Skorzeny* decision, which acquitted a German officer who commanded troops wearing US uniforms, the US and British field manuals took the position that such wear was not unlawful except during engagements with the enemy. This position was not universally accepted, with Germany and some other states retaining an absolute prohibition. However, Article 39(2) of Additional Protocol I later adopted the rule by prohibiting 'use of the flags or military emblems, insignia or uniforms of adverse Parties while engaging in attacks or in order to shield, favour, protect or impede military operations'.

Fleck briefly considers ruses and perfidy in maritime and air warfare, as well as applicability of the norms to non-international armed conflict. He concludes by suggesting that any codification of the rules regarding perfidy will be difficult to draft (although such a rule was included in Additional Protocol I): 'General clauses are subject to erosion by fresh feats of imagination. Any regulation framed in too concrete terms is in danger of being invalidated by international custom' (p. 562). But he perceptively notes that '[t]he more unequivocally the ban on perfidy is stipulated in international law, the more effectively it will be possible to preserve an indispensable minimum of confidence among the parties to a conflict' (ibid.). This observation is equally applicable to any rule of international humanitarian law.

MICHAEL N. SCHMITT

Part I
Weapons

[1]

The Law of Weaponry
at the Start of the New Millennium

Christopher Greenwood

I. Introduction

THE LAW OF WEAPONRY, which seeks to regulate both the means and the methods of warfare, is one of the oldest and best established areas of the laws of war.[1] It is also widely regarded as one of the least effective. The remarkable progress which has been made in the development of weaponry and methods of warfare during the twentieth century has been unmatched by development in the law. The result is that much of the law and the legal literature in this field has a distinctly anachronistic feel. For example, the prohibition of weapons causing unnecessary suffering[2] was first established over a century ago but remains part of the law and was recently applied by the International Court of Justice in considering the legality of nuclear weapons.[3] Yet a 1973 survey of the law on weaponry by the United Nations Secretariat cited bayonets or lances with barbs, irregular shaped bullets, and projectiles filled with glass as examples of weapons considered to be outlawed by the unnecessary suffering principle.[4] Scarcely standard weapons at the beginning of the twentieth century, these were museum pieces by its end. Similarly, leading text books refer to the unnecessary suffering principle meaning that "cannons

The Law of Weaponry

must not be loaded with chain shot, crossbar shot, red-hot balls, and the like."[5] Such examples suggest that the law is firmly rooted in the nineteenth century.

Yet it would be wrong to write off the law on weaponry as unimportant in modern warfare. The twentieth century has seen the adoption of prohibitions on two of the century's most destructive innovations in weaponry—chemical and bacteriological weapons.[6] In the closing years of the century, there has been a burst of activity, unprecedented in this area since the Hague Peace Conferences of 1899 and 1907, which has produced treaties on blinding laser weapons[7] and anti-personnel land mines,[8] as well as a treaty which greatly strengthens the ban on chemical weapons. In addition, the evolution of customary international law regarding the protection of the environment in time of armed conflict has had effects on the law of weaponry, while the discussion of the legality of nuclear weapons by the International Court of Justice, though inconclusive and unsatisfactory in a number of respects, demonstrated that principles established in the last century are capable of being applied well into the next.[9] Finally, wider developments in the laws of armed conflict, in particular the development of the law by the *ad hoc* tribunals for Rwanda and the Former Yugoslavia and the negotiations for the establishment of a permanent international criminal court, have had repercussions for the law on weaponry.[10]

It is therefore a good time at which to take stock of the law relating to weaponry and to consider how that law might develop in the early years of the new millennium. If that is to be done, however, it is important to have a clear understanding of the objectives which the law seeks to achieve in this area and the means by which it has sought, so far, to secure them. Among the reasons why the law on weaponry is so often seen as ineffective are that its objectives are misunderstood and unrealistic expectations are entertained as to what can be achieved. The present paper will accordingly begin with a brief account of the development of the law (Part II) and an analysis of its objectives (Part III). Part IV will then assess the law of weaponry as it stands at the end of the twentieth century. That law does not, however, operate in isolation, and Part V will therefore consider the influence of other parts of international law, in particular those concerned with the restriction of the resort to force, the protection of human rights, and the environment, which may have an impact upon the use of weapons in conflicts. Finally, Part VI will consider how the law is likely to develop in the foreseeable future—and how it might be strengthened.

II. The Development of the Law Relating to Weaponry

The prohibition of certain weapons, particularly poisonous weapons, can be traced back many centuries. The contemporary law on weapons and the

Christopher Greenwood

methods of warfare, however, began to develop only in the mid-nineteenth century. The Lieber Code[11] mentioned the prohibition on the use of poison and, in its emphasis on the principle of necessity, contained an early, albeit implicit, statement of the prohibition of weapons calculated to cause unnecessary suffering.[12] The draft declaration drawn up by the Brussels Conference in 1874[13] and the Oxford Manual prepared by the Institute of International Law in 1880 both contained provisions to the effect that a belligerent State did not possess an unlimited choice of the methods and means of war and prohibited the use of poison, treachery, and weapons causing needless suffering.[14] It is clear, therefore, that by the late nineteenth century there was considerable support for the proposition that international law imposed some constraints upon the weaponry which a belligerent might employ.

The first treaty to that effect was the St. Petersburg Declaration of 1868, which outlawed the employment in hostilities between parties to the Declaration of any "projectile of a weight below 400 grammes, which is either explosive or charged with fulminating or inflammable substances."[15] While the specific prohibition introduced by the Declaration is still in force, a more important feature of the Declaration is the statement in the Preamble of the reasoning behind the specific prohibition, namely:

That the only legitimate object which States should endeavour to accomplish during war is to weaken the military forces of the enemy;

That for this purpose it is sufficient to disable the greatest possible number of men;

That this object would be exceeded by the employment of arms which uselessly aggravate the sufferings of disabled men or render their death inevitable; [and]

That the employment of such arms would, therefore, be contrary to the laws of humanity.

It is this statement which provided the first recognition in treaty form of the prohibition of weapons calculated to cause unnecessary suffering.

The Hague Peace Conferences of 1899 and 1907 built upon these foundations in a number of agreements. Thus, the Regulations on the Laws and Customs of War on Land, adopted at the 1907 Conference,[16] provide that "the right of belligerents to adopt means of injuring the enemy is not unlimited" (Article 22) and go on to declare that it is "especially forbidden" "to employ

The Law of Weaponry

arms, projectiles, or material calculated to cause unnecessary suffering" (Article 23(e)). The Peace Conferences also adopted a number of other treaty provisions relating to weaponry and methods of warfare:

• Hague Declaration No. 2, 1899, banning the use of projectiles the sole object of which is the diffusion of asphyxiating or deleterious gases;[17]

• Hague Declaration No. 3, 1899, prohibiting the use of bullets which expand or flatten easily in the body (especially the so-called soft-headed or "dum-dum" bullets);[18]

• Hague Declaration No. 4, 1899, prohibiting for a period of five years the launching of projectiles and explosives from balloons and other methods of a similar nature;[19]

• Hague Regulations, 1907, Article 23(a), prohibiting the use of poison or poisoned weapons;[20]

• Hague Convention No. VIII, 1907, restricting the use of automatic submarine contact mines.[21]

Subsequent years saw the adoption of the 1925 Geneva Chemical and Bacteriological Weapons Protocol, prohibiting the use of asphyxiating, poisonous or other gases, all analogous liquids, materials or devices, and bacteriological methods of warfare.[22] This prohibition on the use of chemical and biological weapons was reinforced many years later by the 1972 Convention on the Prohibition of Development, Production and Stockpiling of Bacteriological and Toxin Weapons, which prohibited the possession of bacteriological and toxin weapons,[23] and the 1993 Chemical Weapons Convention, which prohibited the possession and use as a means of warfare of chemical weapons.[24] Neither the 1949 Geneva Conventions,[25] nor the two Additional Protocols to those Conventions, adopted in 1977,[26] deal with specific weapons. Additional Protocol I does, however, contain a restatement of the principles that belligerents do not have an unlimited right to choose the methods and means of warfare and may not employ methods or means of warfare of a nature to cause unnecessary suffering,[27] and also codifies important principles of customary international law regarding the protection of civilian life and property which have significant consequences for the freedom of States to select the methods and means of warfare.[28] In addition, the Protocol contains some innovative provisions on the protection of the environment in time of armed conflict.[29] The protection of the environment was also addressed in the 1977 United Nations Convention on the Prohibition of Military or any Other Hostile Use of Environmental Modification Techniques, which prohibited the use of weapons intended to change the environment through the deliberate manipulation of natural processes.[30]

Christopher Greenwood

Finally, a United Nations conference held in 1980 adopted the 1981 United Nations Convention on Prohibitions or Restrictions on the Use of Certain Conventional Weapons, the three original Protocols to which prohibited the use of weapons which injured with fragments which cannot be detected by x-rays (Protocol I) and imposed certain restrictions on the use of mines and booby traps (Protocol II) and incendiary weapons (Protocol III).[31] A subsequent review conference in 1995-96 adopted an amended Protocol II on mines (which will be superseded for some States by the 1997 Land Mines Convention) and a new Protocol IV on laser weapons.[32]

III. The Objectives of the Law Relating to Weaponry

As the law relating to weaponry is a part of the law of armed conflict, it is therefore to be expected that its objectives reflect those of the law of armed conflict as a whole. The law of armed conflict (or international humanitarian law) is primarily concerned with preserving, as far as possible, certain core humanitarian values during hostilities. It is not designed to prevent or deter States from resorting to force, and the constraints which it imposes must not, therefore, be incompatible with the effective conduct of hostilities. Every State has an undoubted right of self-defense under international law and is entitled to use force in order to vindicate that right.[33] While the law of armed conflict imposes limitations upon what a State may do in the exercise of that right, it is not intended to prevent the effective exercise of the right.[34] The law of armed conflict is thus based upon the assumption that States engaged in an armed conflict will necessarily inflict death and injury upon persons and damage to property, and seeks to limit these effects by preventing the infliction of suffering and damage which is unnecessary because it serves no useful military purpose. The law goes beyond that, however, for it requires that, even where destruction does have a military purpose, a balance be struck between the attainment of that purpose and other values, such as the preservation of civilian life; it prohibits the carrying out of an attack when the military benefit which may be expected to ensue is outweighed by the damage to those values.

The principal objective of the law of weaponry is the protection of these values. Thus, the prohibition of indiscriminate weapons and methods of warfare is designed to serve the objective of distinguishing between civilians and civilian objects, on the one hand, and combatants and military objectives, on the other, and protecting the former. Similarly, the principle that belligerents may not employ weapons or methods of warfare of a nature to cause unnecessary suffering serves the objective of protecting even combatants

The Law of Weaponry

from suffering and death which is not necessary for the achievement of legitimate military goals. The principle, which has only recently become a part of the law of weaponry, that limits the use of weapons and methods of warfare which have a substantial adverse effect upon the natural environment[35] also has as its objective the prevention of wanton, unnecessary destruction and the balancing of military needs against the value of environmental preservation.

To that extent, the law of weaponry forms part of an intellectually coherent system. The law has, however, also been used to achieve other objectives which do not so obviously form part of that system. For example, the prohibition of perfidy, which has implications for the choice of methods of warfare (if not the weapons themselves), is designed to serve two very different objectives. In part, it seeks to preserve core humanitarian values by prohibiting the feigning of surrender, protected status, or wounds, because such feints endanger those who genuinely seek to surrender, possess protected status, or are wounded, and whom the law seeks to protect. The prohibition of perfidy has also, however, been used to protect able-bodied combatants from attacks which endanger no one else but which are seen as somehow "unfair." The objective there is the quite distinct one of preserving certain military or chivalric values. Thus, it is easy to see that the prohibition on using the Red Cross and Red Crescent emblems as a shield for military operations[36] serves a humanitarian objective, since abuse of the emblem will endanger genuine medical facilities and personnel. On the other hand, the prohibition on making use of the emblems or uniforms of an adversary while engaging in attacks or in order to assist military operations serves no humanitarian purpose whatsoever; rather, it seeks to ensure that one party to a conflict does not treat the other in a way which is perceived to be contrary to concepts of fair dealing.[37]

In addition, the humanitarian objectives of the law of weaponry have frequently been intertwined with broader concerns about armaments. Thus, the First Hague Peace Conference in 1899 was convened in order to discuss questions of peaceful settlement of disputes, disarmament, and the laws of war, the Russian Government whose initiative had led to the convening of the Conference being particularly concerned to ensure that limits were placed on the introduction of new weapons and the consequent increases in military expenditure which these would entail. In adopting the three declarations banning the use of specific weapons,[38] the Conference clearly had that consideration in mind,[39] but was also influenced by humanitarian considerations. Each of the three Declarations contained a statement to the effect that the Conference had been "inspired by the sentiments" of the 1868 St. Petersburg Declaration, while the debates reveal that humanitarian

Christopher Greenwood

considerations were to the fore in the discussions.[40] Similarly, the attempts to rid the world of chemical and biological weapons which have lasted throughout the twentieth century have involved a mixture of humanitarian and disarmament considerations, the 1993 Chemical Weapons Convention being couched very much in the form of a disarmament agreement with its ban on possession as well as use of chemical weapons and its complex verification system.[41]

There is, of course, no reason why humanitarian and disarmament considerations should not be combined. The outlawing of a weapon as cruel and often indiscriminate as poisonous gas serves the values of disarmament and humanity and the employment of disarmament mechanisms for verification makes a ban far more effective than a simple prohibition on use. It should, however, be borne in mind that the objectives are different. Unlike the law of armed conflict, the disarmament process is intended to make war less likely by achieving a reduction in armaments, irrespective of whether the particular weapons involved are more or less cruel or indiscriminate than others which may not be the subject of disarmament negotiations.

Finally, in considering the objectives which the law of weaponry is designed to serve, it is worth remembering that the process by which those objectives have been applied has not always been one of strict rationality. Consideration of whether a particular weapon or method of warfare causes *unnecessary* suffering or *excessive* harm to civilians requires a comparison between different weapons and methods of warfare. Yet the process of comparison has seldom been a scientific— or even a particularly informed—one. Deep-seated taboos found in many societies regarding certain types of injury or means of inflicting harm have meant that certain types of weapon (those employing or causing fire, for example) have been treated as particularly horrific, without any serious attempt being made to compare their effects with those produced by other weapons.

Moreover, a mixture of humanitarian and disarmament considerations has all too often been used to disguise the pursuit of more self-interested objectives. The attempts to ban the crossbow in the twelfth century were the product of concern not only with the injuries which a crossbow could inflict but also with the way in which this infantry weapon changed the balance of power between mounted knights and infantrymen of a far lower social standing.[42] Likewise, the British proposals eight hundred years later to ban the submarine and the naval mine owed more to the threat which those weapons posed to the supremacy of the Royal Navy's surface fleet than their challenge to the humanitarian values underlying the laws of armed conflict. As Captain (later Admiral) Mahan, one of the United States delegates to the 1899 Peace Conference, explained, new weapons have always been denounced as barbaric.[43]

The Law of Weaponry

IV. The Law of Weaponry at the End of the Twentieth Century

It has already been seen that the law of weaponry consists of general principles, such as that prohibiting weapons of a nature to cause unnecessary suffering, and a number of rules prohibiting, or limiting the use of, specific weapons or methods of warfare. While the relationship between the two is a close one, the specific provisions frequently being an extension of one or other of the general principles, the differences between them are sufficient to justify separate examination here. In particular, the general principles tend to refer to the effects produced by the use of weapons or methods of warfare, whereas the specific provisions usually concentrate upon the means employed. Section 1 of this Part will therefore consider the general principles, while Section 2 will examine some of the rules pertaining to specific weapons. Finally, Section 3 will consider the case of nuclear weapons.

Before turning to the general principles, two preliminary matters call for comment. First, the law of weaponry—both general and specific—has been developed in the context of armed conflicts between States. The treaty provisions have usually been applicable only in conflicts between the parties to the treaty concerned and even the general principles, which apply as part of customary law, have usually been seen as applicable only in international armed conflicts. That assumption is now being challenged. As will be seen, some of the most recent treaties on specific weapons, noticeably the 1993 Chemical Weapons Convention and the two new agreements on land mines (the 1996 Amended Mines Protocol to the Conventional Weapons Convention and the 1997 Land Mines Convention) expressly apply to internal as well as international armed conflicts.[44] In addition, the Appeals Chamber of the International Criminal Tribunal for the Former Yugoslavia has held, in its decision in *Prosecutor* v. *Tadic (Jurisdiction)*, that the customary international law applicable to internal armed conflicts is more extensive than had previously been supposed and, in particular, includes the customary rules regarding methods and means of warfare which apply in international armed conflicts.[45] As the Appeals Chamber put it:

> [E]lementary considerations of humanity and common sense make it preposterous that the use by States of weapons prohibited in armed conflicts between themselves be allowed when States try to put down rebellion by their own nationals on their own territory. What is inhumane, and consequently proscribed, in international wars, cannot but be inhumane and inadmissible in civil strife.[46]

Christopher Greenwood

This aspect of the decision is controversial, not least because the issue of methods and means of warfare did not, in fact, arise on the facts of the *Tadic* case and there is little evidence of State practice to support the conclusion that the rules of customary international law in internal conflicts are as extensive as the Appeals Chamber found. The argument of logic is, however, compelling, and it is likely that the *Tadic* precedent will be followed on this point, particularly if the International Criminal Court is established and given jurisdiction over war crimes committed in internal conflicts. Nevertheless, some differences remain between the law of weaponry in international conflicts and that applicable in internal conflicts because some of the specific provisions on weaponry have not become customary law and, therefore, depend entirely upon treaties as the basis for their applicability.

Secondly, there have sometimes been differences of opinion over whether weapons and methods of warfare are lawful unless prohibited (either expressly or by necessary implication) or whether one should proceed on the basis that the use of at least certain types of weapon is illegal in the absence of a permissive rule to the contrary. An element of uncertainty on this question can be seen in the Opinion of the International Court of Justice in the *Nuclear Weapons* case. The Court stated both that international law contained no "specific authorization of the threat or use of nuclear weapons"[47] and that it contained no "comprehensive and universal prohibition of the threat or use of nuclear weapons as such."[48] Nevertheless, an examination of the whole Opinion demonstrates that the Court did not endorse the argument that nuclear weapons carried a general stigma of illegality which rendered their use unlawful in the absence of a permissive exception to the general rule. Had the Court adopted such an attitude, its finding that there was no rule authorizing the use of nuclear weapons would have disposed of the case. By holding that international law contained neither a comprehensive prohibition of the use of nuclear weapons, nor a specific authorization of their use, all the Court did was to hold that the answer to the General Assembly's question had to be sought in the application of principles of international law which were not specific to nuclear weapons. When the Court came to consider those principles, it looked to see whether they prohibited the use of nuclear weapons, not whether they authorized such use. In commencing its examination of the law of armed conflict, the Court stated that:

> State practice shows that the illegality of the use of certain weapons as such does not result from an absence of authorization but, on the contrary, is formulated in terms of prohibition.

The Law of Weaponry

> The Court must therefore now examine whether there is any prohibition of recourse to nuclear weapons as such ....[49]

This approach, rather than that of seeking a permissive rule, certainly accords better with State practice in relation to all types of weaponry over an extended period.

(1) The General Principles of the Law of Weaponry

(a) The Unnecessary Suffering Principle. The most recent statement of this principle can be found in Article 35(2) of Additional Protocol I, which provides that:

> It is prohibited to employ weapons, projectiles and material and methods of warfare of a nature to cause superfluous injury or unnecessary suffering.

The principle is a long established part of customary international law which can be traced back to the 1868 St. Petersburg Declaration and to the Hague Regulations of 1899 and 1907. As was seen in Part III, the rationale for this principle is to be found in the broader principle of necessity in armed conflict, which prohibits wanton violence that serves no legitimate military purpose.[50] As well as providing a general yardstick against which all weapons and methods of warfare must be judged, the unnecessary suffering principle has provided much of the inspiration for agreements on specific weapons, such as those on explosive, inflammable and soft-headed or expanding bullets,[51] chemical and biological weapons,[52] poison,[53] and weapons which injure with fragments which cannot be detected by x-rays.[54] Some of these agreements go beyond the general principle in that they prohibit the use of such weapons even in circumstances where their use might not have been a violation of the general principle.[55]

The unnecessary suffering principle applies to both the methods and means of warfare. It prohibits outright any weapon (or means of warfare) which is of a nature to cause unnecessary suffering. In addition, where a particular weapon has a legitimate use but is also capable of being used in a way which will, in the circumstances, cause unnecessary suffering (and all weapons can be so used), the principle prohibits the latter use (or method of warfare) even though it does not give rise to an outright ban on the weapon itself.

The fact that a particular weapon or method of warfare causes severe or widespread injuries or death, or inflicts great pain, is not, in itself, sufficient to render its use incompatible with the unnecessary suffering principle. That

Christopher Greenwood

principle does not possess an absolute character; it does not prohibit the use of any weapon or method of warfare which causes extreme suffering or extensive injuries, but only those which cause injuries or suffering that are unnecessary. The application of the unnecessary suffering principle thus requires a balancing of the military advantage which may result from the use of a weapon with the degree of injury and suffering which it is likely to cause. As the Japanese court in the case of *Shimoda* v. *The State* put it, "the use of a certain weapon, great as its inhuman result may be, need not be prohibited by international law if it has a great military effect."[56]

This balancing act is, however, easier to state in the abstract than it is to apply, since one is not comparing like with like and there is considerable uncertainty regarding the factors to be placed on each side of the scales. A 1975 Conference of Experts held at Lucerne which considered this question agreed that the principle "involved some sort of equation between, on the one hand, the degree of injury or suffering inflicted (the humanitarian aspect) and, on the other, the degree of necessity underlying the choice of a particular weapon (the military aspect),"[57] but had more difficulty in agreeing on how this should best be applied. It is important, therefore, to examine the factors which should be taken into account on each side of the equation.

The Military Aspect. In determining what factors may be taken into account on the military side of the equation, the Preamble to the St. Petersburg Declaration provides a useful starting point.[58] The Declaration is based upon the premise that, since the legitimate objective of disabling an enemy combatant could be achieved with ordinary rifle ammunition, the "rifle shell" or exploding bullet merely exacerbated injury or rendered death inevitable and should therefore be prohibited. On the other hand, the high explosive shell, which was far more destructive and just as deadly, was excluded from this prohibition because it offered a distinct military advantage in that it could disable several combatants with one shot or destroy large quantities of property, and thus achieve military goals which ordinary rifle ammunition could not. In taking the decision which they did, the States represented at the 1868 Conference rejected two factors which might have been taken into account on the military side of the equation. First, they expressly rejected the argument that since a disabled enemy might recover and be able to fight again, the fact that a weapon made death inevitable was a legitimate military reason for employing that weapon in preference to others. The same reasoning is reflected more than a century later in the ban on weapons which injure with fragments that cannot be detected with x-rays. Secondly, there was an implicit rejection of the argument that the very savagery

The Law of Weaponry

of a weapon might be a legitimate military advantage because of the effect which it produced upon the morale of enemy combatants.[59]

As the first modern attempt to apply the unnecessary suffering principle in a specific case, the Declaration remains important. Nevertheless, in at least one respect it presents an over-simplified picture. The suggestion that the legitimate objectives of a belligerent can be achieved by disabling the greatest number of men overlooks the fact that there are other equally legitimate objectives, such as:

> [T]he destruction or neutralisation of enemy materiel, restriction of movement, interdiction of lines of communication, weakening of resources and, last but not least, enhancement of the security of friendly forces.[60]

It is generally accepted that the weapons needed to achieve such aims differ, both in character and effect, from those commonly used against personnel and may cause more serious injuries or make death more likely than would typical anti-personnel weapons. Nevertheless, their use does not violate the unnecessary suffering principle, because the advantages which they offer, in terms, for example, of their capacity to destroy materiel, means that this additional suffering cannot be characterized as unnecessary.[61]

The Humanitarian Aspect. Disagreement also exists about what factors should be taken into account on the "suffering" side of the equation. The Lucerne Conference considered that

> [T]his comprised such factors as mortality rates, the painfulness or severeness of wounds, or the incidence of permanent damage or disfigurement. Some experts considered that not only bodily harm but also psychological damage should be taken into account. Another expert could not accept such a wide interpretation of the concept at issue, as all wartime wounds, no matter how slight, could entail severe psychological harm.[62]

The present writer considers that the concept of "injury" or "suffering" includes the totality of a victim's injury, and that a distinction between physical and psychological injuries would be artificial, as well as having no basis in past practice concerning weaponry. A more difficult question is whether the effects of the victim's injuries upon the society from which he or she comes should be taken into account on this side of the equation— for example, the effect upon a society of having to cope with large numbers of limbless or blinded former combatants would invariably be serious and might well be disastrous. Such effects are, however, difficult to quantify and depend more upon the numbers injured than the nature of the injuries in any particular case.

Christopher Greenwood

A report published in 1997 by the International Committee of the Red Cross attempts to specify more precise criteria for determining whether a particular weapon causes unnecessary suffering.[63] The approach taken in this Report is to study the medical effects of existing weapons, i.e., the degree to which they cause death or particular types of injury, and suggest four sets of criteria to be used in determining whether a new weapon is one which violates the unnecessary suffering principle.

• Does the weapon foreseeably cause specific disease, specific abnormal physiological state, specific abnormal psychological state, specific and permanent disability, or specific disfigurement?

• Does the weapon foreseeably cause a field mortality of more than 25% or a hospital mortality of more than 5% (figures substantially in excess of those caused by weapons in use at present)?

• Are the weapons designed to cause particularly large wounds?

• Does the weapon foreseeably exert effects for which there is no well recognized and proven treatment?

The identification of these criteria and the medical study on which they are based is of considerable value in helping to show how the balancing act required by the unnecessary suffering principle can be made more precise and less anecdotal than at present. It is, however, important to realize that the fact that a particular weapon meets one of these criteria is not, in itself, sufficient to brand it as unlawful without consideration of the military advantages which that weapon may offer. For example, the fact that soldiers cannot take cover from a particular type of weapon will, as the report points out, heighten the reaction of abhorrence produced by such a weapon.[64] But it is also the very inability of soldiers to take cover that means that the weapon will, in the language of the 1868 Declaration, disable the greatest possible number of enemy combatants, and which thus gives it its military effectiveness when compared with other weapons.

Comparison Between Weapons. The essence of the unnecessary suffering principle is that it involves a comparison between different weapons in determining whether the injuries and suffering caused by a particular weapon are necessary. As Dr. Hans Blix has noted, "it is unlawful to use a weapon which causes more suffering or injury than another which offers the same or similar military advantages."[65] The 1868 Declaration was based, as has been seen, on precisely such a comparison. In many cases, however, making that comparison will be more difficult than might appear from a glance at the approach taken in 1868.

197

The Law of Weaponry

It is not enough simply to consider the immediate effects of the two weapons (or methods of warfare) which are being compared. It may well be the case that the one weapon offers the same or similar destructive capability and accuracy as another while causing less horrific injuries or a lower level of fatalities. Before it is concluded, however, that the use of the latter weapon would therefore cause unnecessary suffering, it is necessary to consider a number of other factors, in particular the availability (including the expense) of both types of weapon and the logistics of supplying the weapon and its ammunition at the place where it is to be used. A particularly important consideration will be the extent to which each type of weapon protects the security of the troops which employ it, for if the use of the first, more "humane," weapon will lead to significantly higher casualties amongst the force using it, then there is a valid military reason for using the second. A belligerent is not obliged to sacrifice members of its own armed forces in order to spare the enemy's combatants (as opposed to the enemy's civilian population) the effects of the fighting.[66] These considerations are as much part of the military advantages which the weapon offers as the effects which its use produces on the enemy.

Moreover, it has to be remembered that the degree of choice of weapons decreases as one goes down the chain of command. While those who plan or decide upon operations at the highest levels of command are likely to have a large range of weapons at their disposal and the battle group or task force commander retains a significant element of choice, the individual soldier does not, as Professor Kalshoven puts it, carry the military equivalent of a bag of golf clubs from which he can select the weapon appropriate to each task; usually that soldier has no element of choice of weapon at all.[67] This consideration is likely to be of considerable importance if, which has not hitherto been the case, individual servicemen face trial on charges of using illegal weapons.

The Effect of the Unnecessary Suffering Principle. Although it is the oldest principle of the law of weaponry and its continued significance has recently been reaffirmed by the International Court of Justice, in practice the unnecessary suffering principle has only very limited effects. In particular, it is difficult to find a single example of a weapon which has entered into service during the twentieth century and which is generally agreed to fall foul of this principle. There are several reasons why that is the case. First, if the question is whether the weapon itself, as opposed to its use in specific circumstances, contravenes the principle, there is disagreement about the test to be applied. At the Lucerne Conference, a paper submitted by a British military lawyer suggested that the principle would ban a weapon outright only when that weapon was "in practice found inevitably to cause injury or suffering

Christopher Greenwood

disproportionate to its military effectiveness."[68] Other experts contested the use of the word "inevitably" and argued that it was sufficient if the weapon caused such effects in its "normal" use. Article 35(2) of Additional Protocol I speaks of weapons "of a nature" to cause unnecessary suffering. It is doubtful whether the use of this formula offers any greater degree of clarity. In practice, if it can plausibly be argued that there is a significant range of cases in which a weapon can be used without causing unnecessary suffering, the weapon itself is unlikely to be regarded as unlawful under this principle. That conclusion is confirmed by the paucity of examples of contemporary weapons described in the literature as contravening the unnecessary suffering principle.[69] The result is that the unnecessary suffering principle has generally been more important in prohibiting particular uses of weapons (i.e., methods of warfare) than the weapons themselves.

Secondly, as has been seen, the criteria to be employed on both sides of the equation in the unnecessary suffering principle are far from clear. Moreover, even if the criteria themselves were clearer, it is frequently very difficult when a new weapon is developed for anyone outside the circle of those who have been responsible for its development to make an informed assessment of the military advantages which it offers or the medical effects which its use is likely to produce.

Finally, even when sufficient information about the weapon is available, a determination of whether or not its use would violate the unnecessary suffering principle requires a balancing of the likely military advantages and the likely human suffering which its use in the future will entail, and then a comparison between that balance and what would result from the use of alternative weapons. It is scarcely surprising that agreement on the outcome of applying such a test is seldom achieved.

(b) The Principle of Discrimination. The second general principle prohibits the use of indiscriminate weapons or—which is more important in practice—the indiscriminate use of any weapon, irrespective of whether that weapon is inherently indiscriminate. This principle is, in fact, a compound of three separate principles. First, it is well established in customary international law that it is unlawful to direct attacks against the civilian population, individual civilians or civilian property. Under the principle of distinction, a belligerent is required to distinguish between the enemy's combatants and military objectives on the one hand and the civilian population and civilian property on the other, and direct his attacks only against the former.[70] Secondly, even if the target of an attack is a legitimate military objective, the

The Law of Weaponry

principle of proportionality provides that it is prohibited to proceed with the attack if it:

> [M]ay be expected to cause incidental loss of civilian life, injury to civilians, damage to civilian objects or a combination thereof, which would be excessive in relation to the concrete and direct military advantage anticipated.[71]

Finally, if there is a choice of the methods or means of attack, there is a requirement to take all feasible precautions with a view to avoiding or minimizing incidental civilian casualties and damage.[72]

These principles go primarily to the question of targeting, a matter which falls outside the scope of this paper.[73] Nevertheless, they also have an effect upon the law of weaponry. If a weapon is incapable of being used in a way which permits discrimination between military targets and civilians or civilian objects, then it is inherently indiscriminate and these principles render it unlawful. In practice, very few weapons are so inaccurate that they cannot be used in a way which complies with the principles set out in the preceding paragraph, although the V1 and V2 missiles used by Germany in the Second World War probably fell into that category.[74] A far more common case of conduct prohibited by these principles is the indiscriminate use of a weapon which is capable of being used in a discriminating way. Iraq's use of Scud missiles during the Gulf hostilities in 1991 is an example.[75]

These principles are some of the most important cornerstones of the law of armed conflict. They were so widely disregarded during the Second World War that it was open to question whether they could still be regarded as part of the customary law. Since 1945, however, they have been reaffirmed on a number of occasions, most recently in Additional Protocol I, and were applied by, for example, the Coalition States in the operations against Iraq in 1991.[76] Their status as part of the contemporary customary law cannot now be doubted. While difficulties in their application remain, Protocol I has resolved a great many problems. In particular, it has clarified the principle that attacks must be directed only against military objectives by offering a workable definition of a military objective and has made clear that in applying the test of proportionality, only a "concrete and direct military advantage," rather than a nebulous concept such as the effect on enemy morale, is to be weighed against the effect of an attack upon the civilian population.

The principles contain both absolute and relative elements. The principle of distinction possesses an absolute character—civilians and civilian objects must never knowingly be made the object of attack and care must be taken to ensure that any target is, in fact, a legitimate military objective.[77] The principle of

Christopher Greenwood

proportionality, on the other hand, involves a balancing of the military advantages to be gained from an attack upon a military target against expected civilian losses and damage. As with the principle of unnecessary suffering, if those same military advantages can be achieved in different ways, one of which involves likely civilian casualties whereas the other does not, then the choice of the first route will entail a violation of the principle. However, the same qualifications apply here. In determining whether a commander who possesses a choice of weapons or methods of warfare should select one rather than the other, the extent to which both are truly available to him (in the light of such considerations as the likely future calls on precision munitions, the protection of his own forces and the logistic questions considered in the previous section) must be examined. The difference is that, although the security of his own forces remains an important part of this calculation, the need to reduce the risk to the civilian population means that a commander may be required to accept a higher degree of risk to his own forces.

Where the proportionality principle differs from the unnecessary suffering principle is that it is clearly established that it does not stop at the prohibition of unnecessary collateral injury and damage, but also requires a belligerent to abstain from an attack altogether, even if that means losing a military advantage which cannot be obtained by other means, if the military advantage would not be worth the expected civilian casualties and damage. The principle of proportionality is thus a more substantial constraint than the unnecessary suffering principle. Nevertheless, it remains a requirement to balance military gains against civilian losses; it does not possess an absolute character. In this respect, the Commentary on Additional Protocol I published by the International Committee of the Red Cross is misleading when it says that:

> The idea has been put forward that even if they are very high, civilian losses and damage may be justified if the military advantage at stake is of great importance. This idea is contrary to the fundamental rules of the Protocol. . . . The Protocol does not provide any justification for attacks which cause extensive civilian losses and damage. Incidental losses and damage should never be extensive.[78]

What the principle of proportionality (as stated in both customary law and the Protocol) prohibits is the causing of *excessive* civilian losses and damage. By substituting the word *extensive*, the Commentary replaces a term which necessarily implies a balance between two competing considerations with a term which suggests an absolute ceiling on civilian losses. There is no basis in the law for such an approach.

The Law of Weaponry

The Gulf conflict of 1990-91 demonstrated that the principles which are designed to protect the civilian population are workable. That conflict, however, also highlighted the fact that the proportionality test today requires consideration of a wider range of issues than in the past. In the Gulf conflict, Coalition air raids and naval bombardment of military targets appear to have caused relatively few direct civilian losses, but the damage done to the Iraqi power generating system and other parts of Iraq's infrastructure did far more harm to the civilian population. Application of the proportionality test today, at least at the strategic level, requires that less immediate damage of this kind must also be taken into account, although the difficulty of doing so is apparent.

The treaty statements of the discrimination principles do not apply to naval warfare except in so far as it involves the civilian population on land. Nevertheless, it is clear that there are restrictions on targeting in naval warfare.[79] In particular, merchant ships are not automatically to be treated as legitimate targets unless they engage in certain kinds of behaviour. It has therefore been suggested in a recent study that the principles of distinction and proportionality are applicable, *mutatis mutandis*, as part of the customary law of naval warfare, with consequent implications for the law of weaponry in a naval context.[80]

(c) The Prohibition of Perfidy. The principle which prohibits the use of perfidy is well established in both customary international law and Additional Protocol I. The somewhat mixed objectives which this principle seeks to achieve have already been discussed in Part III and little more need be said here. There is probably no weapon which is inherently perfidious,[81] and the principle therefore operates entirely upon the methods of warfare.

The humanitarian rationale of this principle is concisely set out in Article 37(1) of Additional Protocol I as "inviting the confidence of an adversary to lead him to believe that he is entitled to, or is obliged to accord, protection under the rules of international law applicable in armed conflict, with intent to betray that confidence." The provision then goes on to give the following examples of perfidy:

> (a) the feigning of an intent to negotiate under a flag of truce or of a surrender;
> (b) the feigning of an incapacitation by wounds or sickness;
> (c) the feigning of civilian, non-combatant status; and
> (d) the feigning of protected status by the use of signs, emblems or uniforms of the United Nations or of neutral or other States not Parties to the conflict.

202

Christopher Greenwood

Article 38 adds a specific prohibition on the improper use of the emblems (principally the Red Cross and Red Crescent) of the Geneva Conventions and internationally recognized protective emblems, such as the flag of truce, as well as any unauthorized use of the United Nations emblem.[82] By contrast, Article 37(2) provides that:

> Ruses of war are not prohibited. Such ruses are acts which are intended to mislead an adversary or to induce him to act recklessly but which infringe no rule of international law applicable in armed conflict and which are not perfidious because they do not invite the confidence of an adversary with respect to protection under that law. The following are examples of such ruses: the use of camouflage, decoys, mock operations and misinformation.

As has already been seen, these provisions, which reflect customary international law, serve a clear humanitarian objective. The prohibition in Article 39(1) of the use by belligerents of the flags, emblems, and uniforms of neutral States or other States not party to the conflict also serves that objective, since it also seeks to protect persons and objects which would not be legitimate targets of attack. That is not true, however, of the rule in Article 39(2) which forbids the use of *enemy* flags and uniforms by a belligerent while engaging in an attack or in order to shield, favor, protect, or impede military operations. The objective behind the latter rule is quite different and serves no obvious humanitarian purpose.[83]

Traditionally, the law on ruses in naval warfare has been different. In naval warfare, the use of enemy flags and signals is entirely legitimate up to the point at which an attack is commenced.[84] There is, therefore, no equivalent of the rule in Article 39(2) of Additional Protocol I (which is expressly stated not to apply to naval warfare).[85] The principles in Articles 37 and 38 of the Protocol are intended to apply to all forms of warfare, but their application to naval hostilities necessitates some modification to take account of the different conditions of naval warfare. The *San Remo Manual on International Law Applicable to Armed Conflicts at Sea* states the basic principle of perfidy in the same terms used in Additional Protocol I, Article 37(1), and adds, as specific examples of perfidious behavior:

> . . . the launching of an attack while feigning:
>
> (a) exempt, civilian, neutral or protected United Nations status;
> (b) surrender or distress by, e.g., sending a distress signal or by the crew taking to life rafts.[86]

The Law of Weaponry

This provision was supported by a large group of experts and is in accordance with the approach taken in the United States *Naval Commander's Handbook*.[87] It is open to question, however, whether sub-paragraph (a) reflects customary law, since the practice of disguising warships as merchant vessels and the use of Q-ships was extensively practised during the Second World War and there is no clear practice to the contrary since that date.[88]

The *San Remo Manual* also states that:

> Ruses of war are permitted. Warships and auxiliary vessels, however, are prohibited from launching an attack whilst flying a false flag, and at all times from actively simulating the status of:
>
> (a) hospital ships, small coastal rescue craft or medical transports;
> (b) vessels on humanitarian missions;
> (c) passenger vessels carrying civilian passengers;
> (d) vessels protected by the United Nations flag;
> (e) vessels guaranteed safe conduct by prior agreement between the parties, including cartel vessels;
> (f) vessels entitled to be identified by the emblem of the red cross or red crescent; or
> (g) vessels engaged in transporting cultural property under special protection.[89]

(d) The Principle of Environmental Protection. A number of specific rules of the law of armed conflict operate, expressly or impliedly, to protect the natural environment. Thus, the 1977 Environmental Modification Treaty addresses the potential problem of a belligerent seeking to use the environment as a means of warfare in itself by prohibiting the use of environmental modification techniques which have widespread, long-lasting, or severe effects upon the environment.[90] This treaty, however, deals with the exceptional case of the deliberate manipulation of the environment for military purposes, rather than the far more common case of environmental damage inflicted in the course of ordinary military operations. To some extent, the prohibition of the wanton destruction of property and the use of chemical and biological weapons, as well as the restrictions on the use of land mines and incendiary weapons indirectly protect the environment. Today, however, it is argued that there is a broader, general principle of respect for the environment in time of armed conflict.[91]

For States party to Additional Protocol I, such a principle is to be found in Article 35(3), which states that:

Christopher Greenwood

> It is prohibited to employ methods or means of warfare which are intended, or may be expected, to cause widespread, long-term and severe damage to the natural environment.[92]

This provision was, however, an innovation in 1977 and cannot be regarded as forming part of customary international law.[93]

Nevertheless, there are clear indications that a general principle of environmental respect is emerging and may well already form part of customary law. Thus, the 1995 edition of the U.S. *Commander's Handbook on the Law of Naval Operations* stipulates that:

> It is not unlawful to cause collateral damage to the natural environment during an attack upon a legitimate military objective. However, the commander has an affirmative obligation to avoid unnecessary damage to the environment to the extent that it is practicable to do so consistent with mission accomplishment. To that end, and as far as military requirements permit, methods or means of warfare should be employed with due regard to the protection and preservation of the natural environment. Destruction of the natural environment not necessitated by mission accomplishment and carried out wantonly is prohibited. Therefore, a commander should consider the environmental damage which will result from an attack on a legitimate military objective as one of the factors during target analysis.[94]

In its *Advisory Opinion on the Legality of the Threat or Use of Nuclear Weapons*, the International Court of Justice stated that:

> States must take environmental considerations into account when assessing what is necessary and proportionate in the pursuit of legitimate military objectives. Respect for the environment is one of the elements that go to assessing whether an action is in conformity with the principles of necessity and proportionality.[95]

The United Nations General Assembly has expressed similar views.[96] While the language may be different in each case, the general sense is substantially the same.[97]

(e) *Other General Principles.* Before leaving the subject of the general principles, it is necessary to consider whether any other general principle may have become part of the law of weaponry. There is, of course, the principle that the right of the parties to an armed conflict to choose the methods and means of warfare is not unlimited.[98] This principle is not, however, a free-standing norm, since it gives no indication what the limitations upon the right to choose

The Law of Weaponry

might be. It serves only to introduce the limitations, both general and specific, laid down elsewhere in the law.

A more substantial contender is the Martens Clause, which first appeared in the Preamble to Hague Convention No. II of 1899. The most recent version of this clause appears as Article 1(2) of Additional Protocol I:

> In cases not covered by this Protocol or by other international agreements, civilians and combatants remain under the protection and authority of the principles of international law derived from established custom, from the principles of humanity and from the dictates of the public conscience.

It has sometimes been argued that the use of a particular weapon or method of warfare might be unlawful, as a result of the Martens Clause, even though it was not outlawed by any of the general principles or specific provisions of the law of weaponry.[99] According to this approach, a weapon will be unlawful if its effects are so contrary to considerations of humanity and the public conscience that it arouses widespread revulsion. This view is based upon a misunderstanding of the Martens Clause. There is no doubt that one effect of the Clause is that the absence of a specific treaty provision does not mean that a weapon must be lawful; the Clause makes clear that the general principles embodied in customary law still apply and that the use of a weapon contrary to those principles will be unlawful. Furthermore, the Martens Clause undoubtedly states what has frequently been the motivating force behind the adoption of a specific ban (e.g., those on land mines and laser weapons). There is no evidence, however, that the use of any weapon has ever been treated by the international community as unlawful solely on account of the Martens Clause and the Clause should not be regarded as laying down a separate general principle for judging the legality of weapons under existing law.[100]

Finally, it can reasonably be said that the undoubted duty to respect the territorial integrity of neutral States implies the existence of a general principle that the belligerents must abstain from the use of methods and means of warfare which cause disproportionate damage to the territory of neutral States. This principle has only very limited significance for the use of weapons other than nuclear weapons and it is in that context that it will be considered below.

(2) Rules on Specific Weapons. The evolution of the treaty provisions regulating the use of specific weapons has already been outlined in Part II. Unlike the general principles of the law of weaponry, these specific provisions tend to concentrate upon the means used (e.g., exploding bullets of less than 400 grammes weight, laser weapons, chemical weapons), rather than the

Christopher Greenwood

effects produced (e.g., unnecessary suffering, disproportionate civilian casualties). They fall into three broad groups:

- Limitations on the use of a particular weapon which fall short of an outright ban;
- Bans on the use, but not the possession and, perhaps, not the retaliatory use, of a particular weapon; and
- Bans on both use and possession.

It is not intended in this paper to try to analyze all of the specific weapons provisions. Instead, three categories of weapons—laser weapons, land mines, and chemical weapons—which have been the subject of important legal changes in the 1990s, and which illustrate the three categories set out above, will be examined.

(a) The Lasers Protocol. In October 1995, a Conference was convened under the provisions of Article 8(3) of the 1981 Weapons Convention to review the scope and operation of the Convention and its three Protocols. One of the items on the agenda of the Review Conference was a proposal for the adoption of a new protocol to the Weapons Convention to ban the use of anti-personnel laser weapons (a type of weapon not then in common use but which it was believed would be widely available before long) on the ground that such weapons would cause permanent blindness. This issue had been under consideration by the International Committee of the Red Cross for several years.[101] It had been argued by some commentators that the use of laser weapons to blind enemy combatants was already prohibited by the unnecessary suffering principle.[102] That conclusion was challenged, however, by others who argued that a blinding weapon could not be regarded as causing *unnecessary* suffering when the alternative weapons could cause death.[103] In fact, the arguments are finely balanced and the unnecessary suffering principle probably does not outlaw the use of anti-personnel lasers as such, although it might prohibit their use in certain circumstances.[104] In view of this difference of opinion and the uncertainty inherent in the application of the unnecessary suffering principle, the opponents of anti-personnel lasers not surprisingly decided that it was necessary to seek a specific ban.

In this case, the approach of seeking to eliminate an entire category of weapons was never an option. Lasers are used on the battlefield for a wide range of undoubtedly legitimate purposes, including target identification and range finding, which would not normally involve injury to eyesight and which States were not willing to abandon. In addition, several States distinguished between the use of lasers against the human eye and their use against equipment optical systems, where there was a risk of incidental injury to the human eye.

The Law of Weaponry

The new agreement,[105] adopted by the Review Conference as Protocol IV to the Weapons Convention, reflects these views. Article 1 prohibits the employment of "laser weapons specifically designed, as their sole combat function or as one of their combat functions, to cause permanent blindness to unenhanced vision, that is to the naked eye or to the eye with corrective eyesight devices." The use of laser weapons which do not have as one of their combat functions the causing of permanent blindness to the naked eye is not, therefore, prohibited and, if blindness is caused as a collateral consequence of the use of such a weapon, or the use of other laser systems such as range finders, there will be no violation of the Protocol.[106] Article 2 of the Protocol, however, requires the parties to take all feasible precautions, when using laser systems not prohibited by the Protocol, to avoid causing blindness to the unenhanced vision of enemy combatants.

The result is a treaty that bans the use of a fairly narrow category of weapons—laser weapons specifically designed to cause blindness. The use of other types of laser weapon, even if it results in blindness, remains lawful. At the time of writing, the Protocol had not yet entered into force. When it does, it will be binding only upon those States parties to the Weapons Convention which opt to become bound by Protocol IV.

(b) *Land Mines.* Unlike laser weapons, land mines have been the subject of a sustained campaign during the 1990s to achieve a total ban. Whereas the concern about blinding laser weapons centered on the unnecessary suffering principle, the move to ban land mines was motivated more by the effects which their use had been shown to have upon the civilian population, often long after the conflict. Nevertheless, while the indiscriminate use of land mines was a violation of the general principle of distinction, they were also capable of lawful use, against military targets or as a means of denying an adversary access to an area of land.

Protocol II to the Weapons Convention already contained limitations on the use of land mines and booby-traps.[107] So far as mines[108] were concerned, the original Protocol II limited their use in the following ways:

• By prohibiting their use against civilians and their indiscriminate use (Article 3), although this added nothing to the general principles on targeting;

• By imposing a more specific restriction on the use of mines in centers of civilian population where combat was not actually taking place (Article 4);

• By prohibiting the use of remotely delivered mines unless they are used within an area which is itself a military objective and either their location is accurately recorded or they are fitted with a self-neutralizing mechanism which

Christopher Greenwood

will render the mine harmless or destroy it when it no longer serves the military purpose for which it was laid (Article 5); and

• By requiring the recording and publication of the location of minefields and co-operation in their removal after a conflict (Articles 7 and 9).

The provisions of the Protocol are very limited. Only Article 5 imposed a substantial limitation and this is "clumsily worded."[109] Not surprisingly, these provisions were widely regarded as insufficient in view of the devastating effects of land mines—often continuing for many years after the end of active hostilities.[110] A number of States therefore pressed for a complete ban on land mines, while others urged the Review Conference to tighten the restrictions in Protocol II.

The first result was the adoption in 1996 of an amended Protocol II[111] which goes some way towards tightening the restrictions on the use of land mines and increasing the protection of the civilian population. The most important changes introduced by the amendments are as follows:

• A ban on the use of various devices which make mine clearance more dangerous (Article 3(5) and (6));

• A ban on the use of anti-personnel mines which are not detectable, as specified in the technical annex to the Protocol (Article 4);

• Restrictions on the use of mines which do not meet the requirements in the technical annex (Article 5). The technical annex requires that mines produced after 1 January 1997 must meet certain requirements regarding detection and self-neutralization and their location must be carefully recorded;

• Stricter constraints on the use of remotely delivered mines (Article 6);

• Stricter rules for the protection of peacekeepers and others not directly involved in the conflict (Article 12) and for the protection of civilians (Article 3(8) to (11));

• A more extensive obligation regarding mine clearance after the conflict (Articles 10 and 11); and

• A prohibition on the transfer of mines which do not meet the requirements of the Protocol and limitations on the transfer of mines which do meet those requirements (Article 8).

The amended Protocol II is thus considerably more stringent than the original Protocol. Whether it will succeed in significantly reducing the threat posed to civilians by mines is another matter. One of the biggest threats to civilians is the large numbers of old mines, readily available and cheap, which do not meet the requirements of the amended Protocol and which are likely to be used by untrained personnel. This risk is particularly acute in civil wars; indeed, it is in the civil wars in Angola and Cambodia that some of the worst casualties from

The Law of Weaponry

land mines have been sustained. It is therefore an important development that the amended Protocol is expressly applied to internal armed conflicts within the meaning of common Article 3 of the Geneva Conventions, where it applies both to the government and rebel parties.[112] Since the other Protocols to the Weapons Convention contain no provision on the scope of their application, they apply only in the circumstances specified in Article 1 of the Weapons Convention itself, namely international armed conflicts, including wars of "national liberation" as defined in Article 1(4) of Additional Protocol I to the Geneva Conventions. It has, however, been suggested, notwithstanding the absence of any express provision regarding internal conflicts in the new Protocol IV, that Protocol was also intended to apply to internal armed conflicts,[113] although no trace of such an understanding is to be found in its text.

The amended Protocol II did not go far enough for a large body of States. They aimed instead at a complete ban on the use and transfer of land mines and, to that end, adopted a separate treaty in 1997. The United Nations Convention on the Prohibition of the Use, Stockpiling, Production and Transfer of Anti-Personnel Mines and on their Destruction, as its name suggests, is a complete ban on the use of anti-personnel land mines.[114] The Convention, the Preamble of which echoes the language of the Martens Clause and refers specifically to both the unnecessary suffering principle and the principle of distinction, goes beyond a ban on the use of anti-personnel mines "in all circumstances" and bans their production, stockpiling, and possession, as well as the transfer of such mines to others. The definition of an anti-personnel mine, however, excludes mines "designed to be detonated by the presence, proximity or contact of a vehicle as opposed to a person," even if equipped with anti-handling devices.[115] The Convention requires that all parties take steps, including the imposition of penal sanctions, to ensure implementation of its provisions.[116] While the conclusion of this Convention was a triumph for the opponents of land mines, its effectiveness is likely to be limited as a number of major military powers have declined to participate.

Once the 1997 Convention and the amended Protocol II enter into force, there will be a complex network of obligations regarding land mines:

• States party to the 1997 Convention will be obliged not to employ anti-personnel land mines in any circumstances, even in hostilities with States not party to the Convention;

• States party to the 1980 Conventional Weapons Convention which elect to become party to the amended Protocol II will be bound by that Protocol in their relations with other States party to the 1980 Convention which have accepted that Protocol;

Christopher Greenwood

• States party to the 1980 Conventional Weapons Convention which elect not to become party to the amended Protocol II will remain bound by the original Protocol II in their relations with other parties which have made the same choice; and

• States not party to the 1980 Convention or which have not accepted either version of Protocol II will remain subject in their use of land mines only to the customary law general principles on unnecessary suffering and distinction and other States will be subject to the same regime in their relations with such States (unless, of course, they are parties to the 1997 Convention).

As students of the law will doubtless testify, multiplicity of law making bodies has its price.

(c) Chemical Weapons. By far the most important development in the law of weaponry during the last decade of the twentieth century has been the adoption in 1993 of a new Chemical Weapons Convention.[117] The use of chemical weapons in warfare had already been prohibited by the 1925 Geneva Protocol.[118] That prohibition, however, was incomplete in a number of respects. In particular, so many States had entered reservations to the 1925 Protocol, to the effect that they retained the right to use chemical weapons if those weapons were first used against themselves or their allies, that the Protocol was, in reality, only a ban on the first use of such weapons.[119] The use of chemical weapons by Iraq, first against Iranian armed forces and later against parts of Iraq's own civilian population, during the Iran-Iraq war,[120] and the threats by Iraq to use chemical weapons during the Kuwait conflict,[121] highlighted the weakness of the existing legal regime. The prohibition on the use of chemical weapons was reaffirmed by a declaration adopted by 149 States at the Paris Conference in January 1989. Subsequent negotiations led to the adoption of the new convention in 1993. The Convention entered into force in April 1997.

The 1993 Convention establishes a legal regime far more extensive than that contained in the 1925 Protocol and customary international law. While space does not permit a detailed analysis of the provisions of the 1993 Convention here,[122] three points call for comment. First, the scope of the 1993 Convention is broader than that of the 1925 Protocol. The range of weapons covered by the 1925 Protocol had long been the subject of debate, with the United States, and latterly the United Kingdom, arguing that non-lethal riot control agents lay outside the scope of the Protocol,[123] an interpretation contested by many other States. The new Convention expressly prohibits the use of riot control agents "as a method of warfare."[124] While this prohibition still leaves some room for debate about whether a particular use of riot control agents (for example, to suppress a riot at a prisoner of war camp or to deal with

The Law of Weaponry

demonstrators in occupied territory) constitutes their use "as a method of warfare," it clearly outlaws the use of riot control agents against enemy forces in combat or in bombardment of enemy targets. In addition, the obligation placed upon States parties by Article I, paragraph 1, never to use chemical weapons "under any circumstances" applies to non-international armed conflicts, as well as to conflicts between States.[125] While it had been argued by some States and commentators that the prohibition in the 1925 Protocol was also applicable to non-international conflicts,[126] the matter was not free from doubt and the greater clarity of the new Convention is thus most welcome.

Secondly, the 1993 Convention prohibits *all* use of chemical weapons in warfare, not just their *first* use. The obligation never to use chemical weapons in any circumstances, contained in Article I, was intended to exclude the operation of the doctrine of belligerent reprisals as a justification for employing chemical weapons. In addition, Article XXII provides that the Convention is not subject to reservations, so that there is no scope for States to become parties subject to the kind of reservations which many entered on becoming parties to the 1925 Protocol. That does not mean that a State which was the victim of a chemical attack in violation of the Convention may not retaliate. The Convention prohibits retaliation in kind, in the form of a chemical counter-attack, but it does not affect the right of States to retaliate by other means. In this context, a particularly important question is whether a State could lawfully resort to the use of a nuclear weapon in response to a chemical attack. This possibility was considered at some length by Judge Schwebel in his dissenting opinion in the *Nuclear Weapons* case, where he discussed the threat of nuclear retaliation allegedly made by the United States to dissuade Iraq from resorting to chemical weapons during the Kuwait conflict.[127] In the writer's view, the Court's advisory opinion in the *Nuclear Weapons* case leaves open the question whether such a reprisal would be lawful.

Finally, the 1993 Convention goes far beyond a prohibition on the use of chemical weapons and outlaws their manufacture, acquisition, stockpiling, and transfer.[128] It also requires States to destroy their existing stocks.[129] The Convention creates a complex regime of inspection and verification, which goes beyond that envisaged by the Land Mines Convention, the object of which is to guarantee that chemical weapons are completely eliminated. This ambitious project takes the Convention out of the scope of the law of armed conflict and into the realm of arms control. It remains to be seen whether some of the doubts expressed about the effectiveness of this regime can be overcome and the goal of the Convention attained.

Christopher Greenwood

(3) Nuclear Weapons.[130] Nuclear weapons merit separate consideration, both because of their inherent importance and because of the intensity of the debate about whether their use could ever be compatible with the law of weaponry. Those who argue that it could not have tended to base their case on one or more of three propositions.

• That there exists in international law a specific prohibition of the use of nuclear weapons. Since there is evidently no treaty of general application containing such a prohibition, this argument is based upon a series of resolutions adopted by the United Nations General Assembly over the years;[131]

• That one of the other specific prohibitions applies directly, or by analogy, to nuclear weapons. The prohibitions on which reliance is usually placed being those on chemical weapons and poisoned weapons; and

• That any use of nuclear weapons would inevitably violate one or more of the general principles of the law of weaponry.

These arguments have been fully canvassed both in the literature[132] and in the submissions of certain States to the International Court of Justice in the proceedings on the request for an *Advisory Opinion on the Legality of the Threat or Use of Nuclear Weapons.*[133]

Those who take a contrary view do not, for the most part, deny that the law of weaponry is applicable to nuclear weapons. Indeed, it is striking that none of the nuclear-weapon-States which made submissions to the International Court of Justice took such a position.[134] The only respect in which the law of weaponry does not apply to nuclear weapons is that the innovative provisions introduced by Additional Protocol I were adopted on the understanding that they would not apply to the use of nuclear weapons.[135] They maintain, however, that there is no specific prohibition of the use of nuclear weapons in international law, that the prohibitions on chemical weapons and poison do not extend to nuclear weapons, and that it is possible to envisage circumstances in which nuclear weapons could be used without violating the general principles.

In some respects, the Court's Advisory Opinion has clarified the issues in this debate.[136] The Court found (by eleven votes to three) that there was no specific prohibition of nuclear weapons, the majority taking the view that the General Assembly resolutions were insufficient to create a rule of customary international law in view of the strong opposition and contrary practice of a significant number of States.[137] The Court also rejected the argument that nuclear weapons were covered by the prohibitions on chemical weapons or poisoned weapons. The Court found that the various treaties on chemical and biological weapons had "each been adopted in its own context and for its own

The Law of Weaponry

reasons" and concluded that the prohibition of other weapons of mass destruction did not imply the prohibition of nuclear weapons, while the ban on poisoned weapons had never been understood by States to apply to nuclear weapons.[138]

Given the Court's conclusions on these points (which, it is submitted, are manifestly correct), the Court necessarily concentrated on the application to nuclear weapons of the general principles. The Court referred, in particular, to the prohibition of weapons calculated to cause unnecessary suffering, the prohibition of attacks upon civilians and of the use of indiscriminate methods and means of warfare, and the principle protecting neutral States from incursions onto their territory. Although the Court noted that the use of nuclear weapons was "scarcely reconcilable" with respect for these principles, it concluded that it did not have:

> [S]ufficient elements to enable it to conclude with certainty that the use of nuclear weapons would necessarily be at variance with the principles and rules of law applicable in armed conflict in any circumstance.[139]

This passage suggests that the Court should therefore have concluded that the use of nuclear weapons was not unlawful in all circumstances. In fact, however, it adopted, by seven votes to seven on the casting vote of the President, the following conclusion:

> It follows from the above-mentioned requirements that the threat or use of nuclear weapons would generally be contrary to the rules of international law applicable in armed conflict, and in particular the principles and rules of humanitarian law;

> However, in view of the current state of international law, and of the elements of fact at its disposal, the Court cannot conclude definitively whether the threat or use of nuclear weapons would be lawful or unlawful in an extreme circumstance of self-defence, in which the very survival of a State would be at stake.[140]

The Opinion is not easy to follow at this point. In the absence of a specific prohibition of the use of nuclear weapons, the only basis upon which the Court could have concluded, consistently with its own earlier reasoning, that such use was illegal in all circumstances would have been by analyzing the circumstances in which nuclear weapons might be used and then applying the principles of humanitarian law which were relevant. At the heart of any such analysis would have been three questions.

Christopher Greenwood

- Would the use of a nuclear weapon in the particular circumstances inflict *unnecessary* suffering upon combatants?

- Would the use of a nuclear weapon in the particular circumstances be directed against civilians or indiscriminate, or, even if directed against a military target, be likely to cause *disproportionate* civilian casualties ?

- Would the use of a nuclear weapon in the particular circumstances be likely to cause *disproportionate* harmful effects to a neutral State ?

To answer those questions would have required both a factual appreciation of the capabilities of the weapon being used and the circumstances of its use and a value judgement about whether the adverse consequences of that use were "unnecessary" or "disproportionate" when balanced against the military goals which the State using the nuclear weapon was seeking to achieve.

The Court did not, however, attempt that task but merely enumerated the relevant principles, with little discussion, before reaching the conclusions quoted above.[141] It is not clear, therefore, how it arrived at its conclusion that the use of nuclear weapons would "*generally* be contrary to the rules of international law applicable in armed conflict," nor, indeed, what it meant by the term "generally" in this context. It is clear, both from the voting on paragraph 2E of the *dispositif* and from some of the separate and dissenting opinions, that there was a considerable divergence of views within the Court.

Nevertheless, if one looks at the Opinion as a whole, the only interpretation of the first part of paragraph 2E which can be reconciled with the reasoning of the Court is that, even without the qualification in the second part of the paragraph, the Court was not saying that the use of nuclear weapons would be contrary to the law of armed conflict in all cases. It could only have reached such a conclusion if it had found that there were no circumstances in which nuclear weapons could be used without causing unnecessary suffering, striking civilians and military targets indiscriminately (or with excessive civilian casualties), or causing disproportionate damage to neutral States. The Court did not make such an analysis, and the reasoning gives no hint that it reached such a conclusion. Indeed, it is difficult to see how it could have done so. In considering the application of principles of such generality to the use of weapons in an indefinite variety of circumstances, the Court could not have determined that as a matter of *law* a nuclear weapon could not be used without violating one or more of those principles,[142] even if some of its members suspected as a matter of *fact* that that was so.

This reading of the Opinion is reinforced by the fact that there is only one other basis upon which the second part of paragraph 2E of the *dispositif* could make sense. That is that, although the use of nuclear weapons would always be

The Law of Weaponry

contrary to the law of armed conflict, the Court was not prepared to exclude the possibility that there might be circumstances in which the right of a State to self-defense could override the prohibition imposed by the law of armed conflict. Although that interpretation has received a measure of support,[143] it flies in the face of the long established principle that the law of armed conflict applies equally to both sides in a conflict. To hold that the party exercising the right of self-defense can depart from fundamental principles of the law of armed conflict would drive a coach and horses through that principle.[144]

The Court's Opinion has attracted an enormous amount of interest among academic commentators. It is a mark of the ambiguity of the Opinion in general and of paragraph 2E in particular, that some commentators have seen it as largely vindicating the position of the nuclear-weapons States, while others have claimed it as a victory for the anti-nuclear lobby.[145] The present writer finds the analysis of the first group the more persuasive.

V. The Applicability to Weaponry of Other Rules of International Law

It is tempting to take the view that once States resort to the use of force, the law of armed conflict, as *lex specialis*, takes over from all other parts of international law. On this view, the use of methods and means of warfare is governed exclusively by the law of weaponry. In practice, however, that law does not operate in isolation and the rest of international law cannot be disregarded in determining whether the use of a particular weapon is lawful. Three other areas of international law, all of which were considered by the International Court of Justice in its *Advisory Opinion on the Legality of the Threat or Use of Nuclear Weapons*, are potentially relevant.

First, it has sometimes been suggested that the use of particular weapons, especially nuclear weapons, would violate the right to life under human rights treaties.[146] The United Nations Human Rights Committee, for example, has commented that "the designing, testing, manufacture, possession and deployment of nuclear weapons are amongst the greatest threats to the right to life which confront mankind today."[147] However, warfare invariably involves the taking of life and it is clear that the human rights treaties were not intended to outlaw all military action even in self-defense. By prohibiting the *arbitrary* taking of life, Article 6 of the 1966 International Covenant on Civil and Political Rights, and the comparable provisions in other human rights treaties, imply that not all taking of life is prohibited. The *travaux préparatoires* of Article 6 make clear that, in the context of warfare, the term "arbitrary" was intended to mean the taking of life in circumstances which

Christopher Greenwood

were contrary to the law of armed conflict, and killing in the course of a "lawful act of war" was expressly given as an example of a taking of life that would not be arbitrary.[148]

This was the view taken by the International Court of Justice in the *Nuclear Weapons* case. The Court accepted that the protection of the International Covenant (and, by implication, other human rights treaties) did not cease in time of armed conflict but held that:

> The test of what is an arbitrary deprivation of life, however, then falls to be determined by the applicable *lex specialis*, namely, the law applicable in armed conflict, which is designed to regulate the conduct of hostilities. Thus whether a particular loss of life, through the use of a certain weapon in warfare, is to be considered an arbitrary deprivation of life contrary to Article 6 of the Covenant, can only be decided by reference to the law applicable in armed conflict and not deduced from the terms of the Covenant itself.[149]

This conclusion, though no doubt unwelcome to some human rights lawyers, is plainly correct in view both of State practice and the *travaux préparatoires* of the Covenant. Nevertheless, the Court's acceptance that human rights treaties continue to apply in time of war (except insofar as derogation is expressly permitted) may be of considerable importance in other cases. Although the right to life may add nothing to international humanitarian law at the substantive level, human rights treaties contain unique mechanisms for enforcement which may be of great assistance to individuals seeking to rely upon the right to life in order to show that there has been a violation of the law of armed conflict.[150]

Secondly, it has been suggested, again primarily in relation to nuclear weapons, that international environmental law is applicable to the use of weapons.[151] In the *Nuclear Weapons* case, the Court stated that "the issue is not whether the treaties relating to the protection of the environment are or are not applicable during an armed conflict, but rather whether the obligations stemming from these treaties were intended to be obligations of total restraint during military conflict."[152] It rejected the argument that the use of nuclear weapons was prohibited as such by the general environmental treaties or by customary environmental law.[153] It would have been extraordinary for the Court to have concluded that nuclear weapon States, which had so carefully ensured that treaties on weaponry and the law of armed conflict did not outlaw the use of nuclear weapons, had relinquished any possibility of their use by becoming parties to more general environmental agreements. Nevertheless, the Court indicated that the international law on the environment does not

The Law of Weaponry

altogether cease to apply once an armed conflict breaks out, and it seems that it found the origins of what it identified as a customary law duty of regard for the environment in times of war[154] as much in the general law on the environment as in the specific provisions of the law of armed conflict.

Finally, the *Nuclear Weapons* case confirms that:

> A threat or use of force by means of nuclear weapons that is contrary to Article 2, paragraph 4 of the United Nations Charter and that fails to meet all the requirements of Article 51, is unlawful. [155]

This proposition was not contested by any of the States which submitted arguments to the Court.

The Court held that the right of self-defense under Article 51 of the Charter was subject to the limitations of proportionality and necessity which it had earlier held, in the *Nicaragua* case,[156] were part of the right of self-defense at customary international law.[157] It also concluded that, although neither Article 2(4) nor Article 51 refers to specific weapons, the need to ensure that a use of force in self-defense was proportionate had implications for the degree of force and, consequently, for the weaponry which a State might lawfully use. The proportionality requirement of self-defense thus had an effect upon the legality of the way in which a State conducted hostilities. In determining whether the use of a particular weapon in a given case was lawful, it was therefore necessary to look at both international humanitarian law and the requirements of the right of self-defense.

The Court's opinion on this point is of considerable importance. The logic of the Charter and customary law provisions on self-defense means that the modern *jus ad bellum* cannot be regarded as literally a "law on going to war," the importance of which fades into the background once the fighting has started and the *jus in bello* comes into operation.[158] The *jus ad bellum* imposes an additional level of constraint upon a State's conduct of hostilities, affecting, for example, its choice of weapons and targets and the area of conflict. The Court did not, however, accept, as some commentators had argued, that the use of nuclear weapons could never be a proportionate measure of self-defense.[159] In reaching this conclusion, it appears to have accepted that proportionality has to be assessed, as Judge Higgins put it, by considering "what is proportionate to repelling the attack" and not treated as "a requirement of symmetry between the mode of the initial attack and the mode of response."[160]

It is evident, therefore, that the legality of the methods and means of warfare can no longer be considered by reference to the law of weaponry alone.

Christopher Greenwood

Especially when one considers the more destructive weapons, the law of the United Nations Charter will be a significant factor to be borne in mind. Human rights law and international environmental law may also have some importance, although their application is likely to have only a small impact on the substantive law applicable to the use of particular weapons.

VI. The Future of the Law of Weaponry

This stocktaking of the law of weaponry at the end of the twentieth century shows that this part of the law of armed conflict, while not one of the most effective, cannot be disregarded as an anachronism. The adoption of new treaties on weapons of real military significance, such as chemical weapons and land mines, demonstrates that it is possible to develop legal regimes which, if they are made to function properly, can have a significant impact in protecting the values of humanitarian law. Similarly, the Advisory Opinion on *Nuclear Weapons*, whatever its shortcomings, shows that the general principles of the law are capable of developing in such a way that they can be applied to new types of weapon. How then is the law likely to evolve as we enter the new millennium?

The outline of two developments is already visible. First, the trend of extending the law of weaponry from international armed conflicts to conflicts within States is likely to prove irreversible. Application to such conflicts has already been the subject of express provision in the two latest agreements on land mines and the Chemical Weapons Convention. In addition, the logic of the position taken by the International Criminal Tribunal for the Former Yugoslavia in the *Tadic* case and the general trend towards the development of the law of internal conflicts means that most, if not all, of the law of weaponry is likely to become applicable in internal conflicts in time. There is every reason why this should be so. While arguments against extending parts of the law of international armed conflicts, such as those which create the special status of prisoners of war, to internal hostilities have some force, there is no compelling argument for accepting that a government may use weapons against its own citizens which it is forbidden to use against an international adversary, even in an extreme case of national self-defense.

Secondly, it seems probable that the concept of penal sanctions for those who violate the law of weaponry will become far more important in the future. The Chemical Weapons Convention and the 1997 Land Mines Convention both make express provision for the enactment of criminal sanctions.[161] Certain violations of the principle of distinction are included in the grave

219

The Law of Weaponry

breaches regime by Additional Protocol I, Article 85. Moreover, any serious violation of the laws of war is already a war crime and this would include a serious violation of one of the weaponry treaties or a general principle such as that prohibiting unnecessary suffering. However, the existence of the two *ad hoc* criminal tribunals and the development of their jurisprudence, together with the likelihood of a future permanent international criminal court with an extensive war crimes jurisdiction, means that these sanctions are likely to be far more significant in the future. How far this is a desirable development is another matter. While the present writer strongly supports the principle of effective criminal sanctions for violations of the law of armed conflict, it has been seen that the general principles of the law of weaponry—and, indeed, some of the specific provisions—are far from clear or easy to apply. It would be quite wrong to hold individual servicemen, especially low down the chain of command, criminally responsible for the good faith use of weapons with which their government has provided them. Moreover, the preparatory talks on the international criminal court have shown a disturbing tendency to try to use the negotiation of the Court's statute as a way of revising the substantive law on weaponry, thus risking upsetting the work of more specialized conferences.

It is less easy to speculate as to what weapons might be made the subject of new agreements for the prohibition or limitation of their use. Incendiary weapons, fuel-air explosives, and napalm have all attracted considerable opprobrium over the last part of the twentieth century and are likely to face further calls for their limitation or outright prohibition. The precedent of the campaign against land mines, which attracted far greater publicity than do most developments in the law of armed conflict, suggests that future calls for changes in the law of weaponry may come as much from NGOs and public opinion as from governments. Such a change is both desirable and in keeping with the spirit of the Martens Clause. It carries the danger, however, that some of these calls will be unrealistic both in failing to recognize that States must be able to defend themselves and in the expectations which they create about what can be achieved.

One of the most important issues is likely to be the future of nuclear weapons. The inconclusive Opinion of the International Court of Justice included a unanimous finding that:

> There exists an obligation to pursue in good faith and bring to a conclusion negotiations leading to nuclear disarmament in all its aspects under strict and effective international control.[162]

Christopher Greenwood

Although this paragraph adds little of substance to the Non-Proliferation Treaty, it has already led to calls for fresh negotiations on nuclear disarmament. In this writer's view, attempts to achieve a ban on the *use* of nuclear weapons are unlikely to succeed in the foreseeable future and would probably prove counter-productive in that they will block progress in other areas (as happened with attempts to reform the law of armed conflict in the 1950's). As far as the *possession* of nuclear weapons is concerned, a ban is likely to prove possible only if all the nuclear-weapons States (declared and undeclared) support it, and such a result could not be achieved without simultaneous progress on a range of related security issues.

One of the most important developments may well prove to be the application to new types of weaponry of the existing general principles. The Advisory Opinion in the *Nuclear Weapons* case has demonstrated that these principles are capable of being applied to weapons of a kind which was beyond contemplation when those principles were first developed. The flexibility of the general principles thus makes them of broader application than the specific provisions which are all too easily overtaken by new technology. If the speed of change in military technology continues into the next century (as seems almost inevitable),[163] that capacity to adapt is going to be ever more important.

Take one example. Suppose that it became possible for a State to cause havoc to an enemy through the application of electronic measures or the selective planting of computer viruses which brought to a standstill whole computer systems and the infrastructure which depended upon them. Such a method of warfare would appear to be wholly outside the scope of the existing law. Yet that is not really so. The application of those measures, though not necessarily an "attack" within the meaning of Additional Protocol I because no violence need be involved,[164] is still likely to affect the civilian population and possibly to cause great damage and even loss of life amongst that population. As such, it should be subject to the same principles of distinction and proportionality considered above.

The application of the general principles of such forms of warfare would, however, require a measure of refinement of those principles. The place in the concept of proportionality which should be given to indirect, less immediate harm to the civilian population would have to be resolved. Similarly, if the principle of distinction is to be applied to existing, let alone new, weapons of naval warfare, a clearer assessment needs to be made of exactly what constitutes a legitimate target in naval hostilities. Both the military and humanitarian aspects of the unnecessary suffering principle need to be clarified if that principle is to have a significant impact in the assessment of new

The Law of Weaponry

methods and means of warfare. The duty which States have to scrutinize developments in weaponry and to assess whether any new weapons or methods of warfare comply with the law[165] means that the resolution of such questions is a matter of considerable importance.

In this writer's opinion, it is both more probable and more desirable that the law will develop in this evolutionary way than by any radical change. With the law of weaponry, as with most of the law of armed conflict, the most important humanitarian gain would come not from the adoption of new law but the effective implementation of the law that we have. That should be the priority for the next century.

Notes

1. For example, the Second Lateran Council in 1139 attempted to ban the crossbow. Prohibitions of particular weapons or methods of warfare are to be found in several different traditions. *See* UNESCO, INTERNATIONAL DIMENSIONS OF HUMANITARIAN LAW (1988), and Waldemar A. Solf, *Weapons, in* 4 RUDOLF BERNHARDT ET AL., ENCYCLOPAEDIA OF PUBLIC INTERNATIONAL LAW 352 (1982). The more recent history of this area of the law is discussed in Frits Kalshoven, *Arms, Armaments and International Law*, 191 RECUEIL DES COURS 185–341 (1985–II). Strictly speaking, the "means of warfare" refers to the weapons themselves, whereas the "methods of warfare" refers to the ways in which those weapons are used. The term "the law of weaponry" is here used to describe the legal rules and principles relating to methods and means of warfare.

2. This principle is discussed in Part IV, *infra*.

3. Legality of the Threat or Use of Nuclear Weapons (Advisory Opinion of July 8, 1996), 1996 I.C.J. 226.

4. Respect For Human Rights in Armed Conflicts: Existing Rules of International Law Concerning the Prohibition or Restriction of Use of Specific Weapons, U.N. Doc. A/9215, vol. I, at 204 (1973). The list was based upon the entries in national manuals of military law. *See, e.g.,* UNITED KINGDOM WAR OFFICE, THE LAW OF WAR ON LAND (Part III of the Manual of Military Law) 110 (1958).

5. SIR HERSCH LAUTERPACHT, OPPENHEIM'S INTERNATIONAL LAW 340–1 (7th ed. 1952).

6. Geneva Protocol Prohibiting the Use in War of Asphyxiating, Poisonous or other Gases and of Bacteriological Methods of Warfare, June 17, 1925, 26 U.S.T. 571 (1975), 94 L.N.T.S. 65 [hereinafter Geneva Gas Protocol]; Convention on the Prohibition of Development, Production and Stockpiling of Bacteriological (Biological) and Toxin Weapons and their Destruction, April 10, 1972, 26 U.S.T. 583 (1975), 1015 U.N.T.S. 164 [hereinafter Bacteriological and Toxin Weapons Convention]; Convention on the Prohibition of Development, Production, Stockpiling and Use of Chemical Weapons and on their Destruction, Jan. 13, 1993, 32 I.L.M. 800 (1993) [hereinafter Chemical Weapons Convention].

7. Additional Protocol No. IV on Blinding Laser Weapons, Oct. 13, 1995 [hereinafter Lasers Protocol] to the Convention on Prohibitions or Restrictions on Certain Conventional Weapons which may be Deemed to be Excessively Injurious or to Have Indiscriminate Effects,

Christopher Greenwood

35 I.L.M. 1218 (1996) [hereinafter Conventional Weapons Convention]. The Convention itself is at 19 I.L.M. 1523 (1980).

8. Additional Protocol II on Mines, Booby-Traps and Other Devices to the Conventional Weapons Convention, 1980, 19 I.L.M. 1523 (1980) [hereinafter Original Mines Protocol], Amended Additional Protocol II, May 3, 1996, 35 I.L.M. 1206 (1996) [hereinafter Amended Mines Protocol] and the United Nations Convention on the Prohibition of the Use, Stockpiling, Production and Transfer of Anti-Personnel Mines and on their Destruction, Sept. 18, 1997, 36 I.L.M. 1507 (1997) [hereinafter Land Mines Convention].

9. Legality of the Threat or Use of Nuclear Weapons , *supra* note 3.

10. *See* William J. Fenrick, *The Development of the Law of Armed Conflict through the Jurisprudence of the International Criminal Tribunal for the Former Yugoslavia,* and Theodor Meron, *War Crimes Law for the Twenty-First Century,* both in this volume.

11. U.S. War Dep't, General Orders No. 100, April 24, 1863, *reprinted in* THE LAWS OF ARMED CONFLICTS 3 (Dietrich Schindler & Jiri Toman eds., 3d ed. 1988).

12. *Id.,* art. 16. For a discussion of this aspect of the Code, see Burrus M. Carnahan, *Lincoln, Lieber and the Laws of War: The Origins and Limits of the Principle of Military Necessity,* 92 AM. J. INT'L L. 213 (1998).

13. Brussels Conference, Project of an International Declaration Concerning the Laws and Customs of War, 1874, Arts. 12 & 13, 65 Brit. and Foreign State Papers (1873-74) 1005, *reprinted in* THE LAWS OF ARMED CONFLICTS, *supra* note 11, at 25. The declaration never entered into force.

14. Institute of International Law, Manual of the Laws of War on Land, 5 ANNUAIRE DE L'INSITUT DE DROIT INTERNATIONAL 156 (1881–82), *reprinted in* THE LAWS OF ARMED CONFLICTS, *supra* note 11, at 35.

15. Declaration Renouncing the Use, in Time of War, of Explosive Projectiles under 400 Grammes Weight, 1868, 58 Brit. and Foreign State Papers (1867-68) 16 [hereinafter St. Petersburg Declaration], *reprinted in* THE LAWS OF ARMED CONFLICTS, *supra* note 11, at 101.

16. Regulations Respecting the Laws and Customs of War on Land annexed to Hague Convention No. IV, Oct. 18, 1907, 2 U.S.T. 2269, *reprinted in* THE LAWS OF ARMED CONFLICTS, *supra* note 11, at 63 [hereinafter Hague Regulations]. The 1907 Regulations were a revised version of an earlier set of regulations annexed to Hague Convention No. II, July 29, 1899, 2 U.S.T. 2042, *reprinted in* THE LAWS OF ARMED CONFLICTS, *supra* note 11, at 63.

17. 1 AM. J. INT'L L. 155 (1907 Supp.), *reprinted in* THE LAWS OF ARMED CONFLICTS, *supra* note 11, at 105

18. *Id.* at 157, *reprinted in* THE LAWS OF ARMED CONFLICTS, *supra* note 11, at 109.

19. *Id.* at 153, *reprinted in* THE LAWS OF ARMED CONFLICTS, *supra* note 11, at 201. The Declaration was renewed in 1907 until the opening of the Third Peace Conference, an event which has never occurred. 2 AM. J. INT'L L. 216 (1908 Supp.), *reprinted in* THE LAWS OF ARMED CONFLICTS, *supra* note 11, at 201. This Declaration is no longer regarded as being in force and, unlike the other two, is not considered to be declaratory of a rule of customary international law.

20. Hague Regulations, *supra* note 16.

21. T.S. No. 541, *reprinted in* THE LAWS OF ARMED CONFLICTS, *supra* note 11, at 803. For a particularly interesting discussion of this treaty, see HOWARD S. LEVIE, MINE WARFARE AT SEA (1991).

22. *Supra* note 6.

23. *Supra* note 6.

24. *Supra* note 6.

The Law of Weaponry

25. Geneva Convention No. I for the Amelioration of the Condition of the Wounded and Sick in Armed Forces in the Field, Aug. 12, 1949, 6 U.S.T. 3114, 75 U.N.T.S. 31 (1950); Geneva Convention No. II for the Amelioration of the Condition of Wounded, Sick and Shipwrecked Members of the Armed Forces at Sea, Aug. 12, 1949, 6 U.S.T. 3217, 75 U.N.T.S. 85 (1950); Geneva Convention No. III Relative to the Treatment of Prisoners of War, Aug. 12, 1949, 6 U.S.T. 3316, 75 U.N.T.S. 135 (1950); and Geneva Convention No. IV Relative to the Protection of Civilian Persons in Time of War, Aug. 12, 1949, 6 U.S.T. 3516, 75 U.N.T.S. 287 (1950). The four Conventions are *reprinted in* THE LAWS OF ARMED CONFLICT, *supra* note 11, at 373, 401, 423, & 495, respectively.

26. Additional Protocol I, Relating to the Protection of Victims of International Armed Conflicts, 1125 U.N.T.S. 3 (1979), 16 I.L.M. 1391 (1977) [hereinafter Additional Protocol I]; Additional Protocol II, Relating to the Protection of the Victims of Non-International Armed Conflicts, 1125 U.N.T.S. (1979) 609, 16 I.L.M. 1391 (1977), *reprinted in* THE LAWS OF ARMED CONFLICT, *supra* note 11, at 621 & 689.

27. Additional Protocol I, *supra* note 26, art. 35(1) & (2).

28. *Id.*, arts. 51(2)-(5), 52(1) & (2). Most of these provisions reflect customary law, although that is not true of the prohibition of reprisals against civilian objects in Article 52(1) *See* Christopher Greenwood, *The Customary Law Status of the 1977 Additional Protocols*, in HUMANITARIAN LAW OF ARMED CONFLICT: CHALLENGES AHEAD 93 (Astrid Delissen & Gerard Tanja eds., 1991).

29. Additional Protocol I, *supra* note 26, arts. 35(3) & 55.

30. 31 U.S.T. 333, 1108 U.N.T.S. 151 (1978), *reprinted in* THE LAWS OF ARMED CONFLICT, *supra* note 11, at 163 [hereinafter the ENMOD Convention].

31. *Supra* note 7.

32. *Supra* notes 7 & 8.

33. U.N. CHARTER art. 51.

34. *See* Legality of the Threat or Use of Nuclear Weapons, *supra* note 3, at 262–3.

35. This principle, like the others mentioned in the present paragraph, is discussed in greater detail in Part IV, *infra*.

36. Additional Protocol I, *supra* note 26, art. 38.

37. Additional Protocol I, *supra* note 26, art. 39(2). This provision goes beyond the rules of customary law, which prohibited the wearing of enemy uniforms only during an attack itself. *See* United States v. Skorzeny, 9 War Crimes Reports 90. The fact that the law of naval warfare is entirely different from the law of war on land in relation to this matter is a further illustration of the absence of any clear humanitarian purpose behind this rule; *see* text accompanying notes 81–9 *infra*.

38. *See* text accompanying notes 7–8 *supra*.

39. The Conference also unanimously adopted a resolution to the effect that "the Conference is of the opinion that the restriction of military charges, which are at present a heavy burden on the world, is extremely desirable for the increase of the moral and material welfare of mankind." A. PEARCE HIGGINS, THE HAGUE PEACE CONFERENCES 67 (1909).

40. Kalshoven, *supra* note 1, at 214–15.

41. Chemical Weapons Convention, *supra* note 6. *See also* the discussion in Part IV, *infra*.

42. The same was true of the reaction to early firearms. *See* LESLIE C. GREEN, THE CONTEMPORARY LAW OF ARMED CONFLICT 122-3 (1993).

43. Records of the First Hague Peace Conference, published by the Netherlands Ministry of Foreign Affairs, 1907, Part II, at 65.

44. *See* Part IV, sect. 2, *infra*.

Christopher Greenwood

45. Prosecutor v. Tadic (Jurisdiction), 105 I.L.R. 419, 504-20 (1995). For comment, see the article by Fenrick, *supra* note 10, and Christopher Greenwood, *International Humanitarian Law and the Tadic Case*, 7 EUR. J. INT'L L. 265 (1996). For subsequent proceedings in Tadic, see 36 I.L.M. 908 (1997).

46. Prosecutor v. Tadic (Jurisdiction), *supra* note 45, at 516, para. 119.

47. Legality of the Threat or Use of Nuclear Weapons, *supra* note 3, at 266, para. 2(A), of the *dispositif*. The Court was unanimous on this point.

48. *Id.*, para. 2(B) (by eleven votes to three).

49. *Id.* at 247, para. 52.

50. Although the principle of necessity has frequently been seen as justifying violence, in reality it is a restraining principle, requiring belligerents not to injure, kill or damage unless that is necessary for the achievement of legitimate military goals. *See* Carnahan, *supra* note 12.

51. The first two are outlawed by the St. Petersburg Declaration, *supra* note 15, and the last by the 1899 Declaration No. 3, *supra* note 18.

52. The origins of this ban also lie in the principle that civilians should be protected from acts of violence and that indiscriminate weapons are prohibited. However, the influence of the unnecessary suffering principle is evident in the *travaux préparatoires* of both 1899 Declaration No. 2, *supra* note 17, and the 1925 Geneva Gas Protocol, *supra* note 6.

53. Hague Regulations, *supra* note 16, art. 23(a).

54. Protocol I to the Conventional Weapons Convention, *supra* note 30.

55. That would be the case where, for example, no more humane alternative was available.

56. 32 I.L.R. 626 at 634 (1963). *See also* Dissenting Opinion of Judge Higgins, Legality of the Threat or Use of Nuclear Weapons, *supra* note 3, at 585-7, and Kalshoven, *supra* note 1, at 234-6.

57. International Committee of the Red Cross, Conference of Government Experts on the Use of Certain Conventional Weapons (Lucerne, Sept. 9 - Oct. 18, 1974) 9, para. 24 (1975) [hereinafter Lucerne Conference].

58. St. Petersburg Declaration, *supra* note 15, at preamble.

59. For a somewhat extreme example of the "morale" argument, see the article by Major G.V. Fosbery, *Explosive Bullets and their Application to Military Purposes*, 12 J. ROYAL UNITED SERVICES INST. 15–27 (1869), discussed in Kalshoven, *supra* note 1, at 208–13.

60. This was the view of some of the experts at the Lucerne Conference, *supra* note 57, at 9, para. 25. Although this approach was challenged by other experts (*see* Kalshoven, *supra* note 1, at 235) it clearly reflects State practice and, in the view of the present writer, is a correct statement of the law.

61. For example, the use of armor-piercing weapons against tanks and warships has always been accepted as lawful, notwithstanding that they cause more grievous injuries to personnel than do simple anti-personnel weapons. Indeed, the use of inflammable bullets, banned by the 1868 Declaration at a time when they were employed as anti-personnel weapons, came to be accepted as lawful some fifty years later when they were used against aircraft, notwithstanding the effect which they can have upon air crew (although their use in a simple anti-personnel role remains unlawful).

62. Lucerne Conference, *supra* note 57, at 8, para. 23.

63. INTERNATIONAL COMMITTEE OF THE RED CROSS, THE SIRUS PROJECT: TOWARDS A DETERMINATION OF WHICH WEAPONS CAUSE "SUPERFLUOUS INJURY" OR "UNNECESSARY SUFFERING" (Robin Coupland ed., 1997).

64. *Id.* at 27.

The Law of Weaponry

65. Hans Blix, *Methods and Means of Combat, in* UNESCO, INTERNATIONAL DIMENSIONS OF HUMANITARIAN LAW 135, 139 (1988).

66. For that reason, the present writer respectfully disagrees with Professor Françoise Hampson when she argues that Coalition forces in the 1991 Gulf fighting should have used infantry to clear Iraqi trenches rather than bulldozing those trenches and thus condemning large numbers of Iraqi soldiers to a death widely regarded as particularly horrific. In this writer's view, the avoidance of the Coalition casualties which trench fighting would have caused was a military advantage sufficient to ensure that the suffering inflicted upon the Iraqi soldiers manning the trenches was not "unnecessary." *See* Françoise Hampson, *Means and Methods of Warfare in the Conflict in the Gulf, in* THE GULF WAR 1990–91 IN INTERNATIONAL AND ENGLISH LAW 89, 104–7 (Peter Rowe ed., 1993).

67. Frits Kalshoven, *The Soldier and his Golf Clubs, in* STUDIES AND ESSAYS ON INTERNATIONAL HUMANITARIAN LAW AND RED CROSS PRINCIPLES 369–86 (Christophe Swinarski ed., 1986).

68. Unpublished paper submitted by Colonel (later Major-General) Sir David Hughes-Morgan, discussed in the Report of the Lucerne Conference, *supra* note 57, at 7–11.

69. *See* Part I, *supra.*

70. Additional Protocol I, *supra* note 26, arts. 48, 51 (2) & 52 (1). For these purposes, a combatant is a member of the armed forces (with the exception of medical personnel and chaplains) or someone who takes a direct part in hostilities [Art. 51 (3)]. Art. 52 (2) provides that:

> In so far as objects are concerned, military objectives are limited to those objects which by their nature, location, purpose or use make an effective contribution to military action, and whose total or partial destruction, capture or neutralisation, in the circumstances ruling at the time, offers a definite military advantage.

71. *Id.,* art. 51 (5) (b). This principle is also regarded as part of customary international law.

72. *Id.,* art. 57 (2) (a) (ii).

73. On this subject, see ANTHONY P.V. ROGERS, LAW ON THE BATTLEFIELD 7–46 (1996), William Fenrick, *Attacking the Enemy Civilian as a Punishable Offence,* 7 DUKE J. OF COMP. & INT'L L. 539 (1997), and Christopher Greenwood, *Current Issues in the Law of Armed Conflict: Weapons, Targets and International Criminal Liability,* 1 SINGAPORE J. INT'L & COMP. L. 441, 459–62 (1997).

74. The annotated edition of NWP 1-14M gives as an example of an inherently indiscriminate weapon the "bat bomb" developed but never used by the U.S. Navy during the Second World War. This weapon would have consisted of a bat with a small incendiary bomb attached to it. The bats would have been released over Japan, U.S. DEP'T OF THE NAVY, ANNOTATED SUPPLEMENT TO THE COMMANDER'S HANDBOOK ON THE LAW OF NAVAL OPERATIONS (NWP 1-14M/MCWP 5-2.1/COMDTPUB P5800.1), para. 9.1.2, n. 12 (1997) [hereinafter ANNOTATED HANDBOOK]. *See also* JACK COUFFER, BAT BOMB (1992).

75. *But see* the comments of the Trial Chamber of the International Criminal Tribunal for the Former Yugoslavia, Prosecutor v. Martic (Rule 61) 108 I.L.R. 39, 47-52.

76. Christopher Greenwood, *Customary International Law and the First Geneva Protocol of 1977 in the Gulf Conflict, in* Rowe, *supra* note 66, at 63.

77. Additional Protocol I prohibits such attacks even by way of reprisal, but on this point the Protocol is not declaratory of customary law; Greenwood, *supra* note 28, at 110–111, and *Twilight of the Law of Belligerent Reprisals,* 20 NETH. Y.B. INT'L L. 35 (1989). The United Kingdom entered a reservation to the reprisals provisions when ratifying the Protocol in January 1998. Letter of 28 January 1998 to the President of the Swiss Confederation, not yet published.

Christopher Greenwood

78. INTERNATIONAL COMMITTEE OF THE RED CROSS, COMMENTARY ON THE ADDITIONAL PROTOCOLS, para. 1980 (Yves Sandoz et al. eds., 1987).

79. *See* the essays in THE LAW OF NAVAL WARFARE: TARGETING ENEMY MERCHANT SHIPPING (Richard Grunawalt ed., 1993).

80. SAN REMO MANUAL ON INTERNATIONAL LAW APPLICABLE TO ARMED CONFLICTS AT SEA, 114 *et seq.* & 167–8 (Louise Doswald-Beck ed., 1995).

81. Although it has sometimes been suggested that poison and poisoned weapons are perfidious, the prohibition of those weapons, which has long been the subject of a specific rule, probably owes more to perceptions that they cause unnecessary suffering and are difficult to use in a discriminating way.

82. The prohibition of the unauthorized use of the United Nations emblem and the provision in Article 37(1)(d) were intended to apply only where the United Nations was involved in a conflict in a peacekeeping or other impartial role and not where the United Nations itself had committed forces to combat. Sandoz, *supra* note 78, para. 1560.

83. *See* text accompanying note 37, *supra*.

84. ROBERT W. TUCKER, THE LAW OF WAR AND NEUTRALITY AT SEA 138–42 (1955).

85. Additional Protocol I, *supra* note 26, art. 39(3).

86. SAN REMO MANUAL, *supra* note 80, at 186.

87. ANNOTATED HANDBOOK, *supra* note 74, ch. 12, esp. para. 12.7 & n. 23.

88. Contrast the explanation to paragraph 111 of the SAN REMO MANUAL, *supra* note 80, at 186, with TUCKER, *supra* note 84, at 140–1.

89. SAN REMO MANUAL, *supra* note 80, at 185.

90. ENMOD, *supra* note 30.

91. *See, e.g,* the paper by the International Committee of the Red Cross *in* Report of the Secretary-General on the Protection of the Environment in Times of Armed Conflict, United Nations Doc. A/48/269, at 25. *See also* ENVIRONMENTAL PROTECTION AND THE LAW OF WAR (Glen Plant ed., 1992).

92. *See also* art. 55. The terms "widespread, long-term and severe" in the Protocol do not carry the same meaning as "widespread, long-lasting or severe" in the ENMOD Treaty. Not only are the three requirements cumulative in Additional Protocol I, whereas they are alternatives in ENMOD, the *travaux préparatoires* of the two agreements demonstrate that "long-lasting" in the ENMOD Treaty was intended to refer to effects which lasted for approximately a season (*see* the Understanding adopted in relation to this term by the Conference of the Committee on Disarmament, quoted in DOCUMENTS ON THE LAWS OF WAR 377–8 (Adam Roberts and Richard Guelff eds., 1989)), whereas "long-term" in Additional Protocol I was intended to convey a sense of something to be measured "in decades rather than months." Sandoz, *supra* note 78, at 417.

93. See the statement to this effect by the Federal Republic of Germany, VI OFFICIAL RECORDS OF THE DIPLOMATIC CONFERENCE 115 (prepared by the Foreign Ministry of Switzerland). Articles 35(3) and 55 were not included in the list of provisions deemed to be part of customary law which appears in the International Committee of the Red Cross Commentary on the Additional Protocols (Sandoz, *supra* note 78, paras. 1857-9) and the International Court did not treat them as declaratory of custom in the *Nuclear Weapons* case, supra note 3, at 242, para. 31. *See also* Kalshoven, *supra* note 1, at 283.

94. ANNOTATED HANDBOOK, *supra* note 74, para. 8.1.3.

95. Legality of the Threat or Use of Nuclear Weapons, *supra* note note 3, at 242, para. 30.

96. G.A. Res. 47/37 (1992) on the "Protection of the Environment in Times of Armed Conflict." *See also* G.A. Res. 49/50.

The Law of Weaponry

97. *See also* SAN REMO MANUAL, *supra* note 80, at 119; ROGERS, *supra* note 73, at 127-9.

98. Hague Regulations, *supra* note 16, art. 22; Additional Protocol I, *supra* note 26, art. 35(1).

99. See, e.g., the view expressed by some participants at the Lucerne Conference, *supra* note 57, at 11–12. *See also* Helmut Strebel, *Martens Clause*, *in* 3 ENCYCLOPAEDIA OF PUBLIC INTERNATIONAL LAW 252–3 (R. Bernhardt ed., 1982).

100. Kalshoven, *supra* note 1, at 238.

101. On this point, see BLINDING WEAPONS (Louise Doswald-Beck ed., 1993).

102. *See, e.g.,* B. Anderberg, O. Bring, & M. Wolbarsht, *Blinding Laser Weapons and International Humanitarian Law*, 29 J. PEACE RESEARCH 287 (1992).

103. *See, e.g.,* the Memorandum of Law by the U.S. Judge Advocate-General of the Army, *reprinted in* BLINDING WEAPONS, *supra* note 101, at 367.

104. *See* Christopher Greenwood, *Analysis of the Law Applicable to the Use of Battlefield Laser Weapons*, *in id.* at 71, and the ensuing discussion.

105. 35 I.L.M. 1218 (1996). The text of the new protocol is also reproduced, together with a useful commentary, in Louise Doswald-Beck, *The New Protocol on Blinding Laser Weapons*, 36 INT'L REV. RED CROSS 272 (1996). At 30 April 1998 there were 24 parties to the Protocol.

106. *See* art. 3. Doswald-Beck, *supra* note 105, at 298, argues, however, that the use of laser weapons against optics systems is incompatible with the underlying intention of the Protocol.

107. Roberts & Guelff, *supra* note 92, at 479. For a commentary on the original Protocol II, see A.P.V. Rogers, *Mines, Booby-traps and Other Devices*, 30 INT'L REV. RED CROSS 521 (1990).

108. Original Mines Protocol, *supra* note 8, art. 2(1), defines a mine as "any munition placed under, on or near the ground or other surface area and designed to be detonated or exploded by the presence, proximity or contact of a person or vehicle."

109. Rogers, *supra* note 107, at 528.

110. *See, e.g.,* the ICRC booklet, *Mines: A Perverse Use of Technology*; P. CORNISH, ANTI-PERSONNEL MINES: CONTROLLING THE PLAGUE OF "BUTTERFLIES" (R.I.I.A., 1994).

111. Amended Mines Protocol, *supra* note 8. At 30 April 1998 there were 19 parties to the Amended Protocol.

112. *Id.*, arts. 1(2) and (3).

113. Doswald-Beck, *supra* note 105, at 287. Some States have made declarations to this effect when ratifying the new Protocol IV; *see, e.g.,* the declarations by Germany, Ireland and Sweden.

114. The United Nations Convention on the Prohibition of the Use, Stockpiling, Production and Transfer of Anti-Personnel Mines and on their Destruction, 1997, art. 1., 36 I.L.M. 1507 (1997).

115. *Id.*, art. 2.

116. *Id.*, art. 9.

117. Chemical Weapons Convention, *supra* note 6. At 30 April 1998 there were 108 parties.

118. Roberts & Guelff, *supra* note 92, at 137. See also the prohibition on poison and poisoned weapons codified in Article 23(a) of the Hague Regulations in Land Warfare, 1907, and the 1899 Hague Declaration No. 2 Regarding Asphyxiating Gases, notes 17 and 20, *supra*.

119. *See, e.g.,* the United Kingdom Reservation, *reprinted in* Roberts & Guelff, *supra* note 92, at 144. These reservations originally applied to the use of bacteriological weapons as well. For States Party to the 1972 Toxins Convention, however, reservation to the prohibition of such weapons was prohibited, so that the reservation of the right to use bacteriological weapons ceased to have any real substance. Even so, it was not until 1991 that the United Kingdom

Christopher Greenwood

withdrew its reservation of the right to use bacteriological weapons, 63 BRIT. Y.B. INT'L L. 700 (1992).

120. See the reports of a commission of experts established by the UN Secretary-General to inquire into allegations of the use of chemical weapons by Iraq, U.N. Docs. S17130 (April 25, 1985), S/17932 (March 21,1986), and S/18863 (May 14, 1987). The use of chemical weapons by Iraq was condemned in a Statement by the President of the Security Council on 21 March 1986. U.N. Doc. S/PV.2667, *reprinted in* RESOLUTIONS AND STATEMENTS OF THE UNITED NATIONS SECURITY COUNCIL, 1946–92, at 466 (K. Wellens ed., 1993)), but the Council's own resolutions were couched in cautious language and did not formally censure Iraq, let alone impose sanctions upon it. *See* S.C. Res. 598 (1987) & 620 (1988). Not until after the Kuwait conflict did the Security Council take action to seek out and destroy Iraq's stockpiles of chemical weapons. S.C. Res. 687 (1991).

121. See the speech by Iraq's representative to the United Nations in the Security Council on 16 February 1991. U.N. Doc. S/PV.2977.

122. For a detailed commentary, see W. KRUTZSCH & R. TRAPP, A COMMENTARY ON THE CHEMICAL WEAPONS CONVENTION (1994).

123. *See* Roberts & Guelff, *supra* note 92, at 137–8.

124. Chemical Weapons Convention, *supra* note 6, art. I, para. 5. *See also* art. II, paras. 7 & 9; KRUTZSCH & TRAPP, *supra* note 122, at 18 & 42.

125. KRUTZSCH & TRAPP, *supra* note 122, at 13.

126. See, e.g., the statement by the Government of the United Kingdom condemning Iraq's use of gas against Iraqi civilians at Halabja in 1988, 59 BRIT. Y.B. INT'L L. 579 (1988), quoted with approval by the Appeals Chamber of the International Criminal Tribunal for Former Yugoslavia in Prosecutor v. Tadic (Jurisdiction), *supra* note 45, at 517-18.

127. Dissenting Opinion of Judge Schwebel, Legality of the Threat or Use of Nuclear Weapons, *supra* note 3, at 323–29.

128. *See* Chemical Weapons Convention, *supra* note 6, art. I, para. 1.

129. *See id.*, art. I, paras. 3 & 4.

130. The author appeared as one of the counsel for the United Kingdom in the proceedings before the International Court of Justice on the Threat or Use of Nuclear Weapons, *supra* note 3. The views expressed in the present paper are the personal views of the author and should not be taken as representing the position of the Government of the United Kingdom.

131. *See esp.* G.A. Res. 1653 (1961), 2936 (1972), 33/71 B (1978), 35/152 D (1980), 36/92 I (1981), 45/59 B (1990), 46/37 D (1991), 47/53 C (1992), & 48/76 B (1993).

132. *See, e.g.,* N. SINGH & E. MCWHINNEY, NUCLEAR WEAPONS AND CONTEMPORARY INTERNATIONAL LAW (2d ed. 1989), G. SCHWARZENBERGER, THE LEGALITY OF NUCLEAR WEAPONS (1958), and the essays by Falk, Meyrowitz, and Weston in NUCLEAR WEAPONS AND LAW (Miller and Feinrider eds., 1984).

133. *See esp.* Written Observations of India, Malaysia, Nauru and the Solomon Islands.

134. *See* Written Observations of France, the Russian Federation, the United Kingdom and the United States of America. In the case of France, at least, this reflected a change of position. *See also* Kalshoven, *supra* note 1, at 266 *et seq.*; W. Hearn, *The International Legal Regime Regulating Nuclear Deterrence and Warfare*, 61 BRIT. Y.B. INT'L L. 199 (1990); and D. Rauschning, *Nuclear Weapons, in* 4 ENCYCLOPAEDIA OF PUBLIC INTERNATIONAL LAW 44 (R. Bernhardt ed., 1982).

135. *See* Kalshoven, *supra* note 1, at 281–2.

136. For comment, see Richard Falk, *Nuclear Weapons, International Law and the World Court*, 91 AM. J. INT'L L. 64–75 (1997); Michael Matheson, *The Opinions of the International*

The Law of Weaponry

Court of Justice on the Threat or Use of Nuclear Weapons, id. at 417–35; and the symposium in 37 INT'L REV. RED CROSS 4–117 (1997).

137. Legality of the Threat or Use of Nuclear Weapons, *supra* note 3, paras. 71 and 105, part 2(B).

138. *Id.*, paras. 54–7.

139. *Id.*, para. 95.

140. *Id.*, para. 105, part 2(E).

141. See the criticism in the Dissenting Opinion of Judge Higgins, *supra* note 56, at 584–5.

142. Legality of the Threat or Use of Nuclear Weapons, *supra* note 3, paras. 94–5.

143. *See*, in particular, the Separate Opinion of Judge Fleischhauer, 1996 I.C.J. 305.

144. For further discussion of this point, see Christopher Greenwood, *Jus ad Bellum and Jus in Bello in the Advisory Opinion on Nuclear Weapons*, in THE ADVISORY OPINION OF THE INTERNATIONAL COURT OF JUSTICE ON NUCLEAR WEAPONS (P. Sands & L. Boisson de Chazournes eds., 1998).

145. *Compare* Condorelli, 37 INT'L REV. RED CROSS 9 (1997) with David, *id.* at 21.

146. Article 6 of the 1966 International Covenant on Civil and Political Rights, provides that:
Every human being has the inherent right to life. This right shall be protected by law. No one shall be arbitrarily deprived of his life.
Comparable provisions can be found in Article 2 of the European Convention on Human Rights, Article 4 of the American Convention on Human Rights, and Article 4 of the African Charter on Human and People's Rights.

147. General Comment 14(23), U.N. Doc. A/40/40, at 162, para. 4. For comment, see DOMINIC MCGOLDRICK, THE HUMAN RIGHTS COMMITTEE 336 (1994).

148. *See* Written Observations of the Netherlands to the International Court of Justice, para. 27.

149. Legality of the Threat or Use of Nuclear Weapons, *supra* note 3, para. 25.

150. See, e.g., the decisions of the European Court of Human Rights in Loizidou v. Turkey, 103 I.L.R. 622 (1995) and 108 I.L.R. 443 (1996), and the European Commission of Human Rights in Cyprus v. Turkey, 23 E.H.R.R. 244 (1997), where the European Convention on Human Rights was invoked in a case of belligerent occupation.

151. See, e.g., the reliance by Mexico and the Solomon Islands in their Written Observations to the International Court of Justice on the Rio Declaration and other environmental texts.

152. Legality of the Threat or Use of Nuclear Weapons, *supra* note 3, para. 30.

153. *Id.*, paras. 30 and 33.

154. *See* Part IV (1) (d), *supra.*

155. Legality of the Threat or Use of Nuclear Weapons, *supra* note 3, para. 105, part 2(C).

156. 1986 I.C.J. 3.

157. Legality of the Threat or Use of Nuclear Weapons, *supra* note 3, para. 41.

158. *See, e.g.*, Christopher Greenwood, *The Relationship Between Jus ad Bellum and Jus in Bello*, 9 REV. INT'L STUDIES 221 (1982), and *Self-defence and the Conduct of International Armed Conflict, in* INTERNATIONAL LAW AT A TIME OF PERPLEXITY 273 (Yoram Dinstein ed., 1989).

159. Legality of the Threat or Use of Nuclear Weapons, *supra* note 3, paras. 42-43.

160. 1996 I.C.J. 583. See also the views of Judge Ago as Rapporteur on State Responsibility for the International Law Commission, Eighth Report, II(I) Y.B.I.L.C. 69 (1980).
It would be mistaken . . . to think that there must be proportionality between the conduct constituting the armed attack and the opposing conduct. The action needed to halt and

Christopher Greenwood

repulse the attack may well have to assume dimensions disproportionate to those of the attack suffered. What matters in this respect is the result to be achieved by the 'defensive' action, and not the forms, substance and strength of the action itself.

161. *See* Chemical Weapons Convention, *supra* note 6, art. VII. For an example of national implementation, see the United Kingdom's Chemical Weapons Act 1996.

162. Legality of the Threat or Use of Nuclear Weapons, *supra* note 3, para. 105, part 2(F).

163. *See* FRANÇOIS HEISBOURG, THE FUTURE OF WARFARE (1998).

164. Additional Protocol I, *supra* note 26, at art. 49(1).

165. This duty is expressly stated in Additional Protocol I, Article 36, but is regarded as part of customary international law. The United States of America, for example, which is not a party to Additional Protocol I, has long had a scrutiny program of this kind.

[2]

Conventional Weapons Under Legal Prohibitions

R. R. Baxter

The 1860s saw the real beginning of the modern legal regulation of warfare. The carnage of the Battle of Solferino (1859) inspired the first Red Cross Convention of 1864 for the protection of the wounded and sick. Francis Lieber's General Orders No. 100, "Instructions for the Government of Armies of the United States in the Field," of April 1863[1] not only guided the Union forces but were also adopted by a number of foreign countries.

In the wake of these important developments, Russia convened an international military commission at St. Petersburg in 1868. On November 29/December 11, representatives of seventeen countries signed a Declaration which was to form a starting-point for the legal regulation of weapons. The Declaration of St. Petersburg[2] contained three important principles:

The first was "That the only legitimate object which states should endeavor to accomplish during war is to weaken the military force of the enemy." This rule is the basis for the distinction, still fundamental in the law of war, between combatants and non-combatants; the former may naturally be made the object of attack but non-combatants may not.

The second principle took account of the fact that "it is sufficient to disable the greatest possible number of men" and went on to provide "That this object would be exceeded by the employment of arms which uselessly aggravate the sufferings of disabled men, or render their death inevitable." As will be seen, this is the source of a very general principle of law that weapons which cause "unnecessary suffering" are unlawful.

The third principle was specific in its prohibition of one particular weapon:

The contracting parties engage, mutually, to renounce, in case of war among themselves, the employment, by their military or naval forces, of any projec-

---

1. In Leon Friedman, *The Law of War: A Documentary History*, Vol. 1, (New York: Random House, 1972), p. 158.
2. Martens, *Nouveau Recueil général de Traités*, Vol. 18, p. 474, English translation in *American Journal of International Law*, Vol. 1 (1907), Supp., p. 95.

R. R. Baxter is Professor of Law, Harvard University, an Honorary Fellow of Jesus College, Cambridge, and Editor-in-Chief of the American Journal of International Law. *He was an officer in the United States Army and is now Colonel, Judge Advocate General Corps, Army Reserve. He has served as consultant to the United Nations Secretariat on the law of war. Professor Baxter is a member of the United States Delegation to the Conferences of Government Experts on International Humanitarian Law (Geneva), where he serves as Rapporteur of Committee III.*

tile of less weight than four hundred grammes, which is explosive or which is charged with fulminating or inflammable substances.

Although the Declaration was by its terms binding only on the parties to it, it is widely regarded as having passed into general international law and thus to be obligatory for all states. The specific prohibition of projectiles containing explosive or inflammable substances is regarded as applying only to anti-personnel use of such projectiles and as not prohibiting the use of tracer ammunition.

So the matter rested until the Hague Peace Conferences of 1899 and 1907. The Regulations which were annexed to the Convention with respect to the Laws and Customs of Warfare on Land[3] spoke out in more general terms. The basic principle laid down was that "The right of belligerents to adopt means of injuring the enemy is not unlimited."[4] It is, the Regulations said, "especially forbidden" among other things

(a) To employ poison or poisoned weapons;
(b) To kill or wound treacherously individuals belonging to the hostile nation or army;
. . .

(e) To employ arms, projectiles, or material calculated to cause unnecessary suffering;[5]

This last expression has been the source of a vast amount of confusion because the English translation from the authentic French text is inaccurate. The expression used in French was *propres à causer des maux superflus*, which might be more accurately translated as "calculated to cause superfluous (or excessive) injury." In the metaphysical atmosphere in which the legality of certain weapons is often discussed, such niceties count.

The prohibition of poison and poisoned weapons came before the days of chemical warfare and referred to poison in a quite literal sense. There was already a good deal of rather exotic law about such matters as the poisoning of wells—permissible if the adversary was informed of the poisoning, unlawful if he was not. Treacherous killing was originally thought of in terms of misuse of a flag of truce or the feigning of disablement in order to kill, but the phrase must be men-

---

3. Signed at The Hague, October 18, 1907, *United States Statutes at Large*, Vol. 36, p. 2277, Treaty Series No. 539, Bevans, *Treaties and Other International Agreements of the United States of America 1776–1949*, Vol. 1, p. 631.
4. Art. 22.
5. Art. 23.

tioned here because this provision has sometimes been invoked as prohibiting booby traps and mines.

The concept of "unnecessary suffering" or "superfluous injury" (to use the more accurate translation) is the central one. The reasoning was that if one had already put a man out of action by putting a projectile through him, there was no military utility in putting poison on the projectile so that the disabled soldier would die a horrible death from the effect of the poison. The same view lay behind the prohibition in the St. Petersburg Declaration of 1868. If the projectile had knocked out an enemy soldier, nothing more would be achieved by having the projectile explode or burn him. Whether or not one agrees with the reasoning, one must nevertheless concede that the draftsmen of the Conventions were trying to draw a sensible line between what was militarily necessary and what caused injury that had no military advantage.

Several further prohibitions were drafted at The Hague. Inspired by the Declaration of St. Petersburg, the parties to a Declaration Concerning Expanding Bullets agreed "to abstain from the use of bullets which expand or flatten easily in the human body, such as a bullet with a hard envelope which does not entirely cover the core or is pierced with incisions."[6] And, in the first attempt to regulate aerial warfare, the dropping of projectiles from balloons was prohibited for a period of five years.[7] The latter prohibition did not long survive, but the prohibition of "dum-dum" bullets has remained, at least on paper. The justification for the ban on "dum-dums" was derived from other provisions of the Conventions and Declarations; they caused "unnecessary suffering" or "superfluous injury" to the man put out of action.

This was the only law that governed the subject of the prohibition of conventional weapons during both World Wars. The Declaration of St. Petersburg and the various Conventions and Declarations adopted at The Hague acquired a certain foothold in international law, and military manuals and national instructions not infrequently forbade the use of such weapons, even though the particular states were not parties to the instruments. The Regulations annexed to the Hague Convention of 1907 with respect to the Laws and Customs of Warfare on Land were specifically held by the Nuremburg Tribunal to have passed

6. Signed at The Hague, July 29, 1899, cited in James Brown Scott ed., *The Hague Conventions and Declarations of 1899 and 1907* (New York: Oxford, 1915), p. 227.
7. Declaration Prohibiting the Discharge of Projectiles and Explosives from Balloons, signed at The Hague, October 18, 1907, *U.S. Statutes*, Vol. 36, p. 2439, T.S. No. 845, Bevans, Vol. 1, p. 739.

into customary international law by the time of the Second World War.[8] So far as land warfare was concerned, the only additional category of weapons that came under interdiction was chemical and biological weapons (CBW)—under the terms of the Geneva Protocol of 1925 for the Prohibition of the Use in War of Asphixiating, Poisonous or Other Gases, and of Bacteriological Methods of Warfare[9]—to which the United States finally became a party in 1975, a half century after the Protocol was drawn up. But these are not usually regarded as conventional weapons.

What law existed was either pitched on a very high level of abstraction (as was true of the prohibition on weapons causing unnecessary suffering) or was directed to specific weapons or projectiles of marginal military utility (for example "dum-dum" bullets) in comparison with the enormous technological developments that had taken place in the art of warfare.

The stimulus to renewed thought about the prohibition or restriction of use of certain conventional weapons was, not surprisingly, the war in Vietnam, coupled with a renewed concern with the humanitarian law of war in general—the law relating to prisoners of war, the wounded and sick, civilians, and the conduct of warfare, of which the central feature was the Geneva Conventions of 1949 for the Protection of War Victims.[10] The Arab-Israeli Conflict, the civil war in Nigeria, the Korean War, conflict in Cyprus, several outbreaks of conflict between India and China, the United Nations operations in Egypt, the Congo, and in Cyprus had disclosed certain inadequacies in the existing law, much of which was responsive to problems that had been encountered in World War II.

The discussion of new prohibitions on conventional weapons has been ancillary to the wider consideration of new law to supplement the Geneva Conventions of 1949. In order to understand what has been done with respect to weapons, it is necessary to go back to the origins of the present effort, reflected in the work of the Diplomatic Conference on International Humanitarian Law, to add to and to modernize the corpus of the existing treaties on international humanitarian law.[11]

---

8. U.S. Chief of Counsel for the Prosecution of Axis Criminality, *Nazi Conspiracy and Aggression, Opinion and Judgment* (1947), p. 83.
9. Signed June 17, 1925, League of Nations Treaty Series, Vol. 94, p. 65.
10. Signed August 12, 1949, *United States Treaties and Other International Agreements*, Vol. 3, p. 3114, Treaties and Other International Acts Series Nos. 3362–3365.
11. See for a fuller account of this history R. R. Baxter, "Humanitarian Law or Humanitarian Politics? The 1974 Diplomatic Conference on Humanitarian Law," *Harvard International Law Journal*, Vol. 16 (1975), p. 1.

At the International Conference on Human Rights held at Tehran in 1968, as part of the International Year for Human Rights, a resolution was adopted requesting the General Assembly to invite the Secretary-General of the United Nations to study the "steps which could be taken to secure the better application of existing humanitarian international conventions and rules" and "the need for additional humanitarian international conventions or of possible revision of existing conventions."[12] The General Assembly responded, the Secretary-General was requested to survey the law,[13] and three important substantive reports were presented to the General Assembly.[14]

The International Committee of the Red Cross (ICRC), the Geneva-based private international organization which has played a crucial role in developing new international humanitarian law and in seeing to it that the law is applied, saw a threat to its own position with respect to this body of law. It responded by convening two Conferences of Government Experts in 1971 and 1972, the first attended by delegations from forty-one states and the second by delegations from seventy-seven.

In both the General Assembly and in the Conferences of Government Experts, dissatisfaction was expressed that the studies that had been undertaken and the new principles that had been drafted neglected the question of the use of certain forms of weapons against both the civilian population and military personnel. Sweden was the leader in the initiatives that were taken both in the General Assembly and in the Conferences of Government Experts, which was followed by the intergovernmental Diplomatic Conference on International Humanitarian Law. Sweden had for several decades displayed a strong interest in arms control and disarmament, notably with respect to nuclear weapons and CBW, and it was not unnatural that it should turn its efforts to conventional arms as well. In time it gathered about it a core group which consisted of Mexico, Yugoslavia, Austria, Egypt, the Netherlands, Switzerland, and several other medium powers.

The General Assembly and the Secretariat of the United Nations had been watching the work of the two Conferences of Government Experts convened by the ICRC—ready to pounce upon the subject-matter of the law of war if the Conferences or the ICRC should falter in their work. In 1972, the General Assembly

---

12. Resolution XXIII, Final Act of the International Conference on Human Rights, U.N. Doc. A/CONF.32/41, at p. 18 (1968).
13. General Assembly Resolution 2444 (XXIII), December 16, 1968, U.N. GAOR, 23rd Sess., Supp. No. 18, p. 50, U.N. Doc. A/7218 (1969).
14. Respect for Human Rights in Armed Conflicts: Reports of the Secretary-General, U.N. Docs. A/7720 (1969), A/8052 (1970), A/8370 (1971).

adopted a resolution in which it listed what it considered to be the gaps in the work of the Conferences of Government Experts.[15] Among these were the topics of:

—prohibition of the use of weapons and methods of warfare which indiscriminately affect civilians and combatants,

—prohibition or restriction of the use of specific weapons which are deemed to cause unnecessary suffering.

The first of these topics related both to prohibition of weapons per se and to the improper employment of weapons otherwise licit, as, for example, by way of the deliberate bombardment of the civilian population from the air. The Secretary-General was invited to prepare a report on the existing rules of international law concerning the prohibition or restriction of use of specific weapons.

The Secretary-General's report[16] was a fair reflection of the archaic and excessively general character of the existing law. It dealt not only with the prohibition of the use of certain weapons in land warfare but also with the law of bombardment (from the land, sea, or air) and with warfare at sea. If anything, the report demonstrated that the generic rules are very difficult to apply to particular weapons and that the specific rules do not cope with the weapons that are the most likely to do harm to the civilian population or to cause injury and suffering out of proportion to the military advantage to be gained from the use of such weapons. The law was, to put the matter bluntly, an ineffective instrument for establishing some control over the use of weapons, even if a good-faith effort were made to apply it.

The three general criteria for determining the illegality of weapons were identified as (1) whether the weapon causes unnecessary suffering or superfluous injury (the two different versions of the 1907 French text), (2) whether the weapon has indiscriminate effects, and (3) whether the weapon kills through treachery.[17] Behind the criterion of "unnecessary suffering" lay a notion of proportionality—whether the suffering caused is out of proportion to the military advantage to be gained. But the application of that criterion calls for the compari-

---

15. General Assembly Resolution 3032 (XXVII), December 18, 1972, U.N. GAOR, 27th Sess., Supp. No. 30, p. 117, U.N. Doc. A/8730 (1973).

16. *Respect for Human Rights in Armed Conflicts: Existing rules of international law concerning the prohibition or restriction of use of specific weapons: Survey prepared by the Secretariat*, U.N. Doc. A/9215 (Vols. I and II) (1973).

17. For a fuller discussion of these criteria, see R. R. Baxter, "Criteria of the Prohibition of Weapons in International Law," in *Festscrift für Ulrich Scheuner* (Berlin: Duncker & Humblot, 1973), p. 41.

son of two things that are not comparable. No scale of values can establish what suffering is necessary because proportionate with the military advantage gained and what suffering is unnecessary because of disproportionality between the effects of the weapon and what is gained in a military sense from its use. And if one adopts a somewhat impressionistic approach to the question, then it would seem that the more effective a weapon is in disabling and killing, the more likely it is to be "unlawful" because of the suffering that it causes.

The idea of indiscriminacy comes from the law with respect to the manner of employment of weapons rather than the law of illegality of use *per se*. The distinction between combatants and the peaceful civilian population has for long been regarded as fundamental to the protection of the civilian population, particularly from the effects of aerial bombardment. If a weapon directed against military personnel or against military objectives indiscriminately harms civilians because there is no possibility of confining its effects to the military target, the weapon might be stigmatized as unlawful on that account. Even conventional bombardment may fall afoul of this restriction, and various new forms of weapons, such as fragmentation bombs, have on occasion been characterized as unlawful because of their incidental effects on civilians.

The view that weapons may be unlawful because they kill "treacherously" comes from the general prohibition of treacherous killing found in the Regulations annexed to Convention No. IV of The Hague of 1907 respecting the Laws and Customs of Warfare on Land.[18] Delayed action bombs, mines, and booby traps have been cited as instances of weapons forbidden on this account, insofar as they affect the civilian population. When used against military personnel, such devices assume a less heinous aspect.

These are only a few of the considerations bearing upon the attempt to define prohibited weapons by criteria of a very general character. The General Assembly did not pursue the general topic of prohibition of conventional weapons, because by this time it was clear that the question was going to be taken up by the Diplomatic Conference on International Humanitarian Law and by the Conferences of Government Experts that preceded it. But one specific weapon—napalm—continued to be under the attention of the General Assembly.

In 1971 the General Assembly had requested the Secretary-General to prepare a report on napalm and other incendiary weapons and all aspects of their use.[19]

---

18. Art. 23, para. (b).
19. General Assembly Resolution 2852 (XXVII), December 20, 1971,. U.N. GAOR, 26th Sess. Supp. No. 29, p. 90, U.N. Doc. A/8429 (1972).

Conventional Weapons   49

The report,[20] prepared by a group of experts of international composition, found that napalm and other incendiaries have the capacity to cause massive fires, which are largely indiscriminate in their effects. "When there is a difference between the susceptibility to fire of military and civilian targets, it is commonly to the detriment of the latter." Burn injuries are especially grave, and the experts were led to conclude that:

When judged against what is required to put a soldier out of military action, much of the injury caused by incendiary weapons is therefore likely to be superfluous. In terms of damage to the civilian population, incendiaries are particularly cruel in their effects.

And use of incendiaries to kill crops or forests may cause irreversible ecological changes. The conclusion of the experts was that the General Assembly should be aware of "the necessity of working out measures for the prohibition of the use, production, development and stockpiling of napalm and other incendiary weapons."

The General Assembly responded to the invitation in 1974, when it adopted a resolution[21] condemning the use of napalm and other incendiary weapons in armed conflicts in circumstances which might affect human beings or cause damage to the environment and inviting all states to refrain from the production, stockpiling, proliferation and use of such weapons, pending conclusion of agreements on this subject. There were no votes against the resolution, but significantly twenty-seven states, including the Soviet Union and members of the Soviet bloc and the United States and its NATO allies, abstained.

It is now necessary to return to the work on international humanitarian law being conducted under the auspices of the International Committee of the Red Cross. The first rumblings of dissatisfaction with the absence of any consideration of weapons was heard at the second meeting of government experts in 1972, and it was proposed that the subject be placed on the agenda of the Diplomatic Conference which was to be convened by the Swiss Government. The Twenty-second International Conference of the Red Cross, meeting in Tehran in 1973,[22] urged the Diplomatic Conference that was to take up the texts of two Protocols to the Geneva Conventions of 1949 (prepared by the International Com-

---

20. *General and Complete Disarmament: Napalm and other incendiary weapons and all aspects of their use: Report of the Secretary General under General Assembly Resolution 2852 (XXVI)*, U.N. Doc. A/8803 (1972).
21. General Assembly Resolution 3255 B (XXIX).
22. Resolution XIV, Interdiction ou limitation de l'emploi de certaines armes, *Revue Internationale de la Croix-Rouge*, Vol. 56 (1974), p. 35.

mittee of the Red Cross on the basis of the advice received at the two Conferences of Government Experts) to begin consideration of the prohibition or restriction of certain conventional weapons which may cause unnecessary suffering or have indiscriminate effects and invited the ICRC to convene a conference of government experts to study the question. This new task entrusted to the ICRC was the cause of some concern within and outside that body. An organization that had over the years acquired very great expertise in the protection of such war victims as civilians and prisoners of war was now called upon to assist in the assessment of weapons and their effects—to move from humanitarian law to the law of combat. It was feared that to turn to this new subject might slow down the work on the two new draft Protocols on International and Non-international Armed Conflicts which were to be taken up by the Diplomatic Conference which had been convened by the Swiss Government and which was to meet for the first time in 1974. Moreover, this new subject had not undergone the scrutiny of government experts, as had the contents of the two new Protocols, so that the work on weapons was essentially out of phase with the rest of the operation.

But the ICRC rallied round, and the first meeting of the working group of experts was held promptly in 1973.[23] The five categories of weapons considered were those that have continued to occupy the attention of the Diplomatic Conference:
—Incendiary weapons
—Time delay weapons
—Blast and fragmentation weapons
—Small calibre projectiles
—Potential weapons developments (such as the use of lasers).
It became obvious that there was much to be learned about weapons—about their characteristics and their effects. What is the degree of tumbling at various stages in the trajectory of a bullet fired from an M-14 rifle at a muzzle velocity of over 800 meters per second? What effect does such a bullet have on the human body? What happens in human tissue when it is hit by an unstable projectile of high length-to-calibre ratio? Even the recruitment of experts proved to be difficult. Few countries have doctors who are experts in wound traumas caused by gunshots. Even in the case of a country as knowledgeable about weaponry as the United States, it was acknowledged that there were great areas of ignorance, in

---

23. ICRC, *Weapons that may Cause Unnecessary Suffering or have Indiscriminate Effects: Report on the Work of Experts* (Geneva, 1973).

which further inquiries would have to be conducted. There was a task both of re-search and of education to be done.

The hesitancy of a number of states, including the major military powers, about the whole question of control of conventional weapons was reflected in the fact that at the first session of the Diplomatic Conference on International Hu-manitarian Law, held in Geneva in February and March of 1974, there was no "main committee" on weapons—only an Ad Hoc Committee on Weapons. The United States Government viewed the proceedings with a great deal of caution, a natural reaction to the fact that a number of governments, without full informa-tion or consideration of the issues, had apparently already made up their minds what weapons were unlawful.

The discussion of general categories of weapons that should be banned was un-rewarding. The debate turned out to be in large measure one between the "haves" and the "have-nots." The developing countries resented the technological su-periority of the major military powers and of other developed countries, and it was even suggested that the inbalance between the two types of states should be redressed by placing restrictions on the types of weapons that might be em-ployed by developed countries in conflicts with developing countries. The Soviet Union and its allies were placed in a difficult position throughout the negotia-tions. Itself a power of high military technology, the Soviet Union could not welcome placing restraints on weapons, but at the same time as the steadfast ally of Third World states, it found it difficult to take a hard line against the techno-logically-deprived developing states. When the discussion turned to specific weap-ons, such as fragmentation weapons or small calibre projectiles, the Swedish delegation was prepared to speak to the issue, but there were very few other in-terventions. The silence of most of the delegations sitting in the Ad Hoc Com-mittee on Weapons could be traced to ignorance and hesitancy about the direc-tion in which they might be led. No articles were considered or decisions made, and there seemed to be a general sense of relief that there could be a further airing of the issues at the Conference of Government Experts which was to be held in Lucerne.

The discussion at the Lucerne meeting of the Government Experts[24] of the general legal criteria that might be applied to determine the illegality of weap-ons showed how unhelpful these general notions of unnecessary suffering or of

---

24. ICRC, *Conference of Government Experts on the Use of Certain Conventional Weapons (Lucerne, 24.9–18.10.1974): Report* (Geneva, 1975).

indiscriminacy or of treachery actually are. In the face of a great diversity of opinions on these questions, the Government Experts turned to an examination of particular categories of weapons. The discussion was largely conducted on a technical level; the United States, to the satisfaction of the other participants, had sent a team of experts and took an active part in the discussions. Again no articles emerged, although some progress was made toward the definition of the scope of incendiary weapons.

The report of the Government Experts was discussed in the Ad Hoc Committee at the Second Session of the Diplomatic Conference in Geneva in 1975.[25] Although Sweden and six other states (Austria, Egypt, Mexico, Norway, Switzerland, and Yugoslavia) submitted a working paper containing draft prohibitions and restrictions on specific weapons, it was widely understood that yet more study was called for through a second meeting of Government Experts. The Soviet Union took a more active position in the debates by way of drawing attention to difficulties in the Swedish proposals.

A further meeting of Government Experts in Lugano[26] preceded the third session of the Conference in 1976. By this time draft proposals were being circulated on subjects ranging from the use of napalm to a prohibition of projectiles breaking into small fragments not detectable by x-rays. At the 1976 session of the Conference, the Soviet Union adopted a more forthright position of opposition to any controls on conventional weapons, arguing that this was not the proper forum for dealing with the question. The refusal of that country to allow any working groups to be set up meant that any detailed work on the various proposals was impossible, and the meetings of the Ad Hoc Committee, still not yet dignified as one of the main committees of the Conference, involved a good deal of repetition of familiar positions and proposals.[27]

The fourth, and what the Swiss Government vows will be the final session of the Diplomatic Conference will meet in Geneva from March to May of 1977. There seems to be some slight falling off in the interest of some countries in the whole question of the control of conventional weapons, although some still continue to press for action. The participants in the Conference surely must be

---

25. *Report of the Ad Hoc Committee on Conventional Weapons, Second Session*, Doc. CDDH/220/Rev.1 (1975). [The symbol "CDDH" identifies documents of the Diplomatic Conference on the Reaffirmation and Development of International Humanitarian Law Applicable in Armed Conflicts, 1974–1977.]
26. ICRC, *Conference of Government Experts on the Use of Certain Conventional Weapons (Second Session—Lugano, 28.1–26.2.1976): Report* (Geneva, 1976).
27. *Draft Report of the Ad Hoc Committee on Conventional Weapons, Third Session*, Doc. CDDH/IV/216 (1976).

increasingly aware that the complexity and importance of the issues will not permit their resolution in time for articles to be inserted in or added to the Protocols, on which work must be completed in 1977. There is simply not time enough to negotiate the articles, and the intransigence of the Soviet Union and the lack of interest on the part of other major military powers must be discouraging to those states that have been pressing the matter. The probable future course of action seems to be that the work will have to proceed independently of the two Protocols on International and Non-international Armed Conflicts, either under the auspices of the ICRC and the Swiss Government or in some other organization, conference, or forum. The campaign was too late in starting and has, throughout the three sessions of the Diplomatic Conference, had to compete with law-making that was further advanced and probably closer to the interests of the participants in the Conference.

We may now turn to some of the considerations bearing upon the use of particular types of conventional weapons and the proposals that have been made for the prohibition or restriction of their use.

NAPALM AND OTHER INCENDIARY WEAPONS. Incendiary weapons have been defined as comprising,

> any munition which is primarily designed to set fire to objects or to cause burn injury to persons through the action of flame and/or heat produced by a chemical reaction of a substance delivered on the target. Such munitions include flame-throwers, incendiary shells, rockets, grenades, mines and bombs.[28]

Reference has already been made to the severity of the burns produced by incendiaries; the physical and psychological complications which may be caused by burns must also be taken into account. Prejudice against the use of incendiaries could also be traced to the fire-bomb raids of the Second World War against such cities as Dresden and Tokyo, in which hundreds of thousands of civilians perished. On the other hand, incendiaries have proven to be highly useful for various functions, such as destruction of material, attack on strongly entrenched troops and other hardened targets, and in defense. They are also weapons that can be used with a considerable degree of precision. Napalm, whether air-dropped or employed in flame throwers, can be delivered precisely on target. If its use were to be banned, high explosives delivered by air or ground would have to be used in its place, and the danger of collateral injury to civilians would thereby

---

28. Doc. RO 610/4b (1975), in the *Report of the Lugano Conference*, p. 206. See generally on the subject of incendiaries, Stockholm International Peace Research Institute, *Incendiary Weapons* (Cambridge, MA.: MIT Press, and Stockholm: Almqvist & Wiksell, 1975).

be enhanced. Trade-offs such as this complicate simplistic proposals to prohibit the use of particular weapons. "Consider the alternative" is the appropriate warning. In addition, rockets and other projectiles which are today being used against hardened targets such as tanks use intense heat to secure penetration of the projectile. Proposals for prohibition of incendiaries have therefore had to struggle with whether distinctions should be made between their use against civilian and military personnel, against personnel and materiel, against different types of materiel, or between their primary and secondary effects.

Four main trends may be discerned in the proposals for the prohibition of incendiaries. The first is a complete prohibition of the use of all incendiaries. This proposal has been made by Mexico[29] and does not appear to command any appreciable amount of support from other countries. Sweden and a group of its supporters have proposed a general prohibition of incendiaries, to which the following exceptions would be made:

(a) munitions which may have secondary or incidental incendiary effects, such as illuminants, tracers, smoke or signalling systems;

(b) munitions which combine incendiary effects with penetration or fragmentation effects and which are specifically designed for use against aircraft, armoured vehicles and similar targets.[30]

But these exceptions would not meet the objections of those who uphold the military utility of napalm and other oil-based incendiaries and other incendiary agents, such as white phosphorus. The third approach is that of the Netherlands which has attempted to strike a middle path by, in effect, restricting use of these agents to military personnel and subjects.[31] The Netherlands has suggested that the basic rule should be that,

As a consequence of the rules of international law applicable with respect to the protection of the civilian population against the effect of hostilities, it is prohibited to make any city, town, village or other area containing a concentration of civilians the object of attack by means of any incendiary munition.

Norway proposed a similar prohibition on the use of incendiaries against civilians.[32] Both proposals laid out further rules on the precautions that should

---

29. Doc. CDDH/IV/212 (1976).
30. Doc. RO 610/4b (1975), in the *Report of the Lugano Conference*, p. 206, and Doc. CDDH/IV/208 (1976).
31. The proposal was co-sponsored by Denmark and Australia. Doc. CDDH/IV/206 and Adds. 1 & 1(1976).
32. Doc. CDDH/IV/207 (1976).

be taken to assure that civilians are not harmed by these agents. Actually, such rules do not go materially beyond what is already required under the terms of the articles of the Protocol on International Armed Conflicts that have already been adopted in committee. Attacks directed against civilian objects or the civilian population as such are now, and will remain, prohibited, whether by the use of high explosives or incendiaries. The fourth proposal, made by Norway, calls for prohibition of the use of incendiary weapons against personnel generally, which would thus exclude their use against military personnel but not against military objects.

There is such a diversity of opinion in the Diplomatic Conference and such strong feelings are entertained by some states about the military utility of incendiaries that it is unlikely that any prohibition going materially beyond the existing law for the protection of civilian persons and objects will find acceptance by those states that have incendiary weapons in their armories. Unless the major military powers can be persuaded to accept the prohibition, the activity with respect to incendiaries will be an exercise in futility, having only some propaganda and local political value for those who have been hot in pursuit of these restrictions.

SMALL CALIBRE PROJECTILES. Projectiles of small calibre but with a high muzzle velocity have increasingly come to be used in rifles, assault-rifles, and machine-guns. Such projectiles are of great military utility because they have a high probability of hitting and incapacitating enemy personnel. However, they may tumble in a certain portion of their trajectory; they are unstable when they pass from air into human flesh; they create intense hydrodynamic shock waves; and they may break up or deform inside the body. The wounds that they cause are accordingly very severe and resemble those caused by dum-dum bullets. On this account, small calibre projectiles have been thought in some quarters to cause "unnecessary suffering" and to be an appropriate weapon for restriction or prohibition.

The discussion of these weapons in the Diplomatic Conference and more especially in the Conferences of Government Experts,[33] where the really serious consideration of their characteristics and effects has taken place, has indicated how wide a difference of views there is, even among experts, and how much there is to be learned about both the behavior of the projectiles and their effect on human flesh. Various tests and studies have been made by states par-

---

33. See the *Report on the Work of Experts* (1973), pp. 30–38; *Report of the Lucerne Conference*, pp. 37–48; *Report of the Lugano Conference*, pp. 13–16.

ticipating in the work of the Ad Hoc Committee on Weapons, with results that are not decisive. The whole question has turned out to be extremely technical, and even the criteria originally suggested for the identification of these weapons have been demonstrated to be questionable. The criterion of 800 meters or more per second muzzle velocity[34] has been shown to be altogether arbitrary. What was originally seen as a problem of high muzzle velocity came to be identified as a consequence of the use of small calibre projectiles—that is, less than the 7.62 mm rounds that have been in general use in recent wars. Specific criteria have been abandoned in certain proposals made to the Diplomatic Conference,[35] while the most recent Swedish draft has become much more technical and involved than the earlier ones. The text on possible elements of a separate agreement on small calibre projectiles submitted by Sweden in 1976[36] provided:

The states parties to this Protocol have agreed to abstain from use of bullets which:
(a) deform or break easily in the human body, or
(b) tumble rapidly in the human body, or
(c) have a velocity exceeding 1,500 meters per second.
    For the purposes of this Protocol:
—a bullet shall be deemed to deform, or break easily in a human body if, out of a series of ten test shots, performed at any range against a target made of a material of a density and softness comparable to human muscle tissue and of such thickness that the bullet stops in it, any one of the bullets deforms or breaks to an extent detectable without any measuring aids,
—a bullet shall be deemed to tumble rapidly in a human body if, out of a series of ten test shorts at any range exceeding 50 meters against a target of a thickness of 140 mm and made of a material of density and softness comparable to human muscle tissue, the average yaw angle on exit or during passage of the target exceeds X degrees.

The widespread use of small calibre projectiles by a variety of countries, their perceived military utility, and the wide measure of disagreement about their characteristics and effects make it unlikely that any prohibition will be adopted. Any criteria for prohibition would of necessity be largely arbitrary and would call for a technicality of exposition that would make the rule difficult to apply

---

34. The muzzle velocity of the M-14 rifle is 870 meters per second, that of the M-16 Armalite 980 meters per second, and that of the AK–47 rifle 720 meters per second. *Report on the Work of Experts* (1973), p. 34.
35. Working Paper submitted by Austria, Egypt, Mexico, Norway, Sweden, Switzerland and Yugoslavia, Doc. CDDH/IV/201 (1975).
36. Doc. CDDH/IV/214 (1976).

or enforce. The states using low calibre projectiles are unlikely to accept any prohibitions or restrictions, and criticism of such projectiles seems, once again, to be in large measure the defensive reaction of the military "have-nots."

FRAGMENTATION AND BLAST WEAPONS. The weapons that have been considered under this rubric are controlled fragmentation weapons (including the use of cluster bomb units), projectiles breaking up into fragments (for example, of plastic) that are not detectable in the human body, and fuel-air explosives.[37] The starting point was controlled fragmentation weapons. Conventional weapons have long relied on fragmentation effect, as, for example, in the use of shrapnel. There is a quantitative difference but not a qualitative one between the weapons of recent years and modern controlled fragmentation projectiles, which are designed to spread a large quantity of small fragments uniformly over a wide area. Flechettes may also be delivered in great numbers by new forms of munitions. These projectiles may form part of cluster-bomb units (CBUs), which distribute a large number of sub-munitions evenly over the ground. CBUs and controlled fragmentation weapons are of particular utility against troops, antiaircraft guns, radar installations, parked aircraft, unarmored vehicles, and other soft targets. They are used, for example, to attack the crews of antiaircraft artillery or to drive them away from their guns. Sweden and other states have criticized their use on the grounds that such weapons may indiscriminately kill or injure civilians and that the large number of pellets produced may cause unnecessary suffering to military or civilian personnel who are hit by such weapons.

Various charges have been made that bombs producing nondetectable fragments are being used or are in contemplation. Although evidence on the matter is extremely sparse, proposals have been made to ban the use of such projectiles.

A fuel-air explosive involves an explosive device that produces a spray of some inflammable liquid, gas, or powder. The explosive cloud is then detonated. A very high ratio of killed to wounded may be expected as the result of the fire and more especially the blast produced by the explosion. The blast effect has been asserted to bring about particularly painful death or injury, and it is also charged that such weapons will affect military and civilian personnel indiscriminately.

Again, the debate has involved a weighing of the military utility of such

---

37. See the *Report on the Work of Experts* (1973), pp. 39–48; *Report of the Lucerne Conference,* pp. 49–62; *Report of the Lugano Conference,* pp. 17–18.

weapons against their possible effect on civilians and against the "unnecessary suffering" which may be caused to those who are attacked by such weapons. Those who have been in the forefront of the campaign against these weapons have generally proposed blanket prohibitions. Sweden and others proposed in 1975[38] that,

Anti-personnel cluster warheads or other devices with many bomblets which act through the ejection of a great number of small calibred fragments or pellets are prohibited for use.

An outright prohibition was proposed of "any weapon the primary effect of which is to injure by fragments which in the human body escape detection by x-rays."[39] And fuel-air explosives (FAEs) would be dealt with by a prohibition on munitions "which rely for their effects on shock waves caused by the detonation of a cloud created by a substance spread in the air, except when the aim is exclusively to destroy material objects, such as the clearance of mine fields."[40] It will be observed that the use of CBUs and FAEs against materiel is not excluded if personnel are not affected. Personnel and materiel are usually found in close proximity to one another, and any rule which distinguishes between the two has a certain air of unreality about it. Again, there has been no movement toward the acceptance of restrictions by those states that have these munitions at their disposal.

DELAYED ACTION WEAPONS AND TREACHEROUS WEAPONS (INCLUDING MINES AND BOOBY-TRAPS). The concern about these weapons arose largely from their effects upon civilian non-combatants. They were said to violate the criteria of indiscriminacy and perfidy—the latter because certain usages (the mining of dead bodies or the use of booby-traps that might attract civilians, particularly children) were thought to be treacherous. Most of these weapons were not perceived to be unlawful per se; it was rather a question of how they were used.[41] Also, this category of weapons differed from the others under consideration in that guerrillas as well as regular forces employ these weapons. They can range from sharpened spikes or a simple explosive device manufactured in the field to sophisticated naval mines.

One of the central problems about land mines has been that they will be laid

---

38. Doc. CDDH/IV/201 (1975).
39. Doc. CDDH/IV/210 (1976).
40. Doc. CDDH/IV/215 (1976).
41. See *Report on the Work of Experts* (1973), pp. 49–54; *Report of the Lucerne Conference*, pp. 63–72; *Report of the Lugano Conference*, pp. 12–13.

for some legitimate military purpose, but then, as the fighting moves on, civilians, unaware of where the mines are, will venture into areas where mines have been laid and they will be killed or injured. The profitable line of attack on the problem therefore seemed to be a requirement of the recording of the location of mines and an obligation not to employ them where there are large concentrations of civilians. There was some convergence of views between several major military powers and some smaller countries on such a formula.[42] Common ground was found on:

—A prohibition on the use of remotely delivered (e.g., air-dropped) mines without the use of some sort of neutralizing device.

—The recording of where minefields are laid in order to permit their removal when no longer needed, and

—A prohibition on the laying of mines in areas where there are large concentrations of civilians except if the mines are placed in the immediate vicinity of military objectives and/or precautions are taken to keep civilians away.

So far as booby-traps are concerned, some agreement might be found on prohibiting their perfidious use—as, for example, in connection with the wounded and dead, children's toys, and first-aid installations.

There is probably more hope of agreement on some sort of restrictions on delayed action and treacherous weapons than as to any other category of weapons. Nevertheless, no provisions have thus far been adopted.

FUTURE WEAPONS. At the Conferences of Government Experts, there has been some discussion of new forms of "conventional" weapons, such as laser weapons, microwave devices, infra-sound devices, light-flash devices, and electronic warfare, in addition to environmental and geophysical warfare, the last two of which can hardly be placed in the category of conventional weapons.[43] The experts have had relatively little to say about the harm that might be expected to flow from the use of these weapons, and no proposals have been put forward concerning their restriction or prohibition.

What has emerged from the limited consideration that there has been of new weapons has been a sense that there ought to be a review of new weapons in order to determine whether they fall afoul of any of the general standards that

---

42. Cf. Doc. CDDH/211 (1976) (Mexico and Switzerland) and Doc. CDDH/IV/213 (1976) (United Kingdom, France, Denmark, and the Netherlands). At the first session of the Diplomatic Conference, Sweden and a group of fifteen other countries proposed a rule that "Anti-personnel land-mines must not be laid by aircraft." Doc. CDDH/IV/201 (1974).
43. See *Report on the Work of Experts* (1973), pp. 65–69; *Report of the Lucerne Conference*, pp. 73–78; *Report of the Lugano Conference*, pp. 19–20.

have been applied in the past[44] such as the causing of "unnecessary suffering." A policy of this sort was actually put into effect by the United States in 1974 with a Department of Defense Instruction requiring a review by the Judge Advocates General of each Military Department to determine whether the intended use of a new weapon is consistent with international law.[45]

Thus far, at the Diplomatic Conference, there have been only two articles adopted in committee (not in the Ad Hoc Committee on Weapons but in one of the main committees) dealing with weapons, and these two at least will in all likelihood be adopted as articles of the new Protocol on International Armed Conflicts. The two articles[46] provide:

Article 33—Basic rules

1. In any armed conflict, the right of Parties to the conflict to choose methods or means of warfare is not unlimited.

2. It is forbidden to employ weapons, projectiles, and material and methods of warfare of a nature to cause superfluous injury or unnecessary suffering.

3. It is forbidden to employ methods or means of warfare which are intended or may be expected to cause widespread, long-term, and severe damage to the natural environment.

Article 34—New weapons

In the study, development, acquisition, or adoption of a new weapon, means, or method of warfare a High Contracting Party is under an obligation to determine whether its employment would, under some or all circumstances be prohibited by this Protocol or by any other rule of international law applicable to the High Contracting Party.

Paragraph 3 of Article 33 and Article 34 cover new ground but the rest of Article 33, as can readily be seen, is a reiteration of what is already the law.

No one can predict with any certainty what will be the outcome of the present effort to place controls on the use of certain conventional weapons. Some of the momentum seems to have gone out of the campaign once the political points have been scored and states begin to look to the complexities of the use and effect of weapons and to their own national interests in the employment of a wide range of conventional weapons. One might also like to think that there is a heightened awareness that treaty provisions that are not accepted by the states

---

44. Doc. CDDH/IV/201 (1974).
45. Department of Defense Instruction No. 5500.15, "Review of Legality of Weapons under International Law," October 16, 1974.
46. *Report of Committee III, Second Session,* Doc. CDDH/215/Rev.1 (1975).

having the most sophisticated military technology will be of little value. Those countries that have been in the forefront of the effort to place restrictions on weapons will, after the hoped for completion of the Diplomatic Conference in 1977, have to look about for another forum in which to deal with these questions—perhaps either the Conference of the Committee on Disarmament or the General Assembly.

[3]

SOME LEGAL ASPECTS OF THE USE OF NUCLEAR WEAPONS

By

IAN BROWNLIE *

Perspectives

BRITISH jurists have not been attracted to the problems arising from the manufacture, testing, dissemination and use of nuclear weapons, with the notable exception of Professor Schwarzenberger.[1] Two factors may explain a reluctance to take up the problems. The first is broadly political: a certain irritation with the United Nations and particularly with the doings of the General Assembly since its expansion in the years after 1955. The General Assembly has since 1960 produced a number of resolutions trenching on legal questions, and among these the use of nuclear weapons, in a dramatic way. The topics covered have been neglected in the literature of the law and in some cases British sources have failed to report them.[2] One may or may not be pleased with the political developments reflected in the General Assembly but, particularly for lawyers, it is hardly permissible to ignore them. The other factor is probably a feeling of despondency arising from the undoubtedly correct assumption that, where matters of high policy are concerned, the influence of international law is minimal.[3] As a comparative assessment of the role of the law this is incontrovertible and yet it cannot be said to justify the tacit removal of certain subjects from the agenda. Some very important aspects of constitutional and criminal law in the modern State are bound up with matters of high policy; and constitutions are not self-enforcing. Nevertheless, lawyers do not shy away from the " high policy " areas of municipal law. Another

---

* Fellow of Wadham College, Oxford.
[1] *The Legality of Nuclear Weapons*, 1958.
[2] Whilst it is a matter of appreciation and taste, the obvious contemporary source, *The Times*, may be thought to be neglectful of United Nations affairs. Recently the *British Contemporary Practice* has remedied the situation by the inclusion of texts of General Assembly resolutions. The Chatham House publication of *Documents on International Affairs* for particular years appears after a considerable lapse of time. *Keesing* is not geared to legal affairs and often paraphrases important texts.
[3] *Cf.* Article IV of the Test Ban Treaty of 1963: " This Treaty shall be of unlimited duration. Each Party shall in exercising its national sovereignty have the right to withdraw from the Treaty if it decides that extraordinary events, related to the subject-matter of this Treaty, have jeopardised the supreme interests of its country. It shall give notice of such withdrawal to all other Parties to the Treaty three months in advance."

consideration, more important than the first, is that it is very easy to underestimate the relevance of moral arguments in world affairs: the principle of self-determination is an obvious example of the impact of ideas and standards on political and legal developments. The conventional riposte, that appeals to morals by governments are at best aspiration and at worst propaganda, might be regarded as a proof of the *relevance* of morals rather than the reverse, and the riposte certainly does not prove the absolute ineffectiveness of moral standards. The trap is to go forward from a " realist " approach to the view that governments *will* fail to observe moral and legal standards and the corollary that, as the State practice (including treaty commitments) must be assessed apparently on the basis of a presumption of irregularity and an absence of *opinio juris*, therefore there are no legal standards, except perhaps as descriptions of legal powers, for example, to use certain weapons. The consequence is an unattractive nihilism which is often glossed over by implicit reference to the superior appreciation of international affairs which is supposed to grace the " realist." The simple point would seem to be that it is better to uphold a prohibition which *may* be avoided in a crisis than to do away with standards altogether. There is no evidence that, in a crisis, governments deliberately choose instruments of policy outside the law: and to deny the existence of legal standards is to free governments from the burden of justification and to beg any question of the effectiveness of the law.

At any rate the legality of the use of nuclear weapons [4] is a question which has appeared on the agenda of the United Nations General Assembly on several occasions in the recent past and which engages the active interest of a majority of member States. On November 24, 1961, the General Assembly adopted the " Resolution on Prohibition of the Use of Nuclear Weapons for War Purposes " by fifty-five votes to twenty, with twenty-six abstentions.[5] The only vote cast against the resolution from Africa and Asia was that of Nationalist China. The Latin-American States largely abstained,[6]

---

[4] For a treaty definition of " atomic weapons " see the Agreement for Co-operation on the Uses of Atomic Energy for Mutual Defence Purposes, signed July 3, 1958, 326 U.N.T.S., No. 4707, Art. XI, A: " ' Atomic weapon ' means any device utilising atomic energy, exclusive of the means for transporting or propelling the device ' (where such means is a separable and divisible part of the device), the principal purpose of which is for use as, or for development of, a weapon, a weapon prototype, or a weapon test device." Identical definitions appear in other agreements to which the United States is a party.

[5] See Schwarzenberger, " Report on Self-Defence under the Charter of the United Nations and the Use of Prohibited Weapons," *I.L.A., Brussels Conference 1962*, Committee on the Charter of the United Nations, p. 83.

[6] Costa Rica, Guatemala and Nicaragua voted against.

as also did the Scandinavian States, Austria, and certain political associates of the West in Asia. What is interesting about the voting pattern is, however, the fact that States representing a variety of political associations are to be found in the majority vote. This was drawn from the " non-aligned " African and Asian States, some African and Asian States with Western leanings such as Nigeria, Lebanon and Japan, Mexico (the only Latin-American representative on the majority) and the Communist States. Members of NATO (apart from Denmark and Norway), together with Australia, Ireland, New Zealand, Spain, South Africa, three Central American republics and Nationalist China, voted against the resolution. On November 27, 1963, the General Assembly adopted a resolution which asked the eighteen-nation Disarmament Committee in Geneva to study the question of convening a conference to sign a convention banning the use of atomic and hydrogen weapons. In this case the majority consisted of sixty-four votes, there being eighteen votes against and twenty-five abstentions.[7] The General Assembly has also concerned itself with aspects of disarmament relating to nuclear weapons, including the ending of weapon tests[8] and the creation of denuclearised zones in Africa[8a] and Latin America.[9]

The paper presented here is designed to examine the salient features of the legal aspects of the use of nuclear weapons as instruments of international policy. No attempt will be made to tabulate, and comment upon, all the arguments for and against the

---

[7] A/RES/1909(XVIII). See further (1964) *U.N. Monthly Chronicle* 91.

[8] Resol. against Soviet plan to explode a 50-megaton bomb, October 27, 1961, A/RES/1632(XVI); Resol. on continuation of suspension of nuclear tests, November 6, 1961, A/RES/1648(XVI); Resol. on an Undertaking by Countries Possessing no Nuclear Weapons not to have such weapons in their territory, December 4, 1961, A/RES/1664(XVI); Resol. on Prevention of the Wider Dissemination of Nuclear Weapons, same date, A/RES/1665(XVI); Resol. on the Urgent Need for Suspension of Nuclear Tests, Resols. A and B of November 6, 1962, A/RES/1762(XVII); Resol. on Convening a Conference for the purpose of signing a Convention on the Prohibition of the Use of Nuclear Weapons, December 14, 1962, A/RES/1801(XVII); Resol. on the Urgent Need for Suspension of Nuclear and Thermo-Nuclear Tests, November 27, 1963, A/RES/1910(XVIII); Resol. prohibiting the placing in space of weapons of mass destruction, November 17, 1963, A/RES/1884(XVIII). " See also the Decl. of the Conference of Heads of State or Government of Non-Aligned Countries, at Belgrade, of September 6, 1961, *Keesing* 1961–1962, 18601A (25 States participated); and . . ." See also the decisions of the Addis Ababa Conference of the Heads of State and Government of Independent African Countries, May 1963 (a total of 32 States); and the Declaration of the Conference of Heads of State or Government of Non-aligned Countries, Cairo, October 1964, sect. VII (1964) 4 *Indian Journal of Int. Law* 599 (47 States).

[8a] Resol. of November 24, 1961, A/RES/1652(XVI). In favour: 55 votes; none against; 44 abstentions.

[9] Resol. of November 27, 1963; A/RES/1911(XVIII). In favour: 91 votes; none against; 15 abstentions.

440   *International and Comparative Law Quarterly*   [VOL. 14

legality of their use in the literature [10]: only the more valid, or more tenaciously held, positions will be considered. Moreover, the special aspects of the subject, in particular, testing, dissemination of weapons and information, the more detailed implications for the law concerning neutrality, the innocent character of passage of warships through straits and territorial sea,[11] and the criminal responsibility of individuals involved in the preparation and waging of nuclear war, will not be dealt with at any length.[12]

Arguments for Illegality

Though not academically conventional it will be helpful to the presentation if my primary conclusion be stated straightaway. The use of nuclear weapons and, more particularly, of thermonuclear weapons delivered by rocket, is in most conceivable situations illegal under the existing laws of war, which rest on generally accepted customary rules and on conventions to which the United Kingdom is a party. In any case many of the conventions relating to the laws of war are generally regarded as stating the customary law and thus binding on all States. Existing literature provides a comprehensive guide to the factual background and, as a preliminary to the points of law, it is necessary merely to recall two major aspects of these weapons and their use. First, their effects include heat, blast, radiation in the target area and fall-out there and elsewhere. Secondly, the NATO countries and the Soviet Union have threatened each other with policies of deterrence [13] based upon the promise of " massive retaliation " in case of a prior use of nuclear weapons by the other side. The legal considerations are set out in an order dictated by convenience rather than higher considerations of logic.

First, the substantial aspects of the laws of war may be considered. The use of nuclear weapons on any appreciable

---

[10] See in particular Schwarzenberger, *op. cit., supra*; Nagendra Singh, *Nuclear Weapons and International Law* (London, 1959); Charlier (1957-I) 91 *Recueil des Cours* 213,350–378; Menzel, *Legalität oder Illegalität der Anwendung von Atomwaffen* (Tübingen, 1960); *ibid.*, Strupp-Schlochauer, *Wörterbuch*, I, p. 104; Euler, *Die Atomwaffe im Luftkriegsrecht* (Köln-Berlin, 1960); Nahlik (1961) IV *Polish Perspectives* (Aug.–Sept. No. 8–9) 12–32 (In English, trans. from (1961) *Sprawy Miedzynarodowe*, No. 5); Radojkovic (1962) *The Yearbook of World Affairs*, 197–215; Greenspan, *The Modern Law of Land Warfare* (Berkeley and Los Angeles, 1959) 368–377; von der Heydte (1961) 9 *Archiv des Völkerrechts* 162–182; Setalvad (1963) 3 *Indian Journal of Int. Law* 383–395; Meyrowitz (1963) *Revue Générale de droit int. public.*

[11] The existence of the right for warships to pass through the territorial sea is itself the subject of controversy.

[12] On the problem of proportionality in relation to self-defence by nuclear weapons (aside from the issue of illegality as a category of weapon) see Brownlie, *International Law and the Use of Force by States*, pp. 262–264.

[13] There are of course many other strategic uses and considerations but this aspect has always been prominent and consistently emphasised.

scale would involve a refusal to distinguish combatants and non-combatants, and military objectives from other targets. Many of the particular obligations of the laws of war would thus be ignored.[14] Of course it is often said that these distinctions are now obsolete in the conditions of modern warfare. However, the evidence in support of such assertions goes no further than the establishing of the facts that in modern conditions such distinctions may be more difficult to draw and that the categorical extent of the concepts has altered. To suggest that the distinctions have gone is to support a *non sequitur* and to show an unqualified allegiance to military necessity (*Kreigsraison*). The United Kingdom *Manual of Military Law* [15] maintains these distinctions, a circumstance of some importance since the same *Manual* maintains the legality of nuclear weapons in the formula [16]: " In the absence of any rule of international law dealing expressly with it, the use which may be made of a particular weapon will be governed by the ordinary rules and the question of the legality of its use in any particular case will, therefore, involve merely the application of the recognised principles of international law." A large number of States have become parties to the Geneva Conventions of 1949 and new States accede to these conventions in many cases. The *Manual of Military Law* gives force to the provisions of these conventions in the text and later amendments. Yet, as a learned commentator points out [17]:

" If the use of nuclear weapons be prohibited *per se*, or if they cannot be used without violating the customary rules of war or the Geneva Conventions, *e.g.*, because their use means attacking the civilian population, or not protecting and respecting the sick and wounded, medical installations, and the aged and children placed in agreed safety zones, any proposal to use these weapons in the first resort against an aggressor who has

[14] See generally Nagendra Singh, *Nuclear Weapons and International Law*, 1959. In addition, in view of radiation and fall-out effects of nuclear weapons, these weapons are caught by the prohibition of the use of poisoned weapons: see Article 23 (a) of the Rules annexed to the Hague Convention concerning the Laws and Customs of War on Land of 1907. Paragraph (e) of the same article prohibits the employment of " arms, projectiles or material calculated to cause unnecessary suffering."

[15] H.M.S.O., 1958, Part III, " The Law of War on Land." Sir Hersch Lauterpacht had assisted in the revision of this Part of the *Manual* and considerable use was made of the material he had incorporated in his successive editions of Volume II of Oppenheim's *International Law.*

[16] See para. 107, n. 1 (b). *Cf.* para. 113. See also (1961) 10 I.C.L.Q. 586.

[17] G. I. A. D. Draper, *The Red Cross Conventions* (1958), pp. 98–99. See also *ibid.* p. 100. On the fate of a Soviet proposal on the illegality of nuclear weapons *tout court*, made during the diplomatic conference which produced the conventions, see Paul de la Pradelle, *La Conférence diplomatique et les nouvelles Conventions de Genève du 12 Août 1949* (Paris, 1951), pp. 36–41. In April 1950 the C.I.C.R. addressed an appeal to signatories of the Conventions asking them to abolish all weapons causing massive destruction of populations.

not used them, stands condemned as an illegality as serious as, if not more serious than, the aggression."

The effects of a use of nuclear weapons would necessarily involve grave breaches of the Geneva Protocol signed on June 17, 1925, to which thirty-eight States are parties.[18] The Protocol reads in part:

> " The undersigned Plenipotentiaries, in the name of their respective Governments:
> Whereas the use in war of asphyxiating, poisonous or other gases, and of all analogous liquids, materials or devices, has been justly condemned by the general opinion of the civilised world; and
> Whereas the prohibition of such use has been declared in Treaties to which the majority of Powers of the world are Parties; and
> To the end that this prohibition shall be universally accepted as a part of International Law, binding alike the conscience and practice of nations;
> Declare:
> That the High Contracting Parties, so far as they are not already Parties to Treaties prohibiting such use, accept this prohibition, agree to extend this prohibition to the use of bacteriological methods of warfare and agree to be bound as between themselves according to the terms of this declaration."

In so far as the instrument relates to chemical weapons it is without doubt declaratory of the customary law.[19]

---

[18] Hudson, *Int.Legis.*, III, 1670; United Kingdom *Manual*, App. IX, p. 216. The United States is not a party. The United Kingdom and U.S.S.R. are parties on condition of reciprocity. China's accession of August 7, 1929, has been recognised by the People's Republic of China as from August 9, 1952. The Protocol came into force on February 8, 1928. In 1944 ratifications and accessions numbered forty-one, including the three Baltic Republics: *L. of N. Off.Journ., Spec. Suppl.* No. 193, V. Legal. 1944, V. 2, p. 59. Forty-nine States had signed it. On April 13, 1960, Pakistan informed the French Government that she considered herself a party, equally with India. Recent accessions: Hungary, Oct. 21, 1952; Ceylon, Dec. 18, 1953; Tanganyika, April 22, 1963; Rwanda, June 25, 1964. *Cf.* See Council Recs. 7th year, 584th–590th meetings and 7th year, Suppl. April–June 1952, pp. 17, 21–69; and Gen. Ass. Resol. 502 (VI), Jan. 11, 1952.

[19] See Oppenheim, *International Law*, II (7th ed.), p. 344; Schwarzenberger, *The Legality of Nuclear Weapons*, p. 38. See also Art. 171 of the Treaty of Versailles; Art. 135 of the Treaty of St. Germain and especially Art. 5 of the Treaty of Washington, 1922; Hudson, *Int.Legis.*, II, 794. The latter was unratified but may be declaratory in effect. For other condemnations of chemical warfare see Resol. of the Fifth International Conference of American States, May 3, 1923, J. B. Scott, *The International Conferences of American States 1889–1928* (1931), 290; Resol. of the Conference of General Disarmament, July 23, 1932; Resol. of League Council of May 14, 1938; these two resols. are referred to in the Resol. of the League Assembly of September 30, 1938, *L. of N., Off.Journ., Spec.Suppl.* No. 183, 19th Sess., Plen., 1938, p. 135; Final Act of the Consultative Meeting of Foreign Ministers of the American Republics, September 23–October 3, 1939, item vi (1940) 34 A.J.I.L. Suppl. 12. *Cf.* Statement of U.S. President on " poisonous or noxious gases or other inhumane devices of warfare," 8 *Dept. of State Bull.* June 12, 1943, No. 207.

In addition, the use, on any appreciable scale, of nuclear weapons involves the commission of crimes against humanity, declared to be crimes under international law in the Agreement on Military Trials of 1945 which provided for the establishment of an International Military Tribunal at Nuremberg.[20] The Agreement was signed by the United Kingdom, U.S.S.R., the United States and France, and was adhered to by nineteen States.[21] By a unanimous resolution [22] of December 11, 1946, the United Nations General Assembly affirmed " the principles of international law recognised by the Charter of the Nuremberg Tribunal and the Judgment of the Tribunal." In this connection the Convention on the Prevention and Punishment of the Crime of Genocide, adopted by the General Assembly in 1948,[23] has obvious significance. By July 1960 the Convention was in force between sixty-four States. The United Kingdom has refused to ratify it but, on one view at least, Article 1 gives the Convention a declaratory effect and its prescriptions on genocide are binding on all States. The Convention establishes genocide, whether committed in peace or war, as a crime under international law which the parties undertake to prevent and punish. Genocide is defined as acts, such as " killing members of the group," " committed with intent to destroy, in whole or in part, a national, ethnical, racial or religious group as such." *Mens rea* is required, but what is meant by destruction of a group *as such* ? [24] The preparatory materials show a divergence of views on the relevance of motive and one is thrown back on the text. On one view the adoption of a strategy, which in practice will bring about the complete destruction of a nation State, like Norway, or the destruction by tactical nuclear weapons of minorities living in

---

[20] Signed August 8, 1945.   Text: 12 *Dept. of St. Bull.,* p. 222; (1945) 39 A.J.I.L. Suppl., 257.   See also *Judgment of the International Military Tribunal at Nuremberg,* Cmd. 6964, p. 1.   Article 6 (c) of the Charter of the Nuremberg Tribunal defines crimes against humanity as " murder, extermination, enslavement, deportation, and other inhumane acts committed against any civilian population, before or during the war, or persecutions on political, racial or religious grounds in execution of or in connection with any crime within the jurisdiction of the Tribunal, whether or not in violation of the domestic law of the country where perpetrated."   See, generally, Schwelb (1946) 23 B.Y.I.L. 178–226.

[21] Canada and the Philippines were concerned only with the establishment of the International Military Tribunal for the Far East the Charter of which also provided for punishment of crimes against humanity.   Eight States were concerned with the creation of both the International Military Tribunals. See further U.N.W.C.C., *Law Reports of Trials of War Criminals,* XV, 134–138.

[22] Resol. 95.   For further materials on the role of the Nuremberg Charter in State practice see Brownlie, *International Law and the Use of Force by States,* pp. 175–184, 185–188, 191–194.

[23] Resol. 260 (III) of December 9, 1948; 78 U.N.T.S. 278; United Kingdom *Manual,* App. X, p. 217; (1951) 45 A.J.I.L. Suppl. 11.

[24] *Cf. R.* v. *Ahlers* [1915] 1 K.B. 616; *R.* v. *Steane* [1947] K.B. 997; and see Glanville Williams, *Criminal Law, The General Part* (2nd ed.), pp. 40–41.

particular areas of one or more States, is to prepare for the commission of genocide. The other approach would be to say that this is too simple a view because the text, like many other provisions of criminal law, leaves open the question of justification: thus the text is hardly conclusive on the issue of prohibited weapons and a defensive use of nuclear weapons might well be justified. This latter view is probably the more correct, but, even so, the provision must create a presumption of the illegality of resort to nuclear weapons as part of a policy of deterrence and massive retaliation and also, though less obviously, in the case of a large-scale use in other circumstances.

From another point of view, the use of nuclear and thermonuclear weapons in retaliation, in other words, on a large scale in accordance with the policy of the deterrent, would involve extensive fall-out which could inflict great harm on the populations of neutral States. Such a policy contradicts the duties which customary law imposes on belligerents. Moreover, it infringes Article 1 of the Hague Convention of 1907 concerning the Rights and Duties of Neutral Powers and Persons in War on Land,[25] which provides: " The territory of neutral Powers in inviolable." This was not ratified by the United Kingdom but is generally accepted as a statement of general international law, binding all States.

Arguments for Legality

The arguments for legality have varying degrees of ambition. Some are not directed to a proposition of legality but to the weakening of particular planks in the case for illegality. Thus it has been shown effectively enough that the Declaration of St. Petersburg of 1868 [26] was not aimed at weapons of mass destruction since, in the case of projectiles under four hundred grammes in weight, the cruelty of the weapon was out of proportion to its destructive potential. Had their power been to disable large numbers at once, as with projectiles above their weight, there would have been no objection.[27] Again, it could be argued that the chemical weapons referred to in the Geneva Protocol of 1925 have a general aspect which distinguishes them from explosive atomic weapons.[28] This, however, suffers from a comparison with the results of interpreting older statutes on road traffic in such a way as to confine the word " vehicle " to the horse and cart. In any case the deterrent or strategic weapon and, to a lesser extent, other nuclear

---

25 United Kingdom *Manual*, App. VI, p. 210.
26 *Ibid.*, App. I, p. 198.
27 See Schwarzenberger, *Report, op. cit., supra*, 21, 38.
28 See McDougal and Feliciano, *Law and Minimum World Public Order* (1961), pp. 662–668.

weapons, are deployed in part with a view to utilising the destructive effects of radiation and fall-out.[29] Other arguments have a different aspect, that of deflecting attention from technical arguments by pointing to areas of ineffectiveness and acquiescence in the face of wrongdoing. Thus reference is made to the practice of both sets of belligerents in the Second World War of indiscriminate air bombardment of zones of civilian housing.[30] Of course the question of effectiveness arises, as it does everywhere in this part of the law,[31] but reference to it takes the lawyer neither forward nor backward. Even if one accepted that the rules of aerial warfare have disintegrated completely, does it follow that the putatively empty category of " air warfare " affects ground sited rockets aimed at ground targets elsewhere, whether the targets be a few miles away or on another continent? The directed projectile is analogous to artillery rather than to aerial bombardment: indeed, with modern techniques, such a projectile, with a preselected target, is more discriminating than strategic area bombing. Moreover Allied bombing of Germany was indiscriminate but was primarily directed at industrial potential [32]: the prime object of deterrent nuclear weapons is ruthless and unpleasant retaliation—they are instruments of terror rather than weapons of war.

An exception, quite commonly made by jurists who otherwise affirm the illegality of nuclear weapons,[33] depends on the doctrine of reprisal or retaliation. The principle thus offered is that the atomic weapon may be used in reprisal against an unlawful act which itself consists in the use of the atomic weapon.[34] The action taken in reprisal must be proportionate to the original offence and there is some doubt whether non-identical reprisals can be " proportionate." But in the context of nuclear war the argument for reprisals meets two considerable objections. In the first place, it is hardly legitimate to extend a doctrine related to the minutiae of the conventional theatre of war to an exchange of power which, in the case of the strategic and deterrent uses of nuclear weapons, is equivalent to the total of war effort and is the essence of the war aims.[35] Moreover, Article 1 of the Civilian, Prisoners, and Sick and Wounded Conventions of 1949 provides in each case: " The High

---

[29] *A fortiori* if a constituent is placed in the weapon with a view to increasing fall-out.

[30] See the interesting material in Schwarzenberger, *Report*, pp. 23–25, 39–40.

[31] *Supra.*

[32] There is evidence that the bombing *sustained* civilian morale in Germany.

[33] See, for example, Nahlik (1961) IV *Polish Perspectives* (Warsaw: in English) (Aug.–Sept., No. 8–9), 12, 26.

[34] See also Schwarzenberger, *The Legality of Nuclear Weapons*, pp. 40–41; Nagendra Singh, *op. cit., supra*, pp. 218–223.

[35] See Draper, *The Red Cross Conventions*, pp. 98–99.

446   *International and Comparative Law Quarterly*   [VOL. 14

Contracting Parties undertake to respect and to ensure respect for the present Convention in all circumstances." [36] The wording is not of course conclusive of the issue under discussion but the burden of those seeking to establish the exception of nuclear reprisal would seem to be very great. Two other points may be made. First, the reprisal argument does not necessarily involve an admission that nuclear weapons are illegal *per se*.[37] Secondly, whilst reservations of reciprocity may provide for reprisals in the context of prohibitions by treaty, the reservations may not be worth much if the prohibition is, in part at least, declaratory: this point bears on the effect of British and Soviet reservations to the Geneva Protocol.

Conditional Legality: A Primary Conclusion

Some manuals of military law adopt the principle that the use of nuclear weapons is lawful provided that the laws of war are applied.[38] It is true that situations are conceivable in which military targets could be hit without causing suffering to neutral States or population centres, and the possibilities include attacks on vessels in mid-ocean, army brigades in deserts, and a base on the Greenland icecap, and also the destruction of a missile on the fringes of space which threatened territory below. Yet one may feel that the very refinement of these examples tends to prove rather than to disprove the general proposition of illegality set out previously.

However, as a primary conclusion it may be asserted that, even if it is assumed (without prejudice to the examination of other questions below) that the use of nuclear weapons is lawful under certain conditions, the use of nuclear and thermonuclear weapons delivered by bomber and missile in pursuance of a policy of deterrence and involving massive retaliation [39] would still be unlawful for certain compelling reasons. First, the use of these weapons on a large scale could not be reconciled with the general principles of the laws of war in the way envisaged by the United Kingdom *Manual*. Secondly, the deterrent principle rests on the threat of massive retaliation, and this even in reply to attack with conventional weapons according to official Western statements.[40] If put into practice this principle would lead to a lack of proportion

---

[36] *Ibid.* 100.   [37] *Ibid.* 99 for a different view.
[38] See the United Kingdom *Manual* of 1958 quoted *supra*; also the *U.S. Dept. of the Army Field Manual*, FM 27–10, *The Law of Land Warfare*, July 1956, para. 35 (see also para. 38 on the permissibility of chemical and bacteriological weapons); and U.S. *Law of Naval Warfare*, para. 613 (see Tucker, *The Law of War and Neutrality at Sea*, U.S. Naval War College, Int. Law Studies, XLV (1957), sec. 410).
[39] And also with the objective of a strategic knockout blow before the other side moves offensively.
[40] See Brownlie, *op. cit.*, pp. 262–263.

between the actual threat and the reaction to it. Such disproportionate reaction does not constitute self-defence as permitted by Article 51 of the United Nations Charter.[41] Proportionality is always a condition of lawful self-defence. Lastly, massive nuclear strikes would create unreasonable hazards for neutral States, the legal aspects of which have been noticed earlier.

Illegality " Tout Court ": The General Assembly Resolution of November 24, 1961

The adoption by the United Nations General Assembly of the " Resolution on Prohibition of the Use of Nuclear Weapons for War Purposes " has been noticed earlier.[42] Its text is as follows:

" *The General Assembly,*

Mindful of its responsibility under the Charter of the United Nations in the maintenance of international peace and security, as well as in the consideration of principles governing disarmament,

Gravely concerned that, while negotiations on disarmament have not, so far, achieved satisfactory results, the armaments race, particularly in the nuclear and thermonuclear fields, has reached a dangerous stage requiring all possible precautionary measures to protect humanity and its civilisation from the hazard of nuclear and thermonuclear catastrophe,

Recalling that the use of weapons of mass destruction, causing unnecessary human suffering, was, in the past, prohibited as being contrary to the laws of humanity and to the principles of international law, by international declarations and binding agreements, such as the Declaration of St. Petersburg of 1868, the Declaration of the Brussels Conference of 1874, the Conventions of the Hague Peace Conferences of 1899 and 1907, and the Geneva Protocol of 1925, to which the majority of nations are still parties,

Considering that the use of nuclear and thermonuclear weapons would bring about indiscriminate suffering and destruction to mankind and its civilisation to an even greater extent than the use of those weapons declared by the aforementioned international declarations and agreements to be contrary to the laws of humanity and a crime under international law,

Believing that the use of weapons of mass destruction, such as nuclear and thermonuclear weapons, is a direct negation of the high ideals and objectives which the United Nations has been

---

[41] Nor would it fall within the customary rule, based on Webster's correspondence on the *Caroline* incident, which Professor Sir Humphrey Waldock and others regard as having survived the Charter: see Waldock in Brierly, *Law of Nations* (6th ed.), pp. 416–421; and (1962-II) 106 *Recueil des Cours* 5, 232–237; and Bowett, *Self-Defence in International Law*, p. 182 et seq.

[42] *Supra.*

established to achieve through the protection of succeeding generations from the scourge of war and through the preservation and promotion of their cultures,

1. *Declares*:

(a) That the use of nuclear and thermonuclear weapons is contrary to the spirit, letter and aims of the United Nations and, as such, a direct violation of the United Nations Charter;

(b) That the use of nuclear and thermonuclear weapons would exceed even the scope of war and cause indiscriminate suffering and destruction to mankind and its civilisation and, as such, is contrary to the rules of international law and to the laws of humanity;

(c) That the use of nuclear and thermonuclear weapons is a war directed, not against an enemy or enemies alone, but also against mankind in general, since the peoples of the world not involved in such war will be subjected to all the evils generated by the use of such weapons;

(d) That any State using nuclear and thermonuclear weapons is to be considered to violate the Charter of the United Nations, to act contrary to the laws of humanity, and to commit a crime against mankind and its civilisation;

2. *Requests* the Secretary-General to consult the Governments of Member States to ascertain their views on the possibility of convening a special conference for signing a convention on the prohibition of the use of nuclear and thermonuclear weapons for war purposes and to report on the results of such consultation to the seventeenth session of the General Assembly.''

It is trite comment to point out that such a resolution is not of itself binding in law, but the public expression by governments of opinions on matters of law in such an important forum, and in such a forceful manner, provides cogent evidence as to the state of the law.   Out of a hundred and one States, fifty-five voted in favour of the resolution, twenty against it, and there were twenty-six abstentions.[43]   However, in the debates in the First Committee and Plenary Sessions of the General Assembly the differences of opinion related primarily to the appropriateness of the resolution as a measure isolated from disarmament as a whole and preceding the negotiations for a ban on nuclear tests.[44]   Several representatives

---

[43] *Cf.* the voting, and the reasons therefor, at the diplomatic conference which drew up the Geneva Conventions of 1949, on the admissibility of a Soviet proposal on the illegality of atomic weapons: see P. de la Pradelle, *La Conférence Diplomatique et les Nouvelles Conventions de Genève du 12 Août 1949*, pp. 36–41.

[44] General Assembly, 16th Sess., Off.Recs., First Committee, 1171st Meeting *et seq.*; especially 1189th Meeting *et seq.*; 16th Sess., Off.Recs., Plen. Meetings, 1043rd, 1047th, 1049th and 1063rd Meetings.

explained their abstention in these terms.[45] Exceptionally, the United States representative argued that the United Nations Charter placed no limitation on the type of weapon to be used.[46] In general representatives refrained from challenging the conclusions of law in the resolution.

The resolution is a political as well as a legal document and the drafting has many faults from the technical point of view.[47] The enumeration of declarations and binding agreements in the recitals can easily be faulted in detail: thus the Declaration of St. Petersburg may have no relevance at all [48] and the Declaration of Brussels was not ratified by any State. Moreover, the assertion in the substance of the resolution that the " letter " of the Charter of the United Nations forbids the use of nuclear weapons needs some explanation. Yet the existence of such faults hardly reduces the value of the resolution as an expression of the opinion of many governments on the state of the law. Even from the technical point of view, the recital containing the enumeration of declarations and agreements *as a whole* may be thought to make its point. Further, the resolution itself makes the simple but important point that the use of such weapons is irreconcilable with the political and legal rationale of war.[49] The scope of nuclear war is likely to be such that the survival of mankind, or at least of its culture resulting from the works of four millennia, will be placed in issue. It is possible that escalation may not occur, but the risk is sufficiently serious. It is said that the mass raids on Hamburg and Dresden, with their firestorms, involved mass destruction on a scale similar to that of the Hiroshima holocaust.[50] This may be true but vital distinctions remain. First, there is the readiness to inflict such

[45] First Committee, 1193rd Meeting, para. 57 (Venezuela); Plen. Meetings, 1063rd Meeting, paras. 84 (Pakistan), 104 (Thailand).

[46] First Committee, 1192nd Meeting, para. 6. The U.S.S.R. voted for the resolution but has shown itself willing to use nuclear weapons in certain situations: see the Soviet statement on action in the event of an American attack on Cuba, September 11, 1962, *Soviet News*, No. 4738, September 12, 1962.

[47] For a critique: Schwarzenberger, *Report, op. cit., supra*, 38–42.

[48] See *supra*.

[49] The United Kingdom *Manual*, para. 3, in part reads: " The development of the law of war has been determined by three principles: first, the principle that a belligerent is justified in applying compulsion and force of any kind, to the extent necessary for the realisation of the purpose of war, that is, the complete submission of the enemy at the earliest possible moment with the least expenditure of men, resources and money; secondly, the principle of humanity, according to which kinds and degrees of violence which are not necessary for the purpose of war are not permitted to a belligerent; and thirdly, the principle of chivalry, which demands a certain amount of fairness in offence and defence, and a certain mutual respect between the opposing forces."

[50] Of course, it does not follow from this that the mass raids were legal, although this is sometimes the intended inference. The point taken up here is really " plus ça change, plus c'est le même chose."

destruction in a matter of minutes on whole countries, on dozens of conurbations. Secondly, the " like Hamburg " argument ignores the long-term biological effects of nuclear radiation and nuclear warfare.

The legal significance of the resolution does not lie in its value as evidence alone. The resolution takes the firm view that because of their qualities, these weapons are illegal whenever used.[51] At the least, it thus reinforces the " primary conclusion " offered earlier, with the difference that the " primary conclusion " accepted the possibility that certain rather unusual applications of nuclear force might not involve mass destruction and violation of existing legal standards. However, it can be argued that, in view of the risks involved once these weapons are used, it is ridiculous to allow refined examples of putatively lawful use to dominate the legal régime; and further, that the examples offered ignore the general context of a conflict and the risk of escalation. The risk of escalation and the general threat to the viability of mankind, its civilisation and human values justify, whilst they do not in themselves establish, the view that these weapons are illegal *tout court*. If nuclear weapons are within the rationale of the Geneva Protocol of 1925 this view of the law is reinforced. In brief, in any readily foreseeable inter-State conflict these weapons will involve mass destruction, violation of existing legal standards, and the infliction of unnecessary suffering.[52] Alternatively it could be argued that, if the weapons themselves are not unlawful, they are at the moment deployed with a view to the pursuit of strategic and deterrent policies which would necessarily involve illegal use. This alternative view is rather less dogmatic than the first and the more easily sustainable. The difference between this alternative view and that of the United Kingdom *Manual* is in essence that the régime of the *Manual* rests on academically *conceivable* situations (*e.g.*, small weapons used against forces in uninhabited wastes) taken in isolation from a general conflict, whilst the alternative view is based on natural and probable consequences of use in war and " escalation " and on the types of use for which the weapons are declared to be in readiness by governments possessing them.

---

[51] There is a limitation in the term " weapon ": purpose is important. Apparently nuclear devices can be used for ambitious schemes of earth sculpting and excavation.

[52] For views on these lines: Korovin (1955) *Mezhdunarodnoe Zhizn*, No. 5, 48; Menzel, *Legalität oder Illegalität der Anwendung von Atomwaffen* (Tübingen, 1960); Nahlik, *op. cit., supra*; Castrén, *The Present Law of War and Neutrality* (1954), p. 206; Radojkovic (1954) *The Yearbook of World Affairs* 197; Spaight, *Air Power and War Rights* (London, 1947), p. 276; *ibid.*, *The Atomic Problem* (London, 1948).

Practical consequences of illegality tout court

The practical difference between conditional and absolute illegality is in one sense small: any large scale use, any massive retaliation, would be unlawful on either view and the deterrent policy certainly involves the preparation of crimes against humanity. The difference consists in the posing of certain specialised uses and the assumption that these would not lead to escalation. However, the political, " legislative " and moral consequences of choosing one formulation rather than the other are considerable. Governments can always temporise on the facts and use the cloak of military necessity. The avoidance of a firm prohibition, as in the case of the United Kingdom *Manual*, combines too readily with official assertions that these are weapons which are only to be used when " necessary," cant about " modern weapons " and so on, to produce the moral canker of respectability.[53]

The distinction between conditional and absolute illegality has important legal effects. If the conditional view be taken, then preparations for nuclear war, including the testing, deployment and transport of warheads, may not be characterised as illegal—unless they are specifically designed for what would be in any case an illegal threat or use of force. On the principle of absolute illegality normal legal powers and privileges would not extend to preparation and transport of the weapons.[54] Thus, if there is a right of passage for warships through the territorial sea, it could hardly apply to vessels carrying nuclear weapons. Treaties relating to the supply, maintenance or manufacture of these weapons would be void. A war illegal by mode rather than occasion may not draw in its train the privileges of belligerents in respect to neutral States. Apart from the law of neutrality, in this as in other fields not too much reliance can be placed on the maxim *ex injuria non oritur jus*. The argument that the laws of war do not apply in favour of the unlawful belligerent has not found much favour in the context of aggressive war, *i.e.*, war unlawful by occasion,[55] and a similar view of the policy and law applicable should prevail in the case of the other type of unlawful war.[56]

---

[53] The relation between official (and legislative) positions on anti-semitism in the given State and the outlook of the non Jewish population is a case in point. One of the most curious official arguments, often heard in Britain, is that by having nuclear weapons one can then show virtue by negotiating to do away with them.

[54] *Cf.* Ceylonese Note delivered to diplomatic missions on January 23, 1964, prohibiting the entry of warships into Ceylon's seaports and territorial sea and the landing at her airports of warplanes carrying nuclear weapons or equipped for waging nuclear war. The decision was stated to be in pursuance of a policy of preventing the spread of nuclear weapons and supporting the creation of nuclear-free zones. For a report and Soviet reaction: *Soviet News* No. 4957, February 25, 1964.   [55] See Brownlie, *op. cit.*, pp. 406–408.

[56] *Cf.* Belli, *De re militari et bello tractatus*. Part ii, ch. i, 6.

Part II
Persons

[4]

SO-CALLED 'UNPRIVILEGED BELLIGERENCY': SPIES, GUERRILLAS, AND SABOTEURS

By MAJOR RICHARD R. BAXTER, B.A., LL.B.[1]

IN an article in the previous issue of this *Year Book*[2] the duty of the inhabitant of occupied territory to refrain from conduct hostile to the occupant was assessed in the light of recent developments in the law, notably of the prosecutions for war crimes following the Second World War and the Geneva Conventions of 1949. It was suggested there that it is merely the superior power of the occupant rather than a precept of international law which forbids the inhabitant to injure the occupying Power. In arriving at that conclusion it was necessary to assess the roles played in the law of belligerent occupation by the military power of the occupant, by international law, and by municipal law. However, the somewhat perplexing question of the scope to be given to each of these elements is not confined to the law of belligerent occupation alone. It is present in an equally acute form in connexion with the problem of spies, guerrillas, saboteurs, secret agents, and other unlawful belligerents operating in areas which are not under belligerent occupation.

I. *International law applied to war*

Essentially, the outbreak of war[3] creates an area of anarchy in the world order, an area in which the normal law applicable to the peaceful intercourse of states is suspended. The propriety of statements that international law confers a 'right' to resort to war and to exercise 'belligerent rights'[4] is highly questionable, and it is probably more accurate to assert that international

---

[1] Of the Judge Advocate General's Corps, United States Army. Formerly Fulbright Student in the University of Cambridge. The opinions expressed in this article are those of the author and do not necessarily reflect the views of the Secretary of Defence, the Secretary of the Army, or the Judge Advocate General of the Army.

[2] Baxter, 'The Duty of Obedience to the Belligerent Occupant', in this *Year Book*. 27 (1950), p. 235.

[3] The word 'war', as used herein, refers not only to declared war but also to other cases of armed conflict and to the occupation of another state's territory even if the occupation meets with no armed resistance. The law of land warfare was apparently applicable to such situations even before the adoption of the Geneva Conventions of 1949 (see *Judgment of the International Military Tribunal for the Trial of German Major War Criminals* (Cmd. 6964, H.M.S.O., 1946), p. 125, with reference to the occupation of Czechoslovakia), and the Conventions themselves are expressly made applicable to these various types of employment of armed force (common Article 2).

[4] Halleck, *International Law; or, Rules Regulating the Intercourse of States in Peace and War* (1861), p. 312; Hall, *A Treatise on International Law* (7th ed. by Higgins, 1917), pp. 389, 411; and see Jessup, *A Modern Law of Nations* (1948), p. 157. Although the title is somewhat misleading, Dr. Spaight makes plain early in his *War Rights on Land* (1911) that the 'rights' to which he refers are those of individuals to be protected in certain respects from the rigours of war (pp. 1–4).

324   SO-CALLED 'UNPRIVILEGED BELLIGERENCY'

law has dealt with war as a state of fact which it has hitherto been powerless to prevent. Animated by considerations of humanity and by the desire
to prevent unnecessary suffering, states have nevertheless recognized
limits on the unfettered power which they would otherwise actually
enjoy in time of war. The law of war is, in the descriptive words of a war
crimes tribunal, 'prohibitive law',[1] in the sense that it forbids rather than
authorizes certain manifestations of force. During the formative period of
codified international law, delegates to international conferences repeatedly
declared that they would not accept proposed provisions which involved
acquiescence in an enemy's exercise of jurisdiction over nationals of their
state.[2] The report of the committee which dealt with the laws and usages of
war to the Hague Conference of 1899 emphasized that it was not intended
by Convention No. II to sanction the employment of force and that the
purpose of the Convention was rather to restrict the exercise of power
which an enemy might in fact wield over another state.[3]

War, conceived as a condition approximating to a state of international
anarchy, is not an armed conflict between states as abstract entities. It is
rather a conflict between populations, in which each national of one belligerent is pitted against each national of the other. Without the humane
intervention of international law, war would entail death or enslavement
for the combatant or non-combatant overcome by the enemy. To ancient
Greece, all inhabitants of an enemy state were themselves enemies whose
persons were at the mercy of the conqueror, to be killed or made slaves as
expediency might dictate,[4] and it has been said that only considerations of
political policy dissuaded the Romans from following a like course.[5] Even
through the Middle Ages it was the practice to kill infidels and to enslave
Christians captured in war.[6] Since the founders of modern international law
were not prone to overlook the verdict of the past, they were forced to admit
that every enemy could in strict law be subjected to violence and could

---

[1] *United States v. List et Al.* (1948): *Trials of War Criminals*, xi (1950), pp. 1247, 1252, *Law
Reports of Trials of War Criminals* (hereinafter referred to as '*War Crimes Reports*'), viii (1949),
p. 66.

[2] See, for example, the remarks of the Netherlands delegate, concurred in by the Italian and
Belgian delegates, to the Brussels Conference of 1874 (*Actes de la Conférence de Bruxelles* (1874),
pp. 43–44, 204) and those of the Netherlands and Belgian delegates concerning uprisings in
occupied areas (ibid., pp. 158–65).

[3] 'Besides, no member of the subcommission had any idea that the legal authority in an invaded
country should in advance give anything like sanction to force employed by an invading and occupying army. On the contrary, the adoption of precise rules tending to limit the exercise of this
power appeared to be an obvious necessity in the real interests of all peoples whom the fortune of
war might in turn betray' (Report to the Conference from the Second Commission on the Laws
and Customs of War on Land, in *Reports to the Hague Conferences of 1899 and 1907* (ed. by Scott,
1917), p. 140; see also pp. 140, 151 for like statements).

[4] Phillipson, *The International Law and Custom of Ancient Greece and Rome* (1911), vol. ii,
p. 251.

[5] Ibid., p. 253.

[6] Nys, *Le Droit de la guerre et les précurseurs de Grotius* (1882), pp. 115–18, 138–43.

SPIES, GUERRILLAS, AND SABOTEURS   325

only urge that non-combatants be spared from attack as an act of mercy.[1] It is significant that the ancient form of declaration of war, which called upon the subjects of the declarant to do violence to the subjects of the enemy, continued in use even into the eighteenth century.[2] Although the declaration lost much of its literal sense with the passage of time, the view that war makes individuals in belligerent nations enemies one to the other persisted throughout the eighteenth[3] and nineteenth centuries[4] and still perhaps serves as a fundamental assumption of the law.[5] The courts of the United States have been particularly prone to start from the premiss that all inhabitants of the enemy state and all persons adhering to it are enemies, notably in connexion with property rights,[6] treasonable conduct,[7] and commercial intercourse with the enemy at common law.[8]

Despite vast improvements in the lot of those who are without means of defence in war,[9] a number of tendencies are at work the effect of which is once more to extend, rather than to diminish, the extent to which each enemy national is involved in war. The first of these is the fact that

---

[1] Grotius stated that, 'In general, killing is a right of war' (*De Jure Belli ac Pacis* (1646 ed., transl. by Kelsey, 1925), Book iii, ch. iv, v. i), '. . . according to the law of nations, any one who is an enemy may be attacked anywhere' (ibid., viii. 1), and 'How far this right to inflict injury extends may be perceived from the fact that the slaughter even of infants and of women is made with impunity' (ibid., ix. 1). It was the 'bidding of mercy' which called for the protection of certain categories of persons, such as children, women, old men, priests, writers, farmers, merchants, prisoners of war, suppliants, and those who gave themselves up to the victor (ibid., ch. xi, viii–xiv incl.). See also Rachel, *De Jure Naturae et Gentium Dissertationes* (1676), Dissertatio Altera De Jure Gentium, xlvi, xlvii.

[2] '[La Déclaration de Guerre] autorise, à la vérité, il oblige même tous les sujets, de quelque qualité qu'ils soient, à arrêter les personnes & les choses appartenantes à l'Ennemi, quand elles tombent entre leurs mains; mais il ne les invite point à entreprendre aucune expédition offensive, sans Commission, ou sans ordre particulier' (Vattel, *Le Droit des gens* (1758), Book iii, ch. xv, § 227; see Von Martens, *A Compendium of the Law of Nations* (transl. by Cobbett, 1802), p. 287 n. The last formal declaration of war, made by Great Britain in 1762 against Spain, which followed this form of words, is quoted in Twiss, *The Law of Nations considered as Independent Political Communities; On the Rights and Duties of Nations in Time of War* (1863), p. 85.

[3] In *Quaestionum Juris Publici Libri Duo* (1737), Van Bynkershoek declares that although the right of executing the vanquished has 'almost grown obsolete', this result is solely the consequence of clemency (Book i, ch. iii, p. 18).

[4] Twiss, op. cit., p. 84; Halleck, op. cit., p. 411. The texts uniformly stated, however, that usage or custom or law had confined the actual conduct of hostilities to the warring sovereigns and their troops.

[5] The *Manual of Military Law* (1929), Amendments No. 12 (1936), p. 5, takes this view.

[6] *Juragua Iron Co., Ltd. v. United States* (1909), 212 U.S. 297, 306–7; *United States v. Pacific RR. Co.* (1887), 120 U.S. 227, 233, 239; *Young v. United States* (1877), 97 U.S. 39, 61; *Lamar v. Browne et Al.* (1875), 92 U.S. 187, 194.

[7] *Stephan v. United States* (6th Cir. 1943), 133 F. 2d 87, 94, cert. denied (1943), 318 U.S. 781, rehearing denied (1943), 319 U.S. 783; *United States v. Fricke* (S.D.N.Y. 1919), 259 Fed. 673, 675.

[8] *White et Al. v. Burnley* (1857), 20 How. 235, 249; *The Rapid* (1814), 8 Cranch 155, 161; *Griswold v. Waddington* (1819), 16 Johns (N.Y.) 438, 447; *Grinnan et Al. v. Edwards et Al.* (1883), 21 W. Va. 347, 357.

[9] 'Modern American law has come a long way since the time when outbreak of war made every enemy national an outlaw, subject to both public and private slaughter, cruelty and plunder' (*Johnson v. Eisentrager* (1950), 339 U.S. 763, 768).

contemporary conflicts are often fought in pursuance of an ideology. A burning conviction concerning a political or social philosophy may offer both an incitement and a rationalization for the extirpation of all those whose ideas are considered to be evil.[1] The second factor, a technological one, is that it has become increasingly difficult to differentiate between what were once distinguishable as 'military' and 'non-military' objectives, in the choice of target, in the aiming of the weapon, and in the destruction which it causes. That populations are, particularly in the stage of attack and active hostilities, increasingly subjected to the impact of war is a development in warfare of which international law cannot fail to take account.[2] Thirdly, the civilian has often voluntarily become a participant in warfare, as a guerrilla or as a member of the underground or as a secret agent, requiring, *inter alia*, stringent control of his activities or even internment if he is present on the domestic territory of a belligerent.[3]

The law of war has exercised its 'prohibitive' effect with respect to those persons who are in the power of the enemy and would otherwise be subject to the extreme licence of war by extending special protection to certain categories of such individuals. The most familiar of these are the wounded and sick of the armed forces and so-called 'lawful belligerents', who, upon their coming into the hands of the enemy, become prisoners of war endowed with specific rights. Until comparatively recently the protection of civilian non-combatants has been on a somewhat primitive basis, resting as it did upon certain broad principles of international law and scattered provisions of the Hague Regulations, particularly those relating to belligerent occupation. With respect to those actually interned by a belligerent, the protection of the law of nations was so imprecise as to require their being placed in the status of prisoners of war, although they were not belligerents.[4] Such considerations as these, coupled with the suffering to which civilians were exposed during the Second World War, were compelling reasons for the adoption of the Geneva Convention relative to the Protection of Civilian Persons in Time of War of 12 August 1949.

Outside these three classes of persons to whom international law has offered shelter from the extreme violence of war, there are other persons who traditionally have not benefited from a privileged status under

---

[1] Wright, *A Study of War* (1942), vol. ii, p. 160.

[2] Gutteridge, 'The Geneva Conventions of 1949', in this *Year Book*, 26 (1949), pp. 294, 319; Nurick, 'The Distinction between Combatant and Noncombatant in the Law of War', in *American Journal of International Law*, 39 (1945), p. 680.

[3] See Cohn, 'Legal Aspects of Internment', in *Modern Law Review*, 4 (1940–41), p. 200; Parry, 'The Legal Status of Germany and of German Internees', ibid., 10 (1947), p. 403; with respect to the practice of the United States see *Hirabayashi* v. *United States* (1943), 320 U.S. 81.

[4] *R.* v. *Superintendent of Vine St. Police Station; Ex parte Liebmann*, [1916] 1 K.B. 268; *R.* v. *Bottrill; Ex parte Kuechenmeister*, [1947] 1 K.B. 41; the United States followed the same practice during the Second World War (Field Manual 27-10, *Rules of Land Warfare* (1940), par. 70).

international law, namely, guerrillas, partisans, so-called 'war-traitors', *francs-tireurs*, and other persons who, in the face of the enemy or behind his lines, have committed hostile acts without meeting the qualifications prescribed for lawful belligerents.[1] The determination of the requirements to be established for those claiming prisoner-of-war status has not been easy, and it has been equally troublesome to assess the basis on which persons not so qualifying should be penalized or punished—whether as war criminals, or as violators of the laws and customs of war, or merely as persons whose acts have been harmful to the opposing belligerent. It has generally been understood that such persons are subject to the death penalty, and to that extent the law applicable to such combatants has been clear. The Geneva Conventions of 1949 have, however, instead of clarifying the status of these individuals, destroyed what little certainty existed in the law. It is probably safe to say that the Conventions are at their weakest in delineating the various categories of persons who benefit from the protection of each.

Article 4 of the Geneva Prisoners of War Convention of 1949 defines prisoners of war as including the members of the armed forces, militia and volunteer corps conforming with specified requirements, civilians accompanying the armed forces, the crews of merchant ships and civil aircraft, and *levées en masse* in unoccupied territory.[2] Members of resistance movements who are commanded by a responsible person, wear a 'fixed distinctive emblem', carry arms openly, and conform with the law of war, even if operating in occupied territory, were extended the protection of prisoner-of-war status because of difficulties encountered in securing equitable treatment for guerrillas and members of resistance movements during the Second World War.[3] Fears that the opposing belligerent will be put at a military disadvantage by being required to treat such persons as prisoners of war[4] are probably based on the erroneous assumption that all persons engaged in resistance activities will meet the qualifications prescribed in Article 4. It is reasonable to suppose that guerrillas and members of

[1] Oppenheim, *International Law*, vol. ii (6th ed. by Lauterpacht, 1944), p. 454; *Manual of Military Law (1929)*, Amendments No. 12 (1936), p. 82; Hyde, *International Law, Chiefly as Interpreted and Applied by the United States* (1945), vol. iii, p. 1797; Field Manual 27-10, par. 348.

[2] Article 1 of the Geneva Prisoners of War Convention of 1929 and Article 4 of the corresponding 1949 Convention purport to define the persons entitled to be treated as prisoners of war, while Article 1 of the Hague Regulations sets out to define the troops to whom the 'laws, rights, and duties of war apply'. Since persons both civilian and military have been considered to be protected by and subject to the laws, rights, and duties of war in connexion with war crimes prosecutions, there is reason to believe that Article 1 of the Hague Regulations is now to be interpreted only as defining those who are entitled to be prisoners of war upon capture and that, as to the signatories to the Prisoners of War Conventions of 1929 and 1949, the former definition has been superseded.

[3] *Report on the Work of the Conference of Government Experts for the Study of the Conventions for the Protection of War Victims*, International Committee of the Red Cross (1947), pp. 107–8.

[4] Strebel, 'Die Genfer Abkommen vom 12. August 1949—Fragen des Anwendungsbereichs', in *Zeitschrift für Ausländisches Öffentliches Recht und Völkerrecht*, 13 (1950), pp. 133–41.

328   SO-CALLED 'UNPRIVILEGED BELLIGERENCY'

resistance movements will more frequently than not fail to conform to these standards, since secrecy and surprise are the essence of such warfare.

Do then persons engaged in hostilities of a clandestine nature benefit from the protection of any other status? According to the letter of Article 4 of the Geneva Civilians Convention of 1949, persons who 'in any manner whatsoever, find themselves, . . . in the hands of a Party to the conflict' and do not benefit from one of the other Conventions are protected by that Convention. As indicated in the article referred to above,[1] persons guilty of hostile activities in occupied areas are subject to a special régime analogous to a system of municipal law, and spies and guerrillas in such areas are thus in something approaching a protected status. Article 5 of the same Convention, in addition to limiting the extent to which the Convention is applicable to persons guilty of hostile acts in occupied territory, states with respect to the 'territory of a Party to the conflict' that 'an individual protected person' (i.e. any person in enemy hands not otherwise protected) who is engaged in or suspected of hostile activities is not entitled to claim such rights and privileges under the Convention as would imperil the security of the detaining state. This language, and the absence of provisions elsewhere which would preclude strong action against captured unlawful belligerents, are indicative of an intention on the part of the draftsmen of the Convention not to exclude the customary penalties inflicted upon belligerents of this nature. Furthermore, the failure of Article 5 to refer to areas where fighting is in progress outside occupied territory or the territory of the detaining state suggests that both Articles 4 and 5 were directed to the protection of inhabitants of occupied areas and of the mass of enemy aliens on enemy territory and that unlawful belligerents in the zone of operations were not taken into account in connexion with the two articles. It is reasonable to conclude that no provision of the Geneva Conventions of 1949 precludes the death penalty for unlawful belligerents in other than occupied territory[2] and that, *a fortiori*, lesser penalties may be imposed.

A category of persons who are not entitled to treatment either as peaceful civilians or as prisoners of war by reason of the fact that they have engaged in hostile conduct without meeting the qualifications established by Article 4 of the Geneva Prisoners of War Convention of 1949 thus continues to exist and to be subject to the maximum penalty which the detaining belligerent desires to impose. Individuals of this nature taken into custody for hostile conduct in occupied territory are, of course, the beneficiaries of a considerable number of procedural and substantive safeguards. But their counterparts in other areas are less fortunately circumstanced, and it is to this latter group that attention must be directed and to which reference

---

[1] This *Year Book*, 27 (1950), pp. 261, 264.
[2] See Article 68, Geneva Civilians Convention of 1949.

is primarily made hereafter in speaking of spies, guerrillas, and other so-called 'unlawful belligerents'. The first genus to be considered will be the classic form of hostile activity in a guise which conceals the true character of the individual, namely, spies.

II. *Hostile conduct by persons not of the armed forces: Spies*

Over the course of years, much learned discussion has been expended on the question of the conformity of espionage in time of war with international law and with morality. From this consideration has emerged a virtual unanimity of opinion that while the morality of espionage may vary from case to case, some, and probably all, spies do not violate international law. A distinction may, of course, be made with respect to espionage other than in time of war, for such conduct is of doubtful compatibility with the requirements of law governing the peaceful intercourse of states.[1]

The great international lawyers of the past approached espionage, as they did so many other questions, from the standpoints of both law and morals. They were ultimately persuaded by the common view of mankind that persons acting as spies from patriotic motives pursue a moral course of conduct and concluded that the power of a belligerent to punish espionage directed against him arose not from the fact that the law prohibited the activity but from the danger which clandestine acts created and the resulting necessity that they be dealt with severely.[2] How this view was to be reconciled with the safeguards generally accorded enemy soldiers is most persuasively stated in the words of Gentili:

'This also is a reason why you should be unwilling to assume that role [of spy], because it is denied the privileges attaching to military service. And therefore the law against spies seems just, since they have divested themselves of the character which would prevent their being treated in that cruel and degrading fashion.'[3]

At the Brussels Conference of 1874, thorough consideration was given to espionage in war, and the provisions there drafted[4] were carried over, almost without change, into the Hague Regulations of 1899 and 1907.[5] A number of states at the Conference strenuously resisted any suggestion that the proposed code should give legal sanction to an opposing belligerent's exercise of jurisdiction over a spy,[6] and the resulting article provided by

[1] Huybrechts, 'Espionnage et la convention de la Haye', in *Revue de droit pénal et de criminologie*, 31 (1950–1), p. 931.

[2] Belli, *De Re Militari et Bello Tractatus* (1563), Part viii, ch. i, § 42; Grotius, *De Jure Belli ac Pacis* (1646 ed.), Book iii, ch. iv, xviii. 3; Wolff, *Jus Gentium Methodo Scientifica Pertractatum* (1764), ch. vii, §§ 884, 885, 893; Vattel, *Le Droit des gens* (1758), Book iii, ch. x, § 179.

[3] *De Jure Belli Libri Tres* (1612), Book ii, ch. ix, pp. 282–3.

[4] Articles 19–22, *Actes de la Conférence de Bruxelles* (1874), p. 291.

[5] Articles 29–31.

[6] The delegations which were most articulate about this matter were those of Belgium, the Netherlands, and Italy (see p. 324, n. 2). The *Projet* had provided: 'L'espion pris sur le fait, lors même que son intention n'aurait pas été définitivement accomplie ou n'aurait pas été couronnée de succès, est livré à la justice' (*Actes*, p. 13).

330   SO-CALLED 'UNPRIVILEGED BELLIGERENCY'

way of compromise that a spy was to be treated according to the laws in force in the capturing army.[1] A recommendation that a distinction be made between professional agents and volunteers motivated by patriotic fervour met with an unfavourable reception,[2] but the Conference found it impossible to agree whether military and civilian spies were in all respects to be treated in the same manner.[3]

Articles 29 and 30 of the Hague Regulations do not attempt to do more than define the spy and require that he shall not be punished without trial, and it is to be observed that they do not purport to make espionage a violation of the Regulations. A further modification was in fact made in the Brussels draft in order to avoid an implication that a spy is 'to be condemned by virtue of a declaration signed by his own Government'.[4] Moreover, the sanctioning by Article 24 of the 'employment of measures necessary for obtaining information about the enemy' is strongly indicative that espionage falls into the same category as legitimate ruses of war.[5] In accordance with these provisions, recent texts,[6] military manuals,[7] and judicial opinions[8] have normally emphasized that espionage is not in violation of the law of nations but that a belligerent penalizes this conduct because of the danger it presents to him. Frequently military codes incorporate a definition of espionage, conforming to that of the Hague Regulations,[9] and thereby provide a positive legal precept in domestic law to fill up the measure of jurisdiction which international law concedes to be held by the offended state for the protection of its national security. Into this firmly established law some doubt has been interjected by *Ex parte Quirin et Al.*,[10] decided by

---

[1] Article 19, *Actes*, p. 291.

[2] The proposal was made by the Spanish delegate (*Actes*, pp. 42, 203).

[3] The difficulty arose in connexion with the discussion of Article 21, dealing with the spy who had rejoined his army (*Actes*, pp. 44–45).

[4] Proceedings of the Second Subcommission, Second Commission, in *The Proceedings of the Hague Peace Conferences; The Conference of 1899* (ed. by Scott, 1920), p. 489.

[5] *Manual of Military Law (1929)*, Amendments No. 12 (1936), p. 36, n. 4; Field Manual 27–10, *Rules of Land Warfare* (1940), par. 203.

[6] Oppenheim, *International Law*, vol. ii (6th ed. by Lauterpacht, 1944), p. 329; Halleck, op. cit. (3rd Eng. ed. by Baker, 1893), vol. i, p. 571; Wheaton, *International Law*, vol. ii (7th Eng. ed. by Keith, 1944), p. 218; Westlake, *International Law*, Part ii (2nd ed., 1913), p. 90; Hall, *A Treatise on International Law* (7th ed. by Higgins), p. 579; Fauchille, *Traité de droit international public*, vol. ii (1921), p. 150; Calvo, *Le Droit international théorique et pratique* (5th ed., 1896), vol. iv, p. 178; Rolin, *Le Droit moderne de la guerre* (1920), vol. i, p. 366; Waltzog, *Recht der Landkriegsführung* (1942), p. 54; but cf. Hyde, op. cit., vol. iii, p. 1865.

[7] *Manual of Military Law (1929)*, Amendments No. 12 (1936), p. 36; Field Manual 27–10, *Rules of Land Warfare* (1940), par. 203; *Kriegsbrauch im Landkriege* (1902), p. 30.

[8] *United States ex rel. Wessels v. McDonald, Commandant of Brooklyn Navy Yard* (E.D.N.Y., 1920), 265 Fed. 754, dismissed per stipulation (1921), 256 U.S. 705; *United States v. List et Al.* (1948), *Trials of War Criminals*, xi (1950), p. 1245; *War Crimes Reports*, viii (1949), p. 54; see *Opinions of the Attorneys General of the United States*, 31 (1920), p. 356, and 40 (1949), p. 561, concerning the jurisdiction of a United States military tribunal over one Witcke, alias Waberski, a German spy arrested in the vicinity of a military post.

[9] France, *Code de Justice Militaire*, Articles 237, 238; United States, *Uniform Code of Military Justice*, Article 106 (64 Stat. 138; 50 U.S.C. 700).   [10] 317 U.S. 1.

SPIES, GUERRILLAS, AND SABOTEURS   331

the Supreme Court of the United States in 1942. Spies were considered by the Court to be 'offenders against the law of war subject to trial and punishment by military tribunals' for the 'acts which render their belligerency unlawful'.[1] A possible inference from this language is that the Court considered espionage to be subject to punishment as an international crime.[2] There is reason to suppose, however, that the tribunal was led by the somewhat imprecise distinction often made between 'lawful' and 'unlawful' combatants to conclude that failure to qualify as a lawful combatant could be described as a violation of international law. If, indeed, the Court was proceeding on the assumption that the law of nations forbids the employment of spies and espionage itself, that view, it is submitted, fails to find support in contemporary doctrine regarding such activities in wartime.[3]

Article 31 of the Hague Regulations, which provides that a spy who is captured by the enemy after rejoining his army is to be treated as a prisoner of war and incurs no responsibility for his previous acts of espionage, throws considerable light on the juridical status of espionage. Two reasons have been adduced for this limitation in punishment.[4] The first goes to the difficulty of proving the act after the individual has returned to his own army. To this it must be replied that if it is possible to gather and utilize proof of war crimes of the atrocity type years after the event took place, this explanation seems to lack substance. The other, which appears to be the correct reason, is that spying is a ruse of war, which the threat of 'punishment' is designed to deter. Once the act is completed, the deterrent purpose of the death penalty has no room for operation. The limitation of punishment thus offers a strong indication that espionage is not prohibited by the international law of war and that its suppression is instead left to the initiative of the opposing belligerent. Article 31 has been productive of some controversy concerning whether the immunity of the returned spy must be applied to the civilian secret agent as well as the military.[5] References in the

---

[1] 317 U.S. 31.

[2] This is the view adopted by Professor Hyde in 'Aspects of the Saboteur Cases', in *American Journal of International Law*, 37 (1943), p. 88. In commending the 'bold and fresh view' (p. 90) taken by the Supreme Court, he points to the inconsistency between the recognition of the propriety of a state's employment of espionage and the punishment of the spy so employed and suggests that both the act of the state and the act of the individual are equally violative of international law. It would appear, on the contrary, that the appearing inconsistency may be realistically resolved only by an acknowledgement that the act of neither is in contravention of international law.

[3] Although the opinion contains copious citations to Field Manual 27–10, *Rules of Land Warfare* (1940), it does not refer to paragraph 203 of the Manual, which states that spies are *not* punished as 'violators of the law of war'. With respect to espionage, the Court alluded to paragraph 83 of General Orders No. 100, 24 April 1863, but the General Orders, which had been superseded many years previously, stated elsewhere that deception in war is 'a just and necessary means of hostility' (par. 101).

[4] Violle, *L'Espionnage militaire en temps de guerre* (1903), p. 160; Huybrechts, op. cit., pp. 937–8.

[5] In *Re Flesche, Nederlandse Jurisprudentie*, 1949, No. 548, the Dutch Special Court of Cassation

332   SO-CALLED 'UNPRIVILEGED BELLIGERENCY'

article to a rejoining of the *army* and to subsequent treatment as a prisoner of war might seem, from a textual examination alone, to indicate that only a military spy was intended. However, the two possible bases for the limitation on the punishment of spies logically apply with equal force to both the military and civilian agent, and the great difficulty in many cases of establishing whether an individual acted in a military or non-military capacity at the time of his act[1] further suggests that the protection of Article 31 is not confined to the military spy.

Questions of substance concerning spies may also arise in connexion with the limitation of Article 29 of the Hague Regulations to spies taken in the 'zone of operations'. In modern warfare, in which even the remotest town is exposed to the danger of attack by guided missiles, rockets, and parachute troops, the entire territory of a belligerent may with some justice be said to be in a zone of operations.[2] But it is normal to preserve some semblance of distinction between that area and territory which is not subject to military control, if only to provide a line of demarcation between the jurisdiction of the military and civilian authorities.[3] At the same time that military codes frequently contain a specific reference to the type of espionage defined in Article 29, the civil law also contains its own provisions for the protection of official secrets and for the general security of the state in time of war.[4] It is even clearer, however, that espionage falling under this latter type of interdiction cannot be said to be in violation of the law of nations, since its punishment has hitherto been effected without reference to that body of law. An alien enemy engaging in espionage, although divesting himself of the protection he might otherwise enjoy as a prisoner of war, is in turn protected by the safeguards of domestic law, which, by way of securing the liberties of loyal citizens, makes even active enemies benefit from the law's protection. As the difficulty of distinguishing the traitor from the spy and secret agent increases, by reason of the fact that a given act may be treasonable if committed by a citizen and espionage if committed by an

---

held that Article 31 does not apply to civilians, and that the immunity therein provided is confined to military personnel in the zone of operations. On the other hand, the *Manual of Military Law (1929)*, Amendments No. 12 (1936), p. 38, n. 5, and Rolin, op. cit., vol. i, p. 371, take the view that the immunity of the returned spy is a general one, applying to all persons of that character. Article 26 of the Manual prepared by the Institute of International Law extended the immunity to spies who had succeeded in quitting the territory occupied by the enemy (*Annuaire de l'Institut de droit international*, 5 (1881–2), p. 156).

For cases granting immunity to returned military spies see *In re Martin* (1865), 45 Barb. (N.Y.) 142; *In re Rieger* (France, Cass. crim., 29 July 1948), Dalloz, *Hebdomadaire*, 1949, 193, with a note by de Vabres, *Recueil Sirey*, 1950, 1. 37 (under date of 20 July 1948).

[1] Huybrechts, op. cit., p. 941.

[2] *In re Rieger, supra*, recognized that even the unoccupied portion of France could be said to be in a zone of operations; see Waltzog, op. cit., p. 52.

[3] See *Ex parte Milligan* (1867), 4 Wall. 2.

[4] E.g. Official Secrets Act, 1911 and 1920 (1 & 2 Geo. V, c. 28; 10 & 11 Geo. V, c. 75); United States Code, Title 18, Chapter 37.

SPIES, GUERRILLAS, AND SABOTEURS   333

alien,[1] the necessity of subjecting all persons outside the zone of operations to a common law and to a common tribunal grows correspondingly greater. Although problems of this nature have been productive of recommendations that espionage in time of war be the subject of an agreed international definition,[2] it has not been suggested that espionage should itself be interdicted by international law.

As long as espionage is regarded as a conventional weapon of war, being neither treacherous nor productive of unnecessary suffering, the sanctions visited on spies are only penalties to deter the use of that ruse. The actions of a spy are not an international crime, for by his conduct he merely establishes that he is a belligerent with no claim to any of the protected statuses which international law has created.

III. *Hostilities in arms by persons not of the armed forces: Guerrillas*

Hostilities in arms by persons not entitled to be treated as prisoners of war are of tremendously greater practical importance than espionage, but the law applicable to such conduct is, if anything, even less certain. These activities may take the form of individual acts of violence, in which case the expression *franc-tireur* is normally used, or may with greater probability be carried on by armed bands in guerrilla or partisan warfare. For want of a better term, the expression 'guerrilla warfare' will be applied to all such acts, but with the qualification that it is not intended to refer, in the sense in which it is used in military science, to the warfare waged by detached troops of the armed forces, properly so identified, or to armed forces which continue fighting after a surrender, which presents a problem of another nature.[3] The word 'guerrilla' is most usefully applied in a legal context to armed hostilities by private persons or groups of persons who do not meet the qualifications established in Article 4 of the Geneva Prisoners of War Convention of 1949 or corresponding provisions of the earlier Conventions.[4]

The tendency of academic lawyers has been to charge guerrillas with acting in contravention of international law. It has been said that such armed bands carry on 'irregular war' because they are normally self-constituted, lack permanency, do not wear uniforms, carry on pillage and

[1] As in France; see *Code Pénal*, Articles 76 and 77; de Vabres, 'La Répression de l'espionnage et la codification du Droit pénal international', in *Revue de droit international, de sciences diplomatiques et politiques*, 26 (1948), p. 341; Pella, 'La Répression des crimes contre la personnalité de l'état', in *Recueil des cours de l'Académie de droit international de la Haye*, 33 (1930), p. 726.

[2] A suggestion of this nature was made by General Arnaudeau (France) at the Brussels Conference of 1874 (*Actes*, p. 43); see de Vabres, op. cit., p. 350.

[3] Concerning which see Nurick and Barrett, 'Legality of Guerrilla Forces under the Laws of War', in *American Journal of International Law*, 40 (1946), p. 563.

[4] Article 1, Hague Regulations of 1907; Article 1, Geneva Prisoners of War Convention of 1929.

334   SO-CALLED 'UNPRIVILEGED BELLIGERENCY'

destruction, and are disposed to take few prisoners and to deny quarter.[1] The principal accusation which has been made against them is that they eventually degenerate into bandits, engaging in murder and robbery in hope of gain. As a consequence, the texts of the nineteenth and twentieth centuries are disposed to stigmatize guerrilla warfare and any private hostilities in arms as 'war crimes'.[2]

How well this characterization accords with the realities of modern warfare is open to serious question. It must be assumed at the outset that guerrilla activities are an inevitable concomitant of hostilities waged by regularly constituted armed forces.[3] Isolated bodies of regular troops, greatly extended supply lines, and thinly scattered occupation forces offer inviting and advantageous targets to guerrilla columns. By contrast with the armed forces, guerrillas require little logistical support. Their casualties are slight. Above all they have the advantages conferred by the fact that they conceal their character as belligerents and are thus able to exploit to the full the element of surprise.[4]

Strategic and tactical considerations alone do not recruit guerrilla forces, and it must be remembered that the partisan exists in modern warfare because the civilian willingly takes up arms and fights. The guerrilla fighting of today had its forerunners in the resistance of the Spanish Maquis during the Peninsular Campaign[5] and in the hostilities of French civilians in the Franco-Prussian War, which brought the term *franc-tireur* into an undeserved prominence.[6] Resistance activities were an important instrument in the defeat of the Axis during the Second World War, and it is hardly possible to name an armed conflict which has taken place since the conclusion of those hostilities in which guerrillas have not played an important and often decisive role.[7] Only a rigid legal formalism could lead to the characterization of the resistance conducted against Germany, Italy, and

---

[1] Hyde, op. cit., vol. iii, p. 1797; Hyde's sentiments are those of Lieber in *Guerrilla Parties considered with Reference to the Laws and Usages of War* (1862), p. 7.

[2] Oppenheim, op. cit., vol. ii (6th ed. by Lauterpacht, 1944), pp. 451, 454; Fauchille, op. cit., vol. ii, pp. 99 ff.; Hyde, op. cit., vol. iii, pp. 1797–8; Halleck, op. cit., p. 386; Spaight, op. cit., p. 63; Waltzog, op. cit., p. 16; see to like effect the British *Manual of Military Law* (1929), Amendments No. 12 (1936), p. 83, characterizing private hostilities in arms as illegitimate acts 'from the enemy's standpoint', and United States *Rules of Land Warfare* (1940), pars. 348, 351, and 352.

[3] A related problem is that of the use of force by members of civil defence organizations who have not been equipped with uniforms or have not had an opportunity to don them (see *United States* v. *Hangobl* (1945), *War Crimes Reports*, xiv (1949), p. 86).

[4] Miksche, *Secret Forces; The Technique of Underground Movements* (1950).

[5] Napier, *History of the War in the Peninsula* (1828–40).

[6] See Rolin-Jaequemyns, 'Chronique du droit international; Essai complémentaire sur la guerre franco-allemande dans ses rapports avec le droit international', in *Revue de droit international et de la législation comparée*, 3 (1871), p. 288.

[7] United Nations forces in Korea have, for example, encountered guerrilla bands ranging in size from 50 to 2,000 men (*Eighth Report of the United Nations Command Operations in Korea, for the period 16 to 30 October 1950*, U.N.Doc. S/1885).

SPIES, GUERRILLAS, AND SABOTEURS   335

Japan as a violation of international law. Patriotism, nationalism, allegiance to some sort of political authority have replaced the desire for loot, which has traditionally been attributed to the guerrilla, in motivating civilians to take an active part in warfare. And finally, it must not be forgotten that in the Marxist view of the 'people's war', to which a considerable number of important military powers subscribe, popular resistance, including guerrilla warfare, is regarded as a necessary and proper means of defence.[1]

The law of war has had to evolve an uneasy and sometimes unworkable compromise between the legitimate defence of regular belligerent forces and the demands of patriotism. An unwillingness to regard guerrillas as internationally criminal may be discerned at the very threshold of the modern law of war, for the delegations at the Brussels Conference from those countries which had the most often been invaded insisted again and again on the right of the attacked country to call its citizens to arms to resist the enemy.[2] The protected position afforded the members of the *levée en masse*[3] is a monument to these sentiments, but the spontaneous mass uprising in the face of the enemy has lost any real significance. The *levée en masse* is actually an anomaly in the law, for its recognition poses threats not only to the country employing it but to the enemy as well. In an area where a levy exists, the enemy is not without basis in looking upon all inhabitants of the invaded area who are capable of bearing arms as potential enemies to be attacked or, if they surrender, to be made prisoners of war.[4] The very considerations which militate against treating all belligerents as prisoners of war apply with equal force to the members of the *levée en masse*.

The distinction between those forces entitled to be treated as prisoners of war upon capture and those not so qualified which had been worked out at Brussels was preserved in the Hague Regulations of 1899 and 1907.[5] Martens, the president of the 1899 Conference, drew attention to the fact that:

[1] Trainin, 'Questions of Guerrilla Warfare in the Law of War', in *American Journal of International Law*, 40 (1946), p. 534; Kulski, 'Some Soviet Comments on International Law', in *American Journal of International Law*, 45 (1951), p. 347.

[2] The Spanish delegation asserted that defensive war was for Spain a national war to which all the forces of the nation would be directed, regardless of the danger incurred (*Actes de la Conférence de Bruxelles* (1874), pp. 138–9). A member of the Italian delegation expressed the view that the Conference did not wish to indicate that resistance, other than in the form of the *levée en masse*, would be illegitimate (*Actes*, pp. 244–5). General de Leer of Russia expressed his Government's understanding that an attacked state has a right of defence without restriction, so long as it conforms to the law of war (*Actes*, p. 246).

[3] Article 10 of the Brussels Code; Article 2, Hague Regulations of 1907.

[4] *Manual of Military Law* (1929), Amendments No. 12 (1936), p. 11.

[5] A proposed Article recognizing the right of the population of invaded territory to offer 'by all lawful means, the most energetic patriotic resistance against the invaders' was, however, not favourably received (Minutes of the Second Subcommission, Second Commission, Conference of 1899, Eleventh Meeting, 20 June 1899, in *The Proceedings of the Hague Peace Conferences; The Conference of 1899* (ed. by Scott, 1920), pp. 550–5).

336   SO-CALLED 'UNPRIVILEGED BELLIGERENCY'

'The Brussels Conference, therefore, by no means intended to abolish the right of defence, or to create a code which would abolish this right. It was, on the contrary, imbued with the idea that heroes are not created by codes, but that the only code that heroes have is their self-abnegation, their will and their patriotism.

'The Conference understood that its duty was not to try to formulate a code of cases which cannot be foreseen or codified, such as acts of heroism on the part of populations rising against the enemy.

'It simply wished to afford the populations more guaranties than had existed up to that time.'[1]

He went on to assert that the provisions drafted at the Brussels Conference had not been designed to deal with all cases and that they left the door open to 'the heroic sacrifices which nations might be ready to make in their defence'. 'It is not our province', he added, 'to set limits to patriotism.'

It was not, however, until the conclusion of the Second World War that judicial consideration was given to the status of persons falling outside the class of so-called 'lawful belligerents'. In the *Hostages Trial*,[2] guerrillas were actually said, in legal intendment, to resemble spies in that the enemy punished such activities not because of their illegality in an international sense but because of the danger they presented to him. The prevailing view in the trials involving resistance in arms, whether in occupied or other than occupied territory,[3] appears to be in conformity with that expressed in the *Hostages* case. It was also made plain that guerrillas, like spies, may not be punished without trial.[4]

The Geneva Conference of 1949 was well aware of the problem implicit in the existence of guerrilla and partisan warfare and seemed to be under the impression that it had dealt with it in satisfactory fashion.[5] Members of resistance movements who comply with the conditions that they be commanded by a responsible person, wear a fixed distinctive sign, carry arms openly, and comply with the laws of war are, even in occupied areas, entitled to be treated as prisoners of war upon capture.[6] But because guerrilla warfare is in essence secret warfare, it is improbable that the majority of guerrillas will comply with these conditions, particularly those

[1] Minutes of the Second Subcommission, Second Commission, Conference of 1899, Eleventh Meeting, 20 June 1899, in *The Proceedings of the Hague Peace Conferences; The Conference of 1899* (ed. by Scott, 1920), p. 547.

[2] *United States v. List et Al.* (1948), *Trials of War Criminals*, xi (1950), p. 1245; *War Crimes Reports*, viii (1949), p. 58.

[3] *United States v. Ohlendorf et Al.* (1948), *Trials of War Criminals*, iv (1949), p. 492.

[4] *United States v. List et Al.* (1948), *Trials of War Criminals*, xi (1950), p. 1290; *United States v. Von Leeb et Al.* (1948), ibid., p. 530; *War Crimes Reports*, xii (1949), p. 86; see the closing Address for the Prosecution in *United States v. Yamashita* (1945), ibid. iv (1948), p. 31. Article 5 of the Geneva Prisoners of War Convention of 1949 recognizes the necessity of a trial by providing that persons who have committed belligerent acts are to be protected by that Convention 'until such time as their status has been determined by a competent tribunal'.

[5] See Report of Committee II to the Plenary Assembly (CDG/PLEN. 76 Pris, 23 July 1949), p. 7.

[6] Article 4.

SPIES, GUERRILLAS, AND SABOTEURS   337

which relate to the wearing of distinctive insignia and the open carrying of arms.[1] If this is so, the problem of the guerrilla fighter is still one of customary international law. The fact that such persons are still left, subject to the procedural and general safeguards afforded by the Geneva Conventions of 1949, to the mercy of the enemy will in strict law lead to the extreme penalty of death. It may be expected, however, that more favourable treatment, specifically in the form of recognition as prisoners of war, will be held out as an inducement to persuade guerrillas to surrender. The listing of those persons who are entitled as a matter of law to be treated as prisoners cannot reasonably be construed as prohibiting a belligerent from granting that status to persons having no legal right thereto.[2]

When resistance activities in the form of guerrilla warfare are carried out in occupied areas, it would appear, in the light of prosecutions for war crimes and the Geneva Conventions of 1949, that they constitute no violation of any duty imposed by international law and cannot therefore be stigmatized as violative of international law.[3] As guerrilla activities in occupied areas during the Second World War proved to be of considerably greater consequence than those in the face of the enemy, there is reason to suppose that the law applicable to unoccupied areas should correspond to that to be invoked elsewhere, unless some distinction between the two which is of legal significance may be ascertained. But if such warfare within occupied areas, where the power of the enemy is already established, is not in contravention of the law of nations, how much less can similar activities in unoccupied zones, where the fortunes of battle are still in doubt, be said to have that character. Nor can it be argued that a state has no obligation to suppress guerrilla activities on its behalf in that portion of its territory which is occupied but that such a duty does arise where active hostilities are in progress in the face of the enemy. As long as partisan warfare is inspired by genuine allegiance rather than a desire for pillage and as long as guerrilla activities are looked upon as licit and laudable by the state on whose behalf they are undertaken and by third parties to the conflict, it is highly unreal to regard them as internationally criminal.[4]

---

[1] The fear of Strebel that what he characterizes as a legitimation of resistance activities by civilians, particularly those in occupied territory, will put major obstacles in the path of the opposing belligerent (loc. cit., pp. 133 ff.) apparently proceeds from the assumption that large numbers of persons will be affected by those provisions of Article 4 of the Prisoners of War Convention of 1949 pertaining to resistance movements. It is believed that the disputed clauses of Article 4 represent only a slight derogation from the international common law of war and that the problem of guerrillas who are not entitled to be treated as lawful belligerents is still paramount. See also Brandweiner, 'Das Partisanenproblem und die Genfer Konventionen vom 12. August 1949', in *Juristische Blätter*, 72 (1950), p. 261.

[2] This was the view taken by the Danish delegate at the Geneva Conference of 1949 (*Verbatim Report of the Thirteenth Plenary Meeting, 26 July 1949*, CDG/PLEN/CR 13, p. 6).

[3] This *Year Book*, 27 (1950), pp. 253 ff.

[4] The assimilation of guerrillas to 'bandits' and 'pirates', as proposed by Cowles ('Universality of Jurisdiction over War Crimes', in *California Law Review*, 33 (1945), pp. 181–203), is

338   SO-CALLED 'UNPRIVILEGED BELLIGERENCY'

Although guerrilla warfare and private hostilities in arms should not be regarded as violative of international law, this does not necessarily mean that persons carrying on such activities may not be guilty of war crimes in their strict sense. To apply the doctrine of membership in criminal organizations[1] to membership in any guerrilla band because of fears concerning their lawlessness would, of course, constitute an unwarranted extension of the principle, by a legislative rather than a judicial process, from individual organizations within a state to all groups of a specified type. The notion of complicity[2] may, however, involve the responsibility of persons associated with an individual organization of guerrillas members of which have committed criminal acts. Should members of such groups pillage, loot the dead and wounded in the area of battle, refuse to give quarter, or murder prisoners, they would, like members of the regular armed forces, be similarly accountable for their criminal acts.[3]

The guerrilla thus appears, like the spy, to be a belligerent who has failed to meet the conditions established by law for favoured treatment upon capture. The judicial proceeding to which a suspect is subjected is accordingly a determination whether or not he meets the qualifications prescribed for treatment as a prisoner of war or as a peaceful civilian. What formulation of law is necessary to permit his 'punishment' if he fails so to qualify is essentially a matter of domestic law or practice. In Germany, guerrilla warfare against the Reich was defined as a crime by German law.[4] In other countries a purported prosecution for acting in 'violation of the laws and customs of war' is probably to be construed as directed against an offence in violation of the military common law of the state concerned. In any case, the protection of international law, in the sense in which that law safeguards prisoners of war and peaceful civilians, terminates when the judicial proceeding reveals that the individual does not qualify for protected status.

IV. *Other forms of hostile activity by persons not of the armed forces*

Clandestine activities in warfare are not confined to the work of the spy, the armed guerrilla, and the *franc-tireur*. Sabotage, intelligence activities

unwarranted. Although some guerrillas may engage in banditry and thereby become guilty of the war crimes of murder, plunder, and wanton destruction, it is somewhat naïve to suppose that a desire for blood and booty for their own sakes is the sole well-spring of such warfare and that guerrillas never devote themselves to the same missions as the regular armed forces.

[1] *Judgment of the International Military Tribunal for the Trial of German Major War Criminals* (Cmd. 6964, H.M.S.O., 1946), pp. 66 ff.

[2] Article 2 (12) (iv), Draft Code of Offences Against the Peace and Security of Mankind, in *Report of the International Law Commission Covering its Third Session*, 16 May–27 July 1951 (U.N.Doc. A/CN. 4/48, 30 July 1951), par. 59.

[3] I.e. as 'marauders' or 'bandits' in the true sense of those words (see United States *Rules of Land Warfare* (1940), par. 353).

[4] Verordnung über das Sonderstrafrecht im Kriege und bei Besonderem Einsatz (Kriegssonderstrafrechtsverordnung), 17 August 1938, *R.G.Bl.*, 1939, I, 1455, Article 3.

SPIES, GUERRILLAS, AND SABOTEURS 339

other than espionage, propaganda, and psychological warfare may also be carried on by civilians or disguised military personnel, and their importance, by comparison with hostilities in arms, has become so great that partisan warfare has been given the name of 'sabotage with violence'.[1] Since guerrilla bands will depend upon these means of harming the enemy as well as on open combat, guerrilla warfare itself must be understood as embracing this wide range of activities. Such partisan warfare is usually carried on by civilians, as soldiers of the regular armed forces other than those detailed to organize and assist underground warfare derive no advantage in normal circumstances from assuming the garb of civilians. But military personnel will frequently be called upon to serve as secret agents and to perform clandestine functions not calling for the use of armed force. Both they and their counterparts in resistance movements will of necessity disguise themselves or keep in hiding in a manner resembling the clandestine activities of the spy.

To the hostile activities, other than open armed warfare, of those not qualified to be treated as prisoners of war, the term 'war treason' is most frequently applied. If that term, which is highly objectionable as a concept of occupation law,[2] is extended to hostile activities wherever conducted,[3] its use becomes even more difficult to justify. As to the enemy carrying on military operations in other than occupied territory, sabotage behind the lines is not treasonable in an international sense, because no juridical relationship exists between the offending combatant and the state affected. All the inconsistencies inherent in 'war treason' in occupied areas are thus only multiplied if that term is applied to hostile conduct elsewhere. Alternatively, persons carrying on secret warfare have been accused of the offence of 'unlawful combatancy', which the Supreme Court of the United States in *Ex parte Quirin*[4] declared to be violative of international law and presumably on that account a 'war crime'. In that case, eight Germans who had landed secretly in the United States and were bent on a mission of sabotage were held to be within the jurisdiction of a military commission, before which they had been tried on charges which included, *inter alia*, violation of the law of war in the form of 'unlawful belligerency'. The Court distinguished the lawful and unlawful combatant in the following terms:

'Lawful combatants are subject to capture and detention as prisoners of war by opposing military forces. Unlawful combatants are likewise subject to capture and detention, but in addition they are subject to trial and punishment by military tribunals for acts which render their belligerency unlawful.'[5]

The unlawfulness of their conduct was based on the fact that they had

---

[1] Miksche, op. cit., p. 142.   [2] This *Year Book*, 27 (1950), pp. 251–2.
[3] *Manual of Military Law (1929)*, Amendments No. 12 (1936), pp. 37, 83; Field Manual 27–10, *Rules of Land Warfare* (1940), par. 205; Oppenheim, *International Law*, vol. ii (6th ed. by Lauterpacht, 1944), p. 454.   [4] (1942), 317 U.S. 1.   [5] 317 U.S. 31.

340   SO-CALLED 'UNPRIVILEGED BELLIGERENCY'

clandestinely entered the United States on a hostile mission, 'discarding their uniforms upon entry'. While there is no doubt that secret agents of this nature are subject to trial under the statutes or military common law of the captor, the characterization of such conduct as a violation of international law arises, it is submitted, from a fundamental confusion between acts punishable under international law and acts with respect to which international law affords no protection. The German saboteurs were also charged with offences under the United States Articles of War, namely, those defining espionage and aiding the enemy,[1] and it would appear that these provisions of municipal law afforded a surer ground for their punishment than did the offence of 'unlawful belligerency' under international law, to which the Court primarily directed its attention.

It is uncontroverted that a person accused of hostile conduct other than as a member of those forces which are entitled to treatment as prisoners of war must be granted a trial. For the most part, the tribunal would appear to be charged only with the responsibility of determining whether the accused is to be treated as a prisoner of war, as a peaceful and therefore necessarily innocent civilian, or as neither, in which case he may be penalized. Once it has been discovered that the accused is not entitled to treatment as a prisoner of war, there appears in most circumstances to be no reason in law to inquire whether the individual is a civilian or a disguised soldier, for it would appear in the latter case that the soldier, even in occupied territory, is to be regarded as having thrown in his lot with the civilian population and to be subject to the same rights and disabilities. The question of his actual status may, however, be relevant to the penalty to be imposed, since the greater danger presented by the presence of disguised military personnel within or behind the lines may call for a proportionately greater punishment than is meted out to an offending civilian. Special problems are presented only in the case of military personnel seeking to avoid capture and escaped prisoners of war who are captured or recaptured in civilian clothes. The evader, as he is called, is often a member of an air force who has parachuted into territory held by the enemy and has disguised himself in an attempt to escape capture.[2] If he is taken by the enemy, the military tribunal determining his status may with some justification think him to be a spy, and the burden may be upon him to rebut that inference if it is once established that he is in the military service.[3] Dr. Spaight believes that the simple evader who is not a spy should be treated as a prisoner of war.[4]

---

[1] Articles of War 82 and 81, then in effect.

[2] Secret activities to facilitate such escapes were carried on extensively during the Second World War (Hinton, *Air Victory: The Men and the Machines* (1948), p. 325); see *In re Schonfeld et Al.* (British Military Court, Essen, 1946), *War Crimes Reports*, xi (1949), p. 64.

[3] *Manual of Military Law (1929)*, Amendments No. 12 (1936), p. 37.

[4] Spaight, *Air Power and War Rights* (3rd ed., 1947), pp. 102–4.

SPIES, GUERRILLAS, AND SABOTEURS   341

The prisoner of war who escapes will normally attempt to assume protective colouring and thus escape being retaken. It is recognized that prisoners of war have a duty under their own law to escape,[1] and this obligation has been taken into account in placing severe limits on the punishment which may be meted out to a recaptured prisoner who, by the fact of escape, does not remove himself from prisoner-of-war status.[2] Why the evader and the escaping prisoner should benefit from a more favourable régime than their brethren bent on hostile missions within the enemy's lines can probably be explained only by the fact that their conduct in seeking to escape is not regarded as hostile. When, however—as happened in a number of commando and parachute raids—military personnel wear civilian clothes under their uniforms in order that they may assume the guise of civilians when their immediate mission is accomplished, their status is not easily ascertainable.[3] It would seem consistent with the law applicable to ruses and disguised belligerents that such individuals taken while still in uniform should be treated as prisoners of war on the ground that they have only prepared but have not yet executed their deceptive measures. If they should later be captured in civilian clothes, they would appear to be entitled to no better and no worse treatment than falls to the lot of the civilian guerrilla.

Belligerents, both civilian and military, may also assume as disguise the uniform of the enemy. Some authorities regard this as a legitimate ruse before battle,[4] while others contend that the use of the enemy uniform should be absolutely forbidden in all circumstances,[5] save perhaps that of espionage. The view that such deception is permissible if not done in battle is to some extent supported by the outcome of the *Skorzeny* case,[6] which resulted in the acquittal of a number of Germans who had sought to deceive United States forces by the use of American uniforms and equipment. Although such conduct may thus not be a war crime, there is room for the view that individuals so disguising their true character are not entitled to be considered as prisoners of war and are to be treated as if they had been taken in civilian clothes. The fact that hostilities had ceased at the

---

[1] *In re Amberger* (British Military Court, Wuppertal, 1946), *War Crimes Reports*, i (1947), p. 81.

[2] Articles 91–94, Geneva Prisoners of War Convention of 1949.

[3] This question is raised in the annotation (p. 28) to *In re Von Falkenhorst* (British Military Court, Brunswick, 1946), *War Crimes Reports*, xi (1949), p. 18. Spaight states that the outer military garb of such persons might not serve to regularize their position (*Air Power and War Rights* (3rd ed., 1947), p. 314).

[4] Hall, op. cit. (8th ed. by Higgins, 1924), p. 649; Westlake, op. cit., Part ii (1907), p. 73; Fauchille, op. cit., vol. ii, p. 127. The question is essentially, of course, what use of the enemy uniform constitutes 'improper use . . . of the military insignia and uniform of the enemy' within the meaning of Article 23 (f) of the Hague Regulations of 1907.

[5] Spaight, *War Rights on Land* (1911), pp. 106–110 (characterizing a rule which envisages a quick change of uniforms on the battlefield as 'stupid'); Jobst, 'Is the Wearing of the Enemy's Uniform a Violation of the Laws of War?', in *American Journal of International Law*, 35 (1941), p. 435, wherein the whole question is comprehensively discussed.

[6] *United States* v. *Skorzeny et Al.* (1947), *War Crimes Reports*, ix (1949), p. 90.

342   SO-CALLED 'UNPRIVILEGED BELLIGERENCY'

time of the *Skorzeny Trial* may account for the failure of the American authorities to treat these persons in the same way as disguised persons taken in combat. The use of the Red Cross insignia as a means of deception is, of course, absolutely forbidden by the law of war and is a form of ruse punishable as a war crime.[1] With the question of such ruses, the point is reached at which the bearing of war on dissimulation may pass over from a denial of privilege under the law to active prosecution for the violation of the law of war.

V. *Conclusions*

The various types of hostile conduct which have just been described, although outwardly dissimilar, actually share a common characteristic—that of disregard for or deliberate non-compliance with the qualifications established for an individual's recognition as a prisoner of war upon capture. In a sense all of them also constitute ruses of one sort or another, if by ruse is understood any means of deceiving the enemy. Since these qualities are those which most conspicuously inhere in espionage, resistance activities in occupied areas, guerrilla warfare, and private hostilities in arms, they afford grounds for believing that all these acts of warfare, whether or not involving the use of arms and whether performed by military persons or by civilians, are governed by a single legal principle. That this larger category of hostile conduct is not violative of any positive prohibition of international law is demonstrable by much the same considerations as militate against an internationally imposed duty of obedience to the belligerent occupant. In both occupied and unoccupied areas, resistance activities, guerrilla warfare, and sabotage by private persons may be expected to continue on at least as widespread a basis in future warfare as they have in the past. More often than not, patriotism or some sort of political allegiance lies at the root of such activities. Consequently the law of nations has not ventured to require of states that they prevent the belligerent activities of their citizenry or that they refrain from the use of secret agents or that these activities upon the part of their military forces or civilian population be punished. Evidence of the unwillingness of international law to intervene in such matters is found in the failure of those who have compiled lists of 'war crimes' for which persons are actually to be tried to include such acts as espionage or guerrilla fighting. The weight of precedent and history represented by the law applicable to espionage and the importance for practical purposes of the law relating to the hostile conduct of occupied populations together suggest that the supposed illegality of those other types of secret warfare which have been mentioned is based upon a mis-

---

[1] *United States v. Hagendorf* (1946), *War Crimes Reports*, xiii (1949), p. 146.

SPIES, GUERRILLAS, AND SABOTEURS   343

conception. The correct legal formulation is, it is submitted, that armed and unarmed hostilities, wherever occurring, committed by persons other than those entitled to be treated as prisoners of war or peaceful civilians merely deprive such individuals of a protection they might otherwise enjoy under international law and place them virtually at the power of the enemy. 'Unlawful belligerency' is actually 'unprivileged belligerency'.

International law deliberately neglects to protect unprivileged belligerents because of the danger their acts present to their opponent. The peril to the enemy inherent in attempts to obtain secret information or to sabotage his facilities and in attacks by persons whom he often cannot distinguish from the peaceful population is sufficient to require the recognition of wide retaliatory powers. As a rough-and-ready way of distinguishing open warfare and dangerous dissimulation, the character of the clothing worn by the accused has assumed major importance. The soldier in uniform or the member of the volunteer corps with his distinctive sign have a protected status upon capture, whilst other belligerents not so identified do not benefit from any comprehensive scheme of protection. An exception must, of course, be made of the *levée en masse*, which cannot be reconciled on principle with the distinction otherwise made between privileged and unprivileged belligerents. There is considerable justice in the contention that to make the difference between life and death hang on the type of clothes worn by the individual is to create a 'clothes philosophy' of a particularly dangerous character. Indeed, the emphasis on the properly uniformed belligerent may be only a survival from the type of war fought by closely grouped ranks of soldiers, in which firing upon even individual detached soldiers was regarded as violative of international law.[1] As the current tendency of the law of war appears to be to extend the protection of prisoner-of-war status to an ever-increasing group, it is possible to envisage a day when the law will be so retailored as to place all belligerents, however garbed, in a protected status.

The judicial determination which is necessary before a person may be treated as an unprivileged belligerent is in consequence not a determination

---

[1] Article 69, General Orders No. 100, 24 April 1863, prepared by Dr. Francis Lieber for the government of United States forces in the field, stated: 'Outposts, sentinels, or pickets are not to be fired upon, except to drive them in, or when a positive order, special or general, has been issued to that effect.' It is perhaps this distaste for the killing of the detached soldier which accounts for the prohibition of assassination in customary international law. Although this rule is considered to have been incorporated into Article 23 (*b*) of the Hague Regulations, which forbids treacherous killing (Field Manual 27–10, *Rules of Land Warfare* (1940), par. 31), practice must be considered to have given a restrictive interpretation to 'assassination', at least to the extent of not rendering internationally criminal the deliberate killing of individual enemies in battle or in occupied areas. It is, for example, questionable whether the killing of Heydrich in 1942 by three Czech nationals who had parachuted into Czechoslovakia (see Spaight, *Air Power and War Rights* (3rd ed., 1947), p. 305) could be said to be an international crime. But cf. *Opinions of the Attorneys General of the United States*, 11 (1869), p. 297, dealing with the assassination of President Lincoln.

of guilt but of status only and, for the purposes of international law, it is sufficient to ascertain whether the conduct of the individual has been such as to deny him the status of the prisoner or of the peaceful civilian. There is actually no need for the creation of separate categories of offences, since the person bent on espionage will be subject to the same maximum penalty as the individual who transmits information innocently acquired or who engages in secret warfare. The fact that a given individual will, as a matter of practice, carry on a variety of forms of hostile conduct is a further reason why international law need not work out any code of 'offences'. What is thereafter to be done to the individual who is found to lack a privileged status is left to the discretion of the belligerent. It may either, as a belligerent act, cause the execution of the offender or it may require the application of domestic law to determine something denominated in that municipal law as 'guilt'—but a guilt only in the sense of municipal law. In the case of occupied territory Articles 64, 65, and 67 of the Geneva Civilians Convention of 1949 impose a positive requirement that persons in occupied areas be tried only under a municipal law enacted for or applied to the occupied area, and the Convention as a whole so severely restricts the power of the occupant to deal freely with unprivileged belligerency[1] that the resistance worker or guerrilla in occupied territory is actually in a more favourable position than if he had been arrested or captured elsewhere.

A denial that unprivileged belligerency is a violation of international law does not, it must be emphasized, leave the opposing state powerless. Guerrilla warfare may still be met with open warfare and saboteurs and spies captured within the lines may still be penalized, but not for any violation of international law. Except to the extent to which the power to impose the death penalty has been removed by the Geneva Civilians Convention of 1949,[2] the offended state may employ that measure in dealing with clandestine hostile conduct. Moreover, the capturing state is not precluded from punishing an unprivileged belligerent for a war crime *stricti juris*, if he has, for example, killed civilians, or pillaged or refused to give quarter. Although it may be foreseen that in time of war bandits who live by pillage may attempt to contend that they are guerrillas fighting for the defence of their country, the degree to which they comply with the law of war generally applicable to the armed forces will afford the best indication of their purpose, and particularly of their adhesion to one of the belligerents in the conflict rather than to motives of private gain.

As has already been observed, 'unprivileged belligerency' partakes strongly of the nature of a ruse by reason of its clandestine character. The

[1] See Gutteridge, 'The Protection of Civilians in Occupied Territory', in *Year Book of World Affairs* (1951), p. 290.
[2] Article 68.

SPIES, GUERRILLAS, AND SABOTEURS   345

same 'statute of limitations' which forbids the punishment by the enemy of a spy who has returned to his own lines accordingly could be applied to other forms of unprivileged belligerency, and there would appear to be strong reasons of policy for doing so.[1] However, although it is easy to determine that a spy's mission is completed with his return to his own lines, to fix with certainty when the status of 'unprivileged belligerency' in other forms is at an end is extremely difficult. Nevertheless, the principle to be applied would appear to be that if an individual has either returned to his own lines or become part of the regular armed forces or has otherwise indicated the termination of his belligerent status, as by long abstention therefrom, he may not be prosecuted by the opposing state for his previous acts of unprivileged belligerency. In the case of guerrilla warfare or of resistance activities in occupied territory, the cessation of belligerent activity will in all probability be difficult to prove in practice. Furthermore, as the penalizing of the unprivileged belligerent is actually a belligerent act, there is no reason for such action after the definite cessation of hostilities, subject to the exception that new acts occurring thereafter would be punishable on the basis that they had constituted a resumption of hostilities.

[1] It was at one time suggested that the war traitor who had returned to his own lines should benefit from the immunity extended to the spy (Article 104, General Orders No. 100, 24 April 1863), but the contrary view now appears to prevail (*Manual of Military Law* (*1929*), Amendments No. 12 (1936), p. 38; Field Manual 27-10, *Rules of Land Warfare* (1940), par. 213).

[5]

THE STATUS OF COMBATANTS AND THE QUESTION OF GUERILLA WARFARE*

By G. I. A. D. DRAPER

A. History and Theory

A WIDE variety of historical factors led to the emergence of a basic legal principle of the law of arms that the right to bear arms and to participate in acts of public warfare was limited to a particular class of men. According to medieval legal ideas laws could be categorized according to the different callings men performed in society, for the common good. As there was a special law for those who prayed so there could be a special law governing those who fought to protect them and for other good purposes. This was the medieval law of arms (*jus militare*) founded, in the main, on the canon and civil laws. As such it formed part of the *jus gentium* and was universally binding on the knightly and military classes whenever such persons were engaged in their military activities. The law of arms was thus seen as an extension of the canon and civil law just as the latter were, in medieval theory, extensions of the natural law and the law of nations. Thus emerged the idea of a professional military class, subjected to the *jus militare* throughout the length and breadth of Christendom whenever they were engaged in their professional activities.[1]

When to this idea of a special part of the *jus gentium* universally applicable to a special class of men engaged in their specific activities there was added the later elaboration of the 'public and open' war of the fourteenth and fifteenth centuries, we can discern the roots of the idea that combatancy was limited and privileged. In the passage of time the concept of the 'just and public war' became transformed into that of the 'public and open' war. For a war to be 'just' it had to be 'avowed' by a sovereign prince and not a matter of private freebooting, the descendant of the old private, feudal right to make war against which the Church had turned the full force of its anathemas to some effect. The moral element in the 'just and public' war receded in two ways. A war which a prince 'avowed' was not admitted to be other than just. A war which was 'avowed' by a prince was 'public'. If it were 'public' it was not to be admitted that it was other than 'just'. The word 'just' became redundant in this context by the fourteenth century. Conversely, the 'private', i.e. 'unavowed' war was manifestly unjust.[2]

* © G. I. A. D. Draper, 1971.
[1] M. H. Keen, *The Laws of War in the late Middle Ages* (1965), pp. 13–15.
[2] Ibid., pp. 72, 84 et seq.

At the same time the *jus militare* drew much of its practical content, when the precedents of Roman law had been exhausted, from the manners, practices and customs of the knights and the men-at-arms. This was a specialized body of learning with which the heralds and the canon lawyers who practised before the military courts of Christendom were conversant. Their law was professional and technical as betokened the activity, namely fighting, to which that law related. This *jus militare* controlled such vital matters as the right to take prisoners, claim and secure ransom for prisoners, take spoils, conduct sieges, levy 'appatis', i.e. contributions levied in the area of the fighting in return for immunity, and many other matters. Such activities, the essential concomitants of military action, were lawful only within the confines of a 'public and open' war, as known to the heralds and the canonists. If such acts were done outside 'public and open' wars these acts were brigandage and looting. The military courts determined such matters with precision and by the application of technical rules of the *jus militare*. Gradually, and with considerable difficulty, the free companies and *écorcheurs* whose arms were directed against all men irrespective of any 'avowal' by a prince, were brought to some limited account for their actions. The 'open' nature of the public war was seen partly as evidence of its 'public' nature and partly as the antithesis of perfidy and cowardly assassinations, actions repugnant to the conception of chivalry and the membership of the various knightly orders to which many of the knights belonged. An act of perfidy could hardly be redeemed, in the eyes of an order of chivalry, even by later acts of courage and prowess.[1]

It came to be established from the mingling and interplay of such ideas, well understood by those engaged in the professional business of fighting, that fighting was a privilege of a privileged class of men bound by their own law, the *jus militare*, applied and enforced by all military tribunals in Christendom, whether of the enemy prince or of the prince upon whom a knight or man-at-arms depended either in a feudal relationship or as a mercenary. Fighting was thus seen as a business limited as to the occasion upon which it might legitimately be conducted, as to the class of men who might participate in it, and, finally, as to the types of action that might be taken. It must be emphasized that in the fourteenth and fifteenth centuries such restrictions as existed in relation to sparing prisoners, avoiding perfidy, and the like, had no humanitarian qualities. Ransom was lost if a prisoner were not spared, and one's reputation as a knight was in peril of 'dishonouring' if one resorted to perfidy. These were quite powerful factors.

The idea of military honour, so central to the conception of chivalry, did not entertain the idea that all might participate in the fighting. From Germanic sources came that essential link between the concept of honour

---

[1] M. H. Keen, *The Laws of War in the Late Middle Ages* (1965), pp. 69 et seq.

THE QUESTION OF GUERILLA WARFARE   175

and the right to bear arms. The *jus militare* was the law of this exclusive class and it gave little place or mercy to those who were outside its concern. Not only was the *jus militare* severe with those acknowledged members of the military class who fought in wars that were other than 'public and open', but also with those not of that class who had the audacity to participate in 'open and public' wars.

With the break-up of Christendom the medieval law of arms took shape as the embryonic international law of war. The older idea of knights, men-at-arms and mercenaries 'avowed' by a prince changed to that of armed forces in the service of a territorial, secular state. However, many of the ideas and technical rules of the *jus militare* came through into the new international law of war, including the idea of a right or privilege to fight reserved for military classes and the requirement of a certain 'openness' in the manner of fighting. This 'openness' spells out the older idea of a 'public' war and the rejection of perfidy as abhorrent to the knightly classes. Conversely, those who had not the right to fight met short shrift at the hands of those who had. The marauder and the freebooter acted against, and were outside, 'faith and the law of nations' and were early forms of war criminals.[1]

The introduction of standing armies in the seventeenth, and the raising of conscript forces in the late eighteenth and early nineteenth centuries, did not extend, as a matter of the law of war, the classes of persons who had the right to participate in acts of warfare. If anything, the distinction between those who had the right to fight and those who had not became even sharper. By the late eighteenth century a rough and ready balance between military needs and those of minimum humanity had been achieved by the law. Writers, such as Rousseau, in his *Contrat Social*, which appeared in 1762, played an important part in the gradual emergence of humanitarian considerations which he presented with an admixture of reason and sentiment.[2] This principle of balance has come through to the contemporary regulation of fighting in our own time. Not surprisingly, this balance now stands in need of considerable adjustment. The precise degree of this adjustment is, it is suggested, at the centre of the debates taking place in the Conferences of Government Experts on the Reaffirmation and Development of International Humanitarian Principles in Armed Conflicts currently being held in Geneva under the auspices of the International Committee of the Red Cross.[3]

This principle of balance, so far as it has permeated the law governing the right to take part in combat operations in armed conflicts, has taken the

---

[1] Ibid. p. 50, *contra fidem et jus gentium*. This work of Mr. Keen is an invaluable repository of learning upon the theory and content of the medieval law of wars.

[2] *Le contrat social*, Book I, chapter 4.

[3] The first of these was held in Geneva in May–June 1971. The second is to be held in May 1972.

form that only those who have the right to participate may be the human objectives of lawful attack. Those who had come to receive the benefit of the legal immunity from attack, i.e. the non-participant civilian population, received that immunity solely and exclusively on the basis that they retained that capacity and conducted themselves as such. Civilians participating in combat ceased to be immune from attack. They might be killed in combat, and, on capture, were liable to be treated as marauders and executed summarily at the discretion of the captor commander. Such participating civilians had no lawful claim to be treated as prisoners of war. On the contrary, their very participation, however conducted, was in itself a violation of the law of war or, alternatively, conduct that put them outside its protection and left them at the mercy of the enemy.

This dual consequence of civilian participation in armed conflicts, namely, exposure to attack by the opposing belligerent, and a criminal status upon capture, has led to some contemporary division of opinion among jurists. On the one hand, it is claimed that the civilian participant has violated the law of war and may be treated accordingly, upon capture. The other theory, known as that of 'privileged belligerency', adumbrated in the pages of this *Year Book*,[1] is that such civilian participants in the combat, by reason of their admitted capacity to inflict great injury upon their military opponents, may be killed as enemies, subject only to such restrictions as international customary or conventional law may place upon States, e.g. by the requirement of a trial before execution. This theory was, it is thought, first advanced to meet the quite unique legal position of espionage, an activity punishable and punished by belligerents but one lawfully used by them. On balance, the theory that illicit combatants may be killed after capture, as an act of warfare, subject to any restraint imposed by the law of war, is somewhat artificial. There may be some substance in the contention, and it may be more consonant with the war practices of belligerents, the official manuals on the law of war issued by States, and the decisions of national tribunals applying the law of war, that illegal participation in combat is a violation of the law of war exposing the offender to loss of immunity from attack, and, upon capture, to trial and punishment upon conviction. However, the matter is controversial, and there are certain passages in the classical writers on the law of war, such as Grotius, which lend support to the theory of 'unprivileged belligerency'.[2]

---

[1] Baxter, *'So-called "Unprivileged Belligerency"; Spies, Guerillas and Saboteurs'*, this *Year Book*, 28 (1951), p. 323.

[2] *De Jure Belli ac Pacis* (Carnegie, 1925), Book III, Chapter IV, Tit. 3. (Of Spies). However, Grotius distinguishes the case of the spy from that of 'assassins who act treacherously. Not only do they themselves act in a manner inconsistent with the law of nations, but this holds true of those who employ their services.' Grotius considers that the use of the spy is quite different in that the sending of spies 'is beyond doubt permitted by the law of nations'.

The *rationale* of the limitation of the right to bear arms and to kill in combat to the armed forces of a State or other recognized belligerent entity, is that it is partly in the interest of those armed forces themselves and partly in the interest of the civilian population. By so restricting the activity of military engagement, both as to actor and victim, military and humanitarian needs are met within that rough principle of balance previously mentioned. In military terms, the armed forces of a belligerent know their enemies and can identify them. In humane terms the civilian stands outside the lawful ambit of attack, and of capture. It was seen, in the nineteenth century, that the limitation of lawful warfare to the armed forces of a belligerent restricted the effects of warfare and the consequential suffering and destruction, a powerful consideration when the mounting effect of artillery bombardment was a novelty. This is not to deny, as a manifest fact of the history of warfare, that the civilian participating in the combat received short shrift at the hands of the opposing military when he fell into their hands. The ideas of the medieval law of arms and their intimate association with the conception of military honour have lingered long and have not been without influence in determining the pattern of the customary, and later, of the conventional law of war as it emerged in the eighteenth and nineteenth centuries, respectively.

The early nineteenth century witnessed the large-scale participation of bands of civilians in armed combat at a time when their country was being invaded, or the military occupant was being expelled. Such civilians frequently associated and operated with broken military units of the State upon which such civilians depended. The activities of such groups, or loosely organized bands, composed of civilians or of members of military units not operating as part of military formations, or of a mixture of both components, were prominent in the Spanish and Russian campaigns against the armies of Napoleon in the early nineteenth century. In both cases the country upon which the civilian, irregular, fighters depended, had been invaded by the French armies. These groups of irregulars, loosely organized, and acting, normally, without authorization, fought either independently or in varying degrees of association with the armed forces of their own country and its allies, e.g. with the British armed forces under Wellington in Spain.

It was, specifically, this latter activity that has given us the modern name of 'guer(r)illa warfare' and the 'guer(r)illa fighter'. The effectiveness of such irregular fighting against regular formations was very considerable, both from the clandestine and sporadic nature of the offensive operations conducted by guerillas, their knowledge of the fighting terrain, their capacity to move and choose their military position clandestinely, and their like capacity to disappear when pursued, and to obtain shelter, treatment, and sustenance from their own kin and friends in the area. It became readily apparent that such guerilla fighters had many advantages, in military terms, not open to their military opponents. The military harm that they could inflict, based on the element of surprise inherent in their clandestine method of fighting, and their ability to melt away into the countryside and towns with impunity, made them very formidable opponents. The elements of surprise, and their capacity to gain intelligence of enemy movements, vital to military effectiveness, tended to make up for their disadvantage in terms of logistic supply, deficient weaponry and lack of fire-power. When they were captured their fate was certain. The law of war extended no protection over them and placed no prohibitions upon their summary execution or maltreatment beforehand.

Closely allied to their fighting potential, the guerilla fighters carried out a substantial role of sabotage. This activity has become the more pronounced in our own time when the scale and speed of destruction and disruption are commensurate with the technology which has produced the installations and systems exposed to sabotage. Neither can it be dismissed from our consideration that this capacity for effective sabotage has been a contributory factor to the shape of the law governing combatancy as it emerged in the nineteenth century and was codified at its conclusion. In arriving at the principle of balance in the law of war the capacity of the guerilla fighter to inflict large-scale military injury upon their adversaries has not been the exclusive factor. Their equal capacity to inflict sabotage, either in the rear of advancing military forces, or in occupied territory, or on the line of retreating forces, or ahead of advancing forces, has been present in the minds of those intent on securing the traditional balance in the law of war. The sensitive nature of much of our modern communications systems, urban organization generally and power and food supply, enhances the effectiveness of the guerilla fighter at an increasing rate to which the contemporary law of war has not yet adapted itself. This may be seen as one of the areas in which the balance of military and humanitarian needs requires some restoration or readjustment if the law of war is to be an effective instrument.

Further, the guerilla fighter, from his nature, has a capacity to carry out successful espionage either for the purposes of his own guerilla activities or for the benefit of military formations with whom he is associated. The experience of the Napoleonic armies, in advancing or retreating in Russia and in Spain, at the hands of the indigenous populations and guerilla fighters, was not lost upon the governments of the European States.

Contemporaneously, in the nineteenth century, with the awareness of this major threat to the military forces of a State, or other, belligerent, there arose the two strong forces of national patriotism and of humanitarianism.

THE QUESTION OF GUERILLA WARFARE   179

The idea of the entire able-bodied civilian population rising spontaneously to resist an invader, and the idea of loosely organized groups of civilians operating to harass a military occupant, or assisting in driving that occupant out of their country, were seen as part of the powerful current of patriotic feeling, commendable and even heroic. A little later, in the mid-nineteenth century there arose a strong humanitarian sentiment, consequential upon Dunant's famous pamphlet, 'A Souvenir of Solferino' which appeared in 1861 and 1863. As the direct outcome of the effect of these publications there came the first of the Geneva Conventions, in 1864, for the protection of the wounded and sick members of the armed forces in the field and for the limited neutralization of medical personnel, transport and equipment.

At the same time, in 1863, there started the movement to codify the customary law of war on land, with the publication of Francis Lieber's work *Instructions for the Government of the Armies of the United States in the Field*, subsequently issued by President Lincoln as an Official Army Order, styled 'General Orders No. 100'. In 1862, Lieber, a Professor of Law at the Columbia College, had published a work entitled *Guerilla Parties Considered with Reference to the Laws and Usages of War*. It may be claimed that the writings of Lieber were the first major attempt to give written form to the customary rules of land warfare prevailing at the end of the first half of the nineteenth century. The first effective attempt at a modest codification of certain parts of the law of sea warfare had been concluded in the Declaration of Paris of 1856, accepted by a limited number of States at first, but later commanding a more general acceptance by States. So far as the law of war on land is concerned, the work of Lieber on guerilla fighting reflected the prevailing view of the law at that time, namely, that guerilla warfare was a violation of the law of war. His views on this topic are of some importance because they came to be the basis of the abortive Declaration of Brussels of 1874, put before the Conference of States convened by Tsar Alexander II, and designed both to codify and humanize the customs and usages of land warfare.

As is well known, the texts of the proposed codification of the law of war which failed to secure adoption at Brussels in 1874 were brought forward to the First Hague Peace Conference, convened by Tsar Nicholas II in 1899. At this Conference certain of the texts of the Brussels Declaration were adopted as Conventions by the majority of the participating States. At the First Hague Conference of 1899 there was established the Hague Convention Concerning the Laws and Customs of War on Land, based upon the Brussels Declaration of 1874, which had in turn been based largely upon the 'Instructions' drafted by Professor Lieber. This Convention was revised at the Second Hague Peace Conference, convened by

Tsar Nicholas II, in 1907, and, upon acceptance, became established as the Hague Convention No. IV, which is operative today and considered as part of the contemporary customary law of war on land. Hague Convention No. IV of 1907, for the preamble of which the Russian jurist de Martens was responsible, aimed at no more than a partial codification of the then existing customs of war on land and expressly disclaimed, in its preamble, any intention to be comprehensive. It took account of the experience gained during the Franco-Prussian war of 1870 and of the participation, and treatment of, the *franc-tireurs* engaged in fighting the invading Prussian armed forces.[1]

The debates which had taken place at Brussels and at the two Hague Conferences highlighted the current issues surrounding the employment of irregular forces against regular units in warfare. The culmination of this debate led to the establishment of Articles 1 and 2 of the Hague Regulations appended to the Hague Convention No. IV of 1907. Until the Geneva Conventions of 1949, these Articles in the Hague Regulations constituted the sole conventional law concerning lawful irregular combatancy. There remained the customary law for those States not bound by the Hague Convention No. IV. At the close of World War II the International Military Tribunal at Nuremburg was prepared to hold that '. . . by 1939 these rules laid down in the [Hague No. IV] Convention were recognized by all civilized nations and were regarded as being declaratory of the laws and customs of war . . .'.[2] That judgment, including this passage, was the subject of a unanimous Resolution of the General Assembly of the United Nations in 1946. Therein the 'principles of international law recognized by the Charter of the International Tribunal and the Judgment of the Tribunal' were 'reaffirmed'.[3]

In retrospect, it can be seen that the clash of opinions at Brussels and the two Hague Conferences of 1899 and 1907, respectively, led to a compromise solution between the strong opinions of the day. The 'patriots' war', the struggle of smaller countries for independence, e.g. Belgium, the resistance of invaders by civilians, such as Prussia, by the French population operating as *franc-tireurs* and the experience of Russian and Spanish guerilla bands fighting the French invaders, were all persuasive factors for according some lawful combatant status to fighters operating outside the organized armed forces of a belligerent State. Opposed to this position were the policies of powerful military States, such as Prussia, with no less

---

[1] The Prussian practice, during that war, was to consider the *franc-tireurs* as illegal combatants unless they could produce special authorization from the French Government. In default, they were shot. This requirement was not included in the Hague Regulations annexed to Hague Convention No. IV of 1907. See Oppenheim, *International Law*, vol. 2 (7th edn., 1955), pp. 256–7.

[2] *Annual Digest*, 1946, Case No. 92, p. 206.   [3] Resolution 95 (1).

THE QUESTION OF GUERILLA WARFARE   181

powerful military traditions, which denied any such recognition and were fully aware of the menace to orthodox military techniques and ascendancy posed by guerilla methods of fighting. The division of views on this issue between those States which had experienced a military occupation, those which had not and those States which had been successful invaders, formed the core of the debates which led to the provisions now to be found in Articles 1 and 2 of the Hague Regulations of 1907.[1] These provisions governed lawful and unlawful participation in combat until the Geneva (Prisoners of War) Convention of 1949.[2]

Under the Hague Convention No. IV of 1907 the according of combatant status to fighters outside the armies of State belligerents was severely restricted. The widest concession was that granted by Article 2 to members of the *levée en masse*, an institution narrowly defined to meet the situation of a 'last ditch' defence of an invaded State with no time at its disposal to organize and integrate its civilian population into its armies or other formations capable of receiving combatant status under Article 1.

Before considering in detail the present law governing combatancy or the right to participate in armed combat it may be useful to formulate the general principles which underlie the Hague Regulations of 1907, as extended by the Geneva (Prisoners of War) Convention of 1949, in their purported regulation of the modern right of combatancy. These principles are thought to have emerged from the debates mentioned above and to have been reflected in these two Conventions, the former of which governs all States and recognized belligerents engaged in armed conflict and the latter governs 129 States up to date.[3] These general principles are considered to be:

(i) the rights of waging war and engaging in armed combat devolve exclusively upon the armed forces of States and those groups of individuals who, by analogy and concession, have been partially assimilated to such armed forces;

(ii) the duties of those who have the right to engage in armed conflict preclude deliberate military action against innocent civilians as such;

(iii) one of the rights of warfare granted to members of armed forces of belligerents and to those lifted up to that status by concession is that, upon capture, they are entitled to prisoner-of-war status, now governed by the extensive regime of the Geneva (Prisoners of War) Convention, 1949.

It is essential to stress that under the modern law of war this assimilation of the rights of members of the armed forces and of other participants

---

[1] For the texts, see below, p. 186.
[2] Particularly Article 4 A (2), for the text of which see below, p. 191.
[3] 31 December 1971.

accorded combatant status is strictly limited. The concession to the latter group is conditional upon their observance of stringent conditions, default in compliance with which being likely to result in loss of their combatant status, denial of prisoner-of-war status upon capture and exposure to the allegation of war criminality by the very fact of participation in the combat. They derive the benefits of the law of war solely on condition that they meet its requirements. The reasoning is apparent. Such classes of individuals participate in the conflict as a concession. That concession is granted on conditions specified by the law of war and expressly designed to bring them as close to members of the armed forces as possible. The latter have the right to participate when operating as such members of armed forces.[1] Failure to meet the conditions imposed on persons who are not members of the armed forces severs the concession and reduces them to the position of unlawful participants. Such persons fall into an intermediate class to which the law attributes an intermediate status. They are not innocent civilians immune from attack. Such persons are neither liable to be taken, nor entitled to be treated, as prisoners of war. They are not members of the armed forces who have the right to fight provided they operate as such—an 'open' activity conducted as ascertainable members of a military formation dependent upon a State or other recognized belligerent. It is the clandestinity and sporadic nature of guerilla activity which is now proving to be the crux of the debates in progress in the context of the revision of the law governing combatancy.

Guerilla warfare, as has been pointed out by writers, is a method of warfare and not a concept of the law of war. The distinction made by some writers between guerilla warfare and guerilla tactics is not thought to be sustainable today.[2] The former term was meant to convey warfare conducted by irregular combatants not entitled to combatant status under the existing law of war. By the latter was meant special types of warfare carried out by special types of military personnel, commandos, 'Special Service' personnel, and analogous formations, who operate behind the enemy lines carrying out sabotage, general disruption and the giving of false military intelligence. If the latter operate as members of military units, however small the groups, openly and in uniform, with weapons discernible, their operations cannot be considered as guerilla tactics for the purposes of the law of war. Such personnel are entitled to prisoner-of-war status upon capture. Their participation in acts of combat is legitimate, although they,

---

[1] That membership of armed forces is not enough to establish lawful combatancy, unless members operate openly in combat in such capacity, has been illustrated in the recent decision of the Judicial Committee of the Privy Council in *Mohamed Ali and Another* v. *Public Prosecutor*, [1968] 3 All. E.R., 488 (P.C.). See p. 212 n. 5, below, for a fuller note on this case.

[2] For example, Oppenheim, *International Law*, vol. 2 (8th edn., 1955), pp. 212–13, 259–60.

in common with all other lawful combatants, are answerable for breaches of the law of war committed during such lawful participation.[1]

Between the date of the Hague Convention in 1907, and that of the Geneva Conventions of 1949, there had been guerilla activities during the Italian invasion of Ethiopia in 1934 and during the Spanish Civil War of 1936-9. The major experience of large-scale guerilla warfare was during World War II, particularly in countries occupied by the German armed forces which included the greater part of Europe. Substantial and effective resistance was mounted against German occupation forces by partisans in the Soviet Union, Poland, Yugoslavia, and, later, in the countries of western Europe. In the latter the resistance took the form of resistance organizations composed of the indigenous population operating clandestinely, either independently, or under orders of exiled governments, within occupied territories. In eastern Europe, however, partisan forces composed of broken military units and of civilians operated against German occupation forces, either alone or in conjunction with armed forces still operating as such in parts of the country not occupied and where the front had held.[2] The experience gained in the successes and failures of these guerilla formations has been carried forward in the post-1945 era. A new type of guerilla activity has been seen, particularly in the non-international and semi-international armed conflicts of the last quarter of a century. These conflicts have often taken the form of struggles to gain ascendancy within a State or to gain independence, by way of secession from an existing State. More recently guerilla activities have been conducted as a method of securing specific political objectives by groups or organizations disassociated from States or other belligerents, and directed at particular governments, their nationals and property, where and whenever opportunity presents itself. Thus we have arrived at a time when guerilla warfare, in the sense of sporadic and clandestine actions of armed violence for specific political purposes by loosely organized groups in varying degrees of association with, or disassociation from, any government, is a feature of our age. Its manifestations are very diverse and often effective. The capacity of these guerilla groups, however small, to inflict substantial damage upon military formations during an armed conflict, and upon the civilian population in times of relative normality, is not disputable. In times of relative normality the machinery of internal law and order is often inadequate to control the activities of guerillas operating with determination

---

[1] The activities of members of such units led to a number of war crimes trials at the end of World War II, by reason of the policy of liquidating such individuals adopted by Germany, expressed in Hitler's 'Commando Order' of 18 October 1942. For examples of trials of Germans for implementation of this Order, see *In re von Falhkenhorst, Annual Digest*, 1946, p. 282; and *In re Dostler*, ibid., Case No. 116, p. 280.

[2] See Heilbrun, *Partisan Warfare* (1962).

and skill. As the range of political objectives widens this phenomenon expands commensurately. At the same time governments are aware that in time of international armed conflict, particularly when a part of their territory is subject to a military occupation, the activities of such guerillas are of considerable value in securing the liberation of that territory. When such guerillas, in time of internal armed conflict, turn their hostile attention to the government, they are able to reduce politically organized society to chaotic conditions and virtually to frustrate the process of government.

It is an initial and substantial difficulty when considering the legal rules that are to be brought to bear upon guerilla activities that the existing classification, for the purposes of the international law of war, into international and non-international armed conflicts is (i) difficult to determine, and (ii) under fairly consistent attack from some sources with a view to its elimination. So far, that distinction, implicit in the law of war, generally, and explicit in the Geneva Conventions of 1949, has held. In spite of an effort to remove the distinction, particularly in the context of the law governing guerilla activities, between international and non-international armed conflicts, the general consensus of States seems to be in favour of preserving that classification, although some recent Resolutions of the General Assembly of the United Nations may give a contrary impression.[1] The current pressure is for lawful combatant status to be accorded to any guerilla fighters operating for specific political motives such as 'wars of national liberation', 'anti-colonial', 'anti-racist' and 'peoples' wars. We are seeing at the present time two tendencies in this matter. First, the accepted view that common criminals who resort to armed force to achieve their ends, are to be excluded from any attribution of lawful combatancy. Second, we are seeing a widening of the idea of a political struggle carried out by armed force being within the control of the existing law of war. This has the corollary that those who participate in such a struggle, whether openly or clandestinely and sporadically, should be treated as lawful combatants entitled to the full status of prisoners of war upon capture.

It remains to be seen to what extent the law of war will be so revised as to extend its embrace to armed conflicts not conducted between States, or to conflicts within a State between two political and military candidates for power with minimum organization on the non-governmental side. The matter is further complicated by the phenomenon of the armed forces of a third State participating in an internal conflict, e.g. opposed to the government forces and associated with rebel guerillas, or associated with the government forces and opposed to rebel guerillas.

It is readily and generally accepted that the existing law of war stands in

---

[1] For example, Resolutions 2444 (XXIII), operative sect. 2; 2597 (XXIV) operative sect. 1 : 2675 (XXV); and 2676 (XXV).

THE QUESTION OF GUERILLA WARFARE   185

need of revision, but beyond that point consensus is not apparent. The current political tensions tend to aggravate the uncertainties and possible anachronisms of the existing law of combatancy and hence of the legal status of guerilla fighters. It is not easy to secure a detached forum in which the juridical revisions may be considered divorced from their political overtones. In terms of juridical revision the approach might be to start with the existing law of combatancy and work outwards from the limits of its present applicability, itself a debatable matter. The other approach, which may be termed the political approach, is to seek the desirable political goal in new legal rules without regard to the realities of combat conditions and the existing law. Behind such projects of revision there is the salient development with which the law of war has to contend today in the widespread erosion of the distinction between the civilian population and the armed forces of a State. This erosion is due to many factors, but the net result is that the basic premises upon which the existing law of war was constructed are no longer evident. The dilemma of law revision is real. A minimal revision of the existing law of war will leave too wide a gap between the content of the law and the new war practices to which it relates. A major revision of that law which correlates to the gradual obliteration of the distinction between the armed forces and the civilian population, whether in combatancy, in methods of combat, or in targetry, will extend the effects of warfare, to the added misery of mankind. The medieval theologian and canon lawyer were clear that a total war could not be 'just'.[1] In the past quarter of a century we have witnessed the unfolding of the regimes of Human Rights, while at the same time the war practices and combat methods of belligerents have made much of the classical law of war difficult to apply, where not anachronistic. Finally, we are confronted with the position that in International Law it is States, through their governments, that alone have the legal competence to revise the law. Any revision in the direction of an extended lawful combatancy in favour of guerilla fighters is likely to reduce considerably the military effectiveness of the armed forces of States upon which their governments depend for their external and internal security, and, ultimately, for their existence.

B. THE EXISTING LAW OF COMBATANCY AND THE STATUS OF GUERILLAS

The existing rules controlling the classes of individuals who may lawfully participate in armed conflicts of an international character are to be found,

---

[1] See Keen, op. cit. (above, p. 173 n. 1), p. 189. The purpose of war being to establish peace, and to establish right by appeal to divine judgment, its extent was therefore limited by that purpose so that the minimum dislocation of Christian society should be caused. Within such ideas descending through the divine, eternal, natural, canon and civil law, of which the *jus militare* formed part, the law of immunity from acts of 'public and open' wars finds its origins.

186   THE STATUS OF COMBATANTS AND

primarily, in Articles 1, 2, and 3 of the Hague Regulations appended to Hague Convention No. IV of 1907, as impliedly extended by Article 4A of the Geneva (Prisoners of War) Convention, 1949. The Hague Regulations of 1907, as we have seen, bind all States engaged in international armed conflicts, as they are considered to embody the customary law of war on land including the right of participation in that activity. The scheme of the Hague Regulations in regard to combatancy was to specify, definitively and exhaustively, those who had the status of belligerents. The Regulations annexed to the Hague Convention No. IV are divided into sections and the sections into chapters. Section 1 is entitled 'Of Belligerents'. Chapter 1 of that section is entitled 'The Status of Belligerents'. Chapter 2 of that section is entitled 'Prisoners of War'.

Article 1 of the Regulations (Chapter 1, Section 1) is in these terms:

The laws, rights and duties of war apply not only to the army, but also to militia and volunteer corps fulfilling all the following conditions:—

1. They must be commanded by a person responsible for his subordinates;
2. They must have a fixed distinctive sign recognizable at a distance;
3. They must carry arms openly; and
4. They must conduct their operations in accordance with the laws and customs of war.

In countries where militia or volunteer corps constitute the army, or form part of it, they are included under the denomination "army".

Article 2 provides:

The inhabitants of a territory not under occupation, who, on the approach of the enemy, spontaneously take up arms to resist the invading troops without having had time to organise themselves in accordance with Article 1, shall be regarded as belligerents if they carry arms openly and if they respect the laws and customs of war.

Article 3 then continues:

The armed forces of the belligerent may consist of combatants and non-combatants. In the case of capture by the enemy, both have the right to be treated as prisoners of war.

That is the whole of Chapter 1, Section 1, of the Regulations. Chapter 2 is entitled 'Prisoners of War'. Article 13 of that chapter adds 'the followers' of an army to the class entitled to prisoner-of-war status, over and above those enumerated in Article 3 above recited. Article 13 provides:

Individuals following an army without strictly belonging to it, such as newspaper correspondents or reporters,[1] sutlers or constructors, who fall into the enemy's hands

---

[1] There has recently been a strong movement to secure better protection for journalists 'carrying out dangerous missions', which include armed conflicts, e.g. in General Assembly Resolution 2673 (XXV). The particular anxiety seems to be to ensure that they should be issued with 'a universally recognized and guaranteed identification document' (para. 4). A draft Convention designed to carry out the protection of journalists engaged in dangerous missions is under consideration by the Conference of Government Experts at Geneva, referred to above, p. 175 n. 3.

THE QUESTION OF GUERILLA WARFARE   187

and whom the latter thinks it expedient to retain, are entitled to be treated as prisoners of war, provided they are in possession of a certificate from the military authorities of the army which they are accompanying.

The Hague Regulations of 1907 governed the 'status of belligerents' until Articles 1, 2 and 3 thereof were extended by Article 4A (2) and (3) of the Geneva (Prisoners of War) Convention of 1949.[1] In the period between 1907 and 1949 there was not a great deal of authority on the legal significance of these provisions. Neither was there any consensus among the jurists as to their precise meaning. The Hague Regulations, Articles 1, 2 and 3 were operative during World War II and were under judicial scrutiny during the war crimes trials at the close of that war. In so far as these cases dealt with the legal status of irregular combatants, they have only a limited relevance to the contemporary law. Most of the cases decided dealt with the conduct of partisan resistance fighters in guerilla fighting against the German armed forces in occupation of the territory concerned. The cases bear some relevance in regard to the degree of the association of such fighters with, or independence of, the government in exile from the occupied territory, and also from the degree of their organization or lack of it. It was the experience of such irregular fighting, the German authorities' response to it, and the subsequent war crimes trials of Germans for the nature of that response,[2] that led to the present formulation of Article 4A (2) of the Geneva (Prisoners of War) Convention of 1949.

The official Government manuals dealing with the law of war on land do not throw much light on the difficult legal questions arising out of the application of Articles 1, 2 and 3 of the Hague Regulations of 1907. The writings of the jurists show a wide range of views upon these difficulties. The views expressed in Chapter XIV of the British *Manual of Military Law* (1929, as amended in 1936) may be taken as those of the United Kingdom Government on the matter. They are based upon the accepted

---

[1] For the text, see below, p. 191.

[2] A leading case in which the law relating to the response of the German authorities to partisans' resistance activities in occupied territories was fully considered in *In re List and Others* (Hostages Trial), *Annual Digest*, 1948, Case No. 215, p. 632. In the course of the judgment the United States Military Tribunal held: 'We think the rule is established that a civilian who aids, abets or participates in the fighting is liable to punishment as a war criminal under the laws of war. Fighting is legitimate only for the combatant personnel of a country. It is only this group that is entitled to treatment as a prisoner of war [under the then operative Geneva (Prisoners of War) Convention, 1929] and incurs no liability beyond detention after capture or surrender' (p. 640). It was this judgment that formulated the proposition of law, not commanding general assent that: 'The right to kill hostages may be exercised only after a meticulous compliance with . . . safeguards against vindictive or whimsical orders of a military commander' (p. 644). A possible explanation of this part of the judgment is that the taking and shooting of hostages was confused with the exercise of reprisals. The *taking* of hostages and reprisal action against 'protected persons' are now both prohibited by Articles 33 and 34, respectively of the Geneva (Civilians) Convention, 1949, either in the territory of the enemy or in occupied territory.

188   THE STATUS OF COMBATANTS AND

distinction between the enemy's armed forces and its peaceful populations. Thus: 'Both these classes have distinct privileges, duties and
disabilities. It is one of the purposes of the law of war to ensure that an
individual must definitely choose to belong to one class or the other, and
shall not be permitted to enjoy the privileges of both; in particular that an
individual shall not be allowed to kill or wound members of the army of the
opposed nation and subsequently, if captured or in danger of life, pretend
to be a peaceful citizen.'[1] The corresponding paragraph of the current
British Manual on the Law of War on Land (*Manual of Military Law*,
Part III, 1958) repeats this passage with the qualification, 'Subject to the
fact that the distinction between combatants and non-combatants has
become increasingly blurred. . . .'[2]

It will have been observed that the Hague Regulations of 1907, Articles
1, 2 and 3, purport to deal exhaustively with the categories of persons who
may be lifted up so as to become subject to the 'laws, rights and duties of
war', alongside 'the army'. Those who get the benefit of the laws of war
also take the burden. The move away from the exclusive right of armies to
engage in combat action was strictly controlled, although commentators
have not agreed on the precise limits of the conditions imposed upon the
irregular combatants. The four conditions, specified in Article 1, were seen
as being very close to those actually prevailing in armies and in militia or
volunteer corps forming part of the army. There must be: (i) some element
of control, (ii) some element of identifiability, (iii) some element of openness, and (iv) a substantial element of compliance with the law of war
governing military operations. Implicit in the wording of Article 1 are two
further conditions or elements: (v) dependence in some degree, upon the
Government of the State belligerent, and (vi) a measure of organization.

Apart from the difficulty of attributing a core of certainty to these six
conditions there was, and is, a penumbra of uncertainty as to the legal
consequences of failing to comply with all or any of these conditions, and
as to which are applicable to the group, which to the individuals composing
the group, and which to both group and individuals. It is not possible to
say with confidence that any one view is accepted as representing an
established and accepted legal position.

Before treating those matters it is necessary to set out the prevailing
legal rules as to irregular combatancy as they are to be found in the Geneva
(Prisoners of War) Convention, 1949, now in force and binding 129 States,
including the United Kingdom since March 1958. The Geneva Conventions Act, 1957,[3] was enacted on 31 July 1957. This Act effected the
necessary legislative changes in the domestic law of the United Kingdom
required before ratification of the four Geneva Conventions of 1949, the

---

[1] Para. 17, p. 7   [2] Para. 86, p. 30.   [3] 5 and 6 Eliz. 2, c. 53.

THE QUESTION OF GUERILLA WARFARE   189

full texts of which constitute the four Schedules to the Act. Such cases as have been decided by the United Kingdom and other national war crimes tribunals after World War II have only a limited application today in that the bulk of them arose out of partisan activities in occupied territories.[1] It is in that area of activity that the Geneva (Prisoners of War) Convention, 1949, introduced an added category of irregular combatant with combatant status by extending the class of individuals entitled to prisoner-of-war status when they 'have fallen into the power of the enemy'.[2] This class now includes members of 'organized resistance movements, belonging to a Party to the conflict, and operating inside or outside their own territory, even if this territory is occupied' provided that they meet the four conditions set out in Article 1 of the Hague Regulations of 1907, above recited.[3] This is an important extension of lawful combatancy based directly on the experience of partisan activity during World War II and the war crimes trials of those who had killed or tortured them after capture.

This Geneva Convention of 1949 is one of a series of four dealing with various classes of war victims, namely prisoners of war, wounded and sick in the armed forces in the field, wounded, sick and shipwrecked members of such forces at sea, and certain classes of civilians who find themselves in the territory of the enemy or whose country is occupied by the enemy.[4] The Geneva Conventions do not purport to deal with the manner of conducting military operations except tangentially in the sense of securing protection for the war victims above enumerated. The Hague Regulations of 1907, on the other hand, deal with three basic areas of the law of war on land, namely, who may fight, what manner of fighting they may adopt and to whom or what military action may be directed. They also deal with pacific relations between belligerents and the regime of occupied territories. It is the three basic areas just mentioned that have to be kept in mind throughout any consideration of the law which governs who may, and who may not, be accorded the status of lawful combatants. The Hague Regulations of 1907 were framed on the basis of the customary law as it prevailed at that time. Their scheme was relatively simple. Those who had lawful combatant status were thought to be exhaustively defined in Articles 1 and 2. All within the purview of those Articles were accorded prisoner-of-war status, by Article 3, as were the non-combatants forming part of the armed forces of a belligerent, e.g. the medical personnel.[5] At the same time, by Article 13, certain types of army 'followers', namely, newspaper

---

[1] See above, p. 183.

[2] 'Prisoners of war, in the sense of the present Convention, are persons belonging to one of the following categories, who have fallen into the power of the enemy . . .' (Article 4A). For the text of the four Geneva Conventions see *United Nations Treaty Series*, 75 (1950), Nos. 970–3, pp. 31, 85, 135 and 287 respectively.   [3] Ibid., Article 4A (2), p. 138.

[4] See this page, n. 2.   [5] See above, p. 186.

correspondents and reporters, sutlers or contractors, if officially accredited to the armed forces they were accompanying, were given the like status if the enemy 'thinks it expedient to detain them'. It is not thought that the latter qualification meant much in that prisoners of war, members of the armed forces, may always be released, within certain minimal restrictions in the interests of humanity.[1] Today, the Geneva (Prisoners of War) Convention has considerably widened this class of 'followers', in Article 4A (3).[2]

Thus, the class of individuals entitled to prisoner-of-war status upon capture is wider than the class enjoying combatant status.[3] All members of the latter enjoy prisoner-of-war status, but the converse proposition is not true. This, it is thought, expresses the wish of States to extend the humanitarian protection afforded by prisoner-of-war status to as wide a class as possible and at the same time to limit the class entitled to initiate combat action. Non-combatant members of armed forces and civilian 'followers' are thought to enjoy, in common with all others, the essential right of self-defence and, probably, the right to elude capture, as are merchant ships and their crews in the law of sea warfare.[4] Traditionally, there has been a certain generosity in according prisoner-of-war status and a corresponding strictness in the according of combatant status. This was the outcome of the essential balance, which informs the whole of the law of war, between military and humanitarian demands. It is at this precise point that there is a current agitation for the extension of combatant status on more generous terms, analogous to the extension of prisoner-of-war status. This can be seen in recent Resolutions of the General Assembly, e.g. 2674 (XXV) and 2676 (XXV), both of 9 December 1950.[5]

The Geneva (Prisoners of War) Convention, 1949, is, in Article 135, expressed to be 'complementary' to Chapter 11 (Prisoners of War) of the Hague Regulations, 1907, for those States which are Parties to both instruments. Although the Convention of 1949 does not seek directly to extend the category of those entitled to combatant status under Articles 1 and 2 of the Hague Regulations, 1907, that effect has been indirectly achieved by the method of repeating, reframing and extending the categories listed in the Hague Regulations in Article 4 of the Geneva Convention dealing with those entitled to prisoner-of-war status. The reframing is achieved by

[1] Release of prisoners of war in deserts or in mid-ocean may be tantamount to ensuring their death.

[2] Nowhere, in terms, do the Geneva Conventions of 1949 purport to confer combatant status, thus adhering to their purpose of securing the better, i.e. more humanitarian, treatment of war victims, namely those who by definition are not actually engaged in hostilities.

[3] See *United Nations Treaty Series*, 75 (1950), p. 138. By Article 4A (4) members of the crew of the merchant marine and of civil aircraft of the parties to the conflict, are to enjoy prisoner-of-war status if they 'do not benefit by more favourable treatment under any other provisions of international law'; ibid., p. 140.

[4] See Oppenheim, *International Law*, vol. 2 (8th edn., 1955), p. 467.

[5] See this page, n. 2.

reference to 'Members of the armed forces of a Party to the conflict as well as members of militia or volunteer corps forming part of such armed forces'. The relevant extension occurs in Article 4A (2) which is in these terms:

> Members of other militias and members of other volunteer corps, including those of organized resistance movements, belonging to a Party to the conflict and operating within or outside their own territory, even if this territory is occupied, provided that such militias or volunteer corps, including such organized resistance movements, fulfil the following conditions. . . .

Then follow the four conditions appearing in Article 1 of the Hague Regulations previously cited.[1] It is thought that the fourth of these conditions, namely, 'that of conducting their operations in accordance with the laws and customs of war' makes it reasonably clear that those specified in Article 4A (2) as entitled to prisoner-of-war status have been accorded combatant status, including 'members of organized resistance movements operating within or outside their own territory, even if this territory is occupied'. Thus it may be said that the Geneva (Prisoners of War) Convention, 1949, has obliquely amended and extended the class of lawful combatants listed in Article 1 of the Hague Regulations, 1907.[2]

It is also relevant to consider Article 4A (3) of the Convention of 1949 which has accorded prisoner-of-war status to 'Members of regular armed forces who profess allegiance to a government or authority not recognized by the Detaining Power'. This is thought to mean that, apart from the lack of recognition of the authority upon which such individuals depend, they would, in all other respects be considered as members of the armed forces of a State, or other recognized belligerent, engaged in a conflict or occupation to which Article 2, common to the four Geneva Conventions of 1949[3] applies. Having regard to the wide claims that are currently being made for classes of irregular fighters to enjoy combatant and prisoner-of-war status this provision has an important bearing on the current law. Those claims become the more powerful under the impact of the present tendency, not soundly supported in law, to identify prisoners of war with combatant status.

---

[1] See above, p. 186.

[2] It is thought that it is this method of extending humanitarian protection to new classes of individuals to be considered as prisoners of war has led to the current tendency to equate and identify prisoners of war with lawful combatant status. This is part of a more general tendency to accord greater weight to humanitarian needs than to military requirements. Pressed beyond a certain point this tendency becomes self-defeating, and nowhere more so than in the attempt to secure combatant status for secret and sporadic fighters operating as civilians. The fighter-civilian tends to destroy the vestigial distinctions, and hence the immunities of the non-participant civilian in the customary law of war. Such immunity is the latent premise of the Hague Regulations of 1907 and of the Geneva Conventions of 1949.

[3] Common Article 2 is the gateway for the application of the Geneva Conventions, except the common Article 3; see below, pp. 207 et seq.

Likewise, the Geneva (Prisoners of War) Convention 1949 has, in Article 4A (6), expressly extended prisoner of war status to the members of a *levée en masse*. Such persons had been accorded combatant status by Article 2 of the Hague Regulations. They comprise the 'inhabitants of a territory not under occupation, who, on the approach of the enemy, spontaneously take up arms to resist the invading troops without having had time to organize themselves in accordance with Article 1 . . .'. They are to be regarded as 'belligerents if they carry arms openly and if they respect the laws and customs of war'. This is a wide class but narrowly conditioned. The provision has no application in occupied territory. The circumstances in which it may become operative are narrow, being those of a dire national emergency and urgency, but it may well be relied upon today, having regard to the speed and effectiveness of modern armed attacks, e.g. by troops dropped or landed from aircraft. It will be noticed that in the case of the *levée en masse* two of the four conditions required of irregular combatants have been dropped, namely, the wearing of a distinctive sign and of being commanded by a person responsible for his subordinates. It is generally thought that if the *levée en masse* situation becomes applicable the combat operations would be as near to indiscriminate as makes no difference. The members of the *levée en masse* are entitled to prisoner-of-war status upon capture provided that the two conditions mentioned have been met. Their compliance will, it is thought, have to be determined on an individual basis, using the mechanism of Article 5 (2) for such purpose, there being no group requirement of any kind. Under Article 5 (2), 'should any doubt arise as to whether persons, having committed a belligerent act and having fallen into the hands of the enemy, belong to any of the categories listed in Article 4, such persons shall enjoy the protection of the present Convention until such time as their status has been determined by a competent tribunal'.[1] Once the invaded territory is occupied, a matter controlled by Article 42 of the Hague Regulations, 1907, the *levée en masse* provision has no application. Article 42 provides: 'Territory is considered occupied when actually placed under the authority

---

[1] There is no definition of a 'competent tribunal' contained in the Convention. The United Kingdom has issued a Royal Warrant, a form of prerogative legislation, dated 7 August 1958, the First Schedule to which contains regulations for the determination of prisoner-of-war status. (Appendix XXVII to Part III of the *Manual of Military Law* (1958).)

For a case in which the weakness of Article 5 (2) is exposed see *Public Prosecutor* v. *Oie Hee Koi* [1968] 2 W.L.R. 715 (P.C.). No representative of the Protecting Powers appears to have the right to be present at such 'determinations' and the Detaining Power seems to be the sole arbiter, in good faith, of whether a doubt occurs as to the status of the individual concerned, without which doubt there is no requirement for an 'impartial tribunal'. As the consequences of committing hostile acts without combatant status, and hence prisoner status, expose the offender to the death penalty, on trial and conviction, the findings of the impartial tribunal are important. This provision of the Convention, admirable in its humanitarian purpose, seems to be one in need of revision if that intent is to be implemented by Detaining Powers.

THE QUESTION OF GUERILLA WARFARE   193

of the hostile army. The occupation extends only to the territories where such authority has been established and is in a position to assert itself.' It is clear that difficulties will arise in this context. First, there is the question of occupation in areas of disputed territorial claims, although the better opinion may be that occupation is a factual situation, which makes disputed legal claims to the territory irrelevant, at least for the purposes of the law of war.[1] Second, there is the question of the effect of the lawful combatancy of organized resistance groups within 'occupied territory'. Article 64 of the Geneva (Civilians) Convention, 1949, enables the occupant to subject the population to 'provisions which are essential to enable the Occupying Power to fulfil its obligations under the present Convention to maintain the orderly government of the territory and to ensure the security of the Occupying Power, of the members and property of the Occupying forces or administration, and likewise of the establishments and lines of communication used by them'. Organized resistance movements in occupied territory will make it their business to violate such provisions as a daily routine. It looks as if Article 64 will have to work outside the area of lawful combatancy by members of organized resistance movements, but the matter is far from clear. Alternatively the presence of such movements may render the area in which they operate as such territory which is not occupied.

Those participants in combat activities who fail to meet the requirements of Article 4A (2) and (6) of the 1949 Convention not only stand under no benefit of prisoner-of-war status upon capture, but are exposed to allegations of war criminality for their participation in combat. They enjoy the limited protection afforded by Article 5 of the Geneva (Civilians) Convention, 1949, if their hostile actions took place in occupied territory or in that of the enemy. They must 'be treated humanely, and, in case of trial, shall not be deprived of the rights of fair and regular trial prescribed by the present Convention. They shall also be granted the full rights and privileges of a protected person under the present Convention at the earliest date consistent with the security of the State or Occupying Power, as the case may be.'[2] However, no person may claim the benefit of protection under the Civilians Convention, even the limited protection afforded by Article 5, unless he be a national of a State Party to the Convention.[3]

[1] The position adopted by the Israeli Government since 1967 is that certain territories now under the 'control and administration' of the Israeli armed forces are not 'occupied' for the purposes of the application of the Geneva (Civilians) Convention, 1949, to which both Israel and the Arab Republic of Egypt are parties. The formula used in the common Article 2, 'occupation of the territory of a High Contracting Party' has aided the Israeli contention, whereas that employed in Article 42 of the Hague Regulations, 1907: 'territory is considered occupied when actually placed under the authority of the hostile army', eliminates the relevance of territorial claims to the territory in question for the purpose of the law of war.

[2] Article 5 (3).

[3] Article 4 (2). A key concept of the protection afforded by the Geneva (Civilians) Convention, 1949, is that of the 'protected person', defined in Article 4. Here, as in the case of the protection

If the correct legal position be that certain classes of persons enumerated in Article 4 of the Geneva (Prisoners of War) Convention, 1949, now enjoy lawful combatant status, by reason of the overtaking of Articles 1 and 2 of the Hague Regulations, 1907, in that area, for all States bound by the Convention of 1949, it becomes a matter of some importance to determine the exact circumstances in which the Geneva Conventions of 1949 apply. All provisions, except the common Article 3, have their applicability determined by Article 2, i.e. (i) 'all cases of declared war or any other armed conflict which may arise between two or more of the High Contracting Parties, even if the state of war is not recognized by one of them'; (ii) 'cases of total or partial occupation of the territory of a High Contracting Party even if the said occupation meets with no armed resistance'; (iii) 'where one of the Parties in conflict may not be a party to the Convention'. In this latter situation 'the Powers who are parties thereto shall remain bound by it in their mutual relations', and they remain bound thereby in relation to the Power that is not a party to the Convention 'if the latter accepts and applies the provisions thereof'. Article 2 is thus the gateway into each of the Geneva Conventions of 1949, with the sole exception of the common Article 3, which applies to armed conflicts 'not of an international character occurring in the territory of one of the High Contracting Parties'. Thus Article 4, controlling combatant status for some 129 States at the present time, will not apply in Article 3 type armed conflicts, although there is nothing to exclude the parties to such a conflict from expressly agreeing to apply the whole or any part of the remaining provisions of the Convention to the conflict.

In the event of a conflict's occurring in the territory of a Party to the Convention and where recognition has been given to the insurgent faction, it is thought that the Hague Regulations of 1907 will still be applicable as they still represent the customary law regarding combatancy and prisoner-of-war status. Article 3 would not be excluded but would, in certain respects, be superseded. In any event, Article 3 is not primarily concerned with combat activities but with the humane treatment of those who, for specified reasons, are not, or were not, engaged in the combat. In the unlikely event of two States being engaged in an international armed conflict neither of which is Party to the Geneva Conventions of 1949, or the Geneva (Prisoners of War) Convention, 1929, the Hague Regulations would apply

afforded to prisoners of war under the Geneva (Prisoners of War) Convention of 1949, the nationality of the victim may be decisive. Thus those who take hostile actions against the armed forces of the State of their nationality, whilst serving in the armed forces of the adversary State, will be denied prisoner-of-war and lawful combatant status and are liable to be tried, convicted and executed for violation *inter alia* of the municipal law (e.g. unauthorized carrying of arms) of the State of their nationality. Such was the fate of ten of the twelve appellants in *Public Prosecutor* v. *Oie Hee Koi* (see above, p. 192 n. 1), all of whom were Chinese Malays serving in the armed forces of Indonesia, who were captured in civilian clothing.

to determine combatant and prisoner-of-war status. There is nothing to prevent any Party to any armed conflict of any type agreeing with its adversary to apply the whole or any part of the Geneva Convention, 1949, not applicable, *de jure*. What cannot be excluded by the Parties to an international armed conflict is the applicability of Articles 1, 2 and 3 of the Hague Regulations, as forming part of the customary law. However, such a regime would not, it is thought, bring into play the combatant status of members of organized resistance movements operating in occupied territory or elsewhere. As there are now 129 States bound by the Geneva Conventions of 1949, the main lacuna as to combatant status is in relation to internal armed conflicts, so far as the existing law is concerned. Over and above this situation there is a steady pressure within and without the General Assembly of the United Nations for an extension of combatant status in two directions that augment each other. First, that irregular fighters for stated and selected political purposes should be freed from the four restrictions, or some of them, to be found attached to combatant status in Article 1 of the Hague Regulations, 1907, and now reinforced by Article 4A (2) of the Geneva (Prisoner of War) Convention, 1949. Second, there is the like pressure that there should be no distinction as to lawful status as combatants for those engaged in international and non-international armed conflicts. This is, at the moment, perhaps one of the main areas of confrontation in which the future shape of a crucial part of the law of war will have to be resolved in the near future.[1] In this resolution it will be governments that decide. Neither direction of the proposed expansion is likely to be attractive to governments, and particularly to those of the newly created States who are, in general, more conscious of their fragility.

C. GENERAL PRINCIPLES GOVERNING IRREGULAR COMBATANCY

Upon a strict analysis there are six conditions to be met by irregular fighters not fighting as members of a *levée en masse*, i.e. those not forming part of armed forces or of militias or volunteer corps forming part of such forces of a Party to an international conflict. Such a Party must be either a State or a politically organized society which has the actual elements of statehood, but lacks recognition by its adversary. These six conditions are:

(i) they must belong to an organized group;
(ii) the group must belong to a Party to the conflict;
(iii) the group must be commanded by a person responsible for his subordinates;

---

[1] e.g. General Assembly Resolutions 2444 (XXIII), 2597 (XXIV), 2674 (XXV) and 2676 (XXV).

   (iv) the group must ensure that its members have a fixed distinctive sign recognizable at a distance;

   (v) the group must ensure that its members carry their arms openly; and

   (vi) the group must ensure that its members conduct their operations in accordance with the laws of war.

A scrutiny of these conditions indicates that all six are impliedly present in Article 1 of the Hague Regulations, 1907. They are made explicit in Article 4A (2) of the Geneva (Prisoners of War) Convention, 1949. What has divided jurists and commentators is the question as to which of the conditions are collective and which are individual. There is no firm consensus upon this matter which is in need of some attention, particularly in the light of recent types of irregular fighting by groups of guerilla fighters, operating within and outside the territory of the State upon which they depend, and in varying degrees of association or disassociation with the government of that State.

It is suggested that the language and rationale of the provisions, both of the Hague Regulations and of the Geneva (Prisoners of War) Convention, are consistent with the following legal position. The first three of the conditions specified above are, from the nature of their content, applicable to the group collectively, and not to the individual members, i.e. (i) the group must have an organization capable of ensuring that all six conditions are met; (ii) it must belong to a Party to the conflict, whatever the degree of dependence may be; and (iii) the group must be commanded by a person responsible in a manner that can secure compliance with all the conditions.

The remaining three conditions, namely (iv) distinctive sign-bearing, (v) open weapon carrying and (vi) conduct of operations in accordance with the law of war, are—it is suggested—both collectively *and* individually applicable. This means that the obligation of the group, through the commander, is to order, supervise and provide the material means for meeting all six conditions and that this situation must prevail continuously and not intermittently. Further, it means that the overwhelming majority of the individual members of the group must meet conditions (iv), (v) and (vi), set out above, continuously and not intermittently. The final three conditions are thus collective and individual. The first three are addressed to the group collectively and not to the individual members of it.[1]

This distinction becomes apparent when one considers the legal effects of failure to meet any, or some, of the conditions by all, or some, of the members of the organization, at any time or for some of the time. If the members, generally, meet all the conditions all the time, and an individual

---

[1] For the views expressed here see H. Meyrowicz, 'Le statut des saboteurs dans le droit de la guerre', *The Military Law and Law of War Review*, 5 (1966–I), pp. 133–44. The author acknowledges his indebtedness to Dr. Meyrowicz for this part of the article.

THE QUESTION OF GUERILLA WARFARE   197

fails to observe conditions (iv), (v) or (vi), then he does not lose his combatant status or, upon capture, his prisoner-of-war status. He is liable to be tried, as a prisoner of war, for his act of war crime in respect of his individual failure to wear a distinctive sign, carry his arms openly or conduct himself in operations in accord with the law of war, as the case may be, or for all three types of criminality. However, that being said, he still remains a member of a group with combatant status, whose ordinary acts of combat stand as lawful. He enjoys his right to prisoner-of-war status upon capture, but is exposed to trial for his act of war criminality, as a prisoner of war. Articles 85,[1] and 99 to 108 of the Geneva (Prisoners of War) Convention, which afford due process and judicial safeguards to prisoners tried for acts committed before their capture, as in the case of a prisoner tried for a post-capture offence, will therefore enure to the benefit of the irregular fighter under consideration. In other words, he finds himself in the same position and with the same legal protection as a captured member of the armed forces facing a charge of war criminality.

Where, however, the majority of the members of the group, for any reason whatever, fail to meet the conditions (iv), (v) and (vi), or any of them, at any time, then the members of the group, all of them, fail to obtain combatant status. An individual belonging to a group of that kind will, upon capture, be denied a prisoner or combatant status, whatever his individual behaviour may have been. All the members of such a group are then exposed to the legal consequences of illegal combatancy. Part of the evidence of the group failure to meet conditions (i), (ii) and (iii) will lie in the failure of most of the members to meet conditions (iv), (v) and (vi) on any occasion. Such individuals, will, upon capture, be entitled to the limited protection afforded to civilians as a 'protected' person by Article 5 of the Geneva (Civilians) Convention, 1949,[2] assuming that they were operating in occupied territory or in that of the enemy and were nationals of a State Party to that Convention. If they were operating in neither type of territory, their position is far from clear and their protection is speculative. This is a matter which needs attention. They probably remain protected by the general requirement implicit in the de Martens Preamble

---

[1] Article 85 provides: 'Prisoners of war prosecuted under the law of the Detaining Power for acts committed prior to capture shall retain, even if convicted, the benefits of the present Convention.' This is an important and new provision designed to change the previous law under the Geneva (Prisoners of War) Convention of 1929, as applied in cases such as *In re Yamashitu, Annual Digest*, 1945, Case No. 111, p. 255. This case came before the United States Supreme Court on a *habeas corpus* appeal (1946), 327 U.S. 7, which was dismissed on the ground that the requirements as to the judicial proceedings against prisoners of war for offences then contained in Article 60 of the Geneva Convention of 1929 applied only to post-capture offences and not to acts of war criminality. Article 85 of the Geneva Convention of 1949 seeks to reverse that rule. The Soviet bloc of States have made a reservation to Article 85 which substantially negatives its purpose; see *United Nations Treaty Series*, 75 (1950), p. 460.

[2] See above, p. 193.

to the Hague Convention No. IV of 1907, of humane and civilized treatment,[1] as part of the general principles of law recognized by civilized nations. This would, it is thought, demand fair trial and conviction before execution.

If this analysis be correct under the existing law, the fate of the individual irregular is essentially linked with that of the group in which he operates. If the group's members, as a majority, always meet the legal conditions, the individual will answer only for his own misdoings, and then as a prisoner of war who had the right to participate in the combat. If, however, the individual were punctilious in a group in which the majority did not observe the conditions on any one occasion, he would not acquire combatant status or prisoner-of-war status upon capture, and will answer in law as an individual who participated in combat with no legal right to do so, i.e. answerable in municipal law or occupation law, or the law of war. It is apparent that the State upon which the irregulars depend is going to place them in a serious position unless they have been instructed in the law of war including that part which controls their entitlement to a combatant and prisoner-of-war status. It is arguable that condition (iii), a group condition, i.e. 'commanded by a person responsible for his subordinates' carries just that obligation within it. The giving of this instruction, mandatory in the case of members of the armed forces of a State,[2] is allied to that measure of discipline required in the group by that same condition (iii), namely, 'commanded by a person responsible for his subordinates'.

It is apparent that in the circumstances of modern armed conflict many individuals will fall into the hands of the adversary belligerent whose status is as doubtful as their hostile actions are certain. This is particularly the case in the context of the conditions required for irregular fighters to obtain lawful combatant status, whether they be group conditions or group and individual conditions. Article 5 (2) of the Geneva (Prisoners of War) Convention controls that situation and is an invaluable provision if applied in good faith. The complexity of the conditions attaching to combatant status for irregular fighters is met by the certainty of the obligation in Article 5 (2)[3] to accord the individual the benefits of prisoner-of-war status pending the determination of his status. He is not a prisoner of war in the interim, but he is to be treated as if he were.

Over and above this requirement are those contained in Articles 17 and 43 which must be read in conjunction with Article 4A (2) and Article 5 (2) of

---

[1] '. . . in cases not covered by [the Hague Regulations] the inhabitants and the belligerents remain under the protection and governance of the principles of the law of nations, derived from the usages established among civilized peoples from the laws of humanity, and from the dictates of the public conscience.'

[2] Article 127 of the Geneva (Prisoners of War) Convention, 1949, common to all four Conventions.   [3] See above, p. 192.

the Convention. One of the methods of determining cases of doubtful status under Article 5 (2) for the purposes of Article 4A (2) is made manifest in Article 17 (3). This provides that: 'Each Party to the conflict is required to furnish the persons under its jurisdiction who are liable to become prisoners of war with identity cards showing the owner's surname, first names, rank, army, regimental, personal or serial number, or equivalent information, and date of birth.' This document, in effect, is the title of the captured individual to his combatant, and hence prisoner-of-war, status, in case of doubt. Related to this provision is Article 43 (1): 'Upon the outbreak of hostilities, the Parties to the conflict shall communicate to one another the titles and ranks of all the persons mentioned in Article 4 of the present Convention, in order to ensure equality of treatment between prisoners of war of equivalent rank. Titles and ranks which are subsequently created shall form the subject of similar communications.' A government operating in good faith with irregular forces has had its duties made manifest by these related provisions of the Geneva (Prisoners of War) Convention.

It will be observed that there is no legal duty to communicate the nature of any distinctive sign used by irregular forces, under Article 4A (2). It is also clear that the provisions in Article 17 (3) and Article 43 (1) cannot be applied to members of a *levée en masse*. An identity card issued under the former provision—Article 17 (3)—will be of considerable importance to the individual irregular who falls into the hands of the enemy. It will be cogent evidence of his status and the ensuing rights to pay and to particular treatment, e.g. not to be compelled to work if an officer or person of equivalent rank. The system of the Protecting Power's supervision and the transmission of information through the mechanisms of the National Information Bureaux and the Central Prisoners of War Information Agency are closely related to the proper issuing and holding of identity cards by those who seek to establish their status as prisoners.[1] Here we find the very heart of the contrast between clandestine and sporadic fighters and those irregulars who meet the specific and stringent legal requirements necessary for combatant status under Article 4A (2) of the Geneva (Prisoners of War) Convention, 1949.

D. The Specific Conditions Controlling Lawful Irregular Combatancy

(i) *'Organized' bodies*. Those who operate as irregular fighters may be members of broken military units or detached units no longer operating under superior military command, and every sort of civilian, including

---

[1] See Articles 122–4 of the Geneva (Prisoners of War) Convention.

women and children. Often such irregular groups will be composed of both elements. It is clear that irregular fighters operating on their own, as opposed to those operating on a mission detached from the parent group—but within its control and subject to its orders, will not be able to claim combatant status. Such persons appear to stand in no different legal position from that of the marauders of former times. Upon capture and proof of hostile action they are liable to trial as war criminals, or as offenders against the internal security law of the adversary, if caught in its territory, or under occupation penal law, if caught in occupied territory.[1] Although such an individual may be detained without trial, and held incommunicado, he must have humane treatment and, if tried, a fair and regular trial, as specified in Article 5 of the Geneva (Civilians) Convention, 1949. Individuals dispatched on special missions from groups of irregular fighters are normally on intelligence or sabotage assignments and will tend to operate clandestinely and sporadically. Such activities would probably debar the group from having combatant and hence prisoner-of-war status. For the individual to retain combatant and prisoner-of-war status it would have to be determined that he was an individual offender acting contrary to the orders of the group, and the regular compliance of the large majority of its members with the conditions specified in Article 4A (2) of the Geneva (Prisoners of War) Convention. The motive of the individual fighter is not relevant. If he is acting on his own he will be treated as a marauder, however political his purpose. The sole relevance of motive, political or criminal, might be in deciding the sentence to be imposed.

(ii) '*Belonging to a Party to the conflict*'. Even if there be an organized group with its own group commander, the members will not have combatant status if it lacks the necessary nexus with a Party to the conflict. The exact nature or quality of this nexus is far from certain. It is not thought adequate that the group receives logistic support in food, clothing, stores, weaponry and transport, from such a Party. On the other hand, it seems reasonably certain that the triple-stranded subordination of operational command, discipline and logistic dependence, is not necessary. It was a normal feature of para-military formations operating as combat troops in World War II, e.g. *Waffen* (fighting) -*SS* formations, that they were under operational command and logistic supply from the German Armed Forces, but not under disciplinary control of the ordinary military law. Although the situation varied from time to time, personnel of such *Waffen-SS* were, for prolonged periods, not subject to the military law applicable to the armed forces. Special or task-forces (*Einsatzgruppen*) carrying out 'political' roles in the military areas, namely the liquidation of

---

[1] The penal law of an Occupying Power must be established within the limits of Article 64 of the Geneva (Civilians) Convention, 1949.

THE QUESTION OF GUERILLA WARFARE   201

classified 'undesirables', were under logistic dependence upon the German Armed Forces but not under operational or disciplinary control. Such units presented special legal difficulties, upon capture. Normally, they did not engage in combat action. Their criminality was certain. Their status and their capacity to engage the criminal responsibility of the local military commander was uncertain. Such units had their own discipline. It required them to carry out the very criminal acts with which they were charged. Their pay derived from a Party to the conflict, the State of Germany. Their consistent violation of the law of war was the essence of their own special type of operations.

One suggested solution of the question of dependence is that it be resolved by the general principles of international law governing State responsibility. The most manifest proof of 'belonging to a Party to the conflict' is for that Party to make a declaration of its responsibility for the activities of specified groups of fighters not forming part of its armed forces. In humanitarian terms, a declaration of that kind is of value to such fighters in the event of their capture. The military disadvantages in making such a declaration operate solely in cases of illegal combatancy.

(iii) *'Commanded by a person responsible for his subordinates'*. There is surprisingly little authority or certainty as to the legal significance of that expression. It is thought that it means responsibility to some higher authority whether the person concerned be appointed from above or elected from below. It does probably mean that the commander must have sufficient authority to ensure that the conditions applicable to the members of the group, necessary for lawful combatancy, are observed. Part of the evidence of non-compliance with the condition discussed here will be the non-observance of the remaining conditions on the part of the members of the group. It does not mean that the commander must be a commissioned officer of the armed forces of a Party to the conflict, but the form of authority or acknowledgement of his position as commander by some official agency of the Government will be critical in establishing that the group belongs to a Party to the conflict. The internal disciplinary regime of the group must be such that the conditions required for lawful combatancy may be secured in practice. One manifest way of ensuring that result is to make the observance of the conditions required by Article 4A (2) of the Geneva (Prisoners of War) Convention, 1949, a specific part of the disciplinary regime applicable to the group, with a system of penalties for breach. As in all these requirements of the Geneva Conventions the element of good faith is an integral part of the discharge of the obligations contained in them. Departure from his standard of good faith places the members of the group at risk in the event of their capture. It is not, on the other hand, legally requisite that the system of military law of the Party to the conflict should apply to the members of a group of irregular fighters or be imposed by the commander of that group. On the other hand, there is nothing intrinsic to the system of irregular fighters that would preclude military law's being applied to them.[1]

(iv) *'Having a fixed distinctive sign recognizable at a distance'*. This is a severe condition, in practical and operational terms, and the one not generally observed by resistance groups, particularly in occupied territory. However, the experience of World War II is not strictly in point because at that period all such acts of resistance were, in law punishable by the penal law established by the Occupying Power, often with death. It can be seen that the endeavour made in Article 4A (2) of the Geneva (Prisoners of War) Convention, 1949, to lift up organized resistance movements to lawful combatancy if they meet specified conditions, including identifiability, seeks to preserve the military needs of the occupant and the humanitarian treatment of the partisan. However, it is open to doubt whether this purpose has been achieved. The test normally accepted for identifiability is that the individual must be so marked, and permanently, that he is distinguishable from an ordinary peaceful civilian at a distance at which weapons can be brought to bear by, and upon, such individuals. Modern weaponry, and the speed of movement in military operations, has made this condition difficult to apply, but it is none the less essential. It is sometimes suggested that distinctive headgear is the most 'distinctive sign'. This condition does not deny the irregular fighter the right to camouflage himself, as is done by regular troops without committing an illegal ruse. However, camouflage and disguise as an ordinary civilian going about his normal pacific activities are different. At times, the area of distinction will be small. It is the element of permanency that is the major difficulty. If irregular fighters can assume the distinctive sign, without which they appear as ordinary civilians, at a moment of their choosing, their clandestinity is preserved and with it that element of surprise that has proved so effective in the past. Further, the removal of the distinctive sign immediately after the surprise mission is completed enables a successful disengagement in conditions of comparative safety, i.e. the standard method of 'melting away' into the civilian background, whether urban or rural. It is conceded that the borderline between the legal and the illegal ruse or perfidy is very difficult to draw, but no more so than in sea warfare where

---

[1] Most States have provisions in their military penal law systems for the application of certain parts of it to civilians accompanying the regular forces when engaged with an enemy, e.g. the United Kingdom Army Act, 1955, s. 209 (1). Also, certain volunteer corps, such as members of the Home Guard, are made subject to military law on duty, or when the part of it to which he belongs is mustered. See Army Act, 1955, s. 205 (1) (*b*), and the Home Guard Act, 1951, s. 4 (2) (*a*) and (*b*).

the use of flags of deception flown up to the very last minute before opening fire is permitted.[1]

It would seem that there is a considerable need for revision of the law on this matter in order to reassert the balance between military and humanitarian needs in the context of modern weaponry and techniques of fast-moving land fighting. Further, the circumstances are so infinitely various and change so swiftly that it may be unwise to frame any rules other than of the most general kind, designed to avoid perfidy being used as a cover for treacherous killings and woundings. It is probably true that the inhuman treatment of captured partisans in World War II contributed largely to their operations in the guise of innocent civilians. Certain partisan organizations, notably those in Yugoslavia, wore their own partisan uniform with a distinctive head gear and mark. The matter is far from easy but it is open to doubt whether the idea behind the present condition can be disregarded, namely, that there must be a degree of identifiability of the irregular fighter equal to that of the soldier if the former is to have the same combatant status as the latter. During the Hague Peace Conferences of 1899 and 1907 the view was expressed that the best distinctive sign is the open carrying of arms[2] and ammunition. It is doubtful if this view would prevail today. Also, it has to be remembered that if the irregular fighter is not identifiable by his military opponent ordinary civilians will tend to be the first to suffer. The military advantage of the irregular against his regular adversary must not mask the humanitarian risk to the ordinary civilian. This has been a feature of some of the fighting in Vietnam and has undoubtedly caused much loss of innocent civilian life and destruction of civilian property. If one of the purposes of the law of war is to afford a high measure of protection to the innocent civilian, a difficult conception in itself, then the non-identifiability of the irregular fighter will frustrate that purpose in large measure.

(v) *'Carrying arms openly'*. This condition is essentially related to the condition of identifiability, so much so that there is a certain superficial attraction in the view that 'the real distinctive mark of combatants, that which never changes, is the open carrying of arms'. One difficulty in this view is the time factor. When must such weapons be carried openly— when engaged, as well as when about to engage and afterwards? Do not troops, in flight, throw away their weapons or conceal them? It is, perhaps, matter for comment that the detailed implications of lifting up irregular fighters to the rights of members of armed forces, on certain conditions, had never been fully worked out when the Hague Regulations of 1907 first

[1] See Oppenheim, *International Law*, vol. 2, pp. 509–10, and Tucker, 'The Law of War and Neutrality at Sea', *International Law Studies*, 19 (1955), pp. 138–42.

[2] J. B. Scott, *Hague Peace Conferences* (1907), vol. 3, p. 100: Major-General Amourel (France): 'The real distinctive mark of combatants, that which never changes, is the open carrying of arms.'

put the rule into conventional form. The idea still stands, but the uncertainties attending its application have removed much of its value. The demand for revision here is compelling. As a minimum, it may be required that weapons must be carried by irregular fighters in the manner and on the occasions when military units normally do the same and that they must certainly be carried openly when their concealment would amount to treachery or an illegal ruse. The carrying of hand grenades and small explosives, which are concealed and produced only to be used, is probably a breach of the condition. There are many and diverse circumstances in which no more can be expected than the bona fide and rational application of a general rule framed in the light of the purposes of the law of war and current war practices. In the last resort, there may be some value in adhering to the principle that the effects of warfare, a disruption to the normal ordering of civil society, should be minimized. Those who seek the right to participate in such warfare other than as members of armed forces are under the onus of meeting the conditions that have to be observed by such members. The military disadvantage irregular fighters may thereby undergo has to be balanced against the sufferings of innocent civilians who become the victims of clandestine warfare. This is no less the case where women and children are used as clandestine fighters and weapons and explosives carriers.

(vi) '*Conducting their operations in accordance with the laws and customs of war*'. This condition presents considerable difficulties in law and in practice. If an individual member of the group of irregular fighters, contrary to the group order and practice, violates the law of war, e.g. murders or tortures a prisoner, the offender will remain entitled to his combatant and prisoner-of-war status upon capture, but will be liable to be tried for a war crime, as a prisoner of war. If, however, the group, at any time, fails, in the majority of its members, to observe the laws of war, e.g. in one engagement killed their prisoners, then the individual member, even though he himself did not take part, will not be entitled to combatant or prisoner-of-war status. This means that he is exposed to the charge that he is an illegal combatant. He will be debarred from the benefits of the Geneva (Prisoners of War) Convention, but will stand within the lesser measure of protection under Article 5 of the Geneva (Civilians) Convention, assuming that the fighter is a national of a State Party to that Convention and that his participation in the combat took place in occupied territory or in that of the opposing belligerent.[1] If it took place in neither, then it is thought that he will stand under the general protection of humanity accepted as one of the general principles of law recognized by civilized nations, a formulation of which principle may be seen in the Preamble to the Hague Convention

---

[1] See above, p. 193.

THE QUESTION OF GUERILLA WARFARE   205

No. IV of 1907.[1] However, it must also be accepted that he will stand exposed to a charge of illegal participation in combat which may still be a violation of the law of war. That seems, in the state of the present law, to be the price of operating with a group which fails to achieve combatant status because it failed, as a group, to conduct its operations in accordance with the laws and customs of war. Here, again, the law is not likely to command general satisfaction and there will be pressure for revision.

E. THE IRREGULAR FIGHTER AND THE LAW OF HOSTILITIES

The group of irregular fighters must at all times, in the greater number of its members, by practice and order, meet the requirements of the law governing the conduct of hostilities. So far as the customary law of hostilities is concerned part of it can be found in Section II of the Hague Regulations, 1907.[2] This does not exhaust the customary law and, since 1907, certain Conventions have been established which deal with military operations, e.g. the Geneva Gas Protocol of 1925 and the Hague Convention for the Protection of Cultural Property of 1954. Thus, there can be little doubt that irregular fighters must not kill or wound by treachery 'individuals belonging to the hostile nation or army', an activity prohibited by Article 23 (*b*) of the Hague Regulations, 1907. Neither must they kill or wound those who have surrendered (Article 23 (*c*)), or commit illegal ruses (Articles 23 (*f*) and 24). They may not kill or maltreat the wounded, take reprisal action against prisoners of war, or take hostages for any purpose in occupied territory or in that of the enemy. Such activities are today condemned by the Geneva (Sick and Wounded) Convention, 1949, Article 12, the (Prisoners of War) Convention, Article 13, and the (Civilians) Convention, Article 34, respectively. Conversely, irregular fighters who meet the requirements of lawful combatancy may not be subjected to any of the actions forbidden by the customary law of war governing military operations, except in the limited area of reprisal action ordered by a government within the stringent limitations governing their exercise. Captured irregular fighters who do not have lawful combatant status are not to be the object of reprisal action to the extent that they are 'protected persons' for the purposes of Article 4 of the Geneva (Civilians) Convention, 1949. Resort to reprisals against 'protected persons' is expressly prohibited by Article 34 thereof. However, the matter does not rest there because certain acts of reprisal against captured persons, such as killing or torture, will stand outside, and be condemned by, the general principle of humanity recited in the preamble to the Hague Convention No. IV of 1907, even where such irregular fighters continue with the like

---

[1] See above, pp. 197-8.   [2] Hague Regulations, Articles 22-8.

activity and will not desist. Reprisals against those in captivity or in occupied territory or in that of the adversary may today be considered as prohibited by customary law where not expressly prohibited by a Convention. The general inclusion of that prohibition in Conventions now in force has probably lodged such a prohibition within the existing body of the customary law of war. Further, the general principles of law recognized by civilized nations embrace the principles of humanity. This has received recognition in the preamble above referred to, in judicial decisions,[1] and from the natural law theories that have performed a creative function in the development of international law, and the law of arms of the pre-Grotian era.

The difficult question is the extent to which military units must observe the law governing operations when engaged in fighting irregular fighters who do not enjoy combatant status. In the contemporary law of war the general pattern is that reprisal action is prohibited against the victims of war, i.e. those who do not participate, or if they have participated, are now prisoners or wounded or both, but that reprisals still remain as a mechanism of enforcement of the law governing military operations. Its imperfections as a device for law enforcement are manifest, but the absence of other effective mechanisms at the present time may make elimination of reprisal action premature. It is in the context of fighting between armed forces and irregular fighters that the device of reprisals may yet have a purpose to serve in the implementation of the law and its enforcement. Thus, it is a practical question whether clandestine fighters who operate disguised as civilians, or who give no quarter, or kill their prisoners on capture, or take hostages, expose themselves to reprisal action by their adversaries in the manner of conducting operations. What if the armed forces opposed to such illegally operating fighters take the like action against them on the conditions governing the exercise of reprisal action?[2] Thus troops might operate

---

[1] *The Corfu Channel* case, *I.C.J. Reports*, 1949, p. 22. The emergence of crimes against humanity, in the Charter to the London Agreement of 8 August 1945 and the Judgment of the International Military Tribunal at Nuremberg, unanimously reaffirmed in the General Assembly Resolution 95 (I), (see above, p. 180 n. 3) is persuasive of this inclusion. Also see H. Lauterpacht, *International Law: Collected Papers* (ed. by E. Lauterpacht, 1970), vol. 1, pp. 143, 471.

[2] These conditions are considered to be: (i) no reprisal action unless ordered by a government; (ii) no reprisal actions without previous illegality committed by the adversary; (iii) no reprisal action without previous warning and a calling upon the adversary to desist from its previous illegalities; (iv) no reprisal action if the adversary desists in response to that call or otherwise; (v) no continued reprisal action from the moment the adversary desists from its illegality; (vi) reprisal action to be proportionate in quantity and gravity to the illegality of the adversary and designed to ensure that the adversary desists from the illegality; (vii) reprisal action being designed as a device to ensure compliance with the law of the adversary, automatic reciprocal or retaliatory action is inconsistent with a lawful recourse to reprisal action; (viii) no reprisal action against prisoners, detainees, sick, non-defended, non-participant civilians. A reprisal action is an act that if not taken in circumstances that render it a valid reprisal would otherwise be an illegal act. The taking of lawful action, as a retaliatory or reciprocal measure, is not, on this view, an exercise of reprisal.

disguised as civilians against irregular fighters fighting so disguised, until such time as the latter met the requirements of combatant status. This is reprisal action in combat, an area from which it is not yet expelled in law. Once such illegal fighters are reduced to captivity it can be said that the present law, conventional and customary, debars reprisal action against them. Until that time the prohibition of reprisal action, under the existing law, is not manifest. Reprisal action may be taken against lawful combatants, in appropriate circumstances, by acts in operations that might, in the absence of the lawful occasion for reprisals, be illegal. The law would not seem to preclude the like action against illegal combatants. Governments, as a matter of policy, may be restrained in this matter but until reprisal action is prohibited in every part of the law of war, including the law governing military operations, such action would seem to be available against illegal combatants if the purpose be to ensure that they desist from their illegalities and meet the requirements of lawful combatancy.

F. GUERILLA FIGHTERS IN NON-INTERNATIONAL CONFLICTS

The shift to the term 'guerilla fighter' from 'irregular combatancy' at this juncture is not accidental. In the context of non-international armed conflicts, other than those of full-scale civil wars, the international law of combatancy is not in point. Here one is dealing with minimum legal restrictions, designed to secure humanitarian treatment, for armed rebels, when the customary law of war is not applicable. In all other respects the rebels who resort to arms are within the ambit of the internal law, penal and security, of the State concerned. The impact of international law is thought to be confined to that contained in the common Article 3 of the four Geneva Conventions of 1949,[1] the various operative legal regimes of Human Rights, e.g. the European Convention of Human Rights, 1950, Articles 2 (2) (d) and 15, and possibly the customary law relating to the minimum standards for the proper treatment of aliens. Here we are confronted with the situation that international law has made the minimum impact or inroad upon the sovereignty of States in their claim to quell rebellion. Conversely, rebellion is not, *per se*, a violation of international law. The gravity of internal insurrection in municipal law is not reflected in its position in international law. As the handling of internal rebellion lies, traditionally, within the broad competence of the sovereignty accorded to States by international law, that law has not hitherto included rules for the manner of quelling rebellions. It was only in 1949 that the Geneva Conventions of that year attempted the first modest inroads upon the legal

[1] Article 3 applies 'In the case of an armed conflict not of an international character occurring in the territory of one of the High Contracting Parties . . .'.

competence of States to deal with their own rebels in the manner determined by their internal law. The limitation contained in Article 3[1] has proved extremely difficult to achieve. The provision has been a source of uncertainty and controversy since its establishment. What may not have been foreseen by the framers of the Geneva Conventions was that this humanitarian regime for non-international conflicts would assume an importance almost transcending the remainder of those Conventions applicable to international armed conflicts. Internal conflicts have been a feature of political events during the last quarter of a century. On occasions, these internal conflicts have assumed a mixed quality by reason of the adherence of armed forces or guerillas from third States to one side or the other, and sometimes on both sides, of the internal conflicts. In retrospect it cannot be said that Article 3 has done much to clarify the delineation of the law of war or to achieve its own admittedly humanitarian purposes. It has even obscured some areas of the law formerly thought to have enjoyed some measure of certainty.

Customary law lifts certain classes of internal armed conflicts to the international plane so as to bring them within the law of war, where belligerency has been accorded to the insurgent by the government of the State concerned or by third States. Such recognition is rare today. One of the legal requirements for that recognition is that the insurgent element itself complies with the law of war.[2] It is in the case of guerilla fighters, in particular, the insurgents frequently lacking organized armed forces, that there occurs that failure to observe the law of war that inhibits their recognition as lawful belligerents engaged in a civil war. There is a certain logic in this situation in that their lack of resource, in territory, organization and control, which debars the insurgents from employing lawful combatants, is, in the final analysis, the very ground why they are deemed not to be belligerents for the purposes of a civil war. Article 3 of the Geneva Conventions of 1949 will apply when there is an armed conflict not of an

---

[1] 'Each Party to the conflict shall be bound to apply as a minimum . . . : (1) Persons taking no part in the hostilities, including members of armed forces who have laid down their arms and those (*et les personnes*—French text) placed *hors de combat* by sickness, wounds, detention, or any other cause, shall in all circumstances be treated humanely. . . .

To this end, the following acts are and shall remain prohibited at any time and in any place whatsoever with respect to the above mentioned persons:

(*a*) violence to life and person, in particular murder of all kinds, mutilation, cruel treatment and torture;

(*b*) taking of hostages;

(*c*) outrages upon personal dignity, in particular humiliating and degrading treatment;

(*d*) the passing of sentences and the carrying out of executions without previous judgment pronounced by a regularly constituted court, affording all the judicial guarantees which are recognized as indispensable by civilized peoples.

(2) The wounded and sick shall be collected and cared for . . .'.

[2] See Oppenheim, *International Law*, vol. 2, pp. 209–10.

international character occurring in the territory of a party to the Convention and, although this is disputable, both Parties to the conflict, or all Parties if more than two, have the material facilities to carry out the obligations imposed on Parties to such a conflict by that Article.[1] Here lies an area of contemporary controversy both acute and relevant to a number of internal armed struggles that have occurred within States since 1949. Throughout that period no clear view of the proper ambit of the Article's application has emerged. In the view of the International Committee of the Red Cross the Common Article 3 was designed to be a 'microcosm' of the remainder of each Convention and to contain the basic humanitarian prohibitions universally accepted.[2] It would follow from this view that the ambit of Article 3 is wide, excluding only the activities of common criminals resorting to armed violence, and minor tensions and disorders of a social or political nature. If, however, the individual prohibitions are examined, compliance with some of them, e.g. Article 3 (1) (*d*)[3] would demand an administration and organization on the part of both Parties to the conflict of discernible proportions. The obligations contained in Article 3 are to be applied 'as a minimum' and the idea of unilateral, as opposed to reciprocal compliance, seems to pervade the provision. An intermediate view might be that the Parties to an internal conflict must meet all those humanitarian obligations that are not negatived solely by their lack of administrative facilities, e.g. if they lack a judicial apparatus, then trials and punishments have no rightful place. But the other prohibitions, such as those of murder, cruel treatment and the taking of hostages, can always be met. It is also a possible position to adopt that an 'armed conflict', even if 'not of an international character and occurring in the territory of a High Contracting Party', requires some element of military organization and political control on both sides. This view would eliminate exchanges of armed violence with 'tip and run' gunmen not engaged for the purpose of gaining political control in the State, but solely to cause maximum disorder or an anarchical situation.

The Geneva Conventions are framed upon the premise that it is possible to classify all armed conflicts into international and non-international categories. This is open to doubt as the extensive conflict in North and South Vietnam has shown. It is not impossible that certain armed conflicts have an international quality for some of the purposes of the law of war and a non-international character for other parts of that law. This is unfortunate in that it creates complexities and uncertainties. The matter is not eased by the consideration that there is genuine uncertainty as to the minimum level of armed conflict at which Article 3 will apply. The

[1] See above, p. 208 n. 1.   [2] *Commentary*, vol. 4 (ed. by Prictet, 1958), p. 34.
[3] See above, p. 208 n. 1.

difficulty may be reduced in those States which have accepted an international regime of Human Rights, e.g. those which are Parties to the European Convention on Human Rights, 1950. Thereunder, there may be limited derogations from the obligations undertaken in the Convention 'in time of war or other public emergency threatening the life of the nation'.[1] However, the range of application of that Convention is limited and regional. The analogous provisions in the United Nations International Covenant on Civil and Political Rights of 1966 are not yet operative.[2]

Guerilla fighters have been a prominent feature of contemporary non-international armed conflicts. Assuming that there is an armed conflict for the purposes of Article 3 of the Geneva (Prisoners of War) Convention, 1949, in progress, the question will arise whether such guerillas are entitled to the benefit of the prohibitions which it contains. It is clear that the question of prisoner-of-war status, under Article 4, applicable in international armed conflicts, does not arise. The question of lawful combatant status in an internal conflict is, it is thought, irrelevant until such time as there is an ascertainable civil war in which the insurgent element has gained belligerent recognition. Article 3 expressly provides that: 'the application of the preceding provisions shall not affect the legal status of the Parties to the conflict'. The Record of the Diplomatic Conference at Geneva in 1949 shows that without that clause it would probably not have been possible to secure the acceptance of Article 3.[3] This Article was a pioneer provision in a multilateral convention restricting States in their manner of quelling an internal rebellion, and it was accepted with difficulty and considerable caution. The rebels remain, as a matter of law, rebels until such time as they are either successful or granted an amnesty or some other measure of internal law eradicates their rebel status. This position is not conducive to rebels acting in conformity with the terms of Article 3. Under one interpretation Article 3, in spite of its restricted scope, confers the same protection upon insurgent guerilla fighters that it purports to do for the benefit

---

[1] Article 15 (1): 'In time of war or other public emergency threatening the life of the nation any High Contracting Party may take measures derogating from its obligations under this Convention to the extent strictly required by the exigencies of the situation, provided that such measures are not inconsistent with its obligations under international law.' See the case of *Lawless* v. *Government of the Republic of Ireland, I.L.R.* (1961), vol. 31, p. 290, and *Yearbook of the European Convention on Human Rights* (1961), p. 439. It is also necessary to consider Article 2 (2) (c) of that Convention: 'Deprivation of life shall not be regarded as inflicted in contravention of this Article when it results from the use of force which is no more than absolutely necessary . . . (c) in action lawfully taken for the purpose of quelling a riot or insurrection.'

Thus Article 3 of the Geneva Conventions, where properly applicable, will determine the limits of derogation under Article 15 (1) of the European Convention on Human Rights. Deprivation of life under Article 2 (2) (c) of that Convention is not derogation for the purposes of Article 15.

[2] Article 4.

[3] *Commentary*, vol. 3 (ed. by Prictet, 1960), p. 43. And see generally *Final Record of the Diplomatic Conference of Geneva of 1949*, vol. 2-B, pp. 40–8, 75–9, 82–4, 90, 93–5, 97–102.

THE QUESTION OF GUERILLA WARFARE   211

of armed forces, fighting openly as such, against the armed forces of the Government. This view would not import the concept of lawful combatancy, and by contradistinction unlawful combatancy, into the arena of Article 3. The language of Article 3 does not seem to support such a distinction. Another view is that the words used in Article 3 are not apt to embrace irregular guerillas reduced to captivity in that they are not 'Persons taking no active part in the hostilities'. Neither are they 'members of armed forces who have laid down their arms' within the meaning of paragraph 1 of Article 3. This view is consistent with the more limited definitions of Article 3 internal conflicts as confined to those which envisage organized armed forces on both sides. The matter is not clear. There is also a difference in the French and the English texts which does little to clarify the situation.[1] If this latter argument be sound, captured guerilla fighters are outside the humanitarian protection of Article 3, whatever other protection they may attract. It is difficult to derive any such protection from international law, in the absence of human rights provisions being applicable.[2] Perhaps it may be advanced that the intention of making Article 3 a 'microcosm' of the whole of the remainder of each of the four Geneva Conventions would have lifted guerilla fighters into that protection upon capture, and that if the text be imprecise or ambiguous, they are not excluded from it. The intention to make Article 3 a general, basic, minimum, humanitarian provision, within the limits of its proper ambit, seems reasonably clear from the Record of the Conference.[3] What is in debate is whether the words actually used, with the supposed dichotomy between 'persons taking no part in the hostilities' and 'members of armed forces', are sufficient to expel guerilla fighters from the protection of Article 3. This would seem open to doubt because that dichotomy may not be firm or exhaustive. In that case the exclusion of guerillas is ambiguous and the intention may be controlling, i.e. to include them. It must be admitted that the matter is not clear and does expose one of the defects of Article 3. It is perhaps a legitimate criticism of this pioneer humanitarian provision that it has raised substantial uncertainties in areas where uncertainty can be least afforded.[4]

If guerillas are included within Article 3 then they are entitled to humane treatment, proper treatment if wounded, and proper judicial safeguards, if they are brought to trial, before regularly constituted courts. These obligations are not, it is submitted, reciprocal, in accordance with the

[1] See above, p. 208 n. 1.
[2] e.g. Articles 2 (2) (c) and Article 15 of the European Convention on Human Rights, 1950.
[3] *Final Record of the Diplomatic Conference of Geneva of 1949*, pp. 82, 84, and 90.
[4] No less than twenty-eight meetings of the relevant committee were required at the Diplomatic Conference at Geneva in 1949 to establish the present text of Article 3. See *Commentary*, vol. 3 (ed. by Prictet, 1960), p. 28.

system of the Geneva Conventions of which they are a microcosm whereby reprisal or retaliatory action against those protected is expressly prohibited.[1] It is this uncertainty as to the status of the guerilla in non-international conflicts that has contributed to the current agitation expressed in Resolutions of the General Assembly of the United Nations and of other bodies for the granting of prisoner-of-war status to such guerillas upon capture, particularly if they are fighting for certain political purposes, e.g. as 'freedom fighters', 'people's patriots', 'fighters against colonial and racial oppression', and the like.[2]

The extent to which the presence of armed forces or 'volunteer' forces from outside the territory concerned who participate in an existing armed conflict in that territory, render the conflict 'international' for the purpose of the application of the full Geneva Conventions of 1949, is also controversial. One view is that such participation on either side of an internal armed conflict automatically renders it international for the purposes of the application of the law of war in general and the Geneva Conventions of 1949 in particular. This is probably not the legal position at the present time.[3]

Article 4 of the Geneva (Prisoners of War) Convention is not applicable in an Article 3 type of conflict unless the Parties to that conflict agree expressly to make it applicable or one Party decides to treat captives as if it were applicable, *ex concessione*, as was done by the United States Military Command in South Vietnam.[4] Even if Article 4 were applicable, the guerilla fighter normally does not meet its requirements. The attempt to exempt the guerilla fighter from Article 4 conditions in internal conflicts, if he has one of a number of selected political purposes, in order that he may have lawful combatant and prisoner-of-war status in that conflict is an attempt to disrupt any form of balance between military and humanitarian needs and is at variance with the law now operative.[5] The attempt to meet this

---

[1] Article 46 of the (Sick or Wounded) Convention; Article 47 of the (Sick, Wounded or Shipwrecked) Convention; Article 13 of the (Prisoners of War) Convention; and Article 33 of the Geneva (Civilians) Convention.

[2] For example, General Assembly Resolutions 2597 (XXIV) and 2674 (XXV).

[3] For an account of a recent debate on this topic see the *Report on the Work of the Conference of Government Experts on the Reaffirmation and Development of International Humanitarian Law Applicable in Armed Conflicts*, by the International Committee of the Red Cross (Geneva, August 1971), paras. 290–311. The debate was inconclusive.

[4] M.A.C.V. Directive No. 190–3 dated 24 May 1966, para. 3.

[5] Even a member of the armed forces of a belligerent who operates as a concealed fighter, e.g. as a civilian, engaged on a solitary mission, is not entitled to the prisoner-of-war status under Article 4. See the case of *Mohamed Ali and Another* v. *Public Prosecutor*, [1968] 3 All. E.R. 488 (P.C.) in which members of the armed forces of Indonesia, while in civilian clothing, placed a bomb in an office building in Singapore which, upon explosion, killed three civilians. They were tried, convicted of murder and sentenced to death by an ordinary court of penal jurisdiction in Malaysia. On appeal against conviction from the Federal Court of Malaysia to the Judicial Committee of the Privy Council, the Board dismissed the appeal. In the course of its advice the Board held that the appellants had 'forfeited their rights under the Geneva (Prisoners of War)

THE QUESTION OF GUERILLA WARFARE 213

situation by treating General Assembly Resolutions as the expression of the law of the world community, even if in plain discord with existing customary and conventional law, is not persuasive. Perhaps it may be suggested that the balance of the law might be better served by a revision of the existing law which ensures in clear terms humane treatment of guerillas upon capture in a non-international armed conflict.

G. Implementation and Enforcement Measures in Guerilla Warfare

In international armed conflicts States Parties to the Geneva Conventions of 1949 are required to bring before their own courts those who have committed 'grave breaches' of those Conventions,[1] irrespective of their nationality. By customary international law belligerents have the right to try enemy personnel who fall into their hands and who have committed violations of the laws of war. Although 'grave breaches' are widely defined in the Geneva Conventions[2] they do not exhaust the categories of war crimes or deal with crimes against peace or all the forms of crimes against humanity. However, a number of circumstances have to be present before the trials of war criminals become possible. In the period since 1945 there has been little propensity on the part of belligerents to institute such trials. The reasons are diverse, but normally decisive. States prefer to try their own nationals who have committed a 'grave breach' of the Geneva Conventions, or a war crime in the strict sense, before their municipal courts, criminal or military, as the case may be, for the common crime that covers the act of war criminality, e.g. murder or grievous bodily harm.

The central part of the system established for the implementation of the Geneva Conventions of 1949 is the classical device of the Protecting Power. Such a system has not proved effective in the period since World War II. A study of those Conventions leads to the conclusion that without the regular and effective functioning of the system of Protecting Powers a large part of the humanitarian obligations contained in them cannot be supervised. In any particular international armed conflict a triple consensus is required for the Protecting Power to function, namely, the approach by the Power of Origin to the Protecting Power, the positive response of that latter Power to agree to act, and the agreement of the adversary or Detaining

Convention by engaging in sabotage in civilian clothes'. This made it unnecessary for the Board to consider whether they had lost these rights by violating the law of war 'by their attack on a non-military building in which there were civilians'.

For a critical note upon this case and the associated case, *Public Prosecutor* v. *Oie Hee Koi* (see above, p. 192 n. 1), see Baxter, 'The Privy Council on the Qualification of Belligerents', *American Journal of International Law*, 63 (1969), pp. 290–6.

[1] Articles 49, 50, 129 and 146 of the four Geneva Conventions, respectively.
[2] Articles 50, 51, 130 and 147, respectively.

214   THE STATUS OF COMBATANTS AND

Power that the Protecting Power shall so function. No permanent or *ad hoc* international body has yet been established to act as a Protecting Power in spite of proposals to that end made at the Geneva Diplomatic Conference in 1949.[1] It may be said that the failure of the Protecting Power system is, at the present time, the main cause of the failure of the Geneva Conventions, and of the law of war in general, to operate. The activities of guerilla fighters not entitled to combatant status are, from the clandestine nature of their activities, difficult to supervise. If such fighters take prisoners they hold them in secret places and cannot afford to allow access by any supervisory agency. The mechanism of the Protecting Power is thus frustrated in an area where it is particularly necessary.

The two main factors which tend to dissuade irregular fighters from meeting the conditions required of them by Article 4A (2) of the Geneva (Prisoners of War) Convention are the stringency of those conditions and the likelihood of death, or defeat or their capture, if they meet those conditions. As has often been pointed out, an 'open' guerilla is a dead guerilla. The main military advantages for the guerilla lie in failing to meet these conditions, unless the guerillas are numerous, well-trained, armed and supplied. Frequently they are not. They prefer their chances of success by sporadic and clandestine operations giving them the opportunity for escape and identifying themselves with the local population. They are aware that they lack both combatant and prisoner status. They normally prefer to disregard lawful combatancy and to rely upon a successful escape which their experience enables them to make.

Upon capture, the illicit fighter is, by virtue of Article 5 of the Geneva (Civilians) Convention, 1949, shut off from the surveillance of any Protecting Power in that he can be held without trial, excluded from the privileges of the Convention, although he must be treated with humanity. He may be denied rights of communication, on suspicion of activity hostile to the security of an Occupying Power, where absolute military security so requires.[2] This type of detention makes it difficult for a Protecting Power to supervise the requirement of human treatment, assuming that there is such a Power functioning. Experience indicates that the worst types of atrocities occur in places where security suspects are held shut off from all communication. The determination of interrogators to obtain information from such suspects, and the fact that the place of detention is not under the supervision of any outside impartial agency, are normal concomitants of maltreatment and tortures committed on a scale unknown in combat conditions. It is this knowledge that has in the past produced

[1] See Resolution 1 of the Geneva Diplomatic Conference, 1949; *United Nations Treaty Series*, vol. 75, p. 22. For the Declaration by the U.S.S.R. negativing that Resolution, see ibid., pp. 17–18.

[2] Article 5 (2).

THE QUESTION OF GUERILLA WARFARE   215

illegal, rather than lawful, combatancy. Thus the dilemma in any revision of this part of the law of war is real. Is it better to make stricter the conditions required for lawful combatancy or to lower them in the hope that they will be met? A suggested solution is that the conditions of lawful combatancy remain strict but that the conditions for acquiring prisoner-of-war status upon capture be lowered.[1] In the main, however, it may be said that the desire of guerillas to attain the surprise and secrecy of attack outweighs the apprehension of capture, particularly in that many secret fighters are animated with a dedicated political purpose.

If the implementation of the law governing international armed conflicts be weak, the position is much feebler in the case of internal conflicts. Here the Protecting Power has no *locus standi* at all for the system has no place in this context. Any rebel, whether he offers armed violence openly and in all respects as if he were a member of armed forces, or clandestinely and sporadically, is still subject to trial, conviction and execution as a rebel, if he falls into the hands of the Government agencies. Only where the internal conflict attains the dimensions of a civil war between the Parties engaged can the full scale of the customary law of war come into play. By agreement the conventional law can be brought to bear and a Protecting Power system put into operation, but such agreements are not normal. In Article 3 conflicts 'an impartial humanitarian body such as the international Committee of the Red Cross may offer its services to the Parties to the conflict'. Such an offer need not be accepted, nor need it be made. If accepted by one Party, it may be rejected by the other. If the Protecting Power system does not operate regularly in international conflicts one cannot be surprised that it is not mandatory in internal conflicts. However, Article 3 enables the Parties to the conflict to agree to bring into force all or part of the other provisions of each Convention.[2] This is hortatory only. Such an agreement could be made without the authority of the Conventions.

The failure of the Protecting Power mechanism has inclined some writers[3] to advocate a system of collective supervision of the implementation of the Geneva Conventions and even collective enforcement, based on the community of interest of the 129 States Parties to these instruments, the intention to achieve a universal humanitarian rule of law in time of armed conflict and the terms of the common Article 1: 'The High Contracting Parties undertake to respect and to ensure respect for the present Convention in all circumstances.' This argument has been extended to Article 3

---

[1] The difficulty in this suggestion is that it entails according prisoner-of-war status to fighters whose very act of fighting is considered unlawful.

[2] Article 3: 'The Parties to the conflict should further endeavour to bring into force, by means of special agreements, all or part of the other provisions of the present Convention.'

[3] e.g. de la Pradelle, *Annales de droit international médical*, 18 (1968), pp. 24–7, and *Commentary*, vol. 3 (ed. by Prictet, 1960), p. 18.

implementation. The common articles imposing a duty to bring persons accused of committing 'grave breaches' to trial before the ordinary courts, regardless of the nationality of the accused,[1] is also considered to import the idea of collective enforcement. There may be some difficulty in advancing this argument in respect of breaches of the humanitarian obligations in Article 3 which are not 'grave breaches'. However, there may be some substance in the argument that all Parties to these Conventions have a legal interest in the observance of them by other States in the territory of which an internal conflict is in progress. As a matter of law it would not be easy to deny the jurisdiction of a court in a third State to hear and determine a case of breach of Article 3 by a national of a State where an internal conflict occurred in which that national was a participant. That is not the same situation as a mandatory universal jurisdiction such as may exist in the case of 'grave breaches', which can be committed only in the course of an international armed conflict. Political realities will make such a method of enforcement of Article 3 spasmodic and haphazard. In any event, enforcement arises after the violation. What is wanted in the context of Article 3 is that supervision of its implementation which is designed to prevent such violation, and particularly so in the case of guerilla fighting. The assassinations of which guerilla fighters are frequently guilty lead almost inevitably to maltreatment upon their capture. The undoubted and continued status of rebel which every participant in an armed conflict against the Government forces retains makes questions of lawful and unlawful combatancy irrelevant. When there is an equal balance of military power there may be some restraint on the part of both sides to such an internal conflict. The guerilla fighters, on the other hand, see that their method of conducting hostile action is the one most calculated to attain that balance in the quickest possible time. External supervision is not sought, as a rule, by the Government handling an armed rebellion. Where the exception occurs, e.g. where access is granted to the International Committee of the Red Cross, governments will often make clear that that access is granted without any admission that an Article 3 conflict is in progress. Strictly, this proviso is not necessary, but governments are entitled to make their position clear before other States, particularly if the argument in favour of the collective enforceability of Article 3 has any validity.

In practice, the device of amnesty at the close of a rebellion which has not succeeded is a crude and retrospective method of enforcement of Article 3. Thus, rebels who have grossly violated Article 3 may well be excluded, wholly or partially, from the terms of any amnesty granted. It then remains with the Government, as a matter of good faith, whether it

---

[1] See above, p. 213 n. 1.

THE QUESTION OF GUERILLA WARFARE   217

brings its own major offenders to trial and punishment. Other devices, if not those of publicity and debate in the organs of the United Nations, or claims made within any applicable Human Rights regimes, will demand changes in the existing law. Such changes are necessary but they can be made only with the consent of Governments, which are, by definition, the main casualties of a rebellion, successful or otherwise.[1]

H. Conclusions

1. The existing law relating to combatancy is strict. Those who do not meet its requirements render their participation in armed conflict an unlawful activity outside the protection of the law of war and condemned alike by that law, by the municipal law of the State concerned or the penal law of the Occupying Power, as the case may be.

2. Such unlawful participants are not entitled to prisoner-of-war status, as controlled by Article 4A (2) of the Geneva (Prisoners of War) Convention, 1949, unless it is conceded to them by the Detaining Power, *ex gratia.*

3. Such unlawful participants, whether they engage in sabotage or other hostile acts against enemy individuals may, upon capture, have a limited protection under Article 5 of the Geneva (Civilians) Convention, 1949, if their acts took place in enemy territory or in occupied territory.

4. The conditions for lawful combatancy required of individuals not in the armed forces of a State and operating as such are designed to bring them as close as possible to members of such armed forces in order that warfare may be restricted, illegal activities avoided and the indiscriminate killing of non-participating civilians minimized.

5. The existing law has reached a crude balance between the need to limit warfare to military or quasi-military personnel, to identify the enemy in order to spare the innocent civilian and to confer a measure of humanitarian treatment on quasi-military personnel, commensurate with that afforded to members of armed forces, if certain strict conditions are met.

6. Individual hostile activity is prohibited. Only organized group activity in arms can be considered as lawful.

7. The existing law reflects the customary law prevailing at the end of the nineteenth century, adjusted in the light of twentieth-century

[1] The obligation to include the study of the Geneva Conventions of 1949 in the 'programmes of military and, if possible, civil instruction, so that the principles thereof may become known to the entire population' (Articles 47, 48, 127 and 144 respectively) is not strictly applicable in cases of Article 3 conflicts for the reason that only Article 3 applies to non-international armed conflicts. However, there may be some value in including Article 3 as a part of the study rendered mandatory by the Articles previously cited. The rebel element in any State will comprise members of its armed forces or of its civil population or both. The 'educational' mechanism of implementation of the Geneva Conventions, and particularly of the common Article 3, has not yet been fully exploited by the majority of States. It might well be prudent to include a mandatory 'instruction' provision in any extended version of Article 3 that may be in contemplation.

experience, particularly that of partisan activities in World War II. It is open to doubt whether this law is adequate in the light of post-1949 developments in guerilla fighting. Some revision of the law may be necessary to re-adjust the balance between military and humanitarian needs.

8. In non-international armed conflicts there may be some doubt whether the guerilla fighter, operating with the rebel elements, is within the protection of the common Article 3 of the Geneva Conventions of 1949. On balance, there may be some merit in the view that he is so protected. There can be less doubt that he ought to be so protected. His rebel status remains unaffected. He is no more entitled to prisoner-of-war status than members of armed rebel forces, whatever may be granted him by way of concession or amnesty. Rebel status and lawful participation in armed rebellion, even if the former derive from municipal law and the latter from international law, are mutually repugnant.

9. Reprisal action against captured guerilla fighters in international armed conflicts is prohibited, but not equally clearly in the case of internal armed conflicts.

10. Article 3 represented the maximum restraint that States were prepared to accept in 1949, in international law, in the manner of quelling of armed rebellion. Since that date there has been the new approach in the regimes of Human Rights, regional and universal. Human Rights do not dissolve in time of war or public emergency affecting the life of the nation, but are subject to a controlled and limited derogation from specific Human Rights to be justified by the extent of that emergency.

11. The precise relation between the law of war and the regimes of Human Rights has not yet been elaborated.

12. States are not willing to extend the ambit of Article 3's application, but may be willing to amplify the humanitarian content of its provision in major internal conflicts approximating to the dimensions of a civil war as understood by the customary law of war.

[6]

Special Forces' Wear of Non-Standard Uniforms*
W. Hays Parks**

In February 2002, newspapers in the United States and United Kingdom published complaints by some nongovernmental organizations ("NGOs") about US and other Coalition special operations forces operating in Afghanistan in "civilian clothing."[1] The reports sparked debate within the NGO community and among military judge advocates about the legality of such actions.[2] At the US Special Operations Command ("USSOCOM") annual Legal Conference, May 13–17, 2002, the judge advocate debate became intense. While some attendees raised questions of "illegality" and the right or obligation of special operations forces to refuse an "illegal order" to wear "civilian clothing," others urged caution.[3] The discussion was unclassified, and many in the room were not

---

* Copyright © 2003 W. Hays Parks.

** Law of War Chair, Office of General Counsel, Department of Defense; Special Assistant for Law of War Matters to The Judge Advocate General of the Army, 1979–2003; Stockton Chair of International Law, Naval War College, 1984–1985; Colonel, US Marine Corps Reserve (Retired); Adjunct Professor of International Law, Washington College of Law, American University, Washington, DC. The views expressed herein are the personal views of the author and do not necessarily reflect an official position of the Department of Defense or any other agency of the United States government. The author is indebted to Professor Jack L. Goldsmith for his advice and assistance during the research and writing of this article.

1 See, for example, Michelle Kelly and Morten Rostrup, *Identify Yourselves: Coalition Soldiers in Afghanistan Are Endangering Aid Workers*, Guardian (London) 19 (Feb 1, 2002).

2 The judge advocate debate is exemplified by Maj. William H. Ferrell, III, USMC, *No Shirt, No Shoes, No Status: Uniforms, Distinction, and Special Operations in International Armed Conflict* (unpublished paper, 50th Judge Advocate Officer Graduate Course, The Judge Advocate General's School, US Army 2002) (on file with author); Lt. Col. H. Allen Irish, USAR, *Are Soldiers in Civilian Clothes Protected under Geneva-Hague?* (unpublished paper, 2002) (on file with author); and Maj. Robert J. Drone, USAF, *Nontraditional Uniforms Do Accord Prisoner of War Status for Special Operations Forces* (unpublished LLM thesis, George Washington University, 2003) (on file with author).

3 In the debate that ensued over the next year, it was my observation that those most strident in their criticism were most distant from Special Forces ground operations or were judge advocates not serving with or familiar with the missions of Special Forces units.

privy to information regarding Operation ENDURING FREEDOM,[4] Special Forces,[5] its special mission units,[6] or the missions assigned them.

---

4   ENDURING FREEDOM was the US designation for military operations against al Qaeda and Taliban forces in Afghanistan that commenced following the al Qaeda terrorist attack on the World Trade Center and the Pentagon on September 11, 2001. See, for example, Robin Moore, *The Hunt for Bin Laden: Task Force Dagger* (Random House 2003).

5   In official US terms, *Special Operations Forces* are "[t]hose Active and Reserve Component forces of the Military Services designated by the Secretary of Defense and specifically organized, trained, and equipped to conduct and support special operations." Department of Defense, Joint Publication 1-02, *Department of Defense Dictionary of Military and Associated Terms* 493 (April 12, 2001, as amended through May 7, 2002), available online at <http://www.dtic.mil/doctrine/jel/doddict> (visited Oct 6, 2003). Within the US military, this includes US Army Special Forces, Psychological Warfare units, and Civil Affairs units; Naval Special Warfare forces; and Air Force Special Operations forces. *Special Operations* are defined as:

> Operations conducted by specially organized, trained, and equipped military and paramilitary forces to achieve military, political, economic, or informational objectives by unconventional means in hostile, denied, or politically sensitive areas. These operations are conducted across the full range of military operations, independently or in coordination with operations of conventional, non-special operations forces. Political-military considerations frequently shape special operations, requiring clandestine, covert, or low visibility techniques and oversight at the national level. Special operations differ from conventional operations in degree of physical and political risk, operational techniques, mode of employment, independence from friendly support, and dependence on detailed operational intelligence and indigenous assets.

Id at 492–93.

    In the US military, special forces (in the more generic sense of the term) include US Army Special Forces, US Naval Special Warfare units (in particular, SEALs (Sea, Air, Land)) and Air Force Special Tactics units. *Special forces* are "US Army forces organized, trained, and equipped specifically to conduct special operations. Special forces have five primary missions: unconventional warfare, foreign internal defense, direct action, special reconnaissance, and counter-terrorism. Counter-terrorism is a special mission for specially organized, trained and equipped special forces designated in theater contingency plans." Id at 491. *Naval special warfare forces* are "[t]hose Active and Reserve Component Navy forces designated by the Secretary of Defense that are specifically organized, trained and equipped to conduct and support special operations," while *naval special warfare* is defined as "[a] designated naval warfare specialty that conducts operations in the coastal, riverine, and maritime environments. Naval special warfare emphasizes small, flexible, mobile units operating under, on, and from the sea. These operations are characterized by stealth, speed, and precise, violent application of force." Id at 361. Naval Special Warfare includes SEALs, Swimmer Delivery Vehicle Teams, and Special Boat Teams. A *special tactics team* is a:

> US Air Force special operations task-organized element that may include combat control, pararescue, and combat weather personnel who are organized, trained, and equipped to establish and control the air-ground interface at an airhead in the objective area. Functions include assault zone reconnaissance and surveillance, establishment, and terminal control; combat search and rescue; combat casualty care and evacuation staging; and tactical weather observations and forecasting.

Id at 495.

The topic provides lessons and questions for consideration of future issues by judge advocates. The questions are:

> For the history of US Army Special Forces, see Col. Aaron Bank (Ret.), *From OSS to Green Berets: The Birth of Special Forces* (Presidio 1986) (on file with author), and Alfred H. Paddock, Jr., *U.S. Army Special Warfare: Its Origins* (Kansas rev ed 2002) (on file with author). For the SEALs and their Underwater Demolition Team predecessors, see Cdr. Francis Douglas Fane, USNR (Ret.) and Don Moore, *The Naked Warriors: The Story of the U.S. Navy's Frogmen* (Appleton-Century-Crofts 1956) (reprinted by Naval Institute Press 1995); Orr Kelly, *Brave Men, Dark Waters: The Untold Story of the Navy SEALs* (Presidio 1992); T.L. Bosiljevac, *SEALs: UDT/SEAL Operations in Vietnam* (Paladin 1990); and James Douglas O'Dell, *The Water Is Never Cold* (Brassey's 2000). For Air Force Special Tactics Units, see Col. John T. Carney, Jr. and Benjamin F. Schemmer, *No Room for Error: The Covert Operations of America's Special Tactics Units from Iran to Afghanistan* (Ballantine 2002). Coalition special forces that served in Afghanistan have a lineage and missions similar to those of US special forces. See, for example, Philip Warner, *The Special Air Service* (William Kimber 1971); John Strawson, *A History of the S.A.S. Regiment* (Secker & Warburg 1984); Tony Geraghty, *Who Dares Wins: The Story of the SAS, 1950–1992* (Little, Brown, 3d rev ed 1992); David Horner, *SAS: Phantoms of the Jungle: A History of the Australian Special Air Service* (Allen & Unwin 1989); W.D. Baker, *"Dare to Win": The Story of the New Zealand Special Air Service* (Spa 1987), and other references contained in the State Practice sections of this article (Section IV.B. and Appendix). In this article, *special forces* ("SF") includes US Army Special Forces, Naval Special Warfare SEALs, Air Force Special Tactics Units, and coalition special forces, while *special operations forces* ("SOF" or "Special Operations") includes Special Forces, UA Army Psychological Operations units, and Civil Affairs units.
>
>   While the Marine Corps until recently (and at the time of the NGO complaint) was not a part of the special operations community, Marine Corps personnel from 2nd Intelligence Battalion, II Marine Expeditionary Force, assigned to 4th Marine Expeditionary Brigade were operating in Afghanistan in non-standard uniform (indigenous attire with *pakol* and Northern Alliance scarf), as described on pp 5–9, in late winter 2001 and spring 2002. Discussion with Lt. Col. Joseph H. Wheeler III, USMC, Warfighting Faculty, Marine Corps Command & Staff College (September 5, 2003) and e-mail from Lt. Col. Wheeler to author (September 8, 2003), who provided photographs for this author's files. The Marine Corps move to develop a limited special operations capability is described in Lt. Col. Giles Kyser, *Fix Recon, USSOCOM, and the Future of the Corps: Food for Thought*, 87 Marine Corps Gazette 16–21 (July 2003).
>
> 6   *Special mission unit* is "[a] generic term to represent a group of operations and support personnel from designated organizations that is task-organized to perform highly classified activities." Joint Publication 1-02 at 492 (cited in note 5). It should be noted that increased (higher) classification is not a method for engaging in activities beyond the law. As noted in the definition of Special Operations in the preceding paragraph, special operations involve "political-military considerations [that] frequently shape special operations, requiring clandestine, covert, or low visibility techniques and *oversight at the national level.*" Id (emphasis added). It has been the author's personal experience in providing legal support for special missions units for a quarter of a century that special mission unit operations receive more policy and legal oversight—up to the national level—than virtually any other military unit or operation. Because of their sensitive nature and potential risk to individuals operating in denied areas, access to information relating to special mission unit operations necessarily is limited. The judge advocates most strident in their criticism of Special Forces wearing non-standard uniforms were not privy to this information. Those with access necessarily could not discuss the issue in an open forum.

Chicago Journal of International Law

I.   What are the facts?

II. What are the legal issues?

    A. Is it lawful for combatants to wear civilian clothing or non-standard uniforms in combat?

    B. If so, are there legal or other considerations in use of either?

    C. Are there any unique law of war considerations, such as risks, a commander should balance in making his decision?

III. What is the nature of the armed conflict and its armed participants?

    A. Was there something unique about Operation ENDURING FREEDOM with respect to application of the law of war?

    B. If so, how would application of the law of war differ?

IV. What is the relevant law of war?

    A. What is the applicable treaty law and legislative history?

    B. What is state practice, including court decisions?

I. WHAT ARE THE FACTS?

Thirty years ago it was my privilege to serve as the first Marine Corps Representative at The Judge Advocate General's ("JAG") School, US Army, in Charlottesville. As the lone Marine on the faculty, I was expected to attend all major public ceremonies, including the graduation of each Judge Advocate Officers Basic Course—the accession course for new lawyers entering the Army. Course graduation warranted a speech by one of the Army JAG Corps' flag officers. Regardless of who the graduation speaker was, the speech was the same. Written by The Assistant Judge Advocate General of the Army, the late Major General Lawrence H. Williams, it was called "the facts speech." Its message was simple and straightforward: before charging off to tilt at windmills, be sure you have the facts.

There is much to be said for this admonition and its application in the case at hand. Condemning certain actions or declaring them a law of war violation based upon news accounts is not a sound basis for analysis. No lawyer would prepare his case based solely upon news accounts. Indeed, media reports generally are inadmissible as evidence. Regrettably, some rushed to judgment based on less-than-reliable sources.

There are two fundamental issues. The first is what was being worn, and by whom. The second is the motive for the NGO complaints.

In response to the September 11, 2001 al Qaeda terrorist attacks against the World Trade Center and the Pentagon, US and Coalition Special Forces began operations in Afghanistan in late September 2001. At the request—initially insistence—of the leaders of the indigenous forces they supported, they dressed in indigenous attire. For identification purposes within the Northern

Alliance, this included the Massoud *pakol* (a round brownish-tan or gray wool cap) and Massoud checkered scarf, each named for former Northern Alliance leader Ahmad Shah Massoud, who was assassinated days before the al Qaeda attacks on the World Trade Center and Pentagon. This attire was not worn to appear as civilians, or to blend in with the civilian population, but rather to lower the visibility of US forces vis-à-vis the forces they supported. Al Qaeda and the Taliban had announced a $25,000 per head bounty on uniformed US military personnel. Placing a US soldier in Battle Dress Uniform ("BDU") or Desert Camouflaged Uniform ("DCU") in the midst of a Northern Alliance formation would greatly facilitate al Qaeda/Taliban targeting of US Special Forces.[7] As will

---

[7]   Special Forces' wear of Northern Alliance attire was undertaken at the insistence of Northern Alliance General Abdul Rashid Dostum, commander of its 8,000-man Junbishe-Millie, the largest Northern Alliance army. President William J. Clinton ordered the prompt withdrawal of US forces from Somalia following the October 3, 1993 Battle of Mogadishu in which eighteen members of Task Force Ranger died; see Mark Bowden, *Blackhawk Down: A Story of Modern War* (Atlantic Monthly 1999). General Dostum feared US withdrawal from Afghanistan if confronted with US casualties. Multiple Northern Alliance bodyguards were assigned to each US Special Forces soldier. In the early days of fighting, General Dostum told some of his subordinates in Mazar-e-Sharif that he would kill them if they allowed their US charges to be hurt or killed. Once US and coalition forces showed that they were not casualty averse, the bodyguard standards were relaxed. SF wear of the Northern Alliance *pakol*, tribal scarves, and beards prevented them from being singled out for targeting by al Qaeda/Taliban personnel. Wearing indigenous attire also aided SF rapport with the Northern Alliance forces they supported. Special mission unit Special Forces, whose identities are classified, also wore beards to reduce risk of media/public identification.

    The risk is not new. In 1915, serving in the Arabian Peninsula as a military adviser to Wahabi chief Abdul Aziz ibn Saud, British Army Captain William H.I. Shakespear eschewed indigenous attire. During a battle between the forces of Ibn Saud and pro-Turkish tribal leader Ibn Rashid, Shakespear was killed by an enemy sniper when his British Army uniform singled him out and identified him as a high-value target. Jeremy Wilson, *Lawrence of Arabia: The Authorized Biography of T.E. Lawrence* 1043 n 4 (Athenaeum 1990); Robert D. Kaplan, *The Arabists: The Romance of an American Elite* 55–56 (Free Press 1993). The author thanks Max Boot for bringing this to his attention. Knowledge of the circumstances of Captain Shakespear's death prompted T.E. Lawrence to wear Arab clothing as he lead the Arab revolt against Ottoman rule that began June 5, 1916, and to incorporate the lesson into Articles 18–20 of his *Twenty-Seven Articles* published in August 1917 as lessons learned. Wilson at 960, 1043 n 4. Articles 18–20 are discussed below in note 73.

    Indigenous personnel over-protection of US Special Forces personnel is not new. Office of Strategic Services ("OSS") Operational Team MUSKRAT/BEAR experienced the same phenomenon in China in 1945. Frank Mills, Robert Mills, and John W. Brunner, *OSS Special Operations in China* 300, 321 (Phillips 2002) (on file with author).

    In Operation ENDURING FREEDOM, Special Forces wear of the *pakol* was possible because of the Pashtun (Taliban) versus Tajik/Uzbek (Northern Alliance) differences in attire. Special Forces supporting Southern Alliance forces were confronted with a more difficult situation. Southern Alliance soldiers looked and dressed exactly like the Taliban. Afghan Taliban dressed in Pashtun attire since they were from the Pashtun tribes. Other Taliban, from Pakistan predominantly, wore Pakistani attire.

Chicago Journal of International Law

be seen in my review of the law, dressing in this manner more accurately may be described as wearing a "non-standard uniform" than "dressing as civilians." Special Forces personnel who had served in Afghanistan with whom I spoke stated that al Qaeda and the Taliban had no difficulty in distinguishing Northern Alliance or Southern Alliance forces from the civilian population.[8]

The fall of Kandahar in early December 2001 was followed by the collapse of the Taliban regime and the swearing-in of Hamid Karzai as Prime Minister. Another group of US Special Operations Forces—Army Civil Affairs[9]—began to enter Afghanistan. In November 2001, the US Army Central Command ("ARCENT")[10] had established the Coalition and Joint Civil Military Operations Task Force ("CJCMOTF") using soldiers from the 377th Theater Support Command ("TSC"), the 122nd Rear Operations Center, and the 352nd Civil Affairs Command. By January 3, 2002, the CJCMOTF was established in Kabul. It served as liaison with local officials of the Interim government and supervised the humanitarian assistance from US Army Civil Affairs ("CA") teams from the 96th Civil Affairs Battalions, who were beginning to operate throughout Afghanistan. CJCMOTF also was the liaison with the US Embassy, and coordinated coalition humanitarian assistance contributions.

The ARCENT Commanding General made the uniform decision, favoring civilian clothing over DCU. His rationale was based on two factors: (a) the

---

In the south, Special Forces wear of indigenous attire and its distinguishing devices was encouraged by Hamid Karzai to lower US visibility. Accordingly, these Special Forces wore native tops over their DCU. After three days, the Special Forces abandoned the indigenous tops for the balance of their tenure, their leader having convinced Karzai that as everyone knew they were American, there was no reason to pretend otherwise. It also gave the soldiers better access to their DCU pockets and load-bearing equipment.

8   Because neither Taliban/al Qaeda nor Northern or Southern Alliance forces wore a uniform, visual friend or foe identification at a distance was a challenge. Third Battalion, Fifth Special Forces Group, *The Liberation of Mazar-e Sharif: 5th SF Group UW in Afghanistan*, 15 Special Warfare 34, 36 (June 2002). However, this differs from dressing as civilians for the purpose of using the civilian population or civilian status as a means of avoiding detection of combatant status. From the standpoint of possible violation of the law of war, the issue is one of intent. As indicated in the main text, use of non-standard uniform (Massoud *pakol* and/or scarf) by some Special Forces personnel was to appear as members of the Northern Alliance rather than be conspicuous as US soldiers and, as indicated in the preceding footnote, high-value targets.

9   *Civil affairs* refers to "[d]esignated Active and Reserve component forces and units organized, trained and equipped specifically to conduct civil affairs activities and to support civil-military operations," while *Civil affairs activities* are defined as "[a]ctivities performed or supported by civil affairs that (1) enhance the relationship between military forces and civil authorities in areas where military forces are present; and (2) involve application of civil affairs functional specialty skills, in areas normally the responsibility of civil government, to enhance conduct of civil-military operations." Joint Publication 1-02 at 86 (cited in note 5).

10   US Army Central Command is Third US Army, Fort McPherson, Georgia, when not forward deployed.

ability of soldiers to perform humanitarian assistance operations; and (b) the safety of Civil Affairs personnel—that is, force protection.[11] A strong desire

---

11   In *Are Soldiers in Civilian Clothes Protected under Geneva-Hague?* at 31 (cited in note 2), Lieutenant Colonel H. Allen Irish provided the following official rationale for the decision:

> The need to reduce the potential for violence that may be directed at CJCMOTF personnel engaged in humanitarian relief efforts in Afghanistan was the critical factor mandating the decision [to operate in civilian clothing]. In uniform, [CJCMOTF] personnel may be targeted since they could be confused as being engaged in offensive combat operations instead of providing humanitarian assistance. . . . The traditional wear of civilian clothes by unconventional forces for the purpose of humanitarian assistance is time-proven.

This rationale is historically inaccurate and legally flawed. Civil Affairs personnel performing humanitarian assistance in operations short of international armed conflict have been authorized to wear civilian clothing. Civil Affairs personnel have worn standard uniforms only in international armed conflict. US Army and Marine Corps Civic Action (Civil Affairs) personnel operating in the Republic of Vietnam (1964–1971) wore standard field uniforms in threat circumstances similar to those faced by Civil Affairs personnel in Afghanistan. US Army Civil Affairs operating in support of Operation JUST CAUSE (Panama, 1989–1990) and Operations DESERT SHIELD/DESERT STORM/PROVIDE COMFORT (1991) wore standard BDU. These operations were significantly different from Special Forces missions in denied territory.

    From a law of war standpoint, neither "force protection" nor a desire to distinguish soldiers performing "offensive duties" from those engaged in humanitarian assistance constitutes military necessity for soldiers to wear civilian attire in international armed conflict. From the enemy standpoint (particularly the Taliban and al Qaeda), humanitarian assistance to Afghan civilians may constitute as much a threat as a soldier engaged in offensive operations.

    With respect to the force protection argument, US Army Civil Affairs doctrine in preparation at the time of the "force protection" decision (and subsequently approved) is to the contrary. US Army Field Manual 3-05.401, *Civil Affairs Tactics, Techniques and Procedures*, Table 4-2, p 4-40 (on file with author), indicates that Civil Affairs personnel in less than full Battle Dress Uniform, complete with combat equipment, to include Kevlar load bearing vest and individual weapon, risk reduced force protection, while noting that wearing civilian clothing "[g]reatly increases the possibility of fratricide."

    Notwithstanding the eloquence of Lieutenant Colonel Irish's arguments and the outstanding work Civil Affairs units have performed in Afghanistan and Iraq (the latter in Operation IRAQI FREEDOM, the 2003 coalition effort to remove dictator Saddam Hussein), there is no law of war basis for Civil Affairs personnel to wear anything other than standard uniform in an international armed conflict.

    The Bush Administration decision to regard Operation ENDURING FREEDOM as an international armed conflict was not made until early February 2002. It is an example of how good-faith differences may occur between how an on-scene commander views a conflict and the way it may be regarded in Washington. In this case, the Combatant Commander and his subordinate commanders saw the mission as one short of international armed conflict. This difference is commonplace, though the positions of the participants (Washington and the field commander) usually are in reverse. For example, on December 4, 1983, a US Navy air strike was launched against terrorist-related targets in the Beka'a Valley in Lebanon. Poorly executed, two aircraft were lost, and the Syrians captured one serviceman. In a press conference on December 20th, President Ronald Reagan was asked if the man was a prisoner of war. He replied:

Chicago Journal of International Law

existed at US Central Command ("USCENTCOM") headquarters (Tampa) to present a non-confrontational face, as well as a belief that NGOs were reluctant to be seen working with uniformed soldiers. Additionally, 96th Civil Affairs Battalion personnel, who initially operated in Islamabad, Pakistan, were ordered by the United States Ambassador to Pakistan to wear civilian clothing rather than their uniforms, reflecting the sensitive, unique political environment in which US Army forces were operating. This order was not clarified or countermanded on entry into Afghanistan. Civil Affairs personnel continued to wear Western civilian attire. Eventually some adopted Afghan native attire.[12]

Other reasons existed for continued wear of civilian attire. In some areas local governors would not talk to uniformed Civil Affairs personnel. In December 2001, the UN-sanctioned International Security Assistance Force ("ISAF") began arriving in Kabul in accordance with the Bonn Agreement. United Nations representatives refused to meet with US Army Civil Affairs leaders if they were in uniform.

US Army Civil Affairs units have a long, distinguished history. They played an indispensable role in the European Theater of Operations during and after World War II, and in the postwar occupation of Japan. US Army and Marine Corps Civic Action units played an equally indispensable humanitarian assistance role during the Vietnam War.[13] NGO involvement during those conflicts was virtually non-existent (World War II)[14] or extremely limited (Vietnam).[15]

The Syrians claim that he's a prisoner of war. Well, I don't know how you have a prisoner of war when there is no declared war between nations. I don't think that makes you eligible for the Geneva accords [sic].

The White House, *The President's News Conference of December 20, 1983*, 19 Weekly Comp Pres Docs 1729 (Dec 20, 1983). The day after the operation, however, this author cleared on a State Department cable forwarding a demarché to the United States ambassador in Damascus, demanding prisoner of war protection for the captured aviator. Upon receipt of that demarché, the Syrians complied. See Department of State, 3 *Cumulative Digest of United States Practice in International Law, 1981–1988* at 3456 (1995). The one-hour air strike probably did not meet the general criteria for a *war*, but it did cross the threshold for application of the 1949 Geneva Convention Relative to the Treatment of Prisoners of War. Similarly, during the 1999 NATO Kosovo air operations, Serbian forces captured three US Army soldiers. The initial response of the Secretary of State was that these men were not prisoners of war, a point with which every member of the Department of Defense Law of War Working Group strongly disagreed. The Secretary of State subsequently agreed that the men were prisoners of war, another indication that there is more than one threshold. W. Hays Parks, *The United States Military and the Law of War: Inculcating an Ethos*, 69 Social Research 981, 1000 (2002).

12   Unlike their Special Forces counterparts, Civil Affairs personnel in indigenous attire did not necessarily wear the Massoud *pakol* or scarf. Whether wearing western attire or indigenous attire, some concealed their weapons.

13   See, for example, F.S.V. Donnison, *British Military Administration in the Far East, 1943–46* (Her Majesty's Stationary Office ("HMSO") 1956); F.S.V. Donnison, *Civil Affairs and Military Government: North-West Europe, 1944–1946* (HMSO 1961); C.R.S. Harris, *Allied Military Administration of Italy, 1943–1945* (HMSO 1957); and F.S.V. Donnison, *Civil*

Under the terms of the 1949 Geneva Convention Relative to the Protection of Civilian Persons in Time of War ("GC"), NGOs operate subject to the consent of relevant state parties to a conflict.[16] The GC also contemplated a linear battlefield in which NGOs could operate in secure areas, a combat environment different from Afghanistan. Legally and operationally, military operations and requirements take priority over NGO activities. However, NGOs provide valuable services that the military might be expected or required to perform were NGOs not present. Military commanders must give due consideration to this, as NGO absence could add other responsibilities (such as refugee care) to a military commander's burden. At the same time, NGOs cannot expect a risk-free work environment. Military commanders are entitled to make lawful mission-supporting decisions, even if those decisions might place NGOs or other civilians at greater risk.

Service NGOs have become more significant players in areas of armed conflict over the past decade.[17] A service NGO's emphasis is on mission

---

Affairs and Military Government: Central Organization and Planning (HMSO 1966) (each is a part of the official British History of the Second World War, United Kingdom Military Series). US Army Civil Affairs operations in World War II are the subject of Harry L. Coles and Albert K. Weinberg, *Civil Affairs: Soldiers Become Governors* (US Army in World War II, Special Studies series) (Department of the Army 1964) and Earl F. Ziemke, *The U.S. Army in the Occupation of Germany, 1944–1946* (Army Historical Series) (US Army Center for Military History 1975). For Vietnam history, see, for example, Capt. Russel H. Stolfi, *U.S. Marine Corps Civic Action Efforts in Vietnam, March 1965–March 1966* (Historical Branch, US Marine Corps 1968); Capt. William D. Parker, *U.S. Marine Corps Civil Affairs in I Corps, Republic of Vietnam, April 1966 to April 1967* (Historical Division, US Marine Corps 1970).

[14] While the International Committee of the Red Cross does not regard itself as a non-governmental organization, it is in many respects the quintessential NGO and one of few NGOs operating during World War II. For its role in that conflict, see *Report of the International Committee of the Red Cross on Its Activities during the Second World War, September 1, 1939–June 30, 1947* (International Committee of the Red Cross 1948).

[15] See Maj. Gen. George S. Prugh, *Law at War: Vietnam, 1964–1973* at 65–66, 68–72, 76, 78, 116 (Department of the Army 1975), which mentions only work with the International Committee of the Red Cross. The only other NGO seen by this author during his Vietnam service (1968–1969) was the American National Red Cross, which played a limited but important role.

[16] Geneva Convention Relative to the Protection of Civilian Persons in Time of War art 10 (1949), 6 UST 3516. "The provisions of the present Convention constitute no obstacle to the humanitarian activities which the International Committee of the Red Cross or any other impartial humanitarian organization may, *subject to the consent of the Parties to the conflict concerned*, undertake for the protection of civilian persons and for their relief.") (emphasis added). See also Dietrich Schindler and Jiří Toman, eds, *The Laws of Armed Conflicts* 504 (Martinus Nijhoff 3d ed 1988).

[17] The author distinguishes between service NGOs, whose primary purpose is to provide humanitarian assistance in areas of strife and/or natural disaster, and advocacy NGOs, which are solely political action groups (self-proclaimed "human rights groups"). Examples of the former include the International Committee of the Red Cross, *Médecins*

performance following the principles of humanity, impartiality, independence and neutrality. These NGOs feel obliged to maintain independence from the agendas of both the donors that fund them and governments and local authorities that allow them to operate in their territories. In contrast, advocacy NGOs see CA's engagement in assistance activities as driven by political and security objectives.

The US military leadership was not entirely successful in seeking dialogue, much less working relationships, with NGOs in Afghanistan. The relationship was particularly bad as US Army Civil Affairs arrived in Afghanistan. Civil Affairs personnel were denied access to NGO meetings, while some NGOs refused to come to CJCMOTF-hosted meetings. A senior on-scene Army Civil Affairs officer concluded that the key concern was NGO image and market share. NGOs that had worked in Afghanistan since the 1980s feared being upstaged by the Army's Civil Humanitarian and Liaison Cells ("CHLC"). The NGOs also objected to the use of humanitarian projects in support of a military campaign.

The CJCMOTF served as liaison to the interim government and supervised the humanitarian assistance for US Army Civil Affairs teams beginning to operate throughout Afghanistan. Civil Affairs personnel were deployed across Afghanistan to assess and identify projects for some $2 million in initial aid money. The money went directly to local contractors. NGOs wanted to be subcontracted. Based on limited money, the need to have an immediate impact, and concern about whether such use of these funds was permissible, US Army Civil Affairs leadership informed the NGOs that it would not subcontract to them. Moreover, due to security concerns, NGOs were in the main cities but not in the villages where Civil Affairs teams operated. Going directly to local contractors increased the fear of some NGOs that they would lose "market share."

There was friction also with respect to fiscal accountability. US Army Civil Affairs is expected to account for 100 percent of the funds it is allocated. A substantial amount of NGOs' funding—sometimes as much as 60 percent—is directed to "overhead," preventing its allocation toward the designated project and hindering accountability. NGOs resent scrutiny of their financial affairs and high overhead. This resistance increased tension between US Army Civil Affairs and the NGOs.

Social reform was another source of tension. Contrary to claims of neutrality and impartiality,[18] many NGOs in Afghanistan moved into advocacy

---

sans Frontières (Doctors Without Borders), and Vietnam Veterans of America Foundation. Primary examples of the latter are Human Rights Watch and Amnesty International.

18   The International Committee of the Red Cross ("ICRC") defines *neutrality*: "In order to continue to enjoy the confidence of all, the Red Cross may not take sides in hostilities or engage at any time in controversies of a political, racial, religious or ideological nature."

of women's rights and human rights. This caused friction with US Army Civil Affairs, whose role is to provide humanitarian relief without interference in local customs, however objectionable they may be. Civil Affairs work stifled NGOs' agendas on non-humanitarian issues.

An amicable although uneven relationship evolved between CA and NGOs at the working, "grassroots" level. This contrasts with the poor relationship at higher levels due to the conflicts identified above. NGOs' resentment of US Army Civil Affairs and market share concerns apparently prompted the NGO complaint—led by *Médecins sans Frontières*—regarding Civil Affairs wear of civilian clothing.[19] Philosophical differences between NGOs and the military are inevitable. The uniform/civilian clothes issue was symptomatic of a larger issue. It should be noted that not all NGOs agreed with the complaint made by *Médecins sans Frontières*.

In early March 2002, the CJCMOTF commander, desiring to broker a compromise, directed all Civil Affairs personnel in Kabul and Mazar-e-Sharif to return to full uniform. Some Civil Affairs personnel in remote locations (where NGOs would not work due to the risk) were permitted to stay in civilian attire. On March 19th, following its review, USCENTCOM supported CJCMOTF's decision. Guidance and authority were provided to ground force commanders to establish uniform policies based upon local threat conditions and force protection requirements.

As a result of the NGOs' complaints the issue of military wear of civilian clothing was reviewed within the Department of Defense ("DoD"). Following DoD-Joint Chiefs of Staff coordination, guidance was forwarded to

---

Impartiality means that "[the ICRC] makes no discrimination as to nationality, race, religious beliefs, class or political opinions." *International Red Cross Handbook* 17 (ICRC 12th ed 1983). These are fundamental principles of the ICRC, approved by governments at the XX International Conference of the Red Cross, Vienna, 1965. Offering the ICRC definitions is not intended to suggest that the comments contained in the main text sentence are directed at the ICRC.

19   The NGO civilian clothing complaint was directed at Civil Affairs units and personnel only. Speaking at a Harvard University Carr Center Symposium, Army-Navy Club, Washington, October 18, 2002, Nicolas de Torrente, representative of the NGO *Médecins sans Frontières* (Doctors Without Borders) (hereinafter "MSF"), made it clear that the NGO complaint was directed only at US Army Civil Affairs personnel operating in proximity to NGOs. He emphasized that MSF offered no objection as to the attire of US or Coalition Special Forces engaged in counter-terrorist operations against Taliban/al Qaeda (personal knowledge of the author, who was present).

     During the question and answer period, this author offered the counterargument that NGO personnel working in proximity to uniformed CA personnel might be at greater risk of being targeted because of an appearance of overt support for US operations, or as collateral casualties incidental to al Qaeda attacks on uniformed Civil Affairs personnel performing humanitarian relief operations. Mr. Torrente acknowledged the counterargument before stating that MSF objected to the presence of any military personnel in proximity to MSF activities.

Chicago Journal of International Law

USCENTCOM in May 2002 that was consistent with CJCMOTF guidance issued on April 7, 2002. As a result of CENTCOM/CJCMOTF guidance, the number of Civil Affairs and other Special Operations Forces ("SOF") personnel in civilian clothing had diminished substantially prior to DoD-JCS action or the aforementioned USSOCOM Legal Conference.[20]

---

20   Six months later the Commanding General, US Army Special Forces Command ("USASFC") issued an order reinstating standard uniform and grooming practices that received wide media coverage. See, for example, Kitty Kay, *Close Shave for Special Forces*, Times (London) Overseas News 17 (Sept 13, 2002); Mike Mount, *Close Shave for Special Ops Forces in Afghanistan*, CNN (Sept 13, 2002), available online through <http://www.cnn.com> (visited Oct 17, 2003); and Headquarters CJSOTF Afghanistan Memorandum, Subject: Uniform and Appearance Standards Policy – Rescinding of Relaxed Grooming Standards (Sept 6, 2002). According to the Staff Judge Advocate for US Army Special Forces Command, the commander's intent was for field commanders to review the appropriateness of continued wear of non-standard uniforms and beards, particularly by support personnel not engaged in combat missions. This is borne out by reports the author received from special mission units judge advocates, who advised that bearded special mission unit personnel in non-standard uniforms subsequently briefed the Combatant Commander (Commander, US Central Command). The USASFC order was a general tightening of discipline and uniform standards where there was no military necessity for wearing either beards or non-standard uniforms. The author is indebted to Lieutenant Colonel Margaret M. Bedard, JA, USA, and Captain Robert A. Broadbent, JA, USA, US Army Special Forces Command, and Lieutenant Colonel Kevin H. Govern, JA, USA, for the information contained in this footnote.

Special Mission Unit personnel operating against al Qaeda grew beards for several reasons: (1) a dearth of water for daily shaving; (2) for rapport with and to appear like the indigenous personnel with whom they were serving; and (3) to protect them from identification and their families from terrorist attacks. The latter rationale is not new. In 1918, then-Lieutenant Colonel T.E. Lawrence was publicly identified as a leader in the Arab Revolt. His biographer explains:

> As soon as these reports began to appear, the Censorship and Press Committee in London issued a warning to editors which read: "The Press are earnestly requested not to publish any photograph of Lieutenant-Colonel T.E. Lawrence, C.B., D.S.O. This officer is not known by sight to the Turks, who have put a price upon his head, and any photograph or personal description of him may endanger his safety."

Wilson, *Lawrence of Arabia* at 552 (cited in note 7).

As somewhat of an aside and a comparative precedent, the reader is invited to examine the photograph of a bearded Captain Leon DeMers, US Army, a member of OSS Team IBEX in Hainan, northern China, in 1945, which shows him shirtless and in non-standard trousers, with a bandoleer of ammunition across his chest. Bank, *From OSS to Green Berets* at 62–63 (photo section) (cited in note 5). Similarly, British military personnel assigned to Special Operations Executive, changed from civilian clothing into uniform as their individual missions transitioned from clandestine operations into the paramilitary guerrilla phase. Douglas Dodds-Parker, *Setting Europe Ablaze* 145 (Springwood 1983). Similarly, OSS Operational Teams in China wore US uniforms, Chinese uniforms, Chinese Puppet Army (enemy) uniforms, or indigenous civilian attire, depending on the tactical situation. Mills, Mills, and Brunner, *OSS Special Operations in China* at 12, 90, 213–14, 217–18, 234, 270, 281, 284, 287, 294, 392 (cited in note 7). In Lawrence's case and the World War II cases, identification risks were limited to the battlefield. With ease of travel and the global threat of terrorism, the identity of special

II. WHAT ARE THE LEGAL ISSUES?

Considering an issue in the public sector, including the military, is similar to private practice or a law school examination. The legal issues have to be identified and addressed. In weighing the situation at hand, the following legal issues were identified:

A.   Is it lawful for combatants to wear civilian clothing or non-standard uniforms in combat?

B.   If so, are there legal restrictions in use of either?

C.   Are there unique law of war considerations, such as risks, which a commander should balance in making his decision?

Other questions had to be answered prior to answering the above questions.

III. WHAT IS THE NATURE OF THE ARMED CONFLICT, AND ITS ARMED PARTICIPANTS?

The nature of the armed conflict in Afghanistan was an issue that prompted considerable discussion within and outside the government, in large measure due to the nature of the enemy.

References to al Qaeda and the Taliban as separate entities constituted an incomplete and inaccurate picture. The enemy consisted of a loose amalgamation of at least three groups: the Taliban regime (until its December 2001 collapse, following which it reverted to its tribal origins), the al Qaeda terrorist group, used as the Praetorian Guard for the Taliban leadership (both for internal security prior to and following commencement of US/Coalition operations), and foreign Taliban. The picture was further complicated by the tendency of some to refer to the Taliban as the *de facto* government of Afghanistan, because it exercised rough control over 80 percent of Afghanistan. This was open to debate until the collapse of the Taliban, at which time it ceased to be an issue. Until the collapse of the Taliban regime in December 2001, a strong case could be made that this was an internal conflict between non-state actors in a failed state.[21] By the time Army Civil Affairs entered Afghanistan, the case was absolute.

---

mission personnel is classified to protect them and their families. This practice has existed for some time; see, for example, photographs contained in Peter Ratcliffe, with Noel Botham and Brian Hitchen, *Eye of the Storm* (Michael O'Mara 2000), where the faces of current members of Special Air Services ("SAS") are obscured.

21   The section that follows (including the text of this footnote) was prepared from materials provided by the Department of Military Strategy, Planning and Operations, US Army War College, US Army Peacekeeping Institute, the Department of State, and Ahmed Rashid, *Taliban: Militant Islam, Oil and Fundamentalism in Central Asia* (Yale 2000). The author also is indebted to Lieutenant Colonel Kirby Abbott, Chief, International and

Chicago Journal of International Law

Operational Law Division, Office of the Judge Advocate General, Canada, for his contributions to the analysis in this section.

Arguments with respect to the Taliban militia (as they called themselves) depend only so slightly on *who* and *when*. The Taliban was a loose amalgamation of occasional and disparate tribal and other factions. It was a faction engaged in a civil war in a failed state that owed much of its strength and origin to the Pakistani Intelligence Service. It exercised none of the usual activities of a government, other than the negative one of closing down all schools. The Taliban militia never claimed to be the Afghanistan government or armed forces. The Taliban had no uniformed armed forces. The Taliban was structured around tribes rather than as a military unit, recruiting the allegiance of other tribes or personnel from other tribes and private citizens through temporary alliances, defections, bribery, and conscription, while also relying on foreign volunteers.

Since the collapse of the Soviet Union and the break-up of Yugoslavia, the international test has been whether an entity is permitted to sit behind the nameplate in the United Nations (and in other international fora) rather than the previous test of whether it controls population, territory, etc. The Taliban was never permitted to represent Afghanistan at the United Nations or in other international fora.

The UN Security Council never recognized Taliban as the representative of Afghanistan. In a number of UN Security Council resolutions issued against the Taliban, there was discussion as to whether a binding resolution could be issued against a non-state entity. These Security Council resolutions included 1189 (1999), 1267 (1999) and 1363 (2001). Security Council resolution 1189 referred to "the continuing use of Afghan territory, especially areas controlled by the Taliban;" hence the Security Council distinguished between the Taliban and Afghanistan.

Prior to September 11, 2001, the Taliban was recognized only by Saudi Arabia, Pakistan and the United Arab Emirates. All three withdrew their recognition following the terrorist attack. Stated another way, 98.5 percent of the world's governments, including the United States, did not recognize the Taliban as the government of Afghanistan prior to the September 11, 2001 al Qaeda attack. Nor was it recognized by the League of Islamic Nations, nor by Switzerland (depositary of the Geneva Conventions). The Taliban was not invited to the 1999 Conference of Red Cross and Red Crescent Societies as the Afghanistan representative. Had it been invited, it is likely the US and other governments would have prevented it from occupying the Afghanistan delegation seat, as was the case with respect to the FRY in Yugoslavia. By the time Coalition operations began in Afghanistan, no government recognized the Taliban as the government of Afghanistan.

Once US and allied operations began in Afghanistan in October 2001, al Qaeda assumed command of most Taliban militia units. As the battle continued, most Taliban withdrew to their normal areas of Afghanistan, leaving the fighting to al Qaeda and foreign members of the Taliban. Any perception of the Taliban as any sort of a national government dissolved following Taliban abandonment of Kabul (Nov 12, 2001) and the US capture of Kandahar (Dec 10, 2001).

A leading authority, in discussing guerrillas, summed up the Taliban militia and al Qaeda status:

> The law of nations, apart from the Hague Regulations . . . denies belligerent qualifications to guerrilla bands. Such forces wage a warfare which is irregular in point of origin and authority, of discipline, of purpose and procedure. They may be constituted at the beck of a single individual; they lack uniforms; they are given to pillage and destruction; they take few prisoners and are hence disposed to show slight quarter.

Charles Cheney Hyde, 2 *International Law: Chiefly as Interpreted and Applied by the United States* § 652 (Little, Brown 1922).

Another factor was that the United States and its Coalition partners were engaged in military operations in a foreign nation. Hence, regardless of the status of the Taliban, an argument could be made that for certain purposes this was an international armed conflict. However, by the time the uniform issue was raised by NGOs and considered in Washington, the conflict against the Taliban and al Qaeda looked more like a counterinsurgency campaign or counterterrorist operation than an international armed conflict. While the Administration chose to apply the law of war applicable in international armed conflicts as a template for US conduct,[22] it would be incorrect to conclude that all of the law of war for international armed conflicts was applicable. For example, neither the Taliban nor al Qaeda personnel were regarded as entitled to prisoner of war status.[23] Nonetheless, the Geneva Convention Relative to the Treatment of Prisoners of War of August 12, 1949, proved a useful template for their treatment.

This issue was not entirely new. US and other military forces engaged in the various peacekeeping and other peace operations during the 1990s frequently sought to ascertain where they were along the conflict spectrum. From the standpoint of US military conduct, the issue made little difference. DoD policy is that US military personnel will comply with the law of war during all armed conflicts, however such conflicts are characterized, and with the principles and spirit of the law of war during all other operations.[24] The primary issue in US and Coalition operations against al Qaeda and the Taliban was whether captured al Qaeda and Taliban were entitled to prisoner of war status under the Geneva

---

[22]   See, for example, President's Military Order, *Detention, Treatment, and Trial of Certain Non-Citizens in the War on Terrorism*, 66 Fed Reg 57833, § 1(a) (Nov 13, 2001) (hereinafter Military Order).

[23]   Press Briefing by Ari Fleischer (February 7, 2002), available online at <http://www.whitehouse.gov/news/releases/2002/02/20020207-6.html> (visited Sept 21, 2003); Katherine Q. Seelye, *In Shift, Bush Says Geneva Rules Fit Taliban Captives*, NY Times A1 (Feb 8, 2002). The issues are summarized in John C. Yoo and James C. Ho, *International Law and the War on Terrorism*, Va J Intl L (forthcoming Fall 2003).

[24]   *DoD Law of War Program*, DoD Directive 5100.77 at ¶ 5.3.1 (Dec 9, 1998); *Implementation of the DoD Law of War Program*, CJCSI 5810.01A at ¶ 5a (Aug 27, 1999). For this reason, the decision was announced that the United States would apply the law of war applicable in international armed conflict to non-state actors in Operation ENDURING FREEDOM. See Anthony Dworkin, *Excerpt from Interview with Charles Allen, Deputy General Counsel for International Affairs, US Department of Defense*, Crimes of War Project, (Dec 16, 2002), available online at <http://www.crimesofwar.org/onnews/news-pentagon-trans.html> (visited Sept 21, 2003). This announcement was greeted with astonishment by some international law experts. See, for example, Marco Sassoli, *"Unlawful Combatants:" The Existing Law and Whether It Needs to Be Revised*, Conference on Current Issues in International Law and Military Operations 1, US Naval War College (June 25–27, 2003). Comments similar to Professor Sassoli's were offered privately to the author by his foreign military counterparts. As will be indicated, the intention was to use the law of war applicable in international armed conflicts as a template for US conduct in Operation ENDURING FREEDOM.

Convention Relative to the Treatment of Prisoners of War of August 12, 1949 ("GPW")[25] which, as indicated in note 23, had been decided.

IV. WHAT IS THE RELEVANT LAW?

In a speech at the United States Institute of Peace on March 1, 2001, Sir Adam Roberts declared "lawyers stick to the safe anchor of treaties."[26] This perhaps is a more erudite way of expressing the adage, "If the only tool you have is a hammer, every problem is viewed as a nail." So it was in the debate over SOF wear of non-standard uniforms. The argument against non-standard uniforms primarily was cast in terms of the GPW. The author frequently heard critics argue that "in accordance with" the GPW, (a) SOF were required to wear uniforms; (b) failure to wear uniforms was a war crime; and (c) SOF had to wear uniforms and treat captured al Qaeda and Taliban as enemy prisoners of war in the hope of reciprocity should any SOF fall into enemy hands.[27] A closer examination of the law reveals (a) and (b) to be legally incorrect, while (c) was highly speculative at best with respect to al Qaeda and Taliban conduct.

The GPW and its predecessors contain no language requiring military personnel to wear a uniform, nor prohibiting them from fighting in something other than full, standard uniform. Nor does it make it a war crime not to wear a uniform. Article 4 lists persons entitled to prisoner of war status and subject to the protections set forth in the GPW. It states in part:

> A.   Prisoners of war, in the sense of the present Convention, are persons belonging to one of the following categories, who have fallen into the power of the enemy:
>
> > (1)   Members of the armed forces of a Party to the conflict, as well as members of militias and volunteer corps forming part of such armed forces.
> >
> > (2)   Members of other militias and members of other volunteer corps, including those of organized resistance movements, belonging to a Party to the conflict and operating in or outside their own territory, even if this territory is occupied, provided that such militias or volunteer corps, including such organized resistance movements, fulfill the following conditions:
> >
> > > (a)   that of being commanded by a person responsible for his subordinates;
> > >
> > > (b)   that of having a fixed distinctive sign recognizable at a distance;

---

25   6 UST 3316 (hereinafter GPW).

26   Sir Adam Roberts, *Enforcement of International Humanitarian Law: Challenges for the UN Security Council and the USA*, Speech at the US Institute of Peace (Mar 1, 2001) (personal knowledge of author, who was present).

27   Personal knowledge of author as a participant in numerous official meetings and discussions with various NGOs.

involves perfidy, discussed in Section IV.B. Military personnel wearing non-standard uniform or civilian clothing are entitled to prisoner of war status if captured. Those captured wearing civilian clothing may be at risk of denial of prisoner of war status and trial as spies.

There is no doubt that in an international armed conflict any commander will, and should, weigh a decision to authorize the wearing of civilian clothing carefully. That being said, military personnel are in a high-risk profession, and commanders often must make life-and-death decisions. Under most circumstances, a commander ordering a frontal infantry assault on a heavily fortified position understands that in doing so, he has accepted that some soldiers are likely to lose their lives in carrying out his order. Similarly, individuals who join the military should be under no illusion as to the attendant risks. As British Special Operations Executive historian M.R.D. Foot acknowledged, "The truth is that wars are dangerous, and people who fight in them are liable to be killed."[34]

The decision to wear something other than a standard uniform first requires military necessity. At issue then is what constitutes a "non-standard uniform." If a commander provides military necessity for a Special Forces team to conduct operations in international arms conflict in something other than standard uniform, what steps are necessary to comply with the law of war? What guidance, if any, does the law of war provide as to what might constitute a "non-standard uniform?" Also, what is "treacherous" killing, prohibited by Article 23(b), Annex to the 1907 Hague IV?

At the heart of the issue is the law of war principle of *distinction*. The law of war divides the population of nations at war into the belligerent forces and civilians not taking an active or direct part in hostilities.[35] With a single, limited exception,[36] only military forces may engage directly or actively in hostilities, that

---

[34]   M.R.D. Foot, *SOE in France: An Account of the British Special Operations Executive in France, 1940–44* at 20 (HMSO 1966).

[35]   For example, US War Department Field Manual 27-10, *Rules of Land Warfare* 4 states: "The enemy population is divided in war into two general classes, known as the *armed forces* and the *peaceful population*. Both classes have distinct rights, duties, and disabilities, and no person can belong to both classes at one and the same time." (cited in note 31) (emphasis in original). See also War Office [UK], *Manual of Military Law* 7 (War Office 1929) ("The division of the population of a belligerent State into two classes, namely, the armed forces and the peaceful population, has already been mentioned. . . . It is one of the purposes of the laws of war to ensure that an individual who belongs to one class or the other shall not be permitted to enjoy the privileges of both."). See also War Office [UK], *The Law of War on Land, Being Part III of the Manual of Military Law* 30 ¶ 86 (HMSO 1958) (the current British law of war manual). *Belligerent* is the classical term. More recently *belligerents* have been referred to as *combatants*, as medical personnel and chaplains are part of belligerent forces but are non-combatants.

[36]   The *levée en masse* which, as defined in Article 2 of the Annex to the Hague Convention IV (cited in note 29), is "the inhabitants of a territory [not under occupation] who, on the

Chicago Journal of International Law

is, in combatant-like activities. Hostile acts by private citizens are not lawful, and are punishable, in order to protect innocent civilians from harm.[37] Civilians, and the civilian population, are protected from intentional attack so long as they do not take an active or direct part in hostilities. In turn, military forces are obligated to take reasonable measures to separate themselves from the civilian population and civilian objects, to distinguish innocent civilians from civilians engaged in hostile acts, and to distinguish themselves from the civilian population so as not to place the civilian population at undue risk. This includes not only physical separation of military forces and other military objectives from civilian objects and the civilian population as such, but also other actions, such as wearing uniforms. An early 20th century law of war scholar observed:

> The separation of armies and peaceful inhabitants into two distinct classes is perhaps the greatest triumph of International Law. Its effect in mitigating the evils of war has been incalculable.[38]

Another law of war scholar summarizes the principle of *distinction* in the following way:

> It may be said that the principle . . . of distinction between belligerents and civilian population, had found acceptance as a self-evident rule of customary law in the second half of the 19th century. Indeed, it seems no more than a reflection of practice as demonstrated in many of the wars fought in Europe in that period. Soldiers were not merely distinguishable: they were conspicuous in their proud uniforms; and armies fought each other, and preferred the civilian population not to mingle in their business.[39]

State practice and treaty development make it clear that the principle is neither absolute nor rigid. Wearing civilian clothing for intelligence collection is acknowledged in treaty law as a lawful military activity. SOF wearing civilian clothing while serving with partisans was common state practice in World War II and codified in subsequent treaties or their negotiating records, as will be shown in Section IV.B. The ancillary law of war prohibition on "killing treacherously"[40] does not preclude lawful ruses or Special Forces' wearing non-standard uniforms, or openly fighting in civilian attire with no intent to conceal their combatant status.[41]

---

approach of the enemy, spontaneously take up arms to resist the invading troops without having had time to organize themselves." Treaty recognition of the *levée en masse* constituted a first step in relaxation of the principle of *distinction*.

[37]   L. Oppenheim, *Disputes, War and Neutrality*, 2 *International Law: A Treatise* 206 (Longmans, Green 7th ed 1952) (H. Lauterpacht, ed).

[38]   J.M. Spaight, *War Rights on Land* 37 (MacMillan 1911).

[39]   Frits Kalshoven, *The Law of Warfare* 31 (A.W. Sijthoff 1973).

[40]   Article 23(b) of the Annex to the Hague Convention IV (cited in note 29) states that it is prohibited "to kill or wound treacherously individuals belonging to the hostile nation or army."

[41]   Article 24 of the Annex to the Hague Convention IV (cited in note 29) states: "Ruses of war and the employment of measures necessary for obtaining information about the

A. WEAR OF UNIFORMS

Military wear of uniforms during conventional combat operations in international armed conflict reflects the general customary practice of nations, subject to limited exceptions discussed in this section. This practice has a long history, dating at least to the Peloponnesian Wars (431 to 404 BC).[42]

The customary principle of *distinction* is applicable to the regular military forces. Conventional military forces should be distinguishable from the civilian population in international armed conflict between uniformed military forces of the belligerent states. It is an expectation, with codified exceptions, and another exception acknowledged in the negotiating record of the 1977 Additional Protocol I.[43] The criteria set forth for militia and partisan forces not a part of the regular military had as their intention recognition of the generally accepted practice of nations with respect to the characteristics of conventional forces.[44]

---

enemy and the country are considered permissible." See also US Army Field Manual 27-10, *The Law of Land Warfare* ¶ 51 (US Army 1956); War Office [UK], *The Law of War on Land* at 101–02 (cited in note 35).

[42] Where soldiers in international armed conflict lacked proper uniforms through no fault of their own, they were expected to wear a distinctive emblem to distinguish themselves from the civilian population. See Oppenheim, *International Law* at 429–30 (cited in note 37).

[43] The negotiating record exception is discussed in Section IV.B. Two treaty exceptions exist. GPW art 93 (cited in note 25) states in part:

> [O]ffenses committed by prisoners of war with the sole intention of facilitating escape and which do not entail any violence against life or limb, such as offenses against public property, theft without intention of self-enrichment, the drawing up or use of false papers, [and] *the wearing of civilian clothing*, shall occasion disciplinary punishment only.

(Emphasis added.) In its discussion of this provision, the ICRC *Commentary* states:

> [A] prisoner of war retains that legal status until such time as he has made good his escape. It is absolutely forbidden for him to commit any belligerent act, to carry weapons, or to engage in armed resistance, otherwise he will be liable to be treated as a sniper [sic] or saboteur.

Pictet, ed, *Commentary on the Geneva Convention Relative to the Treatment of Prisoners of War* at 454 (cited in note 29). The *Commentary* uses "sniper" in the pejorative sense in which it was formerly used, that is, to denote a civilian who ambushes or "bushwhacks" enemy military personnel. The term was used in this manner during the Franco-Prussian (1870–1871) and Anglo-Boer (1899–1902) Wars; see Spaight, *War Rights on Land* at 52, 62–63 (cited in note 38), for discussion. A military sniper is a lawful combatant. See Headquarters, Department of the Army, Office of The Judge Advocate General, Memorandum, Subject: Legality of Snipers (Sept 29, 1992).

[44] Maj. Richard R. Baxter, JA, USA, *The Juridical Basis of the Distinction between Lawful Combatant and Unprivileged Belligerent* 47–51 (unpublished thesis, The Judge Advocate General's School, US Army, 1959) (on file with author).

Art 4A(2) constituted acknowledgement of the legitimacy of World War II partisan warfare in its amendment of previous treaty categories to "members of other militias and members of other volunteer corps, *including those of organized resistance movements... .*" GPW art 4A(2), 6 UST 3316 (cited in note 25) (emphasis added). This was a further relaxation

No rule exists stating that a complete, standard uniform is the only way by which regular armed forces may make themselves distinguishable from the civilian population.[45] Historically it has been the predominant way by which military personnel, including Special Operations Forces, have distinguished themselves from the civilian population. But it has not been the exclusive way.

A difficulty lies in the lack of definition. There is no international standard as to what constitutes a "uniform."[46] Neither the 1907 Hague Convention IV or the GPW offers a definition or precise standard. In the International Committee of the Red Cross's (ICRC) *Commentary* on Article 4, GPW, its author states:

> The drafters of the 1949 Convention, like those of the Hague Conventions, considered it unnecessary to specify the sign which members of armed forces should have for purposes of recognition. It is the duty of each State to take steps so that members of its armed forces can be immediately recognized as such and to see to it that they are easily distinguishable from . . . civilians.[47]

Similarly, reporting on discussions of the same issue at the 1974–1977 Diplomatic Conference that promulgated Additional Protocol I, the ICRC *Commentary* states:

> What constitutes a uniform, and how can emblems of nationality be distinguished from each other? The Conference in no way intended to define what constitutes a uniform. . . . "[A]ny customary uniform which clearly distinguished the member wearing it from a non-member should suffice." Thus a cap or an armlet etc. worn in a standard way is actually equivalent to a uniform.
>
> The uniform and other emblems of nationality are visible signs. Although certain kinds of battle dress of different countries are very similar nowadays, it is nevertheless possible to distinguish allied armed forces from enemy armed forces by means of characteristics of outfitting and other signs of nationality. Furthermore, this makes it possible to distinguish members of the armed forces from the civilian population . . . .[48]

---

of the principle of distinction. See Pictet, ed, *Commentary on the Geneva Convention Relative to the Treatment of Prisoners of War* at 52–61 (cited in note 29).

45   US Department of War Manual, *Rules of Land Warfare* ¶ 22 (1914, corrected to April 15, 1917), states: "*The distinctive sign.*—This requirement will be satisfied by the wearing of a uniform or even less than a complete uniform." See also Allan Rosas, *The Legal Status of Prisoners of War: A Study in International Humanitarian Law Applicable in Armed Conflict* 348–49 (Suomalainen Tiedeakatemia 1976).

46   See Rosas, *The Legal Status of Prisoners of War* at 348 (cited in note 45) ("[T]he concept of uniforms has never been explicitly defined in international law.").

47   Pictet, ed, *Commentary on the Geneva Convention Relative to the Treatment of Prisoners of War* at 52 (cited in note 29). Spaight, *War Rights on Land* at 57 (cited in note 38), emphasizes that "[t]he 'distinctive emblem' does not mean a uniform."

48   Yves Sandoz, Christophe Swinarski, and Bruno Zimmerman, eds, *Commentary on the Additional Protocols of 8 June 1977 to the Geneva Conventions of 12 August 1949* at 468 (ICRC 1987). The ICRC *Commentary* does not reflect the complexity of the discussions within the Working Group. As three Diplomatic Conference participants indicate in their separate

The ICRC *Commentary* indicates that a state should ensure that its conventional military forces be distinguishable from the civilian population. It does not specify the manner in which this may be accomplished, or state that the complete standard uniform is the only way in which this requirement may be met.

In spite of the clear treaty language in Article 4A(2)(b), GPW ("*fixed* distinctive sign") (emphasis added), the device need not be permanent or fixed. What "fixed distinctive sign" means remains unresolved. In commenting on this, Professor Howard S. Levie notes:

> The ICRC has made several statements attempting to offer acceptable interpretations of the meaning of the term "fixed distinctive sign" [contained in Article 4A(2), GPW]. In 1960 it stated that the sign "must be worn constantly"; but in 1971 it backtracked somewhat when it said that the sign must be "fixed, in the sense that the resistant [partisan or guerrilla] should wear it throughout all the operation in which he takes part." Moreover, at that same time the ICRC stated that the sign "might be an armband, a headdress, part of a uniform, etc." During World War II the listed items were, on various occasions, used by resistance groups; but they were frequently removed and disposed of at critical moments in order to enable the individual to escape being identified as a member of the resistance.[49]

Given generally acceptable "distinctive devices"—a hat, a scarf, or an armband—any device recognizable in daylight with unenhanced vision at a reasonable distance would meet the law of war obligation to be distinguishable from the civilian population.[50]

---

commentary, the Working Group experienced considerable difficulty with the practical details of this issue; see Bothe, Partsch, and Solf, *New Rules for Victims of Armed Conflicts* at 205–06 (cited in note 32).

[49]   Howard S. Levie, *Prisoners of War in International Armed Conflict* 47 (Naval War College 1978) (internal citations omitted). Spaight argued that the distinctive device "must be fixed—externally, so as not to be assumed or concealed at will." *War Rights on Land* at 57 (cited in note 38). This is not consistent with prior or subsequent practice. The original view regarding a distinctive device was expressed by Francis Lieber in his *Guerrilla Parties Considered with Reference to the Laws and Usages of War*. In it he noted, "Nor would it be difficult to adopt something of a badge, *easily put on and off*, and to call it a uniform." Quoted in Richard Shelly Hartigan, *Lieber's Code and the Law of War* 40 (Precedent 1983) (emphasis added).

[50]   Spaight commented:

> At what distance should the sign be recognizable? The German authorities demanded in 1870 that the French irregulars should be distinguishable at rifle range. This, says an eminent English jurist, is "to ask not only for a complete uniform but for a conspicuous one," [citing William Edward Hall, *International Law* 523 (Clarendon 5th ed 1904)]. When rifles are sighted to 2,000 yards and over, the German requirement is clearly unreasonable. If the sign is recognizable at a distance at which the naked eye can distinguish the form and color of a person's dress, all reasonable requirements appear to be met. At the commencement of the Russo-Japanese War, the Russian Government addressed a note to Tokio, stating that Russia had approved the formation of

Chicago Journal of International Law

There are at least five categories of clothing: (a) a uniform such as BDU; (b) uniform worn with some civilian clothing;[51] (c) civilian clothing only, but with a distinctive emblem to distinguish the wearer from the civilian population; (d) civilian clothing only, with arms and other accoutrements (such as load-bearing equipment or body armor) that, combined with actions and circumstances, clearly manifest military status; and (e) civilian clothing, with weapon concealed and no visual indication that the individual is a member of the military.[52] Based upon historical practice and treaty negotiation records, the

---

certain free corps composed of Russian subjects in the seat of war, and that these corps would wear no uniform but only a distinctive sign on the cap or sleeve. Japan replied:[ ]

> The Japanese Government cannot consider as belligerents the free corps mentioned in the Russian Note, unless they can be *distinguishable by the naked eye from the ordinary people* or fulfil the conditions required for militia or volunteers by the Hague *Règlement.*

War Rights on Land at 57 (cited in note 38) (emphasis and punctuation in original, footnotes omitted).

Similarly, US Department of War Manual, *Rules of Land Warfare* (1914, corrected to April 15, 1917) (cited in note 45), followed the Japanese Government's test:

> *The distinctive sign.*—This requirement will be satisfied by the wearing of a uniform, or even less than a complete uniform. The distance that the sign must be visible is left vague and undetermined and the practice is not uniform. This requirement will be satisfied certainly if the sign is "easily *distinguishable by the naked eye of ordinary people*" at a distance at which the form of the individual can be determined.

(Emphasis added). Hyde cites this provision as authority in 2 *International Law* at 291 n 3 (cited in note 21).

The term "unenhanced vision" is utilized in Article 1 of Protocol II (Blinding Laser Weapons) to the 1980 United Nations Conventional Weapons Convention. It means normal vision without enhancements, such as binoculars, or vision corrected to 20/20. For its negotiating history, see Headquarters, Department of the Army, Office of The Judge Advocate General, DAJA-IO Memorandum of Law, Subject: *Travaux Preparatoires* and Legal Analysis of Blinding Laser Weapons Protocol (Dec 20, 1996). On page 8, the memorandum notes the intent of its drafters:

> Unenhanced vision means "the naked eye or . . . the eye with corrective eyesight devices," such as glasses or contact lens. It does not mean binoculars, a telescopic sight, night-vision goggles or similar devices used to increase visual capability above that required by an ordinary person to perform routine tasks, such as reading or driving an automobile.

51 As noted in the text accompanying footnotes 151 and 190, British Special Forces in North Africa in World War II and British and US Special Forces operating behind enemy lines in Iraq during the 1990–1991 war to liberate Kuwait frequently wore indigenous overcoats over their BDUs to counter one of the coldest winters on record, but also as a ruse to reduce immediate, positive identification at a distance by Iraqi military units.

52 Treaty negotiation records suggest participants did not rely upon "carrying arms openly" for regular forces. This is one of the four prerequisites for militias or partisans seeking combatant and prisoner of war status. The phrase "carrying arms only" has itself been plagued with lack of agreement as to its meaning. See, for example, W. Hays Parks, *Air War and the Law of War*, 32 Air Force L Rev 1, 84 (1990) (the debate with regard to Article 44(3), Additional Protocol I). It also was of limited to no value in Afghanistan, as most Afghan civilians carry military weapons. Similarly, following cessation of formal combat

first three constitute a "uniform." The fourth should protect the individual from charges of spying if captured if the individual is distinguishable from the civilian population by physical separation, clearly military duties, and other characteristics.[53] The last is lawful for intelligence gathering or other clandestine activities. As will be indicated, violation of the law of war occurs only when there is treacherous use of civilian clothing that is the proximate cause of death or injury of others. The 1974–1977 Diplomatic Conference did not regard it as serious enough to be classified as a Grave Breach.

The United States is not a State Party to the 1977 Protocol I Additional to the Geneva Conventions of August 12, 1949. Following extensive military, legal and policy review, the United States decided against submission of Additional Protocol I to the United States Senate for its advice and consent to ratification.[54] However, the United States acknowledged that it is bound by Additional Protocol provisions that constitute a codification of customary international law.[55]

---

operations in Iraq on May 1, 2003, private Iraqi citizens were permitted to retain Kalashnikov AK-47 or AK-74 select fire weapons in their homes for personal protection. Coalition Provisional Authority Order No. 3 (May 23, 2003) (on file with author).

[53]   As summarized in this article, there is substantial state practice of Special Forces wear of civilian clothing or non-standard uniforms. As an example of the fourth category, the personal security detail for Commander in Chief, US Central Command ("Combatant Commander"), during Operations DESERT SHIELD and DESERT STORM (1990–1991) wore civilian attire on the basis that VIP protection from terrorist attack is not a traditional military mission. (Attack by conventional Iraqi forces was not regarded as a viable threat.) The personal security detail worked in close proximity to the Combatant Commander, who wore standard BDU. The personal security detail in turn was surrounded by an outer perimeter of uniformed Saudi soldiers. The civilian attire of the personal security detail was dictated in large measure by host nation concerns. Their immediate proximity to the commander and uniformed Saudi military, and their physical separation from the civilian population was consistent with the principle of *distinction*. No reasonable case could be made that their actions were tantamount to *perfidy* (personal knowledge of author and photograph in author's files).

[54]   On January 29, 1987, President Ronald Reagan informed the United States Senate that Additional Protocol I would not be submitted for Senate advice and consent to ratification. Message from the President of the United States Transmitting the Protocol II Additional to the Geneva Conventions of August 12, 1949, and Relating to the Protection of Victims of Noninternational Armed Conflicts, Concluded at Geneva on June 10, 1977, 100th Cong, 1st Sess (1987), 26 ILM 561 (1987).

[55]   Department of State, 3 *Cumulative Digest of United States Practice in International Law, 1981–1988* at 3434–35 (cited in note 11). See also DoD Law of War Working Group, Session One: Memorandum for Assistant Counsel (International), OSD, Subject: 1977 Protocols Additional to the Geneva Conventions; Customary International Law Application (May 9, 1986). See also Michael J. Matheson, *The United States Position on the Relation of Customary International Law to the 1977 Protocols Additional to the 1949 Geneva Conventions*, 2 Am U J Intl L & Poly 419 (1987), based upon a speech Mr. Matheson made at an American University workshop. Mr. Matheson's statements with regard to the provisions of Additional Protocol I regarded by the United States as customary law are based upon the DoD Law of War Working Group memorandum, cited above. Thereafter he expresses

Chicago Journal of International Law

Most paragraphs of Article 44, Additional Protocol I, amended the customary law of war with respect to entitlement to prisoner of war status for private groups (so-called "liberation movements"). For policy, humanitarian, and military reasons, these provisions are regarded as unacceptable by the United States, and were a major reason for the US decision against ratification.

With respect to conventional forces, Article 44, paragraph 7, states:

> This Article is not intended to change the *generally accepted practice* of States with respect to wearing of the uniform by combatants assigned to regular, uniformed armed units of a Party to the conflict.[56]

An authoritative commentary on Additional Protocol I—prepared by individuals directly involved in its drafting and negotiation—offers explanation of this provision:

> Within the Working Group the initial enthusiasm for a single standard applicable both to regular and independent armed forces was dampened when concern was expressed that the ... [new rules] might encourage uniformed regular forces to dress in civilian clothing . . . . Accordingly, para. 7 was developed to overcome this concern. The report of the Working Group, however, states that 'regulars who are assigned to tasks where they must wear civilian clothes, as may be the case ... with advisers assigned to certain resistance units, are not required to wear the uniform.['] The implication of para. 7, construed in the light of the Working Group report is that uniforms continue to be the principal means by which members of regular uniformed units distinguish themselves from the civilian population . . ., but that members of regular armed forces assigned or attached to duty with the forces of resistance or liberation movements may conform to the manner in which irregulars conform to the requirements of para. 3.[57]

---

his personal opinion that "certain provisions of Protocol I reflect customary international law or are positive new developments which should ... become part of that law." Id at 421.

[56]   16 ILM at 1411 (cited in note 32) (emphasis added).

[57]   Bothe, Partsch, and Solf, *New Rules for Victims of Armed Conflicts* at 257 (cited in note 32). The new rules set forth in Article 44, ¶ 3, were among those found unacceptable to the United States in taking its decision against ratification. Paragraph 3 provides:

> In order to promote the protection of the civilian population from the effects of hostilities, combatants are obliged to distinguish themselves from the civilian population while they are engaged in an attack or in a military operation preparatory to an attack. Recognizing, however, that there are situations in armed conflicts where, owing to the nature of the hostilities an armed combatant cannot so distinguish himself, in such situations, he carries his arms openly:
>
> (a)   during each military engagement, and
>
> (b)   during such time as he is visible to the adversary while he is engaged in a military deployment preceding the launching of an attack in which he is to participate.
>
> Acts which comply with the requirements of this paragraph shall not be considered as perfidious . . . .

That being said, another Diplomatic Conference participant offered the following comment as to uniform requirement in light of Article 44, paragraph 7:

> [I]t should be noted that it is apparently not intended to exclude all regular forces from the application of the previous paragraphs of the article. What it does imply, however, is that regular forces whenever possible (notably in "conventional" types of hostilities), should continue to wear uniforms.[58]

Thus, commentaries by participants in the 1974–1977 Diplomatic Conference confirm Additional Protocol I's acknowledgement that, where warranted by military necessity, it may be permissible in international armed conflict[59] for regular military forces to wear civilian clothing. At issue is whether the action is a legitimate ruse or perfidy.

1. Ruses and Perfidy

Ruses of war are lawful deceptive measures employed in military operations in international armed conflict for the purpose of misleading the enemy.[60] The law of war prohibits "killing or wounding treacherously individuals belonging to the hostile nation or army,"[61] commonly known as *perfidy*.[62]

---

[58]   Rosas, *The Legal Status of Prisoners of War* at 333 (cited in note 45). Continuing, the author notes:

> [T]his provision does not seem to imply that all members of regular forces have to wear uniforms in all situations in order to benefit from prisoner-of-war status. On the other hand it serves as a reminder that the uniform continues to be the *normal* way for *regular* combatants to distinguish themselves from the civilian population.

(Emphasis added). The footnote in support thereof states:

> In the 1976 report of Committee III [of the Diplomatic Conference] it is stated that "regulars who are assigned to tasks where they must wear civilian clothes, as may be the case, for example, with advisers assigned to certain resistance units, are not required to wear the uniform when on such assignments."

Id at 349 n 592 (citing CDDH/236/Rev 1, 29). See also Howard S. Levie, 2 *Protection of War Victims: Protocol I to the 1949 Geneva Conventions* 475 (Oceana 1980).

[59]   The uniform requirement has not been codified for military operations short of international armed conflict.

[60]   Hague Convention IV, Annex art 24 (cited in note 29). See also Spaight, *War Rights on Land* at 152–56 (cited in note 38); Oppenheim, 2 *International Law* at 428 (cited in note 37); War Office [UK], *The Law of War on Land* at 101 (cited in note 35).

[61]   Hague Convention IV, Annex art 23(b) (cited in note 29).

[62]   The distinction between a ruse and perfidy is offered as "whenever a belligerent has expressly or tacitly engaged, and is therefore bound by a moral obligation, to speak the truth to an enemy, it is perfidy to betray his confidence, because it constitutes a breach of good faith." Oppenheim, 2 *International Law* at 430 (cited in note 37). See also US Army Field Manual 27-10 at 22, ¶¶ 49–55 (cited in note 41).

Chicago Journal of International Law

Article 23 of the Annex to the 1899 Hague II states:

> 23. Besides the prohibitions provided by special Conventions, it is especially prohibited—
>
> (a) To kill or wound treacherously individuals belonging to the hostile nation or army.[63]

This article, along with Articles 29 and 31, were re-codified with non-substantive changes in the Annex to the 1907 Hague IV. They are important for several reasons. They constitute recognition of the general obligation for military forces to fight in uniform. However, it is not a war crime for military personnel to wear or fight in civilian clothing unless it is done for the purpose of and with the result of killing treacherously. What constituted "killing treacherously" was defined as perfidy in Article 37 of Additional Protocol I:

> It is prohibited to kill, injure or capture an adversary by resort to perfidy. Acts inviting the confidence of an adversary to lead him to believe that he is entitled to, or is obliged to accord, protection under the rules of international law applicable in armed conflict, with intent to betray that confidence, shall constitute perfidy. The following acts are examples of perfidy:
>
> (a)   the feigning of an intent to negotiate under a flag of truce or of a surrender;
>
> (b)   the feigning of an incapacitation by wounds or sickness;
>
> (c)   the feigning of civilian, non-combatant status; and
>
> (d)   the feigning of protected status by the use of signs, emblems or uniforms of the United Nations or of neutral or other States not Parties to the conflict.[64]

In order to be perfidy, the act must be the proximate cause of the killing, injury, or capture of the enemy.[65] But while the Diplomatic Conference codified perfidy, it limited criminal liability. Perfidy was made a Grave Breach only if it involves "the perfidious use ... of the distinctive emblem of the Red Cross, Red Crescent or Red Lion and Sun."[66] Wearing civilian attire or feigning civilian status was not designated a Grave Breach.

Each differs from US and Coalition Special Forces operating in non-standard uniforms as part of heavily armed units clearly known and identifiable by the Taliban and al Qaeda in the war in Afghanistan. Special Forces' wear of non-standard uniforms, whether partial BDU or the indigenous apparel of their

---

[63]   32 Stat 1803 (1899); see also Schindler and Toman, *The Laws of Armed Conflicts* at 82–83 (cited in note 16).

[64]   Id at art 37.

[65]   See Bothe, Partsch, and Solf, *New Rules for Victims of Armed Conflicts* at 204 (cited in note 32). As neither Afghanistan nor the United States is a State Party to Additional Protocol I, the United States is bound by this article only to the extent that it codifies customary law.

[66]   Additional Protocol I art 85, ¶ 3(f), 16 ILM at 1428 (cited in note 32).

Northern Alliance partners, including their distinctive *pakol* hats and/or tribal scarves, did not constitute perfidy. US Army Civil Affairs wearing of Western-style civilian clothing or indigenous attire in Afghanistan would not have constituted perfidy unless it had been done for the purpose of and with the result of killing treacherously. The NGOs' complaint made no such allegation, and no evidence has surfaced to suggest such conduct.

That being said, the devil always has been in the details in drawing the line between perfidy and the allowance for military personnel to operate in denied areas in civilian attire. At the heart of the balance is the law of war principle of distinction. State practice, of which more will be said, suggests that the lines between the two are far from clear.

There is logic to this history. State tolerance of Special Forces' fighting in civilian clothing is limited to special circumstances, such as support for partisans, which is consistent with. humanitarian tolerance for captured guerrillas. It follows efforts by many, including the International Committee of the Red Cross, to provide prisoner of war protection to all and not to prosecute except in the most egregious circumstances, such as terrorism and *treacherous* use of civilian clothing.[67] The drafters of Article 44 had a better sense of state practice than did critics of US and Coalition Special Forces wear of non-standard uniforms.

---

[67] This approach, taken by the United States in Vietnam, was praised by the International Committee of the Red Cross; see Prugh, *Law at War* at 66–67 (cited in note 15).

This legal approach is not new. During the American Civil War (1861–1865) and the Anglo-Boer War (1899–1902), rebel soldiers captured wearing either enemy uniforms or civilian clothing were treated as prisoners of war and not prosecuted unless their actions involved treachery. See, for example, Spaight, *War Rights on Land* at 105–09 (cited in note 38). Boer commandos' wearing of portions of British uniforms produced one of the more sensational historic examples. In 1902 three Australian officers serving with the Bushveldt Carbineers were tried by British court-martial for murder of captured Boers and murder of a civilian. Their plea with regard to the murder of the captured Boers was one of superior orders on the basis that Lord Kitchener had ordered the execution of Boers wearing "British khaki." The prosecution argued that Boer punishment was authorized only if the captured Boers had worn British khaki with intent to deceive. Convicted, two of the three—Captain Harry "Breaker" Morant and Lieutenant Peter Handcock—were executed by British firing squad, resulting in a controversy between Great Britain and Australia that remains to this day. See, for example, Nick Bleszynski, *Shoot Straight, You Bastards!*, (Random House (Australia) 2002) (on file with author) (this title is based upon Morant's last words). The incident was the basis for the 1979 Australian movie *Breaker Morant*, starring Edward Woodward and Bryan Brown. Its screenplay was based upon the novel by Kit Denton, *The Breaker* (Angus & Robertson 1973). Subsequently, Denton authored the non-fiction *Closed File: The True Story behind the Execution of Breaker Morant and Peter Handcock* (Rigby 1983) (on file with author), less sympathetic to Morant than *The Breaker*. Comprehensive, authoritative accounts are contained in Arthur Davey, ed, *Breaker Morant and the Bushveldt Carbineers* (Van Riebeeck Society 1987) and William Woolmore, *The Bushveldt Carbineers and the Pietersburg Light Horse* (Slouch Hat Publications 2000) (on file with author).

Into the midst of this discussion steps the global war on terrorism. Terrorists are not entitled to law of war protection, and the law of war is not applicable as such in counter-terrorist operations.[68] Counter-terrorist units have been authorized to use hollow-point or other expanding ammunition,[69] for example, and have worn civilian clothing or non-standard uniforms on missions.[70] President Bush's radio address to the nation and the world on September 29, 2001,[71] in response to the September 11th terror attacks on the World Trade Center and the Pentagon, may have prompted some in the military to err initially and assume that law of war rules relating to uniform wear were not applicable in the military operations that followed in Afghanistan.

This leads to the proper point for review of State practice.

B. WHAT IS STATE PRACTICE?

State practice is important to answering legal questions because it forms a basis for determining customary international law.[72] State practice—a synonym

---

68   See Toman, *The Status of Al Qaeda/Taliban Detainees* at 287 (cited in note 30).

69   Headquarters, Department of the Army, Office of The Judge Advocate General, DAJA-IA Memorandum 1985/7026, Subject: Use of Expanding Ammunition by US Military Forces in Counterterrorist Incidents (Sept 23, 1985) (on file with author). Hollow-point or expanding small arms ammunition is prohibited in international armed conflict by the Hague Declaration Concerning Expanding Bullets of 29 July 1899. See Schindler and Toman, *The Laws of Armed Conflicts* at 109 (cited in note 16). The United States is not a State Party to this treaty, but has taken the position that it will adhere to its terms in its military operations in international armed conflict to the extent that its application is consistent with the object and purpose of Article 23(e) of the Annex to the Hague Convention IV (cited in note 29), which prohibits employment of "arms, projectiles, or material calculated to cause unnecessary suffering." See, for example, Headquarters, Department of the Army, Office of The Judge Advocate General, DAJA-IO Memorandum, Subject: 5.56mm, 77-grain Sierra MatchKing™ Bullet; Legal Review (May 19, 2000) (on file with author).

70   For example, German counterterrorist *Grenzschutzgruppe 9* ("GSG-9") and British Special Air Service soldiers wore civilian clothing in the October 18, 1977 hostage rescue of Lufthansa flight 181 in Mogadishu, Somalia. Barry Davies, *Fire Magic* (photo section) (Bloomsbury 1994); Rolf Tophoven, *GSG9: The German Response to Terrorism* 66–73 (Bernard & Graefe Verlag 1985). The SAS wore non-standard fireproof uniforms during its hostage rescue operation in the Iranian Embassy at Princes Gate in London on May 6, 1980. Michael Paul Kennedy, *Soldier 'I' SAS* (photo section) (Bloomsbury 1989); General Sir Peter de la Billiere, *Looking for Trouble* 319–3 (photo section) (Harper Collins 1994). Other examples are provided in the State Practice sections of this paper (Section IV.B and Appendix).

71   Available online at <http://www.whitehouse.gov/news/releases/2001/09/20010929.html> (visited Oct 9, 2003).

72   As the United States Supreme Court stated in *The Paquete Habana*, 175 US 677, 700 (1900):

     International law is part of our law, and must be ascertained and administered by the courts of justice . . . [W]here there is no treaty, and no controlling . . .

for military history—reveals how governments interpret, apply, and/or enforce law of war treaty provisions.

As illustrated in the Appendix, state practice in international armed conflict and other military operations contains a significant record of Special Forces wear of civilian attire, non-standard uniforms, and/or enemy uniforms as a ruse or for other reasons. Beginning with Colonel T.E. Lawrence, the celebrated Lawrence of Arabia, state practice reflects an overt tolerance bordering on admiration for special forces wearing civilian clothing when working with indigenous persons in enemy-denied areas, whether for intelligence gathering or combat operations.[73] Special Forces personnel captured while wearing civilian clothing have been treated as spies rather than charged with a war crime, while Special Forces who fought in civilian clothing and returned safely have been honored as heroes.

---

judicial decision, resort must be had to the customs and usages of civilized nations.

[73]   In an experience similar to that of US Special Forces in Afghanistan eighty-five years later, Lawrence donned indigenous attire at the request of the Arab forces he joined, in part because the only soldiers many Arabs had seen wearing khaki were Turkish, the enemy. Mindful of the death of Captain William Shakespear the previous year because he wore his British uniform, Lawrence obliged his hosts. Wilson, *Lawrence of Arabia* at 334–35 (cited in note 7). In August 1917 Lawrence penned his *Twenty-Seven Articles*, lessons learned from his service in the Arab Revolt. They include:

> 18.   Disguise is not advisable. Except in special areas let it be clearly known that you are a British officer and a Christian. At the same time if you can wear Arab kit when with the tribes you will acquire their trust and intimacy to a degree impossible in uniform. It is however dangerous and difficult. They make no special allowances for you when you dress like them. Breaches of etiquette not charged against a foreigner are not condoned to you in Arab clothes. You will be like an actor in a foreign theatre, playing a part day and night for months, without rest, and for an anxious stake. Complete success, which is when the Arabs forget your strangeness and speak naturally before you, counting you one of themselves, is perhaps only attainable in character: while half success (all that most of us strive for—the other costs too much) is easier to win in British things, and you yourself will last longer, physically and mentally, in the comfort that they mean. Also then the Turks will not hang you when you're caught.
>
> 19.   If you wear Arab things, wear the best. Clothes are significant among the tribes, and you must wear the appropriate, and appear at ease in them. Dress like a Sherif—if they agree to it.
>
> 20.   If you wear Arab things at all, go all the way. Leave your English friends and customs on the coast, and fall back on Arab habits entirely.

Id at 963. As Lawrence indicates in Rule 18, he was fully aware of the risks involved in wearing something other than his uniform. He was captured by Turkish forces in Deraa on November 20, 1917, while on a reconnaissance mission in Arab attire. He was well known and sought after by Turkish forces. Identified, he was subjected to severe sexual abuse by his captors before managing to escape. Id at 459–61, 1083 n49.

As noted by James Maloney Spaight, Colonel Lawrence was not alone in wearing civilian clothing on combat missions during World War I. See Spaight, *Air Power and War Rights* at 273–74 (cited in note 31).

Chicago Journal of International Law

The actions of Colonel Lawrence in all likelihood were not the first in which indigenous attire was worn, but one of the more influential. An appreciation of the list that follows necessitates a brief historical overview.

Germany's annexation of Austria in 1938 sparked interest within the British military in the potential necessity for irregular operations. Recalling the Spanish guerrillas in Wellington's campaign against the French in the Peninsular War (1807–1809),[74] Boer commando success against the British in the 1899–1902 Anglo-Boer War,[75] Colonel Lawrence's success, the British experience in facing Sinn Fein in Ireland (1919–1921),[76] Chinese guerrilla operations against Japan in the Sino-Japanese War,[77] and other guerrilla activities in other conflicts, in 1938 the Research Branch of the British General Staff ("GS(R)") began research that led to preparation of Field Service Regulations entitled *The Art of Guerrilla Warfare*, *The Partisan Leaders' Handbook*, and *How to Use High Explosives*, all subsequently noted in *GS(R) Report No. 8 Investigation of the Possibilities of Guerrilla Activities*.[78]

---

[74]   David Gates, *The Spanish Ulcer: A History of the Peninsular War* 35 (W.W. Norton 1986), noting Wellington's comment that because of the guerrillas' activities, "The French armies have no communications and one army has no knowledge of the position or of the circumstances in which others are placed, whereas I have knowledge of all that passes on all sides." The term *guerrilla* is generally regarded as originating from the Peninsular War. See also David G. Chandler, *The Campaigns of Napoleon* 593–660 (MacMillan 1966). Chandler notes: "Although the regular Spanish armies were destroyed or scattered, there were no signs that the will to resist of the Spanish people had been even substantially weakened. Popular patriotism, religious fanaticism and an almost hysterical hatred for the French remained as strong as ever [in January 1809], and over the next five years the world was to see the development of a new type of ruthless war waged by guerrillas who refused to come down into the open plains . . . and . . . defied all efforts to destroy them, in the meantime causing a heavy toll of French casualties." Id at 659–60. See also Don W. Alexander, *Rod of Iron: French Counterinsurgency Policy in Aragon during the Peninsular War* (Scholarly Resources 1985).

[75]   Deneys Reitz, *Commando: A Boer Journal of the Boer War* (Praeger 1970). For general reading, see Byron Farwell, *The Great Anglo-Boer War* (Harper & Row 1976); Thomas Pakenham, *The Boer War* (Random House 1979). The term *commando* originated in Boer use.

[76]   M.R.D. Foot, *The IRA and the Origins of SOE*, in M.R.D. Foot, ed, *War and Society: Historical Essays in Honour and Memory of J.R. Western, 1928–1971* at 57 (Barnes & Noble 1973); M.R.D. Foot, *Resistance: European Resistance to Nazism, 1940–1945*, 7 (McGraw-Hill 1977).

[77]   See generally Frank Dorn, *The Sino-Japanese War, 1937–41* (MacMillan 1974).

[78]   These two publications were distributed free in the hundreds of thousands throughout Europe and Southeast Asia during World War II, either in English or in translated form in Burmese, Chinese, Czech, Danish, Dutch, French, German, Greek, Italian, Malay, Norwegian, Polish, Serbo-Croat, Slovak, Slovene, and Thai. See M.R.D. Foot, *SOE: An Outline History of the Special Operations Executive, 1940–46* at 14 (University Publishers of America 1984).

The association of British thinking with Lawrence's success, the Anglo-Boer War, the Irish War, and the Sino-Japanese War is acknowledged in Jørgen Hæstrup, *Europe Ablaze* 38–39 (Odense 1978); Foot, *SOE in France* at 2–4 (cited at note 34); Foot, *SOE:*

Commencement of the Second World War with the German invasion of Poland on September 1, 1939, revealed Germany's first use of Special Forces in civilian clothing, enemy uniforms, or non-standard attire as a ruse to seize critical objectives.[79] British focus on partisan warfare and Special Forces was renewed with Germany's invasion of Western Europe, the fall of France, and British Army evacuation from Dunkirk in May 1940. Standing alone, the British leadership identified several means for action. In addition to traditional means such as naval blockade and aerial bombing, it directed commando raids and "the undermining of enemy morale and production possibilities through close co-operation with exile governments and through them—or without them—with Resistance Movements in the territories occupied by the enemy."[80] The Charter for the British Special Operations Executive ("SOE") received War Cabinet approval on July 22, 1940.[81] At this time Prime Minister Winston S. Churchill offered his oft-quoted edict: "And now set Europe ablaze."[82] Working closely with exile governments, the British Government began making contact with potential resistance movements throughout Nazi-occupied Europe, ultimately

---

An Outline History at 11–15 (cited above); David Stafford, *Britain and European Resistance, 1940–1945* at 19, 21 (MacMillian 1980); Peter Wilkinson and Joan Bright Ashley, *Gubbins & SOE* 34, 36 (Leo Cooper 1993); W.J.M. Mackenzie, *The Secret History of SOE: The Special Operations Executive, 1940–1945* at 10, 38–39 (St. Ermin's 2000). The Mackenzie volume, the official "in-house" history of the British Special Operations Executive, was compiled in the late 1940s. It remained classified until 1998, and reached open publication in redacted form in 2000.

[79]   James Lucas, *Kommando: German Special Forces of World War Two* (St Martin's 1985). Specific examples are provided on the list in the Appendix.

[80]   Hæstrup, *Europe Ablaze* at 37 (cited in note 78). There is no evidence to suggest establishment of the Special Operations Executive was a reprisal for earlier German actions. A *reprisal* is an act that would be unlawful if not committed for the purpose of reprisal, done for the purpose of compelling the other belligerent to observe the law of war, with strict standards for its execution. W. Hays Parks, *A Few Tools in the Prosecution of War Crimes*, 149 Milit L Rev 73, 84 (1995). See generally, Frits Kalshoven, *Belligerent Reprisals* (A.W. Sijthoff 1971); Andrew D. Mitchell, *Does One Illegality Merit Another? The Law of Belligerent Reprisals in International Law*, 170 Milit L Rev 155 (2001); Shane Darcy, *The Evolution of the Law of Belligerent Reprisals*, 175 Milit L Rev 184 (2003). At the same time, early German operations made it clear to the British leadership that Germany had "set a fashion for subversive activities in countries they proposed to conquer which defied the Queensbury rules of international conduct that staider powers had recently observed. This . . . debased the standards of how countries ought to behave to each other; however reluctant, these powers had to join the new fashion or succumb." Foot, *SOE in France* at 1 (cited in note 34).

[81]   J.R.M. Butler, ed, 1 *History of the Second World War: Grand Strategy* 260–61 (HMSO 1957). The Charter, WP(40)271, can be found in Mackenzie, *The Secret History of SOE* at 753–55 (cited in note 78).

[82]   See Foot, *SOE in France* at 11 (cited in note 34); E.H. Cookridge, *Set Europe Ablaze* 1 (Thomas Y. Crowell 1966). Churchill's early enthusiasm for irregular warfare is acknowledged in Foot, *SOE in France* at 7 (cited in note 34).

providing them personnel and material support, subsequently coordinating their actions to link them directly to the British and Allied war effort.[83]

It is important to understand what SOE was, and what it was not. SOE was an independent secret service.[84] It was not a military service. But SOE relied heavily upon assignment of military officers to it, coordination of operations with the military chiefs of staff, and was dependent on the military services for personnel, support, supply and transportation.[85] Although intelligence was sometimes a by-product of its activities, SOE was not an intelligence collection agency.[86] It was intended for its operatives to engage in clandestine, subversive operations in civilian clothing. The dagger lay concealed beneath the cloak.[87] In Prime Minister Churchill's words, this was "'ungentlemanly warfare' in which the 'Geneva Convention' rules do not apply and the price of failure was often a

---

[83]   See Hæstrup, *Europe Ablaze* at 37, 41 (cited in note 78). For detailed histories by country, see Mackenzie, *The Secret History of SOE* at 133–687 (cited in note 78); Foot, *SOE in France* (cited in note 34); Ian Trenowden, *Operations Most Secret: SOE: The Malayan Theatre* (Crécy 1994); Charles Cruickshank, *SOE in the Far East* (Oxford 1983); Charles Cruickshank, *SOE in Scandinavia* (Oxford 1986); M.R.D. Foot, *SOE in the Low Countries* (St. Ermin's 2001); Knud J.V. Jesperson, *No Small Achievement: Special Operations Executive and the Danish Resistance, 1940–1945* (University of Southern Denmark 2002); Olav Riste and Berit Nökleby, *Norway 1940–1945: The Resistance Movement* (Johan Grundt Tanum Forlag 1973); Tore Gjelsvik, *Norwegian Resistance, 1940–1945* (C. Hurst 1979) (Thomas Kinsgston Derry, trans).

[84]   See Foot, *SOE: An Outline History* at 21 (cited in note 78).

[85]   See Mackenzie, *The Secret History of SOE* at 348–67 (cited in note 78); Foot, *SOE in France* at 74–93 (cited in note 34). SOE was dependent upon the Royal Air Force and Royal Navy for transport. See, for example, Gibb McCall, *Flight Most Secret: Air Missions for SOE and SIS* (William Kimber 1981); Terence O'Brien, *The Moonlight War: The Story of Clandestine Operations in South-East Asia, 1944–45* (William Collins Sons 1987). US Army Air Corps support is discussed in Ben Parnell, *Carpetbaggers: America's Secret War in Europe* (Eakin 1987). Sea transport is described in part in Cruickshank, *SOE in Scandinavia* at 72–92 (Sweden), 91–121 (Norway), and Appendix 1 (cited in note 83). The latter chapter and Appendix 1 summarize "The Shetland Bus Service," which transported agents into Norway—initially by fishing boat, then by submarine chasers furnished by the United States Navy. See also id at 96; David Howarth, *The Shetland Bus* (Thomas Nelson & Sons 1951) (on file with author).

[86]   Responsibility for intelligence collection belonged to the Secret Intelligence Service (SIS). See F.H. Hinsley, et al, 1 *British Intelligence in the Second World War: Its Influence on Strategy and Operations* 277–78 (HMSO 1979).

       No attempt has been made to list or summarize the various British secret agencies during World War II or their missions. The special operations mission of SOE was performed by its SO2 branch, while SO1 was responsible for covert propaganda. A reader interested in the larger picture is invited to read any of the opening chapters of the various books by M.R.D. Foot cited herein and/or *British Intelligence in the Second World War I* at 3–43 and Hinsley et al, 2 *British Intelligence in the Second World War* 3–40 (HMSO 1981).

[87]   Foot, *SOE in France* at 11–12 (cited in note 34).

slow and terrible death."[88] Thus the British Government and SOE operatives consciously entered into this form of operations fully cognizant of its law of war implications.

The "Geneva Conventions" baby had not been tossed out with the bath water. As was the case with US Special Forces in Afghanistan in 2002, restrictions were placed on wearing civilian attire. Military personnel providing transport to SOE personnel to and from an operation were required to be in uniform, for example, while late-war operations enabled some to wear uniforms.[89] For post-D-Day operations, SOE personnel were provided armbands for partisans and British military personnel not in uniform.[90] Prior to and after D-Day, a clear showing of military necessity as it related to the mission was necessary for authorization to wear civilian clothing. For example, on May 30, 1943, the British War Office informed the Commander-in-Chief, India, that the Chief of Staff had decided:

> No member of the armed forces . . . should be sent on military operations, however hazardous, in civilian clothes, except in the case of subversive activities for which civilian clothes are essential.[91]

In addition to SOE, which was to work with underground movements in Axis-controlled nations, the British also recognized the potential of commando units to fight independently and conduct "tip-and-run" raids of not more than forty-eight hours. Their formation began simultaneously with the establishment of SOE.[92] Generally performed in uniform or non-standard uniform, the list of

---

88   Dodds-Parker, *Setting Europe Ablaze* at 36, 76, 198 (cited in note 20). The "Geneva Conventions" were referred to as a general reference to the law of war. Churchill's reference to the "Geneva Convention" otherwise would have been to the Geneva Convention Relative to the Treatment of Prisoners of War of July 27, 1929, 47 UST 2021–73. Article 1 thereof incorporated by reference Article 1 of the Annex to the Hague Convention IV to establish criteria for prisoner of war status.

89   Dodds-Parker, *Setting Europe Ablaze* at 44, 145 (cited in note 20).

90   See Foot, *SOE: An Outline History* at 98 (cited in note 78); Dodds-Parker, *Setting Europe Ablaze* at 85, 124 (cited in note 20).

91   India Office Records L/WS/1/1296, cited in Cruickshank, *SOE in the Far East* at 249 (cited in note 83). Military necessity could change in a moment. For example, British Liaison Officer Major Harvard Gunn was assigned to work with partisans in Southern France in summer 1944. In his official report he noted: "Difficulty in movement, area surrounded by German garrisons; made first recce area BARCELONNETTE-LARCHE, had to travel as Gendarme, uniform hidden." Historian Arthur Layton Funk continues the story while explaining Major Gunn's dilemma: "Gunn's uniform . . . consisted of the kilts of the Seaforth Highlanders, difficult to conceal under any circumstances, but, wishing to let it be known that Allied support had arrived, Gunn and the other British officers (as well as Jedburghs and OGs [Operational Groups]) wore their uniforms as frequently as feasible." Arthur Layton Funk, *Hidden Ally: The French Resistance, Special Operations, and the Landings in Southern France, 1944* at 86 (Greenwood 1992).

92   See Butler, 2 *History of the Second World War: Grand Strategy* 259 (HMSO 1957); Ministry of Defence, *Combined Operations: The Official Story of the Commandos* 3–4 (HMSO 1943); Hilary St. George Saunders, *The Green Beret: The Story of the Commandos, 1940–1945* at 21–25

Chicago Journal of International Law

examples of state practice that follows nonetheless shows that commando units did resort to civilian attire or enemy uniforms on occasion.

Germany invaded Russia on June 22, 1941. In response, Russian Premier Josef Stalin declared that day:

> The struggle against Germany must not be looked upon as an ordinary war. . . . It is not merely a fight between two armies ... in order to engage the enemy there must be bands of partisans and saboteurs working underground everywhere. . . . In territories occupied by the enemy, conditions must be made so impossible that he cannot hold out.[93]

Soviet partisan warfare differed from that of Great Britain and (subsequently) the United States, if perhaps only slightly. Whereas Great Britain and the United States exported support for underground movements in Axis-occupied nations, the Soviet Union supported partisan warfare within its own territory occupied by Germany, operating along interior lines.[94] The partisan movement, organized, trained, and directed by Soviet Army personnel, was

---

(Michael Joseph 1949); Bernard Fergusson, *The Watery Maze: The Story of Combined Operations* 47 (Holt 1961); Charles Messenger, *The Commandos, 1940–1946* at 17–32 (William Kimber 1985). There were distinctions between SOE and Combined Operations. While the former often operated in civilian attire, the latter normally carried out its missions in uniform. Combined Operations raids normally were to be executed by fifty or more British troops, to be withdrawn following the operation. SOE operations were executed primarily by foreign personnel numbering no more than thirty, who would "fade into the landscape" following their mission. See Mackenzie, *The Secret History of SOE* at 94 (cited in note 78). The original commando Independent Companies subsequently were joined by other British special forces, such as the Long Range Desert Group, Special Air Service, Special Boat Service, as well as clandestine reconnaissance units such as the Combined Operations Pilotage Parties. See Roy Farran, *Winged Dagger: Adventures on Special Service* (Collins 1948) (reprinted Cassel 1998); Virginia Cowles, *The Phantom Major: The Story of David Stirling and the S.A.S. Regiment* (Collins 1958); Warner, *The Special Air Service* (cited in note 5); Strawson, *A History of the S.A.S. Regiment* (cited in note 5); Alan Hoe, *David Stirling: The Authorised Biography of the Founder of the SASs* 41–225 (Little, Brown 1992); Derrick Harrison, *These Men Are Dangerous: The Early Years of the S.A.S.* (Blandford Press 1957); W.B. Kennedy Shaw, *Long Range Desert Group: World War II Action in North Africa* (Collins 1945) (reprinted Greenhill 2000); Lt. Col. David Lloyd Owen, *The Desert My Dwelling Place* (Cassell 1957); Michael Crichton-Stuart, *G Patrol* (William Kimber 1958); John W. Gordon, *The Other Desert War: British Special Forces in North Africa, 1940–1943* (Greenwood 1987); Brendan O'Carroll, *Kiwi Scorpions: The Story of the New Zealanders in the Long Range Desert Group* (Token 2000); John Lodwick, *The Filibusters: The Story of the Special Boat Service* (Methuen 1947); C.E. Lucas Phillips, *Cockleshell Heroes* (Heinemann 1956); G.B. Courtney, *SBS in World War Two: The Story of the Original Special Boat Section of the Army Commandos* (Robert Hale 1983); James D. Ladd, *SBS: The Invisible Raiders: The History of the Special Boat Squadron from World War Two to the Present* (Arms and Armour 1983); Bill Strutton and Michael Pearson, *The Secret Invaders* (Hodder and Stoughton 1958); Ian Trenowden, *Stealthily by Night: The COPPists Clandestine Beach Reconnaissance and Operations in World War II* (Crécy 1995).

93   See Stafford, *Britain and European Resistance* at 68 (cited in note 78).

94   Hæstrup notes that the partisan organs worked closely with the General Staff of the Soviet Armies and with the Central Staff of the Partisan Movement. *Europe Ablaze* at 36 (cited in note 78).

substantial. In the month of July 1943, partisan forces carried out 10,000 separate demolitions of track to impede German re-supply efforts.[95] During the night of July 4, 1944 alone, partisans laid 4,110 separate demolition charges on rail lines;[96] on June 19, partisans planted over 5,000 mines on the roads and railroads behind the Second and Fourth German Armies.[97] While it was estimated that 250,000 people were directly engaged in partisan operations by 1944, Soviet authorities boasted that every Soviet civilian in Nazi-occupied territory was at least indirectly involved in partisan activities, and on September 6, 1942, the partisan movement achieved the nominal status of a separate branch of the Soviet military—something thought about in the United Kingdom by some, but never achieved in either the United Kingdom or the United States.[98] Like underground operations supported by the United Kingdom and United States, Soviet partisan operations—with civilians and military personnel fighting in civilian attire—were state approved and directed.

The United States' movement into partisan operations closely followed Russian and British actions. Early in World War II, the Roosevelt Administration established the Office of Strategic Services (OSS). The forerunner of the Central Intelligence Agency, the OSS was a hybrid organization, led by Major General William A. Donovan, a distinguished, decorated former Army officer, under the administrative cognizance of the Joint Chiefs of Staff but under operational control of the theater commander.[99] It was

---

[95]   John Erickson, *The Road to Berlin: Continuing the History of Stalin's War with Germany* 114 (Westview 1983). For a detailed discussion of Soviet partisan warfare, see Earl F. Ziemke and Magna E. Bauer, *Moscow to Stalingrad: Decision in the East* 199–219, 252–54, 330, 434–35 (Military Heritage rev ed 1985) (on file with author); Earl F. Ziemke, *Stalingrad to Berlin* 30, 103–05, 303–08 (Military Heritage 1968) (on file with author).

[96]   Ziemke, *Stalingrad to Berlin* at 141 (cited in note 95). For results in other German-occupied nations, see Henri Michel, *The Shadow War: European Resistance, 1939–1945* at 214 (Harper & Row 1972) (Richard Barry, trans).

[97]   Ziemke, *Stalingrad to Berlin* at 315 (cited in note 95).

[98]   Ziemke and Bauer, *Moscow to Stalingrad* at 330, 435 (cited in note 95); Ziemke, *Stalingrad to Berlin* at 303 (cited in note 95). In June 1944, partisans in Belorussia numbered 150,000 in 150 brigades and 49 detachments. Id at 304.

[99]   Presidential Military Order, Office of Strategic Services, 3 CFR 1308 (1938–1942); JCS 67, Subject: Office of Strategic Services (June 21, 1942) (on file with author). The latter stated in part that "Under direction of the Joint U.S. Chiefs of Staff . . . [OSS will] prepare plans for and . . . execute subversive activities." See also R. Harris Smith, *OSS: The Secret History of America's First Central Intelligence Agency* (California 1972); Edward Hymoff, *The OSS in World War II* (Richardson and Steirman 1972); Richard Dunlop, *Behind Japanese Lines: With the OSS in Burma* (Rand McNally 1979); William Casey, *The Secret War against Hitler* (Regnery Gateway 1988); Roger Hilsman, *American Guerrilla: My War behind Japanese Lines* (Brassey's (US) 1990); Tom Moon, *This Grim and Savage Game: OSS and the Beginning of U.S. Covert Operations in World War II* (Burning Gate 1991) (reprinted Da Capo 2000); Franklin Lindsay, *Beacons in the Night: With the OSS and Tito's Partisans in Wartime Yugoslavia* (Stanford 1993); Mills, Mills, and Brunner, *OSS Special*

Chicago Journal of International Law

an organization focused on espionage, sabotage, and partisan support. US Army personnel provided a major part of the OSS strength, which reached its maximum of 13,000 in December 1944. US Army Special Forces traces its lineage to OSS.[100]

By the spring of 1944, SOE and OSS were operating together in a variety of missions.[101] Some OSS units operated in uniform, while others did not under all circumstances. In one of its major efforts in France, OSS operational units worked in Nazi-occupied territory in direct support of the French Resistance. As a leading history notes:

> The first group consisted of seventy-seven Americans *who wore civilian clothes* as organizers of secret networks, as radio operators, or as instructors in the use of weapons and explosives. Thirty-three members of that group were active in France before 6 June 1944, D-Day.
>
> …
>
> The largest OSS group in France consisted of some 356 Americans who were members of Operational Groups (OGs). All recruits for the OGs were French-speaking volunteers from US Army units, primarily infantry and

---

Operations in China (cited in note 7); Dan Pinck, *Journey to Peking: A Secret Agent in Wartime China* (Naval Institute 2003).

100 Bank, *From OSS to Green Berets* (cited in note 5), traces the OSS to US Army Special Forces lineage, as does Paddock, *U.S. Army Special Warfare* (cited in note 5), and Sutherland, *The OSS Operational Groups*, 2 Special Warfare at 2–13 (cited in note 29). As indicated in the main text, the OSS also was a forerunner of the Central Intelligence Agency. See Thomas F. Troy, *Donovan and the CIA: A History of the Establishment of the Central Intelligence Agency* (CIA 1981); Richard Dunlop, *Donovan: America's Master Spy* (Rand McNally 1982).

101 SOE/Special Operations (SO) became Special Forces Headquarters on May 1, 1944. British SOE and US OSS components in the United Kingdom were amalgamated into the Special Projects Operation Center (SPOC) on May 23, 1944. See Foot, *SOE in France* at 32 (cited in note 34). As described by one authority, SPOC executed six types of missions:

    1.   British SOE missions . . . ;
    2.   French missions . . . ;
    3.   Inter-allied missions, made up of British, French, and American representatives;
    4.   Jedburghs. [discussed in this Section and Appendix];
    5.   Operational Groups. The Operational Groups were an elite OSS mission. They were paratroopers organized into squads of thirty who generally fought in component parts, for example, a half: thirteen men and two officers, all of them American volunteers for "extra hazardous duty" and assigned to OSS for special missions.
    6.   Counterscorch. These counter-sabotage teams consisted of French naval personnel sent to the ports of Marseille, Toulon, and Sète to keep the Germans from sabotaging the docks or blocking the channels.

Funk, *Hidden Ally* at 33–34 (cited in note 91).

engineer (for demolition experts). . . . Working in uniform, these teams parachuted behind the lines after D-Day to perform a variety of missions.[102]

In addition to its Operational Groups, OSS worked with SOE in Jedburgh teams. These teams were intended to be composed of an Englishman, an American, and a continental European member, each military, two of whom were officers; the third was the communications specialist.[103] The initial core contained fifty US officers fluent in French who were to parachute in uniform to resistance groups, initially throughout France during the weeks following the Allied landings on June 6, 1944. They would provide liaison with the underground, arm and train the Maquis, boost "patriotic morale," and coordinate resistance activity with Allied military strategy. Ninety-three Jedburgh teams parachuted into France to join the Maquis after D-Day, numbering three hundred French, British, and US officers. Eventually they served in other Nazi-occupied territory.[104]

While the Jedburghs normally operated in uniform, this was not always possible. In an operation in Nazi-occupied France, Major Horace Fuller, USMC, avoided capture as a result of accepting the advice of his French contact to wear civilian clothing, including during combat operations.[105]

---

[102]   Paddock, *U.S. Army Special Warfare* at 28 (cited in note 5) (emphasis added). As was the case in Great Britain, the United States formed its own commando units, such as the Army Rangers, the short-lived Marine Raiders, the Army's 5307th Composite Unit Provisional (Merrill's Marauders), and the Canadian/American First Special Service Force, all uniformed units and therefore beyond the scope of this article. For their history, see William O. Darby and William H. Baumer, *Darby's Rangers: We Led the Way* (Presidio 1980); Michael J. King, *William Orlando Darby: A Military Biography* (Archon 1981); Michael J. King, *Rangers: Selected Combat Operations in World War II* (Leavenworth Papers No 11, US Army Command and General Staff College 1985) (on file with author); *Merrill's Marauders: February–May 1944* (Historical Division, War Department 1945) (reprinted US Army Center for Military History 1990); Robert D. Burhans, *The First Special Service Force: A War History of the North Americans 1942–1944* (Infantry Journal 1947). First Special Service Force was a combined unit of Canadian and US Army forces. For the history of Marine Corps special operations units, see Charles L. Updegraph, Jr., *U.S. Marine Corps Special Units of World War II* at 1–35 (History and Museums Division, Headquarters, US Marine Corps 1972), and Joseph H. Alexander, *Edson's Raiders: The 1st Marine Raider Battalion in World War II* (Naval Institute 2001).

[103]   This nationality mix became more the exception than the rule. Of the 101 Jedburgh teams deployed to France, only 10 were so composed. Sutherland, *The OSS Operational Groups*, 2 Special Warfare at 13 n11 (cited in note 29); Funk, *Hidden Ally* at 141, 145 (cited in note 91).

[104]   Smith, *OSS: The Secret History of America's First Central Intelligence Agency* at 174–75 (cited in note 99); Bank, *From OSS to Green Berets* at 13–62 (cited in note 5); Cookridge, *Set Europe Ablaze* at 241 (cited in note 82); Stafford, *Britain and European Resistance* at 155 (cited in note 78); Foot, *Resistance* at 247 (cited in note 76); Foot, *SOE: An Outline History* at 151, 191 (cited in note 78); Foot, *SOE in France* at 33–34 (cited in note 34).

[105]   See Maj. Robert E. Mattingly, *Herringbone Cloak—GI Dagger: Marines of the OSS* 140 (US Marine Corps 1989). Another Marine, Captain Peter J. Ortiz, followed the SOE practice of parachuting in civilian clothes, but carried his Marine Corps uniform. In a touch of

Chicago Journal of International Law

Similar operations occurred in other theaters. On May 4, 1942, a US Navy officer formed Naval Group China. Composed of Navy and Marine Corps personnel, its mission was to establish radio intelligence posts, weather-gathering and lookout stations, form, supply, and train indigenous sabotage units, and conduct attacks on Japanese units and equipment. Also known as the Sino-America Cooperative Organization, it executed its operations successfully for the duration of the war, many of them in non-standard uniform or indigenous civilian attire, depending on the mission and situation.[106]

This is not the time to recount Allied support for partisan operations in World War II, nor what then were termed "commando" operations. However, several observations are relevant to the issue at hand. First, partisan operations were universal, occurring in every Axis-occupied nation, actively supported by each of the major Allies—the United Kingdom, the United States, and Soviet Union—and each government in exile.[107] Second, they were significant in their breadth and longevity. For example, the French Resistance Movement began shortly following German conquest in 1940 and continued through the war. By 1944, approximately three million men and women were associated with the various French Resistance organizations.[108] In Yugoslavia, 400,000 were involved in partisan operations.[109]

Resistance activity was dependent upon volunteers—whether partisans from the civilian population of Axis-controlled nations, civilian and military

---

bravado, he frequently wore it in populated areas, thereby alerting the Germans and forcing his team to remain on the move. Foot, *SOE in France* at 357 (cited in note 34). On one occasion Captain Ortiz entered a café dressed in a long (civilian) cape. Hearing a German soldier denigrate Americans, Ortiz drew his weapons—two .45 pistols—then threw back his cape to reveal his Marine uniform before opening fire on the Germans. Mattingly, *Herringbone Cloak—GI Dagger* at 116 (cited above). For his OSS service, Captain Ortiz was awarded two Navy Crosses, a Legion of Merit, made a member of the Order of the British Empire, and received the French Croix de Guerre. *Captain Peter J. Ortiz*, 18 Fortitudine 14 (Marine Corps History and Museums Division Historical Bulletin Fall 1988) (on file with author); Lt. Col. Harry W. Edwards, USMC (ret.), *A Different War: Marines in Europe and North Africa* 12–13 (History and Museums Division, US Marine Corps 1994); Benis Frank, *Colonel Peter Julien Ortiz, US Marine* (unpublished manuscript, on file with author). The author is indebted to Lieutenant Colonel Joseph Wheeler, USMC, for the last two documents.

106   Mills, Mills, and Brunner, *OSS Special Operations in China* at 9 (cited in note 7). Vice Adm. Milton E. Miles, USN, *A Different Kind of War* 274, 371 (Doubleday 1967); Pinck, *Journey to Peking: A Secret Agent in Wartime China* at 134 (cited in note 99); Dale Andrade, *Every Man a Tiger*, Naval Hist 16 (Nov/Dec 1994).

107   Hæstrup, *Europe Ablaze* at 35, 49 (cited in note 78); Michel, *The Shadow War* at 355 (cited in note 96).

108   Hæstrup, *Europe Ablaze* at 14 (cited in note 78).

109   Id at 50. SOE schools graduated 7,500 men and women for operations in Western Europe, and 4,000 for missions in Italy, Yugoslavia, Greece, Albania, Poland, Czechoslovakia, Hungary, Rumania, and elsewhere. See Cookridge, *Set Europe Ablaze* at 26 (cited in note 82).

personnel serving with the SOE or OSS, or members of Special Forces.[110] All were aware of the possible consequences if they were caught, whether in uniform or other attire. At the same time, execution as a spy if captured in something other than standard uniform was not a certainty.[111]

---

[110]   Hæstrup, *Europe Ablaze* at 22 (cited in note 78). See also Cruickshank, *SOE in the Far East* at 249 (cited in note 83), which in noting the Chief of Staff's May 30, 1943 communiqué to the Commander in Chief in India, continues: "The men must be volunteers and warned that if caught they were likely to be shot without trial." Cruickshank adds: "Of course SOE were equally powerless to order men to act as agents."

In his classic and humorous tale of his experience as an Army officer in OSS, Roger Hall repeats the warning provided him at the beginning of his OSS training:

> These units are to be parachuted deep behind enemy lines and carry out work which is designed to accomplish three things. First, organize guerrilla forces and lead them against the enemy. Second, disrupt enemy activity as much as possible. Third, send back by whatever means possible all intelligence that can be gathered. You will operate in uniform, but if you are captured, the chances are fifty to one you will not be treated as a prisoner of war. The work is highly confidential and dangerous. Knowing all this, do you still volunteer?

Roger Hall, *You're Stepping on My Cloak and Dagger* 20 (Norton 1957). See also Bank, *From OSS to Green Berets* at 79–80 (cited in note 5) and Mills, Mills, and Brunner, *OSS Special Operations in China* at 12 (cited in note 7).

[111]   For example, in 1942 two German spies, Johann Eppler and Heinrich Gerd Sandstette, were transported across the Libyan desert and into Cairo to collect intelligence on the British campaign in North Africa. Because they had German military paybooks on them at the time of their apprehension, they were treated as prisoners of war. Saul Kelly, *The Lost Oasis: The Desert War and the Hunt for Zerzura: The True Story behind* The English Patient 226, 228 (Westview 2003). The Eppler-Sanstette mission became the basis for Ken Follett's novel *The Key to Rebecca* (Signet 1981).

Captured SOE and OSS personnel faired unevenly, as noted in Foot, *SOE in France* at 465–69 (cited in note 34); Foot, *SOE in the Low Countries* at 72, 193, 276–77 (cited in note 83); Mackenzie, *The Secret History of SOE* at 636, 664 (cited in note 78); Bank, *From OSS to Green Berets* at 66 (cited in note 5) (noting that one captured OSS officer was executed, while another caught by German troops survived because he was not turned over to the Gestapo). Even when captured in uniform, Special Forces personnel often were murdered. For example, British Special Air Service (SAS) personnel were forced to change into civilian clothing before being taken into the woods to be executed. See Foot, *SOE in France* at 305, 405 (cited in note 34). The individual responsible, Paris *Sicherheitsdienst* ("SD") Leader Josef Keiffer, was captured after the war, tried, convicted, and hanged. See id at 305. Other British commandos captured in uniform suffered the same fate. Mackenzie, *The Secret History of SOE* at 653 (cited in note 78). An SAS War Crimes Investigation Team assisted in the capture of Germans suspected of murdering SOE or SAS personnel. See Anthony Kemp, *The Secret Hunters* (Michael O'Mara 1986).

Others fared better. Captured in North Africa in 1943, OSS officer Jerry Sage was sent to a prisoner of war camp after successfully concealing his OSS status and claiming to be a downed aviator. Jerry Sage, *Sage* (Miles Standish 1985) (on file with author). An SOE agent captured in Norway successfully employed the same cover story. See Mackenzie, *The Secret History of SOE* at 659 (cited in note 78). Similarly, David Stirling, a founder of the British Special Air Service, survived his capture. See Hoe, *David Stirling* at 223–57 (cited in note 92).

Chicago Journal of International Law

Partisan sabotage operations were regarded as a valuable alternative to highly inaccurate strategic bombing in Nazi-occupied territory, as the Allies sought to reduce collateral civilian casualties to friendly populations.[112] Partisan sabotage was the "smart bomb" of World War II. In its employment of very precise means, it was the epitome of the second facet of the fundamental law of war principle of distinction.[113] In some cases, the evidence was clear that

---

[112] The French, Dutch, Belgian, and Norwegian governments-in-exile expressed concern over collateral civilian damage and injuries resulting from Allied air attacks. See Michel, *The Shadow War* at 212, 216–17 (cited in note 96). As its author notes, "The Allies undoubtedly committed a major error in disregarding such appeals and in persisting to bomb Europe—including their friends in the Resistance." Id at 217. Sabotage vis-à-vis air attacks did reduce civilian casualties. An example is the successful SOE attack on the SCNF (French national railways) locomotive works at Fives, described as one of the largest and most important in France, on June 27, 1943. The factory was in a heavily populated area, and bombing would have caused many collateral civilian casualties. Dressed as gendarmerie with the raid leader disguised as Gestapo, the factory was attacked successfully with no loss of life. Foot, *SOE in France* at 266 (cited in note 34). Another example—the Peugeot factory at Sochaux near Montbéliard, which manufactured tank turrets—was taken out of action by an SOE-delivered satchel charge after an earlier Royal Air Force attack missed the target and resulted in heavy civilian casualties nearby. Foot, *SOE: An Outline History* at 219–20 (cited in note 78). For a list of key SOE industrial sabotage, see Foot, *SOE in France* at 505–17 (cited in note 34). Benjamin F. Jones, *The Moon is Down: The Jedburghs and Support to the French Resistance* (unpublished MA thesis, University of Nebraska, 1999) describes the Resistance process for infiltrating and attacking these targets. Foot, *SOE in France* at 505 (cited in note 34), notes that the industrial sabotage listed was accomplished with a total of approximately 3,000 pounds of explosive. In contrast, a single Royal Air Force Lancaster bomber could carry 14,000 pounds of bombs, with some modified to carry the 22,000 pound Grand Slam bomb. Sir Charles Webster and Noble Frankland, 1 *The Strategic Air Offensive against Germany, 1939–1945* at 452–53 (Sir James Butler, ed, History of the Second World War, United Kingdom Military Series) (HMSO 1961) (on file with author). For heavy bomber accuracy, see W. Hays Parks, *"Precision" and "Area" Bombing: Who Did Which, and When?*, 18 J Strategic Stud 147 (1995). In contrast to SOE accuracy through industrial sabotage, it took 9,070 bombs dropped by 3,024 US heavy bomber aircraft to achieve a 90 percent probability of a single hit on a target 60 by 100 feet in size. Richard P. Hallion, *Storm over Iraq: Air Power and the Gulf War* 283, Table 2 (Smithsonian 1992).

[113] *Distinction* is the customary international law obligation of parties to a conflict to engage only in military operations the effects of which distinguish between the civilian population (or individuals not taking a direct part in hostilities), and combatant forces or military objectives, directing the application of force solely against the latter.

The principle of distinction was acknowledged in the 1863 US Army General Orders No 100 (the Lieber Code). Articles 20 through 23 state:

20.   Public war is a state of armed hostility between sovereign nations or governments. It is a law and requisite of civilized existence that men live in political, continuous societies, forming organized units, called states or nations, whose constituents bear, enjoy, suffer, advance and retrograde together, in peace and in war.

21.   The citizen or native of a hostile country is thus an enemy, as one of the constituents of the hostile state or nation, and as such is subjected to the hardships of the war.

partisan/Special Forces sabotage often was more effective than air operations against the same targets,[114] while in other instances OSS-led partisans were able

---

22. Nevertheless, as civilization has advanced during the last centuries, so has likewise steadily advanced, especially in war on land, the distinction between the private individual belonging to a hostile country and the hostile country itself, with its men in arms. The principle has been more and more acknowledged that the unarmed citizen is to be spared in person, property, and honor as much as the exigencies of war will admit.

23. Private citizens are no longer murdered, enslaved, or carried off to distant parts, and the inoffensive individual is as little disturbed in his private relations as the commander of the hostile troops can afford to grant in the overruling demands of a vigorous war.

Schindler and Toman, *The Laws of Armed Conflicts* at 6–7 (cited in note 16).

Similarly, two UN General Assembly Resolutions acknowledge the principle. UN General Assembly Resolution No 2444 (XXIII 1968), adopted unanimously, states in part:

— That it is prohibited to launch attacks against the civilian population as such; [and]

— That distinction must be made at all times between persons taking part in the hostilities and members of the civilian population to the effect that the latter be spared as much as possible.

Schindler and Toman, *The Laws of Armed Conflicts* at 263 (cited in note 16).

UN General Assembly Resolution No 2675 (XXV 1970), adopted by a vote of 109–0, with 18 States abstaining or absent, states in part:

(2) In the conduct of military operations during armed conflicts, a distinction must be made at all times between persons actively taking part in the hostilities and civilian populations.

(3) In the conduct of military operations, every effort should be made to spare the civilian populations from the ravages of war, and all necessary precautions should be taken to avoid injury, loss or damage to civilian populations.

(4) Civilian populations as such should not be the object of military operations.

(5) Dwellings and other installations that are used only by civilian populations should not be the object of military operations.

Schindler and Toman, *The Laws of Armed Conflicts* at 267 (cited in note 16).

114 See Mackenzie, *The Secret History of SOE* at 599 (cited in note 78), which provides the following report from a French railway engineer who reached England in December 1943:

Aircraft attacks on Locomotives

Since the beginning of 1943 650 locomotives have been hit (an average of 70 a month) out of 10,200 in service.

The damage is very slight and the average period of repair is a fortnight. There are therefore on an average 35 locomotives under repair, about 0.34 percent of the total.

In order to achieve this derisory result 78 railwaymen have been killed and 378 wounded. . . .

Sabotage of Locomotives

40 locomotives on an average were sabotaged each month, but the repairs required were much more serious. The average time required has not yet been established. But if we take it as six months, this means 240 locomotives under

to destroy heavily defended targets that had resisted air attack.[115] While the rationale for partisan or Special Forces attacks may have been selected over aerial attack more for political than law of war reasons,[116] it offers evidence of why governments chose not to condemn attacks in civilian clothing as a Grave Breach in Additional Protocol I. Special Forces/partisan unconventional warfare operations tied down Axis units that could have been used more effectively engaging Allied forces but for the partisan threat,[117] and significantly impaired German efforts to reinforce their defenses at Allied points of offensive ground operations.[118] Special Forces and their partisan allies performed other life-saving actions, such as the rescue of downed Allied aircrew and assistance in running escape routes.[119] Special Forces served as on-the-scene ambassadors where Allied combat operations killed innocent civilians.[120]

---

            repair, 2.40 percent of the total, eight times as many as those damaged by aircraft.

          See also Michel, *The Shadow War* at 215–16 (cited in note 96), describing the SOE attack on the Vermork heavy water facility in Norway.

[115]   Mills, Mills, and Brunner, *OSS Special Operations in China* at 45, 47, 186–203 (cited in note 7) describes one such case. The Yellow River Bridge carrying Ping-Han railway traffic had been attacked repeatedly but unsuccessfully by the 311th (US) Air Force, with heavy friendly losses. OSS Operational Team Jackal severed the bridge on August 9, 1945.

[116]   As a matter of policy, Great Britain prohibited area bombing attacks in Nazi-occupied territories. Webster and Frankland, *The Strategic Air Offensive against Germany* at 463 (cited in note 112); Robin Neillands, *The Bomber War: The Allied Air Offensive against Nazi Germany* 288–89 (Overlook 2001).

[117]   See, for example, Michel, *The Shadow War* at 289 (cited in note 96), which notes that in Russia in the summer of 1942, it was necessary for Germany to employ fifteen divisions in counter-partisan operations.

[118]   See Foot, *SOE: An Outline History* at 225–27 (cited in note 78); Stafford, *Britain and European Resistance* at 153–54 (cited in note 78); Hæstrup, *Europe Ablaze* at 434–35 (cited in note 78). Hæstrup notes on page 435, for example, that:

        On D-Day itself, about 950 actions were carried through, out of a planned 1050, and German Divisions which relied upon railway transport were delayed in their movements towards the [Allied] bridgehead in Normandy for up to two weeks, by which time the bridgehead had been consolidated.

[119]   See Hæstrup, *Europe Ablaze* at 373–74 (cited in note 78); Airey Neave, *The Escape Room* (Doubleday 1970); M.R.D. Foot and J.M. Langley, *MI9: The British Secret Service That Fostered Escape and Evasion 1939–1945 and Its American Counterpart* (Bodley Head 1979).

[120]   For example, on August 13, 1944, a US Fifteenth Air Force heavy bomber attack on a bridge across the Drôme River in southern France missed the bridge and struck the town of Crest, killing 280 civilians, wounding 200, and destroying 480 buildings. OSS Operational Group ALICE arrived on the scene, and reported:

        Upon arriving they were greeted by a very downhearted and somewhat belligerent group of people. The damage consisted of destruction of about one-fourth of the town . . . . Lt. Barnard and Lt. Meeks talked with the people, visited the hospital and encouraged the people that the bombing was a mistake and would not occur again.

        Funk, *Hidden Ally* at 77–79, 153 (cited in note 91); Kit C. Carter and Robert Mueller, eds, *The Army Air Forces in World War II: Combat Chronology, 1941–1945* at 424 (Center for Air Force History 1973).

Partisan operations, including sabotage and direct attacks on Axis personnel, were executed primarily in civilian attire, occasionally (after the Allied return to Europe on June 6, 1944) wearing a distinctive device, sometimes in a partial uniform, but seldom in full uniform. "Uniform" varied, often being more like modern "gang" colors than a traditional military uniform.[121] The same was true for SOE and OSS military personnel serving with resistance movements and, in some cases, Special Forces.

Finally, partisan operations were successful. Danish historian Jørgen Hæstrup concludes: "[T]he Resistance Movements, seen in their entirety, deeply influenced the course of the war, psychologically, militarily and politically."[122] In support thereof, he quotes Russian historian E. Boltin:

> History has never known a popular fight of such huge dimensions as was apparent during the 1939–1945 war. Furthermore the masses had never before taken so directly part in the military combat, as was the case in the last war in Europe.[123]

V. CONCLUSION

The preceding comments are offered to show that the wearing of civilian attire by partisans or military personnel in Special Forces units or in the SOE or OSS was neither unique, occasional, nor limited in time and space. In the examples listed in the Appendix, it is clear that the wearing of civilian attire or non-standard uniform (and, in some cases, enemy uniform) was a deliberate act based upon a decision made at the highest levels of government. State practice provides several points for fine-tuning a general principle:

First, treacherous killing involves more than wearing or fighting in civilian clothing. Colonel Lawrence wore indigenous attire while leading the Arab uprising against the Ottoman Empire in the Hejaz Province of Arabia (Syria) in 1916. Fighting in large, armed groups against the Turkish Army, his actions parallel those of Coalition Special Forces aligned with Northern Alliance and Southern Alliance forces in Afghanistan, suggesting a nuance to the law of war principle of distinction: an armed military group recognizable at a distance and readily identifiable to the enemy by its size and other characteristics, even when wearing indigenous attire with or without distinctive devices, is acting lawfully.

Second, non-standard uniforms or indigenous attire may be adopted for practical rather than perfidious reasons. The British/Commonwealth Long Range Desert Group ("LRDG"), operating behind enemy lines in North Africa

---

121   See, for example, Roy Farran, *Operation Tombola* 22, 32, 33, 35, 59 (Arms and Armour 1960).

122   Hæstrup, *Europe Ablaze* at 9, 421–31 (cited in note 78).

123   Id at 7. On pp 42–43, the same author attributes emphasis on partisan warfare to several factors, not the least of which were technical advances in aircraft and radios that facilitated partisan operations.

Chicago Journal of International Law

from 1940–1943, adopted the *kaffiyeh* and *agal* as a standard part of their uniform for utilitarian purposes, for example.[124] The LRDG wore native sheep or goatskin coats to ward off the nighttime desert cold, as did British and US Special Forces operating behind Iraqi lines in the 1991 Coalition effort to liberate Kuwait.[125] Wear of the latter by the LRDG served partially as a ruse against casual observation, such as by enemy aircraft. However, their identity clearly was recognizable at a distance by enemy ground forces.[126]

Third, law of war compliance with something as simple as wearing a distinctive device may not be practical where the enemy is known to punish rather than reward compliance. For example, immediately prior to D-Day (June 6, 1944), British air-delivered supplies included armbands for partisan and supporting Special Forces' use once Allied conventional forces returned to the continent.[127] However, distinctive emblem wear was viewed with skepticism in

---

124 Gordon, *The Other Desert War* at 50 (cited in note 92).

125 Ratcliffe, Botham, and Hitchen, *Eye of the Storm* at 214, 305, 326 (cited in note 20).

126 See Shaw, *Long Range Desert Group* at 27 (cited in note 92); O'Carroll, *Kiwi Scorpions* at 14–15, 75–79 (cited in note 92).

127 See Foot, *SOE: An Outline History* at 98 (cited in note 78); Dodds-Parker, *Setting Europe Ablaze* at 85, 124 (cited in note 20). This pessimism was confirmed in a number of cases. Four uniformed British soldiers captured during a failed attack on the German heavy water plant at Vermork, Norway, were executed in compliance with this order on November 20, 1942. See Richard Wiggan, *Operation Freshman: The Rjukan Heavy Water Raid, 1942* at 81–82 (William Kimber 1986). During the night of March 22, 1944, a uniformed US Army special operations team landed along the Italian coast about sixty miles north of La Spezia. Captured two days later, they were executed on the orders of General Anton Dostler who, in turn, was following Hitler's *Führerbefehl* (Commando Order) of October 18, 1942, which ordered all SOF to be executed, even if captured in uniform. Dostler was tried and convicted by a US Military Commission on October 8–12, 1945, sentenced to death, and executed. *In re Dostler*, in 1 *Law Reports of Trials of War Criminals* 22 (cited in note 29).

The background to Hitler's *Führerbefehl* is contained in Foot, *SOE in France* at 186–87 (cited in note 34). The *Führerbefehl* declared:

> [A]ll enemies on so-called commando missions in Europe or Africa challenged by German troops, even if they are to all appearances soldiers in uniforms or demolition troops, whether armed or unarmed, in battle or in flight, are to be slaughtered to the last man . . . . Even if these individuals when found should apparently be prepared to give themselves up, no pardon is to be granted them.

At a minimum the Commando Order violated Article 23(d) of the Annex to the Hague Convention IV (prohibiting denial of quarter) (cited in note 29). The Commando Order is contained in its entirety in *United States v Wilhelm von Leeb* ("High Command Case"), 11 *Trials of War Criminals* 73–75, 525–27 (GPO 1951), with additional implementing orders at pp 76–110. The Court's judgment that the *Führerbefehl* was "criminal on its face" is on 527. The *Führerbefehl* also is discussed in 11 *International Military Tribunal* 26 (GPO 1946), and 15 *International Military Tribunal* 296–306, 403–10, the trial of major German war criminals.

In Operation COLD COMFORT, two members of a British SAS team captured in uniform in Italy in February 1945 were executed. See Farran, *Operation Tombola* at 7–8

light of Hitler's Commando Order denying quarter to any partisans or Special Operations Forces.[128]

Fourth, perfidy requires *mens rea*, that is, the donning of civilian attire with the clear intent to deceive. A group of alert, fit young men, heavily and openly armed, surrounding an individual in military uniform, and themselves surrounded by host nation military personnel in uniform, clearly are a personal protection detail, and are not attempting to mask their status nor gain an advantage over some unsuspecting enemy soldier.

The law of war regards a uniform as the principal way in which conventional military forces distinguish themselves from the civilian population in international armed conflict. State practice (including US practice), treaty negotiation history, and the views of recognized law of war experts reveal (a) that the law of war obligation is one of *distinction* that otherwise has eluded precise statement in all circumstances; (b) there is no agreed definition of *uniform*; (c) the uniform "requirement" is less stringent with respect to Special Forces working with indigenous forces or executing a mission of strategic importance; and (d) a law of war violation occurs only where an act is perfidious, that is, done with an intent to deceive, and the act is the proximate cause of the killing, wounding, or capture of the enemy. My review of state practice found no

---

(cited in note 121); and Strawson, *A History of the S.A.S. Regiment* at 275 (cited in note 5). Similarly, German Security Forces ("SD") leader Josef Keiffer was tried and executed for the murder of captured uniformed British Special Air Service troops. See Foot, *SOE in France* at 305 (cited in note 34). See also *Trial of Karl Buck and Ten Others*, 5 *Law Reports of Trials of War Criminals* 39 (HMSO 1948); *Trial of Karl Adam Golkel and Thirteen Others*, 5 *Law Reports of Trials of War Criminals* at 45 (murder of captured uniformed SAS pursuant to *Führerbefehl*); *Trial of Generaloberst Nickolaus von Falkenhorst*, 11 *Law Reports of Trials of War Criminals* 18 (HMSO 1949); E.H. Stevens, ed, *Trial of Nikolaus von Falkenhorst: Formerly Generaloberst in the German Army*, in Sir David Maxwell Fyfe, ed, 6 *War Crimes Trials* (William Hodge 1949) (murder of captured uniformed British commandoes pursuant to *Führerbefehl*); *Trial of Werner Rohde and Eight Others*, 5 *Law Reports of Trials of War Criminals* at 54 (murder of captured female SOE).

The Japanese issued similar orders directing the execution of aviators and/or SOF. In 1944 members of a combined British-Australian SOF team captured in uniform were executed or died as a result of illegal medical experimentation, pursuant to such an order. As a result of postwar proceedings, Japanese General Dihihara was hanged, while other participants received lesser sentences. See Lynette Ramsay Silver, *The Heroes of Rimau: Unravelling the Mystery of One of World War II's Most Daring Raids* 225 (Sally Milner 1990). See also *The Jaluit Atoll Case*, 1 *Law Reports of Trials of War Criminals* 71 (HMSO 1947); *Trial of Lieutenant General Shigeru Sawada and Three Others*, 5 *Law Reports of Trials of War Criminals* 1 (HMSO 1948) (execution/murder of three captured US airmen); *Trial of Lieutenant General Harukei Isayama and Seven Others*, 5 *Law Reports of Trials of War Criminals* 60 (HMSO 1948) (murder of captured US aircrew).

[128]   For an example of the skepticism of field agents, see Farran, *Operation Tombola* at 70 (cited in note 121).

Chicago Journal of International Law

enforcement by a government against its own personnel.[129] Enemy combatants captured *in flagrante delicto* were prosecuted as spies rather than for law of war violations, with the exception of *Ex parte Quirin* and the unsuccessful post-World War II US prosecution of *SS-Obersturmbannführer* Otto Skorzeny.

In international armed conflict, the wearing of standard uniforms by conventional military forces, including special operations forces, is the normal and expected standard. Wearing civilian attire or a non-standard uniform is an exception that should be exercised only in extreme cases determined by competent authority.

In international armed conflict military necessity for wearing non-standard uniforms or civilian clothing has been regarded by governments as extremely restricted. It has been limited to intelligence collection or Special Forces operations in denied areas. No valid military necessity exists for conventional military forces, whether combat (combat arms, such as infantry, armor, or artillery), combat support (such as Civil Affairs), or combat service support personnel to wear non-standard uniforms or civilian attire in international armed conflict.

The codified law of war for international armed conflict does not prohibit the wearing of a non-standard uniform. It does not prohibit the wearing of civilian clothing so long as military personnel distinguish themselves from the civilian population, and provided there is legitimate military necessity for wearing something other than standard uniform. The generally recognized manner of *distinction* when wearing something other than standard uniform is through a distinctive device, such as a hat, scarf, or armband, recognizable at a distance.

Violation of the law of war (*perfidy*) occurs when a soldier wears civilian clothing—*not* a non-standard uniform—with intent to deceive, and the deception is the proximate cause of the killing, wounding, or capture of the enemy. Perfidy does not exist when a soldier in civilian attire or non-standard uniform remains identifiable as a combatant, and there is no intent to deceive.

Discussion of the issue raises an appearance of a double standard in considering Taliban militia/al Qaeda (in Afghanistan) or Saddam Fedayeen (in Iraq) wear of civilian clothing while justifying SOF wear of Western civilian attire or indigenous attire. A "double standard" exists within the law of war for regular forces of a recognized government vis-à-vis unauthorized combatant acts by private individuals or non-state actors. The issue was complicated by the

---

129   The inevitable reaction of some would be to suggest new legislation beyond the prohibition of perfidy, or to make any act of perfidy a Grave Breach. History shows that successful means and methods of warfare elude efforts at prohibiting them. See W. Hays Parks, *Making Law of War Treaties: Lessons from Submarine Warfare Regulation*, in Michael N. Schmitt, ed, *International Law across the Spectrum of Conflict: Essays in Honor of Professor L.C. Green on the Occasion of his Eightieth Birthday*, 75 International Law Studies 339 (US Naval War College 2000).

unique nature of operations in Afghanistan, that is, counter-terrorist operations against non-state actors in a failed state, and the increased role of NGOs in a non-linear combat environment.

The law of war principle of distinction cannot be taken lightly. The standard military field uniform should be worn absent compelling military necessity for wear of a non-standard uniform or civilian clothing. *Military convenience* should not be mistaken for *military necessity*. That military personnel may be at greater risk in wearing a uniform is not in and of itself sufficient basis to justify wearing civilian clothing. "Force protection" is not a legitimate basis for wearing a non-standard uniform or civilian attire. Risk is an inherent part of military missions, and does not constitute military necessity for wear of civilian attire. But the law of war requirement to wear a complete, "standard" uniform is not as absolute as some recently suggested.

IN SUMMARY

The law of war requires military units and personnel to distinguish themselves from the civilian population in international armed conflict.[130] Article 4(A)2 of the Geneva Convention Relative to the Treatment of Prisoners of War of August 12, 1949 sets forth standards all combatants are expected to satisfy. However, military personnel may distinguish themselves from the civilian population in other ways, such as physical separation.

Standard US military uniforms satisfy the requirements of Art 4A, GPW. "Standard military uniform" refers to battle dress uniform ("BDU"), desert camouflage uniform ("DCU"), official flight suit, or other obvious military apparel.[131] The presumption should be that all US armed forces operate in standard uniforms during military operations in international armed conflict.

When authorized, the requirements of GPW Art 4(A)2 may be satisfied by other than complete standard military uniform. For example, a visible part of the standard military uniform, or a fixed, distinctive sign will satisfy the requirements provided that the forces are recognizable as combatants with unenhanced vision at a distance.

Neither the Global War on Terrorism nor the fact that one is a member of Special Operations Forces offers *carte blanche* for military personnel to wear something other than the full, standard uniform. The wearing of a partial uniform or non-standard uniform with fixed, distinctive sign should be reserved for exceptional circumstances when required by military necessity. Force

---

130   Stating the obvious, special operations missions outside international armed conflict, such as counterterrorism, are not subject to these legal obligations.

131   For example, a heavily-armed Navy SEAL attired in a wet suit, fins, and face mask would be distinctive from the civilian population except, perhaps, in the annual zany Bay-to-Breakers foot race in San Francisco.

protection does not constitute military necessity. Authority should be regarded as extremely limited, mission- and unit-specific, and decided by a senior commander or higher, such as (in the US military) the Combatant Commander responsible for the mission.

While a hat, scarf, or armband would meet the fixed distinctive sign requirement, a permanently affixed distinctive sign such as an American flag sewn onto body armor or clothing is more prudent.

Forces operating in other than complete standard uniform should receive training in the law of war to ensure that they understand the requirements of distinction and are fully aware of the risks they may face if captured if they fail to comply with the law of war.

Captured US military personnel (other than escaping prisoners of war) wearing civilian apparel without a fixed distinctive sign and without visible weapons may be considered spies by their captor. The captor may try them for domestic law violations (for example, spying). Unless they otherwise commit an independent law of war violation (for example, perfidy), history indicates that the acts will not be regarded as violation of the law of war.

APPENDIX

The list that follows is illustrative rather than exhaustive, and is offered for historical purposes rather than necessarily with approval or condemnation of the missions listed. With the exception of US action in *Ex parte Quirin*[132] and the unsuccessful prosecution of Otto Skorzeny,[133] the list reveals that state practice in international armed conflict has tended not to treat wear of civilian attire, non-standard uniforms, and/or enemy uniforms by regular military forces as a

---

[132]   317 US 1 (1942) (discussed in note 31).

[133]   *Trial of Otto Skorzeny and Others*, 9 *Law Reports of Trials of War Criminals* 90 (HMSO 1949). *SS-Obersturmbannführer* (Lieutenant Colonel) Otto Skorzeny commanded a commando mission during the last-ditch December 1944 German Ardennes Offensive to infiltrate US lines wearing US Army uniforms. Eighteen members of his forty-four man team were captured in US uniform; each was executed as a spy. Skorzeny was arrested in 1947. As he was not captured *in flagrante delicto*, he could not be charged as a spy. See Hague Convention IV, Annex art 31 (cited in note 29). Nor, however, was he charged with violation of Hague Convention IV, Annex art 23(b), that is, "killing treacherously."

    The court delivered its acquittal without explanation. Popular speculation has been that the court accepted Skorzeny's claim that his men did not fight in US uniforms. Skorzeny's defense was less that he and his men did not fight in US uniforms nor necessarily *tu quoque* ("you also"), but rather based upon the international law principle of *rebus sic stantibus* ("substantial change of circumstances"). James J. Weingartner, *Otto Skorzeny and the Laws of War*, 55 J Milit Hist 207, 217–18 (1991). A major contribution to Skorzeny's acquittal was the testimony of Royal Air Force Wing Commander Forest Yeo-Thomas, a highly decorated veteran of British Special Operations Executive service, who acknowledged that British Special Operations Executive engaged in similar conduct. Other evidence was offered of similar US and British operations. Otto Skorzeny, *My Commando Operations: The Memoirs of Hitler's Most Daring Commando* 450–51 (Schiffer Milit Hist 1995) (David Johnston, trans); and Weingartner, 55 J Milit Hist at 219 (cited above).

    Restatement (Second) of Foreign Relations Law of the United States § 153 (1965) states that *rebus sic stantibus* means in part that:

> An international agreement is subject to the implied condition that a substantial change of a temporary or permanent nature, in a state of facts existing at the time when the agreement became effective, suspends or terminates, as the case may be, the obligations of the parties under the agreement to the extent that the continuation of the state of facts was of such importance to the achievement of the objectives of the agreement that the parties would not have intended the obligations to be applicable under the changed circumstances.

See also Wolfgang Friedman, Oliver J. Lissityn, and Richard C. Pugh, *International Law, Cases and Materials* 417–21 (West 1969) (on file with author).

    Based upon information known today, as exhibited in the state practice section of this paper, a defense of *rebus sic stantibus* was plausible. It also is possible that the court accepted the evidence more as the *tu quoque* defense, as was the case in the prosecution of Admiral Karl Dönitz. Charged with conducting unrestricted submarine warfare, the court declined to find Admiral Dönitz guilty of the charge when his defense presented a statement by Admiral Chester Nimitz, USN, Commander in Chief, US Forces Pacific, acknowledging that US submarines had conducted unrestricted submarine warfare throughout World War II. See Peter Padfield, *Dönitz: The Last Führer* 463–68 (Harper & Row 1984).

war crime.[134] Personnel caught *in flagrante delicto* in civilian attire or enemy uniforms have been treated as spies, sometimes (but not always) with severe consequences.[135] However, those who returned safely were decorated rather than punished, manifesting an endorsement of their actions by their government.

The wearing of enemy uniforms is not directly within the scope of the issue under consideration. However, State practice is germane regarding the prohibition on "killing treacherously" contained in Article 23(b) of the Annex to the 1907 Hague Convention IV. State practice shows that governments have been willing to deploy Special Forces in civilian attire or enemy uniforms where a major advantage is anticipated, and where the gain is greater than the risk to the deployed personnel. Such actions have not been regarded as a war crime either by the government ordering them or the government against which such forces were employed.[136]

---

134   As indicated in the preceding footnote, members of Skorzeny's commando team captured wearing US Army uniforms were executed as spies. They were not charged with violation of Article 23(b) of the Annex to the Hague Convention IV. Skorzeny could not be charged as a spy, as he was arrested long after completion of his mission. His prosecution as a spy was precluded by Article 31 of the Annex to the Hague Convention IV, and no consideration was given to alleging a violation of Article 23(b). At the time of the Skorzeny trial, law of war experts disagreed as to whether or not wearing an enemy uniform in battle was illegal. Weingartner, 55 J Milit Hist at 213–14 (cited in note 133), and Spaight, *War Rights on Land* at 105–06 (cited in note 38).

135   Michel, *The Shadow War* at 121 (cited in note 96), offers perspective on numbers:

> Of 250 [SOE] agents who left London for Belgium . . . 145 returned to Great Britain but 105 were arrested; of the latter 25 were executed, 20 died from maltreatment and 40 were deported, of whom only 20 survived. The casualty rate therefore was a full 25 per cent.

136   Special forces' wear of enemy uniforms is more commonplace than generally known. For example, summarizing the practice of the German special operations Brandenburg Regiment, one study concluded, "Throughout the period 1941–1943, the *usual* operational technique was the use of disguise in enemy uniforms." Edward N. Luttwak, Steven L. Canby, and David L. Thomas, *A Systematic Review of "Commando" (Special) Operations, 1939–1980,* II-188 (C&L Associates unpublished report) (on file with author). Efforts at summarizing pre-Protocol I law as to the wearing of enemy uniforms include Valentine Jobst III, *Is the Wearing of the Enemy's Uniform a Violation of the Laws of War?*, 35 Am J Intl L No 3 435 (July 1941); and R.C. Hingorani, *Prisoners of War* 28–30 (N.M. Tripathi 1963).

Article 39, ¶ 2 of the 1977 Additional Protocol I states:

> It is prohibited to make use of the flags or military emblems, insignia or uniforms of adverse Parties while engaging in attacks or in order to shield, favour, protect or impede military operations.

16 ILM at 1409 (cited in note 32). This new law has not been tested. In addition to the list in Section IV.B., there is considerable historical evidence to the contrary, including since 1977. See Parks, 32 Air Force L Rev at 76 n259 (cited in note 52). The list that follows shows that this provision is new law rather than a codification of customary practice. Canada took a reservation to Article 39(2) on ratification. The Canadian reservation, available online at <http://www.icrc.org/ihl.nsf/677558c021ecf2c14

Table of Historical State Practice

Who	When	Where	Disposition (if any)
Japan[137] Japanese officers in Chinese civilian clothing	1904	Manchuria (Russo-Japanese War)	Captured and executed as spies.
Russia[138] Russian soldiers in Chinese civilian attire attacked Japanese units	1904 (Russo-Japanese War)	Manchuria	Japanese diplomatic protest

1256739003e6370/172ffec04adc80f2c1256402003fb314?OpenDocument> (visited Sept 21, 2003), states:

> Article 39—Emblems of nationality (Enemy uniforms). The Government of Canada does not intend to be bound by the prohibitions contained in paragraph 2 of Article 39 to make use of military emblems, insignia or uniforms of adverse parties in order to shield, favor, protect or impede military operations.

One may speculate on why the Diplomatic Conference supported this provision. Part of the reason is that state practice was neither acknowledged nor well known. Aside from personal accounts and the official works of M.R.D. Foot and Charles Cruickshank cited herein, OSS records were not declassified until 1985, and the official SOE history, see Mackenzie, *The Secret History of SOE* (cited in note 78), was not declassified until 1998. Speaking from this author's experience, a "wall" between special operations forces and the negotiating process existed that does not exist within the US government today. While US negotiation guidance was coordinated within the Department of Defense, in all likelihood it did not reach the closed-door, Cold War special operations environment that prevailed at that time. Even if it had, it is entirely probable that the decision was taken not to comment. The author's work with counterparts in other governments suggests that this wall persists to this day within many governments.

137 See Spaight, *War Rights on Land* at 110 (cited at note 38).

138 Sakuyé Takahashi, *International Law Applied to the Russo-Japanese War* 174–78 (Banks Law 1908).

Chicago Journal of International Law

Who	When	Where	Disposition (if any)
United Kingdom[139] Colonel T.E. Lawrence (Lawrence of Arabia) wore Arab attire while leading the Arab uprising against the Ottoman Empire, fighting the Turkish Army	· 1916–18 (WWI)	Hejaz Province, Arabia (Syria)	Lawrence decorated
Germany[140] Special Forces dressed as Polish civilians faked a raid on customs house as a pretext for the German invasion of Poland	1939	Germany	None
United Kingdom[141] Special Operations Executive ("SOE") personnel in civilian clothing supported partisan operations in Axis-controlled nations	1940–45	Europe, Asia	SOE agents captured *in flagrante delicto* were incarcerated, not always executed[142]
Germany[143] Danish-speaking SF dressed as Danish soldiers seize key bridge to initiate invasion	1940	Denmark	None
Germany[144] SF dressed as Dutch military policemen seize key bridge at start of German invasion	1940	Netherlands	None

---

139   Lt. Col. W. F. Stirling, *Safety Last* 81, 94 (Hollis and Carter 1953); Wilson, *Lawrence of Arabia* at 279–568 (cited at note 7). Lawrence served in the ranks of lieutenant to colonel. Lawrence's awards included the French Legion d'Honneur, Companion of the Order of the Bath (in lieu of a recommended Victoria Cross, denied on a technicality), and Distinguished Service Order. Id at 251–52, 424–25, 492. He declined a recommendation by King George V for a knighthood. Id at 577.

140   Lucas, *Kommando* at 29–39 (cited in note 79).

141   Mackenzie, *The Secret History of SOE* at 334 (cited in note 78).

142   Where captured SOE personnel were executed without trial, those responsible were prosecuted following World War II. See, for example, *Trial of Wolfgang Zeuss (The Natzweiler Trial)*, 5 War Crimes Trials (HMSO 1949).

143   Lucas, *Kommando* at 45 (cited in note 79).

144   Id at 49.

Special Forces' Wear of Non-Standard Uniforms *Parks*

Who	When	Where	Disposition (if any)
Germany[145] SF wearing Belgium Army overcoats over their uniforms seize key bridge at start of German invasion	1940	Belgium	None
United Kingdom[146] Long Range Desert Group ("LRDG") wore Arab *kaffiyeh* and *agal*, sometimes worn over their uniforms	1940–43	Libya	None. *Kaffiyeh/agal* adopted by LRDG as official uniform
France[147] Free French commander wore indigenous attire in attack on Italian fort at Murzuk, January 11, 1941	1941	Libya	Killed in action during attack
Germany[148] SF wearing Russian Army overcoats, carrying Russian weapons, driving Russian vehicles, spearhead German invasion	1941	Russia	None
Germany[149] SF dressed in British Army uniforms and indigenous attire, driving British vehicles, attempt reconnaissance to Suez	1941	Libya	None
Soviet Union[150] Russian partisans and military operative groups deployed to support them fought in civilian clothing	1941–45	German-occupied territory in Soviet Union	Partisans captured were executed. Survivors decorated by Russia post-war

---

145   Id at 71–73.

146   Shaw, *Long Range Desert Group* at 27 (cited in note 92); Gordon, *The Other Desert War* at 50 (cited in note 92); O'Carroll, *Kiwi Scorpions* at 75, 79 (cited in note 92).

147   Crichton-Stuart, *G Patrol* at 27, 38, 42 (cited in note 92).

148   Lucas, *Kommando* at 77 (cited in note 79).

149   Id at 84–85.

150   John Erickson, *The Road to Stalingrad*, 1 *Stalin's War with Germany* 240–48 (Harper & Row 1975); Erickson, *The Road to Berlin* at 114–15, 147 (cited in note 95); Ziemke and Bauer, *Moscow to Stalingrad* at 199–219 (cited in note 95); Ziemke, *Stalingrad to Berlin* at 303–09,

Chicago Journal of International Law

Who	When	Where	Disposition (if any)
United Kingdom[151] SF in German uniforms infiltrated Tobruk as part of Operation AGREEMENT. Mission executed with infiltration by another officer in indigenous attire	1942	Libya	None
United Kingdom[152] SOE-trained, equipped, and transported partisans kill *Obergruppenführer* Reinhard Heydrich, Nazi Governor of Czechoslovakia	1942	Czechoslovakia	Partisans committed suicide rather than surrender
Soviet Union[153] Naval *Spetsnaz* conduct operations in civilian clothing and enemy uniforms	1942–45	German-occupied territory in Soviet Union	Partisans captured were executed. Survivors decorated by Russia post-war

315–16 (cited in note 95). These histories show that Soviet partisan units reached a peak strength of 250,000 in 1943 and 1944, consisting of 40 percent civilians, 40 percent Russian soldiers left behind German lines during Germany's invasion of Russia, and 20 percent Special Forces parachuted in to augment, organize, and direct partisan operations.

[151] Gordon Landsborough, *Tobruk Commando* 29–31, 35, 64–66 (Cassell 1956); Shaw, *Long Range Desert Group* at 185–95 (cited in note 92); Owen, *The Desert My Dwelling Place* at 224–27 (cited in note 92); Gordon, *The Other Desert War* at 119–26 (cited in note 92); Kelly, *The Lost Oasis* at 233–34 (cited in note 111); Maj. Gen. I.S.O. Playfair and Brig. C.J.C. Molony, *The Mediterannean and Middle East: The Destruction of the Axis Forces in Africa*, 4 *History of the Second World War: United Kingdom Military Series* 20–23 (HMSO 1966). The raiding party consisted of uniformed SAS posing as British prisoners of war guarded by German-speaking Palestinian Jews, members of the British Special Identification Group ("SIG"), dressed in German uniforms. While Saul Kelly states that the German-uniformed escort changed into British uniforms following infiltration and before fighting, (see Kelly, *The Lost Oasis* at 233 (cited in note 111)), Lansborough indicates only the three British officers who donned German uniforms at the last moment changed back into British uniform, see id at 98. The raid proved a disaster, and captured SIG were executed. Author's discussion with Saul Kelly, June 21, 2003. The raid was the basis for the movie *Tobruk* (1967) starring Rock Hudson and George Peppard.

[152] Callum MacDonald, *The Killing of SS Obergruppenführer Reinhard Heydrich* (Free Press 1989).

[153] Yuriy Fedorovich Strekhnin, *Commandos from the Sea: Soviet Naval Spetsnaz in World War II* at 3, 58, 66, 71, 89–90 (Naval Institute, 1996) (James F. Gebhardt, trans).

Special Forces' Wear of Non-Standard Uniforms   *Parks*

Who	When	Where	Disposition (if any)
Japan[154] Used English-speaking Germans (French Foreign Legion) captured in Thailand in Feb. 1941 dressed in uniforms resembling British khaki to penetrate British lines	1942	Malaya	None
Germany[155] Eight German soldiers on sabotage mission captured in civilian clothing	1942	US	Tried by military commission for violation of the laws of war
United Kingdom/ Australia[156] Operation JAYWICK, combined SOF team navigated to Singapore in Japanese fishing boat *Kofuku Mara*, flying Japanese flag and dressed in native sarongs. Attacked and sunk seven ships (38,000 tons)	1943	Singapore	Participants commended
Poland[157] SOE-trained partisans, one dressed in SS uniform, raided Pinsk prison near Brest-Litovsk, freed prisoners and killed commandant	1943	Poland	None

---

154   Peter Elphick, *Singapore: The Pregnable Fortress* 356–60 (Hodder and Stoughton 1995).

155   *Ex parte Quirin*, 317 US at 1. The eight German saboteurs were civilians. They wore German naval uniforms when they boarded the submarine, and again at the time of their landings in the United States. After landing, they changed into civilian clothing. The uniforms were sent back to the U-boat. Fisher, *Nazi Saboteurs on Trial* at 23, 26, 35 (cited at note 31).

156   Brian Connell, *Return of the Tiger* 84, 122 (Doubleday 1961); Ronald McKie, *The Heroes* 58, 99, 146, 175 (Harcourt, Brace 1961); Lynette Ramsey Silver, *Krait: The Fishing Boat that Went to War* (Sally Milner 1992). Illegal Japanese reprisals against Allied prisoners of war and civilian internees held in Singapore was the basis for the postwar *Trial of Sumida Haruzo and Twenty Others (The "Double Tenth" Trial)*, in Colin Sleeman and S.C. Silkin, eds, 8 *War Crimes Trials* (William Hodge 1951).

157   Foot, *SOE: An Outline History* at 193 (cited in note 78).

Chicago Journal of International Law

Who	When	Where	Disposition (if any)
United Kingdom[158] SOE-trained, equipped, and transported partisans sabotaged German heavy water plant at Vermok	1943	Norway	None
Japan[159] Formed Indian National Army from captured Indian Army personnel, who fought in Indian Army uniforms against British and Commonwealth forces in Burma	1943	Burma	Post-war trials of soldiers captured under India Army Act or Indian Penal Code rather than charges of war crimes
United Kingdom[160] Lt. B.J. Barton, No. 2 Commando, penetrated German defenses wearing indigenous attire and killed German commandant	1944	Brac (Aegaen)	Awarded Military Cross

---

[158]   Riste and Nökleby, *Norway 1940–1945* at 59–60 (cited in note 83); Thomas Gallagher, *Assault in Norway: Sabotaging in the Nazi Nuclear Bomb* (Harcourt Brace Jovanovich 1975); and Dan Kurzman, *Blood and Water: Sabotaging Hitler's Bomb* 144–58 (Henry Holt 1997).

[159]   A detailed and fascinating account is contained in Leslie C. Green, *Essays on the Modern Law of War* 41–434 (Transnational 2d ed 1999), based upon Professor Green's personal participation in the post-war trials. The Indian National Army (Azad Hind Fauj) was formed from Indian Army personnel captured during the 1942 Japanese conquest of Hong Kong, Malaya, and Singapore. Subsequently the Japanese "recruited" its Indian prisoners of war—through inducements as well as threats of violence and torture—to enlist in the Indian National Army ("INA") to fight against British forces. Some, but not all, did so. As Professor Green explains on page 411:

> These "Volunteers" had indulged in infiltration and propaganda on behalf of Free India among Indian Army personnel, often operating through Burma and the Malayan advance behind British lines which, in view of their uniforms and language, they were easily able to infiltrate, [sic] In addition, they were able to indicate to the Japanese where British or Indian troops were hiding.

Professor Green notes that British military authorities began the prosecution of personnel captured while fighting on behalf of the INA as early as the middle of 1943. See id at 414–15. These prosecutions continued through the post-war period, gradually becoming more selective with respect to those brought to trial. See id at 418. However, accused were brought before courts martial for violations of the Indian Army Act or the Indian Penal Code rather than being charged with a war crime for fighting in Indian Army uniforms. See id at 431.

The role of the INA in Japanese operations against British forces in Burma is described in Field Marshal, The Viscount Slim, *Defeat into Victory* (David McKay 1961), and Louis Allen, *Burma: The Longest War, 1941–1945* (St. Martin's 1985).

Who	When	Where	Disposition (if any)
United Kingdom[161] British officers dressed as German soldiers, with partisan assistance, abducted Major General Karl Kreipe, Commander, 22nd Panzer Division on Crete	1944	Crete	None
United Kingdom[162] SAS wore mixed dress of British, German, and Italian uniforms and civilian clothing	1944	Aegaen	One Victoria Cross, numerous other awards
United Kingdom[163] Operation RIMAU, combined SF team in uniform attacked Japanese ships	1944	Singapore	Captured, died from illegal medical experiment-ation or were executed
United Kingdom[164] Special Boat Squadron ("SBS") officer dressed as priest led successful attack on German units	1944	Nisiros (Aegaen)	None

160   Saunders, *The Green Beret* at 244–45 (cited in note 92); Messenger, *The Commandos* at 331–32, 335 (cited in note 92); and William Seymour, *British Special Forces* 49–50 (Sidgwick & Jackson 1985).

161   W. Stanley Moss, *Ill Met by Moonlight* (MacMillan 1950). While SOE historian M.R.D. Foot states that "SOE never attempted in France to do what the *Lehr-Regiment Brandenburg* did on the other side in Russia: operate tactical or even strategic reconnaissance and fighting patrols behind the lines in enemy uniform." Foot, *SOE in France* at 390 (cited in note 34). While Stanley Moss never acknowledged his mission to have been SOE-sponsored, the official SOE history acknowledges it as an SOE mission, Mackenzie, *The Secret History of SOE* at 483 (cited in note 78). Moss's book is an early one, but the team's priority of dispatch—a dozen parachute attempts before being delivered by ship—his communications capabilities, his liaison with SOE operatives on Crete, and his less-than-credible procurement of well-fitting German military police uniforms (the book contains a photograph of Moss and his teammate in German uniforms) suggests that Foot's statement denying any such activity "in France" was carefully crafted. A summary of Moss's mission in Patrick Howarth, *Undercover: The Men and Women of the SOE* 162–65 (Phoenix 1980), adds to the official SOE acknowledgement. *Lehr-Regiment Brandenburg* operations are the subject of Lucas, *Kommando* (cited in note 79).

162   Suzanne Lassen, *Anders Lassen VC* 121, 176 (Muller 1965) (Inge Hack, trans).

163   Silver, *The Heroes of Rimau* (cited in note 127) details the mission. In 1951, those responsible for the illegal medical experimentation and execution of the captured Allied personnel were convicted of war crimes by an Australian military court sitting on Admiralty Island of Los Negros. Id at 228–29.

164   Ladd, *SBS: The Invisible Raiders* 64–66 (cited at note 92).

Chicago Journal of International Law

Who	When	Where	Disposition (if any)
United Kingdom[165] SOE-trained/equipped partisans sabotaged and sunk ferry carrying German heavy water	1944	Norway	None
United States[166] Office of Strategic Service ("OSS") teams entered Nazi-occupied Europe, conducted operations in civilian clothing and German uniform.	1944	France, Yugoslavia	None
United States[167] US Naval Group China wearing civilian clothing collected intelligence and executed direct action missions against Japanese	1944	China	None
United States[168] Army Rangers dressed as German soldiers to penetrate and fight in Aachen (OSS operation)	1944	Germany	None
United States/ United Kingdom[169] JEDBURGH teams operate post-D-Day in support of partisans, not always in uniform	1944–45	France, Italy, Yugoslavia, Albania, Netherlands	None

---

[165]   Riste and Nökleby, *Norway 1940–1945* at 60–61 (cited in note 83); Kurzman, *Blood and Water: Sabotaging Hitler's Bomb* 224–38 (cited in note 158).

[166]   Joseph E. Persico, *Piercing the Reich: The Penetration of Nazi Germany by American Secret Agents during World War II* at 12–115, 120–21, 126–27, 140–41 (Viking 1979); Paddock, *U.S. Army Special Warfare: Its Origins* at 28 (cited in note 5).

[167]   Miles, *A Different Kind of War* at 274, 371 (cited in note 106).

[168]   Charles Whiting, *Bloody Aachen* 143–46 (Stein and Day 1976). The US Army use of German uniforms in the battle for Aachen was specifically mentioned in the defense of *SS-Obersturmbannführer* Otto Skorzeny. See Weingartner, 55 J Milit Hist at 217–218 (cited in note 133).

[169]   David Schoenbrun, *Soldiers of the Night: The Story of the French Resistance* 331 (Dutton 1980); Hymoff, *The OSS in World War II* at 247–50 (cited in note 99); Casey, *The Secret War against Hitler* at 74–75, 92, 94–95, 122–23, 146, 148, 154 (cited in note 99); Mackenzie, *The Secret History of SOE* at 603–04, 642 (cited in note 78). Jedburgh teams were planned for Belgium, but were not deployed. Id at 604.

Who	When	Where	Disposition (if any)
Germany[170] German Kommando unit dressed in US uniforms and driving US vehicles penetrated US lines in Ardennes	1944	Belgium	Members captured in US uniforms executed; mission commander Otto Skorzeny and ten others acquitted in war crimes trial
Germany[171] Partisan operation by German SF in civilian clothing	1944–45	Germany	None
United Kingdom[172] Operation TOMBOLA, SAS operation with Italian partisans. Civilian attire with mixed uniform	1945	Italy	None
United States[173] OSS team in German uniforms to conduct Operation IRON CROSS to execute subversion missions and capture or kill Nazi officials	1945	Germany	Mission aborted by end of war

---

[170]   *Trial of Otto Skorzeny and Others,* 9 *Law Reports of Trials of War Criminals* at 90–94 (cited in note 133); Hugh M. Cole, *The Ardennes: Battle of the Bulge,* Stetson Conn, ed, 8 *United States Army in World War II: European Theater of Operations* 269–71 (Department of the Army 1965). See also discussion in note 133.

[171]   Lucas, *Kommando* at 205–06 (cited in note 79).

[172]   See Farran, *Winged Dagger* at 282–339 (cited at note 92); Farran, *Operation Tombola* at 13, 22, 25, 33, 59–60 (cited in note 121). The latter narrative suggests that some partisans wore distinctive emblems relating to their communist or non-communist affiliation, or allegiance to the group with whom they were associated (somewhat akin to modern day gang "colors") rather than as distinctive devices in the traditional law of war sense.

[173]   Persico, *Piercing the Reich* at 253 (cited in note 166); Bank, *From OSS to Green Berets* at 73–99 (cited in note 5). A photograph of the London OSS fitting room, showing an OSS agent being outfitted in German *Wermacht* uniform, is in Francis Russell, *The Secret War* 106 (Time-Life 1981).

Chicago Journal of International Law

Who	When	Where	Disposition (if any)
United States[174] OSS Operations Groups operated in US uniforms, indigenous attire, and Chinese Puppet Army uniforms	1945	China	None
Indonesia (I)[175] Soldiers dressed in civilian attire while attacking civilian objects	1965	Singapore	Captured and tried under domestic law
Indonesia (II)[176] Soldiers in civilian attire captured while on mission to attack civilian objects	1965	Singapore	Captured and tried under domestic law
United States[177] Military Assistance Command (Vietnam) Studies and Operations Group teams wore non-standard uniforms while operating in denied areas	1965–71	Southeast Asia	None
United States[178] SF soldier fought in civilian clothing in response to Tet Offensive enemy attacks	1968	Vietnam	Awarded Medal of Honor

---

174   Mills, Mills, and Brunner, *OSS Special Operations in China* (cited in note 7).

175   *Krofan*, 1 Malayan L J at 133 (cited in note 31).

176   *Osman bin Haji Mohamed Ali v Public Prosecutor*, 1 AC 430 (Privy Council 1969) (appeal taken from Malaysia) (UK).

177   John Plaster, *SOG: The Secret Wars of America's Commands in Vietnam* 143 (Simon and Schuster 1997). Some, including US Road Runner teams operating in North Vietnam, wore sterile field uniforms or indigenous straw conical hats to delay positive enemy identification at a distance. Interview with Lt. Col. L.H. Burruss, SF, USA (June 12, 2002).

178   The Medal of Honor citation of Sgt. Drew D. Dix, USA, reads as follows:

> Learning that a nurse was trapped in a house near the center of the city, S/Sgt. Dix organized a relief force, successfully rescued the nurse, and returned her to the safety of the Tactical Operations Center. Being informed of other trapped civilians within the city, S/Sgt. Dix voluntarily led another force to rescue 8 civilian employees located in a building which was under heavy mortar and small-arms fire. S/Sgt. Dix then returned to the center of the city. Upon approaching a building, he was subjected to intense automatic rifle and machine gun fire from an unknown number of Viet Cong. He personally assaulted the building, killing six Viet Cong, and rescuing two Filipinos. The following day S/Sgt. Dix, still on his own volition, assembled a 20-man force and though under intense enemy fire cleared the Viet Cong out of the hotel, theater, and other adjacent buildings within the city. During this portion of the attack, Army Republic of Vietnam soldiers inspired by the heroism and

Who	When	Where	Disposition (if any)
Soviet Union[179] *Spetsnaz* dressed as tourists disabled the Prague airport before disembarkation of planes carrying Soviet troops.	1968	Czechoslovakia	None
United States[180] Navy SEAL officer switched from uniform to indigenous attire to fight way in and out of encircled aircrew to rescue him	1972	South Vietnam	Awarded Medal of Honor

success of S/Sgt. Dix, rallied and commenced firing upon the Viet Cong. S/Sgt. Dix captured 20 prisoners, including a high ranking Viet Cong official. He then attacked enemy troops who had entered the residence of the Deputy Province Chief and was successful in rescuing the official's wife and children. S/Sgt. Dix's personal heroic actions resulted in 14 Viet Cong killed in action and possibly 25 more, the capture of 20 prisoners, 15 weapons, and the rescue of 14 United States and free world civilians. The heroism of S/Sgt. Dix was in the highest tradition and reflects great credit upon the US Army.

Available online at <http://www.army.mil/cmh-pg/mohviet.htm> under "Dix, Drew Dennis" (visited Oct 11, 2003).

[179] Viktor Suvorov, *Spetsnaz: The Inside Story of the Soviet Special Forces* 131, 161 (Norton 1987).

[180] This was the famous rescue by Lieutenant Thomas R. Norris, USN, of Lieutenant Colonel Iceal E. Hambleton, USAF, commonly referred to as Bat 21, the designation of the B66 in which Lieutenant Colonel Hambleton served as navigator. (Lieutenant Colonel Hambleton actually was Bat 21B.) See Darrel D. Whitcomb, *The Rescue of Bat 21* (Naval Institute 1998). The Vietnamese mentioned in Norris' citation was Nguyen Van Kiet, a South Vietnamese frogman. For his actions, he became the only Vietnamese in the war to be awarded the US Navy Cross. See Bosiljevac, *SEALs: UDT/SEAL Operation in Vietnam* at 211–213 (cited in note 5). The 1988 movie *Bat-21*, starring Danny Glover and Gene Hackman, errs in depicting this as solely an Air Force rescue. Lieutenant Norris' Medal of Honor citation clearly acknowledges his fighting in civilian clothing, and the US Government's approval of his actions:

> Lt. Norris completed an unprecedented ground rescue of 2 downed pilots deep within heavily controlled enemy territory in Quang Tri Province. Lt. Norris, on the night of 10 April, led a 5-man patrol through 2,000 meters of heavily controlled enemy territory, located 1 of the downed pilots at daybreak, and returned to the Forward Operating Base (FOB). On 11 April, after a devastating mortar and rocket attack on the small FOB, Lt. Norris led a 3-man team on 2 unsuccessful rescue attempts for the second pilot. On the afternoon of the 12th, a forward air controller located the pilot and notified Lt. Norris. *Dressed in fishermen disguises and using a sampan,* Lt. Norris and 1 Vietnamese traveled throughout that night and found the injured pilot at dawn. Covering the pilot with bamboo and vegetation, they began the return journey, successfully evading a North Vietnamese patrol. Approaching the FOB, they came under heavy machinegun fire. Lt. Norris called in an air strike which provided suppression fire and a smoke screen, allowing the rescue party to reach the FOB. By his outstanding display of decisive leadership, undaunted courage, and selfless dedication in the face of extreme danger, Lt. Norris enhanced the finest traditions of the U.S. Naval Service.

Chicago Journal of International Law

Who	When	Where	Disposition (if any)
Israel[181] Operation Aviv Neurim, Israeli Defense Force ("IDF") SF team dressed in civilian clothing raided PLO Beirut targets	1973	Lebanon	Team commander Ehud Barak eventually became IDF Chief of Staff, Israeli Prime Minister
Israel[182] Entebbe rescue force included commandos dressed as Uganda soldiers	1976	Uganda	Mission successful in rescuing hijacked aircrew and passengers held hostage

Available online at <http://www.army.mil/cmh-pg/mohviet2.htm> (under "Norris, Thomas R.") (visited Oct 11, 2003) (emphasis added).

[181] Yeshayahu Ben-Porat, Eiten Haber, and Zeev Schiff, *Entebbe Rescue* 210 (Delacorte 1976) (Louis Williams, trans); Neil C. Livingstone and David Halevy, *Inside the PLO: Covert Units, Secret Funds, and the War against Israel in the United States* 36–37 (Morrow 1990); Israeli Defence Forces Weekly *Ba'Machaneh* (1998) (on file with author); e-mail message to author from David H. Halevy, Global Options, Inc (July 8, 2003) (on file with author). The operation took place during the night of April 9–10, 1973. Barak was dressed as a woman, with a long, dark wig, false breasts, and women's clothing. An interview with retired Brigadier General Emanuel Shaked, commander of the actual operation, tells the story:

> The task of killing the three senior members of the PLO was entrusted to the Sayeret Matkal people. They walked singly and in pairs at a distance of ten meters one from the other as if there was no relationship between them, wrote Moshe Zondar in his book "Sayeret Matkal". Four of the warriors were disguised as women. Ehud Barak's wig was black. Amiram Levine (destined to become Commanding General of the Northern Command and Deputy Head of the Mossad) boasted a red hairpiece. Loni Rafaeli and Danny Bar looked like blond women. In accordance with the dictates of fashion, Barak wore widening pants and within his large breasts, artificial of course, he hid explosive blocks.
>
> Barak walked in front with "her" partner, Muki Betzer, who wore a civilian suit. To the Lebanese passerby the two looked like a man and a woman, normal citizens. In fact, a pair of Lebanese Gendarmieres, who strode towards them on the sidewalk, gave them a close look, and Betzer, who strengthened his lovers hug, dared even to rub shoulders with the Lebanese uniform bearer, who was forced to give in and to step down to the road with his partner. The Lebanese did not know that in front of them was a deadly couple, leading the force forward.

The attack on three separate Palestine Liberation Organization targets was successful. E-mail message to author from Col. Daniel Reisner, Israeli Defence Force, (Aug 6, 2003) (on file with author).

[182] William Stevenson, *90 Minutes at Entebbe* 109, 112 (Bantam 1976).

Special Forces' Wear of Non-Standard Uniforms   *Parks*

Who	When	Where	Disposition (if any)
Soviet Union[183] *Spetsnaz* dressed in civilian clothing neutralized senior Afghan officers, then secured Kabul Airport wearing Afghan Army uniforms	1979	Afghanistan	None
United States[184] Team for rescue of US hostages in American Embasssy in Tehran wore non-standard uniforms approved by the Joint Chiefs of Staff and President	1980	Iran	Mission aborted due to helicopter failures
Soviet Union,[185] **East Germany** *Spetsnaz* dressed in civilian clothing or NATO uniforms trained/planned to penetrate/operate in NATO rear, attack high-value targets	Cold War	NATO nations	Never executed
North Korea[186] SF infiltrated South Korea wearing civilian clothing or South Korean uniforms	1950–88	South Korea	Treated as spies when caught

---

[183]   Michael G. Welham and Bruce Quarrie, *Operation Spetsnaz: The Aims, Tactics and Techniques of Soviet Special Forces* 40 (Patrick Stephens 1989); Department of Defense, *Soviet Military Power* 72 (1985).

[184]   Personal knowledge of the author. Each aircraft carried Iranian markings to be stuck on the fuselage in the event an aircraft had to be abandoned. For the history of the mission, see Paul B. Ryan, *The Iranian Rescue Mission: Why It Failed* (Naval Institute 1985), and Col. James H. Kyle, *The Guts to Try* (Orion 1990).

[185]   Welham and Quarrie, *Operation Spetsnaz* at 31–32 (cited in note 183); Ross S. Kelly, *Spetsnaz: Special Operations Forces of the USSR*, 12 Def & Foreign Aff 28–29 (Dec 1984) (on file with author); Dale Van Atta, *Spetsnaz: The Soviets' Sinister Strike Force*, 65 Reader's Digest 72 (Apr 1986).

[186]   Joseph S. Bermudez, Jr., *North Korea Special Forces* 21, 33, 53, 54, 70 (Jane's 1988). North Korean Special Forces' disguises included dressing as civilian males and females; see id at 37, 70. North Korean use of South Korean uniforms or civilian clothing cannot be documented to present, but is likely.

Chicago Journal of International Law

Who	When	Where	Disposition (if any)
Israel[187] *Sarayet Maktal* wearing non-standard uniforms carried out successful direct action mission to kill Abu Jihad, PLO military commander, in Tunis	1988	Sidi-bou-Said, Tunisia	None
Panama[188] 7th Infantry Company (*Macho de* Monte), Panamanian Defense Forces, fought in civilian attire of shorts, t-shirts, and straw hats	1989	Panama (Operation JUST CAUSE)	Captured members treated as prisoners of war by US
United States[189] Commander-in-Chief's SF personal security detail wore civilian attire	1990–91	Saudi Arabia	None
United Kingdom/ United States[190] SF wore *kaffiyeh/agal* and indigenous coats over uniforms during operations in Iraq	1991	Iraq	None

---

187   See Livingstone and Halevy, *Inside the PLO* at 31–58 (cited in note 181). Team members wore unmarked black fireproof coveralls. Id at 50.

188   E-mail message to author from Lt. Col. Kevin H. Govern, JA, USA (June 18, 2003) (on file with author).

189   Personal knowledge of the author, photograph in author's files.

190   See Ratcliffe, Botham, and Hitchen, *Eye of the Storm* at 214, 305 (cited in note 20).

[7]

UNLAWFUL COMBATANCY

*By Yoram Dinstein**

I. COMBATANTS AND CIVILIANS

Under the *jus in bello*, combatants are persons who are either members of the armed forces (except medical and religious personnel) or – irrespective of such membership – take an active part in hostilities in an international armed conflict.[1] The *jus in bello* posits a fundamental principle of distinction between combatants and non-combatants (*i.e.*, civilians).[2] The goal is to ensure in every feasible manner that inter-State armed conflicts be waged solely among the combatants of the belligerent Parties. Lawful combatants can attack enemy combatants or military objectives, causing death, injury and destruction. By contrast, civilians are not allowed to participate in the fighting. As a complementary norm, civilians "enjoy general protection against dangers arising from military operations".[3]

It is not always easy to define what an active participation in hostilities denotes. Sometimes, the reference is to "direct" participation in hostilities.[4] But the adjective "direct" does not shed much light on the extent of participation required. For instance, a person who gathers military intelligence in enemy controlled territory and a driver delivering ammunition to firing positions are generally acknowledged as actively taking part in hostilities (although merely assisting in the general war effort does not suffice).[5]

A civilian may convert himself into a combatant. In fact, every combatant is a former civilian: nobody is born a combatant. In the same vein, a

---

* M.Jur., LL.M., Dr.Jur. Yanowicz Professor of Human Rights, Pro-President, Tel Aviv University (Israel); Member, *Institut de Droit International*.

1 *See* A.P.V. Rogers & P. Malherbe, *Model Manual on the Law of Armed Conflict* 29 (ICRC, 1999).

2 *See* Advisory Opinion on Legality of the Threat or Use of Nuclear Weapons, [1996] *I.C.J. Rep.* 226, 257.

3 Protocol Additional to the Geneva Conventions of 12 August 1949, and Relating to the Protection of Victims of International Armed Conflicts (Protocol I), 1977, *The Laws of Armed Conflicts: A Collection of Conventions, Resolutions and Other Documents* 621, 651 (D. Schindler & J. Toman eds., 3rd ed., 1988) (Art. 51(1)).

4 *See* Rogers & Malherbe, *supra* note 1, at 29. *Cf.* Art. 51(3) of Protocol I, *supra* note 3, at 651.

5 *See* Rogers & Malherbe, *supra* note 1, at 29.

combatant may retire and become a civilian. But at any given point a person is either a combatant or a civilian: he cannot (and is not allowed to) be both at the same time, nor can he constantly shift from one position to the other.

Whether on land, by sea or in the air, one cannot fight the enemy and remain a civilian. Interestingly, this general norm first consolidated in the law of sea warfare. Already in Article 1 of the Declaration of Paris of 1856, it is proclaimed:

> Privateering is, and remains, abolished.[6]

Privateers were private persons (at times known as corsairs, not to be confused with pirates) who obtained official letters of marque from a Government, allowing them to attack enemy merchant ships.[7] As the language of the Declaration of Paris indicates, it merely confirms the abolition of privateering as "an already established situation" under customary international law.[8] The law of land (and air) warfare ultimately adjusted to proscribe parallel modes of behaviour.

Combatants can withdraw from the hostilities not only by retiring and becoming civilians, but also by becoming *hors de combat*. This can happen either by choice (through laying down of arms and surrendering) or by force of circumstances (by getting wounded, sick or shipwrecked). A combatant who is *hors de combat* and falls into the hands of the enemy is in principle entitled to the status of a prisoner of war. Being a prisoner of war means denial of liberty, *i.e.*, detention for the duration of the hostilities (which may go on for many years). However, that detention has only one purpose: to preclude the further participation of the prisoner of war in the ongoing hostilities. The detention is not due to any criminal act committed by the prisoner of war, and he cannot be prosecuted and punished "simply for having taken part in hostilities".[9] While his liberty is temporarily denied, the decisive point is that the life, health and dignity of a prisoner of war are guaranteed. Detailed provisions to that end are incorporated in Geneva Convention (III) of 1949.[10]

---

6   Paris Declaration Respecting Maritime Law, 1856, *The Laws of Armed Conflicts, supra* note 3, at 787, 788.

7   *See* U. Scheuner, "Privateering", 3 *Encyclopedia of Public International Law* 1120, 1120-21 (R. Bernhardt ed., 1997).

8   *Ibid.*, 1122.

9   A. Rosas, *The Legal Status of Prisoners of War: A Study in International Humanitarian Law Applicable in Armed Conflicts* 82 (1976).

10 Geneva Convention (III) Relative to the Treatment of Prisoners of War, 1949, *The Laws of Armed Conflicts, supra* note 3, at 423.

II. LAWFUL AND UNLAWFUL COMBATANTS

Entitlement to the status of a prisoner of war – upon being captured by the enemy – is vouchsafed to every combatant, subject to the *conditio sine qua non* that he is a lawful combatant. The distinction between lawful and unlawful combatants complements the fundamental distinction between combatants and civilians: the primary goal of the former is to preserve the latter.[11] The *jus in bello* can effectively protect civilians from being objects of attack in war only if and when they can be identified by the enemy as non-combatants. Combatants "may try to become invisible in the landscape, but not in the crowd".[12] Blurring the lines of division between combatants and civilians is bound to result in civilians suffering the consequences of being suspected as covert combatants. Hence, under customary international law, a sanction (deprivation of the privileges of prisoners of war) is imposed on any combatant masquerading as a civilian in order to mislead the enemy and avoid detection.

An enemy civilian who does not take arms, and does not otherwise participate actively in the hostilities, is guaranteed by the *jus in bello* not only his life, health and dignity (as is done with respect to prisoners of war), but even his personal liberty which cannot be deprived (through detention) without cause. But a person is not allowed to wear simultaneously two caps: the hat of a civilian and the helmet of a soldier. A person who engages in military raids by night, while purporting to be an innocent civilian by day, is a combatant in the sense that he can be lawfully targeted by the enemy. Yet, he is an unlawful combatant. Hence, he will not be accorded the privileges attached to lawful combatancy.

Upon being captured by the enemy, an unlawful combatant – like a lawful combatant (and unlike a civilian) – is subject to automatic detention. But in contradistinction to a lawful combatant, an unlawful combatant fails to enjoy the benefits of the status of a prisoner of war. Hence, although he cannot be executed without trial, he is susceptible to being prosecuted and severely punished for any acts of violence committed in the course of the hostilities in which he has participated. The legal position was summed up by the Supreme Court of the United States, in the *Quirin* case of 1942 (per Chief Justice Stone):

---

[11] *See* T. Meron, "Some Legal Aspects of Arab Terrorists' Claims to Privileged Combatancy", 40 *Nordisk Tidsskrift for International Ret* 47, 62 (1970).

[12] D. Bindschedler-Robert, "A Reconsideration of the Law of Armed Conflicts", *The Law of Armed Conflicts: Report of the Conference on Contemporary Problems of the Law of Armed Conflict, 1969* 1, 43 (Carnegie Endowment, 1971).

> By universal agreement and practice, the law of war draws a distinction
> between the armed forces and the peaceful populations of belligerent
> nations and also between those who are lawful and unlawful combatants.
> Lawful combatants are subject to capture and detention as prisoners of
> war by opposing military forces. Unlawful combatants are likewise
> subject to capture and detention, but in addition they are subject to trial
> and punishment by military tribunals for acts which render their
> belligerency unlawful.[13]

With the exception of the last few words, this is an accurate reflection of the
jus in bello.

What can unlawful combatants be prosecuted and punished for? The
Quirin judgment refers to "trial and punishment by military tribunals for acts
which render their belligerency unlawful". Admittedly, sometimes the act
which turns a person into an unlawful combatant constitutes by itself an
offence (under either domestic or international law) and can be prosecuted
and punished as such before a military tribunal. But on other occasions the
judicial proceedings may be conducted before regular courts and, more
significantly, they are likely to pertain to acts other than those that divested
the person of the status of lawful combatant. Even when the act negating the
status as a lawful combatant does not constitute a crime *per se* (under either
domestic or international law), it can expose the perpetrator to ordinary penal
sanctions (pursuant to the domestic legal system) for other acts committed by
him that are branded as criminal. Unlawful combatants "may be punished
under the internal criminal legislation of the adversary for having committed
hostile acts in violation of its provisions (e.g., for murder), even if these acts
do not constitute war crimes under international law".[14]

At bottom, warfare by its very nature consists of a series of acts of
violence (like homicide, assault, battery and arson) ordinarily penalized by
the criminal codes of all countries. When a combatant, John Doe, holds a
rifle, aims it at Richard Roe (a soldier belonging to the enemy's armed forces)
with intent to kill, pulls the trigger, and causes Richard Roe's death, what we
have is a premeditated homicide fitting the definition of murder in virtually
all domestic penal codes. If, upon being captured by the enemy, John Doe is
not prosecuted for murder, this is due to one reason only. The *jus in bello*
provides John Doe with a legal shield, protecting him from trial and
punishment, by conferring upon him the status of a prisoner of war. Yet, the
shield is available only on condition that John Doe is a lawful combatant. If

---

[13]   *Ex parte Quirin et al.* (1942), 317 *U.S.* 1, 30-31.
[14]   Rosas, *supra* note 9, at 305.

John Doe acts as he does beyond the pale of legal combatancy, the *jus in bello* simply removes the protective shield. Thereby, it subjects John Doe to the full rigor of the enemy's domestic legal system, and the ordinary penal sanctions provided by that law will become applicable to him.

There are several differences between prosecution of war criminals and that of unlawful combatants.[15] The principal distinction is derived from the active or passive role of the *jus in bello*. War criminals are brought to trial for serious violations of the *jus in bello* itself. With unlawful combatants, the *jus in bello* refrains from stigmatizing the acts as criminal. It merely takes off a mantle of immunity from the defendant, who is therefore accessible to penal charges for any offence committed against the domestic legal system.

It is also noteworthy that, unlike war criminals (who must be brought to trial), unlawful combatants may simply be subjected to administrative detention without trial. Detention of unlawful combatants without trial was specifically mentioned as an option in the *Quirin* case (as quoted above), and the option has indeed been used widely by the United States in the war in Afghanistan (see *infra*, V).

Detention of unlawful combatants is also the subject of special legislation of Israel, passed by the Knesset in 2002.[16] This Detention of Unlawful Combatants Law defines an unlawful combatant as anyone taking part – directly or indirectly – in hostilities against the State of Israel, who is not entitled to a prisoner of war status under Geneva Convention (III).[17] Detention is based on the decision of the Chief of Staff of the armed forces, on grounds of State security, but it is subject to judicial review by a (civilian) District Court (both initially and every six months thereafter).[18] The Law emphasizes that detention is just one option, and that an unlawful combatant can equally be brought to trial under any criminal law.[19] An important point addressed by the Law is the maximum duration of the detention. An unlawful combatant can be held in detention as long as the hostilities of the force to which he belongs have not been terminated.[20]

Admittedly, the sanction of detention and/or prosecution (under the domestic legal system) is irrelevant to a prime category of unlawful

---

[15] *See* Y. Dinstein, "The Distinction between Unlawful Combatants and War Criminals", *International Law at a Time of Perplexity* 103-16 (Essays in Honour of Shabtai Rosenne, Y. Dinstein ed., 1989).

[16] *See* Detention of Unlawful Combatants Law-2002, 1834 *Sefer Hahukim* [Laws of the State of Israel, Hebrew] 192. An English translation of this Law appears as s Special Supplement in the present Volume.

[17] *Ibid., id.* (Sec. 2).

[18] *Ibid., id.* (Secs. 3, 5).

[19] *Ibid.*, 193 (Sec. 9).

[20] *Ibid., id.* (Secs. 7-8).

combatants, *i.e.*, successful suicide bombers. A person who merely prepares himself to become a suicide bomber but is thwarted in the attempt can still be subject to detention or prosecution. However, once the act is executed, the perpetrator is beyond the reach of the law. The question as to which measures can be taken by way of deterrence against potential suicide bombers is by no means resolved at the time of writing, especially in light of the generally upheld principle that nobody can be punished for an offence he has not personally committed.[21] Accomplices and accessories to the terrorist act can evidently be prosecuted or detained, but members of the perpetrator's family – or others closely associated with him – cannot be held responsible for his conduct.

III. THE ENTITLEMENT TO PRISONER OF WAR STATUS UNDER CUSTOMARY INTERNATIONAL LAW

Article 1 of the Regulations Respecting the Laws and Customs of War on Land, Annexed to Hague Convention (II) of 1899 and Hague Convention (IV) of 1907, proclaims:

The laws, rights, and duties of war apply not only to armies, but also to militia and volunteer corps fulfilling the following conditions:
1. To be commanded by a person responsible for his subordinates;
2. To have a fixed distinctive emblem recognizable at a distance;
3. To carry arms openly; and
4. To conduct their operations in accordance with the laws and customs of war.[22]

Article 2 adds a provision entitled "Levée en masse", which reads in the revised 1907 version:

The inhabitants of a territory which has not been occupied, who, on the approach of the enemy, spontaneously take up arms to resist the invading troops without having had time to organize themselves in accordance with

---

[21] *See* Art. 33, first Paragraph, of Geneva Convention (IV) Relative to the Protection of Civilian Persons in Time of War, 1949, *The Laws of Armed Conflicts, supra* note 3, at 495, 511.

[22] Regulations Respecting the Laws and Customs of War on Land, Annexed to Hague Convention (II) of 1899 and Hague Convention (IV) of 1907, *The Laws of Armed Conflicts, supra* note 3, at 63, 75, *id.*

Article 1, shall be regarded as belligerents if they carry arms openly and if they respect the laws and customs of war.[23]

Article 3 prescribes further:

The armed forces of the belligerent parties may consist of combatants and non-combatants. In the case of capture by the enemy, both have a right to be treated as prisoners of war.[24]

As far as civilians who are not employed by the armed forces, yet accompany them, Article 13 stipulates:

Individuals who follow an army without directly belonging to it, such as newspaper correspondents and reporters, sutlers and contractors, who fall into the enemy's hands and whom the latter thinks expedient to detain, are entitled to be treated as prisoners of war, provided they are in possession of a certificate from the military authorities of the army which they were accompanying.[25]

The Hague formula thus establishes four general – and cumulative – conditions for lawful combatancy: (i) subordination to responsible command, (ii) a fixed distinctive emblem, (iii) carrying arms openly, and (iv) conduct in accordance with the *jus in bello*. In the special setting of a "levée en masse", conditions (i) and (ii) are dispensed with, and only conditions (iii) and (iv) remain valid. These provisions of the Hague Regulations (like others) "are considered to embody the customary law of war on land".[26]

The Geneva Conventions of 1949 retain the Hague formula, making it even more stringent. Article 4(A) of Geneva Convention (III) sets forth:

Prisoners of war, in the sense of the present Convention, are persons belonging to one of the following categories, who have fallen into the power of the enemy:
(1) Members of the armed forces of a Party to the conflict, as well as members of militias or volunteer corps forming part of such armed forces.

---

[23] *Ibid.*, 75-76.

[24] *Ibid.*, 76.

[25] *Ibid.*, 79.

[26] *See* G.I.A.D. Draper, "The Status of Combatants and the Question of Guerilla Warfare", 45 *Brit. Y.B. Int'l L.* 173, 186 (1971).

(2) Members of other militias and members of other volunteer corps, including those of organized resistance movements, belonging to a Party to the conflict and operating in or outside their own territory, even if this territory is occupied, provided that such militias or volunteer corps, including such organized resistance movements, fulfil the following conditions:

    (a) that of being commanded by a person responsible for his subordinates;

    (b) that of having a fixed distinctive sign recognizable at a distance;

    (c) that of carrying arms openly;

    (d) that of conducting their operations in accordance with the laws and customs of war.

(3) Members of regular armed forces who profess allegiance to a government or an authority not recognized by the Detaining Power.

(4) Persons who accompany the armed forces without actually being members thereof, such as civilian members of military aircraft crews, war correspondents, supply contractors, members of labor units or of services responsible for the welfare of the armed forces, provided that they have received authorization from the armed forces which they accompany, who shall provide them for that purpose with an identity card similar to the annexed model.

(5) Members of crews, including masters, pilots and apprentices, of the merchant marine and the crews of civil aircraft of the Parties to the conflict, who do not benefit by more favorable treatment under any other provisions of international law.

(6) Inhabitants of a non-occupied territory, who on the approach of the enemy spontaneously take up arms to resist the invading forces, without having had time to form themselves into regular armed units, provided they carry arms openly and respect the laws and customs of war.[27]

This language is replicated in Article 13 of both Geneva Convention (I)[28] and Geneva Convention (II).[29] Article 4(B) of Geneva Convention (III) goes on to create two further categories of persons that should be treated as

---

[27] Geneva Convention (III), *supra* note 10, at 430-31.

[28] Geneva Convention (I) for the Amelioration of the Condition of the Wounded and Sick in Armed Forces in the Field, 1949, *The Laws of Armed Conflicts*, *supra* note 3, at 373, 379-80.

[29] Geneva Convention (II) for the Amelioration of the Condition of Wounded, Sick and Shipwrecked Members of Armed Forces at Sea, 1949, *The Laws of Armed Conflicts*, *supra* note 3, at 401, 408.

UNLAWFUL COMBATANCY

prisoners of war: one relating to occupied territories (members of armed forces who have been released from detention in an occupied territory and are then reinterned),[30] and the other pertaining to neutral countries (members of armed forces of belligerents who reach neutral territory and have to be interned there under international law).[31] Article 4(C) states that nothing in the above provisions affects the status of medical personnel and chaplains,[32] who under Article 33 of Geneva Convention (III) cannot be taken prisoners of war, but may be retained by the Detaining Power with a view to assisting prisoners of war.[33]

The first and foremost category of persons entitled to the status of prisoners of war covers members of the armed forces of the belligerent Parties, including all their different components. These are the regular forces of the belligerents. It does not matter what the semantic appellation of regular forces is (they may function, e.g., under the technical designation of militias); how they are structured; whether military service is compulsory or voluntary; and whether the units are part of standing armed forces or consist of reservists called to action. The distinction is between regular forces of all types, on the one hand, and irregular forces in the sense of partisans or guerrilla forces, on the other.

On the face of it, the Geneva Conventions do not pose any conditions to the eligibility of regular forces to prisoners of war status. Nevertheless, regular forces are not absolved from meeting the cumulative conditions binding irregular forces. There is simply a presumption that regular forces would naturally meet those conditions. But the presumption can definitely be rebutted. The issue came to the fore in the *Mohamed Ali* case of 1968, where the Privy Council held (per Viscount Dilhorne) that it is not enough to establish that a person belongs to the regular armed forces, in order to guarantee to him the status of a prisoner of war.[34] The Privy Council pronounced that even members of the armed forces must observe the cumulative conditions imposed on irregular forces, although this is not stated *expressis verbis* in the Geneva Conventions or in the Hague Regulations.[35] The facts of the case related to Indonesian soldiers who – at a time of a "confrontation" between Indonesia and Malaysia – planted explosives in a

---

[30] This special category makes it "impossible for an occupying Power to deprive prisoners of war of the benefit of the convention through the subterfuge of release and subsequent arrest". R.T. Yingling & R.W. Ginnane, "The Geneva Conventions of 1949", 46 *Am. J. Int'l L.* 393, 405-406 (1952).

[31] Geneva Convention (III), *supra* note 10, at 431-32.

[32] *Ibid.*, 432.

[33] *Ibid.*, 442-43.

[34] Mohamed Ali *et al.* v. Public Prosecutor (1968), [1969] *A.C.* 430, 449.

[35] *Ibid.*, 449-50.

building in Singapore (then a part of Malaysia) while wearing civilian clothes. The Privy Council confirmed the Appellants' death sentence for murder, on the ground that a regular soldier committing an act of sabotage while not in uniform loses the entitlement to a prisoner of war status.[36] The earlier *Quirin* judgment – concerning German members of the armed forces who took off their uniforms when on a sabotage mission in the United States (where they had landed by submarine) – is to the same effect.[37]

The second category of prisoners of war under the Geneva Conventions pertains to irregular forces: guerrillas, partisans and the like, however they call themselves. This is the most problematic category, given the proliferation of such forces in modern warfare. The Geneva Conventions repeat the four Hague conditions verbatim. However, two additional conditions are implied from the *chapeau* of Article 4(A)(2): (v) organization, and (vi) belonging to a Party to the conflict. One more condition is distilled in the case law from the text of the Geneva Conventions: (vii) lack of duty of allegiance to the Detaining Power.

Each of the four Hague conditions, and the additional three conditions, deserves a few words of explanation:

(i)   The first condition – of subordination to a responsible commander – is designed to exclude the possibility of activities of individuals (known in French as "franc-tireurs") on their own. The operation of small units of irregular forces is permissible, provided that the other conditions are fulfilled, but there is no room for individual initiatives. John Doe or Richard Roe – especially in an occupied territory – cannot legitimately conduct a private war against the enemy.

(ii) The second condition – of having a fixed distinct emblem recognizable at a distance – is predicated on two elements. The emblem in question must meet the dual requirement of distinction (*i.e.*, it must identify and characterize the force using it) and fixity (to wit, the force is not allowed to confuse the enemy by ceaselessly changing its distinctive emblem). The most obvious fixed distinct emblem of regular armed forces is that of a particular uniform. But irregular armed forces need not have any uniform, and it suffices for them to possess a less complex distinctive emblem: part of the clothing (like a special shirt or particular headgear) or certain insignia.[38]

The fixed distinctive emblem must be worn throughout every military operation against the enemy in which the combatant takes part (throughout means from start to finish, namely, from the beginning of

---

[36]   *Ibid.*, 451-54.

[37]   *Ex parte* Quirin *et al.*, *supra* note 13, at 35-36.

[38]   *See Commentary, III Geneva Convention* 60 (J. de Preux ed., 1960).

UNLAWFUL COMBATANCY

deployment to the end of disengagement), and the emblem must not be deliberately removed at any time in the course of the operation.[39] Still, combatants are not bound to wear the distinctive emblem when discharging duties not linked to military operations (such as training or administration).[40]

The condition of having a fixed distinctive emblem raises a number of questions owing to its language. Thus, it is not easy to fully understand the obligation that the distinctive emblem will be recognizable at a distance. The phraseology must be reasonably interpreted. Combatants seeking to stay alive do not attempt to draw attention to themselves. On the contrary, even soldiers in uniform are prone to use camouflage. This is a legitimate ruse of war,[41] as long as the combatant merely exploits the topographical conditions: the physical as distinct from the demographic landscape of civilians.[42] Another question is germane to night warfare. Needless to say, if the combatant does not carry an illuminated distinctive emblem, that emblem will not be recognisable at a distance in the dark. Again, it is important that the terse and imperfect wording would not overshadow the thrust of the condition, which is crystal clear. Just as regular forces wear uniforms, so must irregular forces use a fixed emblem which will distinguish them – in ordinary circumstances and in a reasonable fashion – from the civilian population. The issue is not whether combatants can be seen, but the lack of desire on their part to create the false impression that they are civilians.

It should be added that when combatants go to (or from) battle in a vehicle or a tank – and, similarly, if they sail in a vessel or fly in an aircraft – it is not enough for each individual person to carry the distinctive emblem: the vehicle or other platform must itself be properly identified.[43] By the same token, the external marking of the vehicle or platform does not absolve the combatants on board from carrying their personal distinctive emblems. As for members of the crew of a military aircraft, there is a specific provision to that effect in Article 15 of the (non-binding) 1923 Hague Rules of Air Warfare, where it is explained

---

[39] *See* H.S. Levie, *Prisoners of War in International Armed Conflict*, 59 *Int'l L. Stud.* 47 (1978).

[40] *See* W.A. Solf, "Article 44", *New Rules for Victims of Armed Conflicts: Commentary on the Two 1977 Protocols Additional to the Geneva Conventions of 1949* 241, 252 (M. Bothe, K.J. Partsch & W.A. Solf eds., 1982).

[41] *See* Art. 37(2) of Protocol I, *supra* note 3, at 645.

[42] *See* Bindschedler-Robert, *supra* note 12, at 43.

[43] *See Commentary*, *supra* note 38, at 60.

that this is required in case the members of the crew "become separated from their aircraft".[44]

(iii) The third condition – of carrying arms openly – brings up similar issues as the second. Does this mean that a combatant is barred from carrying a handgun in a holster or hand grenades in a pouch? The question is patently rhetorical. Once more, what counts is not the ambiguous language but the gist of the condition. A lawful combatant must abstain from purporting to be an innocent civilian, with a view to facilitating access to the enemy by stealth. He must carry his arms openly in a reasonable way, depending on the nature of the weapon and the circumstances at hand.

(iv) The fourth condition – conduct in accordance with the *jus in bello* – is the key to lawful combatancy. Unless a combatant is willing himself to respect the *jus in bello*, he is estopped from relying on that body of law when desirous of enjoying its benefits.[45]

These are the original Hague conditions, endorsed by the Geneva Conventions. As mentioned, the following additional conditions are derived from the Conventions:

(v) The fifth condition – organization – actually reinvigorates the first condition in a somewhat different way. Lawful combatants must act within a hierarchic framework, embedded in discipline, and subject to supervision by upper echelons of what is being done by subordinate units in the field.

(vi) The sixth condition – belonging to a Party to the conflict – got a practical expression in the 1969 Judgment of an Israeli Military Court in the *Kassem* case.[46] Here a number of persons who belonged to an organization calling itself the "Popular Front for the Liberation of Palestine" crossed the Jordan River from the East Bank (the Kingdom of Jordan) to the West Bank (Israeli occupied territory) for sabotage purposes. When captured and charged with security offences, they claimed entitlement to prisoners of war status. The Israeli Military Court held that irregular forces must belong to a Party to the conflict.[47] Since no Arab Government at war with Israel had assumed responsibility for the activities of the Popular Front – which was indeed illegal in the Kingdom of Jordan – the condition was not fulfilled.[48] The judgment

---

[44] Hague Rules of Air Warfare, 1923, *The Laws of Armed Conflicts*, *supra* note 3, at 207, 209.

[45] *See* Levie, *supra* note 39, at 50-51.

[46] Military Prosecutor v. Kassem and Others (Israel, Military Court, 1969), 42 *I.L.R.* 470.

[47] *Ibid.*, 476.

[48] *Ibid.*, 477-78.

UNLAWFUL COMBATANCY 259

was criticized by G. Schwarzenberger on the ground that the Geneva Conventions were not meant to limit the scope of lawful combatancy under preexisting rules of international law.[49] However, even prior to the Geneva Conventions, the premise was that the Hague conditions apply only to combatants acting on behalf of a State Party to the conflict.[50] It is evident that the members of an independent band of guerrillas cannot be regarded as lawful combatants, even if they observe the *jus in bello*, use a fixed distinctive emblem, and carry their arms openly. One way or another, "a certain relationship with a belligerent government is necessary".[51] One can, of course, argue whether Palestinian guerrillas factually belonged at the time to a Party to the conflict. But the condition itself is irreproachable.

(vii) The seventh and last condition – of non-allegiance to the Detaining Power – is not specifically mentioned in the Geneva Conventions, and is derived from the case law. The principal authority is the 1967 judgement of the Privy Council in the *Koi* case,[52] in which captured Indonesian paratroopers – landing in Malaysia – included a number of Malays convicted and sentenced to death for having unlawfully possessed arms in a security zone. The question on appeal before the Privy Council was whether they were entitled to prisoners of war status. The Privy Council held (per Lord Hodson) that nationals of the Detaining Power, as well as other persons owing it a duty of allegiance, are not entitled to such status.[53] This was viewed by the Privy Council as a rule of customary international law.[54] Although the condition does not appear in the text of Article 4(A), the Privy Council found other provisions of Geneva Convention (III) – specifically Articles 87 and 100[55] – in which it is clearly stated that prisoners of war are not nationals of the Detaining Power and do not owe it any duty of allegiance.[56]

The requirement of nationality (or allegiance) has to be approached carefully. The fact that a combatant belonging to State A – captured by State B – is a national of State C, does not make any difference. A German soldier in the French Foreign Legion was entitled to a prisoner

---

[49] *See* G. Schwarzenberger, "Human Rights and Guerrilla Warfare", 1 *Israel Y.B. Hum. Rts.* 246, 252 (1971).

[50] *See* L. Nurick & R.W. Barrett, "Legality of Guerrilla Forces under the Laws of War", 40 *Am. J. Int'l L.* 563, 567-69 (1946).

[51] Bindschedler-Robert, *supra* note 12, at 40.

[52] Public Prosecutor v. Koi *et al.* (1967), [1968] *A.C.* 829.

[53] *Ibid.*, 856-58.

[54] *Ibid.*, 856-57.

[55] Geneva Convention (III), *supra* note 10, at 460, 464.

[56] Public Prosecutor v. Koi *et al.*, *supra* note 52, at 857.

The Conduct of Hostilities in International Humanitarian Law II

ISRAEL YEARBOOK ON HUMAN RIGHTS

of war status in the Indo-China War. But such a soldier would not have been entitled to the same status if fighting in a war against Germany.

The *Koi* case also occasions a question of the law of evidence. Under Article 5 (second paragraph) of Geneva Convention (III) – quoted in full *infra*, V – should any doubt arise as to whether certain persons belong to any of the categories enumerated in Article 4, they enjoy the Convention's protection until their status is determined by a competent tribunal. Opinions in the Privy Council were divided as to whether the mere allegation by a defendant that he is a foreign national generates doubt in accordance with Article 5: the majority held that that was the legal position, but a minority dissented.[57] The more central issue is that of the burden of proof. The minority opined that the burden of proof lies on the defendant, who must show that he is entitled to a prisoner of war status (and consequently that he is not a national of the Detaining Power).[58] The majority did not address the point. But the correct position apparently is that, once a defendant persuades the court that he is a member of the enemy armed forces, the burden of proof that he owes allegiance to the Detaining Power (and is therefore not entitled to a prisoner of war status) falls on the prosecution.[59] Incontestably, the defendant first has to establish that he is a member of the enemy armed forces.

It is not easy for irregular forces to observe cumulatively the seven conditions catalogued or – for that matter – even the core four Hague conditions. These conditions are actually patterned after the operations of regular forces (to which they do not explicitly allude). Regular forces are organized, are subject to hierarchical discipline, and naturally belong to a Party to the conflict; they have a proud tradition of wearing uniforms and carrying their arms openly; they are trained to observe the *jus in bello*; and the issue of allegiance scarcely arises. However, with irregular forces (to whom the conditions expressly refer), the position is not so simple. Even if other problems are ignored, the difficulty to meet both the second and third conditions (of a fixed distinctive emblem and carrying arms openly) is blatant, "since secrecy and surprise are the essence" of guerrilla warfare.[60] Most of the partisan (resistance) movements of World War II did not fulfil all

---

[57] *Ibid.*, 855, 865.

[58] *Ibid.*, 864.

[59] *See* R.R. Baxter, "The Privy Council on the Qualifications of Belligerents", 63 *Am. J. Int'l L.* 290, 293 (1969).

[60] *See* R.R. Baxter, "So-Called 'Unprivileged Belligerency': Spies, Guerrillas, and Saboteurs", 28 *Brit. Y.B. Int'l L.* 323, 328 (1951).

UNLAWFUL COMBATANCY   261

the cumulative conditions.[61] From a practical standpoint, many believe that "obedience to these rules would be tantamount to committing suicide, as far as most guerrillas would be concerned".[62] Still, these are the norms of the Hague Regulations, the Geneva Conventions, and customary international law.

Under the Hague Regulations, the Geneva Conventions, and customary international law, the only time that the cumulative conditions are eased is that of "levée en masse". It must be accentuated that this category applies only to the inhabitants of unoccupied areas, so that there is no "levée en masse" in occupied territories. The idea (originating in the French Revolution[63]) is that at the point of invasion – and in order to forestall occupation – the civilian population takes arms spontaneously, without an opportunity to organize. This is an extraordinary situation in the course of which – for a short while and as an interim stage in the fighting – there is no need to meet all seven cumulative conditions to the status of lawful combatancy. The Hague Regulations and Geneva Conventions enumerate only two cumulative conditions: carrying arms openly and respect for the *jus in bello* (conditions (iii) and (iv)). It follows that there is no need to meet the two other Hague conditions of subordination to a responsible commander and using a fixed distinctive emblem (conditions (i) and (ii)). Given the postulate that there was no time to organize, condition (v) is inapplicable. Condition (vi) is also irrelevant: when the civilian population resists invasion, the problem of belonging to a Party to the conflict is moot. On the other hand, it is arguable that condition (vii) of nationality (or allegiance) remains in place. In any event, the transitional phase of "levée en masse" lapses *ex hypothesi* after a relatively short duration. One of three things is bound to happen: either the territory will be occupied (despite the "levée en masse"); or the invading force will be repulsed (thanks to the "levée en masse" or to the timely arrival of reinforcements); or the battle of defence will stabilize, and then there is ample opportunity for organization.

Both the Hague Regulations and the Geneva Conventions equate the position of certain civilians – employed by or accompanying the armed forces – to that of lawful combatants as far as prisoners of war status is concerned. Evidently, the fact that a civilian is employed by or accompanies the armed forces does not turn him into a combatant. Hence, the question of

---

[61]   *See* J.S. Pictet, "The New Geneva Conventions for the Protection of War Victims", 45 *Am. J. Int'l L.* 462, 472 (1951).

[62]   G. von Glahn, "The Protection of Human Rights in Time of Armed Conflicts", 1 *Israel Y.B. Hum. Rts.* 208, 223 (1971).

[63]   On the origins of the institution, *see* W.G. Rabus, "A New Definition of the 'Levée en Masse'", 24 *Netherlands Int'l L. Rev.* 232, *id.* (1977).

the fulfillment of most of the cumulative conditions does not arise. Yet, in all instances condition (iv) must be regarded as paramount: anybody seeking the privileges of the *jus in bello* must himself respect the laws from which he proposes to benefit. Condition (vii) of nationality – or allegiance – is also relevant to civilians. Should the civilian bear light arms for self-defence, condition (iii) relating to carrying the arms openly will apply.

Who should observe the seven conditions: the individual or the group of which he is a member? The issue does not arise with respect to regular troops. The assumption is that these forces collectively fulfil all the conditions, and to the extent that there is doubt in the concrete case, it affects John Doe but not an entire army. In the *Mohamed Ali* and *Koi* cases, there was no doubt that members of the armed forces of Indonesia generally wear uniforms and do not owe allegiance to Malaysia, although the defendants in the dock failed to meet these conditions (and were therefore denied prisoners of war status). However, where irregular forces are concerned, the question of whether the conditions of lawful combatancy are met may relate both to a guerrilla movement collectively and to each of its members individually. The answer to the question is contingent on the various conditions.

The addressee of conditions (i), (v) and (vi) is clearly the group collectively, and not any of the members individually. It is necessary to ascertain that the group as a whole is organized, has a responsible commander and belongs to a Party to the conflict. Should that be the case, the same yardsticks must be applied to all members of the group.[64] The reverse applies to condition (vii), directed at each member of the group rather than the group as a collective: the link of nationality is determined individually. In between are the other conditions: (ii), (iii) and (iv). Condition (ii) on a fixed distinctive emblem requires some preliminary action on the part of the group, which must adopt its identifying emblem; if it does not do that, no member of the group is capable of meeting the condition. Still, even if the group adopts a fixed distinctive emblem, that does not mean that John Doe will use it at the critical time (just as the defendants in the *Mohamed Ali* case did not wear their uniforms at the critical time). If John Does fails to do that, his misconduct does not contaminate the entire group, but the personal consequences are liable to be dire.

As for conditions (iii) and (iv) – carrying arms openly and observance of the *jus in bello* – the present writer believes that the correct approach is that their fulfillment should be monitored primarily on an individual basis and only secondarily on a group basis. That is to say, if observance of these conditions in the individual case comes to a test in reality, John Doe has to

---

[64] *See* Draper, *supra* note 26, at 196.

answer for his actual behavior. However, if no opportunity for such individual verification presents itself – for instance, when John Doe is captured in possession of arms but before setting out to accomplish any hostile mission – it is possible to establish how the group behaves in general and extrapolate from the collectivity to the individual. If the group as a whole has a record of disrespect for the *jus in bello*, there is no need to accord John Doe a prisoner of war status. Conversely, if the group as a whole generally acts in compliance with the *jus in bello*, John Doe should be allowed to benefit from doubt. It has been contended that – even if John Doe actually observes the *jus in bello* – he should not be deemed a lawful combatant when the group as a whole generally acts in breach of that body of law.[65] This is unassailable in extreme cases like Al Qaeda (see *infra*, V, 2). But if the conduct of the members of the group is uneven, John Doe should be judged on the merits of his own case and not on the demerits of that of some of his comrades at arms.

IV. THE LEGAL POSITION UNDER PROTOCOL I OF 1977

The legal position is radically changed pursuant to Additional Protocol I of 1977. Article 43 of the Protocol promulgates:

1. The armed forces of a Party to a conflict consist of organized armed forces, groups and units which are under a command responsible to that Party for the conduct of its subordinates, even if that Party is represented by a government or an authority not recognized by an adverse Party. Such armed forces shall be subject to an internal disciplinary system which, *inter alia*, shall enforce compliance with the rules of international law applicable in armed conflict.
2. Members of the armed forces of a Party to a conflict (other than medical personnel and chaplains covered by Article 33 of the Third Convention) are combatants, that is to say, they have the right to participate directly in hostilities.
3. Whenever a Party to the conflict incorporates a paramilitary or armed law enforcement agency into its armed forces it shall so notify the other Parties to the conflict.[66]

By itself, Article 43 appears to follow in the footsteps of the Hague and Geneva rules, as reflected in customary international law. Indeed, it reaffirms four of the seven conditions for (lawful) combatancy: condition (i)

---

[65] *See ibid.*, 197; and Meron, *supra* note 11, at 65.
[66] Protocol I, *supra* note 3, at 647.

concerning the existence of a command responsible for the conduct of its subordinates; condition (iv) about compliance with the rules of the *jus in bello*; condition (v) stressing the need for organization and discipline; and condition (vi) pertaining to the need to belong to a Party to the conflict.[67]

Unfortunately, Article 44 goes much further:

1.   Any combatant, as defined in Article 43, who falls into the power of an adverse Party shall be a prisoner of war.

2.   While all combatants are obliged to comply with the rules of international law applicable in armed conflict, violations of these rules shall not deprive a combatant of his right to be a combatant or, if he falls into the power of an adverse Party, of his right to be a prisoner of war, except as provided in paragraphs 3 and 4.

3.   In order to promote the protection of the civilian population from the effects of hostilities, combatants are obliged to distinguish themselves from the civilian population while they are engaged in an attack or in a military operation preparatory to an attack. Recognizing, however, that there are situations in armed conflicts where, owing to the nature of the hostilities an armed combatant cannot so distinguish himself, he shall retain his status as a combatant, provided that, in such situations, he carries his arms openly:

(a)   during each military engagement, and

(b)   during such time as he is visible to the adversary while he is engaged in a military deployment preceding the launching of an attack in which he is to participate.

Acts which comply with the requirements of this paragraph shall not be considered as perfidious within the meaning of Article 37, paragraph 1(c).

4.   A combatant who falls into the power of an adverse Party while failing to meet the requirements set forth in the second sentence of paragraph 3 shall forfeit his right to be a prisoner of war, but he shall, nevertheless, be given protections equivalent in all respects to those accorded to prisoners of war by the Third Convention and by this Protocol. The protection includes protections equivalent to those accorded to prisoners of war by the Third Convention in the case where such a person is tried and punished for any offences he has committed.

5.   Any combatant who falls into the power of an adverse Party while not engaged in an attack or in a military operation preparatory to an attack

---

[67] *See* J. de Preux, "Article 43", *Commentary on the Additional Protocols of 8 June 1977 to the Geneva Conventions of 12 August 1949* 505, 517 (Y. Sandoz *et al.* eds., ICRC, 1987).

shall not forfeit his rights to be a combatant and a prisoner of war by virtue of his prior activities.

6.   This article is without prejudice to the right of any person to be a prisoner of war pursuant to Article 4 of the Third Convention.

7.   This article is not intended to change the generally accepted practice of States with respect to the wearing of the uniform by combatants assigned to the regular, uniformed armed units of a Party to the conflict.

8.   In addition to the categories of persons mentioned in Article 13 of the First and Second Conventions, all members of the armed forces of a Party to the conflict, as defined in Article 43 of this Protocol, shall be entitled to protection under those Conventions if they are wounded or sick or, in the case of the Second Convention, shipwrecked at sea or in other waters.[68]

The language of this verbose text is quite convoluted, not to say obscure. But when a serious attempt is made to reconcile its disparate paragraphs with one another, a distressing picture emerges. Notwithstanding the provision of Article 43, Article 44(2) does away – to all intents and purposes – with condition (iv): whether or not in compliance with the *jus in bello*, all combatants (*i.e.*, those taking a direct part in hostilities) are entitled to the status of lawful combatancy and to the attendant privileges of prisoners of war. Paragraph (3) of Article 44, while paying lip service to the principle of distinction, retains only a truncated version of condition (iii): the duty to carry arms openly is restricted to the duration of the battle itself and to the preliminary phase of deployment in preparation for the launching of an attack, while being visible to the enemy. The issue of visibility to the enemy is complex, implying that if the combatant neither knows nor should know that he is visible, the obligation does not apply.[69] It is not clear whether visibility is determined solely by the naked eye or it also includes observation by means of binoculars and even infra-red equipment.[70] More significantly, there is no agreement as to when deployment begins: at the original assembly point (from which the combatants proceed to their destination) or only moments before the attack is launched.[71] But these and other points are quite moot, since – in a most enigmatic fashion[72] – paragraph (4) mandates that, albeit technically deprived of prisoners of war status, transgressors must be

---

[68]   Protocol I, *supra* note 3, at 647-48.

[69]   *See* J. de Preux, "Article 44", *Commentary on the Additional Protocols*, *supra* note 67, at 519, 535.

[70]   Solf, *supra* note 40, at 254-55.

[71]   *See* de Preux, *supra* note 69, at 534-35.

[72]   *See* R. Lapidoth, "Qui a Droit au Statut de Prisonnier de Guerre?", 82 *R.G.D.I.P.* 170, 204 (1978).

accorded every protection conferred on prisoners of war. Thus, in terms of practicality, condition (iii) – however circumscribed – is vitiated by Article 44. As far as condition (ii) is concerned, the sole reference to it is made in paragraph (7), articulating an intention to not affect the practice of wearing uniforms by regular armies. Thereby, Article 44 only underscores the elimination of condition (ii) where it really counts, namely, when irregular forces take part in hostilities. In fact, the consequence is "to tip the balance of protection in favor of irregular combatants to the detriment of the regular soldier and the civilian".[73] In the final analysis, it is the civilians who will suffer. "Inevitably, regular forces would treat civilians more harshly and with less restraint if they believed that their opponents were free to pose as civilians while retaining their right to act as combatants and their POW status if captured".[74]

As pointed out above, the seven cumulative conditions of lawful combatancy are onerous for irregular forces. Hence, it would have made sense to alleviate the conditions to some extent. For instance, conditions (ii) and (iii) could become alternative rather than cumulative in their application, considering that when one is fulfilled the other may be looked at as redundant.[75] Still, the pendulum in Article 44 has swung from one extreme to the other, reducing *ad absurdum* the conditions of lawful combatancy. The outcome is that, for contracting Parties to the Protocol, the general distinction between lawful and unlawful combatants becomes nominal in value.

Objections to the new legal regime created in Article 44 are among the key reasons why the leading military Power of the day – the United States – declines to ratify Protocol I (while recognizing that many of its other provisions reflect customary international law),[76] and this negative assessment is shared by an array of other States.

V. THE WAR IN AFGHANISTAN

The war in Afghanistan, waged by the United States and several allied countries against the Taliban regime and the Al Qaeda terrorist network – following the armed attacks of 11 September 2001 – raises multiple issues germane to the status of lawful/unlawful combatancy:

---

[73] G.B. Roberts, "The New Rules for Waging War: The Case against Ratification of Additional Protocol I", 26 *Va. J. Int'l L.* 109, 129 (1985-86).

[74] A.D. Sofaer, "The Rationale for the United States Decision", 82 *Am. J. Int'l L.* 784, 786 (1988).

[75] *See* W.J. Ford, "Members of Resistance Movements", 24 *Netherlands Int'l L. Rev.* 92, 104 (1977).

[76] *See Operational Law Handbook* 5-3 (US Army Judge Advocate General, 2000).

UNLAWFUL COMBATANCY   267

1.   The first problem relates to the standing of Taliban fighters. On the one hand, the Taliban regime – on the eve of the war -- was in *de facto* control of as much as 90% of the territory of Afghanistan. On the other hand, the regime was unrecognized by the overwhelming majority of the international community. This lack of recognition does not by itself alter the legal position of combatants under customary international law. According to Article 4(A)(3) of Geneva Convention (III) – quoted *supra*, III – members of regular armed forces professing allegiance to a government unrecognized by the Detaining Power (the paradigmatic case being that of the "Free France" forces of General De Gaulle in World War II, unrecognized by Nazi Germany[77]) are entitled to prisoners of war status. Yet, inasmuch as the underlying idea is the equivalence of armed forces of recognized and unrecognized governments, the latter – no less than the former – are bound by the seven cumulative conditions of lawful combatancy. The proper question, therefore, is not whether the Taliban regime was recognized, but whether the Taliban forces actually observed all these conditions.

In light of close scrutiny of the war in Afghanistan by the world media – and, in particular, the live coverage by television of literally thousands of Taliban troops before and after their surrender – it is undeniable that, whereas Taliban forces were carrying their arms openly (condition (iii)) and possibly meeting other conditions of lawful combatancy, they did not wear uniforms nor did they display any other fixed distinctive emblem (condition (ii)). Since the conditions are cumulative, members of the Taliban forces failed to qualify as prisoners of war under the customary international law criteria. These criteria admit of no exception, not even in the unusual circumstances of Afghanistan as run by the Taliban regime. To say that "[t]he Taliban do not wear uniform in the traditional western sense"[78] is quite misleading, for the Taliban forces did not wear any uniform in any sense at all, Western or Eastern (nor even any special headgear that would single them out from civilians). All armed forces – including those belonging to the Taliban regime – are required to wear uniforms or use some other fixed distinctive emblem. If they do not, they cannot claim prisoners of war status.

The legal position seems singularly clear to the present writer. But since some observers appear to entertain doubt in the matter (perhaps because the case of governmental forces not wearing any uniform is so extraordinary), the issue could be put to judicial test. Article 5 (Second Paragraph) of Geneva Convention (III) enunciates:

---

[77] *See Commentary, supra* note 38, at 62.
[78] R. Cryer, "The Fine Art of Friendship: *Jus in Bello* in Afghanistan", 7 *J. Conflict & Sec. L.* 37, 70 (2002).

Should any doubt arise as to whether persons, having committed a belligerent act and having fallen into the hands of the enemy, belong to any of the categories enumerated in Article 4, such persons shall enjoy the protection of the present Convention until such time as their status has been determined by a competent tribunal.[79]

Ex abundante cautela, the United States might be well advised to have the status of Taliban forces determined by a competent tribunal. A competent tribunal for this purpose can be a military commission.[80]

2.   The legal position of Al Qaeda fighters must not be confused with that of Taliban forces. Al Qaeda fighters constitute irregular forces. They easily satisfy the requirement of belonging to a Party to the conflict (condition (vi)): in reality, in the relations between Al Qaeda and the Taliban regime there were times when it appeared that "the tail was wagging the dog", in other words, that the Party to the conflict (Afghanistan) belonged to Al Qaeda rather than the reverse. Incontrovertibly, Al Qaeda is a well-organized group (condition (v)), with subordination to command structure (condition (i)), and in the hostilities in Afghanistan its members carried their arms openly (condition (iii)). However, apart from the fact that Al Qaeda (like the Taliban regime) has declined to use a uniform or possess a fixed distinctive emblem (condition (ii)), the group has displayed utter disdain towards the *jus in bello* in brazen disregard of condition (iv).[81] Al Qaeda's contempt for this paramount prerequisite qualification of lawful combatancy was flaunted in the execution of the original armed attack of 9/11. Not only did the Al Qaeda terrorists, wearing civilian clothes, hijack US civilian passenger planes. The most striking aspects of the shocking events of 9/11 are that (i) the hijacked planes (with their explosive fuel load) were used as weapons, in total oblivion to the fate of the civilian passengers on board; and (ii) the primary objective targeted (the World Trade Center in New York City) was manifestly a civilian object rather than a military objective.[82] The net result was a carnage in which some 3,000 innocent civilians lost their lives. No group conducting attacks in such an egregious fashion can claim for its fighters prisoners of war status. Whatever the lingering doubt which may

---

[79]   Geneva Convention (III), *supra* note 10, at 432.

[80]   *See* K. Anderson, "What to Do with Bin Laden and Al Qaeda Terrorists? A Qualified Defense of Military Commissions and United States Policy on Detainees at Guantanamo Bay Naval Base", 25 *Harv. J. L. & Pub. Pol'y* 591, 619-20 (2002).

[81]   *See* C. Greenwood, "International Law and the 'War against Terrorism'", 78 *Int'l Aff.* 301, 316 (2002).

[82]   On the principle of military objectives, *see* Y. Dinstein, "Legitimate Military Objectives under the Current *Jus in Bello*", 31 *Israel Y.B. Hum. Rts.* 1-34 (2001).

UNLAWFUL COMBATANCY   269

exist with respect to the entitlement of Taliban forces to prisoners of war status, there is – and there can be – none as regards Al Qaeda terrorists.

3.   The Al Qaeda involvement raises another issue. Whereas the Taliban forces were composed of Afghan (and some Pakistani) nationals, Al Qaeda is an assemblage of Moslem fanatics from all parts of the world. Most of them are apparently Arabs, but some have come from Western countries, and there were at least two cases of renegade American nationals. Without getting here into the question how the US should have handled the situation from the standpoint of its domestic – constitutional and criminal – legal system, the salient point is that, under the *jus in bello*, irrespective of all other considerations, nobody owing allegiance to the Detaining Power can expect to be treated as a prisoner of war (condition (vii)).

4.   The constraints of the conditions of lawful combatancy must not, however, be seen as binding on only one Party to the conflict in Afghanistan. As the hostilities progressed, it became all too evident (again, thanks to the ubiquitous TV cameras) that some American combatants – Special Forces units, CIA agents in the field, and conceivably others – were not wearing uniforms while in combat. It must be underscored that observance by even 99% of the armed forces of a Party to a conflict of the seven conditions of lawful combatancy – including the condition relating to having a fixed distinctive emblem, such as a uniform (condition (ii)) – does not absolve the remaining 1% from the unshakable obligation to conduct themselves pursuant to the same conditions. Consequently, had any American combatants in civilian clothing been captured by the enemy, they would not be any more entitled to prisoners of war status than Taliban and Al Qaeda fighters in a similar situation.

5.   Perhaps "the primary focus of debate and controversy" in this field has been the detention of Al Qaeda terrorists transferred by the US from Afghanistan to Guantanamo Bay (on the island of Cuba).[83] Since unlawful combatants are not entitled to prisoners of war status, most criticisms against conditions of detention in Guantanamo are beside the point. However, it must be understood that – assuming that the detainees are not charged with any crime in judicial proceedings – detention (as a purely administrative measure) cannot go on beyond the termination of hostilities: hostilities in Afghanistan as regards Taliban personnel; hostilities in which Al Qaeda is involved in the case of its incarcerated fighters.

---

[83]   Anderson, *supra* note 80, at 621.

VI. CONCLUSION

Surely, unlawful combatancy is a matter of great practical significance in present-day international law. Unlawful combatants can be tried for violations of ordinary domestic laws and they can also be detained without trial (as long as the hostilities by the force to whom they belong go on). The seven cumulative conditions of lawful combatancy are no doubt stringent. But as the Afghanistan case amply demonstrates, the need for maintaining the distinction between lawful and unlawful combatants is as imperative as ever. Otherwise, compliance with the basic rule of distinction between civilians and combatants would be in jeopardy.

[8]

The legal situation of "unlawful/unprivileged combatants"

KNUT DÖRMANN*

While the discussion on the legal situation of unlawful combatants is not new, it has nevertheless become the subject of intensive debate in recent publications, statements and reports following the US-led military campaign in Afghanistan. Without dealing with the specifics of that armed conflict, this article is intended to shed some light on the legal protections of "unlawful/unprivileged combatants" under international humanitarian law.[1] In view of the increasingly frequent assertion that such persons do not have any protection whatsoever under international humanitarian law, it will consider in particular whether they are a category of persons outside the scope of either the Third Geneva Convention (GC III)[2] or the Fourth Geneva Convention (GC IV) of 1949.[3] On the basis of this assessment the applicable protections will be analysed. Before answering these questions, a few remarks on the terminology would seem appropriate.

Terminology

In international armed conflicts, the term "combatants" denotes the right to participate directly in hostilities.[4] As the Inter-American Commission has stated, "the combatant's privilege (...) is in essence a licence to kill or wound enemy combatants and destroy other enemy military objectives."[5] Consequently (lawful) combatants cannot be prosecuted for lawful acts of war in the course of military operations even if their behaviour would constitute a serious crime in peacetime. They can be prosecuted only for violations of international humanitarian law, in particular for war crimes. Once captured, combatants are entitled to prisoner-of-war status and to benefit from the protection of the Third Geneva Convention. Combatants are lawful military targets. Generally speaking, members of the armed forces (other

---

* Knut Dörmann is a Legal Advisor at the Legal Division of the International Committee of the Red Cross. The article reflects the views of the author alone and not necessarily those of the ICRC.

than medical personnel and chaplains) are combatants. The conditions for combatant/prisoner-of-war status can be derived from Article 4 of GC III and from Articles 43 and 44 of PI, which developed the said Article 4.[6]

Generally speaking, a civilian is any person who does not belong to one of the categories of persons referred to in Article 4A (1), (2), (3) and (6) of GC III and Article 43 of PI (see PI, Article 50). Under the law governing the conduct of hostilities, as contained especially in Articles 48 *et seq.* of PI, and under customary international law, civilians are entitled to general protection against the dangers arising from military operations; in particular they may not be made the object of an attack. Except for the relatively rare case of a *levée en masse*, civilians do not have the right to participate directly in hostilities. If they nevertheless take direct part, they remain civilians but become lawful targets of attacks for as long as they do so. Their legal situation once they find themselves in enemy hands will be the crux of the following analysis.

Whereas the terms "combatant", "prisoner of war" and "civilian" are generally used and defined in the treaties of international humanitarian law, the terms "unlawful combatant", "unprivileged combatant/belligerent" do not appear in them. They have, however, been frequently used at least since the beginning of the last century in legal literature, military manuals and case law. The connotations given to these terms and their consequences for the applicable protection regime are not always very clear.

For the purposes of this article the term "unlawful/unprivileged combatant/belligerent" is understood as describing all persons taking a direct part in hostilities without being entitled to do so and who therefore cannot be classified as prisoners of war on falling into the power of the enemy. This seems to be the most commonly shared understanding.[7] It would include for

---

1   This article does not address protection deriving from other bodies of law, in particular human rights law.

2   Convention (III) relative to the Treatment of Prisoners of War. Geneva, 12 August 1949.

3   Convention (IV) relative to the Protection of Civilian Persons in Time of War. Geneva, 12 August 1949.

4   See Article 43(2) of the 1977 Protocol Additional to the Geneva Conventions of 12 August 1949, and relating to the Protection of Victims of International Armed Conflicts (Protocol I) (PI).

5   Inter-American Commission on Human Rights, Report on Terrorism and Human Rights, OEA/Ser.L/-V/II.116 Doc. 5 rev. 1 corr., 22 October 2002, para. 68.

6   Article 44 of PI sets the standard for parties to the Protocol. Its status under customary international law is more doubtful.

7   See for example G. Aldrich, "The Taliban, Al Qaeda, and the determination of illegal combatants". *American Journal of International Law*, Vol. 96, 2002, p. 892; Report on Terrorism and Human Rights, *op. cit* (note 5), para. 69.

example civilians taking a direct part in hostilities, as well as members of militias and of other volunteer corps — including those of organized resistance movements — not being integrated in the regular armed forces but belonging to a party to conflict, provided that they do not comply with the conditions of Article 4A (2) of GC III. In the following text, for reasons of convenience, only the term "unlawful combatant" will be used.

If a person who has participated directly in hostilities is captured on the battlefield, it may not be obvious to which category that person belongs. For such types of situations Article 5 of GC III (PI, Article 45) provides for a special procedure (competent tribunal) to determine the captive's status.

The notion "unlawful combatant" has a place only within the context of the law applicable to international armed conflicts as defined in the 1949 Geneva Conventions and Additional Protocol I. The law applicable in non-international armed conflicts does not foresee a combatant's privilege (i.e. the right to participate in hostilities and impunity for lawful acts of hostility).[8] Once captured or detained, all persons taking no active/direct part in hostilities or who have ceased to take such a part come under the relevant provisions of international humanitarian law (i.e. Article 3 common to the four Geneva Conventions, and Additional Protocol II, in particular Articles 4-6), as well as the relevant customary international law.[9]

---

8 See also Report on Terrorism and Human Rights, *op. cit* (note 5), para. 70.

9 This may clearly be seen from the following excerpts (emphasis added):
GC I-IV, common Art. 3: "(1) *Persons taking no active part in the hostilities*, including members of armed forces who have laid down their arms and those placed hors de combat by sickness, wounds, detention, or any other cause, shall *in all circumstances* be treated humanely, *without any adverse distinction* founded on race, colour, religion or faith, sex, birth or wealth, or any other similar criteria. (...)"

PII, Art. 2: "1. This Protocol *shall be applied without any adverse distinction* founded on race, colour, sex, language, religion or belief, political or other opinion, national or social origin, wealth, birth or other status, or on any other similar criteria (hereinafter referred to as 'adverse distinction') *to all persons affected by an armed conflict* as defined in Article 1.

2. At the end of the armed conflict, *all the persons who have been deprived of their liberty or whose liberty has been restricted for reasons related to such conflict*, as well as those deprived of their liberty or whose liberty is restricted after the conflict for the same reasons, shall enjoy the protection of Articles 5 and 6 until the end of such deprivation or restriction of liberty."

PII, Art. 4 (1): "*All persons who do not take a direct part or who have ceased to take part in hostilities* (...)"

PII, Art. 5 (1): "shall be respected as a minimum with regard to *persons deprived of their liberty for reasons related to the armed conflict*, whether they are interned or detained"

PII, Art. 6 (1): "This Article applies to the prosecution and punishment of criminal offences related to the armed conflict."

The protective rules apply regardless of the way in which such persons have participated in hostilities (e.g. in accordance with IHL or not; in accordance with national law or not; etc.). Nor does it matter whether the person was a member of an armed rebel group, a member of the armed forces of a State or a civilian who (temporarily) took a direct/active part in hostilities.

The legal protection of unlawful combatants under GC IV

Given that unlawful combatants as defined in the previous section do not meet the conditions to qualify as prisoners of war and thus are not protected by GC III, this analysis will first examine whether unlawful combatants fall within the personal scope of application of GC IV. It will then consider to what particular protections they are entitled once they are in enemy hands. Lastly, the implications of the law on the conduct of hostilities will be briefly discussed.

In accordance with the rules of interpretation of international treaties, the main focus will be on the "ordinary meaning to be given to the terms of the treaty in their context and in the light of its object and purpose".[10] Subsidiarily, the *travaux préparatoires* and legal writings will also be analysed.

Personal field of application of GC IV as defined in Article 4 thereof

The personal field of application of GC IV is defined in the following terms. Article 4 (1) specifies:

"Persons protected by the Convention are those who, at a given moment and in any manner whatsoever, find themselves, in case of a conflict or occupation, in the hands of a Party to the conflict or Occupying Power of which they are not nationals."

This definition seems all-embracing. According to this paragraph *any person* would be protected once he/she finds himself/herself in the hands of a Party to a conflict or occupying Power. Only nationals of that Party/Power are excluded.[11] The very broad wording of the paragraph, read in isolation, would not only include civilians but even members of the armed forces.[12]

The scope of application is, however, reduced by specific exceptions. The following persons are excluded by the subsequent paragraphs of Article 4:

---

10 Art. 31 of the Vienna Convention on the Law of Treaties.

11 The provisions of Part II are, however, wider in application, as defined in Article 13.

12 J. Pictet (ed.), *Commentary: IV Geneva Convention relative to the Protection of Civilian Persons in Time of War*, ICRC, Geneva, 1958, (hereinafter *Commentary IV*), p. 46.

According to its paragraph 2:

- "Nationals of a State which is not bound by the Convention" are not protected (this is a highly theoretical restriction, since the 1949 Conventions have virtually universal participation);
- "Nationals of a neutral State who find themselves in the territory of a belligerent State, and nationals of a co-belligerent State," are not protected "while the State of which they are nationals has normal diplomatic representation in the State in whose hands they are".

For the latter exception the wording is not absolutely clear. According to the ICRC Commentary to Article 4 of GC IV — which is confirmed by the *travaux préparatoires* — the following distinction is required:

On the territory of belligerent States nationals of a neutral or co-belligerent State, so long as the State in question has normal diplomatic representation in the State in whose territory they are, are excluded. In occupied territories nationals of a co-belligerent State, so long as the State in question has normal diplomatic representation in the occupying State, are excluded. However, in this situation, nationals of neutral States are protected persons and the Convention is applicable to them. Its application in this case does not depend on the existence or non-existence of normal diplomatic representation.[13]

According to Article 4 (4), GC IV does not protect persons protected by GC I-III.

A textual interpretation of the Conventions can only lead to the conclusion that all persons who are not protected by GC I-III, thus also persons who do not respect the conditions which would entitle them to POW status/treatment, are covered by GC IV provided that they are not:

- nationals of a State which is not party to the Convention;
- nationals of the Party/Power in which hands they are; or
- nationals of a neutral State (only if they are in the territory of a belligerent State) or co-belligerent State with normal diplomatic representation (for details see the foregoing quotation from the ICRC Commentary).

---

13 *Commentary IV, op. cit* (note 12), p. 46. Commentaries concerning the draft Convention, Final Record of the Diplomatic Conference of 1949 (hereinafter Final Record), Vol. II A, p. 814. See also the explanation by the Swiss Rapporteur at the Diplomatic Conference, who confirmed that interpretation, Final Record, Vol. II A, p. 793. See also the statement by the US, *ibid.*, p. 794.

The fact that a person has unlawfully participated in hostilities is not a criterion for excluding the application of GC IV. On the contrary, Article 5 of GC IV, which allows for some derogations — under strict conditions — from the protections of GC IV, uses the term "protected persons" with regard to persons detained as spies or saboteurs as well as persons definitely suspected of or engaged in activities hostile to the security of the State/Occupying Power. Both the concepts of "activity hostile to the security of the State/Occupying Power" and of "sabotage" [14] certainly encompass direct participation (without entitlement) in hostilities. Thus, this article would apply in particular to persons who do not fulfil the criteria of GC I-III and take a direct part in hostilities, i.e. persons labelled "unlawful combatants". [15]

A further argument for the application of GC IV to "unlawful combatants" can be drawn from Article 45 (3) of PI. The provision reads as follows:

"Any person who has taken part in hostilities, who is not entitled to prisoner-of-war status and who does not benefit from more favourable treatment in accordance with the Fourth Convention shall have the right at all times to the protection of Article 75 of this Protocol. In occupied territory, any such person, unless he is held as a spy, shall also be entitled, notwithstanding Article 5 of the Fourth Convention, to his rights of communication under that Convention."

This provision of Additional Protocol I, which was adopted by consensus, [16] contains an implicit confirmation of our interpretation of GC IV that "unlawful combatants" are protected persons under GC IV if they fulfil the above-mentioned nationality criteria. By stating in Article 45 (3) of PI that "any person who has taken part in hostilities, who is not entitled to prisoner-of-war status and who does not benefit from more favourable treatment in

---

14 See E. Rosenblad, "Guerrilla warfare and international law". *Revue de droit pénal militaire et de droit de la guerre*, 1973, pp. 110 *et seq.* Rosenblad further states: "A saboteur, who is [sic] unlawful combatant, is on the one hand punished in accordance with the Civilians Convention. Granted that he is a "protected person" (Article 4) and that in this capacity he shall be unconditionally "treated with humanity" (third paragraph of Article 5). A protected person can, however, if 'imperative reasons of security' make this necessary, be subjected to assigned residence or to internment (Article 78). Furthermore, the Occupying Power can under certain circumstances retain a saboteur without judgement (second paragraph of Article 5) and, in the case of prosecution, sentence him to death (second paragraph of Article 68)."

15 See F. Kalshoven, "The position of guerrilla fighters under the law of war". *Revue de droit pénal militaire et de droit de la guerre*, 1972, p. 72, for guerrilla fighters whom he defines as persons (taking a direct part in hostilities) not regarded as prisoners of war, *ibid.*, pp. 65, 69.

16 CDDH/SR.41, O.R. Vol. VI, p. 155.

RICR Mars   IRRC March   2003   Vol. 85   N° 849   **51**

accordance with the Fourth Convention shall have the right at all times to the protection of Article 75 of this Protocol", it recognizes that GC IV is in fact applicable to some categories of unlawful combatants — otherwise the formulation "who does not benefit from more favourable treatment in accordance with the Fourth Convention" would be meaningless. The second sentence of that paragraph ("In occupied territory, any such person, unless he is held as a spy, shall also be entitled, notwithstanding Article 5 of the Fourth Convention, to his rights of communication under that Convention") implicitly recognizes that especially unlawful combatants in occupied territory (i.e. protected persons participating directly in hostilities in occupied territory without being entitled to POW status) are protected by GC IV. If unlawful combatants in occupied territories were not covered by GC IV, there would be no reason to restrict the scope of its Article 5.[17]

Further support for our interpretation may also be found in Military Manuals. For example in the US Military Manual FM 27-10, The Law of Land Warfare, 1956, pp. 31, 98 *et seq.*, the law is developed as follows (emphasis added):

> "72. Certain Persons in Occupied Areas
> Persons in occupied areas not falling within the categories set forth in Article 4 [GC III], who commit acts hostile to the occupant or prejudicial to his security are subject to a special regime [reference is made to the provisions of GC IV, Part III, Section III] ...
> 73. Persons Committing Hostile Acts Not Entitled To Be Treated as Prisoners of War
> *If a person is determined by a competent tribunal, acting in conformity with Article 5 [GC III] not to fall within any of the categories listed in Article 4 [GC III], he is not entitled to be treated as a prisoner of war. He is, however, a "protected person" within the meaning of Article 4 [GC IV]. ...*
> 247. Definition of Protected Persons
> [quotation of GC IV, Art. 4]
> *Interpretation. Subject to qualifications set forth in paragraph 248, those protected by [GC IV] also include all persons who have engaged in hostile or belligerent conduct but who are not entitled to treatment as prisoners of war.*

---

17 See in this regard M. Bothe, K. Partsch and W. Solf, *New Rules for Victims of Armed Conflicts: Commentary on the Two 1977 Protocols Additional to the Geneva Conventions of 1949*, Martinus Nijhoff, The Hague, 1982, pp. 261 *et seq.*

248. Derogations
a. Domestic and Occupied Territory
[reference is made to GC IV, Art. 5]
b. Other Areas. Where, in territories other than those mentioned in a. above, a Party to the conflict is satisfied that an individual protected person is definitely suspected of or engaged in activities hostile to the security of the State, such individual person is similarly not entitled to claim such rights and privileges under [GC IV] as would, if exercised in favour of such individual person, be prejudicial to the security of such a State."

See also the British Manual Part III—The Law of War on Land, 1957, n°. 96:

«Should regular combatants fail to comply with these four conditions [of GC III, Art. 4], they may in certain cases become unprivileged belligerents. This would mean that they would not be entitled to the status of prisoners of war upon their capture. Thus regular members of the armed forces who are caught as spies are not entitled to be treated as prisoners of war. But they would appear to be entitled, as a minimum, to the limited privileges conferred upon civilian spies or saboteurs by the Civilian Convention, Art. 5. (...) Members of the armed forces caught in civilian clothing while acting as saboteurs in enemy territory are in a position analogous to that of spies."

Travaux préparatoires

The issue of persons qualifying as unlawful combatants, as defined for the purposes of this article, was touched upon in two committees dealing with GC III and GC IV. On the basis of the Final Records it is difficult to reach a definite conclusion, although there might be good reason to believe that "unlawful combatants" meeting the nationality criteria of Article 4 of GC IV are protected by GC IV (and that this protection is subject to derogations). The difficulty of reaching a positive conclusion lies in the fact that first of all, the recorded statements can hardly be considered representative, since they reflect only the views of some delegations. Secondly, they were made in different committees and at different stages of the negotiations; in particular, some statements relating to GC III were made at a time when Article 5 of GC IV had not yet been proposed. Thirdly, the terms "unlawful combatants"/"unprivileged belligerents" were generally not used; instead, references are found to persons violating the laws of war, saboteurs and spies. In Committee II, discussing GC III, the underlying view seems primarily to have been that "unlawful combatants" should not be entitled to the same protection as prisoners of war, nor to all the protections accorded to "peaceful" civilians,[18] but that they should be entitled to a humane treatment and not be summarily executed.[19]

The draft Convention III, as approved by the International Red Cross Conference in Stockholm and submitted to the Diplomatic Conference of 1949, contained the following paragraph in Article 3 defining POWs:

> "The present Convention shall also provide a minimum standard of protection for any other category of persons who are captured or detained as the result of an armed conflict and whose protection is not specifically provided for in any other Convention."

The ICRC delegate Mr Wilhelm explained this paragraph as follows:

> "The ICRC was uncertain which category of persons it was desired to cover. The present Conference was engaged in framing a Convention to protect members of armed forces and similar categories of persons, such as members of organized resistance movements, and another convention to protect civilians. Although the two Conventions might appear to cover all the categories concerned, irregular belligerents were not actually protected. It was an open question whether it was desirable to give protection to persons who did not conform to the laws and customs of war; but in view of the fact that isolated cases might arise which deserved to be taken into account, it would appear necessary to provide for a general clause of protection, similar to the one contained in the Hague Convention of 1907, to which the Soviet Delegate had referred. It did not however seem expedient to introduce this conception into an Article, the main object of which was to define clearly all the categories of persons who should be protected by the present Convention [III]." [20]

---

18 See for example Colonel Hodgson (Australia): "In his opinion, the rights of the State in relation to certain persons such as spies, saboteurs, fifth columnists and traitors, had been insufficiently defined. (...) It was desirable to provide for the necessary exceptions to the rules for protection contained in the Convention." (Committee III (Civilians), 2nd meeting, 26.4.1949), Final Record, Vol. II A, p. 622.

19 Wilhelm (ICRC), Cohn (Denmark), Final Record, Vol. II A, p. 433; Brigadier Page (UK): "The whole conception of the Civilians Convention was the protection of civilian victims of war and not the protection of illegitimate bearers of arms, who could not expect full protection under rules of war to which they did not conform. Such persons should no doubt be accorded certain standards of treatment, but should not be entitled to all the benefits of the Convention. (...) To sum up, the United Kingdom Delegation considered that (...) civilians who violated those rules should cease to be entitled to the treatment provided for law-abiding citizens. The United Kingdom Delegation would not however oppose any reasonable proposal to ensure that such civilians were humanely treated." (Committee III (Civilians), 2nd meeting, 26.4.1949), Final Record, Vol. II A, p. 621; General Dillon (USA): "Clearly, the persons not enumerated in Article 3 [Art. 4 GC III] were not to be deprived of all rights". Final Record, Vol. II A, p. 409.

20 Final Record, Vol. II A, p. 433.

From this statement, three essential points can be singled out:

First, Mr Wilhelm interpreted the Stockholm drafts of GC III and IV as not protecting irregular belligerents or "persons who did not conform to the laws and customs of war". This is rather surprising, given that the personal scope of application of GC IV was very broadly defined,[21] unless he meant that such persons might be covered by the personal field of application but that the substantive provisions did not really accord protection (if he limited his statement to unlawful combatants on the battlefield as defended nowadays in the legal literature by, for example, Baxter, Draper and Kalshoven).

Second, he recognized the need for minimum protection of such persons, which can be derived from the Martens Clause.

Third, this protection should not be spelled out in a convention dealing with POWs.

The Danish delegate responded by saying that "it was not a question of granting the persons referred to in the paragraph the same rights and privileges as those of prisoners of war, but simply of affording "a minimum of protection", "of preventing such persons from being subjected to inhuman treatment or summarily shot".[22]

Other delegates were not opposed to providing a minimum of protection, but could not agree that such a protection clause be introduced in GC III. Thus the proposed paragraph 3 of draft Article 3 [GC III, Art. 4] was not retained.[23] Instead the Conference essentially agreed upon what became the substance of Article 5 of GC III (i.e. protection as POWs for "persons resisting the enemy" until a competent tribunal determines their status). The second part of the latter proposal, which read: "Even in cases where the decision of the above-mentioned authorities would not allow these persons to benefit under the present Convention, they shall nevertheless remain under the safeguard and rule of the principles of International Law as derived

---

21 "Persons protected under the present Convention are those who, at a given moment and in whatever manner, find themselves, in the case of a conflict or occupation, in the hands of a Power of which they are not nationals; (...) Persons such as prisoners of war, the sick and wounded, the members of medical personnel, who are subject to other international conventions, remain protected by the said conventions." Art. 3, *Revised and New Draft Conventions for the Protection of War Victims*, texts approved and amended by the XVIIth International Red Cross Conference, Geneva, 1948, pp. 114-115.

22 Final Record, Vol. II A, p. 433.

23 Final Record, Vol. II A, p. 480.

RICR Mars   IRRC March   2003   Vol. 85   N° 849　　　　　　　　　　　　　**55**

from the usages prevailing among civilized nations, of human rights and the demands of the public conscience", was likewise not retained.[24] In the end, the Danish delegate only asked as cited in the quotation below, for the Summary Record to mention that his view regarding interpretation of Article 3 had met with no objections.[25] The Committee's discussions were summarized as follows in the Report to the Plenary Assembly:

"Certain Delegations wished to extend the application of the Convention to cover still other categories of persons. They had particularly in mind civilians who had taken up arms to defend their life, their health, their near ones, their livelihood, under an attack which violated the laws and conditions of war and desired to ensure that such civilians falling into enemy hands should not be shot after summary judgment but should be treated according to the provisions or at least the humanitarian principles of the Convention. Numerous possible solutions of this problem were carefully considered but in the end a majority of the Committee came to the conclusion that it would be difficult to take the course proposed without the risk of indirectly weakening the protection afforded to persons coming under the various categories of Article 3 [GC III, Art. 4]. One Delegation pointed out, in particular, that the acceptance of the proposed extension would be tantamount to rejecting the principles generally accepted at The Hague, and recognized in the Prisoner of War Convention. It was, according to the views of this Delegation, essential that war, even illegal war, should be governed by those principles. Nevertheless, another Delegation asked that the Summary Record should mention that no objections had been raised, during the discussion in the Special Committee, against his view that Article 3 should not be interpreted in such a way as to deprive persons, not covered by the provisions of Article 3, of their human rights or of their right of self-defence against illegal acts."[26]

In the plenary debates on Article 5 of GC III (decision by a competent tribunal in case of doubt) the issue of persons not fulfilling the conditions to qualify as POWs, but participating nevertheless in hostilities (i.e. unlawful combatants), arose again. Captain Mouton (Netherlands), arguing in favour of

---

24 Final Record, Vol. III, p. 63.

25 Final Record, Vol. II A, p. 481.

26 Final Record, Vol. II A, p. 562. The last two sentences of the Report to the Plenary Assembly, which touch upon separate issues but were nevertheless intermingled, gave rise to controversy in the Plenary. See Final Record, Vol. II B, p. 268.

a court decision instead of a decision by a "competent authority", claimed that the latter approach would mean "in practice that (...) the military commander on the spot ... decides whether a person who has fallen into his hands comes under Article 3 [GC III] or does not belong to Article 3. (...) It means that if he decides that he does not belong to Article 3 he will be considered to be a *franc tireur* and be put against the wall and shot on the spot." Mr. Morosov (USSR) responded: "Where is it laid down that any person not protected by Article 3 should be shot? I do not know of any law to this effect, and I do not know of anybody who would wish to devise a clause of that kind. ... If a person is not recognized as a prisoner of war under the terms of Article 3, such a person would then be a civilian and would enjoy the full protection afforded by the Civilians Convention." The Dutch delegate did not accept that view and said: "That persons who do not fall under Article 3 are automatically protected by other Conventions is certainly untrue. The Civilian Convention, for instance, deals only with civilians under certain circumstances; such as civilians in an occupied country or civilians who are living in a belligerent country, but it certainly does not protect civilians who are in the battlefield, taking up arms against the adverse party. These people, if they do not belong to Article 3, and if they fall into the hands of the adverse party, might be shot (...)."[27]

To sum up, in the debates on GC III one statement (Russia) is recorded that GC IV automatically applies when the conditions of Article 4 of GC III are not met. The efforts by the Danish delegation focused on ensuring a minimum of protection for civilians resisting an aggressor in the exercise of self-defence without fulfilling the conditions of a *levée en masse*. The Dutch delegation rejected the Russian view as regards civilians on the battlefield taking up arms against the adverse party. Their statement can, however, be interpreted as implying that civilians taking up arms against the enemy in occupied territory or in enemy territory protected by GC IV.

The discussions in connection with GC IV must be assessed against this background. The drafting history of GC IV seems to support the view that "unlawful combatants" fulfilling the nationality criteria of its Article 4 are protected, but that the protection is subject to derogations. While certain delegations took the view that GC IV should not protect persons violating the laws of war, saboteurs and spies (who would be unlawful combatants[28] — although the

---

27 Final Record, Vol. II B, pp. 271 *et seq.*

28 The term "sabotage" in a military context has been said to denote acts committed in order to damage or destroy the infrastructure material of the enemy, "lines of communication" and "military installations" (GC IV, Articles 64 and 68). See Rosenblad, *op. cit* (note 14), p. 109.

RICR MARS   IRRC MARCH   2003   VOL. 85   N° 849   **57**

term was never used in the Final Record),[29] other delegations disagreed.[30] As stated by the Australian delegate, "two schools of thought had become evident during the discussion — that of those delegations which wished for a broad and 'elastic' Convention, and that of those which wanted a restricted Convention."[31] In order to overcome the divergent views the Committee adopted, as a compromise, draft Article 3A (which became Article 5 of GC IV). This provision treated persons violating the laws of war, saboteurs and spies as "protected persons", but allowed States in certain circumstances to deprive such persons of some of the protections of GC IV.[32] This compromise solution was finally adopted overwhelmingly by the Diplomatic Conference.[33]

29 *Commentary IV, op. cit* (note 12), p. 52 ("Some people considered that the Convention should apply without exception to all the persons to whom it referred, while to others it seemed obvious that persons guilty of violating the laws of war were not entitled to claim its benefits. These divergent views had not been expressed [during preliminary discussions], however, and the problem did not arise until after the Stockholm Conference. It arose then because the Conference had adopted a definition of protected persons which covered those who committed hostile acts without being members of the regular combatant forces.").

30 Mr. Castberg (Norway): "Saboteurs could not of course claim protection under the Prisoners of War Convention; they should nevertheless be protected against criminal treatment and torture." Mr. Söderbolm (Sweden) and Mr. Dahl (Denmark) supported this view. Colonel Du Pasquier (Switzerland) remained somewhat ambiguous in saying "In regard to the legal status of those who violated the laws of war, the Convention could not of course cover criminals or saboteurs. Moreover, Article 55 [Art. 64 of GC IV] and those following established the principle that an occupying Power was entitled to lay down penal regulations to protect its troops. On the other hand, Article 29 [Arts 31/32 of GC IV] and those following fixed the limits of such penal legislation and in particular prohibited torture and the taking of hostages." He was in favour of the revised form of Article 3 as drawn up by the International Committee of the Red Cross [which would have covered unlawful combatants! Therefore, the Italian delegate Mr. Maresca, while expressing support for the ICRC proposal, suggested that a clause be added providing that protected persons were under an obligation not to act in such a way as to violate the rules of war.]. General Schepers (Netherlands) agreed with the Scandinavian delegates. (Committee III (Civilians), 2nd meeting, 26.4.1949), Final Record, Vol. II A, pp. 621 *et seq*.

31 Final Record, Vol. II A, p. 622.

32 See Final Record, Vol. II A, p. 796; Commentaries concerning the draft Convention, *ibid.*, p. 814: "Modern warfare does not take place on the battlefield alone; it also filters into the domestic life of the belligerent; enemy secret agents penetrate into the inner workings of the war machine, either to spy or to damage its mechanism. [...] Many Delegations have therefore felt the fear that, under cover of the protection offered by our convention, spies, saboteurs or other persons dangerous to the State may be able to abuse the rights which it provides for them. The Delegations have considered it their duty to prevent the guarantees of the Convention acting to the advantage of surreptitious activities. The idea has thus arisen that, with respect to persons who are a secret threat to the security of the State, the benefit of the Convention should be restricted to a certain extent. Owing to the very great difficulty in tracking down these underground activities, it is intended to allow the State a free hand in its defence measures without imposing any obligations under the Convention other than the duty to ensure humane and legal treatment. It was these considerations which resulted in Article 3A [Art. 5 of GC IV] (...)."

33 Final Record, Vol. II B, pp. 377, 384: 31 votes in favour, 9 abstentions (GC IV, Art. 4); 25 votes in favour, 9 against, 6 abstentions (GC IV, Art. 5).

If the interpretation expressed by the UK delegate[34] of the initial draft of GC IV's Article 4[35] is correct ("[i]n its present form, Article 3 would mean that persons who were not entitled to protection under the Prisoners of War Convention would receive exactly the same protection by virtue of the Civilians Convention, so that all persons participating in hostilities would be protected, whether they conformed to the laws of war or not"), and since no fundamental changes were made to that draft text, there are strong reasons to believe that in the end delegations accepted that GC IV is applicable to unlawful combatants if they fulfil the conditions set forth in Article 4 thereof. The aim of a somewhat reduced protection for such persons is achieved by means of its Article 5, which was inserted at a later stage and allows for derogations for the types of persons often referred to as unlawful combatants. In short, the drafting history of GC IV — in particular the UK statement cited above — justifies the conclusion that it covers unlawful combatants and that the extent of this coverage is subject to the limitations outlined in its Article 5. The drafting history as a whole — namely the discussions on GC III and IV — shows that the issue of persons not fulfilling the conditions to qualify as POWs but participating nevertheless in hostilities was controversial at the time. There are no indications that — contrary to the adopted wording of its Article 4 — there was general agreement that GC IV should not cover "unlawful combatants". Its broad personal scope of application was finally accepted, despite obvious hesitations, by the Diplomatic Conference. The price for this was the insertion of Article 5.

Legal literature

In legal writings divergent opinions are expressed about the applicability of GC IV to unlawful combatants. A number of authors clearly share our view that GC IV does cover unlawful combatants if they fulfil the nationality

---

34 Brigadier Page (UK), Committee III (Civilians), 2nd meeting, 26.4.1949, Final Record, Vol. II A, p. 621.

35 "Persons protected under the present Convention are those who, at a given moment and in whatever manner, find themselves, in the case of a conflict or occupation, in the hands of a Power of which they are not nationals; (...) The provisions of Part II are, however, wider in application, as defined in Article II. Persons such as prisoners of war, the sick and wounded, the members of medical personnel, who are subject to other international conventions, remain protected by the said conventions." Art. 3, *Revised and New Draft Conventions for the Protection of War Victims*, texts approved and amended by the XVIIth International Red Cross Conference, Geneva, 1948, pp. 114-115.

RICR Mars IRRC March 2003 Vol. 85 N° 849   **59**

criteria.[36] Baxter apparently limits the scope of application of GC IV to unlawful combatants who operate in occupied territory.[37] The fact that he does not extend the protection to unlawful combatants operating in the territories of the parties to a conflict (Part III, Section 1) and in enemy territory (Part III, Section 2) is not consistent, given that the definition of protected persons is the same. Despite the clear indications in the wording of GC IV, some legal commentators seemingly do not recognize the applicability of GC IV to unlawful combatants at all.[38] However, they do not give any legal reasoning for their position. It is merely asserted that GC IV does not cover unlawful combatants; an analysis of its Article 4 is not provided. When these authorities refer to case law (in particular *ex parte Quirin*[39]), it is case law that predates GC IV. Considering that the issue was simply not specifically regulated in any instrument of international humanitarian law before the adoption of GC IV, this approach is somewhat doubtful. More recent case law correctly adopts a rather different view. In the *Delalic* case, the ICTY found that:

---

36 K. Ipsen, in D. Fleck (ed.), *The Handbook of Humanitarian Law in Armed Conflicts*, Oxford University Press, 1995, p. 301; H. McCoubrey, *International Humanitarian Law: Modern Developments in the Limitation of Warfare*, Dartmouth, Aldershot, 2nd ed., 1998, p. 137; E. David, *Principes de droit des conflits armés*, Bruylant, Brussels, 2nd ed., 1999, pp. 397 *et seq.*; Bothe, Partsch and Solf, *op. cit* (note 17), pp. 261 *et seq.*; Aldrich, *op. cit* (note 7), p. 893, footnote 12; G.I.A.D. Draper, "The status of combatants and the question of guerrilla warfare". *British Yearbook of International Law*, 1971, p. 197 (recognizes the applicability of GC IV to persons who do not fulfil the conditions of GC III, Art. 4, but participate in hostilities in enemy territory or in occupied territory, within the limits of GC IV, Art. 5); Rosenblad, *op. cit* (note 14), p. 98 (recognizes the applicability of GC IV to members of organized resistance movements who do not fulfil the conditions of GC III, Art. 4, within the limits of GC IV, Art. 5); Kalshoven, *op. cit* (note 15), p. 71 (recognizes the applicability of GC IV to persons who do not fulfil the conditions of GC III, Art. 4, but participate in hostilities in enemy territory or in occupied territory. In situations other than fighting in enemy territory or occupied territory, "the guerrilla fighter who falls into enemy hands will not enjoy the full protection extended to protected persons in occupied territory. It is submitted, however, that he will not be entirely without protection. The principle expounded in Article 3 for non-international armed conflict provide at the same time a minimum below which belligerents may not go in other situations either (...) To my mind, the strongest argument in favour of this thesis lies precisely in the element of their foreign nationality and, hence, allegiance to the opposite Party from the one which holds them in its power."

37 R.R. Baxter, "So-called 'unprivileged belligerency': Spies, guerrillas, and saboteurs". *British Yearbook of International Law*, 1951, pp. 328 *et seq.*, 343 *et seq.*; R.R. Baxter, "The duties of combatants and the conduct of hostilities (Law of The Hague)", in Henry Dunant Institute and UNESCO (ed.), *International Dimensions of Humanitarian Law*, Martinus Nijhoff, The Hague, 1988, pp. 105 *et seq.*

38 For example I. Detter, *The Law of War*, Cambridge University Press, 2000, p. 136; R.K. Goldmann/B.D. Tittemore, "Unprivileged combatants and the hostilities in Afghanistan: Their status and rights under international humanitarian and human rights law". http://asil.org/taskforce/goldman.pdf, p. 38; C. Greenwood, "International law and the "war against terrorism". *International Affairs 2002*, p. 316; Report on Terrorism and Human Rights, *op. cit* (note 5), para. 74.

39 317 U.S. 1, 63 S.Ct. 2 (1942).

"271. [...] If an individual is not entitled to the protections of the Third Convention as a prisoner of war (or of the First or Second Conventions) he or she necessarily falls within the ambit of Convention IV, *provided that its article 4 requirements are satisfied.*" [40]

In 1949, GC IV was adopted in the knowledge of the problems associated with unlawful combatants (see the discussions during the Diplomatic Conference). It is therefore in our view hardly defendable to maintain that unlawful combatants were generally excluded from the scope of application of GC IV, contrary to the rather comprehensive wording of its Article 4. The same would be true of claims that there is coexisting customary international law which comprehensively covers unlawful combatants and would constitute a sort of *lex specialis* (the US Manual quoted above would be contrary to such a rule of customary international law!). In this connection it should also be recalled that the drafters of PI apparently had an understanding of the scope of application of GC IV which would include at least certain types of unlawful combatants.

Substantive protections for unlawful combatants under GC IV

With regard to the treatment of protected persons, GC IV provides for various standards of protection depending on the situation in which they find themselves in the hands of another Party/Power. Part III thereof defines the material scope of protection for protected persons within the meaning of GC IV's Article 4. Its first section contains provisions common to the territories of the parties to conflict and to occupied territories. These include:

rules on humane treatment; special protection for women; non-discrimination; prohibition of the use of protected persons as human; prohibition of coercion and of corporal punishment, torture, etc.; individual responsibility; and prohibition of collective punishment, pillage, reprisals and hostage taking.

This section is followed by specific provisions on the treatment of aliens in the territory of a party to conflict (Section II), which deal *inter alia* with:

the right to leave the territory; the treatment of persons in confinement; the right to individual/collective relief, to medical attention and to

---

40 ICTY, Judgment, *The Prosecutor v. Delalic* et al., IT-96-21-T, 16 November 1998, para. 271 (emphasis added).

practise their religion; employment; measures of control, i.e. assigned residence and internment, and the procedure to be followed; and transfer to another Power.

Section III, on protected persons in occupied territory, includes rules on:

deportation and transfers; children; labour; food and medical supplies for the population; hygiene and public health; relief operations; penal legislation; penal procedure; treatment of detainees; and security measures.

Section IV contains regulations for the treatment of internees, *inter alia* on:

places of internment; food and clothing; hygiene and medical attention; religious, intellectual and physical activities; personal property and financial resources; administration and discipline; relations with the outside; penal and disciplinary sanctions; transfers of internees; deaths; and release, repatriation and accommodation in neutral countries.

Article 79 of that section stipulates that protected persons may not be interned, except in accordance with the provisions of Articles 41-43 (aliens in the territory of a party to conflict) and Articles 68 and 78 (protected persons in occupied territory).

Since unlawful combatants are protected by GC IV if they fulfil the nationality criteria set out in Article 4 thereof, the above forms of protection also apply to them. In addition to the general protections of Part III, Section 1, applicable to the territories of Parties to the conflict and to occupied territories, specific protections are foreseen for unlawful combatants operating in occupied territory and for unlawful combatants in enemy territory. These protections may, however, be subject to derogations under Article 5 of GC IV (see below).

The fact that GC IV only provides for different *specific* protections to aliens in the territory of an enemy party to the conflict and persons in occupied territory, who are in the hands of the adverse party, may have led some experts to conclude that the situation of unlawful combatants in the zone of military operations (at the front/on the battlefield in their own country, which is not occupied) was not taken into account in the drafting of GC IV, and in particular of Articles 4 and 5.[41]

If, however, the interpretation of GC IV's Article 6 proposed in the Commentary edited by J.S. Pictet is accepted, this approach would be difficult to defend:

---

41 See A. Rosas, *The Legal Status of Prisoners of War*, Helsinki, Suomalainen Tiedeakatemia, 1976, p. 411; Baxter, "Unprivileged belligerency", *op. cit* (note 37), pp. 329 *et seq.*

"It follows from this that the word "occupation". as used in the Article, has a wider meaning than it has in Article 42 of the Regulations annexed to the Fourth Hague Convention of 1907. So far as individuals are concerned, the application of the Fourth Geneva Convention does not depend upon the existence of a state of occupation within the meaning of the Article 42 referred to above. The relations between the civilian population of a territory and troops advancing into that territory, whether fighting or not, are governed by the present Convention. There is no intermediate period between what might be termed the invasion phase and the inauguration of a stable regime of occupation. Even a patrol which penetrates into enemy territory without any intention of staying there must respect the Conventions in its dealings with the civilians it meets. (…) The Convention is quite definite on this point: all persons who find themselves in the hands of a Party to the conflict or an Occupying Power of which they are not nationals are protected persons. No loophole is left."

Under the foregoing interpretation, every person who fulfils the nationality criteria as set out above and is captured while enemy armed forces are present (from the moment of invasion until the withdrawal) would be protected by the provisions of GC IV (Part III, Sections I, III and IV).

This interpretation of the concept of occupation, however, is not universally shared. The German Military Manual for example states: "Occupied territory does not include battle areas, i.e. areas which are still embattled and not subject to permanent occupational authority (area of invasion, withdrawal area)." In the commentary to that provision of the manual it is further explained: "The law of occupation is not applicable until the armed forces invading a foreign country have established actual control over a certain territory (after invasion), and ceases to apply when they no longer have such control (after withdrawal). The rules are intended to apply in stable situations." [42] Similarly, the distinction proposed by Draper, Baxter and Kalshoven[43] can be of significance only if they have a different understanding of occupation, which for them would probably require a minimum control of territory for some time by the adverse party.

As a consequence of that interpretation, persons who fulfil the nationality criteria as set out above, and who find themselves in enemy hands in battle areas where no actual control has been established, would not be covered by the provisions of Part III, Sections III and IV, of GC IV. They would

42 H.P. Gasser, in Fleck (ed.), *op. cit* (note 36), p. 528.
43 See footnotes 30 and 31.

be protected by the rather general provisions of GC IV, Part II,[44] and should also come within the protections of its Part III, Section I.[45]

But what will their protection be once they are taken from the battle area to enemy territory or occupied territory, or if the battle area itself becomes occupied territory (i.e. foreign troops have established actual control)? Does it matter that these persons were not in enemy territory or occupied territory at the time they were captured? The normal reflex would possibly be that the law applicable to the place where they are held should apply, i.e.:

- Part III, Sections I, III and IV, of GC IV for persons who end up in occupied territory;
- Part III, Sections I, II and IV, of GC IV for persons who end up in enemy territory.

The very broad wording of Article 4 of GC IV points in that direction by specifying that the Convention protects "those who, *at a given moment and in any manner whatsoever*, find themselves, in case of a conflict or occupation, in the hands of a Party to the conflict or Occupying Power".[46] Support for our position

---

44 Provisions on:
– the establishment of hospital and safety zones and neutralized zones;
– the conclusion of agreements for the evacuation of especially vulnerable categories of persons;
– the protection of civilian hospitals;
– the protection of medical personnel;
– the protection of transports of sick and wounded civilians and other especially vulnerable categories of persons on land, by sea or by air;
– the free passage of aid consignments;
– the special protection of children;
– permission to exchange family news; and
– facilitating enquiries relating to missing family members.
For the purpose of this article they are not relevant because they do not regulate the treatment/detention/prosecution of protected persons.

45 In addition Art. 3 common to GC I-V, the application of which is recognized in any type of armed conflict as a matter of customary international law (see the International Court of Justice in *Military and Paramilitary Activities in and against Nicaragua (Nicaragua v. United States of America)*, Merits, Judgment, ICJ Reports 1986, p. 14 at p. 114, para. 218), would also apply, as well as other minimum guarantees which will be discussed below.

46 In the *Rajic* case (Review of the Indictment, *Prosecutor v. Ivica Rajic*, IT-95-12-R61, paras. 35-37), the ICTY held that:
"The International Committee of the Red Cross's Commentary on Geneva Convention IV suggests that the protected person requirement should be interpreted to provide broad coverage. The Commentary states that the words 'at a given moment and in any manner whatsoever' were 'intended to ensure that all situations and all cases were covered'. International Committee of the Red Cross, Commentary: IV Geneva Convention Relative to the Protection of Civilian Persons in Time of War 47 (Geneva 1958) (...). At page 47 it further notes that the expression 'in the hands of' is used in an extremely general sense.
It is not merely a question of being in enemy hands directly, as a prisoner is ... In other words, the expression 'in the hands of' need not necessarily be understood in the physical sense; it simply means that the person is in territory under the control of the Power in question."

may be found in the Commentary edited by Pictet, which states: "The Article refers both to people who were in the territory before the outbreak of war (or the beginning of the occupation) and to those who go or are taken there as a result of circumstances: travellers, tourists, people who have been shipwrecked and even, it may be, spies or saboteurs." [47]

However, those authors who agree that GC IV is applicable to unlawful combatants in occupied territory or in enemy territory do not further pursue that line of thought. They seem to limit the specific protections of GC IV to unlawful combatants operating in occupied territory or in enemy territory at the time of their capture.[48] In the words of Draper: "If they were *operating in neither type of territory*, their position is far from clear and their protection is speculative." [49]

If that approach is agreed with, there should be no doubt that at least Article 75 of PI and Article 3 common to GC I-IV do as customary international law provide for a minimum of protection.

Derogations

The rights and privileges defined in particular in Part III of GC IV are not absolute. Article 5 of GC IV provides for derogations in specific circumstances:

"Where in the territory of a Party to the conflict, the latter is satisfied that an individual *protected person is definitely suspected of or engaged in activities hostile to the security of the State*, such individual person shall not be entitled to claim such rights and privileges under the present Convention as would, if exercised in the favour of such individual person, *be prejudicial to the security of such State*.

Where in occupied territory an individual *protected person is detained as a spy or saboteur, or as a person under definite suspicion of activity hostile to the security of the Occupying Power*, such person shall, in those cases where

---

47 *Commentary IV, op. cit* (note 12), p. 47.

48 Draper, *op. cit* (note 36), p. 197; Baxter, "Unprivileged belligerency", *op. cit* (note 37), pp. 328 and 343 *et seq.*; Baxter, "Duties of combatants". *op. cit* (note 37), pp. 105 *et seq.*; Kalshoven, *op. cit* (note 15), pp. 70 *et seq.*, 73; Rosas, *op. cit* (note 41), pp. 411 *et seq.* In one of its publications the ICRC has also chosen such a formulation, which could point to such an interpretation: "thus guerrillas who do not meet these conditions [of GC III, Art. 4] and who operate in occupied territory are protected by Geneva Convention IV". *Rules Applicable in Guerrilla Warfare*, Conference of Government Experts on the Reaffirmation and Development of International Humanitarian Law Applicable in Armed Conflicts, Geneva, 24 May – 12 June 1971, Paper submitted by the International Committee of the Red Cross, Geneva, January 1971, p. 19.

49 Draper, *op. cit* (note 36), p. 197.

absolute military security so requires, be regarded as having forfeited rights of communication under the present Convention.

In each case, such persons shall nevertheless be treated with humanity and, in case of trial, shall not be deprived of the rights of fair and regular trial prescribed by the present Convention. They shall also be granted the full rights and privileges of a protected person under the present Convention at the earliest date consistent with the security of the State or Occupying Power, as the case may be." (Emphasis added.)

On reading this article it could be taken to apply in particular to persons who take a direct part in hostilities without fulfilling the criteria of GC I-III, i.e. such persons as are labelled "unlawful combatants".[50] As pointed out above, both the concepts of "activity hostile to the security of the State/Occupying Power" and of "sabotage"[51] certainly do encompass direct participation in hostilities (without being entitled thereto).

Article 5 contains the following distinction:

- in the territory of a Party to conflict, such persons are not entitled to claim such rights and privileges under GC IV as would, if exercised in the favour of such individual person, be prejudicial to the security of such State;[52]
- in occupied territory, such persons are, in those cases where absolute military security so requires, regarded as having forfeited rights of communication under GC IV.

---

50 See Kalshoven, *op. cit* (note 15), p. 72, for guerrilla fighters whom he defines as persons (taking a direct part in hostilities) not regarded as prisoners of war, *ibid.*, pp. 65, 69.

51 See references in note 10.

52 As for possible derogations under para. 1, *Commentary IV, op. cit* (note 12), p. 55, indicates the following: "The rights referred to are not very extensive in the case of protected persons under detention; they consist essentially of the right to correspond, the right to receive individual or collective relief, the right to spiritual assistance from ministers of their faith and the right to receive visits from representatives of the Protecting Power and the International Committee of the Red Cross. The security of the State could not conceivably be put forward as a reason for depriving such persons of the benefit of other provisions — for example, the provision in Article 37 that they are to be humanely treated when they are confined pending proceedings or subject to a sentence involving loss of liberty, or the stipulation in Article 38 that they shall receive medical attention, if their state of health so requires. Furthermore, it would be really inhuman to refuse to let a chaplain visit a detained person who was seriously ill. Torture and recourse to reprisals are of course prohibited. It should, moreover, be noted that this provision cannot release the Detaining Power from its obligations towards the adverse Party. It remains fully bound by the obligation, imposed on it by Article 136, to transmit to the official Information Bureau particulars of any protected person who is kept in custody for more than two weeks. This is not, in fact, a right or privilege of the protected person, but an obligation of the Detaining Power."

Apart from problems of interpretation of concepts such as "definitely suspected"[53], "hostile to the security of the State". "such rights and privileges ... as would be prejudicial to the security of such State". "absolute military security so requires", the meaning of Article 5 (2), which gives a right to derogate only from the provisions relating to communication, is rendered somewhat unclear by paragraph 3, according to which "in each case" (i.e. both in the situations referred to in paragraph 1 and in those referred to in paragraph 2) the protected persons "shall nevertheless be treated with humanity and, in case of trial, shall not be deprived of the rights of fair and regular trial prescribed by the present Convention".[54] If only provisions relating to communication can be derogated from, why is there a need to indicate as minimum protections humane treatment and fair trial?[55]

The two categories of non-derogable protections include: the right to "humane treatment" as defined in Articles 27 and 37, and thus the prohibition of torture and ill-treatment;[56] as well as the fair trial rights contained in Articles 71-76,[57] which are made applicable to internees in non-occupied territory by Article 126 in the event of criminal proceedings.[58]

Minimum guarantees under customary international law

As we have seen, the protection of unlawful combatants under GC IV depends on whether they fulfil the nationality criteria set out in Article 4.

---

53 As far as suspicion is concerned, it is important to emphasize that "[t]he suspicion must not rest on a whole class of people; collective measures cannot be taken under this Article; there must be grounds justifying action in each individual case". *Commentary IV, op. cit* (note 12), p. 55. See also Final Record, Vol. II A, p. 815 (Committee III report to the Plenary).

54 Rosas, *op. cit* (note 41), p. 412.

55 See debate at the Diplomatic Conference between the representatives of the USSR and the UK, Final Record, Vol. II B, pp. 379 *et seq.*

56 GC IV, Art. 32. See also Final Record, Vol. II A, p. 815 (Committee III report to the Plenary): "The third paragraph defines what was left somewhat vague by the first two paragraphs. It confirms the obligations of the State as regards humane treatment and correct penal procedure; it does nothing to weaken the force of the prohibition of torture or brutal treatment." See also the findings of the ICTY in the *Delalic* case, which were adopted "in order to determine the essence of the offence of inhuman treatment [under the Geneva Conventions], the terminology must be placed within the context of the relevant provisions of the Geneva Conventions and Additional Protocols". It considered the prohibition of inhuman treatment in the context of GC II, Art. 12; GC III, Arts 13, 20 and 46; GC IV, Arts 27 and 32; GC I-IV, common Art. 3; PI, Art. 75; and PII, Arts 4 and 7; according to which protected persons "shall be humanely treated". Any conduct contrary to the behaviour prescribed in these provisions shall constitute inhuman treatment.

57 *Commentary IV, op. cit* (note 12), p. 58.

58 *Ibid.*, Art. 126, p. 497; Kalshoven, *op. cit* (note 15), p. 72. Otherwise common Article 3 would be the basis, *Commentary IV, op. cit* (note 12), Article 5, p. 58.

The question remains as to how far the protections of GC IV are supplemented by other rules of international law and to what extent such rules apply to unlawful combatants who do not fulfil those criteria.

The minimum guarantees applicable to all persons in the power of a party to conflict are defined nowadays in Article 75 of PI. The scope of application is defined as follows:

> "1. In so far as they are affected by a situation referred to in Article 1 of this Protocol, persons who are in the power of a Party to the conflict and who do not benefit from more favourable treatment under the Conventions or under this Protocol shall be treated humanely in all circumstances and shall enjoy, as a minimum, the protection provided by this Article without any adverse distinction based upon race, colour, sex, language, religion or belief, political or other opinion, national or social origin, wealth, birth or other status, or on any other similar criteria. Each Party shall respect the person, honour, convictions and religious practices of all such persons."

This article clearly ensures that no person in the power of a Party to an international armed conflict is outside the protection of international humanitarian law.[59] It defines the minimum standards that apply to any such person and thus increases existing protection, for example in the situations referred to in Article 5 of GC IV. As pointed out above, Article 45 (3) of PI explicitly recognizes the application of Article 75 to unlawful combatants.

The said Article 45[60] not only contains an implicit confirmation of our interpretation of the personal field of application of GC IV but, in connection with Article 75 of PI, it supplements the protection of unlawful combatants. This is done in two ways:

First, Article 45 (3) in conjunction with Article 75 provides for a minimum of protection for those unlawful combatants not covered by GC IV because they do not fulfil the nationality criteria of GC IV's Article 4 and — if the interpretation defended by Baxter, Draper and Kalshoven is followed

---

59 See statement by the ICRC at the Diplomatic Conference of 1974-1977, CDDH/III/SR.43, OR Vol. XV, pp. 25 *et seq.*; Finland, *ibid.*, p. 27, Belgium, *ibid.*, p. 31, Holy See, *ibid.*, p. 34.

60 This paragraph does not cover combatants who are denied prisoner-of-war status by application of paragraph 4 of Article 44 (i.e. members of the armed forces who do not comply with the minimum standards of distinction). The latter in fact continue to come within the scope of the procedural guarantees of the Third Convention, whereas the provision under consideration here concerns persons who are refused these guarantees.

— for those who fall into enemy hands in the battle area.[61] Previously, these types of unlawful combatants were protected solely on the basis of common Article 3 as customary international law or of the Martens Clause.

Second, for those unlawful combatants who are protected by GC IV it complements that protection by defining minimum guarantees which must be respected in all circumstances. More specifically:

(1) For unlawful combatants in enemy hands on enemy territory, Article 75 of PI specifically ensures that various judicial guarantees are respected (para. 4). Before the adoption of PI this was possible only on the basis of common Article 3 as customary international law[62] or of GC IV's Article 126.[63] In addition, Article 75 of PI lays down other protections in relation to treatment (paras 1 and 2) and to arrest, detention and internment (para. 3), which in certain cases increase the protections contained in Part III, Sections I, II and IV, of GC IV.

(2) For unlawful combatants in enemy hands in occupied territory, Article 75 PI adds a few more judicial guarantees, such as the presumption of innocence. The protections in relation to treatment, arrest, detention and internment are supplemented. In addition, Article 45 (3) of PI restricts the possibility for derogations under GC IV's Article 5.

This interpretation is largely shared by Bothe, Partsch and Solf in their commentary on PI:

> "Paragraph 3 applies the safeguards and protections of Art. 75 to any person who has taken part in hostilities, but who is not entitled to prisoner-of-war status or treatment, and who does not qualify for more favourable treatment under the Fourth Convention. This class of persons includes: members of the armed forces who forfeit both entitlement to prisoner-of-

---

61 See also the ICRC's commentary on the Draft Additional Protocols to the Geneva Conventions of August 12, 1949 (October 1973), on draft Article 65 [Art.75 of PI]: "The purpose of this draft is to rectify an omission in the existing treaty law; on the one hand, persons who are not protected by the First, Second and Third Conventions are not necessarily always protected by the Fourth Convention, as is shown by its Article 4; on the other hand, Article 5 of the Fourth Convention relating to derogations is fairly difficult to interpret and appears to restrict unduly the rights of the persons protected.". pp. 81 *et seq.*

62 "[T]he following acts are and shall remain prohibited at any time and in any place whatsoever (...) (d) the passing of sentences and the carrying out of executions without previous judgment pronounced by a regularly constituted court, affording all the judicial guarantees which are recognized as indispensable (...)"

63 "The provisions of Articles 71 to 76 inclusive shall apply, by analogy, to proceedings against internees who are in the national territory of the Detaining Power."

war status and treatment [e.g. spying under PI, Art. 46, or failure to distinguish themselves from the civilian population, as required by PI, Art. 44 (3)], nationals of States not bound by the Fourth Convention, nationals of the Detaining Power, and nationals of a neutral or co-belligerent State with which the Detaining Power maintains normal diplomatic relations [see the exclusions based on nationality in GC IV, Art. 4], spies, and mercenaries. Notwithstanding the derogations permitted by Art. 5 of the Fourth Convention, this paragraph also makes the protections of Art. 75 the minimum humanitarian standard applicable to civilians protected under the Fourth Conventions who participate directly in hostilities in the territory of a Party to the conflict or in any other area other than occupied territory. In occupied territory it virtually neutralizes the derogations permitted under Art. 5 of the Fourth Convention except for persons held as spies." [64]

See also the ICRC Commentary on Article 45 of PI:

"In armed conflict with an international character, *a person of enemy nationality who is not entitled to prisoner-of-war status is, in principle, a civilian protected by the Fourth Convention, so that there are no gaps in protection.* However, things are *not always so straightforward in the context of the armed conflicts of Article 1 (General principles and scope of application), paragraph 4, as the adversaries can have the same nationality. Moreover, the concept of alien occupation often becomes rather fluid in guerrilla operations as no fixed legal border delineates the areas held by either Party,* and this may result in insurmountable technical difficulties with regard to the application of some of the provisions of the fourth Convention. This is one of the reasons why the paragraph under consideration here provides that in the absence of more favourable treatment in accordance with the fourth Convention, the accused is entitled at all times to the protection of Article 75 of the Protocol (Fundamental guarantees). This rule is confirmed in paragraph 7 (b) of the said Article 75. However, it is also possible that, without being denied the protection of the fourth Convention, the accused may fall under the scope of Article 5 of the same Convention, which lays down some important derogations. In this case the guarantees of Article 75 (Fundamental guarantees) continue to apply in their entirety. Finally, the latter also apply to the person concerned when the

---

64 Bothe, Partsch and Solf, *op. cit* (note 17), pp. 261 *et seq.*

fourth Convention as a whole applies to him, whenever the treatment resulting from this would be more favourable to him, whether or not the crimes of which he is accused are grave breaches of the Conventions or the Protocol (Article 75 — Fundamental guarantees, paragraph 7 (b)). This also applies, for example, to aliens in the territory of a Party to the conflict who may have taken part in hostilities against this Party, as the fourth Convention does not indicate what judicial guarantees they are entitled to."[65] (Emphasis added.)

The protections of PI, Article 75, now constitute customary international law.[66] Most of the authors who do not seem to recognize the applicability of GC IV to unlawful combatants share the view that Article 75 of PI is applicable to unlawful combatants.[67] The authors who limit the applicability of GC IV to some types of unlawful combatants equally recognize the applicability of the said Article 75 to all unlawful combatants.[68] Those authors who wrote before the adoption of PI recognized that some minimum humanitarian guarantees apply to all unlawful combatants. They derived those guarantees either from Article 3 common to GC I-IV, Article 5 (3) of GC IV or the Martens Clause, depending on whether they accepted the applicability of GC IV to unlawful combatants or not.[69]

Penal prosecution of unlawful combatants

It is generally accepted that unlawful combatants may be prosecuted for their mere participation in hostilities, even if they respect all the rules of international humanitarian law.[70] National legislation must, however, first

---

65 Commentary on Art. 45, in Y. Sandoz, Ch. Swinarski and B. Zimmermann (eds), *Commentary on the Additional Protocols of 8 June 1977 to the Geneva Conventions of 12 August 1949*, ICRC, Martinus Nijhoff, Geneva, 1987, no. 1761. See also Commentary on Art. 51, in *ibid.*, no. 1942.

66 See Greenwood, *op. cit* (note 38), p. 316; Report on Terrorism and Human Rights, *op. cit* (note 5), para. 76; Aldrich, *op. cit* (note 7), p. 893.

67 Report on Terrorism and Human Rights, *op. cit* (note 5), para. 74; Y. Dinstein, "The distinction between unlawful combatants and war criminals", in Y. Dinstein (ed.), *International Law at a Time of Perplexity*, 1989, p. 112.

68 Ipsen, in Fleck (ed.), *op. cit* (note 36), p. 301; McCoubrey, *op. cit* (note 36), p. 137; David, *op. cit* (note 36), pp. 397 *et seq.*; Bothe, Partsch and Solf, *op. cit* (note 17), pp. 261 *et seq.*; Aldrich, *op. cit* (note 7), p. 893, footnote 12.

69 G. Schwarzenberger, *International Law as applied by International Courts and Tribunals*, Vol. II, Stevens, London, 1968, pp. 115 *et seq.*; Draper, *op. cit* (note 36), p. 197; Rosenblad, *op. cit* (note 14), p. 98; Kalshoven, *op. cit* (note 15), p. 71.

70 C. Rousseau, *Le droit des conflits armés*, A. Pedone, Paris, 1983, p. 68; Dinstein, *op. cit* (note 67), p. 105; *Commentary IV*, *op. cit* (note 12), p. 50; Kalshoven, *op. cit* (note 15), pp. 73 *et seq.*

provide for such a possibility.[71] If unlawful combatants furthermore commit serious violations of international humanitarian law, they may be prosecuted for war crimes.[72] In any such proceedings they are entitled to fair trial guarantees as contained in GC IV if applicable (i.e. if they comply with the nationality requirements of its Article 4), or at least to those contained in Article 75 of PI, which reflects customary international law. There seems to be general agreement that once in the hands of the enemy they may not be executed/punished without proper trial.[73] It is interesting to note that Dinstein considerably limits the competence of a capturing State to punish unlawful combatants for mere participation in hostilities when he claims "[a]n unlawful combatant may be put on trial only for an act committed in the course of the same mission that ended up in his capture by the adversary. (…) Hence, should the enemy capture [him] at a later stage, it may not prosecute him for the misdeeds of the past." [74] Thus, Dinstein applies to unlawful combatants the rules of the Hague Regulations relating to spies. This restriction has also been included in Article 44 (5) of PI (which stipulates that "[a]ny combatant who falls into the power of an adverse Party while not engaged in an attack or in a military operation preparatory to an attack shall not forfeit his rights to be a combatant and a prisoner of war by virtue of his prior activities") for members of the armed forces who have not distinguished themselves from the civilian population as required by that article's paragraph 3.[75]

---

71 Dinstein, *op. cit* (note 67), p. 114; Kalshoven, *op. cit* (note 15), p. 73.

72 Baxter, "Unprivileged Belligerency", *op. cit* (note 37), p. 344.

73 Draper, *op. cit* (note 36), pp. 197-198; Baxter, "Unprivileged Belligerency", *op. cit* (note 37), pp. 336, 337, 340; Baxter, "Duties of Combatants". *op. cit* (note 37), pp. 105 *et seq.*; Schwarzenberger, *op. cit* (note 69), pp. 115 *et seq.*; M.H.F. Clarke, T. Glynn and A.P.V. Rogers, "Combatant and Prisoner of War Status", in M.A. Meyer (ed.), *Armed Conflict and the New Law: aspects of the 1977 Geneva Protocols and the 1981 Weapons Convention*, British Institute of International and Comparative Law, London, 1989, p. 125; Rousseau, *op. cit* (note 70), p. 68; Dinstein, *op. cit* (note 67), p. 112; Kalshoven, *op. cit* (note 15), pp. 73 *et seq.*

74 Dinstein, *op. cit* (note 67), p. 112.

75 See Commentary on Art. 44, in Sandoz, Swinarski and Zimmermann (eds), *op. cit* (note 65), nos. 1721 *et seq.* (footnotes omitted):

"The Rapporteur explains this provision as follows:

'Paragraph 5 is an important innovation developed within the Working Group. It would ensure that any combatant who is captured while not engaged in an attack or a military operation preparatory to an attack retains his rights as a combatant and a prisoner of war whether or not he may have violated in the past the rule of the second sentence of paragraph 3. This rule should, in many cases, cover the great majority of prisoners and will protect them from any efforts to find or to fabricate past histories to deprive them of their protection.'

Thus only a member of the armed forces captured in the act can be deprived of his status as a combatant and of his right to be a prisoner of war. For paragraph 4 to be applicable, it is necessary that the violation was

"Protections" of unlawful combatants in the conduct of hostilities

Only the civilian population and individual civilians enjoy general protection against dangers arising from military operations. They are protected against direct attacks, unless and during the time that they take a direct part in hostilities. A civilian is any person who does not belong to "one of the categories of persons referred to in Article 4 (A) (1),[76] (2),[77] (3)[78] and (6)[79] of the Third Convention and in Article 43 of this Protocol" (i.e. members of the armed forces). Thus for the purposes of the law on the conduct of hostilities, there is no gap.[80] Either a person is a combatant or a civilian. Given that unlawful combatants by definition do not fulfil the criteria of either Article 4 (A) (1), (2), (3) and (6) of GC III or Article 43 of PI, this means that they are civilians. For such time as they directly participate in hostilities they are lawful targets of an attack. When they do not directly par-

committed at the time of capture or directly before the capture. The link in time between violation and capture must be so close as to permit those making the capture to take note of it themselves. Thus this is a case of 'flagrante delicto'. There is no doubt that this is, 'mutatis mutandis,' analogous to the situation of the spy, and consequently there is some relationship with the concept of an unprivileged belligerent. Like a spy, the combatant who does not carry his arms openly must be caught in the act for the sanction to be applicable to him. Similarly, like him, the combatant who is captured while he is not committing this breach, does not incur any responsibility for acts which he committed previously. However, it should be noted that in contrast to espionage, which is not prohibited by the law of armed conflict, but is merely made punishable, it is prohibited in the Protocol for a combatant not to carry his arms openly, and in principle the Protocol makes him responsible for this. However, in practical terms the adversary cannot do anything against him as a matter of criminal law unless he has surprised him 'flagrante delicto' at the moment of capture. The prohibition exists, but the sanction can only be applied under this condition. A combatant who commits this breach preserves, at least temporarily, his status as a combatant, and his right to prisoner-of-war status. If he is captured while he is not committing this breach, he is a prisoner of war and punishment can only be meted out in accordance with paragraph 2."

76 Members of regular armed forces.

77 Members of militias and volunteer corps, including organized resistance movements, not included in the regular armed forces.

78 Members of regular armed forces of a non recognized government/authority.

79 Levée en masse.

80 For the different approaches in GC IV and PI see Commentary on Art. 50, in Sandoz, Swinarski and Zimmermann (eds), *op. cit* (note 65), no. 1908: "Article 4 of the fourth Geneva Convention of 1949 relative to the Protection of Civilian Persons in Time of War contains a definition of the persons protected by that Convention against arbitrary and wanton enemy action when they are in the power of the enemy; this is the main object of the Convention. However, Part II, entitled "General protection of populations against certain consequences of war" has a wider field of application; according to Article 13, that Part covers "the whole of the populations of the countries in conflict". That definition is close to the definition of the civilian population given in Article 50 of the Protocol under consideration here."

ticipate in hostilities they are protected as civilians and may not be directly targeted. It must be stressed that the fact that civilians have at some time taken direct part in the hostilities does not make them lose their immunity from direct attacks once and for all.[81]

If unlawful combatants who have laid down their arms or no longer have means of defence surrender at discretion, they must not be killed or wounded.[82] It is likewise prohibited to declare that no quarter will be given.[83]

Conclusion

As this article has shown, it can hardly be maintained that unlawful combatants are not entitled to any protection whatsoever under international humanitarian law. If they fulfil the nationality criteria of GC IV's Article 4, they are clearly protected by that convention. The fact that a person has unlawfully participated in hostilities is not a criterion for excluding the application of GC IV, though it may be a reason for derogating from certain rights in accordance with Article 5 thereof. The specific protections of GC IV depend on the situation in which such persons find themselves in enemy hands. They are most extensive if unlawful combatants are in enemy hands in occupied territory. For those in enemy hands in enemy territory the protections of international humanitarian law are also quite well developed, whereas on the battlefield, where no actual control is established — depending on the interpretation of occupation — they may be the least developed. The guarantees contained in Article 75 of PI constitute the minimum protections that apply to all persons, including unlawful combatants, in the hands of a Party to an international armed conflict, irrespective of whether they are covered by GC IV or not.

---

81 See Art. 51 (3) PI: "Civilians shall enjoy the protection afforded by this Section, unless and *for such time as* they take a direct part in hostilities" (emphasis added). Commentary on Art. 51, in Sandoz, Swinarski and Zimmermann (eds.), *op. cit* (note 65), no. 1944; Bothe, Partsch and Solf, *op. cit* (note 17), p. 301.

82 Art. 23 (c) 1907 Hague Regulations. See also ICRC, *Rules Applicable in Guerrilla Warfare, op. cit* (note 48), p. 19.

83 Art. 23 (d) 1907 Hague Regulations. See also ICRC, *Rules Applicable in Guerrilla Warfare, op. cit* (note 48), p. 19; Kalshoven, *op. cit* (note 15), pp. 67 *et seq.*

[9]

Humanitarian Law and Direct Participation in Hostilities by Private Contractors or Civilian Employees

Michael N. Schmitt*

Over the past decade, many military affairs analysts have touted the advent of a "revolution in military affairs."[1] Although generally framed in the context of those technological advances that make possible four-dimensional, network-centric warfare, it is the dramatic "civilianization" of conflict that may prove normatively more revolutionary.[2]

In no conflict has the civilian footprint supporting military operations been larger than in Iraq.[3] This paper begins by examining civilian employee and private contractor involvement in Operation Iraqi Freedom ("OIF") as a case study in the contemporary nature of such participation. It then assesses the possibility of either de jure or de facto integration of civilians into the armed forces. Concluding that integration will be rare, the article turns to the issue of when it is that civilians can be classified as "directly participating in hostilities," thereby becoming both lawful targets of attack and prosecutable for their

---

*   Professor of International Law and Director, Program in Advanced Security Studies, George C. Marshall European Center for Security Studies, Garmisch-Partenkirchen, Germany. The views expressed herein are those of the author in his personal capacity and should not be construed as the official position of either the Federal Republic of Germany or the United States.

1   For a comprehensive compilation of material on the "revolution in military affairs," see The RMA Debate website created by the Project on Defense Alternatives, available online at <http://www.comw.org/rma/> (visited Nov 18, 2004).

2   The four dimensions are air and space, land, sea, and cyberspace. Network-centric warfare must be distinguished from "platform-centric" warfare, in which military assets, like ships, operate as separate entities (albeit sometimes cooperatively). In network-centric warfare, various platforms are linked such that they share the same battlefield "picture" and operate as parts of an integrated whole. It is the development and networking of information, sensor, command and control, and engagement grids that has enabled this transformation in warfare.

3   David Phinney, *Dangerous Business: Sending Contractors to War Zone Poses New Problems for DoD*, Fed Times (Feb 24, 2003), available online at <http://federaltimes.com/index.php?S=232833> (visited Dec 6, 2004).

Chicago Journal of International Law

actions. Finally, it concludes with an analysis of various scenarios involving civilian participation.

I. CIVILIANS AND THE WAR IN IRAQ

Estimates of the number of government civilian employees and contractor personnel present in Iraq range from twenty to thirty thousand, making civilian workers the second largest contingent in-country.[4] These figures do not include the thousands of nonmilitary personnel who support OIF from outside the country.

The scope of conflict-related activities which civilians perform today is unprecedented. Of greatest importance is their centrality to the complex logistics system that supports the Coalition armies. For instance, civilian contract employees drive the nearly seven hundred trucks that deliver supplies daily to the sixty military bases across Iraq.[5] They also provide most of the combat service support (for example, feeding troops and maintaining billeting facilities).

Closer to the fight, civilians maintain complex weapons systems such as the F-117 Nighthawk fighter, B-2 Spirit bomber, M1 Abrams tank, and TOW missile system, and operate the Global Hawk and Predator unmanned aerial vehicles ("UAV"). Civilians also conduct intelligence collection (especially with remote sensors) and analysis, although often from outside the area of operations. Contractors and government civilians have even interrogated prisoners of war and other detainees, regrettably participating in the now-infamous abuse incidents.[6] By September 2004, investigators had recommended referral of six

---

4   Estimates on the number of contractors vary widely as there is no central registry documenting their presence. However, most estimates are in this range. See, for example, Edward Cody, *Contractor Immunity a Divisive Issue*, Wash Post A1 (June 14, 2004); Roseanne Gerin, 'No Withdrawal' – Contractors vow to stay course in Iraq, 19 Wash Tech (May 10, 2004), available online at <http://www.washingtontechnology.com/news/19_3/cover-stories/23484-1.html> (visited Nov 19, 2004). They far outnumber the United Kingdom's 8,361 troops (as of October 21, 2004). GlobalSecurity.org, *Non-US Forces in Iraq – early December 2004*, available online at <http://www.globalsecurity.org/military/ops/iraq_orbat_coalition.htm> (visited Nov 19, 2004).

5   James Glanz, *For Truckers in Iraq, 'It's All about Money,'* Intl Herald Trib 1 (Sept 28, 2004).

6   See the formal investigations of detainee abuse: US Army, Antonio M. Taguba, Investigating Officer, *Article 15-6 Investigation of the 800th Military Police Brigade*, available online at <http://www.npr.org/iraq/2004/prison_abuse_report.pdf> (visited Nov 19, 2004); US Army, Anthony R. Jones, Investigating Officer, *AR 15-6 Investigation of the Abu Ghraib Prison and 205th Military Intelligence Brigade*; US Army, George R. Fay, Investigating Officer, *AR 15-6 Investigation of the Abu Ghraib Detention Facility and 205th Military Intelligence Brigade*, available online at <http://news.findlaw.com/nytimes/docs/dod/fay82504rpt.pdf> (visited Nov 19, 2004).

cases of alleged contractor abuse to the US Department of Justice for possible prosecution.[7]

Private security companies ("PSCs") have even been protecting employees and facilities of the US government, other governments, and private companies.[8] PSCs (over fifty operate in Iraq) range in size from a few individuals to hundreds. Global Risks, for example, employs 1100 personnel, including 500 Gurkha and 500 Fijian troops, thereby making it one of the larger "military" contingents in Iraq.[9] Contractors provided personal security for Coalition Provisional Authority ("CPA") Administrator L. Paul Bremer, as they currently do for senior civilians and distinguished visitors. They also guard nonmilitary facilities at the Baghdad airport and inside the Green Zone, protect convoys, and shoulder the lion's share of training for the New Iraqi Army, paramilitary forces, and law enforcement organizations.[10]

---

[7]   Fay, *AR 15-6 Investigation of the Abu Ghraib Detention Facility* at 131 (cited in note 6). The alleged participation in torture of detainees has generated a class action suit in a US District Court against the companies involved, principally Titan Corporation and CACI International, for their role in the alleged torture, rape, and summary execution of detainees. See *Saleh v Titan Corp*, No 04 CV 1143 R (NLS) (SD Cal), 2d amended complaint at 2, available online at <http://www.ccr-ny.org/v2/legal/docs/Saleh%20v%20Titan%20Corp%20 Second%20Amended%20Complaint.pdf> (visited Nov 19, 2004). An attempt to ban the practice of using private contractors in military interrogations was tabled in the US Senate. See National Defense Authorization Act for Fiscal Year 2005, S 2400, Amend No 3313, 108th Cong, 2d Sess (June 14, 2004), in 150 Cong Rec S 6831 (June 16, 2004).

[8]   See Letter from Donald H. Rumsfeld, Secretary of Defense, to The Honorable Ike Skelton (May 4, 2004), available online at <http://www.house.gov/skelton/5-4-04_Rumsfeld_letter_on_contractors.pdf> (visited Nov 19, 2004). The Coalition Provisional Authority defines PSCs as "non-Iraqi legal entities or individuals not normally resident in Iraq, including their non-Iraqi employees and Subcontractors not normally resident in Iraq, that provide security services to Foreign Liaison Missions and their Personnel, Diplomatic and Consular missions and their personnel, the MNF and its Personnel, International Consultants and other Contractors." Coalition Provisional Authority Order Number 17 (Revised), *Status of the Coalition Provisional Authority, MNF – Iraq, Certain Missions and Personnel in Iraq*, CPA/ORD/27 June 2004/17 § 1.14, available online at <http://www.cpa-iraq.org/regulations/ 20040627_CPAORD_17_Status_of_Coalition__Rev__with_Annex_A.pdf> (visited Dec 6, 2004). On the topic generally, see P.W. Singer, *War, Profits, and the Vacuum of Law: Privatized Military Firms and International Law*, 42 Colum J Transnatl L 521 (2004).

[9]   P.W. Singer, *Warriors for Hire in Iraq* (Apr 15, 2004), available online at <http://archive.salon.com/news/feature/2004/04/15/warriors/print.html> (visited Nov 2, 2004).

[10]   And contractors are often used at home to free up military personnel for combat overseas. Currently, 4,300 private security contractor employees guard some fifty US Army installations in the United States pursuant to contracts worth well in excess of $1 billion. T. Christian Miller, *Army Turns to Private Guards; The Military Is Criticized for Risking Security at Bases and for a Process that Awarded $1 Billion in Contracts without Competitive Bidding*, LA Times A1 (Aug 12, 2004).

Chicago Journal of International Law

Secretary of Defense Rumsfeld has asserted that PSCs in Iraq "provide only defensive services,"[11] but some of their activities appear indistinguishable from military operations.[12] Consider an incident in April 2003 during which employees of Blackwater USA engaged in an intense battle with insurgents who were attacking the CPA headquarters in Najaf. Thousands of rounds of ammunition and hundreds of 40mm grenades were expended in the firefight, and the company used its own helicopters to resupply employees during the battle.[13]

And contractors, particularly those in the security sector, do not come cheap.[14] By July 2004, Kellogg, Brown & Root (Halliburton) alone had been awarded $11.4 billion in contracts for Iraq and Afghanistan.[15] In light of the number of contractors and contract values, critics have taken to calling the Pentagon-contractor relationship a coalition "of the billing."[16]

---

[11]   See Rumsfeld letter (cited in note 8). A CPA order and memorandum limited contractors and other nonmilitary security personnel to possession of "'Small Arms and Defensive Weapons . . . including pistols, shotguns, and rifles firing ammunition up to an [sic] including 7.62mm and Defensive Weapons including crew-served machine guns, non-lethal weapons and riot control agents." CPA Memorandum Number 5, *Implementation of Weapons Control Order No. 3 (CPA/ORD/23 May 2003/03)* § 1, CPA/MEM/22 August 2003/05, available online at <http://www.cpa-iraq.org/regulations/20030822_CPAMEMO_5_Implementation_of_Weapons_Control_with_Annex_A.pdf> (visited Dec 6, 2004); CPA Order Number 3 (Revised) (Amended), *Weapons Control*, CPA/ORD/31 Dec 2003/03, available online at <http://www.cpa-iraq.org/regulations/20031231_CPAORD3_REV__AMD_.pdf> (visited Dec 6, 2004).

[12]   An attempt to "prohibit contractors from participating in most combat operations except in cases of self-defense, and . . . prevent U.S. moneys from being used to pay contractors for those purposes" was tabled in the Senate. See National Defense Authorization Act for Fiscal Year 2005, S 2400, Amend No 3313, 108th Cong, 2d Sess (June 14, 2004), in 150 Cong Rec S 6706 (June 14, 2004); Amend No 3313, 150 Cong Rec S at 6831 (cited in note 7).

[13]   Dana Priest, *Private Guards Repel Attack on U.S. Headquarters*, Wash Post A1 (Apr 6, 2004).

[14]   Aegis Defense Services, for example, is charging $430 million to guard Iraqi oil installations over three years. Jeremy Lovell, *Private Affair*, Melb Herald Sun 84 (Sept 25, 2004). Private military companies are earning an estimated $100 billion a year in government contracts. Jim Krane, *A Private Army Grows Around the U.S. Mission in Iraq and Around the World*, Cnews (Oct 29, 2003) available online at <http://cnews.canoe.ca/CNEWS/World/Iraq/2003/10/29/240886-ap.html> (visited Dec 6, 2004).

[15]   The Center for Public Integrity, *Post-War Contractors Ranked by Total Contract Value in Iraq and Afghanistan from 2002 through July 1, 2004*, available online at <http://www.publicintegrity.org/wow/resources.aspx?act=total> (visited Nov 20, 2004). For a regularly updated listing of contracts regarding Iraq and Afghanistan, see The Center For Public Integrity, *Contractors: All*, available online at <http://www.publicintegrity.org/wow/bio.aspx?act=pro> (visited Nov 20, 2004).

[16]   Tom Engelhardt, *Everything's Private: Private Contractors in Iraq Might Be the Largest U.S. Coalition Partner* (Nov 4, 2003), available online at <http://www.motherjones.com/news/dailymojo/2003/11/we_601_02a.html> (visited Nov 20, 2004).

The financial rewards for individual civilians serving in Iraq can be substantial. Senior PSC personnel regularly earn in the $20,000 a month range, sometimes more.[17] Blue-collar workers pull in approximately $80,000 to $100,000 annually.[18] The pay is so good relative to military salaries that the US Special Forces are experiencing a "brain drain" as well-trained troops depart for more lucrative positions with civilian contractors.[19]

But, at the same time, the risks can be deadly. Recall the dramatic April 2004 incident in Fallujah, during which crowds dragged the bodies of four Blackwater employees through the streets in scenes reminiscent of Mogadishu circa 1993.[20] And by September 2004, Kellogg, Brown & Root had suffered forty-six employee deaths.[21] Overall, contractors have experienced more casualties than any Coalition contingent except the US: more than 100 by August 2004.[22] Sadly, by September 2004, in excess of 140 foreign hostages have also been seized, the vast majority civilians; 26 were later murdered.

There are practical problems with the use of contractors or civilian government employees in an area of combat operations. For instance, PSC activities are limited by the terms of their respective contracts, thereby limiting the flexibility of military commanders overseeing them when responding to evolving situations. Indeed, contractors may simply refuse to perform contractual functions, preferring contract penalties or termination to the assumption of risks incident to compliance. The decision of numerous companies to withdraw from Iraq in the face of the deteriorating security situation, especially in the wake of hostage takings, is illustrative.

Further, PSC employees may lack adequate training or be of questionable background. Backwater, as an illustration, has admitted that 30 percent of its employees do not have military training. Additionally, it hired thirty Chilean soldiers in February 2003, most reportedly with ties to the Pinochet regime.[23] Not surprisingly, professional military personnel have expressed concern about

---

17   Neil King Jr. and Yochi J. Dreazen, *Amid Chaos in Iraq, Tiny Security Firm Found Opportunity*, Wall St J A1 (Aug 13, 2004).

18   Russell Gold, The *Temps of War: Blue-Collar Workers Ship Out for Iraq*, Wall St J A1 (Feb 5, 2004).

19   Pauline Jelinek, *Many Elite Soldiers Leave for Better Pay*, Christian Broadcasting Network (July 21, 2004), available online at <http://www.cbn.com/cbnnews/wire/040721h.asp> (visited Nov 2, 2004).

20   Mike Farhi, *Progress is Ongoing in Iraq, White House Says*, Wash Post A20 (Apr 1, 2004).

21   Glanz, *For Truckers in Iraq* (cited in note 5).

22   Renae Merle, *Contract Workers Are War's Forgotten: Iraq Deaths Create Subculture of Loss*, Wash Post A1 (July 31, 2004).

23   Singer, *Warriors for Hire in Iraq* (cited in note 9).

Chicago Journal of International Law

armed civilians operating in close proximity to combat operations.[24] Many worry that misconduct by civilian contractors may cause reprisals against uniformed forces. They also question the rules of engagement under which civilians operate.[25] Most fundamentally, the presence of armed civilian groups operating independently, even if only "defensively," violates the unity of command principle of war.[26]

Problematically, civilians are far less accountable than their military counterparts. Consider US mechanisms for handling misconduct. Government civilian employees are subject to civil service disciplinary measures, but the system is administrative, not judicial. Contractors are even less accountable, for the contracting officer, and not the military commander, exercises "supervisory" control over them. In the event of misconduct, the contracting officer may impose pecuniary penalties on the firm, but has no authority vis-à-vis the employee. Rather, discipline is the company's responsibility.[27] This absence of genuine command and control over contract personnel invites abuses. Tellingly, some US judge advocates have reportedly charged that contractors were used during interrogations of detainees in Iraq to keep aggressive techniques quiet.[28]

Of course, when civilians commit crimes, penal sanctions should be imposed. However, status of forces and related agreements often determine whether the country in which a civilian commits a crime has jurisdiction.[29] In Iraq, civilian government employees and government contractor personnel enjoyed immunity from prosecution during the occupation. As occupation ended, Ambassador Bremer issued CPA Order 17, which grants continued immunity from Iraqi jurisdiction to civilians of the Multinational Force and "international consultants" provided to the Iraqi Transitional Government by other states: contractor personnel enjoy immunity "with respect to acts

---

24   This comment is based on numerous conversations I have had with military officers deployed to Iraq.

25   Borzou Daragahi, *In Iraq, Private Firms Lighten Load on U.S. Troops: For Profit, Private Firms Train Iraqi Soldiers, Provide Security and Much More*, Pitt Post-Gazette (Sept 28, 2003), available online at <http://www.post-gazette.com/pg/03271/226368.stm> (visited Nov 20, 2004).

26   "Unity of command means that all forces operate under a single commander with the requisite authority to direct all forces employed in pursuit of a common purpose." Joint Chiefs of Staff, *Joint Publication 3-0 Doctrine for Joint Operations* A-2 (Sept 10, 2001), available online at <http://www.dtic.mil/doctrine/jel/new_pubs/jp3_0.pdf> (visited Nov 20, 2004). The other principles of war are objective, offensive, mass, economy of force, maneuver, security, surprise, and simplicity. Id at Appendix A.

27   Rumsfeld letter (cited in note 8).

28   This assertion has been denied by a Pentagon spokesperson. Joshua Chaffin, *Contract Interrogators Hired to Avoid Supervision*, Lon Fin Times 9 (May 21, 2004).

29   See generally Dieter Fleck, ed, *The Handbook of the Law of Visiting Forces* (Oxford 2001).

performed by them pursuant to the terms and conditions of a Contract or any sub-contract thereto," although the "Sending State" may waive said immunity.[30]

To fill the jurisdictional vacuum, some States have established domestic criminal jurisdiction over their civilians on the battlefield. US legislation, for instance, includes the Military Extraterritorial Jurisdiction Act, which subjects individuals employed by the US military abroad, whether directly or as contractors, to federal jurisdiction.[31]

What accounts for the explosion of contractor personnel and civilian government employees on or near the battlefield? Cost is one factor. In the aftermath of the Cold War, most governments sought to realize the "peace dividend" by drawing down legacy armies sized and equipped to fight a global conflict.[32] But the dividend never materialized; on the contrary, many states found their security environment complicated by the demise of (stabilizing) bipolarity and the emergence of new threats like transnational terrorism and internal unrest. Yet, for domestic political reasons, downsizing was a process that usually proved irreversible.

In light of this dilemma, the use of civilians in support roles proved especially appealing because it freed up military personnel to perform combat missions. In this way, armed forces avoided a straight-line relationship between reduced numbers and reduced combat effectiveness. In the US, the consequent civilianization was labeled "Transformation."[33]

Civilians are also typically less costly than their military counterparts. Although salaries may exceed those of uniformed personnel, overhead pales by

---

[30]   CPA Ord No 17 at §§ 4.3, 5.2 (cited in note 8). Pursuant to Article 26(C) of the Law of Administration for the State of Iraq for the Transitional Period (hereinafter Transitional Administrative Law), "[t]he laws, regulations, orders, and directives issued by the Coalition Provisional Authority . . . shall remain in force until rescinded or amended by legislation duly enacted and having the force of law." Law of Administration for the State of Iraq for the Transitional Period, art 26(C) (Mar 8, 2004), available online at <http://www.cpa-iraq.org/government/TAL.html> (visited Nov 20, 2004). The UN Security Council endorsed the transitional arrangements as set forth in the Transitional Administrative Law. Security Council Res No 1546, UN Doc S/RES/1546 (2004).

[31]   Military Extraterritorial Jurisdiction Act, 10 USC § 3261 (2000). This Statute was primarily designed to address crimes by contractors against US military personnel and their dependents abroad. Also providing possible jurisdiction is the War Crimes Act of 1996, 18 USC § 2441 (2004), and the federal torture statute, 18 USC § 2340A (2000).

[32]   In the United States, the size of the military dropped to its present 1.4 million from 2 million a decade ago. Robert Burns, *Downsizing of Military Now Unlikely*, Seattle Post-Intelligencer (Sept 1, 2001), available online at <http://seattlepi.nwsource.com/national/37341_military01.shtml> (visited Nov 23, 2004).

[33]   On transformation, see material compiled by the Department of Defense on its Transformation website, available online at <http://www.defenselink.mil/transformation/> (visited Nov 20, 2004).

Chicago Journal of International Law

comparison. Civilians, especially contractors, perform discrete tasks rather than operate within a system in which they are expected to acquire the skills and experience necessary to advance through the ranks. Therefore, they can devote a much greater percentage of their time to the core undertaking, without having to also complete training and education or provide the same to others. Further, the military does not have to fund frequent transfers to acquire the experiential base necessary for assumption of greater responsibility, nor compensate for efficiency loss while new personnel learn their jobs. Perhaps most significant is the fact that civilians do not require the extensive support structure that many militaries provide their uniformed personnel (for example, commissaries, housing, dining halls, recreational and fitness facilities, hospitals, off-duty education, etc.).

An additional motivator is that the technology of modern warfare often exceeds the ability of militaries to train their personnel. This phenomenon has two facets. First, while some technology is so complex that only highly trained individuals can operate it, most military personnel lack the aptitude or length of service to develop the requisite skills. Second, some hi-tech military equipment exists in small numbers in the inventory. Thus, the training thereon is extraordinarily expensive because it benefits from no economies of scale. Both dynamics have led to "package deals" in which the military purchases not only the weapon system, but also contracts for training and maintenance support, and, in some cases, even operation of the system.[34]

In Iraq, the dynamic impelling the widespread use of civilians is simple. With US forces deployed to the Balkans, Afghanistan, and elsewhere, the number of troops available for combat, occupation, and transition duties in Iraq has been limited. At the same time, the security situation in Iraq has stretched combat troops to the breaking point.[35] It should, therefore, come as little surprise that duties usually shouldered by uniformed troops, such as guarding convoys or airports, have been outsourced. Furthermore, in light of the unstable security situation, reconstruction projects have created additional security burdens that cannot be met by military forces.

---

[34]   For instance, civilian contract personnel flew aboard the E-8 J-Stars (Joint Surveillance Target Attack Radar System) during operations over the Balkans from 1995–99 and have manned ground stations for Predator unmanned aerial vehicle operations (although USAF personnel have now assumed full responsibility).

[35]   Ambassador L. Paul Bremer has opined that the size of the US occupation force was too small. Robin Wright and Thomas E. Hicks, *Bremer Criticizes Troop Levels: Ex-Overseer of Iraq Says U.S. Effort Was Hampered Early On*, Wash Post A1 (Oct 5, 2004).

II. LEGAL CONSEQUENCES OF CIVILIAN PARTICIPATION IN CONFLICT

It is not the purpose here to exhaustively explore the legal consequences of civilian government employee or private contractor participation in hostilities. Rather, the intent is to consider when they attach. However, a brief review of consequences will place the subsequent discussion in context.[36]

Most significantly, pursuant to Article 51.3 of the 1977 Protocol Additional I to the Geneva Conventions ("Protocol I"), civilians enjoy immunity from attack during international armed conflict "unless and for such time as they take a *direct part in hostilities.*"[37] Those who do directly participate may be legally targeted and their injury or death does not bear on such conduct of hostility issues as proportionality or precautions in attack.[38] Civilian direct participants are labeled either "unlawful combatants" or "unprivileged belligerents."[39]

Secondly, those who participate in hostilities without the status of lawful combatant do not benefit from prisoners of war protections, particularly those of the Third Geneva Convention.[40] While combatants may forfeit their right to

---

[36]   See Jéan-François Quéguiner, Working Paper, *Direct Participation in Hostilities Under International Humanitarian Law* (Nov 2003), available online at <http://www.ihlresearch.org/ihl/pdfs/briefing3297.pdf> (visited Nov 20, 2004).

[37]   Protocol Additional to the Geneva Conventions of 12 August 1949, and Relating to the Protection of Victims of International Armed Conflicts, art 51.3, 16 ILM 1391 (1977) (emphasis added).

[38]   The principle of proportionality prohibits attacks "which may be expected to cause incidental loss of civilian life, injury to civilians, damage to civilian objects, or a combination thereof, which would be excessive in relation to the concrete and direct military advantage anticipated" from the operation. Id, art 51.5(b). See also id, art 57.2. Even if an attack is proportional, those who plan, decide on, or execute an attack must take precautions to further spare the civilian population. For example, "[w]hen a choice is possible between several military objectives for obtaining a similar military advantage, the objective to be selected shall be that the attack on which may be expected to cause the least danger to civilian lives and to civilian objects." Id, art 57.3.

[39]   "Unlawful combatant" is the better term because: (1) it preserves the distinction between combatants and civilians; and (2) the term "belligerents" generally refers to states which are party to a conflict, not individuals. On the topic generally, see Knut Dörmann, *The Legal Situation of "Unlawful/Unprivileged Combatants"*, 85 Intl Rev Red Cross 45 (2003); Jason Callen, *Unlawful Combatants and the Geneva Conventions*, 44 Va J Intl L 1025 (2004); K.W. Watkin, Working Paper, *Combatants, Unprivileged Belligerents and Conflicts in the 21st Century* (June 2003), available online at <http://www.ihlresearch.org/ihl/pdfs/Session2.pdf> (visited Nov 4, 2004).

[40]   Geneva Convention (III) Relative to the Treatment of Prisoners of War (1949), art 4, 6 UST 3316 (1956) (hereinafter Geneva Convention III).

Chicago Journal of International Law

be a prisoner of war (for example, by failure to wear a uniform),[41] civilians who participate directly in hostilities generally lack that right in the first place.[42]

Finally, civilians who directly participate may be punished for their actions because they lack the "combatant privilege" to use force against lawful targets. Currently contentious is the issue of whether mere direct participation, without more, is a war crime.

Consider the case of David Hicks, the Australian detainee being tried before a Guantanamo Military Commission for, inter alia, "attempted murder" (of "American, British, Canadian, Australian, Afghan, and other Coalition forces") "by an unprivileged belligerent."[43] This charge is somewhat curious. In humanitarian law, combatants enjoy no general protection from attack,[44] so attacking them cannot be a war crime (absent more).

Perhaps, then, prosecution is based on Hick's alleged status as an unprivileged belligerent. Despite dated support for the assertion that being an unprivileged belligerent can constitute a war crime,[45] the better position is that

---

[41]   Protocol I, art 44.4 (cited in note 37).

[42]   An exception exists for certain persons who accompany the armed forces without being members thereof, certain crews of aircraft and vessels, and members of a *levee en masse*. The first two categories are discussed in Section III. A *levee en masse* occurs when "[i]nhabitants of a non-occupied territory, who on the approach of the enemy spontaneously take up arms to resist the invading forces, without having had time to form themselves into regular armed units, provided they carry arms openly and respect the laws and customs of war." Geneva Convention III, art 4A(6) (cited in note 40).

[43]   Military Commission Charges, *United States v Hicks* (June 2004), available online at <http://news.findlaw.com/wp/docs/gitmo/ushicks604chrg.html> (visited Dec 6, 2004). Although the accused is not a civilian employee or contractor, the case is instructive.

[44]   No treaty (including the statutes governing international courts such as the International Criminal Court, International Criminal Tribunal for the Former Yugoslavia, and International Criminal Tribunal for Rwanda) suggests that targeting a combatant is unlawful. Rather, combatants are only protected from attack when they are *hors de combat* because they have surrendered, are sick or wounded and not carrying on the fight, are shipwrecked, or have parachuted from a disabled aircraft. Convention between the United States and Other Powers Respecting the Laws and Customs of War on Land, art 23(c), 36 Stat 2277 (1907) (hereinafter HIVR); Protocol I, art 41 (cited in note 37); Geneva Convention (I) for the Amelioration of the Condition of the Wounded and Sick in Armed Forces in the Field (1949), art 12, 6 UST 3114 (1956) (hereinafter Geneva Convention I); Geneva Convention (II) for the Amelioration of the Condition of Wounded, Sick and Shipwrecked Members of the Armed Forces at Sea (1949), art 12, 6 UST 3217 (1956) (hereinafter Geneva Convention II); Protocol I, arts 10, 42. They are also immune from attack when serving as *parlementaires* conducting negotiations with the enemy or as medical or religious personnel. HIVR, art 32; Geneva Convention I, arts 24, 25; Protocol I, art 15. Note that medical or religious personnel are not considered combatants. Protocol I, art 43.

[45]   In the *Hostages Trial*, a post-World War II war crimes trial, a military tribunal held that "[w]e think the rule is established that a civilian who aids, abets or participates in the fighting is liable to punishment as a war criminal. Fighting is legitimate only for the combatant personnel of a

only the acts underlying direct participation are punishable. If they amount to war crimes (for example, killing civilians), the acts may be tried as such. Further, because civilians who directly participate lack combatant immunity, they may be convicted for offenses against the domestic law of a State that enjoys both subject matter and personal jurisdiction. This is the position proffered by leading scholars,[46] as well as that in operational guidance such as the US Army's *Operational Law Handbook (2004)*.[47]

In noninternational armed conflict, civilians who participate in armed conflict also forfeit certain protections. Common Article 3 to the four 1949 Geneva Conventions applies only to "[p]ersons taking no active part in the

---

country." The United Nations War Crimes Commission, 15 *Law Reports of Trials of War Criminals* 112 (HMSO 1949). Many embracing this position also cite the US Supreme Court's decision in *Ex parte Quirin*, 317 US 1 (1942). There the Court held that:

> those who during time of war pass surreptitiously from enemy territory into our own, discarding their uniforms upon entry, for the commission of hostile acts involving destruction of life or property, have the status of unlawful combatants punishable as such by military commission. This precept of the law of war has been so recognized in practice both here and abroad, and has so generally been accepted as valid by authorities on international law that we think it must be regarded as a rule or principle of the law of war.

Quirin, 317 US at 35–36 (footnotes omitted). The reasoning in both decisions is flawed, particularly to the extent that they apply analogies to spying, which is clearly not a violation of the law of war. See, for example, *In re Flesche*, 16 Ann Dig 266, 267 (Spec Ct Cass 1949) (Holland) (stating that espionage "is a recognized means of warfare and therefore is neither an international delinquency on the part of the State employing the spy nor a war crime proper on the part of the individual concerned"). Commentators are in accord, as are the military manuals such as those of the US Army and UK Forces. See Yoram Dinstein, *The Conduct of Hostilities under the Law of International Armed Conflict* 210–13 (Cambridge 2004); Richard R. Baxter, *So-Called 'Unprivileged Belligerency': Spies, Guerrillas, and Saboteurs*, 27 Milit L Rev 487 (1975); Department of the Army Field Manual 27-10, *The Law of Land Warfare* ¶ 77 (1956) ("resort to [espionage] involves no offense against international law."); UK Ministry of Defence, *The Manual of the Law of Armed Conflict* ¶ 4.9.7 (2004) ("Spies are usually tried by civilian courts under the domestic legislation of the territory in which they are captured."). The *Quirin* decision has been criticized for its deviation from law of war principles by several top scholars and practitioners in the field. For instance, W. Hays Parks has noted that "*Quirin* is lacking with respect to some of its law of war scholarship." W. Hays Parks, *Special Forces' Wear of Non-Standard Uniforms*, 4 Chi J Intl L 493, 510 n 31 (2003).

46   Dinstein, *Conduct of Hostilities* at 234 (cited in note 45); Baxter, 27 Milit L Rev at 487 (cited in note 45); Julius Stone, *Legal Controls of International Conflict* 567 (Rinehart 1954). See also Derek Jinks, *The Declining Significance of POW Status*, 45 Harv Intl L J 367, 436–39 (Summer 2004) (taking an even more permissive view of the issue).

47   "Unprivileged belligerents may include spies, saboteurs, or civilians who are participating in the hostilities or who otherwise engage in unauthorized attacks or other combatant acts. Unprivileged belligerents are not entitled to prisoner of war status, and may be prosecuted under the domestic law of the captor." US Army, Judge Advocate General's Legal Center and School, *Operational Law Handbook (2004)* 17 (US Army 2004).

Chicago Journal of International Law

hostilities,"[48] thereby depriving those who do of the limited protections therein. Although Protocol Additional II to the Geneva Conventions ("Protocol II") augments the Common Article protections, Article 13.3 thereof deprives civilians of both the "general protection against the dangers arising from military operations" and immunity from attack "for such time as they take a direct part in hostilities."[49]

The participation of civilian employees and private contractors in noninternational armed conflict poses only marginally distinct legal issues from participation in international armed conflict. In the first place, rebel forces are unlikely to hire civilians or contractors. Further, because rebel forces lack combatant immunity, violence they direct at their government opponents is wrongful per se regardless of the status of the victim. This being so, the central issue is whether the government civilian employee or government contractor harmed by the rebel was "taking no active part in the hostilities."[50] If so, the rebel will have committed a war crime; if not, only a domestic crime will have been committed. But one assesses participation using the same analysis as in international armed conflict. Therefore, the focus here shall be on that genre of conflict.

III. THE LEGAL STATUS OF CIVILIANS INVOLVED IN ARMED CONFLICT

There are but two categories of individuals in an armed conflict, combatants and civilians. Combatants include members of a belligerent's armed forces and others who are directly participating in a conflict. As noted, the latter are labeled unlawful combatants or unprivileged belligerents; they are either civilians who have joined the conflict or members of a purported military organization who do not meet the requirements for lawful combatant status. Everyone else is a civilian, and as such enjoys immunity from attack.

---

48   See, for example, Geneva Convention I, art 3(1) (cited in note 44); Geneva Convention II, art 3(1) (cited in note 44); Geneva Convention III, art 3(1) (cited in note 40).

49   Protocol (II) Additional to the Geneva Conventions of 12 August 1949, and Relating to the Protection of Victims of Non-International Armed Conflicts, arts 13.1, 13.3, 16 ILM 1442 (1977) (hereinafter Protocol II). Although the Geneva Conventions employ the term "active" rather than "direct," the International Criminal Tribunal for Rwanda appropriately found the terms so similar that they should be treated synonymously. Article 3 of the Geneva Conventions, Geneva Convention I, art 3(1) (cited in note 44); Geneva Convention II, art 3(1) (cited in note 44); Geneva Convention III, art 3(1) (cited in note 40); *Prosecutor v Akayesu*, Case No ICTR-96-4-T, ¶ 629 (ICTR 1998).

50   Rome Statute of the International Criminal Court, arts 8.2(c), 8.2(e)(i), 37 ILM 999 (1998) (hereinafter Rome Statute).

A. CIVILIAN EMPLOYEES AND PRIVATE CONTRACTORS AS LAWFUL COMBATANTS

If civilian employees and private contractors qualify as lawful combatants, the aforementioned legal consequences never befall them.[51] Thus, before turning to the notion of direct participation, it is necessary to query how civilians might acquire lawful combatant status. This is one of several issues the International Committee of the Red Cross has focused on during its ongoing direct participation project.[52] It is a red herring.[53]

Combatant and civilian status are opposite sides of the same coin. Article 50.1 of Protocol I provides that "[a] civilian is any person who does not belong to one of the categories of persons referred to in Article 4 (A) (1), (2), (3), and (6) of the Third Convention and in Article 43 of this Protocol."[54] The relevant provisions of Article 4 exclude the following from civilian status:

(1) Members of the armed forces of a Party to the conflict, as well as members of militias or volunteer corps forming part of such armed forces.

(2) Members of other militias and members of other volunteer corps, including those of organized resistance movements, belonging to a Party to the conflict and operating in or outside their own territory, even if this territory is occupied, provided that such militias or volunteer corps, including such organized resistance movements, fulfil the following conditions:

   (a) that of being commanded by a person responsible for his subordinates;

   (b) that of having a fixed distinctive sign recognizable at a distance;

   (c) that of carrying arms openly;

---

[51]   Article 43.2 of Protocol I defines participation with reference to direct participation: "Members of the armed forces of a Party to a conflict (other than medical personnel and chaplains covered by Article 33 of the Third Convention) are combatants, that is to say, they have the right to participate directly in hostilities." Protocol I, art 43.2 (cited in note 37).

[52]   The ongoing multiyear project being conducted in collaboration with the Asser Institute began in 2003.

[53]   US doctrine expressly rules out the possibility: "In all instances, contractor employees cannot lawfully perform military functions and should not be working in scenarios that involve military combat operations where they might be conceived as combatants." Joint Chiefs of Staff, *4-0 Doctrine for Logistics Support of Joint Operations* § V-1(d) (Apr 6, 2000), available online at <http://www.dtic.mil/doctrine/jel/new_pubs/jp4_0.pdf> (visited Nov 20, 2004). See also US Army Field Manual 3-100.21, *Contractors on the Battlefield* ch 1 (Jan 2003), available online at <http://www.globalsecurity.org/military/library/policy/army/fm/3-100-21/index.html> (visited Nov 20, 2004); US Army Regulation 715-9, *Contractors Accompanying the Force* § 2-3(a) (Oct 29, 1999), available online at <http://www.army.mil/usapa/epubs/pdf/r715_9.pdf> (visited Nov 20, 2004).

[54]   Protocol I, art 50.1 (cited in note 37).

Chicago Journal of International Law

(d) that of conducting their operations in accordance with the laws and customs of war.[55]

Article 43 provides that:

[t]he armed forces of a Party to a conflict consist of all organized armed forces, groups and units which are under a command responsible to that Party for the conduct of its subordinates, even if that Party is represented by a government or an authority not recognized by an adverse Party. Such armed forces shall be subject to an internal disciplinary system which, *inter alia*, shall enforce compliance with the rules of international law applicable in armed conflict.[56]

It also notes that a "paramilitary or armed law enforcement agency" may be incorporated into the armed forces; the party doing so is required to notify the opposing side of such incorporation.[57]

Subparagraph (1) of Article 4 addresses de jure combatant status—in other words, formal incorporation into the armed forces by a state—whereas (2) involves combatant status that derives from the nature and actions of a group. Article 43 encompasses both categories.

It is difficult to imagine a situation in which individual government civilian or contractor employees might qualify as formal members of the armed forces, regardless of the duties they perform. In the first place, most armed forces have set procedures for enlistment or conscription. An individual failing to comply with them cannot individually become a member thereof. Admittedly, some militaries have de minimis procedural prerequisites, sometimes even permitting an individual to acquire "membership" by simply joining the fighting.[58] However, the very fact that a civilian is separately employed in a government "civilian" post or works for a company with a contractual relationship to the government would by definition rule this possibility out. Moreover, if a state wished to formally draw individual civilians into the armed forces, it could readily do so. For instance, some countries require certain civilian employees in key positions to serve as reservists; this facilitates their rapid change of status in the event of armed conflict. Thus, vis-à-vis individual civilians, the fact that no formal recruitment has occurred is dispositive evidence of a state's understanding that the civilian in question does not enjoy Article 4(A)(1) status.

---

55   Geneva Convention III, art 4(A) (cited in note 40). This listing appears in Article 13 of both Geneva Convention I and Geneva Convention II. Geneva Convention I, art 13 (cited in note 44); Geneva Convention II, art 13 (cited in note 44). Article 4(A)(6) of Geneva Convention III also deals with the *levee en masse* and is irrelevant to this inquiry.

56   Protocol I, art 43.1 (cited in note 37).

57   Id, art 43.3.

58   For example, there were no formal procedures or prerequisites for joining the Taliban armed forces in Afghanistan.

Might the *group* to which such civilians belong qualify as part of the armed forces? After all, many perform functions indistinguishable from those performed by military units, sometimes even units in the same armed force that employs or contracts them.

Again, logic would dictate otherwise. First, such groups coexist alongside, not within, the armed forces and are thereby distinguishable on that fact alone. It would be incongruent to suggest that a group with a clearly distinct civilian identity (conditions of employment, supervisory chain, disciplinary system, etc.) could somehow transmogrify into an element of the armed services merely because of the function it performs.

More significantly, recall the Article 43.3 proviso on incorporation of paramilitary and law enforcement forces, which confirms the requirement for states to affirmatively act to incorporate groups into the military before they acquire the status of armed forces. This makes it patent that unincorporated paramilitary and law enforcement agencies are civilian in nature for the purposes of humanitarian law. Thus, any of their members who engage in hostile action against enemy forces prior to notification of incorporation are directly participating as civilians. For instance, paramilitary forces of the Central Intelligence Agency cannot be characterized as members of the armed forces absent incorporation and notification. To the extent that this is so for formal organized standing paramilitary and law enforcement entities of the government, it is even more so for other groups of government employees, private military companies, or other entities acting to maintain law and order or provide security.

Nor does Article 4(A)(1)'s "militias or volunteer corps forming part of such armed forces" verbiage offer an alternative route to membership. The official Commentary to the Third Geneva Convention notes the comment referred to groups that "although *part of the armed forces*, were quite distinct from the army as such."[59] This unambiguously suggests a requirement for formal affiliation with the armed forces beyond a mere term contract.

A further practical obstacle to de jure armed forces status is the requirement that the group in question meet four criteria. Specifically, the conditions set forth for militia forces in Article 4(A)(2), which mirror those contained in the 1899 and 1907 Hague Conventions,[60] also apply to components of the armed forces. Although this is a somewhat controversial position, and while textually it would appear they do not, the better position is that the

---

[59]   Jean de Preux, *Commentary: III Geneva Convention Relative to the Treatment of Prisoners of War* 52 (ICRC 1960) (emphasis added) (hereinafter GCIII Commentary).

[60]   Convention with Respect to the Laws and Customs of War on Land (1899), art 1, reprinted in 1 Am J Intl L 129, 132 (Supp 1907); HIVR (cited in note 44).

conditions are implicit in the meaning of armed forces.[61] Simple logic supports this interpretation. For instance, the requirements to wear a uniform and carry arms openly serve to distinguish combatants from civilians, thereby enhancing protection for the latter. Suggesting that military personnel need not comply with them would fly in the face of this rationale.

Article 44.3 of Protocol I further confirms the approach's validity when it (albeit relaxing the standards of combatancy in ways objectionable to some states[62]) provides that to *retain* combatant status, a soldier must minimally carry arms openly during a military engagement and during such time as he is visible to the enemy in the deployment phase of an attack.[63] The ICRC Commentary specifically opines that an individual who does not comply loses combatant status. In language paralleling the normative consequences of direct participation by civilians, it explains: "Thus criminal prosecution becomes possible, even for hostile acts which would not be punishable in other circumstances. In other words, such a prisoner can be made subject to the provisions of the ordinary penal code of the Party to the conflict which has captured him."[64]

Since civilian employees and private contractors do not wear uniforms denoting combatant status, seldom fall under the formal command of military personnel, and generally lie beyond the reach of military discipline that the armed forces use to enforce adherence to the "laws and customs of war," it would be a stretch to style them members of the armed forces.

In sum, it is highly unlikely that civilian government employees or private contractors, whether individually or as a group, would ever qualify for combatant status under Article 4(A)(1), particularly in light of Article 43.1 of Protocol I. To do so, they would have to individually enlist (or be conscripted)

---

[61]   As has been noted, "[i]t is generally assumed that these conditions were deemed, by the 1874 Brussels Conference and the 1899 and 1907 Hague Peace Conferences, to be inherent in the regular armed forces of States. Accordingly, it was considered to be unnecessary and redundant to spell them out in the Conventions." Michael Bothe, Karl Josef Partsch, and Waldemar A. Solf, *New Rules for Victims of Armed Conflicts: Commentary on the Two 1977 Protocols Additional to the Geneva Conventions of 1949*, 234 (Martinus Nijhoff 1982).

[62]   The US position on Protocol I provisions is authoritatively set out in Office of the Secretary of Defense, Memorandum for Mr. John H. McNeill, Assistant General Counsel (International), *1977 Protocols Additional to the Geneva Conventions: Customary International Law Implications* (May 8, 1986) (on file with author). See also Michael J. Matheson, *Remarks at the 1987 Humanitarian Law Conference on the United States Position on the Relation of Customary International Law to the 1977 Protocols Additional to the 1949 Geneva Conventions* (Jan 22, 1987), 2 Am U J Intl L & Poly 419 (1987).

[63]   Protocol I, art 44.3 (cited in note 37).

[64]   Yves Sandoz, Christophe Swinarski, and Bruno Zimmermann, eds, *Commentary on the Additional Protocols of 8 June 1977 to the Geneva Conventions of 12 August 1949* ¶ 1719 (ICRC 1987) (hereinafter Protocols Commentary). It does caveat this assertion with mention that "this is the view of the majority of the delegations."

or be formally incorporated as a group. Additionally, the requirements inferred from Article 4(A)(2) would usually act as a further bar to characterization as members of the armed forces, and thereby combatants.

But might civilian employees and private contractors be integrated de facto into the armed forces in the sense of Article 4(A)(2) and Article 43.1?[65] Article 4(A)(2) resulted from efforts at the 1949 Diplomatic Conference to address the partisan operations of the Second World War.[66] The four conditions included therein reflected a delicate balance between the concerns of occupying powers and the desires of occupied countries.[67]

In assessing the Article 4(A)(2) conditions, it must be borne in mind that they apply to groups, not individuals. Moreover, such groups cannot consist of government employees, except in the unusual circumstance that they become resistance fighters upon isolation from the government. Simple logic dictates that if paramilitary and law enforcement agencies must be formally incorporated, other groups of government employees cannot circumvent this requirement by complying with the less stringent requirements of 4(A)(2). The 4(A)(2) inquiry is thus limited to private contractors.

Before moving to the four express criteria, it is useful to examine the nature of the groups that might be affected. As noted in the official Commentary, the threshold question is whether a group is "fighting on behalf of a 'Party to the conflict.'"[68] Although pre-twentieth century practice was that the sovereign had to formally authorize fighting units outside the armed forces, by the time of the 1899 and 1907 Hague Conferences, this traditional requirement had faded away. Instead, there needed merely to be a de facto relationship between the group and a party to the conflict, one that makes it apparent for whom the group is fighting. That the relationship did not have to be formal is evident from the fact that such a criterion would have excluded some of the very

---

[65]   As noted, Article 43.1 relaxes the Geneva conditions by dispensing with the requirement to distinguish oneself from the civilian population in situations where doing so is not possible, so long as the individual carries arms openly while deploying to an engagement and during the battle. This relaxation, which is opposed most notably by the United States, cannot be said to reflect customary international law. See Office of the Secretary of Defense, Memorandum (cited in note 62); Matheson, 2 Am U J Intl L & Poly at 419 (cited in note 62).

[66]   The existing 1899 and 1907 Hague Regulations only embraced "militia and volunteer corps." Regulations Concerning the Laws and Customs on Land, art 1, annex to Convention with Respect to the Laws and Customs of War on Land (1899), art 1, 32 Stat 1803 (1903); Convention Respecting the Laws and Customs of War on Land, annex to Hague Convention (IV) Respecting the Laws and Customs of War on Land (1907), art 1, 36 Stat 2277, 1 Bevans 631, 639 (1968).

[67]   de Preux, *GCIII Commentary* at 53 (cited in note 59).

[68]   Id at 57. See also Dinstein, *The Conduct of Hostilities* at 39 n 55 (cited in note 45), citing *Prosecutor v Kassem*, 42 ILR 470 (Milit Ct 1969) (Israel).

World War II partisan groups which motivated inclusion of Article 4(A)(2) in the Geneva Conventions. The requirement is simply that the group be fighting in support of, in concert with, or in a complementary fashion to the government forces (or the aims thereof if those forces have been vanquished).

To the extent a group is employed directly by, or under contract to, a party to the conflict, this requirement should pose no obstacle to 4(A)(2) combatant status. More tenuous is the situation where a government contractor subcontracts the firm in question, a prevalent practice in Iraq today. For instance, the prime contractor may be under contract to rebuild infrastructure, but then subcontract security for its operations to a PSC. Alternatively, the prime contractor may have been awarded a broad contract that includes security of various government facilities in the contractual specifications. Yet, so long as the activities the subcontractor engages in are integral to contract performance, they further the objectives of a party to the conflict.

But consider the case of a PSC contracted by other than a party to the conflict, for instance a private mining or drilling firm operating in the conflict zone. Maintaining security for such firms may necessitate engaging in combat operations with forces of one or more of the Parties, but such operations would not be on behalf of the other side. In other words, the determinative question is not whom you are fighting, but rather are you fighting in order that one side might prevail.[69] Contractors hired by a private entity to support one side in order to bolster the chances of the other might qualify; those hired for any other purpose would not. Obviously, the former is a fairly far-fetched scenario, one made even more implausible by limits on mercenaries.[70]

A second threshold requirement is independence from the armed forces. In crafting Article 4, the drafters adhered to the distinction contained in Article 1 of the 1907 Hague Regulations between "militia and volunteer corps forming part of the army and those which are independent"—hence, Article 4(A)(1) *and* 4(A)(2).

---

69   This begs the question of the group which is fighting for its own purposes in order to defeat one side, in the hope, for instance, that it will come to power upon expulsion of an occupying force, an interesting scenario which lies beyond the scope of this article.

70   The contract firms in Iraq would not qualify for mercenary status. By Article 47.2(a) of Protocol I, mercenaries are "specially recruited . . . to fight in an armed conflict," that is, direct participation is their express purpose. Protocol I, art 47.2(a) (cited in note 37). They must also be motivated by private gain and promised compensation in excess of that received by the armed forces, be neither a national of a party to the conflict nor a resident of territory a party controls, not be a member of the armed forces of a party, and not been sent by a nonparty as a member of its own armed forces. Id, art 47.2(c)–(f). See also International Convention against the Recruitment, Use, Financing and Training of Mercenaries, art 1, General Assembly Res No 44/34, UN Doc A/44/49/306 (1989).

Independence is measured by the extent to which a group operates autonomously, for if it does not to some degree, it would be indistinguishable from Article 4(A)(1) militia and volunteer corps (in other words, it would form part of the military). Many contractors and subcontractors would run afoul of this provision in that they provide services specified by the armed forces; thus, they are not meaningfully independent. Of course, the degree of independence grows as one moves from contractor to subcontractor to firms without affiliation to a party to the conflict. The catch-22 is that the greater their independence in operational matters, the less likely contractors are to be acting on behalf of a party.[71] But in the improbable event that a contractor operated with the requisite independence and on behalf of a party to the conflict, it would need to meet the four explicit criteria set forth in Article 4(A)(2).

Subordination to a commander, the first criterion, excludes individuals acting alone or in small, unstructured groups. Consider Iraq. Some Coalition contractors, particularly the large PSCs, might meet this criterion, for they are generally subject to some form of supervisory direction analogous to command.[72] It is not necessary that military personnel exercise command.[73] Rather, the question is the extent of accountability and authority wielded by the person in control. As noted in the official Commentary:

> [the leader] is responsible for action taken on his orders as well as for action which he was unable to prevent. His competence must be considered in the same way as that of a military commander. Respect for this rule is moreover in itself a guarantee of the discipline which must prevail in volunteer corps and should therefore provide reasonable assurance that the other conditions referred to below will be observed.[74]

As Yoram Dinstein has noted, "[l]awful combatants must act within a hierarchic framework, embedded in discipline, and subject to supervision by

---

[71] Lest the discussion appear more significant than it is, this analysis only pertains to groups that would be characterized as directly participating in hostilities (see discussion below). If the contractor is not directly participating, and most do not, it is by definition not the sort of group envisaged by Article 4A(2).

[72] "Command" is defined as:

> [t]he authority that a commander in the Armed Forces lawfully exercises over subordinates by virtue of rank or assignment. Command includes the authority and responsibility for effectively using available resources and for planning the employment of, organizing, directing, coordinating, and controlling military forces for the accomplishment of assigned missions. It also includes responsibility for health, welfare, morale, and discipline of assigned personnel.

Department of Defense, *DOD Dictionary of Military and Associated Terms*, available online at <http://www.dtic.mil/doctrine/jel/doddict/> (visited Nov 20, 2004).

[73] de Preux, *GCIII Commentary* at 59 (cited in note 59).

[74] Id.

Chicago Journal of International Law

upper echelons of what is being done by subordinate units in the field."[75] Arguably, some contractors could meet this standard. Most are organized and controlled along military lines, an unsurprising fact given that so many of their employees are ex-military. Whether their employees are sufficiently subject to a leader's discipline would be a case-specific determination. Of particular relevance is the degree to which they are subject to criminal prosecution for abuses of which superiors become aware. State practice demonstrates that a leader need not play a formal role in this process, for, in many militaries, soldiers who commit crimes are referred for prosecution to civilian judicial authorities. That said, to enforce "command" discipline, the leader should have this option available.

The second and third criteria require distinction from the civilian population. Although many contractors do carry arms openly, contractors generally do not wear distinctive attire that distinguishes them from civilians such as aid and relief workers.[76] On the contrary, as noted by a senior US Marine Corps officer with combat experience in Iraq, "many private US Armies that work there wear a bewildering and amusing hodgepodge of 'tough guy' attire."[77]

---

[75]   Dinstein, *The Conduct of Hostilities* at 39 (cited in note 45).

[76]   Note that in Iraq the relaxed standards of Protocol I, Article 43, do not apply, as neither the United States nor Iraq are party states. US Department of the Army regulations allow deployed government civilians to be issued BDUs (battle dress uniforms), NBC (nuclear, biological, chemical) equipment, Kevlar helmets, and load-bearing personal equipment "as necessary to perform assigned duties during hostilities." The uniforms have special insignia intended to identify the wearer as a civilian. Department of the Army, *Pamphlet 690-47: DA Civilian Employee Deployment Guide* (Nov 1, 1995), available online at <http://www.hq.usace.army.mil/cere/civiliandeploymentguide.htm> (visited Nov 20, 2004). In the Air Force, that insignia is an olive green triangular patch with the letters "US" in the center on their left shoulder. Department of the Air Force, *AFI36-801: Uniforms For Civilian Employees* § 6.7 (Apr 29, 1994), available online at <http://www.e-publishing.af.mil/pubfiles/af/36/afi36-801/afi36-801.pdf> (visited Nov 20, 2004).

[77]   Along these lines, a Marine lieutenant in Iraq provided the following vignette:

While we were waiting for the delegation of IZs (Iraqis) to arrive, the Ambassador and the generals went into a small room to chat . . . . I was hanging out outside . . . . The place was crawling with the Ambassador's and generals' PSDs (personal security detail). The generals' . . . . are made up of Marines, but the Ambassador's is made up of private contractors. They all look exactly alike. Merrill low-top trail shoe-boots, REI or J. Peterman light weight safari pants, a muted single color t-shirt, highspeed chest rig/flack vest with lots of magazines, a couple little gadgets, an American flag Velcro patch, a Glock pistol, an M-4 with some ridiculous scope almost as big as the rifle, a battered baseball cap, the mandatory goatee, and the clear, spiraled fiber-optic cord running out of their ear. So they're all walking around, looking concerned at everyone, talking into their wrists, and oozing with seriousness. One of the guys starts shooting the shit with me. Nice guy from upstate New York. After a few minutes, he says, "So, who are those guys over there?" and points at a small group of PSD guys across the courtyard. I said, "I thought they were with you." He said . . . they weren't. I said, "well who are you with?" He said

Adherence to the laws and customs of war comprises the fourth criterion. Iraq represents an interesting case study in this regard. Recall that the 4(A)(2) assessment is of the group, not the individual. There is no question that some Coalition contractor employees have egregiously violated the laws of war, particularly vis-à-vis detainee treatment. However, on the whole, firms have not engaged in systematic violations that would suggest a disregard for the law. In order to forfeit combatant status on this count, the company as a unit would have to engage in violations of humanitarian law.[78]

Taken together, the aforementioned criteria make it highly unlikely that private contractors could qualify for Article 4(A)(2) combatant status. This is unsurprising, for the provision was never meant to address them. On the contrary, it was specifically crafted to build on the Hague Regulations' reference to "militia and volunteer corps" through addition of resistance movements. The very independence of such groups distinguishes them from the regular armed forces; private contractors, by contrast, are typically dependent on the armed forces, if only for fiscal survival.

B. CIVILIAN EMPLOYEES AND PRIVATE CONTRACTORS AS UNLAWFUL COMBATANTS

If civilian employees and private contractors seldom, if ever, qualify for lawful combatant status, what are the limits on their participation in hostilities? In other words, when will their participation rise to the level of "direct" participation such that they not only are lawfully targetable, but also punishable for their participation?[79]

Unfortunately, the meaning of direct participation, whether in international or noninternational armed conflict, is highly ambiguous. Articles 4(A)(4) and (5) of the Third Geneva Convention constitute the only authoritative delineation of activities barred from characterization as direct participation. Recall that Article 50.1 of Protocol I defines civilians by excluding those encompassed in subparagraphs 1–3 and 6 of Article 4(A)(2). Thus, individuals falling within the

---

he was with the Ambassador. I said, "Well who do you work for?" He said, "Blackwater." I said, "Well, I think those guys work for Triple Canopy . . . . Who could they be here with?" He said he didn't know. I didn't either. So here we are in Iraq, in a courtyard full of mercenaries, but no one can figure out exactly who is working for who. And they all look so alike, there's no way to tell. Typical.

Correspondence in possession of author.

[78] Note that the requirement involves violations of humanitarian law, not the higher standard of war crimes.

[79] Assuming the actions had been privileged if conducted by a lawful combatant.

remaining two subparagraphs are by definition civilians, albeit ones entitled to POW status upon capture. They include:

> (4) Persons who accompany the armed forces without actually being members thereof, such as civilian members of military aircraft crews, war correspondents, supply contractors, members of labour units or of services responsible for the welfare of the armed forces, provided that they have received authorization from the armed forces which they accompany, who shall provide them for that purpose with an identity card similar to the annexed model.[80]

> (5) Members of crews, including masters, pilots and apprentices, of the merchant marine and the crews of civil aircraft of the Parties to the conflict, who do not benefit by more favourable treatment under any other provisions of international law.[81]

The "such as" language in Article 4(A)(4) demonstrates that the list is merely illustrative. Unfortunately, the official Commentary does not expound more fully on the matter beyond indicating "the text could therefore cover other categories of persons or services who might be called upon, in similar conditions, to follow the armed forces during any future conflict."[82] But note that none of the individuals cited are involved in any direct way with the application of force. Nor do the provisions distinguish between government employees and contractors. The sole relationship criterion is that they "accompany" the armed forces.

In acknowledging the ambiguity inherent in the notion of direct participation, the International Committee of the Red Cross has noted:

> Undoubtedly there is room here for some margin of judgment: to restrict this concept to combat and to active military operations would be too narrow, while extending it to the entire war effort would be too broad, as in modern warfare the whole population participates in the war effort to some extent, albeit indirectly.[83]

Thus, there is a participation continuum that runs from general support for the war effort to the conduct of combat operations. W. Hays Parks has

---

80 Geneva Convention III, art 4(A)(4) (cited in note 40). This provision is based on Article 81 of the 1929 Geneva Convention that in turn derived from Article 13 of the 1907 Hague Regulations. Convention Relative to the Treatment of Prisoners of War (1929), art 81, 118 LNTS 343, 389–90 (1931–32); HIVR (cited in note 44).

81 Geneva Convention III, art 4(A)(5) (cited in note 40). The mention of more favorable treatment under international law is a reference to Article 6 of the Eleventh Hague Convention, which prohibited merchant seamen from being made prisoners of war. Very few countries are party to that treaty. Convention Relative to Certain Restrictions with Regard to the Exercise of the Right of Capture in Naval War (1907), 1 Bevans 711 (1968).

82 de Preux, *GCIII Commentary* at 64 (cited in note 59).

83 Sandoz, Swinarski, and Zimmerman, eds, *Protocols Commentary* at ¶ 1679 (footnotes omitted) (cited in note 64).

profitably dissected this continuum into war effort (which is protected under both customary law and Protocol I), military effort such as military research by civilians (which he suggests is not protected under customary law, but is protected by the Protocol), and military operations (unprotected under either customary or treaty law). Conceived in this manner, Parks suggests that Protocol I sets a fairly high threshold for direct participation.[84]

The Commentary appears to support the premise of a high threshold: "[d]irect participation in hostilities implies a *direct causal relationship* between the activity engaged in and the *harm done* to the enemy at the *time and the place where the activity takes place.*"[85] It also describes direct participation as "acts which by their nature and purpose are *intended to cause actual harm* to the personnel and equipment of the armed forces"[86] and defines hostilities as "acts of war which are intended by their nature or their purpose to *hit specifically* the personnel and the matériel of the armed forces of the adverse Party."[87] In much the same vein, the Commentary to Protocol II notes that in noninternational armed conflict the notion of direct participation in hostilities "implies that there is a sufficient causal relationship between the act of participation and its immediate consequences."[88]

Direct participation, therefore, seemingly requires "but for" causation (in other words, the consequences would not have occurred but for the act), causal proximity (albeit not direct causation) to the foreseeable consequences of the act, and a mens rea of intent. In other words, the civilian must have engaged in an action that he or she knew would harm (or otherwise disadvantage) the enemy in a relatively direct and immediate way. The participation must have been part of the process by which a particular use of force was rendered possible, either through preparation or execution. It is not necessary that the individual foresaw the eventual result of the operation, but only that he or she knew his or her participation was indispensable to a discrete hostile act or series of related acts.[89]

---

84   W. Hays Parks, *Air Law and the Law of War*, 32 AF L Rev 1, 133 (1990).

85   Sandoz, Swinarski, and Zimmerman, eds, *Protocols Commentary* at ¶ 1679 (emphasis added) (cited in note 64).

86   Id at ¶ 1942 (emphasis added).

87   Id at ¶ 1679 (emphasis added).

88   Id at ¶ 4787.

89   Some have labeled this approach the "kill chain"; in other words, if a particular activity is necessary to accomplish the "kill" in a specific situation, the activity is direct participation. The kill chain notion is overly restrictive in that it limits activities to those related to the application of deadly force; not all military operations seek to weaken the enemy in this fashion. However, most kill chain activities would unquestionably qualify as direct participation; as such, the

Chicago Journal of International Law

In the end, direct participation determinations are necessarily contextual, typically requiring a case-by-case analysis. But case-by-case determinations need not be eschewed. On the contrary, sometimes they more precisely balance military requirements and humanitarian ends than mechanical applications of set formulae. Moreover, armed forces have embraced them. The US Navy's *Commander's Handbook on the Law of Naval Operations*, for example, states that "[c]ombatants in the field must make an honest determination as to whether a particular civilian is or is not subject to deliberate attack based on the person's behavior, location and attire, and other information at the time."[90] Similarly, in the *Tadic* case, the International Criminal Tribunal for the Former Yugoslavia adopted a contextual framework:

> It is unnecessary to define exactly the line dividing those taking an active part in hostilities and those who are not so involved. It is sufficient to examine the relevant facts of each victim and to ascertain whether, in each individual's circumstances, that person was actively involved in hostilities at the relevant time.[91]

Perhaps the best tack when analyzing a particular act is assessing the criticality of the act to the direct application of violence against the enemy. Consider intelligence. Rendering strategic-level geopolitical estimates is certainly central to the war effort, but will have little bearing on specific combat missions. By contrast, tactical intelligence designed to locate and identify fleeting targets is the sine qua non of time-sensitive targeting; it is an integral component of the application of force against particular targets. Civilians providing strategic analysis would not be directly participating in hostilities, whereas those involved in the creation, analysis, and dissemination of tactical intelligence to the "shooter" generally would.

Many activities lie between the extremes. In such cases, the methodology that best approximates the underlying intent of the direct participation notion is to interpret the term liberally, in other words, in favor of finding direct participation. That distinction is a seminal principle in humanitarian law.[92] An interpretation of direct participation that allows civilians to retain their immunity

---

notion of a kill chain is a useful analytical construct when making direct participation assessments.

90   Oceans Law and Policy Department, *Annotated Supplement to the Commander's Handbook on the Law of Naval Operations* § 11.3 (1997).

91   *Prosecutor v Tadic*, Case No IT-94-1-T, ¶ 616 (ICTY 1997), available online at <http://www.un.org/icty/tadic/trialc2/judgement/index.htm> (visited Nov 20, 2004). The issue was crimes against persons taking no direct part in hostilities.

92   International Court of Justice, Advisory Opinion, *Legality of the Threat or Use of Nuclear Weapons* ¶ 78, 1996 ICJ 257 (July 8, 1996) ("The first [cardinal principle of humanitarian law] is aimed at the protection of the civilian population . . . and establishes the distinction between combatants and non-combatants.").

even though inextricably involved in the conduct of ongoing hostilities will engender disrespect for the law on the part of combatants endangered by their activities. Moreover, the liberal approach provides an incentive for civilians to remain as distant from the conflict as possible because they can thereby avoid being directly targeted and are less susceptible to being charged criminally for their acts of participation. While broadly interpreting the activities that subject civilians to attack might seem counterintuitive from a humanitarian perspective, it actually enhances the protection of the civilian population as a whole by encouraging distance from hostile operations.[93]

The temporal aspects of direct participation also lack precision. Recall that Article 51.3 immunizes civilians from attack "unless and for such time as they take a direct part in hostilities."[94] The Commentary on the provision notes that several delegations expressed their view that direct participation includes "preparations for combat and the return from combat,"[95] but it further provides that "[o]nce he ceases to participate, the civilian regains his right to the protection."[96] With regard to noninternational armed conflict, Article 13.3 of Protocol II repeats the "unless and for such time" verbiage, while the Commentary thereon states that protection is denied "for as long as his participation lasts. Thereafter, as he no longer presents any danger for the adversary, he may not be attacked."[97] Neither provision can be deemed to be customary international law.[98]

The "unless and for such time" clause has resulted in what has come to be known as the "revolving door" debate, popularly characterized by the image of the civilian who is a guerrilla by night and a farmer by day. Can it possibly be that those who directly participate in hostilities regain their civilian immunity whenever they successfully return from an operation even though they fully intend to subsequently recommence hostile action? This scenario is particularly

---

93   One approach that does not hold water, but surfaces regularly in discussions on the subject, is basing direct participation determinations on whether military personnel typically perform a function that has been converted to civilian status. In the first place, soldiers often perform functions that would not constitute direct participation by civilians: cooking, medical treatment, providing personal legal advice, playing musical instruments, etc. Moreover, the functions typically performed by military personnel vary widely from military to military. Therefore, it is neither possible to convert a military position to a civilian billet and thereby immunize the function from attack, nor deem everyone filling such a position a direct participant in hostilities.

94   Protocol I, art 51.3 (cited in note 37).

95   Sandoz, Swinarski, and Zimmerman, eds, *Protocols Commentary* at ¶ 1943 (cited in note 64).

96   Id at ¶ 1944.

97   Id at ¶ 4789.

98   US unwillingness to take such a position is exemplified by Office of the Secretary of Defense, Memorandum (cited in note 62).

Chicago Journal of International Law

ill-fitting in the case of civilian employees and private contractors. For instance, is the requirement simply to return to duties that do not amount to direct participation? Or does the end of the duty day mark return from hostilities?

More significantly, the revolving door standard flies in the face of logic grounded in the realities of armed conflict. Military forces facing attacks from civilians who can acquire sanctuary simply by returning home, a known location where they may be best targetable, will soon conclude that their survival dictates ignoring the purported revolving door. And ignoring individual aspects of humanitarian law invites disrespect for that body of law more generally, thereby exposing the civilian population to increased danger. Furthermore, a revolving door heightens the likelihood of direct participation by civilians in that it lessens the risk to them of such participation.

The sole practical interpretation of direct participation's temporal aspect is one in which a civilian who participates in hostilities remains a valid military objective until unambiguously opting out through extended nonparticipation or an affirmative act of withdrawal. Although the difficulty of ascertaining when the unlawful combatant has withdrawn from further participation is marked, it is reasonable that he or she bear the risk that the other side is unaware of the withdrawal. After all, the unlawful combatant volitionally joined the fray without enjoying any privilege to do so.

A final issue is whether mere employment by a particular civilian entity or private contractor can constitute direct participation. Generally, it should not. Even assuming a firm that is retained solely for duties that would be direct participation, there would likely be employees therein who engage in other activities, like cooks or personnel managers. Of course, such individuals run a high risk of being incidentally injured in legitimate attacks on their colleagues who have become targetable by virtue of their direct participation.

IV. ILLUSTRATIVE SCENARIOS

As noted, each instance of direct participation must be evaluated on its own merits. That said, it may be useful to briefly examine major categories of participation in hostilities, if only to engender further in-depth analysis.

A. ATTACKING MILITARY PERSONNEL AND MILITARY OBJECTIVES

Any attack by civilians on military personnel or military objectives constitutes direct participation so long as there is a nexus between the attack and the armed conflict. The nexus need not be a battle itself. For instance, combatants may be attacked anywhere they are found outside neutral territory. As an example, if a civilian attacks a combatant who is on leave at a resort because of his or her membership in the armed forces of a party to the conflict, the civilian has directly participated in hostilities.

On the other hand, if the same civilian attacks the combatant out of motives unrelated to the conflict (for example, to steal his money), the requisite nexus is absent. Similarly, civil disturbances would generally not qualify unless directed at the occupying force, for it is the motivation of the participants that determines the existence of a nexus. Obviously, though, soldiers have the right to use even deadly force in self-defense if they or others are threatened with death or serious bodily injury.

The means used to conduct the attack are relevant only to the extent they evidence motivation.[99] For example, use of a rocket-propelled grenade against soldiers in a military vehicle suggests direct participation, whereas using one's fists to batter a soldier in a bar would not. But perhaps the first incident is a murder related to a passenger's involvement in organized crime, whereas the latter is an attempt to kill a soldier as such. It is also usually irrelevant that the means of injury or destruction are delayed or indirect (for example, remotely controlled explosive bombs, mines, booby traps, and the like) so long as the ultimate aim is to directly affect the military capacity of one party to the conflict.

Nor are the nature of the injuries caused generally dispositive. Of course, an individual who merely slaps a soldier can hardly be deemed to be directly participating. But when an act causes death or serious injury, or was intended to but failed, one must still ask why the attack occurred.

Finally, proximity of the act to the combat zone indicates direct participation, but is in no sense determinative. For instance, a devastating computer network attack may be launched from continents away. So too may air and missile attacks. Civilians who are an essential link in the conduct of specific missions from great distances are no less directly participating than their counterparts near the battlefront. Distance does not provide civilians sanctuary from which to directly participate.

The same general approach would apply to attacks on military objectives. It is the intent of the civilian that matters. Moreover, because military objectives are defined in part by whether their "total or *partial* destruction, *capture or neutralization*" yields a definite military advantage,[100] the hostile act need not be calculated to permanently damage the object. It is enough that the action diminishes its military utility. So long as that is the intent, the civilian has directly

---

[99]   This position is supported by the Commentary to Article 51.3 of Protocol I: "It seems that the word 'hostilities' covers . . . situations in which [a civilian] undertakes hostile acts without using a weapon." Sandoz, Swinarski, and Zimmerman, eds, *Protocols Commentary* at ¶ 1943 (cited in note 64).

[100]   Protocol I, art 52.2 (emphasis added) (cited in note 37).

participated. This approach applies equally to dual-use facilities, in other words, objects with both a military and civilian use. If the civilian's action is intended to affect the former, it is direct participation; if the latter, it is not.

Reduced to basics, then, the mens rea of the civilian involved is the seminal factor in assessing whether an attack or other act against military personnel or military objects is direct participation. In this regard, direct participation would certainly also require some actus reus; a mere threat would not suffice. On the other hand, preparation for and deployment to the attack certainly qualify, for it would be unreasonable to expect the victim of the wrongful attack to sit idly by while the civilian finalized preparations and commenced the operation. Although the revolving door issue remains, surely the civilian can be engaged until making good his escape.[101] Again, it would be strange to require victims of a wrongful attack to break contact with their attackers following a strike.

B. SELF-DEFENSE, DEFENSE OF OTHERS, AND DEFENSE OF PROPERTY

A civilian government employee or private contractor defending military personnel or military objectives from enemy attack directly participates in hostilities. His or her actions are indistinguishable from the quintessential duties of combat personnel. Thus, for instance, civilians may not claim defense of others when they provide cover or assistance to military forces under attack, even in cases of ambush. Additionally, performing such functions frees up soldiers for other combat missions, thereby further contributing to hostile action. Unfortunately, the absence of agreement on what constitutes a military objective complicates matters. Nevertheless, the *principle* that guarding a military objective against enemy action amounts to direct participation remains.[102]

On the other hand, defending *any* personnel or property against looters or others (including lawful combatants) engaged in criminal activity or war crimes does not comprise direct participation. The trickiest scenario is defense of

---

101   This is the position adopted in the Commentary to Article 51.3: "[T]he word 'hostilities' covers not only the time that the civilian actually makes use of a weapon, but also, for example, the time that he is carrying it." Sandoz, Swinarski, and Zimmerman, eds, *Protocols Commentary* at ¶ 1943 (cited in note 64).

102   In the Central Command (CENTCOM) area of operations, contractors are prohibited from being armed by General Order No 1A. However, subordinate commanders may request an exception to the policy in order to arm government contractor employees either for personal protection or contracted security duties. Exceptions are not allowed "where the intent is to guard U.S. or Coalition MSRs [main supply routes], military personnel, military facilities, or military property, including property destined for military use." Headquarters, Multi-National Corps – Iraq, *Information Paper: Procedures to Obtain CENTCOM Authority to Arm Government Contractor Employees* (July 29, 2004) (on file with author).

military objectives against attacks by civilians or other unlawful combatants. In these cases, the key is whether there is a direct nexus between the threat and the ongoing hostilities. If so, civilians must avoid becoming involved. Civilians may also always defend themselves (because they are not legitimate targets under humanitarian law).[103]

In such cases, the civilian is acting either to enforce the law or in accordance with the right to defend persons and property in domestic and international criminal law. It would be absurd to hold that the law disallows defense against illegal actions by the victims thereof or by those who might come to their aid. After all, recall that law enforcement agencies are not part of the armed forces, an indication that law enforcement and other activities designed to maintain civil order during an armed conflict are appropriate. Of course, any lawful use of force must be necessary and proportionate. In a hostile combat environment, more force than would seem necessary in a benign peacetime environment might be justified. For instance, civilians may "shoot their way out" of a dangerous situation if reasonably necessary to ensure their safety.

Despite the right to defense against unlawful actions, the presence of civilians armed for defense in a war zone is highly problematic. The more armed civilians in an area, the more difficult it is for lawful combatants to distinguish between unlawful combatants and those who are merely armed for defensive purposes. This in turn endangers the civilian population by eroding the practical implementation of the principle of distinction. Soldiers may be more inclined to employ force against civilians who they feel pose a threat. Alternatively, soldiers may refrain from the use of force when it is appropriate, thereby assuming greater risk than necessary.

C. RESCUE OPERATIONS

Operations to rescue military personnel would be direct participation in hostilities, an inevitable conclusion drawn from the fact that combat search and rescue ("CSAR") is widely deemed a combat activity.[104] Similarly, rescuing

---

[103]   The Rome Statute provides that there is no criminal responsibility when:

> [t]he person acts reasonably to defend himself or herself or another person or, in the case of war crimes, property which is essential for the survival of the person or another person or property which is essential for accomplishing a military mission, against an imminent and unlawful use of force in a manner proportionate to the degree of danger to the person or the other person or property protected.

Rome Statute, art 31.1(c) (cited in note 50). See also *Prosecutor v Kordic*, Case No IT-95-14/2-T, ¶¶ 449–51 (ICTY 2001).

[104]   UK Ministry of Defense, *The Manual of the Law of Armed Conflict* at ¶ 12.69 (cited in note 45).

Chicago Journal of International Law

prisoners of war is combat action that may only be undertaken by military personnel.

However, the widespread hostage taking in Iraq raises the question of rescuing military or civilian hostages. A hostage is an individual who has been unlawfully deprived of his or her liberty and faces threat of death, injury, or further detention in order to compel a third party to act or abstain to act as a condition for the release of the hostage.[105] Geneva Convention IV, Article 34, prohibits taking civilians hostage, while Article 147 makes doing so a grave breach.[106] Protocol I similarly outlaws hostage taking as a grave breach.[107] Common Article 3 to the four Geneva Conventions prohibits seizing individuals who are "taking no part in the hostilities" during noninternational armed conflict,[108] a prohibition echoed in Protocol II.[109] The Statutes of the International Criminal Tribunal for the Former Yugoslavia,[110] the International Criminal Tribunal for Rwanda,[111] and the International Criminal Court[112] characterize hostage taking as a war crime. Although the prohibition is usually understood as the taking of civilians, it logically extends to military personnel[113] who have been unlawfully deprived of their liberty, for instance through seizure by civilians who have no right to participate directly in hostilities.

Since virtually every act of hostage taking during an armed conflict is a war crime and also probably a violation of applicable domestic law, the rescue of hostages is a law enforcement or defense of others measure, not direct participation in hostilities. This interpretation corresponds to reality because most hostage rescue expertise resides in civilian law enforcement agencies.

---

[105]   See discussion of the elements of the offense of hostage taking under the ICC Statute. Knut Dörmann, *Elements of War Crimes under the Rome Statute of the International Criminal Court: Sources and Commentary* 124–27 (Cambridge 2002). The elements rely heavily on the International Convention Against the Taking of Hostages (1979), 1316 UNTS 205 (1983).

[106]   Geneva Convention (IV) relative to the Protection of Civilian Persons in Time of War (1949), 6 UST 3516 (1956).

[107]   Protocol I, arts 75.2(c), 85.2 (cited in note 37).

[108]   See, for example, Geneva Convention I, art 3(1)(b) (cited in note 44); Geneva Convention II, art 3(1)(b) (cited in note 44); Geneva Convention III, art 3(1)(b) (cited in note 40).

[109]   Protocol II, art 4.2(c) (cited in note 49).

[110]   United Nations, *Report of the Secretary-General Pursuant to Paragraph 2 of Security Council Resolution 808 (1993)*, UN Doc S/25704 at art 2(h) (1993), 32 ILM 1159, 1171 (1993).

[111]   Security Council Res No 955, UN Doc S/RES/955 at art 4(c) (1994), 33 ILM 1598 (1994).

[112]   Rome Statute, art 8.2(a)(viii), (c)(iii) (cited in note 50).

[113]   See Dinstein, *Conduct of Hostilities* at 227 (cited in note 45).

D. HUMAN SHIELDS

The fact that individuals have been compelled to act as human shields does not render them direct participants in hostilities, even though it is undeniable that their presence may deter attack on a legitimate target. Rather, they remain protected civilians, and any likely harm to them must be factored into the requisite proportionality analysis when determining whether the attack may be executed.[114] This position tracks Article 51.8 of Protocol I, which further bolsters their status as nonparticipants by providing that "[a]ny violation of these prohibitions [in this context, the obligation of states to separate civilians from military objectives] shall not release the Parties to the conflict from their legal obligations with respect to the civilian population and civilians [that is, proportionality]."[115]

It is sometimes claimed that voluntary shields also are not direct participants because "[t]heir actions do not pose a direct risk to opposing forces" and they are not "directly engaged in hostilities."[116] Such an assertion ignores the fact that the human shields are deliberately attempting to preserve a valid military objective for use by the enemy. In this sense, they are no different from point air defenses, which serve to protect the target rather than destroy inbound aircraft.[117] Voluntary shielding is unquestionably direct participation.

---

[114]   The principle of proportionality prohibits attacks that "may be expected to cause incidental loss of civilian life, injury to civilians, damage to civilian objects, or a combination thereof, which would be excessive in relation to the concrete and direct military advantage anticipated." Protocol I, art 57.2(a)(iii) (cited in note 37). See also id, arts 51.5(a), 57.2(b).

[115]   Protocol I, art 51.8 (cited in note 37). It is also the position adopted in US joint doctrine. Joint Publication 3–60 specifically provides that:

> Civilians may not be used as human shields in an attempt to protect, conceal, or render military objects immune from military operations. Neither may civilians be forced to leave their homes or shelters to disrupt the movement of an adversary. Joint force responsibilities during such situations are driven by the principle of proportionality as mentioned above. When an adversary employs illegal means to shield legitimate targets, the decision to attack should be reviewed by higher authority in light of military considerations, international law, and precedent.

Joint Chiefs of Staff, Joint Publication 3–60, *Joint Doctrine for Targeting* A2–A3 (Jan 17, 2002), available online at <http://www.dtic.mil/doctrine/jel/new_pubs/jp3_60.pdf> (visited Dec 6, 2004).

[116]   Human Rights Watch, Briefing Paper, *International Humanitarian Law Issues in a Potential War in Iraq* (Feb 20, 2003), available online at <http://www.hrw.org/backgrounder/arms/iraq0202003.htm> (visited Nov 20, 2004).

[117]   In most cases, it will serve no valid military purpose to directly target the voluntary human shields. After all, the objective is the target they are shielding. However, the fact that they are directly participating means that their injury or death would not factor into the required proportionality calculation. Children who act as voluntary shields would be an exception to this

Chicago Journal of International Law

E. Computer Network Attack and Other Forms of Electronic Warfare

Although electronic warfare does not involve kinetic force, it can be just as devastating to enemy forces as traditional warfare. Military equipment may be neutralized or destroyed, enemy troops may be injured or killed, command and control may be disrupted, logistics may be interfered with, intelligence may be altered or blocked, and so forth. Undeniably, in twenty-first century conflict, electronic warfare can be as integral to the conduct of hostilities as kinetic operations. Therefore, it makes little sense to distinguish direct from indirect participation on this basis. Rather, the key, as with most participation, is to ascertain the extent to which the electronic warfare in question factors into ongoing or immediately prospective operations.

It has been suggested that computer network attack is not direct participation unless it "kills, injures, captures or damages." This assertion confuses the notion of "attack" with "participation." A computer network attack that does not result in these consequences is not an attack as that term is understood in humanitarian law,[118] but this fact has little to do with whether or not an individual is directly participating. On the contrary, many types of military operations do not involve an attack *strictu sensu*, but nevertheless are integral to the conduct of hostilities.[119]

F. Planning

Planning occurs at the strategic, operational, and tactical levels.[120] Civilian government employees are regularly involved in planning at the strategic level,

---

rule, for as a general matter of law they lack the mental capacity to form the intent necessary to voluntarily shield military objectives.

118   Michael N. Schmitt, *Wired Warfare: Computer Network Attack and* Jus in Bello, 84 Intl Rev Red Cross 365, 375–78 (2002).

119   For example, collection of tactical intelligence.

120   The US Department of Defense defines these concepts as follows:

> *Strategic Level of War.* The level of war at which a nation, often as a member of a group of nations, determines national or multinational (alliance or coalition) security objectives and guidance, and develops and uses national resources to accomplish these objectives. Activities at this level establish national and multinational military objectives; sequence initiatives; define limits and assess risks for the use of military and other instruments of national power; develop global plans or theater war plans to achieve these objectives; and provide military forces and other capabilities in accordance with strategic plans. See also operational level of war; tactical level of war.
>
> *Operational Level of War.* The level of war at which campaigns and major operations are planned, conducted, and sustained to accomplish strategic objectives within theaters or other operational areas. Activities at this level link tactics and strategy by establishing operational objectives needed to

which involves the setting of national security strategy, national military strategy, and national resource allocation. Indeed, involvement in such planning is a core tenet of democratic control of the armed forces through balanced civil-military relations. A typical strategic level planning decision would involve, for instance, composition of a coalition of the willing.

By contrast, planning at the operational level entails decisions about the conduct of particular military campaigns or operations, whereas tactical planning encompasses individual battles or engagements. All tactical level planning, such as mission planning for aerial operations, amounts to direct participation because specific military operations could not occur but for that planning. The same is generally true of operational level planning regarding employment of forces, although operational level logistics planning is generally remote enough from the hostilities to avoid characterization as direct participation.

A recurring question involves civilian leaders who engage in military decision making. If they qualify as combatants (for instance, by serving as the commander of the armed forces), they are targetable as such. If they do not qualify, the question is whether or not they are directly participating in hostilities. The strategic/operational/tactical paradigm of decisionmaking serves as a useful starting point in this regard. In particular, civilian leaders who engage in tactical level planning or approval are directly participating and thereby legitimate targets.[121]

G. INTELLIGENCE

As suggested earlier, one distinguisher regarding intelligence operations is the level of war the intelligence is designed to affect. Gathering, analyzing, and disseminating tactical intelligence usually amounts to direct participation because the relationship between the intelligence and the immediate conduct of

---

accomplish the strategic objectives, sequencing events to achieve the operational objectives, initiating actions, and applying resources to bring about and sustain these events. These activities imply a broader dimension of time or space than do tactics; they ensure the logistic and administrative support of tactical forces, and provide the means by which tactical successes are exploited to achieve strategic objectives. See also strategic level of war; tactical level of war.

Tactical Level of War. The level of war at which battles and engagements are planned and executed to accomplish military objectives assigned to tactical units or task forces. Activities at this level focus on the ordered arrangement and maneuver of combat elements in relation to each other and to the enemy to achieve combat objectives. See also operational level of war; strategic level of war.

Department of Defense, *DOD Dictionary of Military and Associated Terms* (cited in note 72).

[121] See Michael N. Schmitt, *State Sponsored Assassination in International and Domestic Law*, 17 Yale J Intl L 609 (1992).

Chicago Journal of International Law

hostilities is close, whereas strategic intelligence would not be sufficiently related to the hostilities to render related activities direct participation. Operational level activities constitute the gray area.

It is essential to emphasize the situational nature of the determination. Technology now permits the gathering of tactically useful data from great distances, often by satellite or airborne platform. Few would suggest that involvement in the launch or control of reconnaissance satellites is direct participation. However, as that data is processed, analyzed, and disseminated to troops in the field, the likelihood of civilian involvement being characterized as direct participation grows.

Lastly, detainee interrogations often result in the development of time-sensitive tactical and operational level intelligence. To the extent civilian government employees or private contractors participate in interrogations designed to elicit such information, as in Iraq, they are directly participating in hostilities.

H. LOGISTICS AND SUPPORT

Most logistics and support functions would not constitute direct participation. For instance, driving supply convoy trucks or feeding and housing troops are legitimate activities for civilian employees and private contractors. However, immediate battlefield logistics functions (for example, directly supplying troops engaged in combat with ammunition) would be direct participation. After all, resupply during a firefight, or the lack thereof, may well determine the victor. The battle involving contractors in Najaf cited earlier forcefully illustrates this point.

I. MAINTENANCE OR OPERATION

The operation of a weapons system by a civilian is unambiguously direct participation. So too is operation of any nonweapons system, or component thereof, that is integral to ongoing or imminent hostilities, such as an unarmed UAV used to locate fleeting targets.[122]

Maintenance is increasingly being outsourced to contractors. Depot maintenance of military equipment, in other words, maintenance conducted away from the battle zone, is relatively remote from the hostilities and clearly not

---

[122]   Lisa L. Turner and Lynn G. Norton, *Civilians at the Tip of the Spear*, 51 AF L Rev 1, 31 (2001) (stating that the Judge Advocate General School of the Army adopts the position that "the contract technical advisor that spends each day working with members of an armed force to make a weapon system more effective . . . is integrated with [the] force, [and taking an] active role in hostilities, [and therefore] may be targeted.").

direct participation. Similarly, routine, regularly scheduled maintenance on equipment, even near the front, does not directly impact on specific operations.

On the other hand, preparing equipment for battle has a direct impact on the course of battle. Thus, activities such as fueling aircraft, loading weapons, conducting preflight checks, performing life-support functions, and locally repairing minor battle damage would meet the direct participation threshold. Between these two extremes, as with all other cases cited above, the analysis must be case specific.

J. PROVIDING TRAINING AND MILITARY ADVICE

In Iraq, much of the generalized military advice (for instance, on structuring the New Iraqi Army and other military and law enforcement forces) and most of the training has been outsourced to private firms. Such training and advice has little immediate impact on military operations. On the other hand, if civilians are providing advice on the conduct of actual military operations at the tactical level, then they are directly participating because the flow of hostilities is greatly determined by their input. At the operational level, the evaluation of such advice would have to be conducted on a case-by-case basis. To the extent it involves the deployment of forces into combat for specific operations, it is likely to amount to direct participation. By contrast, merely offering general advice on military matters in the area of operations would not. The distinguisher is the extent of nexus to, and impact on, specific combat operations.

K. RECONSTRUCTION

Many of the government civilians and private contractors in Iraq during the occupation engaged in reconstruction efforts. Reconstruction of civilian or dual-use facilities is designed to benefit the civilian population, not to improve the military wherewithal of a party to the conflict. In fact, in the case of Iraq, there are multiple UN Security Council Resolutions that encourage reconstruction efforts.[123] The suggestion that such efforts amount to direct participation is unconvincing.

Even general construction or reconstruction of military facilities would be permissible because there is no immediate impact on ongoing military operations. However, construction that directly relates to immediate combat operations might well amount to direct participation. For instance, workers who

---

[123] See, for example, Security Council Res No 1483, UN Doc S/RES/1483 (2003); Security Council Res No 1511, UN Doc S/RES/1511 (2003). See also generally Michael N. Schmitt and Charles H.B. Garraway, *Occupation Policy in Iraq and International Law*, 9 YB Intl Peacekeeping 27 (2004).

conduct rapid runway repair following an attack in order to launch aircraft are directly participating because but for their efforts, no further missions are possible.

V. CONCLUDING OBSERVATIONS

Participation by civilian government employees and private contractors in armed conflict is growing exponentially, with no end in sight. Therefore, it is imperative that agreement be reached on the terms of reference for such participation. In doing so, it is necessary to balance military good sense, state practice, and humanitarian concerns. Unfortunately, the increasing tendency of states to rely on civilians (for reasons that are paradoxically very sensible) creates a confusing and dangerous environment for military forces engaged in combat. It also places the civilian population at great risk. Hopefully, time remains to establish reasonable normative lines of demarcation, ones that protect civilians and enhance military operations, but which states can accept.

[10]

THE STATUS OF MERCENARIES IN INTERNATIONAL LAW†

L. C. GREEN*

The activities of white mercenaries during the Congolese and Angolan civil wars, the trial of a number of them at Luanda after the establishment of an independent Angolan government, and the inclusion of a special article denying them combatant status in *Protocol I Additional to the Geneva Conventions of 1949 relating to the Protection of Victims of International Armed Conflicts*[1] have focused attention on what has long been a reality in so far as the armed forces of a number of countries are concerned. The uproar that these events caused might well lead one to assume that the problem is new. To adopt such an attitude, however, not only indicates a lack of historical knowledge, but also an ignorance of classical international law.

The Classical View of Mercenaries

While modern writers on the law of war have not drawn any distinction between the status of mercenaries and others and have not seen any need to make any specific reference to their existence, many of the classical writers were concerned since princes often made use of foreign troops to fight their wars,[2] even it would seem against their own sovereign. Thus, Bynkershoek records that

> at the beginning of the second English war when the States-General gave permission to some Scotch mercenaries to depart if they did not wish to serve in the Netherlands, some remained in the service of the States-General, ready to serve against any and every enemy, even the English. Charles II, however, issued an edict proscribing these men as traitors. But when peace was made with England the men requested the States-General to use their influence with the English King to have the edict repealed so that they might again acquire property in England by right of inheritance and by the other customary practices in vogue in England. The States-General did as requested on October 24, 1688. . . .[3]

It is true that Ayala was of opinion that "sovereigns should be urged to employ as soldiers in war natives rather than foreigners, for the latter serve for pay rather than glory."[4] His reason for arguing thus did not depend on any doubt as to the right of a foreigner to be a soldier, but he feared that such foreigners might not be easy to disband at the end of hostilities, and he cites the instance of

---

†   Paper originally prepared for Vol. 8, Israel Yearbook on Human Rights (1978).
*   LL.B., LL.D., University Professor, University of Alberta.
1.   Art. 47 in (1977), 16 Int'l. Legal Materials 1391.
2.   *See e.g.*, A. Mockler, *The Mercenaries* (1969), ch. 2-5; C.C. Bayley, *Mercenaries for the Crimea* (1977).
3.   Bynkershoek, *Quaestionum Juris Publici* (1737) found in Bk. II ch. XXV, s. vi, J. B. Scott (ed.), *Carnegie Endowment for International Peace* (T. Frank trans. 1930) 279-80.
4.   Ayala, *De Jure et Officius Bellicis et Disciplina Militari* (1582) found in Bk. III, ch. 4, s. 16, J. B. Scott (ed.), *Carnegie Institute of Washington* (J. Bate trans. 1912) 188.

> the Emperor of Constantinople [who having] no forces of his own, . . . summoned Turkish auxiliaries to protect him from his neighbours; but he could not get rid of them at the end of the war; and that is how the whole of Greece fell under the rule of Turkey.
>
> I, therefore, do not approve of the policy of Cyprus, who declared that soldiers should not be selected out of citizens, but be brought from afar like the best horses, nor of that ancient custom of the Alexandrians, who would not allow of any but foreign soldiers.[5]

Ayala, thus, pays no attention to the justness of the cause or the motive of the alien soldier, but is merely concerned with the ultimate safety of the prince in whose service he is.

Others among the classicists were more concerned with the justness of the cause than in the safety of the country of enlistment or the status or nationality of any of the soldiers who enlisted. They also tended to be more condemnatory of the alien than of the liege national who might be involved in an unjust cause. Thus Vitoria was prepared to argue that

> if it is evident that the war is unjust, or if this is known to be the case, or if the subjects are conscious that the war is unjust, they may not fight, even when the prince exercises compulsion upon them. The reason for this is that such a prince is committing a mortal sin, and one must obey God rather than him. . . . I also maintain that those who are prepared to go forth to every war, who have no care as to whether or not a war is just, but follow him who provides the more pay, and who are, moreover, not subjects, commit a mortal sin, not only when they actually go to battle, but whenever they are thus willing. I further contend that, when the case is doubtful, allies . . . may not, when they themselves are subjects, furnish aid to the other side. However, it should be observed in this connection that there may exist a doubt as to the right of the matter — as to whether a particular city belongs to France. But *let us suppose the city is in the possession of our king; it is then indubitable that the war in which the city is defended by the Spanish king, is a just war; and accordingly, any person whosoever may offer aid to the Spanish king.*[6]

Grotius, too, condemned any ally who fought without regard to the justice of the cause and since

> those Alliances which are entered into, with the Design and Promise of Assistance in any War, without regarding the Merit of the Cause, are altogether unlawful; so there is no Course of Life more abominable and to be detested, than that of mercenary Soldiers, who without ever considering the Justice of what they are undertaking, fight for the Pay; who *By their Wages the Goodness of the Cause compute*. . . .The Case of a Soldier . . . is really a miserable one, *Who to support his Life to Death resorts*. . . .Did they sell only their own Lives it were no great Matter: but they sell also the Lives of many an harmless inoffensive Creature: . . . by how much it is worse to kill without a Reason, than with one. . . .Phillip of Macedon said of that sort of Men, *who got their Livelihood by fighting, that War was Peace to them, and Peace War*. . . . *To bear Arms is . . . no Crime, but to bear Arms on the account of Booty is Wickedness with a Witness*. Nay, it is so to fight for Pay, if that be the sole and principal View; tho' it is otherwise very justifiable to receive Pay, for *who ever goes to War at his own Cost?*[7]

---

5.   *Id.*, 188-89; *see also* Mockler, *Supra* n. 2, at 181 *et seq* in reference to the mercenary revolt in the Congo.

6.   *De Bello*, Art. 1, para. 8, in J. B. Scott, *Francisco de Vitoria and His Law of Nations* (1934), App. F., cxviii, cxix-cxx.

7.   Grotius, *De Jure Belli ac Pacis* (1625), found in Bk. II, ch. XXV, ss. ix,x. (Eng. trans. 1738). In his notes, Barbeyrac disagrees with the interpretation Grotius gives to the classical authorities he cites. J. B. Scott (ed.), *Carnegie Endowment for International Peace* (F. Kelsey trans. 1930) 585-86.

It has been said that Suarez developed the law of nations as elaborated at Salamanca by Vitoria out of the teachings of Aquinas.[8] While he believes that the cause should be just, he is somewhat more charitable than either Vitoria, his predecessor, or Grotius, his Protestant successor, towards the individual soldier.[9] Thus, he asserts that

> common soldiers, as subjects of princes, are in no wise bound to make diligent investigation, but rather may go to war when summoned to do so, provided it is not clear to them that the war is unjust. This conclusion may be proved by the following arguments: first, when the injustice of the war is not evident to these soldiers, the united opinion of the prince and of the realm is sufficient to move them to this action; secondly, subjects when in doubt . . . are bound to obey their superiors.[10]
> . . .

---

8.   J. B. Scott, *The Catholic Conception of International Law* (1934), 128-30.
9.   F. Suarez, *De Triplici Virtate Theologica* (1621) found in Disp. XIII: On War, s. vi, para. 8, J. B. Scott (ed.), *Carnegie Endowment for International Peace, Suarez: Selections from Three Works* (G. Williams and others trans. 1944) 832.
10.   *Id.*, paras. 10, 11, 12, at 833-36. He goes on to say:

> A greater difficulty arises with soldiers who are not subjects and who are called mercenaries. The opinion commonly held seems to be that these soldiers are bound to inquire into the justice of a war, before they enlist. . . . However, such an opinion comes into conflict with the following difficulties.
>
> First, it would be necessary for each individual mercenary soldier to inquire into the cause of the war. But such an investigation is contrary to all custom, and humanly speaking, is impossible; for . . . the reason for the war cannot be explained to all, nor are all capable of appreciating that explanation.
>
> Secondly, (if the opinion in question were valid,) even soldiers who were subjects could not take part in a doubtful war without examining the cause, save when they were under strict orders of such sort that they would be disobedient in not going; for in that case their obedience would alone excuse them. But as long as they were not under orders, it would be (morally) safer not to fight. However, this consequent is contrary to all custom, and that obligation (to investigate the cause of war) would be harmful to the state.
>
> Thirdly, if permanent mercenaries could, previously to a war, bind themselves to fight even in doubtful cases by giving their consciences into the keeping of the prince's conscience, why could not those mercenaries do the same who enlist at the outbreak of a war? For, from a moral standpoint, the same principle is involved in the performance of an action and in binding oneself to perform it.
>
> The confirmation of this argument lies in the fact that just as one is not allowed to proceed to an unjust war, neither is he allowed to undertake the obligation of serving in such a war, nor even in any war indiscriminately, whether just or unjust; and the reason for these restrictions is that to fight in an unjust war is to act unjustly. Therefore, conversely, if one is permitted to bind himself to service in a doubtful war, the obligation involved in such a case is not wicked; and therefore, it would be permissible so to bind oneself for pay, here and now, although no previous obligation exists. Nor does it seem to be of much importance that a given (mercenary) was already regarded as a subject before the war, by reason of his pay. For one might say the same thing . . . of a contract made on the eve of the outbreak of the war, since, at such a time also, soldiers bind themselves to obedience in all matters in which obedience is legitimate; so that it makes no difference from the standpoint of justice, whether this contract was made before the war, or whether it is made now, (at the moment when the conflict begins).
>
> Fourthly, in a similar doubtful situation, any person is permitted to sell arms to these princes and to the soldiers; nevertheless, if they do so, the same danger is present, namely, that the act may contribute to the injury of innocent persons, if by any chance, the war is in fact unjust. The antecedent is commonly accepted as true. The proof of the consequent is, that both kinds of co-operation are very pertinent to actual wars; and although soldiers seem . . . to co-operate more immediately, nevertheless the persons who furnish arms are ordinarily able to do more harm. . . .
>
> Lastly, . . . the first and essential element is that one who is not a subject, submits himself to another for the sake of payment, and in so doing, inflicts no injury

Another early writer who was concerned with the justness of a war, and particularly with the safety of the soul of the soldier participating in an unjust war, whether as a mercenary or otherwise, was Belli, who although among the classicists of international law, is not normally regarded as one of the great writers thereon. Writing earlier than any of those already mentioned, Belli proclaimed that

> Volunteers . . . should beware . . . of putting themselves in jeopardy . . . because of peril to their souls; for . . . it is not lawful to serve in an unjust war. . . .
>
> Furthermore, the mercenary soldiers, too, should have a care — who, . . . the instant they hear the mention and tumult of war, rush to the clinking coin, with never a thought about justice or injustice. For such . . . are manifestly doomed to endless perdition, if they do not reform. . . . [S]uch soldiers should not be absolved, unless they renounce their calling, or at any rate return to the service of justice. [11]

Having expressed his concern for the soul of a serviceman engaged in an unjust war, Belli reaffirms that distinctions cannot be drawn between the volunteer and the hired man, for both are soldiers. [12] He is, unlike Ayala, not concerned that they may be difficult to disband when hostilities cease, but rather with the fear that they may desert and so cause the defeat of their employer. He cites in this connection the defeat of Scipio the Elder by Hasdrubal and "almost in our times, [the case of] Ludovico Sforza, [who] . . . through the defection of the Swiss lost Milan, and [in 1500] fell into the hands of Louis XII, King of France." [13]

---

upon any person; neither, generally speaking, does he expose himself to the danger of any wrongdoing. And for the rest, he is. . . exercising his right, when he sells his own property or his own labour, a right of which he . . . is not bound to deprive himself to his own detriment. With regard to these (mercenary) soldiers, there is, in addition, a special argument; for each of them has the authority of the prince and that of the whole state to support him, a fact which involves a great probability (that their conduct is just).

Hence, all the circumstances being weighed, it would by no means seem that mercenaries who serve in that contingency (when there is great probability that the war is just), are choosing the course that is (morally) less safe.

These arguments are clearly convincing; nor do I find any difference in actual fact between subjects and non-subjects. So it is that Vitoria, . . . too, speaks simply of 'soldiers', without distinction . . . [I]f the doubt (as to the justice of a war) is purely negative, it is probable that the soldiers in question may . . . take part in that war without having made any examination of the question, all responsibility being thrown upon the prince to whom they are subject.

. . . If, however, the doubt is positive . . ., then . . . (those who are about to enlist) should make an inquiry into the truth of the matter. If they are unable to ascertain the truth, they will be bound to follow the course of action which is more probably just, and to aid him who is more probably in the right . . . Finally, if the arguments on both sides contain an equal. . . probability, the soldiers may under such circumstances conduct themselves as if the doubt were purely negative; for the balance is . . . equal, and the authority of the prince turns the scale.

11.   Belli, *De Re Militari et Bello Tractatus* (1563) found in Pt. II, ch. II, ss. 4-5, J.B. Scott (ed.), *Carnegie Endowment for International Peace* (H. Nutting trans. 1936), 64.
12.   *Id.*, Pt. III, ch. 1, s. 12, at 106.
13.   *Id.*, Pt. VIII, ch. 1, ss. 28-29, at 228; *see also* Mockler *Supra* n.2, at 96-98, who points out that both parties were aided by Swiss mercenaries.

It is often pointed out that the Peace of Westphalia, 1648,[14] marks a watershed in the European law of nations. It is interesting to note therefore that Pufendorf, writing some 25 years later in 1672, had nothing detrimental to say of the use of mercenaries. He comments that it is frequently said, in respect of the use in war of the help of any persons whose support may be secured, "that a distinction should be drawn between traitors to and deserters from their masters, who voluntarily offer their services, and those who are led by promises or rewards to break their faith," and confesses that he does not understand the reason why the former is considered legitimate, but not the latter, for "when I am permitted to kill a man with an iron lance, why may I not attack him as well with one of silver?"[15] He reminds us, however, that he who has once shown perfidy towards his liege lord cannot be expected to remain completely faithful to his new master. It is perhaps of interest that he does not deal with the problem of mercenaries from a third state, although it would appear that he is fully aware of their existence, for when discussing who may take booty under a declaration to this effect, he states that this relates only to citizens, for "mercenary troops are owed nothing beyond their pay, unless it be the desire to use them generously, or to reward them for some distinguished service, or to incite them to great fortitude."[16]

A somewhat different approach — perhaps more practical and less philosophical — is to be found in the writings of the eighteenth century. Wolff, almost foretelling German views on expansionism, pointed out that

> [T]he greater its power for resisting foreign attack, the more powerful the nation is. And since for resisting foreign attack, . . . or even for obtaining by force its own right from another nation which refuses to concede it, both a number of soldiers . . . and enormous expenditures are required . . . the power of a nation depends upon the number of men who can perform military service, and upon its wealth. And since it is just the same whether the soldiers are natives or foreigners hired for a price, a nation is still rated as powerful, if it is rich enough to hire for a price as many foreign soldiers as it needs.[17]

Perhaps the country which is best known as a source of mercenaries is Switzerland. It is interesting, therefore, to note the views of Vattel on the subject, and one cannot but be impressed by the chauvinism which underlies much of his comments:

---

14. *See e.g.*, L. Gross, "The Peace of Westphalia 1648-1948" (1948), 42 Am. J. Int'l. Law 20.
15. Pufendorf, *De Jure Naturae et Gentium* (1688) found in Bk. VIII, ch. VI, ss. 18, 20 J. B. Scott (ed.), *Carnegie Endowment for International Peace* (C. Oldfather and W. Oldfather trans. 1934) 1308.
16. *Id.*, at 1311.
17. Wolff, *Jus Gentium Methodo Scientifica Pertractatum* (1764) Ch. 1, s.69, found in J. B. Scott (ed.), *Carnegie Endowment for International Peace* (J. Drake trans. 1934) 41.

Mercenary soldiers are foreigners who voluntarily enter into the service of the State for a stipulated pay. As they are not subjects of the sovereign they owe him no service in that capacity, and consequently the pay he offers them is the motive of their service. By their contract they bind themselves to serve him, and the Prince on his part agrees to certain conditions set down in the terms of enlistment. These terms are the rule and measure of the respective rights and obligations of the contracting parties, and they should be scrupulously observed. . . . [Vattel then takes issue with French commentators who have criticised Swiss mercenaries for having left their employment on the employing prince's failure to pay.] But . . . the Swiss . . . have never quit service at the first payment overdue; and when they have found a sovereign sincerely desirous to pay them, but actually unable to do so, their patience and their zeal have always kept them faithful to him. Henry IV owed them immense sums, but they never forsook him in his greatest necessity, and that brave man found the Swiss Nation as generous as it was courageous.[18]

Vattel's reference to Swiss whom he describes as "auxiliaries," since they serve with permission of their sovereign by virtue of alliances, typified the situation prevailing in Europe up until the Crimean War. It has already been pointed out that Swiss mercenaries served on both sides during the conflict between Louis XII and Sforza, and, during the years immediately following, enabled the Confederacy almost to create a powerful central European state, "but as always with the Swiss, their mercenary spirit ruined their

---

18.   E. de Vattel, *Le Droit des Gens, ou Principes de la Loi Naturelle* (1758) found in Bk. III, ch. II, ss. 13-14, J. B. Scott (ed.), *Carnegie Institute of Washington Translation* (C. Fenwick trans. 1916) 239-40. Vattel then goes on to state:

I mention the Swiss in this connection because, in fact, they were often mere mercenaries. But troops of that sort are not to be confused with the Swiss who at the present day serve various powers with the permission of their sovereign and in virtue of alliances existing between those powers and the Swiss Confederation or some individual canton. These latter troops are real auxiliaries, although paid by the sovereign whom they serve.

The question has been much discussed whether the profession of a mercenary soldier be legitimate or not, whether individuals may, for money or other rewards, engage as soldiers in the service of a foreign prince? The question does not seem to me very difficult of solution. Those who enter into such contracts without the express or implied consent of their sovereign are wanting in their duty as citizens. But when the sovereign leaves them at liberty to follow their inclination for the profession of arms, they become free in that respect. Now, every free man may join whatever society pleases him best and seems most to his advantage, and may make common cause with it and take up its quarrels. He becomes in some measure, at least for a time, a citizen of the State into whose service he enters; and as ordinarily an officer is free to leave the service when he thinks fit, and a private soldier at the expiration of his term, if that State should enter upon a war that is manifestly unjust, the foreigner may leave its service. *Such mercenary soldiers, by learning the art of war, will render themselves more capable of serving their country,* if ever it has need of them. This last consideration furnishes us the answer to a question proposed at this point: Can the sovereign properly allow his subjects to serve foreign powers indiscriminately as mercenaries? He can, and for this simple reason — that in this way his subjects learn an art the knowledge of which is both useful and necessary. *The tranquility, the profound peace which Switzerland has so long enjoyed in the midst of wars which have agitated Europe, would soon become disastrous to her if her citizens did not enter into the service of foreign princes and thereby train themselves in the art of war and keep alive their martial spirit.*

Mercenary soldiers enlist freely. A sovereign . . . should not even resort to deceit or stratagem to lead [foreigners] to enter into a contract which, like every other, should be founded upon good faith.

political enterprises."[19] By virtue of the *Perpetual Peace of 1516*[20] Switzerland became virtually a mercenary recruiting ground for France, with the Swiss agreeing never to supply mercenaries to the enemies of France, although Swiss regiments did serve in the armies of Savoy, Holland, Spain, Austria, and England. However, the French connection remained supreme until the massacre of the Swiss Guard during the French Revolution and Napoleon's intervention in Swiss affairs at the time of the Helvetic Republic. Now, in accordance with the Swiss Constitution,[21] military capitulations, that is to say agreements for the supply of mercenary troops to foreign countries, may not be concluded. While, if Vattel's views are accepted, only alien volunteers should be used as mercenary troops, by the time of the American War of Independence, England, at least, was arranging with the various German princes for the wholesale employment of entire regiments, for "many of the small princes depended for almost their entire revenue upon hiring out their subjects at exorbitant prices."[22] Despite the fact that George II complained that "this giving commissions to German officers to get men . . . in plain English amounts to making me a kidnapper which I cannot think a very honourable occupation,"[23] German troops were in fact employed against the American rebels, when the United Provinces refused to make its Scots Brigade available.[24]

National Experiences

The European View — England and France

The English traditionally were opposed to a standing army on British soil and it was always difficult to secure sufficient local recruits. It therefore became necessary to recruit abroad and in 1695 "approximately ¼ of the grand total was made up of Dutch, Danish, and Hanoverians and by the end of the century this proportion had risen to one half . . ., while by the middle of the Seven Years' War the national army of 97,000 was supplemented by some 60,000 foreign troops."[25] The English attitude is well expressed by Lord Egremont in 1756: "I shall never be for carrying a war upon the continent of Europe by a large body of national troops, because we can always get foreign troops to hire. This should be our adopted method in any war on the continent of Europe."[26]

---

19. Mockler, *Supra* n.2, at 102.
20. 4 Dumont, *Corps Universel Diplomatique*, Pt. 1, cxi, 248.
21. Constitution of Switzerland, Art. 11.
22. Mockler, *Supra* n. 2, at 115.
23. *Id. See* Ch. 5 for a full discussion.
24. *Id.*, at 114; *see also* Bayley, *Supra* n. 2, at 5.
25. Bayley, *Supra* n. 2, at 4-5.
26. W. Cobbett, *Parliamentary History* (1753) XIV, col. 1283; Bayley, *Supra* n.2, at 4.

Typical of the period is the treaty of 1776 between George III and the Landgrave of Hesse-Cassel[27], whereby

> His Brittanic Majesty, being desirous of employing in his service a body of 12,000 men, of the troops of his most serene highness the reigning landgrave of Hesse Cassel; and that prince, full of attachment for his Majesty, desiring nothing more than to give him proofs of it. . . .[28]

it was agreed that fully equipped troops of fit men should be made available immediately for "there is no time to be lost,"[29] and

> this body of troops shall not be separated, unless reasons of war require it, but shall remain under the orders of the general, to whom his most serene highness has entrusted the command. . . .[30]

While George III undertook to pay to the Landgrave a fixed sum in respect of every man supplied, together with certain additional items, as well as an annual subsidy,

> with regard to the pay and treatment, as well ordinary as extraordinary, of the said troops, they shall be put on the same foot in all respects with the national British troops, and his Majesty's department of war shall deliver, without delay, to that of his most serene highness, an exact and faithful state of the pay and treatment enjoyed by those troops.[31]

The treaty was not popular with Parliament, both on account of its expense and in view of the unpopularity of the American war. Perhaps it is enough to cite the comments of the Duke of Manchester, comments which have a familiar ring today:

> Let us consider the means we have to prosecute this war. The British troops, we find, fail not, my Lords, in point of courage, but they show an honest backwardness to engage . . . their fellow citizens. To Germany we have recourse for assistance: 17,000 German mercenaries [— he clearly made no distinction, as did Vattel, between individual hirelings and 'auxiliaries' obtained under treaty —] are at last obtained; with these and a small British army, many of whose regiments consist entirely of recruits some of whom are of the worst description — for I have been told that even the prisons have been ransacked to augment their numbers — is this country to engage a nation who are enthusiastic in their case, have no hopes but in success, are united in every tie, have every stimulative to courage that shame or ambition can give an army of brothers? . . . The mercenaries we employ, . . . for they may be justly called so since that man must be deemed a mercenary soldier who fights for pay in the cause in which he has no concern, are a motley barrel of various nations who are yet in Germany, are yet to be conveyed across the Atlantic; some will perish on the way, some desert, but I will suppose the remnant landed on the American shore. Will conquest immediately follow? Impossible to expect it.[32]

It hardly needs mentioning that the presence of the German mercenaries ultimately made no difference to the result of the war.

---

27. 46 C. Parry (ed.), *Consolidated Treaty Series (C.T.S.)* 1127; *see* Mockler *Supra* n.2, at 292 for translation. *See also*, Treaty with Brunswick for 3964 men (46 *C.T.S.* 119) and with Hesse-Hanau for 668 men (46 *C.T.S.* 163).
28. Mockler, *Supra* n. 2, at 292.
29. *Id.*, at 293.
30. *Ibid.*
31. *Id.*, at 294.
32. *Id.*, at 122-23.

During the Crimean War, in view of the difficulty in securing allies, Britain considered the advisability of raising a foreign legion. This had been done under the authority of statute during the Napoleonic wars, although then, it could be argued, the Germanic Legion was fighting for the liberation of its own soil, since George III was a Germanic king *vis-à-vis* Hanover. *The Foreign Enlistment Act of 1854*[33] authorized the enlistment of foreign volunteers in separate regiments, not to be employed in the United Kingdom other than during the period of training. The number in the United Kingdom was not to exceed 10,000; they were not to be billeted in private households; and they were to be amenable to the British articles of war. Problems arose, since some European countries, for example, Switzerland and the German *Bund*, fearing for their neutrality, had made recruitment by foreign powers within their territory a criminal act. Nevertheless, British-German, British-Swiss and British-Italian Legions of 9682, 3294, and 3581 officers and men respectively were ultimately raised and saw service under the British flag.[34] While the British Army continued to employ foreign units, *e.g.* the Gurkha Regiments, as part of its regular armed forces, this was the last occasion on which governmental efforts were directed at securing the services of mercenary units.

In so far as France was concerned, the need to make use of mercenaries was not the same, since general conscription provided a much larger solid core of trained personnel. For foreign service, particularly in colonial territories, the Foreign Legion, comprised of foreign personnel serving under French authority and on personal contract, had been available from 1831. While by an extended application of the definition both the Gurkhas and the Foreign Legion might be considered as mercenaries — and this term has even been applied by one writer to the International Brigade in Spain as well as British officers seconded to the Arab Legion[35] — they would hardly fall within the term as currently used, or perhaps even as used by the classicists, for they were serving as embodied personnel within the regular forces of those under whose flag they served. However, at times it would appear that even today the Foreign Legion is being used almost as a traditional mercenary unit, although not for the purpose of a foreign war but for suppressing a rebellion. Thus, in April 1978, some 300 Foreign Legion troops were sent by France to assist Chad in combatting Chad National Liberation Front rebels.[36] This

---

33.   *The Foreign Enlistment Act (1854)* 18 & 19 Vict., c.2 (U.K.).
34.   House of Commons Sessional Papers, xxvii, 151; found in Bayley *Supra* n.2, at 149.
35..   Mockler, *Supra* n. 2, at 14.
36.   *The Times* (London), Apr. 21, 1978, at 6, col. 8. In May, the Legion went to Zaire to rescue Europeans and suppress a rebellion.

may perhaps be compared with the actions of Louis-Philippe who, in 1835, during the Carlist war hired the Legion to Queen Cristina.[37] However, there is no evidence of any hire arrangement with Chad, merely the provision of aid by an ally.

The Crimean War seems to have proved a watershed in both the doctrinal writing and state practice with regard to the service of non-nationals in conflict situations. In his *Institutes of the Law of Nations*, Lorimer proposed some rules concerning the enlistment of neutrals based on the distinction "between the position of the neutral State in its corporate capacity, and when viewed as an aggregate of private persons."[38] This distinction is now becoming more and more disregarded, not only as regards the problem of state trading, but also more generally,[39] and particularly in the attitude of third world countries when assessing the activities of nationals of the first world. Lorimer saw nothing wrong in a neutral national's enlisting in belligerent forces and was of the opinion that by so doing he abandoned all claim to protection by his own nation, being regarded from the moment of enlistment as a citizen of the belligerent State concerned.[40] In his view there was to be no distinction between volunteering and enlisting, so that presumably both were to be treated alike. Moreover, enlistment was to be permitted even within the neutral State, and it was not to be considered a breach of neutrality that the State in question permitted the enlistee to retain his domicile and enjoy any private rights resulting therefrom. Calvo, too, seemed to see nothing wrong in the employment of foreign mercenaries, whom he regarded as being entitled to full rights under international law.[41]

The general view of nineteenth century writers seems to have been that the use and enlistment of foreign volunteers was legitimate, and there was a tendency to accept that the provision of such personnel under an agreement made between a non-belligerent sovereign and a country at war, or about to enter into war, was not incompatible with neutrality. It was, of course, open to the belligerent against whom such 'treaty' mercenaries were operating to regard the arrangement as an unneutral act amounting to a *casus belli* authorizing warlike acts against the *soi-disant* neutral.

---

37. Mockler, *Supra* n. 2, at 135.
38. 2 J. Lorimer, *Institutes of the Law of Nations* (1884) 179-80.
39. *See e.g.,* M. Garcia-Mora, *International Responsibility for Hostile Acts by Private Persons against Foreign States* (1962) 68.
40. *See e.g.,* 1 G. Schwarzenberger, *International Law*, (3d ed. 1957) 593.
41. 1 *Derecho Internacional* (1868), s.387, at 483.

The American View

Whether nationals would be allowed to serve in a foreign army depended, in the absence of specific treaty[42] between two states seeking to protect themselves, not on the requirements of international law but on the provisions of municipal law. A good many countries, concerned about the danger of the presence of foreign troops upon their own territory, had passed legislation forbidding the stationing within the territory of such personnel, if enlisted.[43] Some countries went further and forbade their nationals from enlisting in alien armies and alien causes. Thus, as early as 1794,[44] the United States Congress enacted, and this is still law today[45]:

> Every citizen of the United States who, within the territory or jurisdiction thereof, accepts and exercises a commission to serve a foreign prince, state, colony, district, or people, in war, by land or by sea against any prince, state, colony, district, or people, with whom the United States are at peace, shall be guilty of a high misdemeanor.

In practice, it would seem that this Act was primarily concerned with the fitting out of raiding naval vessels,[46] a matter which was eventually dealt with by the *Declaration of Paris, 1856,*[47] having over centuries been regarded as an act of extreme infamy and akin to piracy.[48]

The present law of the United States is wider than that originally enacted, for it now forbids anyone in the United States, regardless of nationality, from recruiting or enlisting or leaving the United States to serve "any foreign prince, state, colony, district or people as a soldier or as a marine or seaman,"[49] but there is no reference to the service being in a campaign against a state with which the United States is at peace. There are certain exceptions. The ban does not apply to nationals of a belligerent allied to the United States, unless he "shall hire or solicit a citizen of the United States to enlist or go beyond the jurisdiction of the United States with intent to enlist or

---

42.   *See, e.g., Jay Treaty* (1794), United States — Great Britain, Art. 21; in 52 *C.T.S., Supra* n. 27, at 243,260. *See also General Treaty of Peace and Amity of the Central American States* (1923), Art. 14, in 2 M. Hudson *Int'l. Leg.,* 901, 906; *Habana Convention on Duties and Rights of State in the Event of Civil Strife* (1928), Art. 1, in 4 M. Hudson *Int'l. Leg.,* 2416, 2418; *Habana Convention on Maritime Neutrality* (1928), Art 23, in 4 M. Hudson *Int'l. Leg.,* 2401, 2410:

> Neutral States shall not oppose the voluntary departure of nationals of belligerent states *even though they leave simultaneously in great numbers;* but they *may* oppose the voluntary departure of their own nationals going to enlist in the armed forces."
> (italics added).

43.   *See, The Foreign Enlistment Act (1854),* 18 & 19 Vict., c.2. (U.K.).
44.   2nd Cong., 1st Sess., c. 50, s. 3.
45.   18 U.S.C.A. s. 958 (1976).
46.   *See e.g., The Charming Betsy* 6 U.S. (2 Cranch) 64, 2 L. Ed. 208 (1804) *See also, The Alabama Arbitration* (1872), 1 J.B. Moore *Int'l. Arbitrations* (1898) 653, in which Great Britain was held liable for having allowed such fitting out.
47.   D. Schindler and J. Roman, *The Laws of Armed Conflicts* (1973), 567.
48.   Sir Geoffrey Butler and S. Maccoby, *The Development of International Law* (1928) 165.
49.   18 U.S.C.A. s. 959(a), (1976).

enter the service of a foreign country."[50] Equally no offence is committed by

> any subject or citizen of any foreign prince, state, colony, district, or people who is transiently within the United States and enlists or enters himself on board any vessel of war, letter of marque, or privateer, which at the time of its arrival within the United States was fitted and equipped as such, or hires or retains another subject or citizen of the same foreign prince, state, colony, district, or people who is transiently within the United States to enlist or enter himself to serve such foreign prince, state, colony, district, or people on board such vessel of war, letter of marque, or privateer, if the United States shall then be at peace with such foreign prince, state, colony, district, or people.[51]

This would suggest that it might be possible for the subjects of a belligerent with which the United States is at peace to time their arrival in the United States to coincide with that of a vessel visiting the United States with the sole purpose of enlisting such nationals, and it would appear not to matter that the United States might be at peace with the state against which the enlistment is directed.

Finally, an offence is committed by

> Whoever, within the United States, knowingly begins or sets on foot or provides or prepares a means for or furnishes the money for, or takes part in, any military or naval expedition or enterprise to be carried on from thence against the territory or dominion of any foreign prince or state, or of any colony, district, or people with whom the United States is at peace . . .[52]

This would seem to cover the advertising for and recruiting of mercenaries to serve in such places as the Congo or Angola[53] subject to the question of whether the liberation movement against which they were operating could be considered as a district or people with whom the United States was at peace.

Perhaps more important than the fine or imprisonment envisaged by these provisions, at least in the case of United States citizens, is the provision in the 1952 *Immigration and Nationality Act*,[54] providing for the loss of nationality by any United States national, whether by birth or naturalization, who enters or serves in the armed forces of a foreign state without the prior written authorization of the Secretary of State and Secretary of Defense.

In practice, the United States has appeared hesitant to apply the penal clauses referred to. During the First World War before the United States became a belligerent, United States citizens formed the Escadrille Américaine, which became the Escadrille Lafayette after

---

50.   18 U.S.C.A. s. 959(b), (1976).
51.   18 U.S.C.A. s. 959(c), (1976).
52.   18 U.S.C.A. s. 960, (1976).
53.   *See e.g.*, W. Burchett and D. Roebuck, *The Whores of War, Mercenaries Today* (1977), ch. 6 and 10; *see also, The Times* (London), May 9, 1978, at 9, col. 2-5, citing J. Stockwell, *In Search of Enemies: A CIA Story* (1978).
54.   8 U.S.C.A. s. 1481(a) (3) (1976).

German protests at the presence of an American squadron with the French air force. No action was taken against these "citoyens Américains volontaires pour la durée de la guerre,"[55] and after the United States joined the Allies, the Lafayette Squadron became 103rd Pursuit Squadron U.S. Air Service.[56] There was a similar group of American airmen with the R.A.F, the Eagle Squadron, prior to Pearl Harbour, while Chennault's Flying Tigers became part of the U.S.A.A.F. only in the summer of 1942.[58]

During the Middle East crisis of 1956, when it was known that American Jews were joining the Israeli forces, the Department of State pointed out that no authorization had been issued "in any individual case and there is no intention of departing from this policy."[59] There is, however, no record of any prosecution. A somewhat different attitude has been adopted towards service in revolutionary forces. After the victory of the Castro forces in Cuba the United States Embassy stated that while citizens who fought with the Revolutionary Forces would not necessarily be expatriated, "such persons who continue voluntarily to serve with these forces, if and when they become an integral part of the armed forces of the Republic of Cuba" are so liable, and this was reiterated by the State Department shortly thereafter. "Thus, a distinction was made between serving in the revolutionary forces of Castro and serving in the armed forces of a foreign State."[60] The significance of this became clear in *Marks* v. *Esperdy*[61] in which an equally divided Supreme Court[62] upheld a decision expatriating Marks by reason of his service in the Cuban armed forces after the conclusion of the revolution and the establishment of the Castro Government. It would seem, however, that since *Afroyim* v. *Rusk*[63] this would no longer be the case, for the Supreme Court held that non-voluntary expatriation was unconstitutional. While this decision arose out of the exercise of the franchise by a citizen during a foreign election, it seemingly is of general application[64] and would indicate that *Marks* would not be followed.

---

55.   J. M. Spaight, *Air Power and War Rights* (3d ed, 1947) 463.
56.   *Ibid.*
57.   *Id.*, at 463-64.
58.   *Id.*, at 465.
59.   8 M. Whiteman, *Digest of International Law* (1967) 171.
60.   *Id.*, at 174.
61.   (1964), 377 U.S. 214; aff'g. (1963), 315 F. 2d 673 (2d Cir.).
62.   Four votes to four, Mr. Justice Brennan not participating.
63.   (1967), 387 U.S. 253.
64.   [1975] *Digest of United States Practice in International Law*, 817.

Modern English Legislation

Twenty-five years after the American precedent, and as a result of activities on behalf of the rebellious Spanish American colonies,[65] England passed its first Act "to prevent the enlisting or engagement of His Majesty's subjects to serve in Foreign Service, and the fitting out or equipping, in His Majesty's Dominions, vessels for warlike purposes, without His Majesty's licence."[66] The Preamble declared that such action

> in or against the Dominions or Territories of any foreign prince, state, potentate, or persons exercising or assuming to exercise the powers of government in or over any foreign country, colony, province or part of any province, or against the ships, goods, or merchandise of any foreign prince, state, potentate or persons as aforesaid, or their subjects, may be prejudicial to and endanger the peace and welfare of this Kingdom.[67]

This being so, the Act repealed previous legislation, such as the *Act of 1754*[68] forbidding service as officers in the French forces and that of 1769[69] requiring British subjects accepting commission in the "Scotch Brigade in the Service of the States General of the United Provinces" to take the oath of allegiance. To take such service as was proscribed by the *Act* without royal licence was made a misdemeanor, punishable by fine and/or imprisonment at the discretion of the Court. The *Act* was not made retroactive so that persons already serving were able to continue. The *Act* further provided that any vessel at a British port with such persons aboard might be detained, while any vessel fitted out in British territory for this purpose was made liable to forfeiture, and any person who added to or changed the military equipment of any warship was equally guilty of a misdemeanor. The *Act* made no reference to any requirement that the foreign ruler be at peace with England, and clearly forbade enlistment in foreign service whether the ruler concerned was at peace or war. *Prima facie*, the wording of the *Act* was such that it would apply to any government *de facto* or *de jure* and to any band of rebels describing itself as a government provided it controlled some territory, and it would appear that recognition by England was irrelevant.

---

65.   2 Lord McNair, *International Law Opinions* (1956) 328 ff.
66.   *Foreign Enlistment Act*, 1819, 59 Geo. 3, c. 69 (U.K.).
67.   *Ibid.*
68.   *Foreign Enlistment Act*, 1754, 29 Geo. 2, c. 17 (U.K.). The full name of this statute is:
       "An act to prevent His Majesty's Subjects from serving under the French King and for better enforcing an act passed in the Ninth year of His present Majesty's Reign to prevent the enlisting His Majesty's Subjects to serve as soldiers without His Majesty's licence and for obliging such of His Majesty's Subject as shall accept commissions in the Scotch Brigade in the service of the States General of the United Provinces, to take the oaths of Allegiance and Abjuration."
69.   *The Militia Act*, 1769, 9 Geo. 3, c. 42 (U.K.).

Problems affecting the *Act* arose during the American Civil War, particularly with regard to the fitting out of ships for the Confederacy, culminating in *The Alabama Arbitration*.[70] To some extent the award could not have been completely unexpected, for in a Report by the Law Officers of August 11, 1862, it is stated:

> [I]n the event of war breaking out, an act prohibited by the Foreign Enlistment Act would be illegal, and would be punishable by the law of this country, even though it might be done in fulfilment of some contract entered into before the breaking out of war: and it might probably be the duty of Her Majesty's Government, either of its own accord or on the requisition of either belligerent, to exercise the powers given to them by that statute, in order to prevent and to punish any such act. And we must add, that we think it hardly probable that a contract with a foreign Government, for building in this country an armour-plated ship could be completed, after the breaking out of war between that Government and another foreign State, without some acts amounting to an 'equipping, furnishing, fitting-out, or arming', within the meaning of the 7th section of the Foreign Enlistment Act, and therefore punishable by the laws of this country.[71]

It was partly as a result of the experience of the American Civil War that a new *Foreign Enlistment Act* was passed in 1870[72] and it is still the law of Great Britain on this matter. It should be pointed out, however, that

> [T]he Foreign Enlistment Act is no measure of the international obligations of Great Britain. It goes far beyond them, and its extreme stringency is presumably designed to arm Her Majesty's Government with power to interpose in possible contingencies which it would be difficult to anticipate . . .[73]

By virtue of the new *Act*, it is a misdemeanor punishable at the discretion of the court by fine and/or imprisonment, to a maximum of two years, for

> any person [who], without the license of Her Majesty, being a British subject, within or without Her Majesty's dominions, accepts or agrees to accept any commission or engagement in the military or naval service or any foreign state at war with any foreign state at peace with Her Majesty, and in this Act referred to as a friendly state, or whether a British subject or not within Her Majesty's dominions, induces any other person to accept or agree to accept any commission or engagement in the military or naval service of any such foreign state as aforesaid. . . .[74]

The *Act* then contains a number of detailed provisions with regard to the use of ships for this purpose, including the obligation to remove immediately any illegally enlisted persons who shall not be allowed to return to the ship. If a ship is built to the order of a belligerent state at war with a friendly state or is delivered to the order of such state or its agent and is employed in the military or naval service of such state, it shall, until the contrary is proved, be deemed to have been built for

---

70. *See Supra* n. 46; 3 Lord McNair, *International Law Opinions* (1956) 171 ff.
71. *Id.*, at 224-25.
72. *Foreign Enlistment Act, 1870,* 33 & 34 Vict., c. 90 (U.K.).
73. *See* McNair *Supra* n. 70, at 170 (Law Officers' Report, February 12, 1895).
74. *Foreign Enlistment Act, 1870,* 33 & 34 Vict., c. 90, s. 4 (U.K.).

that purpose and the burden of proof is upon the builder. Perhaps more important at the present time is the provision that forbids in British territory the preparation or fitting out of "any naval or military expedition to proceed against the dominions of any friendly state . . . [and] every person engaged in such preparation or fitting out, or assisting therein, or employed in any capacity in such expedition . . ."[75] equally commits an offence. This wording is probably wide enough to cover any British subject volunteering in any capacity as a member of a force engaged in hostilities against a foreign friendly state, while any ship, arms or munitions used in or forming part of such an expedition is forfeit to the Crown. Reflecting the embarrassment of the British government over the *Alabama*, if the Secretary of State is satisfied that a ship is being built, commissioned or equipped contrary to the *Act*, and is to be taken out of the jurisdiction he may order the ship to be seized, detained and searched, and if the suspicions are justified then it may be detained until its release is ordered. The *Act* does not apply to any commissioned ship of any foreign state, which is in accord with the view expressed by the Law Officers in 1866 that

> the Peruvian warship *Independencia*, supposing that she had violated the Foreign Enlistment Act of 1819 in recruiting British subjects within British jurisdiction and taking on board arms and ammunition within British jurisdiction, with a view to warlike operations against Spain, would, if she returned within British jurisdiction under a regular commission from the Peruvian Government, be entitled to the immunity of a foreign public armed ship.[76]

It might be possible to argue, however, that if such a ship had in fact recruited British nationals while lying in British waters she had abused her status by exercising a sovereign act in Britain without the consent of the Crown, and had therefore subjected herself to the same sort of treatment as had been threatened against the Chinese Embassy in 1896 when Sun Yat Sen was wrongly detained.[77] It is also possible that such a ship would not be granted permission to return to British waters, at least for some time.

The most important section of the *Act* is Section 30, the interpretation section:

> 'foreign state' includes any foreign prince, colony, province, or part of any province or people, or any person or persons exercising or assuming to exercise the powers of government in or over any foreign country, colony, province, or part of any province or people.

In the opinion of the Law Officers as reported on December 7, 1877, this definition would include rebels as "a foreign state at peace with

---

75.   *Foreign Enlistment Act, 1870*, 33 & 34 Vict., c. 90, s. 11 (U.K.).
76.   1 Lord McNair, *International Law Opinions* (1956) 103.
77.   E. Satow, *Guide to Diplomatic Practice* (N. Bland ed., 1957) 218; *see also ibid.* for incident affecting Soviet embassy in Paris in 1929.

Her Majesty,''[78] so as to make it an offence for a British ship to be employed in the military or naval service of the Peruvian Government for the purpose of suppressing a rebellion. In the instant case, the Commander of the British Pacific Station had cautioned the ship which he had found in Peruvian waters, as the master and crew "were engaged in the commission of a breach of neutrality, [and] Admiral de Horsey would, on the high seas, have been justified in stopping the vessel and preventing her proceeding on her voyage whilst the Peruvian troops remained on board.''[79] It would also seem to be the case that rebels would be regarded as a foreign friendly state even though there had been no recognition of insurgency or belligerency, and the Law Officers doubted whether a British ship, "fitted out as a privateer and to be used in the service of an unrecognized nationality, could be dealt with as a piratical vessel.''[80] The Law Officers also pointed out that for the purposes of the *Foreign Enlistment Act,* a protectorate, engaged in hostilities against the protecting state, is a friendly foreign state, so that "when a state of hostilities exists between two such states, and they are recognized by Her Majesty's Government as belligerents, the Foreign Enlistment Act would apply to either.''[81] They considered, however, that since British interests had not yet been affected by the instant hostilities there was no obligation upon Britain to apply the *Act.* They did not say that recognition of belligerency was a prerequisite, but they did interpret the 1877 Report concerning the Peruvian rebellion:

> It would seem that the term 'rebels' was probably meant only to cover such 'rebels' as by establishing a more or less stable Government, and, by obtaining general recognition as belligerents, might fairly be said to have constituted themselves into a separate 'State' within the meaning of that expression as generally employed.[82]

The other definition which is of importance in Section 30 is that of "military service," for this includes "any employment whatever, in or in connection with any military operation." This definition is wide enough to include service in an air force, but the *Act* only refers to military and naval forces and expeditions and "as a penal statute falls to be construed with strict regard to the statutory language used. It is not permissible for courts of law to extend the definitions of statutory offences by analogy in order to deal with new situations which they regard as equally reprehensible.''[83]

---

78.   H. Lauterpacht, *Recognition in International Law* (1947) 267.
79.   *Id.,* at 268.
80.   *Supra* n. 65, at 368.
81.   *Supra* n. 76, at 61. In this case, Madagascar was fighting against France.
82.   *Id.,* at 60.
83.   *Report of the Committee of Privy Councillors appointed to inquire into the Recruitment of Mercenaries,* Cmnd. 6569 (1976), para. 25 (hereinafter referred to as the Diplock Report).

While the Reports of the Law Officers of the Crown are important and may affect government policy in a particular case, their significance must not be exaggerated. True, a Report may serve as a precedent or guideline or give an indication of what the government considers the law to be, and may well be followed in the future. It is not, however, an authoritative and binding interpretation of the law, while its contents are, generally speaking, not even known to the general public. For such a definitive statement, reference must be made to the courts but the judgments in both the United Kingdom and the United States are somewhat sparse, at least in so far as individual volunteers or the preparation and equipping of a military expedition are concerned. What decisions there have been, have for the most part related to ships.[84] The unwillingness to prosecute is brought home quite clearly by the experience of the Spanish Civil War. While British volunteers served on both sides, and while Britain pursued a policy of non-intervention and the Foreign Office issued a public warning that the *Act* applied,[85] no volunteer was ever prosecuted. The English case which does deal with an armed expedition is *R. v. Jameson*[86] arising out of the Jameson Raid against the South African Republic. Although the judgment was concerned with technical details affecting the validity of the indictment rather than the substance of the charge, Jameson was subsequently sentenced to fifteen months in jail, although he only served six.

The Commonwealth View

It is, of course, not only the United Kingdom and the United States which have legislation directed against foreign enlistment. In so far as Commonwealth countries are concerned, the British *Act* was extended to most of them and still prevails. Some, however, have enacted their own legislation. For example, Ghana has made it a felony punishable by life imprisonment "to accept or induce any engagement in the military service of any other country."[87] The Canadian *Act* is very similar to its English forebear, the definition of "foreign state" in whose service enlistment may be forbidden being identical.[88] Unlike the English *Act* of 1870, the Canadian *Act* makes no reference to a state at peace with Canada, but uses instead the phrase "a friendly foreign state" which is clearly a synonym, and the *Act* provides that it is an offence for any Canadian, wherever he may happen to be, to accept an engagement in the armed forces of "any

---

84.   For a list of cases, *see* Burchett and Roebuck, *Supra* n. 53, at 184 n. 10.
85.   *Supra* n. 78, at 273 (The warning was issued January 10, 1937, before any recognition of the Nationalists.)
86.   [1896] 2 Q.B. 425.
87.   *Foreign Enlistment Act*, (Ghana) 1961.
88.   *Foreign Enlistment Act*, R.S.C. 1970, c.F-29, s. 2.

foreign state at war with any friendly foreign state." Any person in Canada, regardless of nationality, who induces another to leave with such intent equally commits an offence.[89] The *Act* likewise forbids any Canadian from leaving Canada for this purpose[90] and also forbids any person within Canada from fitting out any army, naval or air expedition to proceed against the dominions of any friendly state.[91] The *Act* thus reflects the development since 1870 of war in the third dimension. As regards recruiting, this is forbidden within Canada in so far as it relates to the "armed forces of any foreign state or other armed forces operating in such a state."[92] It is clear, therefore, that there can be no doubt as to the application of the *Act* as regards rebels, whether recognized or not, and whether a state of belligerency is recognized.

Moreover, since the *Act* relates to operations by "other armed forces operating in a state,"[93] it would appear that it would operate in an area where the governing power, *e.g.* a foreign ruler, had withdrawn and fighting was being conducted between a variety of forces each describing itself as a national liberation movement. This interpretation finds support in the provision that the Governor General in Council may by order or regulation provide for the application of the *Act* "to any case in which there is a state of armed conflict, civil or otherwise, either within a foreign country or between foreign countries."[94] It should be noticed that the *Act* again recognizes modernity, in that it uses the generic term "armed conflict" rather than the technical term "war." The Governor General is also authorized to provide for the requirement of consent before any prosecution is launched, and may, in addition to the normal punishment of fine and/or two years imprisonment, provide for the restriction, cancellation or impounding of passports, whether within Canada or elsewhere, should that be considered necessary.[95] Such a provision, of course, is rather more formal than real. Strictly speaking, there is nothing to stop a Canadian from leaving Canada without a passport, and it depends on foreign not Canadian law whether any country will admit him if he has no passport. It is hardly likely that the authorities in whose service he is seeking to enlist will be unduly worried as to whether he does or does not carry a passport.

The Penal Codes of Belgium, France and Sweden all forbid recruiting for foreign service, while Sweden and Belgium both

---

89.   *Foreign Enlistment Act*, R.S.C. 1970, c.F-29, s. 3.
90.   *Foreign Enlistment Act*, R.S.C. 1970, c.F-29, s. 4.
91.   *Foreign Enlistment Act*, R.S.C. 1970, c.F-29, s. 10.
92.   *Foreign Enlistment Act*, R.S.C. 1970, c.F-29, s. 11.
93.   *Foreign Enlistment Act*, R.S.C. 1970, c.F-29, s. 11.
94.   *Foreign Enlistment Act*, R.S.C. 1970, c.F-29, s. 19(a).
95.   *Foreign Enlistment Act*, R.S.C. 1970, c.F-29, s. 19(e).

enacted special legislation during the Spanish Civil War. Perhaps not surprisingly in view of her special relationship to the area, Belgium passed no such legislation during the Congo Civil War[96] when a number of Belgian nationals, both *colons*[97] and others, played a significant role, sometimes as specially enlisted mercenaries.[98] However, all these national enactments are of local significance only and do not as such have any importance in international law unless there is some rule of the latter which would be infringed if the states in question failed to enforce their criminal law in this regard.

International Law

In assessing whether international law has any bearing in this regard it is necessary to avoid political assessements or subjective analysis. International law applies universally and not on an eclectic basis. Moreover, in examining the activities of mercenaries nothing is to be gained by the use of such language as would imply that those on the ''wrong'' side were fighting for loot and reward, while those who were on the ''right'' side were motivated by some higher ideal. Thus, we read in one violent attack on mercenaries that as ''whores of war'' they were ''hijacking a country,''[99] with ''economic power. . .abused to hire human bodies with the specific intentions of avoiding public association with them and responsibility for their welfare, and using money to exploit moral weakness.''[100] What does one say of the validity of a work which attempts to discriminate among the whites who were fighting for the various nationalist movements in Angola in 1976:

> [T]here were plenty of white Angolans fighting with the MPLA, which led the mercenaries to assume that they were often confronted by Cubans when they were not . . . [These] fought for what they believed in: true independence, an end to colonialist oppression and exploitation. . . . If [the blacks with the FNLA] . . . went back to their villages or rallied to the MPLA, it was because their sympathies were with those who really fought to end oppression and exploitation.[101]

It is equally difficult to accept as objective comment anything written by those who can say of two mercenaries charged at the Luanda trial,[102] one of whom testified that he had probably killed FAPLA personnel, while the other had not, that the former ''succeeded in

---

96. Burchett and Roebuck, *Supra* n. 53, at 220-23.
97. Mockler *Supra*, n. 2, at 177. Mockler condemns as mercenary, Schramme who, in 1964 and 1966, ''was pacifying the area where he owned plantations. . .'' and who regarded himself as ''. . . a planter and administrator, in uniform only through force of circumstances.'' *Id.*, at 206.
98. *Id.*, ch. 8.
99. Burchett and Roebuck, *Supra* n. 53, at 37.
100. *Id.*, at 6.
101. *Id.*, at 117.
102. *Id.*, at 74-75.

convincing the Tribunal that he sincerely regretted what he had done and recognized the enormity of the use of mercenaries," and was sentenced to thirty years, while the latter's "demeanour, if not his actual words, betrayed regret that his efforts had not succeeded. He never displayed any regret for his own activies" and was executed. The former was "a money-motivated mercenary," the other "a political mercenary"[103] but he believed in the wrong politics.

Traditional Views

What does international law say of those who enlist in foreign service? Does it regard such persons as committing any illegality and does their country of origin carry any liability? As we have seen, the "fathers of international law" were somewhat divided in their views. So, also, were some countries which were affected by mercenary activities. For example, in 1818 before the passage of the first British *Foreign Enlistment Act*, the Law Officers were called upon to advise on the status of British nationals serving the Spanish-American colonial insurgents. Spain intimated that it intended treating any such aliens they might capture as insurgents. According to the Report of July 21, 1818:

> The Spanish Government has undoubtedly the Right of War against such Persons, and the letter of the Spanish Minister describes 'the Foreigners as *waging War against His Majesty*', but the ordinary laws of War would not justify severity in the nature of punishment, which appears to be the measure in the contemplation of the Spanish Government. It is certain also, that Foreigners may be guilty of Treason, against the Sovereign of a State in which they have only an occasional residence. But cases of that kind have usually been very distinguishable in principle from the present case, which is merely that of Individuals joining the Forces of Persons exercising the powers of Government, in Provinces, that have been in a state of Revolt, asserting their Independence for some Years.[104]

A somewhat similar problem arose, after the enactment of the modern *Act*, when it was learned in 1895 that the French military authorities engaged in fighting a civil war in Madagascar considered themselves "justified in treating as 'condottieri' the British subjects who have taken service with the Hovas, and, if captured, in at once shooting them," while apparently not intending to treat captured Hovas in the same way. In their Report of April 16, 1895, the Law Officers stated

> [T]he French authorities are *not* entitled to discriminate between British subjects serving in the armed forces of the Malagasy Government and Hovas in the like service to the prejudice of the former.
> [T]he French authorities are *not* entitled to shoot British subjects serving in the Hova forces whom they may take prisoners in open fight during the pendency of the present hostilities in Madagascar. We assume that the British subjects are regularly incorporated in the regular forces of the Hovas.

---

103. *Ibid.*
104. *Supra* n. 65, at 335.

[I]t is open to, and . . . desirable, for Her Majesty's Government to communicate with the French Government upon the subject . . . with a view to preventing what . . . would be a violation of international law.

[I]f the fighting now in progress between the French and the Hovas were merely a civil brawl, or a local popular tumult, the French might legitimately treat persons who take part in it as rioters and murderers. Or, if British subjects took part in hostilities against the French without being incorporated in any regular forces, they might be treated as private individuals unwarrantably engaged in lawless warfare . . . .

[B]ut . . . a state of war does exist between France and Madagascar. Her Majesty's Government, as a neutral Power, have not thought fit to recognize belligerency. . . . But the duties imposed upon belligerents by international law are in no sense dependent upon, and have no relation to the action of, neutral Powers which is dictated by their policy and interests. If a state of war exists as distinguishable from a civil brawl, the authorized soldiers of one belligerent when captured by the other belligerent must be treated as prisoners of war to whatever nationality they belong, subject always to the risk of such reprisals as are recognized by international law, in case the Government they serve has violated the law.[105]

While the activities and attitudes of neutral powers are "dictated by their policy and interests," by the end of the nineteenth century the European powers were involved in codifying the international law regarding neutrality. As to the practice almost immediately prior to this, perhaps one might refer to the Swiss decision in 1870 at the time of the Franco-German War to allow French and German nationals to traverse Switzerland in order to join their units so long as they were in civilian clothing and unarmed. She would not, however, permit France to open an office for the purpose of sending Alsatian volunteers through Switzerland to the south of France.[106] By the end of the century

[t]he majority of writers maintained that the duty of impartiality must prevent a neutral from allowing the levy of troops. . . . if the levy and passage of troops . . . must be prevented by a neutral he is all the more required to prevent the organisation of a hostile expedition from his territory against either belligerent. This takes place when a band of men combine under a commander for the purpose of starting from the neutral territory and joining the belligerent forces. Different however, is the case in which a number of individuals, not organized into a body under a commander, start in company from a neutral State for the purpose of enlisting with one of the belligerents. Thus in 1870, during the Franco-German War, 1200 Frenchmen started from New York in two French steamers [the *Lafayette* and the *Ville de Paris*] for the purpose of joining the French Army. Although the vessels carried also 96,000 rifles and 11,000,000 cartridges, the United States did not interfere, since the men were not organized in a body, and since, on the other hand, the arms and ammunition were carried in the way of ordinary commerce.[107]

That Oppenheim's view was, broadly speaking, an expression of the by then generally accepted view of international law is shown by

---

105.   *Id.*, at 371.
106.   2 *Oppenheim's International Law* (H. Lauterpacht, ed.) (7th ed. 1952) 704, reproducing 1st ed. 1906, 352-53.
107.   *Id.*, (1st ed. 1906) 353; (7th ed. 1952), at 703-04. *But see Wiborg* v. *U.S.* (1896), 163 U.S. 632, at 654, in which it was held that "the elements of the expedition . . . were combined or in process of combination; there was a concert of action. . . ."

the terms of *Hague Convention V respecting the Rights and Duties of Neutral Powers and Persons in War on Land:*

> Art. 4. Corps of combatants cannot be formed nor recruiting agencies opened on the territory of a neutral Power to assist the belligerents.
> Art. 5. A neutral Power must not allow any [such] acts to occur on its territory.
> Art. 6. The responsibility of a neutral Power is not engaged by the fact of persons crossing the frontier separately to offer their services to one of the belligerents.[108]

There is no clarification in the *Convention* as to the meaning of the word "separately" or how many individuals may be allowed to cross at any one time. Presumably so long as they do not constitute an organized corps of combatants no liability on the part of the neutral state concerned could arise. As to any individual who does cross and enlist, Article 17 confirms the views of the British Law Officers:

> Art. 17. A neutral cannot avail himself of his neutrality . . . particularly if he voluntarily enlists in the ranks of the armed force of the parties. In such a case, the neutral shall not be more severely treated by the belligerent as against whom he has abandoned his neutrality than a national of the other belligerent State could be for the same act.[109]

Thus, such a "neutral" national enjoys all the rights of a normal combatant, including those of a prisoner of war. In so far as the fitting out of ships to assist belligerents is concerned, *Hague Convention XIII concerning the Rights and Duties of Neutral Powers in Naval War*[110] reflects the limitations and restrictions of the foreign enlistment enactments of the United States and the United Kingdom, but it makes no reference to criminal liability. The neutral state is required "to employ the means at its disposal to prevent the fitting out . . . [and] to display the same vigilance to prevent" departure.[111] Apparently, since failure to take such steps would constitute a breach of neutrality, a belligerent whose rights had been adversely affected would be entitled to regard such failure as a *casus belli.*

As has already been pointed out, no action was taken against those who volunteered during the Spanish Civil War, regardless of whether they joined the International Brigade supporting the government or served with the rebels. This was probably due to the fact that the Republic and the Nationalist authorities represented a political cleavage that crossed frontiers and found some support in most of the countries from which the foreign fighters — be they called volunteers, mercenaries or conscripts — originated. Again, as has been seen, in the case of the Eagle Squadron between 1939 and 1941, or the volunteers serving with Israel in the Middle East, no authority, private individual, or organ of the media seemed unduly worried by such activists or their doings.

---

108.   *See Supra* n. 47, at 715.
109.   *Id.*, at 717.
110.   *Id.*, at 721.
111.   *Id.*, at 723, Art. 8.

A Change in Attitude

It was only when white settlers struggling against the activities of local rebels, described as National Liberation Movements, became involved, by assisting one of the local rebel movements, usually the less radical, that the problem took on a new aspect. The term "mercenary" suddenly acquired an obscene flavour, and the profession of arms as conducted by professionals prepared to serve an alien master came to be regarded with such obloquy that it seemed almost to have sunk to the level of the supreme crime against mankind.

The first intimation of this change in attitude came during the struggle for independence in the Belgian Congo, the United Nations having decided in 1960 to take steps to provide the Republic with such military assistance as it might require and calling upon third States to do nothing to impede the government's efforts to restore order, while urging Belgium to withdraw its forces as speedily as possible. While the United Nations Force was operating, an attempt was made by the Province of Katanga to secede, which automatically raised the possibility of United Nations military involvement in an internal armed conflict. The Katangese secessionists were assisted by foreign mercenaries, some of whom were in fact Belgian local landowners,[112] but a number of African states strongly objected to their presence, contending that they were interfering with the activities of the United Nations force; were unlawfully interfering in the internal affairs of an African country; were using the activities of the Katangese as a cover for a possible return of European imperialism; and, probably more importantly, because many of them feared possible secessionist activities by tribal minorities within their own countries.

In its resolution of February 21, 1961, the U.N. Security Council, with France and the Soviet Union abstaining, reiterated its concern at the situation in the Congo, and urged "that measures be taken for the immediate withdrawal and evacuation from the Congo of all Belgian and other paramilitary personnel and political advisers not under the United Nations command, and mercenaries."[113] By November, not much having been done to this end, and with the General Assembly having resolved[114] that the "central factor" was the continued presence of Belgian and other foreign military and paramilitary personnel, political advisers and mercenaries, the Security Council, with France and the United Kingdom abstaining, resolved "to secure the immediate withdrawal and evacuation from the Congo of all foreign military, paramilitary and advisory person-

---

112.   *Supra* n. 97.
113.   S/4741, 1.
114.   A/Res/1599 (XV) (adopted by vote of 61-5-33).

nel not under the United Nations Command, and all mercenaries,'' deprecated "the secessionist activities illegally carried out by the provincial administration of Katanga, with the aid of external resources and manned by foreign mercenaries,'' and authorized the Secretary-General "to take vigorous action, including the use of requisite measures of force, if necessary, for the immediate apprehension, detention pending legal action and/or deportation of all foreign military and paramilitary personnel and political advisers not under the United Nations command, and mercenaries . . . [and] prevent the entry or return of such elements under whatever guise. . ."[115]

It is essential to note that in these Resolutions the Security Council was not concerned with the status of mercenaries and in fact was treating them in exactly the same way as any other foreign military personnel in the Congo other than as part of the United Nations command. The main thrust of the resolutions was the prevention of Katangese secession and the termination of the civil war, with the concomitant consolidation of the power and authority of the Republic. The Council's condemnation of the mercenaries, as of other foreign military personnel, was solely on the basis that they formed one of the resources being employed to secure Katanga's secession and thus to thwart the resolutions of the Council and the purpose for which its Force had been sent to the Congo. Any attempt to use these Resolutions as a ground for condemning mercenaries or their employment *per se* is fraudulent misrepresentation of the activities and objectives of the Security Council. It was not until the beginning of 1963, after military confrontations between the mercenaries and the United Nations forces, that the United Nations was able to declare that the Katanga revolt was over.[116] In 1964, however, a further revolt took place against the authority of the Republican Government and the mercenaries were back again. This culminated in 1966 in a further attempt by the Katangese to secede, although on this occasion it appeared that the mercenaries were prepared to serve on either side.[117] In 1967, there was a revolt by the mercenaries themselves which appeared likely to overthrow President Mobutu. The Security Council's resolution was again non-committal in so far as the mercenaries as such were concerned. Having condemned

> any State which persists in permitting or tolerating the recruitment of mercenaries and the provision of facilities for them, with the objective of overthrowing the Governments of States Members of the United Nations, [called] . . . upon

---

115. S/5002.
116. Mockler, *Supra* n. 2, at 168-71.
117. *Id.*, at 171-93.

Governments to ensure that their territory and other territories under their control, as well as their nationals, are not used for the planning of subversion, and the recruitment, training and transit of mercenaries designed to overthrow the Government of the Democratic Republic of the Congo.

The council decided to remain seized of the question and requested the Secretary-General to "follow closely the implementation of this Resolution,"[118] which was hardly one that could be implemented in any way that the United Nations could inspire or control. What the Security Council meant by implementation became a little clearer by the end of the year. It had been known for some time that the mercenaries were using the Portuguese colony of Angola as their marshalling area and the base from which attacks against the Congo were being launched. In November 1967, without a vote, the Security Council condemned the failure of Portugal to prevent the mercenaries from using Angola in this way, and called "upon all countries receiving mercenaries who have participated in the armed attacks against the Democratic Republic of the Congo to take appropriate measures to prevent them from renewing their activities against any State."[119] It is clear that the Security Council was not prepared to state that mercenarism was a crime or that mercenaries were not entitled to treatment as prisoners of war or the protection of the international law of armed conflict. All it was willing to do was call upon member states to take the measures they might consider necessary to prevent mercenaries from taking action against any state. In other words, the most that can be said of the action of the Security Council at this time is that it called upon members to enforce their foreign enlistment legislation.

The General Assembly too had passed resolutions concerning the Congo, but these are of less significance than those of the Security Council. There is no need at this juncture to consider how far such resolutions, even if constantly reiterated, are binding in law. What is more important is that, with the presence of the United Nations force in the Congo, and the constant consideration of the problem by the Security Council, the role of the Assembly was somewhat reduced. Moreover, attempts to condemn the mercenaries as such failed to secure the requisite two-thirds majority in the Assembly. Further, to some extent the African members of the United Nations were able to express their views through the Organization of African Unity where they were free of western pressures and could give vent to their ideological concerns for national liberation. It soon became clear that from the point of view of this Organization, whatever be the actual issue that led the members to pass a condemnatory resolution,

118.   S/Res/239 (1967) 1.
119.   S/Res/241 (1967) 1.

they were really only concerned with those mercenaries who were engaged in hostilities against forces that the Organization regarded as struggling for their self-determination and national liberation.

From 1964 until 1971 the Organization passed a series of resolutions condemning the recruitment and use of mercenaries, and by 1971 had resolved that it was time to draft a convention condemning mercenarism as a crime, especially when directed against African Liberation movements. [120] While these resolutions and proposals may have had some moral effect upon the members of the Organization, they were of course completely irrelevant as regards any state not such a member, even though that state might itself promote the recruitment of mercenaries for service in Africa.

Both the Organization of African Unity and the United Nations became concerned with the problem again during the civil war in Angola. As early as 1966, problems had arisen between Portugal and the Congo, with the latter accusing Portugal of allowing mercenaries to operate from its colonial territories against the Congo. Portugal stated that there were no mercenaries in Angola and no camps for operations against the Congo. The Security Council, having called upon all states not to interfere in the domestic affairs of the Congo, simply urged Portugal "not to allow foreign mercenaries" to use Angola as a base. [121] A further resolution pretty well to the same effect was passed in 1967 when the Council called upon "all countries receiving mercenaries who have participated in the armed attacks against the Democratic Republic of the Congo to take appropriate measures to prevent them from renewing their activities against any State." [122] More substantively, it condemned Portugal, for having failed in violation of earlier resolutions, to prevent the mercenaries from using the territory of Angola under its administration as a base for operations against the Congo.

Within a year the scene of activity had shifted. The military operations were now being carried on in Portugal's colonial territories and the scene of international concern was the General Assembly. Thus, in 1968, having condemned the Portuguese failure to grant independence to "territories under Portuguese domination," and "the collaboration between Portugal, the minority racist regime of South Africa and the illegal racist minority regime in Southern Rhodesia, which is designed to perpetuate colonialism and oppression in Southern Africa," [123] the General Assembly called upon all states as a matter of urgency "to take all measures to pre-

---

120.   Burchett and Roebuck, *Supra* n. 53, at 233-34.
121.   S/Res/226 (1966).
122.   *Supra* n. 119.
123.   A/Res/2395 (XXIII) 2.

vent the recruitment or training in their territories of any persons as mercenaries for the colonial war being waged in the Territories under Portuguese domination and for violations of the territorial integrity and sovereignty of the independent African States.''[124] The Resolution, continuing with its anti-colonial bias, deplored the Portuguese policy of settling "foreign immigrants" in the colonial territories.

In addition, there was one new feature in the Resolution. Traditionally, colonial powers have been allowed to treat their dependent territories as "private property" and what they have done therein has been regarded as falling within the reserved domain of domestic jurisdiction. This has, of course, been affected on the political level by the series of General Assembly resolutions, and in some cases conventions, on human rights and independence for non-self-governing territories, but these did not introduce any rules of international law regulating the conduct of internal conflicts. The *Geneva Conventions of 1949* relating to humanitarian principles in armed conflict made only the slightest inroads into this position by including in each of them, what is known as Common Article 3. This is to apply in the case of armed conflict not of an international character occurring in the territory of one of the High Contracting Parties, and which is binding on all parties to the conflict. By its Resolution, the General Assembly called upon Portugal to observe the provisions of the *Prisoners of War Convention.*[125] It should be pointed out that this merely imposes observance of the minimal conditions of humanity and requires reciprocal application. There is, however, nothing to indicate that the rebels applied its provisions to their prisoners. Moreover, the Assembly completely ignored the fact that when Portugal ratified the Conventions she made a reservation concerning Article 3, to which no opposition appears to have been expressed:

> As there is no actual definition of what is meant by a conflict not of an international character, and as, in case this term is intended to refer solely to civil war, it is not clearly laid down at what moment an armed rebellion within a country should be considered as having become a civil war, Portugal reserves the right not to apply the provisions of Article 3, in so far as they may be contrary to the provisions of Portuguese law, in all territories subject to her sovereignty in any part of the world.[126]

Again it should be noted that the resolution is not general in character and does not condemn mercenarism as such nor the use of mercenaries. It is only concerned with their use by Portugal in its African territories and against African States. The same is true of the 1973 resolution concerning Guinea: "The use of mercenaries by colonial and racist regimes against the national liberation movements

---

124. *Ibid.*
125. *See Supra* n. 47, at 345 (for Art. 3, at 352.).
126. *Id.,* at 500-01.

struggling for their freedom and independence from the yoke of colonialism and alien domination is considered to be a criminal act and the mercenaries should accordingly be punished as criminals."[127]

It must not be thought that the General Assembly always looked at the problem of mercenaries in the context of a particular struggle. In 1965, when considering the need for a condemnation of intervention in the affairs of third states, the Assembly may be considered to have dealt with the problem in a somewhat indirect fashion, when it stated that "no State shall organize, assist, foment, finance, incite or tolerate subversive, terrorist or armed activities directed towards the overthrow of the régime of another State, or interfere in civil strife in another State."[128] The ideological background for this is to be seen in the Preamble which reaffirms

> the principle of non-intervention, proclaimed in the charters of the Organization of American States, the League of Arab States and the Organization of African Unity and affirmed at the conferences held at Montevideo, Buenos Aires, Chapultepec and Bogotá, as well as in the decisions of the Asian-African Conference at Bandung, the First Conference of Heads of State or Government of Non-Aligned Countries at Belgrade, in the Programme for Peace and International Co-operation adopted at the end of the Second Conference of Heads of State or Government of Non-Aligned Countries at Cairo, and in the declaration on subversion adopted at Accra by the Heads of State and Government of the African States.[129]

That this resolution was not regarded with excessive seriousness by some members of the United Nations, even though it had been adopted by 109 to 1, with only the United Kingdom abstaining, became clear when it was reaffirmed a year later by 114 to 0, with 2 abstentions.[130] Then, in 1969, by 78 to 5 with 16 abstentions, the Assembly reaffirmed[131] its *Declaration on the Granting of Independence to Colonial Countries and Peoples*,[132] which by its very title indicates that its provisions are not of general application, but solely concerned with colonial independence. Within this context the Assembly found it possible to state in general terms, that is to say not in relation to any particular conflict, that

> the practice of using mercenaries against movements for national liberation and independence is punishable as a criminal act and that the mercenaries themselves are outlaws, and calls upon the Governments of all countries to enact legislation declaring the recruitment, financing and training of mercenaries in their territory to be a punishable offence and prohibiting their nationals from serving as mercenaries.[133]

---

127. A/Res/3103 (XXVIII) 3.
128. A/Res/2131 (XX).
129. *Ibid.*
130. A/Res/2225 (XXI).
131. *See* A/Res/2548 (XXIV).
132. A/Res/1514 (XV).
133. A/Res/2548 (XXIV).

While the Resolution condemns mercenaries as outlaws, this is only true if they are opposing national liberation and independence. In addition, the Assembly, aware that its Resolutions are only *voeux* did no more than call upon states to make recruitment and enlistment of mercenaries for such campaigns criminal offences. It did not even go to the extent of calling upon the International Law Commission to codify the law on mercenaries, nor on the members of the United Nations to enter into negotiations for a treaty to this end. Without the will to act, a mere affirmation is as empty as the original resolution, and in 1970 to mark the tenth anniversary of the adoption of the aforesaid *Declaration*, the Assembly, after deploring the fact that the colonial powers, particularly Portugal, South Africa and Southern Rhodesia were still "colonial" or racist rulers, and noting with grave concern that many territories were still under "colonial domination and racist regimes," reiterated its declaration that

> the practice of using mercenaries against national liberation movements in the colonial Territories constitutes a criminal act and the Assembly calls upon all States to take the necessary measures to prevent the recruitment, financing and training of mercenaries in their territory and to prohibit their nationals from serving as mercenaries.[134]

Could anything be clearer that the General Assembly is not concerned in mercenarism or mercenaries as such, but only when they are employed against national liberation movements in colonial territories? On this basis, presumably, the General Assembly is not concerned with mercenaries who may be serving on behalf of a national liberation movement — seemingly it agrees with the view that such persons have the right ideological approach[135] — nor if they are serving on one or both sides in a traditional type of armed conflict. Here it should be remembered, however, that the General Assembly's definition of colonialism, imperialism, foreign rule, racism, and the like, is highly subjective, so that since 1975, when it was decided[136] by the barest majority (72 to 35, and 32 abstaining) that Zionism is racism it would seem that Jewish and other non-Israelis going to fight for Israel would be "criminal" mercenaries, while non-Palestinians fighting in the Palestinian cause would be looked upon as fighters in the twentieth century version of a just war.

The somewhat jaundiced attitude of the United Nations towards issues when it might be possible to argue that national liberation is in question, is to be seen also in the definition of aggression.[137] Among the acts in Article 3 described as constituting aggression is "the

---

134.   A/Res/2707 (XXV).
135.   *See* Burchett and Roebuck, *Supra* n. 53, at 117.
136.   A/Res/3379 (XXX).
137.   A/Res/3314 (XXIX).

sending by or on behalf of a State of armed bands, groups, irregulars or mercenaries, which carry out acts of armed force against another State."[138] However,

> [n]othing in this definition, and in particular article 3, could in any way prejudice the right to self-determination, freedom and independence . . . of peoples forcibly deprived of that right . . ., particularly peoples under colonial and racist régimes or other forms of alien domination; nor the right of these peoples to struggle to that end and to seek and receive support.[139]

It is clear, therefore, that a people allegedly engaged in or supporting a struggle for national liberation would be able to argue that, far from acting as an aggressor by employing mercenaries, it was in fact acting in a perfectly lawful fashion, while the mercenaries and the countries from which they were coming, were carrying out obligations imposed upon them by the United Nations.

While the members of the United Nations were not prepared to carry any of these resolutions into effect so as to make mercenarism a crime, the same end was reached in some countries in so far as Rhodesia was concerned, by reason of legislation consequent upon resolutions condemning the white régime in that country — Zimbabwe — whereby nationals were forbidden from having relations with that régime, but such measures do not refer to mercenaries specifically and have to be read in the context of the Zimbabwe issue.[140]

The Angolan Civil War

Matters took a new turn in 1976 because of the events connected with the Angolan civil war. In November, the General Assembly, reflecting the emotions occasioned by Angola, carried its prejudicial discrimination to its logical conclusion, for it now bluntly declared not only "that the practice of using mercenaries against movements for national liberation and independence constitutes a crime [but also] that the mercenaries are criminals."[141] If one recalls the number of members of the Organization of African Unity which are in the United Nations it is only surprising that such a declaration had not been made much earlier. In 1972, the Organization had prepared a

---

138. *Ibid.*
139. *Id.*, at Art. 7.
140. *See e.g.*, statement by Prime Minister Callaghan in British House of Commons, March 10, 1976, ("Political aspirations of Africans in Rhodesia must be met if there is to be peaceful progress" *The Times* (London), March 11, 1976, at 4, col. 1); proceedings under the *Southern Rhodesia Act 1956* and the 1968 Order in Council (U.N. Sanctions Order No. 2) against Roy Dovaston for advertising for 'emigrants.' ("Anti-Communist on Rhodesia Charges" *The Times* (London), Apr. 14, 1977, at 3, col. 7 and " 'Emigrate to Rhodesia' campaigner cleared" *The Times* (London), Apr. 16, 1977, at 3, col. 4); and the report of Rhodesian Commission of Justice and Peace (summarized by Louis Herin, "Breaking the Rhodesian Spiral of Violence" *The Times* (London), Apr. 23, 1977, at 14, col. 1).
141. Res. 31/34 [G.A.O.R. Supp. 39 (A/31/39), 93].

draft *Convention for the Elimination of Mercenaries in Africa.* In so far as the draft condemns the employment of aliens to overthrow the government of any Member State or undermine its independence there is perhaps nothing with which to quarrel. But the definition goes on to include any such person who

> is employed, enrols or links himself willingly to a person, group or organization whose aim is . . . to block by any means the activities of any liberation movement recognized by the Organization of African Unity . . . [and] the actions of [such] a mercenary . . . constitute offences considered as crimes against the peace and security of Africa and punishable as such.[142]

The clear meaning of this is that such persons will not be regarded as legitimate combatants or, in so far as they are, would be liable to trial for crimes against peace. Such a policy is clearly discriminatory and runs counter to the whole trend of international humanitarian law which regards all combatants, regardless of nationality, as entitled to equal treatment when captured.[143] That this was also the effect of the General Assembly's 1976 resolution becomes clear from the statement made by the United States representative in Committee III:

> [The] paragraph . . . is contrary to the 1949 Geneva Conventions and general international law in suggesting that individual combatants can be treated as 'criminals' solely on the basis of the political acceptability of the cause for which they are fighting or the fact that they may be regarded as 'mercenaries' by other parties to the issue in question.[144]

Others must have had similar views, for the resolution, while carried by 109 to 4, had 24 abstentions.

It is time now to refer to the events in Angola.

By the time the Portuguese announced their intention to withdraw from Angola, there were three distinct liberation movements and fighting soon broke out among them for the reins of power. The MPLA (Popular Movement for the Liberation of Angola) proclaimed a government and this received recognition from the majority of the members of the Organization of African Unity, but the FNLA (National Front for the Libertion of Angola) and UNITA (National Unity for the Total Independence of Angola) continued the struggle.[145] The two movements opposed to the MPLA recruited a number of non-African 'white' mercenaries who were promised high wages and were organized in a separate unit under their own command, and apparently with their own disciplinary code. It was reported that these mercenaries had committed a

---

142.   O.A.U., Doc. CM/433/Rev. L, Annex 1 found in Burchett and Roebuck *Supra* n. 53, at 234.
143.   *See Supra* n. 65, at 370.
144.   [1976] *Digest of United States Practice in International Law* 13.
145.   It is perhaps worth pointing out here that both the FNLA and MPLA had been admitted to the first two sessions of the Geneva Conference on Humanitarian Law 1974 and 1975, as fully recognized national liberation movements.

number of atrocities against Angolan citizens on both sides, and also that their commander had killed or ordered the killing of a number of his own men who had refused to fight. Some of these mercenaries were captured and the Government of Angola brought ten British and three United States nationals to trial for the crime of mercenarism, crimes against peace, murder, brutality, looting and the like. The trial was held in accordance with Angolan law, namely, the 1966 Code of Discipline of the MPLA which had become Angolan law by the Constitution of November 1975. It is hard to see how the accused were subject to this law, although it is possible that in so far as murder and the like were involved, even the Angolan government might have been able to try them for war crimes.

From our point of view what is important is the charge concerning mercenarism. According to the indictment, this was based on declarations by the heads of state and governments of the Organization of African Unity, and on General Assembly resolutions, most of which, as we have seen, referred to the employment of mercenaries in specific conflicts. None of these resolutions or declarations created law. The introductory paragraphs of the Organization of African Unity's draft *Convention* itself suggested that existing laws do not really cover the specific problem of mercenarism.[146] The judgment of the court states:

> Mercenarism was not unknown in traditional penal law, where it was always dealt with in relation to homicide. . . . Yet it is important that in modern penal law, and in the field of comparative law, the mercenary crime lost all autonomous existence and was seen as a common crime, generally speaking aggravated by the profit motive which prompts it. And this mercenary crime, which is known today as 'paid crime to order', comes within the laws of criminal complicity, it being through them that the responsibility of he who orders and he who is ordered is evaluated. . . .[147]

The judgment then states that mercenarism is therefore provided for in Article 20(4) of the Penal Code:

> This annuls the objection of the defence that the crime of mercenarism has not been defined and that there is no penalty for it. It is in fact provided for with penalty in most evolved penal systems. As a material crime, of course![148]

This would seem to imply that if mercenarism is a crime it can only be so if another common crime has also been committed to which it can be associated as an inherent part. This does not seem to have been possible in the case of Gearhart, the American executed for mercenarism, and this led American spokesmen to comment on this execution in the light of the legal status of mercenarism. Then Secretary of State Kissinger stated:

---

146. *Supra* n. 142.
147. G. H. Lockwood, Q.C., "Report on the Trial of Mercenaries: Luanda, Angola, June 1976" (1977), 7 Man. L. J. 183, at 198-99.
148. *Id.*, at 199.

> [T]here is absolutely no basis in national or international law for the action now taken by the Angolan authorities. The 'law' under which Mr. Gearhart was executed was nothing more than an internal ordinance of the MPLA issued in 1966, when the MPLA was only one of many guerrilla groups operating in Angola. Furthermore, no evidence whatsoever was produced during the trial of Mr. Gearhart in Luanda that he had even fired a shot during the few days he was in Angola before his capture.[149]

Somewhat similar arguments were put forward by Assistant Secretary of State Schaufele in testimony before the House International Relations Committee's Special Subcommittee on Investigations:

> The recruitment of mercenaries within the territory of the United States to serve in the armed forces of a foreign country is an offense under our Neutrality Laws.[150] . . . [A] legally accepted definition of what constitutes a mercenary does not exist in international law. Nor is the act of serving as a mercenary a crime in international law, not to mention Angolan law where the Angolan authorities were forced to use a set of guidelines for their combatants the MPLA issued in 1966. The general international practice appears to consider mercenaries in the same status as other combatants and therefore to be treated as such under the terms of the Geneva Convention of 1949 [on Prisoners of War]. This has certainly been American practice back to the Revolutionary War and was reflected in our treatment of captured Hessian troops. This was also the case in the Civil War when there had been combatants on both sides who fought for hire, adventure, or beliefs and who could be considered by some as mercenaries. . . . [T]he act of being a mercenary is not a crime in international law and mercenaries were entitled to the same status and protection as other combatants under the 1949 Geneva Conventions and the rules of warfare. Mr. Gearhart was not charged with any other specific crime. No evidence was presented that he had harmed anyone during the few days he was in Angola before his capture.[151]

Even authors who have condemned the use of mercenaries, especially in Angola, treating them as below contempt, and condemning Gearhart as a monetary mercenary, have tended to agree that his sole crime was that of mercenarism, aggravated by a refusal to express humility at this fact.[152]

The Diplock Report

It was not only in the United States that the reports of mercenary activities in Angola and the trial in Luanda had repercussions, generally condemning mercenaries and those who acted as recruiting agents. Almost simultaneously with the opening of the trial, a Labour Member of the British Parliament was given leave by 184 votes to 89 to introduce the *Advertisement for the Recruitment of Mercenaries (Prohibition) Bill,*[153] with the aim of ending mercenary recruitment in Britain, although it did not forbid Britons from going as mercenaries, even though Mr. Hughes had described the trade of

---

149. *Supra* n. 144, at 714.
150. *See* text *Supra* n. 44.
151. *Supra* n. 144, at 714-15.
152. *See* Burchett and Roebuck, *Supra* n. 53, at 74-75.
153. "Labour MP's Bill aims to ban advertising for mercenaries" *The Times* (London), June 16, 1976, at 7, col. 3.

mercenary as ''obscene. It reduces man below the level of beasts, for animals do not kill without purpose or reason, as a mercenary does. We owe a duty to end this despicable trade.''[154]

The House of Commons was saved the need of further consideration of this Bill by reason of the fact that the Diplock Committee established in February delivered its report in August, 1976.[155] The Commission defined ''mercenaries'' in the ''broad sense'' as ''persons who serve voluntarily for pay in armed forces other than the regular forces of their own country,'' and recognized that this was wide enough to include the Gurkha Regiments in the British Army, the International Brigade, the Eagle Squadron, British Jews in the Israeli Army, as well as the *condottiere* of Renaissance Italy.[156] The Committee pointed out that mercenaries were motivated by a variety of reasons, not always monetary, for they might include

[a] conscientious conviction that the merits of [the] cause are so great as to justify his sacrificing his own life if need be in order to ensure that it will triumph. The soldier of conscience may be found fighting side by side with the soldier of fortune — in the same ranks and for the same rate of pay. . . .

[A]ny definition of mercenaries which required positive proof of motivation would . . . either be unworkable, or so haphazard in its application as between comparable individuals as to be unacceptable. . . . To serve as a mercenary is not an offence under international law. Under the Geneva Conventions . . . a mercenary serving as a member of an organised armed force of one party to a conflict which would be recognised in international law as involving a 'state of war' between the parties to it, is entitled to the same treatment as a combatant and as a prisoner of war as any other member of that force. . . .

. . . [W]e do not think there are any means by which it would be practicable to prevent a United Kingdom citizen from volunteering while he is abroad to serve as a mercenary and from leaving the United Kingdom to do so, we should regard any attempt to impose such a prohibition upon him by law as involving a deprivation of his freedom to do as he will which would require to be justified by a much more compelling reason of public policy than the prohibition of active recruiting of mercenaries within the United Kingdom.

. . . No administrative action can stop a United Kingdom citizen from volunteering for service as a mercenary once he is abroad, but his journey from this country to a foreign destination, though it cannot be prevented, can be hindered and made more difficult for him by his not possessing a valid passport.

At common law, . . . a citizen of the United Kingdom has the right to leave this country and to return to it unhindered and at his own free will. A similar right in every human being is recognised by Article 13(2) of the Universal Declaration of Human Rights. . . . A passport. . . . merely makes it easier for him to exercise that right. . . . [and] if he establishes his identity by other means, an immigration officer has no legal power to prevent his embarkation.[157]

Since there is no legal right in a person to receive a passport and, since when granted it remains the property of the Crown, it may be refused or withdrawn. In fact, passports were withdrawn from 8 per-

---

154. *Ibid.*
155. *Supra* n. 83.
156. *Id.*, para. 5.
157. *Id.*, paras. 6, 7, and 17.

sons who had served as mercenaries in the Congo in 1961, from three who served there in 1967-68, four who served in Nigeria in 1968, and 54 who served in Angola, but in each case "the stable door was shut after the horse had gone," and there was nothing to stop the person involved from leaving again, especially as "an applicant for a passport is not required to state why he wants it."[158]

As has already been pointed out, the Diplock Report emphasized that as the *Foreign Enlistment Act* was a penal statute it had to be interpreted narrowly, and

> [T]he statutory language used in the Act . . . is adapted to conditions as they existed in 1870 as respects relations between sovereign states, the kinds of armed conflict that had taken place in foreign territory during the previous decades and the means of transport and of waging war that were then available. The immense changes in those conditions which have taken place in the last hundred years and particularly since World War II have resulted in there being important omissions from the Act and a number of obscurities in the statutory language affecting most of the ingredients of the offences. These make the application of the Act to United Kingdom citizens who participate in a particular internal conflict in a foreign state a matter of grave legal doubt and the commission of an offence almost incapable of satisfactory proof.[159]

The Committee pointed out that the *Act* referred to foreign enlistment, and therefore could have no application to enlistment in the forces of a Commonwealth country, even though that country might be at war. Equally, since by the *Ireland Act*[160] the Republic of Ireland is not a "foreign state", the *Act* would not apply in that case either. It then stated that *"A fortiori* the *Act* would have no application to service in the army or air force of the régime in Southern Rhodesia, since this still remains, *de jure*, a Crown colony."[161] One cannot refrain from enquiring why the Report fails to mention that enlistment in these forces would therefore amount to treason.[162]

One of the problems that arose in connection with Angola, as it has and will in similar cases, related to the status of the parties to the conflict, a question which concerned the Legal Officers of the Crown on earlier occasions.[163] On this matter the Report was rather full and tended to illustrate a continuity in the official interpretation:

> The expanded definition of 'foreign state' prevents its being confined to a government that is recognised by HM Government as the *de jure* sovereign government over a particular area. It is . . . broad enough to make it an offence to enlist in armed forces raised by rival governments . . . or forces . . . raised by insurgents . . . in their . . . struggles for independence. But the questions of whether and, . . .when, the Act becomes applicable to particular cases of internal struggles for power between rival forces within a state in the varied circumstances in

---

158.   *Id.*, para. 20.
159.   *Id.*, para. 26.
160.   12, 13 & 14 Geo. 6, c. 41, s. 2 (U.K.).
161.   *Supra* n. 83, para. 32.
162.   *See e.g.*, L. C. Green, "Southern Rhodesian Independence" (1969), 14 *Archiv des Völkerrechts* 155.
163.   *See Supra* n. 80-82.

which such struggles may arise today, are capable of raising so many doubts as to make this part of the Act unsuitable . . . to continue to be used as a penal statute. The expanded definition . . . is capable of including within its ambit armed forces raised by groups of persons who are *de facto* exercising governmental powers over a particular identifiable area even though their right to do so *de jure* is recognized neither by Her Majesty's Government nor by any other sovereign state. But the description of the offences requires that the persons on whose behalf the force is raised should also constitute an entity possessed of characteristics which in international law entitle it to recognition as being 'at war' with another state and so enable it to exercise belligerent rights vis-à-vis neutral states. . . . [T]his requires not only that the persons controlling the force should be claiming to be entitled to act as an independent sovereign government but that they should also have been actually exercising effectively and with some degree of permanence exclusive governmental powers over an identifiable part of the territory to which they lay claim; and their opponents must either be a government which is recognised *de jure* by Her Majesty's Government or must also satisfy the same criteria as a *de facto* government,[164]

and it is extremely doubtful whether these conditions were in fact satisfied at the time of the Angola situation. In fact, the Committee commented that

[U]ntil the status in international law of each of the parties to the struggle in Angola was clear, the United Kingdom Government had no power in law to stop the enlistment or recruitment of mercenaries for service on behalf of any of those parties.

[Further,] it would be necessary to prove that Her Majesty's Government had recognised the persons on whose behalf the armed force was raised and the persons against whom they were fighting as being *de facto* or *de jure* at the time that the accused enlisted. So in practice no offence can be committed until Her Majesty's Government . . . is prepared to accord that recognition formally [— a view that does not appear to tally with earlier interpretations]; and it would be a breach of the United Kingdom's own obligations under international law to grant this recognition to a *de facto* government before the criteria were satisfied.[165]

Since, in its practice, the United Kingdom tends to base its recognition policy on political rather than legal criteria, and since there is no record of any country ever having been held liable for premature recognition, it is perhaps unfortunate that the Committee did not give any indication of the basis for this last assertion.

Many of the recent conflicts, particularly in Africa, have been fought between, or have involved the use of guerrilla forces, and in the light of its above comments the Diplock Committee considered it

doubtful whether the Act could ever apply to enlistment in guerrilla forces or in security forces engaged in their suppression if the guerrillas were not purporting to act as the regular government of a particular part of the state's territory but were seeking to bring down the existing régime throughout the territory by force of arms.[166]

In the light of this statement it would appear that the *Foreign Enlistment Act* could probably not be invoked against any mercenaries participating in the activities of SWAPO (South West African

---

164.   *Supra* n. 83, paras. 34-36.
165.   *Id.*, paras. 39 & 35.
166.   *Id.*, para. 36.

People's Organisation) or the ANC or PAC (African National and Panafricanist Congress) against South Africa.

> [Moreover], since the offence consists of enlistment and not a continuing offence of service as a mercenary the applicability of the Act to a particular mercenary might depend upon the stage that had been reached in an internal struggle between rival factions at the time he enlisted. A mercenary who had enlisted before the group on whose behalf the force was raised had won and exercised control over an identifiable area of the disputed territory and had been formally recognised . . . as a *de facto* government would have committed no offence, while his comrade-in-arms who had enlisted in the same force after that event would be liable to conviction.[167]

It is highly probable that however carefully legislation was worded, the same practical difficulties would exist and the same loopholes present themselves. This led the Committee to the conclusion that it would not be

> practicable or just to try to define an offence of enlisting as a mercenary in such a way that guilt would depend upon proof . . . of a particular motive as activating the accused to do so. . . . [A] penal prohibition sought to be imposed by the State upon what an individual does abroad involves a restriction on the liberty of the individual which can only be justified on compelling grounds of public interest. . . . Accordingly we would *recommend the abolition of any statutory offence by a United Kingdom citizen of enlisting as a mercenary while abroad or of leaving the United Kingdom in order to do so.* . . . [W]e see *no advantage in retaining a statutory offence of enlisting in the United Kingdom for service as a mercenary abroad.* . . . We do not think that it can be justified . . . to impose a general prohibition on United Kingdom citizens from serving . . . in the armed forces of a foreign state at a time when there are no hostilities in which that force is engaged. To make it a criminal offence . . . for him not to desert that force as soon as it became involved in external or internal conflict, to which the United Kingdom was not itself a party, would . . . be an impermissible affront to the sovereignty of the foreign state concerned[168]

and the Committee was, therefore, opposed to the idea of making mercenarism criminal. On the other hand, it was opposed to recruitment and advertising therefor, so that

> any fresh legislation creating . . . new offences in relation to recruitment . . . should take the form of an enabling Act empowering Her Majesty's Government . . . by Order in Council . . . requiring affirmative resolutions by both Houses of Parliament to apply the provisions of the Act to the armed forces specified in the Order. . . . The description of proscribed forces need not necessarily be by reference to the name that they bore; it could be by reference to the area in which they were operating. . . .[169]

If such an Act were passed, the concept that service would need to be on behalf of a 'foreign' state would end, for the proscribed forces could be operating equally in a Commonwealth country or a colony.

As yet, there is no indication that the British Government has accepted the recommendations in the Diplock Report. Equally, there

---

167. *Id.*, para. 36.
168. *Id.*, paras. 42 & 44.
169. *Id.*, para. 49.

has been no official indication of any intent to pass legislation making enlistment as a mercenary illegal or taking any steps to forbid recruitment or advertising. In Australia, on the other hand, the government itself introduced legislation[170] forbidding recruitment and advertisement for service with the armed forces of a foreign country, as well as the preparing for or engaging in incursions into foreign countries. But it does not prohibit enlistment of mercenaries outside Australia.

The "International Commission of Enquiry on Mercenaries"

While third states were considering the problems arising from the employment of their nationals in Angola, other developments on an international level were taking place. In an effort to give credibility to their show trial, the Government of Angola invited 51 'Commissioners' from 37 countries to attend the proceedings and draft an international convention on the suppression of mercenarism, prepare a general declaration on the subject and report on the fairness of the trial. Some of the members of the Commission were appointed by governments friendly to the MPLA, some were nominated by political parties, while some were personal invitees known for their sympathy for left-wing political movements.

What is important is that this so-called 'International Commission of Enquiry on Mercenaries' had no official international status, cannot be regarded as a normal international body representing any countries or learned bodies, and has about as much credibility as the so-called Russell Trial of Lyndon Johnson.[171] In the normal way, one would be able to ignore it as a pure propaganda effort, despite the fact that some of its members may truly have been imposed-upon 'innocents abroad.' However, some politicians from the third world have given its findings almost an official status.

The only thing that need be said of the relation between the Commission and the trial is that the former produced its general declaration and the draft convention before the judgment was delivered. Despite the comment that the trial was fair[172] one cannot but feel that its condemnation of mercenarism as such must have contributed to the attitude of a tribunal which did not consist solely of trained judges or lawyers. In its Declaration[173] the Commission ac-

---

170. *Crimes (Foreign Incursions and Recruitment) Act*, in *Commonwealth of Australia Acts* (1978), no. 13.
171. J. Duffet (ed.), *Against the Crime of Silence* (1968).
172. *Supra* n. 147, at 193. Mr. Lockwood here states that he is commenting from a purely procedural point of view; it could hardly have been otherwise, since his Committee on 'fairness' started 3 days after the trial opened and he left before it concluded.
173. Original French text supplied by Dr. Al-Faluji, Head, Iraqi Delegation, Geneva Conference on Humanitarian Law in Armed Conflict.

cepted as truth the allegations made against the mercenaries at their trial, accepting the Angolan government's propaganda statement that the recruitment, despatch and equipment of the mercenaries could not have been effected without the tacit approval of the countries where they had been recruited or equipped, and Great Britain and the United States were specifically mentioned — allegations which both governments vehemently denied. It then proceeded to allege that mercenaries were being recruited all over the world, in defiance of international public opinion, and to confront liberation movements as part of an imperialistic counter-offensive against the progress of freedom and world peace. Since it was considered that Namibia and Zimbabwe were in imminent danger of mercenary activities the Commission called upon the world, its organisations, its governments and its people to adopt without delay the proposed Convention making mercenarism criminal. The draft taking as its basis the variety of resolutions and declarations concerning Africa already referred to, which were regarded as "indicative of the development of new rules on international law making mercenarism an international crime," declares that

> The crime of mercenarism is committed by the individual, group or association, representatives of states and the State itself which, with the aim of opposing by armed violence a process of self-determination, practises any of the following acts:
>> (a) organises, finances, supplies, equips, trains, promotes, supports or employs in any way military forces consisting of or including persons who are not nationals of the country where they are going to act, for personal gain, through the payment of a salary or any other kind of material recompense;
>> (b) enlists, enrols or tries to enrol in the said forces;
>> (c) allows the activities mentioned in paragraph (a) to be carried out in any territory under its jurisdiction or in any place under its control or affords facilities for transit, transport or other operation of the above mentioned forces.[174]

This makes no reference to increased pay as an inducement to enlistment, so that an alien serving in a regular armed force only becomes a mercenary if that armed force is engaged in activities against the "process of self-determination," and no attempt is made to indicate how one decides that the operations against which such forces are sent are in fact in aid of this process.

Since, at present, no state recognizes the existence of Rhodesia, it is probably true to say that there is no Rhodesian nationality, so that its military forces consist of people who do not possess the nationality of the country where they are acting, namely Zimbabwe, and since it would appear that the African countries at least recognize the 'Popular Front' as engaged in the 'process of self-determination' logically every member of the Rhodesian forces is guilty of the crime

---

174.   Original French text supplied by Dr. Al-Faluji; English translation found in Burchett and Roebuck, *Supra* n. 53, at 237-40.

of mercenarism. Since a number of countries in the Third World have equated the Palestine Liberation Organization with a popular liberation movement and having secured the passing of a General Assembly resolution equating Zionism with imperialism, [175] one is compelled to assume that the same would be considered true of all members of the Israel armed forces, at least those of them fighting against the P.L.O., for it might be possible to argue that Israeli forces engaged against Egyptian forces in, for example, Sinai, are engaged in a regular armed conflict, even though there is little doubt that in such circumstances Egypt and its Arab and African friends would maintain that it was fulfilling its obligations as a member of the United Nations on behalf of self-determination.

Perhaps the most striking feature of the definition is that it includes states and declares that they, too, if their governments allow the recruitment of mercenaries, are guilty of crime — a somewhat new development in international law, and probably one that could only have been invented by a body not terribly concerned with, or competent in, the realities of international law and politics. When a state representative becomes a criminal under this definition, he is to be punished for his acts or omissions. As to the state, "any other State may invoke such responsibility: (a) in its relations with the State responsible, and (b) before competent international organisations." At present, it is somewhat doubtful whether the International Court of Justice would be willing to take on this jurisdictional responsibility, and whether there would be mutual declarations under the 'Optional Clause' to grant jurisdiction. The draft makes no provision for a competent tribunal to be established, merely providing that in the event of a dispute as to interpretation or application the issue shall be settled by negotiation or a competent international tribunal or arbitrator acceptable to all parties — does this include the national liberation movement involved?

Assuming one is prepared to accept the view that mercenarism is a crime in itself, there could be little quarrel with the provision that the individual concerned is personally responsible for all other criminal acts he may have committed, nor perhaps with the principle that the maxim *aut punire aut dedere* is to operate. While one might agree that war crimes and other common crimes are not to be regarded as political offences, [176] this becomes more difficult to accept when mercenarism within this wide definition is equally regarded as a common crime. The position is made even more unacceptable by Ar-

---

175. *See Supra* n. 136.
176. *See* L. C. Green, "Political Offences, War Crimes and Extradition" (1962), 11 Int. & Comp. Law Q. 329.

ticle 4 which postulates that "mercenaries are not lawful combatants. If captured they are not entitled to prisoner of war status." Not only does this discriminate among those engaged in armed conflict, but it means that until such time as the conflict becomes one opposed to self-determination the individual soldier is a protected combatant. After the conflict changes its character, any legitimate act of war committed by him becomes illegal and he may find himself on trial, not merely for mercenarism but for murder in respect of any member of the national liberation movement concerned that he may have killed in the course of battle.

The only thing that may be said in favour of this draft is that, since it is tied in with the concept of self-determination, it may be short-lived, for, hopefully, it will not be long before all peoples have achieved this, and this twentieth century version of a political "Sermon on the Mount" will have dropped from the vocabulary of international law. Unfortunately, however, the concept is subjective and every revolutionary movement, and its supporters, claim to be engaged in a struggle for self-determination and national liberation, as has been made clear by the Soviet reaction in June 1978 to the possible creation of a Pan-African Peacekeeping Force supported by the western powers and directed to preserving some, at least, of the African governments against foreign subversion and incursions.

At one time it appeared as if this draft might be peddled at the Geneva Conference on Humanitarian Law in Armed Conflict. However, general support was given to a more modified version put forward by Nigeria which omitted the objectionable ideological features of the Luanda draft. It is true that Article 47 of Protocol I additional to the *Geneva Conventions of 1949,* relating to the *Protection of Victims of International Armed Conflicts,* 1977,[177] retains the undesirable discriminatory provision denying a mercenary his status as a combatant or a prisoner of war. However, the definition of a mercenary is less objectionable. The most important change from Luanda lies in the fact that the definition is now general in scope and no longer has any reference to struggles for national liberation, even though these by Article 1 have been elevated to the level of international armed conflicts.[178] What is perhaps of great significance is that there is no provision on mercenaries in Protocol II[179] concerning non-international conflicts. While this may clarify some of the issues with regard to internal conflict and guerrilla activities mentioned in the Diplock Report[180] the matter remains confused in that the

177.   *Supra* n. 1.
178.   *See* L. C. Green, "The New Law of Armed Conflict" (1977), 15 Can. Y. B. Int'l. Law 3.
179.   *Supra* n. 177, at 1442.
180.   *See Supra* n. 164.

borderline between a Protocol I and a Protocol II situation is not clear, and all one dare say is that if the movement concerned is not in control of part of the national territory, and not operating from outside, Protocol I might not apply — this fact was seemingly not sufficiently appreciated by some of the third world countries at Geneva, and would probably have excluded many of the incidents in which mercenaries were engaged in Africa between 1960 and 1977. According to Article 47

> A mercenary is a person who:
> (a) is specially recruited locally or abroad in order to fight in an armed conflict;
> (b) does, in fact, take a direct part in the hostilities;
> (c) is motivated to take part in the hostilities essentially by the desire for private gain and, in fact, is promised by or on behalf of a Party to the conflict, material compensation substantially in excess of that promised or paid to combatants of similar ranks and functions in the armed forces of that Party;
> (d) is neither a national of a Party to the conflict nor a resident of territory controlled by a Party to the conflict;
> (e) is not a member of the armed forces to the conflict, and
> (f) has not been sent by a State which is not a Party to the conflict on official duty as a member of the armed forces.[181]

Perhaps the most notable aspect of the article is that it no longer describes the mercenary as a criminal, although it does lay him open to proceedings as an unprivileged person taking part in hostilities when he is not granted the status of combatant. There is no suggestion that the state involved in any way in his recruitment is itself criminally liable. Nor does it require the parties to the Protocol to make mercenarism a crime or forbid enlistment within their territory.

In addition, the segments of the definition are cumulative, so that embodiment of the mercenaries within the armed forces of a party to the conflict would remove from those persons the slur of mercenarism, subject to the contention, of course, that they only enlisted for reasons of reward and were paid on a higher scale than nationals holding the same rank and performing the same task. It is probable, however, that mercenaries enlisted into technical units may well hold the same rank and be described as performing the same tasks, but since they hold abilities not possessed by the locals their pay might in fact be higher. Since the mercenary is one who takes a direct part in the hostilities and has been specially recruited for this purpose, 'advisers' would not fall within the condemning rubric. However, Polisario — the national liberation movement in the Sahara — has announced its intention to treat French technicians captured in Mauretania as mercenaries, an announcement that was bitterly condemned by France.[182] Equally exempt are members of the

---

181. *Supra* n. 177.
182. "Le Polisario traite en 'mercenaires' les Techniciens français de Mauritanie" *Le Monde*, May 24-25, 1977, at 1, col. 3-5.

armed forces sent by their government, even if they are described —
as were the German and Italian supporters of Franco's Nationalists
in Spain — as volunteers. Thus, Cubans in Angola or Ethiopia would
not be mercenaries, nor for that matter would be the 'traditional
mercenary' of the critics, namely the French Foreign Legion
operating on behalf of the Government of Zaire in 1978. Nor would
it include the Gurkha units of the British Army, or officers seconded
to, or on contract as members of, foreign units. Since residents are
not regarded as mercenaries even though they are specially recruited
and receive a higher pay than the regular servicemen, it would seem
that, for example, non-Israelis wishing to serve in the Israeli forces
would merely be required to take up residence for such period of time
as is prescribed by Israeli law in order to become lawful combatants.
The same is not true for the Rhodesians, for the Protocol definition
still involves nationality considerations. Their situation is not helped
by the decision of the World Council of Churches, seeking apparently to plug the loophole in the Protocol concerning punishment, at
least in so far as Rhodesia is concerned, calling on member-churches
"to urge their government to treat enlistment in the armed forces of
Rhodesia regime as a criminal offence, to punish offenders accordingly, and to outlaw any recruitment for this purpose."[183]

While the Protocol definition may have omitted some of the
most unpleasant parts of the Luanda formula, it retains the motive
test. A mercenary "is motivated essentially by the desire for private
gain," so that any non-national captured would have to be examined
as to the motive which led him to enlist. His comrade, paid the same,
but motivated — at least, so he says — by ideological sympathy,
though this of course could not protect him in a campaign against national liberation, would not be considered a mercenary and would be
a lawful combatant entitled to prisoner of war status. One should not
overlook the warning of Brian C.J. in 1477, "It is common
knowledge that the thought of man shall not be tried, for the Devil
himself knoweth not the thought of man."[184] or as it has been expressed more recently "I do not see how intent can make infringement of what otherwise is not. The less legal rights depend on
someone's state of mind, the better."[185]

---

183. "Churches urged to put pressure on oil firms" *The Times* (London), Aug. 6, 1977, at 3, col. 6-7.
184. Y. B. 17 Edw. 4, Pasch., fo. 2, cited with approval in *Brogden* v. *Metropolitan Ry. Co.* (1877), 2 App. Cas. 692 (H.L.) (per Lord Blackburn).
185. *Mercoid Corp.* v. *Mid-Continent Investment Co.* (1944), 320 U.S. 661, at 679-80. (per Justice Jackson).

Conclusion

The Protocol is in force only for those ratifying, while the various resolutions of the United Nations and other international organizations in this area are not law-making, and since it is of the essence of humanitarian law and of the law of war that it should be even-handed, so that even those engaged in an unlawful war remain protected by the law,[186] mercenaries at this moment, are still legally combatants, entitled to treatment as prisoners of war and only liable to trial for such crimes against the law of war or the criminal law that they may commit. International law, as yet, does not regard mercenarism as an offence. Moreover, since the drafting of Protocol I it has become noticeable that the African countries, the very countries that led the campaign against mercenaries, are no longer so concerned when alien troops, even so mercenary a unit as the French Foreign Legion, are engaged in keeping a recognised African government in power. True, it would seem that ideology is here important. If the proposed Pan-African Peacekeeping Force comes into existence, it may no longer be necessary for the Foreign Legion to play a part on the African stage. But will the role of such a force be any different from that of, for example, the Cubans operating on behalf of left-wing governments in Africa, ostensibly at the invitation of such governments? If the British Foreign Secretary can say at the 1978 Lord Mayor's Banquet that "[they] are like private armies in the Middle Ages, which moved around 'tilting the military balance indiscriminately at the whim of the feudal barony,' "[187] then the Soviet Union is equally entitled to describe the western-sponsored and supported Pan-African Peacekeeping Force as a tool of the imperialists directed at destroying the national liberation movements of Africa — it is, of course, unfortunate, as the Soviet and Cuban role in Ethiopia and Somalia illustrate, that today's idealists are yesterday's neo-colonialists, and *vice-versa*. So long as the present political temper prevails, with its rival power interests, it will matter little how the treaty text defines mercenaries.

In any case, if the Diplock Report and events in Africa since the signature of Protocol I are any indication, it may well be that Article 47 will be subject to reservation. Since there were hints at Geneva that if such a politically motivated provision were in fact reserved, the majority of third world states would not ratify the Protocol as such, it may well be the law will remain as it has always been. The

---

186. *See e.g.*, H. Lauterpacht, "Rules of Warfare in an Unlawful War," in Lipsky (ed.), *Law and Politics in the World Community* (1953) 89, at 112, and in 2 L. Oppenheim *International Law* (1952) 231, at 299; *see also* "The Law of Armed Conflict" 2 G. Schwarzenberger, *International Law* (1968) 98-99 and 105-06, and G. Schwarzenberger, *International Law and Order* (1971) 235.
187. "Russian role in Africa denounced by Dr. Owen" *The Times* (London), Apr. 6, 1978, at 1, col. 1-2.

new threats to independence in Africa may herald a period in which the African states themselves strengthen their Pan-African Peacekeeping Force, with a leavening of white mercenaries, leading us back to a period when the profession of arms is again like any other, open to those who wish to follow it, and made use of by those employers who require the services of such professionals. Morality, particularly when fed by propaganda and pseudo-idealism, may condemn the profession. While law should reflect the morality of those it governs, it should not be affected by the vagaries of the season, nor should it hesitate when morality runs away from justice to be the medium through which level-handed justice and humanity remain supreme.

[11]

THE INTERNATIONAL LEGAL PROTECTION OF CHILDREN IN ARMED CONFLICTS

GERALDINE VAN BUEREN*

I. INTRODUCTION

THE conflicts in Angola, Somalia, Sudan and former Yugoslavia[1] have focused attention on the plight of children[2] caught up in armed conflicts and it is tempting to assume—as the Jesuit philosopher, Bernard Lonergan, once said about the Church—that international law arrives at the place of action a little late and somewhat out of breath. Hence, to protect children in armed conflicts international law must be able to respond to the changing nature of wars and strife. In the past hundred years open warfare between sovereign States has, with notable exceptions, given way to internal armed conflicts often with covert support from outside the State. There has been a similar change in military strategy. Modern tactics seek to obscure the differences between those who fight and those who do not by camouflaging combatants within the overall population. In addition, there are increasing risks to children because many internal armed conflicts are perpetrated on a tribal or zonal basis with the result that any person outside that particular group is regarded as the enemy.[3] Consequently, the proportion of civilian casualties in armed conflicts has been rising. In the First World War only 5 per cent, approximately, of all casualties were civilian.[4] By the end of the Second World War this figure

---

* Director of the Programme on International Rights of the Child, Faculty of Laws, Queen Mary and Westfield College, London.

1. See the report on the situation on human rights in the territory of the former Yugoslavia submitted by Mazowiecki, Special Rapporteur of the Commission on Human Rights, pursuant to Commission Res.1992/S–1/1 (UN Doc.E/CN.4/1993/50), who highlights the particular suffering of children. For the impact of conflicts in Central America see Ernesto and Cohn, *Children and War: Report on the Psychosocial Impact of Violence on Children in Central America* (UNICEF, 1990); in relation to Southern Africa see UNICEF, *Children on the Front Line: The Impact of Apartheid, Destabilisation and Warfare on Children in Southern and South Africa* (1987) and for the global impact see Rosenblatt, *Children of War* (1983).

2. Throughout this article the terms "child" and "children" are applied to all those under the age of 18.

3. In Sierra Leone the army's counter-insurgency operation involves the systematic detention of men, women and children found in areas recaptured from rebels. Children have been among those arbitrarily detained by the military in areas where rebel forces have been active; see Amnesty International Sierra Leone, *Prisoners of War? Children Detained in Barracks and Prison*, Amnesty International AFR 51/06/93.

4. According to studies undertaken for the International Symposium on Children and War held in Finland in 1983, cited in UNICEF Dec. 1985 C/1, Annex 1. See also Kahnert, Pitt and Taipale (Eds), *Children and War, Proceedings of Symposium at Siuntio Baths, Finland 1983*, p.5.

810 *International and Comparative Law Quarterly* [VOL. 43

had arisen to approximately 50 per cent and continues to rise. Out of the 20 million killed in the 150 armed conflicts between 1945 and 1982, the majority of deaths were women and children.[5] In the past ten years alone internal armed conflicts have led to 1.5 million child deaths, 4 million children disabled as a result of war wounds and 5 million children living in refugee camps to escape conflicts.[6]

There also has been a general geographical shift in the territories where armed conflicts take place. The majority now occur in developing States. According to Makamure, "the poorly developed economic resources in Africa are such that the outbreak of war leads to economic dislocation and consequent large scale hunger and starvation among the civilian population, mostly among women and children".[7] In 1986 in Angola and Mozambique, for example, 140,000 children (representing 45 per cent of the total infant and young child mortality in these States)[8] died from the conflict and the consequential destabilisation. Hence, rather than appearing on the fringe of the concerns of international humanitarian law, as is often assumed to be the case, the international legal regulation of armed conflicts has particular significance for children. The issues which this article addresses are whether the existing distinction between child recruitment into the armed forces and the participation of children in armed conflicts is justifiable and whether military considerations, as a matter of international law, now take precedence over the physical safety and best interests of the child. The decision whether to evacuate children is also considered, as is an analysis of the potential of the duty upon States to provide recovery and reintegration services for war-traumatised children.

II. THE HISTORICAL DEVELOPMENT OF THE INTERNATIONAL LEGAL PROTECTION OF CHILDREN IN ARMED CONFLICTS

THE protection of children in armed conflicts was one of the earliest concerns of the international law on the rights of the child; the standard of protection was, however, minimal. The Hague Convention Respecting the Laws and Customs of War on Land 1907 incorporated only the principle of respect for family life without considering whether children with or separated from their families were entitled to additional levels of protection.[9] Furthermore, even though the Declaration of the Rights of the

---

5. According to Kahnert *et al., ibid,* the proportion of civilian deaths in Lebanon may have been as high as 97%.

6. In Bosnia and Herzegovina alone 1,000 children have died and 30,000 wounded: UNICEF figures presented to the Committee on the Rights of the Child (UN Doc.CRC/C/SR.38, Oct. 1992). At the time of writing no accurate information is available for Somalia.

7. Makamure, paper presented to the Nairobi Conference on Children in Situations of Armed Conflict.

8. Wilson and Mamphela, in UNICEF (1987), *op. cit. supra* n.1 at p.21. See also Jupp, "Apartheid Violence against Children" (1986) 10 Cultural Survival Q. 34.

9. Hague Convention No.4, Art.46: "Family honour and rights, the lives of persons ... must be respected." Arts.42–56 apply to civilians generally.

Child 1924 owed its origins to the concern for children affected by armed conflicts in the Balkans, it provided only that in times of distress children should be the first to receive relief.[10] In 1938, however, the International Conference of the Red Cross asked the International Committee of the Red Cross to co-operate with the International Union for Child Welfare to study the possibility of providing protection under a convention, and in 1939 they produced a draft Convention for the Protection of Children in Emergency and Armed Conflict.[11] On 12 January 1939 the draft was accepted but work to secure its adoption was somewhat overtaken by events. The issue re-emerged in 1946 when a draft Convention for the Protection of Children in the Event of International Conflict or Civil War was submitted by the Bolivian Red Cross to the Preliminary Conference of Red Cross Societies for the Study of the Geneva Conventions. The resolution recommended that the provisions of the draft Convention should be incorporated into the future Geneva Convention on the Protection of Civilians in preference to an additional fifth treaty.[12]

The Geneva Convention on the Protection of Civilians 1949, Geneva Convention 4, incorporates 17 articles of specific concern to children, affording general protection to children as civilians and special protection for children living in both unoccupied and occupied territory.[13] The considerable achievements of the Geneva Diplomatic Conference in 1949 in reaching sufficient consensus to codify and regulate the conduct of armed conflicts ought not be underestimated, but the changes in warfare since the Conventions were adopted in 1949 revealed several lacunae in relation to children. Of particular concern were the absence of any prescribed minimum age for child participation in hostilities and the lack of specific additional protection for children caught up in an increasing number of internal armed conflicts. The General Assembly of the United Nations attempted to address several of these issues in 1974 when it adopted the Declaration on the Protection of Women and Children in Emergency and Armed Conflict.[14] According to the Preamble the Declaration was drafted: "Bearing in mind the need to provide special protection of women and children belonging to the civilian population." hence the issue of child combatants was beyond its scope. In retrospect the Declaration proved to be of greater value in terms of its overall strategic importance than in its normative status. The adoption of the Declaration assisted in the acceptance of provisions relating to the special protection of children in the two Additional Protocols to the Geneva Conventions.[15]

10. Art.3: in Van Bueren, *International Documents on Children* (1993).
11. Res.13(1938).
12. A decision approved by the Conference of Government Experts 1947. The Convention does not abrogate Hague Convention No.4, which still remains in force.
13. Arts.14, 17, 23–27, 40, 50, 51, 68, 76, 81, 82, 89, 94 and 132.
14. See Van Bueren, *op. cit. supra* n.10.
15. Adopted in 1977 by the Diplomatic Conference, which held its first session in 1974.

812   *International and Comparative Law Quarterly*   [VOL. 43

However, although the two Protocols provide greater protection for children against the effects of hostilities[16] and for the first time regulate the participation of children in the conflict, the potential of the Protocols is at present somewhat limited for children because fewer States are party to the Protocols than to the Geneva Conventions themselves.[17] Hence, the drafting of the Convention on the Rights of the Child presented an ideal opportunity to seek to raise the standards within a less contentious framework. It was an opportunity, however, which was not fully seized: standards were not raised, and in one significant area they were arguably lowered.[18] In sharp contrast the African Charter on the Rights and Welfare of the Child, which is not yet in force, does break new ground by extending the ambit of international humanitarian law as it applies to children.[19] Article 22(3) of the African Charter applies not only to children caught up in armed conflicts but also to "tension and strife", thus importantly protecting children caught up in lower levels of violence. The drafters of the African Charter, in contrast with those who drew up the Geneva Protocols and the Convention on the Rights of the Child, proved to be sufficiently far-sighted to recognise that the best interests of the child ought to predominate in international law and not the form and level of the conflict. Despite, or perhaps because of, its increased standards the African Charter is not yet in force and there does not appear to be significant pressure within the Organisation of African Unity or the United Nations for its implementation. Yet significant pressure could be applied to the member States of the former, if the recently proposed study on improving the protection of children in armed conflicts were to include a recommendation for the implementation of regional standards protecting children in armed conflicts.[20]

III. THE PARTICIPATION OF CHILDREN IN HOSTILITIES

CHILDREN participate in conflicts directly by engaging in combat and indirectly through an infinite variety of means including seeking and send-

The Conference was convened by the Swiss government in its capacity as the depository of the Geneva Conventions.

16. See Plattner, "The Protection of Children in International Humanitarian Law" (1984) 240 Int. Rev. Red Cross 140 and Singer, "The Protection of Children During Armed Conflict Situations" (1986) 252 Int. Rev. Red Cross 133.

17. For reasons not exclusively related to children. The four Geneva Conventions have 181 States parties, whereas Protocol I has 125 and Protocol II has 116 parties as at 10 June 1993: (1993) 294 Int. Rev. Red Cross 256.

18. See further *infra*.

19. Thompson, "Africa's Charter on Children's Rights—A Normative Break with Cultural Traditionalism" (1992) 41 I.C.L.Q. 43; Van Bueren, "The African Charter on the Rights and Welfare of the Child—A New Children's Treaty" (1991) 8 Int. Children's Rights Monitor 20.

20. In Res.A/C.3/48/L.40 of 23 Nov. 1993 the G.A. called upon the UN Secretary-General to undertake a study on the ways and means of improving the protection of children from the adverse effects of armed conflicts.

ing military information and transporting arms and munitions. There are at least 20 States in which children from 10 to 18 are involved in military training, and 25 States permit children to go to war before they can vote.[21] Their participation in armed conflict brings into focus two issues: first, whether children ought to be recruited into the armed forces; and, second, whether they ought to be permitted to participate in armed conflicts. The issue is of grave concern to many States, not only because it has been estimated that there are approximately 200,000 child soldiers in the world,[22] but because there are a number of States in which children form the majority of the population. According to the Canadian delegation during the drafting of Article 77 of Protocol 1, young people aged 16 to 18 are often better equipped physically for fighting than were their fathers.[23] If international law were to oblige States to prohibit child recruitment and participation, many would be at risk of depriving themselves of a significant pool of potential combatants. The possibility of such a loss to some States is particularly influential for several governments as child soldiers have proven themselves to be effective combatants. During the Iran–Iraq war children under 15 participated in the fighting and were regarded as a powerful fighting force, as the testimony of Iraqi soldiers demonstrates. They found that the Iranian child soldiers against whom they fought were the most difficult because "they had not fear", and an army without fear is the most dangerous army in the world.[24] The Iraqi experience is consistent with that of Cambodia. According to one Khmer Rouge officer: "It usually takes a little time but eventually the younger ones become the most efficient soldiers of them all."[25]

The four Geneva Conventions 1949 are silent both on the recruitment of children into the armed forces and on their direct or indirect participation in military operations. It was not until the entry into force of the two Protocols that this situation was partly remedied. For both international and internal armed conflicts the Protocols establish 15[26] as the minimum age of recruitment, although, in international conflicts, when recruiting children aged between 15 and 18 the oldest should be recruited first.[27] This standard is reiterated in the Convention on the Rights of the Child.[28] There does, however, seem to be some uncertainty about the pre-

21. See works mentioned *supra* n.4.

22. UN Doc.E/CN.4/Sub.2/AC.21 (1988).

23. In the debates prompted by Brazil's attempts to set the minimum age at 18. See CDDH/111/325 and 328.

24. Condor, Terres des Hommes, paper presented at the International Congress for the Prevention of Child Abuse and Neglect, Hamburg, 1990.

25. See Boothby, "Children and War" (1986) 10 Cultural Survival Q. 28.

26. Art.77(2) Protocol 1, Art.4(3)(c) Protocol 2: see Van Bueren, *op. cit. supra* n.10. See also Mann, "International Law and the Child Soldier" (1987) 36 I.C.L.Q. 50.

27. Art.77(2) Protocol 1.

28. Art.38(3).

cise definition of recruitment. According to Dulti the word "recruitment" includes both compulsory and voluntary enrolment, so that parties to the conflict would also be under a duty to refrain from enrolling children under 15 years of age who volunteer to join the armed forces.[29] During the drafting of Article 77(2) of Protocol 1 the International Committee of the Red Cross (ICRC) had initially proposed that States should refrain not only from recruiting children under 15 in their armed forces but also from accepting their voluntary enrolment, and a similar point was made by Finland and Austria during the second reading of the Convention on the Rights of the Child. Both countries stated categorically that a prohibition also included a prohibition on accepting voluntary enlistment. Algeria, however, adopted the opposite approach, arguing that setting a minimum age for recruitment did not entail States dissuading children who wished to volunteer, particularly for wars of national liberation.[30] Algeria's position, however undesirable to some, appears to be supported by the text of Geneva Convention IV, which expressly uses the term "voluntary enlistment" elsewhere, thereby implying a difference between recruitment and voluntary enlistment.[31]

During the lengthy negotiations over Article 38 of the Convention on the Rights of the Child, a number of States, principally Latin American and Scandinavian, wished to see the existing standards raised and 18 established as the minimum age of recruitment. Their position was opposed by the United States and the United Kingdom. The negotiations at one stage appeared more akin to a game of bingo, with the Netherlands suggesting a minimum age of 16 as a compromise.[32] Despite the frequent communications, particularly between the American delegate and the State Department, Article 38 merely reiterates the existing standards of 15 as the minimum age of recruitment and the oldest to be recruited first from those aged between 15 and 18. Several States have expressed their discontent with the lack of progress in the form of declarations appended to their ratifications and accessions to the Convention.[33] This is consistent with the practice in those States where the minimum age of recruitment is 18. It is also consistent with the evolving standards in international human rights law, where the most recently drafted child rights treaty—the Afri-

29. Dulti, "Captured Child Combatants" (1990) 278 Int. Rev. Red Cross 424.
30. UN Doc.E/CN.4/1986/39. The Algerian delegate did not state her reasons but it may not have been unconnected to Algeria's support of the Polisari.
31. See e.g. *infra* in relation to Art.51 Geneva Convention 4 (1949). That there is a distinction appears also to be supported by the wording of a draft declaration of minimum standards drawn up by a group of independent experts convened by the Institute for Human Rights, Abo Akademi University, Finland, which in Art.10 recommends: "Children who have not yet attained the age of 15 years shall not be recruited in or allowed to join armed forces."
32. UN Doc.E/CN.4/1989/48.
33. See e.g. Argentina and Spain (UN Doc.CRC/C/2).

can Charter on the Rights and Welfare of the Child—sets the standard of 18 as the minimum age for recruitment.[34]

Recruitment, however, does not necessarily imply that children will directly participate in armed conflicts, merely that they will be part of the armed forces. In respect of international armed conflicts Protocol I provides only that children under 15 should not take "a direct part in hostilities".[35] The ICRC had opposed the insertion of the word "direct" because it would appear to exclude indirect acts of participation which are capable of being as life-threatening and dangerous as direct combat. The ICRC approach was rejected in relation to Protocol I but accepted and incorporated into Protocol II: children under 15 are prohibited from any type of participation in non-international armed conflicts. Hence, States appear to assume that indirect participation in international conflicts is safer than indirect participation in civil wars: an assumption which deserves Bentham's epithet of "nonsense upon stilts".[36] The Convention on the Rights of the Child does not remedy satisfactorily this discrepancy as it only places a duty on States parties to ensure that children under 15 do not participate directly in hostilities.[37] Although the African Charter on the Rights and Welfare of the Child links recruitment and participation and prohibits all those under 18 from participating in armed conflicts, the treaty law currently in force sets only 15 as the minimum age for child participation. This standard appears to be consistent with Islamic law, as those under 15 are not permitted to participate in *jihad*.[38]

Ironically, in setting the minimum age of 15, States ignored one of only two direct interventions by children in the drafting of the Convention on the Rights of the Child. The Working Group on the Question of a Convention on the Rights of the Child ignored a petition presented to them on behalf of 654 organisations representing 95,698,415 young people from 118 States.[39] Included in the petition was a demand to end the participation of all children in the armed services. The non-governmental organisations sought to draw a comparison with the minimum age (18) set by the International Labour Organisation for working with hazardous materials.[40] Ammunition, it was argued by the non-governmental organisations, was a hazardous material and there are very few events in life more hazardous than having to face bullets from a semi-automatic rifle. This

---

34. By reading Arts.2 and 22(2) together.
35. Art.77(2) Protocol 1.
36. Bentham, "Anarchical Fallacies", in Bowring (Ed.), *Complete Works*, Vol.2.
37. Art.38(2).
38. See further Elahi, "The Rights of the Child under Islamic Law: Prohibition of the Child Soldier" (1988) 19 Col. Human Rights Rev. 274.
39. Presented to the Working Group by Swedish Red Cross Youth.
40. Art.3 ILO Convention No.138: in Van Bueren, *op. cit. supra* n.10.

approach also failed. As with the age of recruitment, several States refused to accept the issue as determined and attached declarations to Article 38 that they will not authorise those within their jurisdictions under the age of 18 to participate directly in armed conflicts.[41]

Philosophically, child participation in armed conflicts raises fundamental problems for those advocating a greater participation by children in decisions affecting their own lives. Those who have coherently and consistently argued for the recognition of greater child autonomy in international instruments fall back on the welfare and best interests of the child, which traditionally have been used to justify restrictions on child autonomy.[42] Yet it can be argued that the restrictions placed by treaties on the minimum age of recruitment interfere with the rights of children to freedom of association and arguably also raise issues of freedom of expression,[43] particularly since children have proved themselves to be competent soldiers. The issue becomes even more complex when children believe the only contribution they can make is to fight in wars of liberation,[44] as occurred among some of the Ugandan child soldiers. Such loyalty is not always due to cynical manipulation by the fighting forces. Although there have been occasions when their lack of experience has been exploited and they have been sent ill-prepared into the front line of battle, children whose entire family and social structures have been destroyed by the opposing forces may well find that the army provides them with a replacement structure in which they are fed and are given the basic necessities of life such as food and shoes.[45] Hence, to regard the issue as only that of protection versus participation is too simplistic; some children will not survive unless taken into the armed forces.

For those who argue for greater participatory rights of children the answer may lie in equating the participation of children in armed conflicts with their participation in specific forms of exploitation. Thus, armed conflicts are inherently brutalising and their very nature makes it impossible for those under 18 to give free and informed consent. There are, however,

---

41. See *supra* n.33.

42. See the discussions in *Children of War*, Report from the Conference on Children in War, Raoul Wallenberg Institute, Report No.10 (1991).

43. A more persuasive argument may be that prohibiting the recruitment of child volunteers violates the children's right to associate with the army or specific armed groups. The argument that the interference may be justifiable under Art.15(2), Convention on the Rights of the Child, or any regional equivalent, has not yet been tested.

44. A point noted by the Democratic Republic of Vietnam in its unsuccessful amendment to Art.77(1), Protocol 1: "Persons under eighteen who have been arrested for their patriotism or for their political non-submission shall be set free as soon as possible and before other citizens" (CDDH/111/304).

45. See the evidence of the Quakers in UN Doc.E/CN.4/Sub.2/1989 on the use of child soldiers by the Iranians and also by the Contras in Nicaragua.

OCTOBER 1994]   *Protection of Children in Armed Conflicts*   817

both legal and philosophical limits to the exploitation comparison. The European Commission of Human Rights has observed that the use of children aged over 15 in the military did not amount to forced labour provided there is parental consent to the original recruitment.[46] The exploitation argument admittedly does possess superficial moral attractions. Yet a deeper line of enquiry would raise the question that if armed conflicts are so brutalising that children are unable to consent, why are adults able to consent? For those who advocate the non-participation of children in armed conflict as opposed to the non-participation of all, adults and children, are applying the age-old concept of welfarism, albeit heavily disguised. As Ruskin noted, the aim of soldiering "is not slaying but being slayn".[47]

IV. THE PROTECTION OF CHILD CIVILIANS IN INTERNATIONAL AND INTERNAL ARMED CONFLICTS

THE majority of children become caught up in armed conflicts as civilians. In Cambodia, in 1991, in the three provincial hospitals the ICRC calculated that 10 per cent of the injured were children under the age of 14, and in Thailand, for the first six months of 1992, 15 per cent of 596 mine injuries were to children under 14 years of age. Armed conflicts also claim child victims indirectly.[48] During the Gulf conflict the destruction of canalisation systems caused a proliferation of epidemics and intestinal diseases.[49] According to Iraqi figures, in November 1989, prior to the conflict, 52 children under the age of five died from malnutrition, 96 from diarrhoea and 110 from pneumonia. In November 1992, 592 children under five died from malnutrition, 1,102 from diarrhoea and 1,272 from pneumonia. The figures represent increases of 52, 1,148 and 1,156 per cent.[50] Consequently, it is rather strange that a disproportionate percentage of the world's attention appears to be focused on child soldiers. As Gardam observes, there are few war memorials honouring dead civilian women and children in comparison to the number paying homage to the military dead.[51] More

46. The European Commission found that the young age at which a person enters into military service cannot itself attach the character of servitude to normal military service: *X, Y and Z* v. *United Kingdom* (Applications Nos.3435–38/67 CD 28, 109). However, in this particular case the Commission laid stress on the fact that recruitment had occurred with parental consent.

47. Ruskin, "The Roots of Honour", in *Unto this Last* (1862).

48. UN Doc.E/CN.4/Sub.2/1992/NGO/16.

49. *Ibid.* For indirect effects of conflict generally see Kent, *War and Children's Survival* (1990).

50. All the figures are taken from UN Doc.E/CN.4/1993/77.

51. Gardam, "The Law of Armed Conflict: A Feminist Perspective", in Mahoney and Mahoney (Eds), *Human Rights in the Twenty First Century. A Global Challenge* (1993). The few exceptions are haunting—the single child's shoe in Yad Vashem, Jerusalem where visitors leave the museum and enter the memorial terrace. Only 11% of European Jewish children survived from 1939 to 1945: Dwork, *Children with a Star* (1991).

818   *International and Comparative Law Quarterly*   [VOL. 43

controversially, Morgan postulates that the rationale for the atomic bombing of Hiroshima was that soldiers' lives would be saved but that "women and children were expendable".[52] Hence even during the drafting of the Convention on the Rights of the Child most of the States' attention was focused on the protection of child combatants, the majority of whom are male. Although it is arguable that sufficient safeguards to protect child civilians already exist in Protocols I and II, the blinkered vision of the drafters of the Convention may have contributed to the weakening of standards in respect of child civilians.

Prior to the adoption of the Convention on the Rights of the Child international humanitarian law had begun both to provide special legislative measures to protect child civilians and to implement innovative attempts to protect them in both international and internal armed conflicts. Child civilians benefit from provisions aimed at protecting the civilian population as a whole and from specific provisions found in Protocols I and II providing special measures.[53] In particular, the ICRC and the United Nations Childrens Fund (UNICEF) had built upon the concept of hospital zones,[54] promoting the idea that children caught up in armed conflicts should be regarded as bridges of peace or zones of peace. Broadly defined, this means that both sides have a mutual concern for children so that their needs can be seen as a bridge which all parties to the conflict have an interest in protecting. This adaptation of the concept of a safety zone to be applied not to a specific area but to a specific group of the population requires an imaginative and constructive use of international law. It combines the principles of international humanitarian law with those of international human rights law; specifically Principle 8 of the Declaration of the Rights of the Child 1959, which provides: "The child shall in all circumstances be amongst the first to receive protection and relief."[55] Declaring children as zones of peace, with the consequential cease-fires to allow children to be brought from all over Lebanon and El Salvador for innoculation against life-threatening diseases, is important because it allows for the possibility that if fighting factions are willing, albeit in limited cases, to agree to cease-fires on the basis of respecting the right of the child to health, then the United Nations and its non-governmental partners ought to consider seeking to extend this principle to protect additional rights of children.[56] In addition to zones of peace, inter-governmental organis-

---

52. Morgan, *The Demon Lover: On the Sexuality of Terrorism* (1989), p.132.
53. Arts.77 and 78 Protocol 1 and Art.4(3) Protocol 2: in Van Bueren, *op. cit. supra* n.10.
54. See further Art.14 Geneva Convention 4 establishing hospital and safety zones.
55. The standard is lower than Art.3 Declaration of the Rights of the Child 1924 but was amended to allow relief to be given to medical personnel and others first so that more children could receive the necessary assistance.
56. See e.g. the importance of the right to leisure for children in armed conflict, in Dawson, "Children and the Right to Play" (1993) 1 Int. J. Children's Rights 33.

ations have sought to establish corridors of tranquillity, routes through which food and medical supplies can be transported to those in need of relief.[57] During 1989 Operation Lifeline in Sudan was originally intended to have occurred during a "month of tranquillity", but agreement was not reached between the government and the rebels and a corridor of tranquillity was established instead. The potential of both these approaches ought to be developed further, although only if they are implemented sufficiently early and without some of the publicity stunts, noted by Buckoke, which in the past have risked their devaluation.[58]

Because of contemporary, practical and sometimes successful applications of international humanitarian law concerning child civilians, the expectation was that in incorporating provisions on armed conflicts in the Convention on the Rights of the Child the standards would be raised or at the very least maintained. However, it has been convincingly argued both by the ICRC and by governments and non-governmental organisations that Article 38(4) significantly lowers the standard of protection. Child civilians ought to benefit from the range of international laws which regulate the conduct of hostilities on civilian populations in general. The basic principles which ought to apply include: limitations placed on the means of injuring the enemy; distinctions made between the civilian population and those participating in hostilities (in the conduct of military operations every effort should be made to spare the civilian population); and a prohibition on civilian populations being the objects of reprisals, forcible transfers or other assaults upon their dignity.[59] The principles relating to the protection of the general civilian population from attack are found in the Regulations to Hague Convention 4 (1907) and are reaffirmed and developed in the Geneva Conventions and Protocols. Article 48 of Protocol I (1977) enshrines the basic principle that to protect the civilian population conflicting parties should distinguish not only between the civilian population and combatants but also between "civilian objects and military objectives and accordingly shall direct their operations only against military objectives".[60] These approaches are reiterated, albeit only in nonbinding form, in the Declaration on the Protection of Women and Children in Emergency and Armed Conflict. Article 4 of the Declaration

57. See Art.20(8) World Declaration on the Survival, Protection and Development of Children 1990: in Van Bueren, *op. cit. supra* n.10.

58. For a critical analysis of the role of the Director of Operation Lifeline see Buckoke, *Fishing in Africa—A Guide to War and Corruption* (1991).

59. See Kalshoven, *The Laws of Warfare* (1973), p.28 on the distinctions between civilians and combatants and civilian and military targets. See generally Pictet, *The Principles of International Humanitarian Law* (1966).

60. For a comprehensive analysis see Sandoz, Swinarski and Zimmerman (Eds), *Commentary on the Additional Protocols of 8 June 1977 to the Geneva Conventions of 12 August 1949* (1987). For the relevant treaty provisions see Roberts and Guelff (Eds), *Documents on the Laws of War* (1989).

provides: "All efforts shall be made by States involved in armed conflicts ... to spare women and children from the ravages of war. All the necessary steps shall be taken." Under the Declaration the recommendation is to take "all necessary steps". In unwelcome contrast, Article 38(4) of the Convention on the Rights of the Child incorporates the phrase "all feasible measures" rather than "all necessary measures" as the standard by which States parties are obliged to ensure the protection of children affected by armed conflict.[61] Although Article 38(4) links this duty with their existing obligations under international humanitarian law, and places States parties under a duty to "ensure" children's protection, at the very least, in the heat of battle, Article 38(4) muddies the waters at a time when clarity is most needed. It is also clear from the *travaux préparatoires* that this lowering of standards was brought to the drafting States' attention and, despite being contrary to the best interests of the child and to the principle that children should be the object of special respect, was acceptable to them.[62] Those seeking to protect child civilians are forced to rely upon either international customary law[63] or the provisions of Article 41, which states that nothing in the Convention on the Rights of the Child "shall affect" any provisions in applicable international law which are "more conducive to the realisation of the rights of the child". For States which are party to the Geneva Conventions and Protocols the higher standard will apply. However, the alarm bell ought to begin to ring when the majority of States negotiating a treaty on children's rights are willing to risk giving children's lives a lower priority than military feasibility.

V. CHILDREN, FAMILY LIFE AND ARMED CONFLICTS

THE principle of family unity is undoubtedly easier to apply in times of peace than during armed conflicts. Any decision to allow children to remain with their families in danger in conflict zones or to remove children from the conflict, thus separating the family, is fraught with difficulty. Unlike deportation or forcible transfers evacuation is a provisional measure which should be taken only in the best interests of the child, because

61. "In accordance with their obligations under international humanitarian law to protect the civilian population in armed conflicts, States Parties shall take all feasible measures to ensure protection and care of children who are affected by an armed conflict."
62. See in particular the comments of Sweden and Switzerland at UN Doc.E/CN.4/1987/25. The principle that children should be the object of special respect is found in Art. 77(1) Protocol I.
63. See the remarks by Lt.-Col. B. Carnahan (of the Joint Chiefs of Staff in his personal capacity) that Arts.77 and 78 of Protocol I "were likely candidates eventually to reflect general practice recognised as law". Cited in Meron, *Human Rights and Humanitarian Norms* (1989), p.66.

children have to leave their home and family environment and move into an unknown environment. In assessing the best interests of the child, the starting point for Geneva Convention IV is the physical safety of the child. States balanced the damage to a child through family separation against the risks of injury in a conflict zone and believed that less harm would come to children through evacuation. They recognised that, no matter how well organised, child welfare measures may not be able to guarantee the safety of children in countries at war. Hence Article 17 encourages the conflicting parties to conclude local agreements to provide for the evacuation of children from besieged and encircled areas. In the light of Article 24, if appropriate, such agreements may help facilitate the evacuation of children under 15 and those orphaned or separated from their families to a neutral country. Two safeguards are incorporated. First, all children both national and alien can be evacuated only if the country of reception can provide for their maintenance, education and the exercise of their religion.[64] Second, the consent of the protecting powers is required before children of enemy nationality are evacuated, so as to prevent children from being evacuated to countries from which they may never return.

At the end of the Greek Civil War (1945–6) 30,000 Greek children were evacuated to a number of foreign countries and, although the repatriation negotiations began in 1948, it was not until the early 1950s that several thousand children were returned.[65] Partly because of the period of time involved an uncertainty developed as to whether evacuation was, as had been assumed, in the best interests of the child. UNESCO commissioned a study, *War Handicapped Children*, which found that:[66]

> it is not the fact of war itself—such as bombings, military operations—which have affected him emotionally ... It is the repercussion of events on the family affective ties and the separation of his customary framework of life which affects the child and more than anything the abrupt separation from his mother.

Thus, although the Convention does not make evacuation compulsory, Brosse's findings undermine the belief, incorporated in Geneva Convention IV, that remaining in situations of physical danger is frequently contrary to the best interests of the child. Brosse's report was commissioned, unfortunately, only after the drafting and adoption of the four Geneva

---

64. Art.24 Geneva Convention 4.

65. See generally Ressler, Boothby and Steinbock, *Unaccompanied Children—Care and Protection in Wars, Natural Disasters and Refugee Movements* (1988).

66. Brosse, *War Handicapped Children* (UNESCO, 1950). See also Freud and Burlingham, *War and Children* (1943) and Bryce, *Cries of Children in Lebanon: As Voiced by their Mothers* (UNICEF, 1986).

822 *International and Comparative Law Quarterly* [VOL. 43

Conventions, and its conclusions were therefore unable to exert any influence on the substance of the evacuation provisions. The report's conclusions, however, were presented to the Conference of Government Experts in 1972 and its influence is reflected in Article 78 of Protocol I, which begins with a resounding negative and incorporates the word "temporary".[67] The Article places greater weight on the psychological consequences of the separation of children, and provides an exhaustive list of reasons for evacuation—health, medical treatment or safety—which must be fulfilled. As exceptions they are specific and narrowly drawn. Even narrower are the grounds for evacuation of children in occupied territories, who may be evacuated by the occupying power only for reasons of medical treatment or health. It was felt that the dangers of an occupying power abusing its discretion are greater than the dangers of prohibiting evacuation for safety reasons.[68] An additional safeguard is that both in the State's own territory and in occupied territory the written consent of the parents or guardians is required.

In Bosnia and Herzegovina a particular problem has arisen with regard to family unity as it affects "the children who have been born or are expected to be born in the near future, as a result of rape".[69] In the past, errors have been made with the placement of children for adoption in relation to both Cambodia and Operation Babylift out of Vietnam. Children were placed in cultures alien to their own and some subsequently discovered that they had living family members.[70] The current international standards require that inter-country adoption may be considered only if a child cannot be cared for in a suitable manner in the child's country of origin.[71] As Ressler observes, no course of action will be ideal but in relation to the children in Bosnia and Herzegovina, of whom there are more than 600,000 under six years of age, 281,000 of them in besieged cities, it is clear that all children cannot be evacuated.[72] The emphasis away from evacuation together with current international instruments concerning inter-country adoptions, including the recently adopted Hague Convention on Protection of Children and Cooperation in Respect of

67. "No party to the conflict shall arrange for the evacuation of children other than its own nationals to a foreign country except for a temporary evacuation where compelling reasons of the health of or medical treatment of the children or except in occupied territory, their safety so requires."
68. O.R.vx 466. CDDH/407/rev.1, para.66.
69. See Special Rapporteur's report, *supra* n.1, at p.21.
70. Ressler, *Evacuation of Children from Conflict Areas; Considerations and Guidelines* (1992).
71. Art.21(b) Convention on the Rights of the Child: in Van Bueren, *op. cit. supra* n.10. See also Williamson and Moser, *Unaccompanied Children in Emergencies: A Field Guide for their Care and Protection* (1987) for recommendations to avoid similar errors.
72. Ressler, "Considerations in the Evacuation of Children in the Former Yugoslavia" (1993) 1 Int. J. Children's Rights 331.

Intercountry Adoption,[73] seek to avoid such errors as well as minimising the risk of trafficking in babies born as a result of rape; a risk which will diminish provided these babies are not stigmatised.[74]

VI.   THE PROVISION OF RECOVERY AND REINTEGRATION SERVICES FOR CHILD VICTIMS OF ARMED CONFLICTS

THE potential of the Convention on the Rights of the Child to assist child victims of armed conflict by obliging States parties to promote the provision of psychological recovery and social reintegration for child victims of war is an innovation in international law.[75] The breadth of the provision means that it is capable of applying to child soldiers and civilians, and such services have been recommended as benefiting the child victims of rape in the territory of the former Yugoslavia.[76] The guiding principle for all recovery and reintegration programmes for war-traumatised children is that they should take place in environments which foster the health, self-respect and dignity of the children.[77] Since the Convention has been adopted UNICEF has initiated programmes in Croatia and Serbia training professionals to identify and counsel children displaying symptoms of war.[78]

The scope of Article 39 is illustrated by several pioneering pilot schemes which predated the Convention. In Uganda, after the end of the civil war the government was faced with the integration of 3,000 child soldiers into the school system.[79] There was much debate over whether the children should be educated with other children or in military academies. Partly because of the difficulties that these children faced in reintegrating into the schools and the effect upon the other children, they stayed in the military academies where they continued their education. In Mozambique the government together with Save the Children established a rehabilitation centre to assist children who were abducted into the Mozambique National Resistance and forced to witness and participate in killings. The centre's staff—medical practitioners, psychologists and

73. Adopted 28 May 1993; see further Duncan, "Regulating Intercountry Adoption—An International Perspective", in Bainham and Pearl (Eds), *Frontiers of Family Law* (1993). For a critical analysis see Cantwell, "The Hague Convention on Intercountry Adoption—Will it Work?" (1993) 10 Int. Children's Rights Monitor 22.

74. Recommendation B2 in *For the Protection of the Rights of Unaccompanied Children in Former Yugoslavia*, Report of the Joint Mission of UNICEF, UNHCR and DCI in collaboration with the Hague Conference on Private International Law 1993.

75. Art.39 Convention on the Rights of the Child, which is far broader than Art.14 Convention Against Torture and Other Cruel, Inhuman or Degrading Treatment or Punishment 1984.

76. For rehabilitation generally see UN Doc.E/CN.4/1993/NGO/1.

77. Art.39 Convention on the Rights of the Child.

78. *UNICEF News*, April/May 1993.

79. Cole, *War, Violence and Children in Uganda* (1987).

social workers—work with children so that they are able to resume fuller lives back in the community.[80]

There are, however, inherent dangers with rehabilitation. Indoctrination can masquerade as recovery and reintegration. In Afghanistan boys who had been trained as spies by the Soviet Afghan authorities and were captured by the Mujahadin were "rehabilitated" and trained to spy for the Mujahadin.[81]

One of the serious impediments to States implementing Article 39 is that governments are not always willing to acknowledge the need for rehabilitative services, particularly if they concern children who are in the State's care as prisoners of war.[82] Criticism has been levelled at governments for the lengthy periods of time for which children are detained as child prisoners of war. In Iraq, in Ramadi 8 Prisoner of War Camp near Baghdad, Terres des Hommes and Defence for Children International provided educational instruction for 150 of the 800 Iranian child prisoners of war.[83] The instruction was both general and vocational. In 1989, however, the Iraqi authorities terminated the project as the government maintained, despite objections from the non-governmental organisations, that there were insufficient child prisoners of war to merit the continuation of the programme.[84]

Because of the recent origins of the legal duty upon States to provide recovery and reintegration services for child victims of armed conflict, information is scarce. Hence this is one area where the comparative data produced by States parties' reports under the Convention on the Rights of the Child may prove of particular value.[85]

VII.   IMPROVING THE IMPLEMENTATION OF THE RIGHTS OF THE CHILD IN ARMED CONFLICT[86]

THE Committee on the Rights of the Child held a special session on children in armed conflicts which concluded, *inter alia*,[87] in a recommendation for an additional Protocol to the Convention seeking to raise the mini-

---

80. See further Hammarberg, Benigno Aquino Human Rights Lecture, Yale University, 1989; Boothby, "Reclaiming the Killing Field", *Duke Perspectives* (Duke University, 1990).

81. "To Win the Children: Afghanistan's Other War" *Helsinki/Asia Watch* (1986), p.19.

82. There is no minimum age above which an individual qualifies as a prisoner of war.

83. Van Bueren, "Special Features of the Assistance and Protection of Children as Victims of Armed Conflict", in Kalshoven (Ed.), *Assisting the Victims of Armed Conflict and Other Disasters* (1989), p.129.

84. Condor, Terres des Hommes, unpublished paper at International Congress for the Prevention of Child Abuse and Neglect 1990.

85. States parties have a duty to submit to the Committee on the Rights of the Child reports on the progress made: Art.44 Convention on the Rights of the Child.

86. Kent, "Implementing the Rights of Children in Armed Conflict", Working Paper No.1. University of Hawaii (1992).

87. In addition, the Committee requested the Secretary-General to undertake a study of the protection of the rights of children in armed conflict. UN Doc.CRC/C/16.

mum ages for child recruitment and participation. However, such an approach is too simplistic. El Salvador, for example, which is party both to Protocol II and to the Convention on the Rights of the Child, has established the age of 18 as the minimum age of recruitment, yet eyewitness reports allege conscription of boys as young as 14.[88] Sometimes a disproportionate amount of energy is expended in seeking to raise standards, leaving less resources for their implementation.[89] Building upon his experience as a former Secretary-General of Amnesty International, the Swedish member of the Committee on the Rights of the Child has advocated the creation of a procedure allowing "urgent responses",[90] which would be an exceptional measure to be used by the Committee in serious, urgent situations entailing a risk of further violations and hence particularly suited to armed conflicts.[91] In such situations the Committee would address a letter to the government concerned, setting out the information available, referring to the relevant articles of the Convention and requesting a response. The response would be regarded as part of the dialogue between the State party and the Committee. Such interim measures are particularly necessary as, after their initial reports, States parties are under a duty to report only every five years.[92]

It is this type of constructive approach, working within the boundaries of the treaty, which needs to be explored more fully before seeking to raise minimum ages, which even at their present levels are not always honoured. The first application by the Committee on the Rights of the Child of its powers under Article 45(c), in calling for a report by the Secretary-General[93] on a study of the ways and means of improving the protection of children from the adverse effects of armed conflicts, ought to provide an excellent opportunity for such an examination.[94] Instead of focusing exclusively on treaty amendment alternatives need to be provided so that children are not attracted to army life because it provides them with basic necessities and a replacement for a lost family structure. Similarly, provision has to be made for children to feel they are making some form of alternative valuable contribution.[95] Although there are areas requiring a

88. The Friends World Committee for Consultation Society of Friends (Quakers) publishes a regular newsletter (Ed. Woods) detailing such incidents.
89. See discussions in *op. cit. supra* n.42.
90. Urgent responses rather than urgent appeals to distinguish the actions of the Committee from those of non-governmental organisations.
91. Hammarberg at CRC/C/SR 42.
92. Art.44(1)(b).
93. UN Doc.CRC/C/16.
94. Similarly, Res.4(1993) of the Council of Delegates of the International Red Cross and Red Crescent Movement calling for the ICRC and the International Federation of Red Cross and Red Crescent Societies in co-operation with the Henri Dunant Institute to draw up and implement a plan of action aimed at the promoting the non-recruitment and non-participation of children below 18: in (1993) 297 Int. Rev. Red Cross 493.
95. Such as the driving of ambulances, as occurred in Lebanon.

raising of standards, particularly the distinctions between recruitment and participation and direct and indirect participation, the proposed draft Protocol additional to the Convention on the Rights of the Child will represent a squandered opportunity if its sole purpose is the raising of minimum ages.[96]

96. This is at present the case: see the Preliminary Draft Optional Protocol on Involvement of Children in Armed Conflicts Annex VII at UN Doc.CRC/C/16.

[12]

Protection of Women
in Armed Conflict

Judith Gardam* & Hilary Charlesworth**

I. INTRODUCTION

Women increasingly bear the major burden of armed conflict.[1] In recent
years particular attention has been given to the question of violence against
women in armed conflict.[2] The significance of these developments is
considerable. However, the focus on violence—in particular on sexual

* *Judith Gardam* is Reader in Law, The University of Adelaide.
** *Hilary Charlesworth* is Director of the Centre for International and Public Law, The
Australian National University.
    The authors are grateful to Michelle Jarvis for the valuable contribution she made to this
paper and to Susannah Reddick for her research assistance. The preparation of this paper
was assisted by a grant from the Australian Research Council.

1. *See* Statement of Renée Guisan, Member of the Int'l Comm. of the Red Cross, to the
    Fourth World Conference on Women, Beijing, China, 4 Sept. 1995, *available on* <http://
    www.icrc.org/icrceng.nsf/3c31e92a906daf86412561f60050d211/8a19d95f10b98fe
    641256251002d8360?OpenDocument> (visited 18 Nov. 1999); *Fourth World Confer-
    ence on Women: Action for Equality, Development, and Peace, Beijing Declaration and
    Platform for Action,* U.N. GAOR, U.N. Doc. A/CONF.177/20 (1995), *reprinted in* Report
    of the Fourth World Conference on Women (1995) (recommended to the UN General
    Assembly by the Committee on the Status of Women on 7 Oct. 1995) [hereinafter
    Beijing Platform for Action]. *See also Report to the Secretary-General on Humanitarian
    Needs in Kuwait and Iraq in the Immediate Post-Crisis Environment by a Mission to the
    Area Led by Mr. Martti Ahtisaari, Under-Secretary-General for Administration and
    Management, Dated 20 March 1991,* U.N. SCOR, U.N. Doc. S/22366 (1991); Amnesty
    International, Report on the Gulf War (1991); Human Rights Watch, Needless Deaths in the
    Gulf War (1991), Harvard Study Team Report: Public Health in Iraq After the Gulf War
    (1991); Harvard Study Team Report: Health and Welfare in Iraq After the Gulf Crisis (1991)
    [hereinafter Health and Welfare in Iraq].
2. *See, e.g., Report of the Special Rapporteur on Violence Against Women, Its Causes and
    Consequences, Ms. Radhika Coomaraswamy, Submitted in Accordance with Commis-
    sion on Human Rights Resolution 1997/44,* U.N. ESCOR, Comm'n on Hum. Rts., 54th
    Sess., Agenda Item 9(a), U.N. Doc. E/CN.4/1998/54 (1998); *Preliminary Report of the*

violence[3]—tends to obscure other important aspects of women's experience of armed conflict that to date have been largely ignored.[4] The purpose of this comment is to consider a range of ways in which women are affected by armed conflict and to assess the adequacy of international law in protecting them. This issue is, in theory, on the international agenda. For example, the 1995 Beijing Platform for Action calls on "[g]overnments, the international community and civil society, including non-governmental organisations and the private sector . . . to take strategic action" in relation

---

Special Rapporteur on the Situation of Systematic Rape, Sexual Slavery and Slavery-like Practices During Periods of Armed Conflict, Ms. Linda Chavez, U.N. ESCOR, Comm'n on Hum. Rts., 48th Sess., Agenda Item 15, U.N. Doc. E/CN.4/Sub.2/1996/26 (1996). See also Vienna Declaration and Programme of Action, U.N. GAOR, World Conf. on Hum. Rts., 48th Sess., 22d plen. mtg., part I, U.N. Doc. A/CONF.157/24 (1993), reprinted in 32 I.L.M. 1661 (1993); Declaration on the Elimination of Violence Against Women, adopted 20 Dec. 1993, G.A. Res. 48/104, U.N. GAOR, 48th Sess., 85th plen. mtg., U.N. Doc. A/RES/48/104 (1993), reprinted in Human Rights and Disabled Persons: Essays and Relevant Human Rights Instruments *416 (Theresia Degener & Yolan Koster-Dreese eds., 1995); Beijing Platform for Action, supra note 1, ¶¶ 131, 136.*

3. *See, e.g.,* Human Rights Watch, Untold Terror: Violence Against Women in Peru's Armed Conflict: A Report by Americas Watch and Women's Rights Project (1992); Amnesty International, Bosnia-Herzegovina: Rape and Sexual Abuse by Armed Forces (1993); 2 Helsinki Watch, War Crimes in Bosnia-Hercegovina 18, 163–86 (1992); *Final Report of the Commission of Experts Established Pursuant to Security Council Resolution 780 (1992),* U.N. SCOR, U.N. Doc. S/1994/674/Annex (1994) (considering the issue of rape and sexual assault at ¶¶ 58–60, 232–53); African Rights, Rwanda: Death, Despair and Defiance, (rev. ed. 1995); Human Rights Watch Women's Rights Project, Human Rights Watch Global Report on Women's Human Rights 100–38 (1995) (relating to sexual assault of refugees and displaced women); Human Rights Watch, Shattered Lives: Sexual Violence During the Rwandan Genocide and its Aftermath (1996) [hereinafter Shattered Lives].

4. An exception to this focus on sexual violence is the work of ECOSOC, particularly in relation to Palestinian women and children in occupied territories. *See, e.g., Situation of Women and Children in the Occupied Arab Territories,* U.N. ESCOR, Comm'n on Hum. Rts., 22d plen. mtg., U.N. Doc. E/RES/1982/18 (1982); *Situation of Palestinians Within and Outside the Occupied Territories,* U.N. ESCOR, Comm'n on Hum. Rts., 19th plen. mtg., U.N. Doc. E/RES/1984/18 (1984); *Situation of Palestinian Women,* U.N. ESCOR, Comm'n on Hum. Rts., 15th plen. mtg., U.N. Doc. E/RES/1988/25 (1988); *Situation of Palestinian Women,* U.N. ESCOR, Comm'n on Hum. Rts., 13th plen. mtg., U.N. Doc. E/RES/1990/11 (1990); *Situation of and Assistance to Palestinian Women,* U.N. ESCOR, Comm'n on Hum. Rts., 12th plen. mtg., U.N. Doc. E/RES/1991/19 (1991); *Situation of and Assistance to Palestinian Women,* U.N. ESCOR, Comm'n on Hum. Rts., 40th plen. mtg., U.N. Doc. E/RES/1992/16 (1992); *Situation of and Assistance to Palestinian Women,* U.N. ESCOR, Comm'n on the Status of Women, 43d plen. mtg., U.N. Doc. E/RES/1993/15 (1993); *Palestinian Women,* U.N. ESCOR, Comm'n on the Status of Women, 51st plen. mtg., U.N. Doc. E/RES/1995/30 (1995). See also ECOSOC resolutions dealing with women and children in Namibia. *E.g., Women and Children in Namibia,* U.N. ESCOR, Comm'n on the Status of Women, 15th plen. mtg., U.N. Doc. E/RES/1988/24 (1988); *Women and Children in Namibia,* U.N. ESCOR, Comm'n on the Status of Women, 15th plen. mtg., U.N. Doc. E/RES/1989/31 (1989); *Women and Children in Namibia,* U.N. ESCOR, Comm'n on the Status of Women, 13th plen. mtg., U.N. Doc. E/RES/1990/6 (1990). *See also* Human Rights Watch, The Human Rights Watch Global Report on Women's Human Rights 1–96 (1995).

to the "[t]he effects of armed or other kinds of conflict on women, including those living under foreign occupation."[5] However, the available information is fragmented, making "strategic action" difficult to formulate.

Considerable work has been done regarding women and armed conflict by institutions concerned with human rights violations against women generally. Indeed, the process of identifying women's particular experiences and demonstrating the failure of the law to acknowledge them is more advanced in this context than in organizations focusing solely on armed conflict.[6] However, even when gender-based violence is addressed in these fora, the wider aspect of the problem is ignored.[7] Traditionally, reports and studies on the effects of armed conflict tend to incorporate women in the general category of civilians without regard to the different experiences of men and women civilians. The particular concerns of women have, to date, been regarded as peripheral in such analyses. For example, until recently, sexual violence against women was regarded as an inevitable aspect of armed conflict.[8]

We now have evidence that women experience armed conflict in a different way than men.[9] These effects differ widely across cultures depending upon the role of women in particular societies. One thing is clear: armed conflict often exacerbates inequalities (in this context, those based on gender) that exist in different forms and to varying degrees in all societies[10] and that make women particularly vulnerable when armed conflict breaks out. Of the more than one billion people living in poverty

---

5. *Beijing Platform for Action, supra* note 1, ¶ 44.
6. This process is particularly marked in the context of the work of the United Nations High Commission on Refugees (UNHCR) in relation to refugee women. *See* UNHCR, *Policy on Refugee Women, in* UNHCR Guidelines on the Protection of Refugee Women (1991) [hereinafter UNHCR Guidelines]; UNHCR, Sexual Violence Against Refugees: Guidelines on Prevention and Response (1995) [hereinafter Sexual Violence Against Refugees]. *See also* Christine Chinkin, *Feminist Interventions into International Law,* 19 Adel. L. Rev. 13, 16 (1997).
7. *See generally* Julie Mertus & Pamela Goldberg, *A Perspective on Women and International Human Rights after the Vienna Declaration: The Inside/Outside Construct,* 26 N.Y.U.J. Int'l L. & Pol. 201 (1994).
8. *See* Christine Chinkin, *Rape and Sexual Abuse of Women in International Law Issues,* 5 Eur. J. Int'l L. 326 (1994). Many other examples exist of the invisibility of women's experience of armed conflict. *See* Judith Gardam, *Women and the Law of Armed Conflict: Why the Silence?, in* 46 Int'l & Comp. L.Q. 55, 59–61 (1997).
9. Interview with Dorothy Thomas, Human Rights Watch, New York (June 1996); Interview with Louise Doswald-Beck, ICRC, Geneva (June 1997); Interview with Ariane Brunet, Women's Rights Coordinator, Canada Programme, International Centre for Human Rights and Democratic Development, Montreal (Nov. 1997).
10. Interview with Marco Sassoli, formerly of the Division for Promotion of International Humanitarian Law, Delegate to Academic Circles, ICRC, Geneva (June 1997). *See also Beijing Platform for Action, supra* note 1, ¶ 136.

today, the great majority are women.[11] They are, moreover, generally disadvantaged in terms of education and are considerably less mobile because of their traditional role in caring for others.[12] Further, these inequalities continue after the cessation of hostilities. Women are often excluded from the reconstruction processes that take place after armed conflict as well as from peacebuilding initiatives.[13]

The rules of International Humanitarian Law (IHL) are intended to provide protection for victims of armed conflict.[14] This regime has been criticized as inadequate in performing its task in modern-day armed conflict. In addition, many practitioners and academics regard law as largely irrelevant in armed conflict or place more confidence in the ability of human rights law, rather than IHL, to adapt itself to provide effective safeguards for the protection of the victims of armed conflict. Whatever the

---

11. The feminization of poverty was a key area of concern at the Beijing Conference. *See Beijing Platform for Action, supra* note 1, ¶¶ 47–59. *See also African Platform for Action adopted by the Fifth Regional Conference on Women, held at Dakar from 16 to 23 November 1994,* U.N. ESCOR, Comm'n on the Status of Women, 39th Sess., ¶ 25, U.N. Doc. E/CN.6/1995/5/Add.2 (1994); *Report of the Secretary-General, Second Review and Appraisal of the Implementation of the Nairobi Forward-looking Strategies for the Advancement of Women,* U.N. ESCOR, Comm'n on the Status of Women, 39th Sess., Agenda Item 3(b), ¶ 92, U.N. Doc. E/CN.6/1995/3/Add.1 (1995).

12. *See* INT'L COMM. OF THE RED CROSS, WOMEN & WAR (1995), *available on* <http://www.icrc.org/icrceng.nsf/8ec4e051a8621595c12564670032d7ef/63fa9b7bbd8e677e4125622d0033e0d9?OpenDocument> (visited 18 Nov. 1999).

13. In the context of Palestinian women, see Hilary Charlesworth, *International Human Rights Law: Prospects and Problems for Palestinian Women, in* HUMAN RIGHTS: SELF-DETERMINATION AND POLITICAL CHANGE IN THE OCCUPIED PALESTINIAN TERRITORIES 79, 81–85 (Stephen Bowen ed., 1997). *See also* Anonymous, *Stop Press: Emergency Appeal, Women in Somalia,* 3–4 CHANGING THE WORLD: A NEWS BULLETIN ON WOMEN'S MOVEMENTS AROUND THE WORLD AND CHANGE'S ACTIVITIES 8 (1992); Tosca Looby, *Women in Bougainville,* 42 REFRACTORY GIRL 66, 66–67 (1992).

14. *See* Geneva Convention (I) for the Amelioration of the Condition of the Wounded and Sick in Armed Forces in the field, 12 Aug. 1949, 6 U.S.T. 3114, 75 U.N.T.S. 31 (*entered into force* 21 Oct. 1950) (*entered into force for U.S.* 2 Feb. 1956) [hereinafter Geneva I]; Geneva Convention (II) for the Amelioration of the Condition of Wounded, Sick and Shipwrecked Members of Armed Forces at Sea, 12 Aug. 1949, 6 U.S.T. 3217, 75 U.N.T.S. 85 (*entered into force* 21 Oct. 1950) (*entered into force for U.S.* 2 Feb. 1956) [hereinafter Geneva II]; Geneva Convention (III) Relative to the Treatment of Prisoners of War, 12 Aug. 1949, 6 U.S.T. 3316, 75 U.N.T.S. 135 (*entered into force* 21 Oct. 1950) (*entered into force for U.S.* 2 Feb. 1956) [hereinafter Geneva III]; Geneva Convention (IV) Relative to the Protection of Civilian Persons in Time of War, 12 Aug. 1948, 6 U.S.T. 3516, 75 U.N.T.S. 287 (*entered into force* 21 Oct. 1950) (*entered into force for U.S.* 2 Feb. 1956) [hereinafter Geneva IV]. Protocol (I) Additional to the Geneva Conventions of 12 August 1949, and Relating to the Protection of Victims of International Armed Conflicts (Protocol I), 8 June 1977, 1125 U.N.T.S. 3 (*entered into force* 7 Dec. 1978), *reprinted in* 16 I.L.M. 1391 (1977) [hereinafter Protocol I]; Protocol (II) Additional to the Geneva Conventions of 12 August 1949, and Relating to the Protection of Victims of Non-International Armed Conflicts (Protocol II), 8 June 1977, 1125 U.N.T.S. 609 (*entered into force* 7 Dec. 1978), *reprinted in* 16 I.L.M. 1442 (1977) [hereinafter Protocol II].

general inadequacies of IHL, it is clear that its provisions operate in a discriminatory fashion in relation to women.[15]

II. WOMEN'S EXPERIENCE OF ARMED CONFLICT

Armed conflict is by no means always negative in its impact on women. Indeed for some women it can be a time of empowerment as they take over roles traditionally performed by men.[16] In some cases armed conflict removes abusive partners from the home and allows women the opportunity to develop new skills.[17] Upon the cessation of hostilities, however, many of these advantages are lost.[18] Overall, an assessment of the effect of armed conflict on women requires a consideration of a wide variety of factors, the relevance and impact of which differ considerably among cultures and individual women within those cultures. It is easy to over-simplify the issues, and to misinterpret the impact on women of events that take place in conflict situations. Nevertheless, it is possible to identify some common themes that warrant closer scrutiny.

Overall, women are most likely to experience conflict as civilians. Many armed struggles, however, do involve a significant number of female combatants.[19] Their treatment by the military institution reflects the subordinate position of women in society generally.[20] The experiences and needs of women combatants during captivity differ from that of men. Although the

---

15. *See* Gardam, *supra* note 8, at 67–77.
16. *See* Gail Braybon & Penny Summerfield, Out of the Cage: Women's Experiences in Two World Wars (1987); Sarah Fishman, *Waiting for the Captive Sons of France: Prisoner of War Wives, 1940–1945, in* Behind the Lines 182 (Margaret Randolph Higonnet et al. eds., 1987); Janna Thompson, *Women and War,* 14 Women's Stud. Int'l F. 63 (1991).
17. *See* Alexandra McLeod, *Marking Time in Tuzla* Manchester Guardian Wkly., 26 May 1996.
18. *See* Hibaaq I. Osman, *Somalia: Will Reconstruction Threaten Women's Progress?,* Ms. Magazine, Mar./Apr. 1993, at 12; *Report of the Expert of the Secretary–General, Ms. Graça Machel, Submitted Pursuant to General Assembly Resolution 48/157,* U.N. GAOR, 51st Sess., ¶ 88, U.N. Doc. A/51/306 (1996) [hereinafter *Machel*]; Fishman, *supra* note 16, at 193; Penny Summerfield, *Women in the Two World Wars,* 23 Historian 3 (1989).
19. *See* United Nations, *Women: Victims of Violence, Advocates of Peace, in* Women: Challenges to the Year 2000, at 65, U.N. Sales No. E.91.I.21 (1991); Francoise Krill, *The Protection of Women in International Humanitarian Law,* 249 Int'l Rev. Red Cross 337 (1985).
20. *See Gender-based Persecution: Report of the Expert Group Meeting,* U.N. GAOR, Division for the Advancement of Women, ¶ 52, U.N. Doc. EGM/GBP/1997/Report (1997), *available on* <gopher://gopher.un.org:70/00/esc/cn6/1998/armedcon/GBP97.EN> (visited 18 Nov. 1999) [hereinafter *Report of the Expert Group Meeting*]. *See also* Canadian Centre For Foreign Policy and Development, Options: Report on the Roundtable on Gender and Peacebuilding 36 (1997) (discussing the different needs of women with regard to demobilization).

Third Geneva Convention provides for such matters as separate dormitories and conveniences for women prisoners of war, it does not deal adequately with issues such as reproductive health.[21]

As members of the civilian population women experience distinctive economic problems in armed conflict. In many cases women are separated from the men who traditionally may be their source of income. Lack of education and training, their role in caring for others, and general community attitudes makes it extremely difficult for women to support themselves financially.[22] In many cultures, moreover, it is women who have the most to gain from economic development, and are thus particularly disadvantaged when these resources are diverted during armed conflict.[23]

Many other cultural factors exacerbate the economic problems suffered by women in armed conflict. For instance, armed conflict often forces women from their homes. In fact, women civilians are generally the first to be evacuated when hostilities break out. Evacuation, although desirable in many ways, can lead to considerable hardship. Evacuees are generally exposed to foreign—and often inadequate—living conditions and, consequently, tend to be more prone to accidents, injuries, and disease. There may also be an increased risk of pregnancy as contraception is generally not readily available, and women are likely to be dislocated from many basic health services.[24] Further, refugees and internally displaced persons—a large percentage of whom are women and girl children[25]—are an almost inevitable result of armed conflict, and the problem is growing.[26] Evidence exists of widespread mistreatment of women in refugee camps.[27] These women also face distinctive problems that are largely unacknowledged as they attempt to rebuild their lives as refugees in a new country.[28]

---

21. *See* Geneva III, *supra* note 14, arts. 14, 25, 29.
22. *See Report of the Special Rapporteur on Violence Against Women, Its Causes and Consequences, Ms. Radhika Coomaraswamy, Submitted in Accordance with Commission on Human Rights Resolution 1995/85, Economic and Social Consequences*, U.N. ESCOR, Comm'n on Hum. Rts., 52d Sess., Agenda Item 9(a), addendum 2, ¶ 1, U.N. Doc. E/CN.4/1996/53/Add. 2 (1996). *See also Beijing Platform for Action, supra* note 1, ¶¶ 72–81, 152–66 (detailing the inadequacy of the education of women, not just during armed conflict).
23. *See* Jeanne Vickers, Women and War 25, 90 (1993).
24. *See* UNHCR Guidelines, *supra* note 6, at 7, 51–54.
25. *See Beijing Platform for Action, supra* note 1, ¶ 136 (estimating that 80 percent of refugees are women). *See also* Carolyn Moorhead, *Hostage to the Male Agenda*, Index on Censorship, July/Aug. 1995, at 68; Adam Jones, *Gender and Ethnic Conflict in Ex-Yugoslavia*, 17 Ethnic & Racial Stud. 115, 119 (1994).
26. *See Machel, supra* note 18, ¶¶ 26, 62–64.
27. *See* UNHCR, The State of the World's Refugees, ¶ 76 (1993) [hereinafter The State of the World's Refugees]; Sexual Violence Against Refugees, *supra* note 6; Anonymous, *Human Rights are Women's Rights*, 25 Amnesty Int'l Report, 1995, at 3–4.
28. *See, e.g.,* Susan Forbes Martin, Refugee Women 6–15 (1991). *See also Beijing Platform for Action, supra* note 1, ¶ 137.

The reproductive role of women generally makes them particularly vulnerable to shortages in medicine, reliable birth control, and medical treatment.[29] The absence of medical services and basic supplies has vastly different implications for women than for men. Male relief workers and officials have treated the provision of sanitary towels (or the appropriate items given the cultural practices of the women concerned) as a minor concern. This is not the reality for women—for women such matters are basic to their dignity and well being. Despite some resistance within the organization, The Office of the UN High Commissioner for Refugees (UNHCR) now ensures that sanitary towels are included in supplies to refugees.

Where food is scarce, women are more prone to malnutrition than men.[30] Cultural factors may contribute to this situation. For example, tradition often dictates that men are to eat first, followed by women.[31] The imposition of economic sanctions associated with armed conflict, moreover, exacerbates the special difficulties experienced by women during times of conflict. This phenomenon has been convincingly demonstrated by the sanctions regime imposed on Iraq during and after the Persian Gulf War.[32] Some have called for compulsory and continuous monitoring of the impact of sanctions upon children.[33] The same should apply for women.

A significant proportion of official and non-governmental aid fails to reach women survivors.[34] Almost invariably, men are placed in charge of the decision-making process regarding humanitarian assistance and its

---

29. See *European Community Investigative Mission into the Treatment of Muslim Women in the Former Yugoslavia: Report to European Community Foreign Ministers*, U.N. SCOR, Annex I, U.N. Doc. S/25240 (1993); FORBES MARTIN, *supra* note 28.
30. See Anonymous, *Sisterhood is Global*, 3 Ms. MAGAZINE, Sept./Oct. 1992, at 10; Looby, *supra* note 13, at 67. *See also Implementation of Article 21 of the Convention on the Elimination of All Forms of Discrimination Against Women: Report to the Committee on the Elimination of Discrimination Against Women on the Work of the World Health Organization in the Area of Women, Health and Development*, U.N. GAOR, Comm. on the Elimination of Discrimination Against Women, Annex, ¶ 8, U.N. Doc. CEDAW/C/1996/3/Add.1 (1995), *available on* <gopher://gopher.un.org:70/00/ga/cedaw/15/1996-3a1.en> (visited 18 Nov. 1999).
31. In 1995, the International Committee of the Red Cross (ICRC) reported that 38 percent of Kabul's residents surveyed in January of that year suffered from malnutrition. The figure was much higher amongst girls, because in Afghan culture boys are fed first, and girls frequently receive only leftovers. *See* UNHCR GUIDELINES, *supra* note 6, at 49.
32. See, e.g., Bela Bhatia et al., *Unheard Voices: Iraqi Women on War and Sanctions*, CHANGE INTERNATIONAL REPORTS: THINKBOOK VIII (1992). *See also* HEALTH AND WELFARE IN IRAQ, *supra* note 1 (detailing the impact of the Gulf conflict on women's everyday lives).
33. See Machel, *supra* note 18, ¶ ¶ 127–30.
34. See Joan Fitzpatrick, *The Use of International Human Rights Norms to Combat Violence Against Women*, in HUMAN RIGHTS OF WOMEN: NATIONAL AND INTERNATIONAL PERSPECTIVES 532 (Rebecca J. Cook ed., 1994); Fred Pelka, *Voices from the War Zone*, 55 THE HUMANIST, Mar./Apr. 1995, at 6–10.

distribution, despite the fact that women are generally far more experienced in food production, distribution, and preparation than men.[35] Consequently, women are frequently disadvantaged, either deliberately or because their needs are not properly understood.[36] Further, the balance of sexes in the teams of experts sent to provide humanitarian assistance contributes to the unequal treatment of women in such situations. UNHCR stresses the need to involve women in their operations in the field and confirms the difference that their involvement makes to the perception of women's particular problems.[37] However, to date the teams of experts have been dominated by male personnel who may not be particularly sensitive to problems faced by female survivors.

Similarly, the balance of sexes in fact-finding investigation teams dealing with sexual violence in armed conflict is determinative of whether women's stories are to be told. Methods of investigating and documenting human rights abuses often obscure abuses against women. For example, the UN "fact-finding" mission in Rwanda in 1994 somehow did not detect systematic sexual violence against women until nine months after the genocide when women began to give birth in unprecedented numbers.[38] It has been suggested in the context of the Rwandan conflict that due to the significance of rape in that culture it is not possible to investigate incidents of sexual violence as the women concerned are not willing to discuss their ordeals.[39] However, Human Rights Watch has found that the use of female investigators and interpreters makes a considerable difference to whether or not women are willing to speak out.[40]

Documentation of sexual abuse of women during and after warfare has increased,[41] and the trauma suffered by victims of sexual abuse is now receiving greater consideration.[42] However, more support services need to

---

35.   *See* UNHCR Guidelines, *supra* note 6, at 49.

36.   *See* The State of the World's Refugees, *supra* note 27, at 87 (detailing the vulnerability of households headed by women); *Machel, supra* note 18, ¶ 77.

37.   *See* UNHCR Guidelines, *supra* note 6; *Machel, supra* note 18, ¶ 71 (recommending that women should be the initial point of control for food distribution systems undertaken by the World Food Program). *See also* Human Rights Watch, Shattered Lives, *supra* note 3, at 25.

38.   *See* Anne Gallagher, *Ending the Marginalization: Strategies for Incorporating Women into the United Nations Human Rights System,* 19 Hum. Rts. Q. 283, 292 n.31 (1997).

39.   *See* Shattered Lives, *supra* note 3, at 25.

40.   See UNHCR Guidelines, *supra* note 6, at 50.

41.   For an account of rape in warfare over the centuries, see Susan Brownmiller, Against Our Will: Men, Women and Rape 31–132 (1975).

42.   *See, e.g.,* UNHCR, Draft Guidelines on Evaluation and Care of Victims of Trauma and Violence (1993); *Machel, supra* note 18, ¶ 107. *But see* Ustinia Dolgopol, *A Feminist Appraisal of the Dayton Peace Accords,* 19 Adel. L. Rev. 59, 66–68 (1997) (criticizing the Dayton Peace Accords for the lack of support offered to victims of sexual violence in the Former Yugoslavia).

be provided to women, particularly for dealing with the physical and psychological effects of their injuries. Some of the common issues women have to deal with are abortion (if it is available), abandonment of babies conceived during rape, and HIV and other infections.

Despite the fact that women are generally responsible for trying to rebuild families and communities after conflict, they are almost always excluded from decision-making processes regarding reconstruction.[43] This absence of women reflects the situation that exists in all cultures during times of peace and, moreover, in the United Nations system itself.[44] The inappropriateness of not taking into account the views of women is particularly marked in post-conflict situations where, typically, a high percentage of households are headed by women.[45]

Girl children are vulnerable in armed conflict in many of the same ways as women, but there are also factors that affect them specifically. To date, little attention has been given to this issue.[46] The primary focus in relation to children has been on raising the minimum age of participation in hostilities, an issue predominantly affecting boy children.[47] However, a recent study of children in armed conflict commissioned by the UN General Assembly has addressed some of these issues, although its focus is sexual violence against girl children.[48]

In more recent times, the media has fundamentally changed the way that armed conflict is viewed throughout the world. This has a particular impact on women.[49] A positive effect of this development has been the presence of women journalists in the conflict in the Former Yugoslavia, which is thought to have contributed to attention being focused on the incidence of sexual violence during those hostilities.[50] Nevertheless, overall

---

43. For example, Palestinian women were excluded from the transitional process to self-rule. *See, e.g., Palestinian Women's Organizations Struggle Against the Exclusion of Women from the Transitional Process,* Women's Watch, June 1996, at 3.

44. *See* Hilary Charlesworth, *Transforming the United Men's Club: Feminist Futures for the United Nations,* 4 Transnat'l L. & Contemp. Probs. 421 (1994).

45. It is estimated that women make up 50 percent of heads of households in Rwanda. *See* Shattered Lives, *supra* note 3, at 2.

46. *See* Rebecca J. Cook, *Elimination of Sexual Apartheid: Prospects for the Fourth World Conference on Women,* Issue Papers on World Conferences, No. 5, June 1995. *See also Report of the Administrative Committee on Coordination: Social, Humanitarian and Human Rights Questions: Advancement of Women,* U.N. ESCOR, Agenda Item 5(e), U.N. Doc. E/1996/16 (1996) (dealing with the advancement of women).

47. *See* Machel, *supra* note 18, ¶ 62; Stéphane Jeannet & Joël Mermet, *The Involvement of Children in Armed Conflict,* 322 Int'l Rev. Red Cross 105 (1998).

48. *See* Machel, *supra* note 18, ¶¶ 67, 76, 89–107.

49. *See* Anonymous, *supra* note 13, at 8; Simona Sharoni, *Every Woman is an Occupied Territory: the Politics of Militarism and Sexism and the Israeli-Palestinian Conflict,* 1 J. Gender Stud. 459 (1992).

50. *See* Cynthia Enloe, *Afterword, Have the Bosnian Rapes Opened up a New Era of Feminist Consciousness?, in* Mass Rape: The War Against Women in Bosnia-Herzegovina 219 (Alexandra Stiglmayer ed., 1994).

the emphasis has traditionally been placed on the suffering and heroism of men. The glorification of the combatant is an integral part of the culture of warfare.[51] Generally, the trauma, experiences, and death of women as a result of armed conflict are disregarded. When, on the other hand, attention is paid to the experiences of women in armed conflict, it is frequently exploitative and damaging to the women concerned.[52]

The peacekeeping forces of the United Nations have kept up the unfortunate tradition of abuse of women. There are many reports of rape and sexual harassment by UN Peacekeepers—for example in Cambodia—as well as complicity in sexual abuse perpetrated by parties to the conflict.[53] These incidents raise unresolved questions regarding the extent to which the United Nations is bound by the provisions of IHL. The International Committee of the Red Cross (ICRC) has consistently argued for a broad approach to the applicable law and regards all the provisions of IHL as applicable when UN contingents resort to force, whether through peace-keeping or peace enforcement forces.[54] The United Nations, by contrast, continues to maintain its longstanding view that it is bound by the "fundamental principles and rules of international humanitarian law."[55]

The issue of compensation, although of significance to all victims of armed conflict, has particular manifestations in the context of women.[56] Compensation for individuals for the effects of armed conflict is not specifically addressed by IHL. Its provisions protect individuals within the confines of the traditional rules of state responsibility. In other words, harm to individuals is considered an injury to the state and is pursued on that

---

51. *See* Judith Gardam, *Gender and Non-Combatant Immunity*, 3 Transnat'l. L. & Contemp. Probs. 345, 348–49 (1993).

52. *See* Sexual Violence Against Refugees, *supra* note 6, at 71.

53. *See* Anne Orford, *The Politics of Collective Security*, 17 Mich. J. Int'l L. 373, 377–79 (1995); Julianne Peck, *The U.N. and the Laws of War: How Can the World's Peacekeepers Be Held Accountable?*, 21 Syracuse J. Int'l L. & Com. 283, 283 (1995) (detailing allegations of rape by UN soldiers in Bosnia-Hercegovina).

54. *See* International Committee of the Red Cross, International Conference for the Protection of War Victims: Report on the Protection of War Victims, *reprinted in* 296 Int'l Rev. Red Cross 391, 428–29 (1993).

55. *E.g.*, Kofi A. Annan, Secretary-General, *Observance by United Nations Forces of International Humanitarian Law*, Secretary-General's Bull., 6 Aug. 1999, ¶ 1.1, U.N. Doc. ST/SGB/1999/13. Section 7 of the Bulletin includes protections for women against attacks, including rape and other forms of sexual violence. *Id.* ¶¶ 7.2–7.3.

56. The importance of compensation for women victims of armed conflict has been acknowledged on several occasions. *See, e.g., Beijing Platform for Action, supra* note 1, ¶ 124(c), (d) & (h); *Peace: Measures to Eradicate Violence Against Women in the Family and Society: Report by the Secretary-General*, U.N. ESCOR, Comm'n on the Status of Women, 38th Sess., Agenda Item 5(c), ¶ 72, U.N. Doc. E/CN.6/1994/4 (1994); Chavez, *supra* note 2, ¶¶ 74–79; *Report on the Situation of Human Rights in Rwanda Submitted by Mr. René Degni-Sequi, Special Rapporteur of the Commission on Human Rights, Under Paragraph 20 of Resolution S-3/1 of 25 May 1994*, U.N. ESCOR, Comm'n on Hum. Rts., 52d Sess., Agenda Item 10, ¶ 141, U.N. Doc. E/CN.4/1996/68 (1996).

level. States, however, are generally not willing to pursue claims where the individuals concerned have little political or economic status, which is the case with women.[57] Where particular States have adopted measures to provide compensation to victims of armed conflict, a gender perspective has been missing. One exception in this area is the United Nations Compensation Commission established by the Security Council to deal with claims arising from the Persian Gulf conflict of 1990 and 1991.[58] The Commission recognizes claims for "serious personal injury," defined so as to include "mental pain and anguish" arising from sexual assault.[59]

In the context of enforcement, some progress has been made in taking particular concerns of women into account in the prosecution of sexual offenses. Such matters as the anonymity of victims and witnesses in trials for sexual assault and provision of victim support and counseling have been addressed.[60] These changes have not been readily accepted. For example, a perceived conflict exists between the demands of a fair trial and the protection of women as victims and witnesses.[61] The two are not necessarily inconsistent; it is the appropriate balance that should be addressed.[62] It is also important that there be gender balance in the composition of enforcement tribunals and their support staff.[63]

---

57. *See* Chinkin, *supra* note 8, at 326.
58. *See Determination of Ceilings for Compensation for Mental Pain and Anguish (Decision No. 8)*, U.N. SCOR, U.N. Compensation Comm'n, Governing Council, 4th Sess., U.N. Doc. S/AC.26/1992/8 (1992), *reprinted in* United Nations Compensation Commission 421 (Richard B. Lillich ed., 1995).
59. *Id.*
60. *See Prosecutor v. Tadic, Decision on the Prosecutor's Motion Requesting Protective Measures For Victims and Witnesses*, Int'l Crim. Tribunal for the Former Yugoslavia, U.N. Doc. IT-94-1 (1995), *available on* <http://www.un.org/icty/tadic/trialc2/decision-e/100895pm.htm> (visited 18 Nov. 1999); Rome Statute of the International Criminal Court, U.N. Diplomatic Conf. of Plenipotentiaries on the Establishment of an Int'l Crim. Ct., arts. 43(6) & 57(3)(c), U.N. Doc A/CONF.183/9 (1998), *reprinted in* 37 I.L.M. 999 (1998) [hereinafter Rome Statute]. *See also* Christine Chinkin, *Due Process and Witness Anonymity*, 91 Am. J. Int'l L. 75, 78–79 (1997); Patricia Viseur Sellers & Kaoru Okuizumi, *Intentional Prosecution of Sexual Offences*, 7 Transnat'l L. & Contemp. Probs. 47 (1997); Netherlands Ministry of Foreign Affairs, Conference Report Summary: Report of the International Conference of Experts: 50 Years Universal Declaration of Human Rights: Preventing and Combating Violence Against Women 5, ¶ 14 (1998).
61. *See* Theodor Meron, *The Yugoslav Tribunal: Use of Unnamed Witnesses Against Accused*, 90 Am. J. Int'l L. 235 (1996).
62. Chinkin, *supra* note 6, at 78–79.
63. *See Report of the Expert Group Meeting, supra* note 20, ¶ 51; Rome Statute, *supra* note 60, art. 36(8)(a)(iii).

III. HOW INTERNATIONAL LAW RESPONDS TO WOMEN AND ARMED CONFLICT

How has the law responded to women's experience of armed conflict? IHL contains general provisions protecting all civilians and a number of provisions affording women "special protection" during armed conflict.[64] Forty-three provisions of the Geneva Conventions and Protocols specifically deal with women and the effects of armed conflict.[65] However, they all deal with women in their relationships with others, not as individuals in their own right. Nineteen are, in fact, designed to protect children.[66] Those that deal with sexual offenses are couched in terms of offenses against women's honor.[67] Women's honor, as depicted in IHL, is constituted solely on the basis of certain sexual attributes, the characterizing features of which are what is seen as important to men, namely the chastity and modesty of women.[68] In contrast, the honor of men is a much more complex concept in IHL, encompassing both mind and bodily attributes.[69] The rules dealing with women are presented as less important than others. They are drafted in different language than the provisions protecting combatants and civilians generally, using the concept of "protection" rather than prohibition.[70] Their breach, moreover, is not treated as serious within the rules themselves in that they are not considered "grave breaches" of the Conventions and, until recently, no attempt had been made to enforce these rules, despite widespread breaches.[71]

When questions are raised as to the adequacy of these provisions the

---

64. For a description of the system of IHL in relation to women, see Mala Tabory, *The Status of Women in Humanitarian Law, in* International Law at a Time of Perplexity 941 (Yoram Dinstein ed., 1989); Krill, *supra* note 19.

65. *Id.*

66. *See, e.g.,* Protocol I, *supra* note 14, arts. 70(1), 76(2). *See also* Commentary on the Additional Protocols of 8 June 1977 to the Geneva Conventions of 12 August 1949, 822, 893–95 (Yves Sandoz et al. eds., 1987); Michael Bothe et al., New Rules for Victims of Armed Conflicts: Commentary on the Two 1977 Protocols Additional to the Geneva Conventions of 1949 470 (1982) (relating to Protocol I, art. 76(2)).

67. *See* Geneva IV, *supra* note 14, art. 27(2) (stating that "[w]omen shall be especially protected against any attack of their honor, in particular against rape, enforced prostitution, or any form of indecent assault.")

68. *See* Geneva I, *supra* note 14, art. 12 (stating that "women shall be treated with all consideration due to their sex"). One commentator defines this article as the "consideration which is accorded in every civilized country to beings who are weaker than oneself and whose honor and modesty call for respect." Int'l Comm. of the Red Cross, Commentary: I Geneva Convention for the Amelioration of the Condition of the Wounded and Sick in Armed Forces in the Field 140 (Jean S. Pictet ed., 1952) (eng. trans.).

69. *See* Judith G. Gardam, *An Alien's Encounter With the Law of Armed Conflict, in* Sexing the Subject of Law 233, 250 (Ngaire Naffine & Rosemary J. Owens eds., 1997).

70. *See* Gardam, *supra* note 8, at 57.

71. *Id.*

most frequent response is that the rules are sufficient and that what is needed is better enforcement.[72] Certainly better enforcement of all the rules of IHL is necessary. However, the basic problem is that the provisions are inherently discriminatory. No amount of enforcement can overcome this fundamental flaw in the system.

IHL fails to take account of women as subjects in their own right. It takes the experience of men as the starting point. In a world where women are not equals of men, a general category of rules based on the experience of men cannot respond to their situation.[73] Armed conflict affects men and women in fundamentally different ways, and laws that take the experience of men as the norm against which to construct the rules are unjust. Women may already receive special protection under IHL—for example when they are pregnant or prisoners of war.[74] But these rules relate only to the sexual and reproductive aspects of women's lives viewed from a male perspective.

The failure to address many of the problems experienced by women as a result of armed conflict can be attributed to the boundaries of IHL. Increasingly, scholars are focusing on the unreality of the rigid divisions between human rights law, IHL, and refugee law.[75] Modern armed conflict involves the whole population and its effects are far reaching and long-term. IHL, with the exception of the Fourth Geneva Convention dealing with occupied territories, only applies while armed conflict continues.[76] For women in particular, the cessation of hostilities often marks just the beginning of their battle for survival, a process that is markedly different than the post-conflict experience of men.

Two examples of the operation of the boundaries of IHL illustrate how the law fails to consider the reality of warfare for women. The first illustration concerns the way in which a component of the rules themselves, the principle of proportionality, has been applied. The second example relates to economic sanctions.

---

72. *See, e.g.,* Advancement of Women and Implementation of the Outcome of the Fourth World Conference on Women, Statement by the ICRC to the General Assembly 3d Comm., 53d Sess., Agenda Items 103–04 (15 Oct. 1998), *available on* <http://www .icrc.org/icrceng.nsf/c1256212004ce24e4125621200524882/d366866e92d 18001412566a4004eb94c?OpenDocument> (visited 18 Nov. 1999).

73. Equality theory is still the preferred mode of liberal theorists for accommodating the demands of women for change. In the area of international law see, for example, Fernando R. Teson, *Feminism and International Law: A Reply*, 33 Va. J. Int'l L. 647 (1993).

74. *See generally* Krill, *supra* note 19.

75. *See generally* The Problem of Refugees in the Light of Contemporary International Law Issues (Vera Gowlland-Debbas ed., 1995).

76. *See* Edward K. Kwakwa, The International Law of Armed Conflict: Personal and Material Fields of Application 18 (1992).

The principle of proportionality is a central aspect of IHL. The treaty rule of proportionality can be found in Article 51 (5)(b) of Protocol I, where indiscriminate attacks are defined so as to include those "which may be expected to cause incidental loss of civilian life, injury to civilians, damage to civilian objects, or a combination thereof, which would be excessive in relation to the concrete and direct military advantage anticipated."[77] This provision does not require that factors such as long-term civilian casualties, either from injuries at the time of attack or from resulting starvation and disease, be taken into account in determining what is a proportionate attack. Neither are commanders required to assess to what extent attacks will lead to the displacement of the civilian population and the creation of a refugee problem.[78] To some extent these factors might be regarded as more appropriately the province of the law on the use of force. That is, in the overall planning of a military campaign leaders should always consider whether such results are warranted by the requirements of self-defense or the restoration of international peace and security.[79] As things stand, however, long-term effects of attacks and the potential dislocation of civilians are not limiting factors in either the law on the use of force or IHL. This failure to recognize and take account of the whole picture of what happens after an armed attack affects women particularly.

The use of economic sanctions illustrates the increasingly random impact of the boundaries within which IHL operates. The effects of this phenomenon on women are distinctive and unacknowledged.[80] On several recent occasions, sanctions have been associated with enforcement actions of the Security Council as an integral part of the overall solution to international conflict.[81] The deleterious impact of economic sanctions on

---

77. *See,* Protocol I, *supra* note 14, art. 51(5)(b). *See also* Judith Gail Gardam, *Proportionality and Force in International Law,* 87 Am. J. Int'l L. 391, 406–10 (1993) (for a discussion of proportionality requirements in the law on the use of force).

78. For a discussion of the situation of refugee women, many of whom acquire this status as a result of armed conflict, see Lucy Bonnerjea, Shaming the World: The Needs of Women Refugees 5–6 (1995); Christiane Berthiaume, *Do We Really Care?,* 100 UNHCR Refugee Women 11 (1995).

79. *See* Gardam, *supra* note 77 (for a discussion of the relationship between proportionality in the law on the use of force and IHL).

80. *See The Relationship between Economic Sanctions and Respect for Economic, Social and Cultural Rights,* General Comment No. 8, U.N. ESCOR, Comm. on Econ., Soc. & Cult. Rts., 17th Sess., U.N. Doc. E/C.12/1997/8 (1997) (discussing transcending the boundaries of human rights law in the context of economic sanctions).

81. *See* Sebastian Bohr, *Sanctions by the United Nations Security Council and the European Community,* 4 Eur. J. Int'l L. 256 (1993); W. Michael Reisman & Douglas L. Stevick, *The Applicability of International Law Standards to United Nations Economic Sanctions Programmes,* 9 Eur. J. Int'l L. 86, 101–24 (1998).

the civilian population is documented.[82] The particular effects of such measures on women, however, is largely overlooked although well-illustrated by the Persian Gulf conflict where a mandatory sanctions regime has continued long after the cessation of armed hostilities.[83]

There are no rules of IHL that specifically regulate economic sanctions during armed conflict.[84] Some provisions of IHL are, however, relevant in this context. Starvation is a prohibited method of warfare under Articles 54 of Protocol I and 14 of Protocol II; this principle is arguably a customary rule.[85] Article 70 of Protocol I provides for relief actions in certain circumstances.[86] Additionally, Articles 23 and 55 of the Fourth Geneva Convention impose certain obligations on contracting States or occupying powers in relation to the provision of essential supplies to the civilian population.[87] However, these rules only apply while the armed conflict is in progress or, in the case of the Fourth Convention, during occupation. After the conflict, arguably, no relevant law applies.[88]

Thus the economic sanctions still in place against Iraq, as part of the overall solution to the threat to international peace and security posed by that state, are outside any rules of armed conflict. Furthermore, the source of these sanctions is the powers of the Security Council under Chapter VII of the United Nations Charter.[89] Decisions of the Security Council under Chapter VII impose mandatory obligations on states. Under Article 103 of

---

82. *See generally* Vera Gowlland-Debbas, Collective Responses to Illegal Acts in International Law: United Nations Action in the Question of Southern Rhodesia (1990); Lori Fisler Damrosch, *The Civilian Impact of Economic Sanctions, in* Enforcing Restraint: Collective Intervention in Internal Conflicts 274 (Lori Fisler Damrosch ed., 1993); Reisman & Stevick, *supra* note 81, at 96–124.

83. *See* Anonymous, *supra* note 30.

84. The general question of the compatibility of sanctions with the requirements of IHL, and in particular the prohibition against starvation as a method of warfare, indicates that the requirements of IHL are being breached in spirit if not in fact. For a discussion of the Security Council's practice in relation to sanctions and the requirements of IHL, see Hans Peter Gasser, *Collective Economic Sanctions and International Humanitarian Law: An Enforcement Measure under the United Nations Charter and the Right of Civilians to Immunity: an Unavoidable Clash of Policy Goals?*, 56 Zeitschrift Für Ausländiches Öffentliches Recht Und Völkerrecht 871, 884–90 (1996). *See also* Reisman & Stevick, *supra* note 81 (discussing the application of the principles of necessity, proportionality, and discrimination to the imposition of economic sanctions by the United Nations).

85. *See* Protocol I, *supra* note 14, art. 54; Protocol II, *supra* note 14, art. 14. *See also* René Provost, *Starvation as a Weapon: Legal Implications of the United Nations Food Blockade Against Iraq and Kuwait,* 30 Colum. J. Transnat'l L. 577, 628–34 (1992).

86. *See* Protocol I, *supra* note 14, art. 70.

87. *See* Geneva IV, *supra* note 14, arts. 23, 55.

88. *See* Universal Declaration on the Eradication of Hunger and Malnutrition, *adopted* 17 Dec. 1974, G.A. Res. 3348, U.N. GAOR, 29th Sess., U.N. Doc. E/Conf.65/20 (1974), *reprinted in* Human Rights; Sixty Major Global Instruments (Winston E. Langley ed., 1992).

89. *See* U.N. Charter art. 41, *signed* 26 June 1945, 59 Stat. 1031, T.S. No. 993, 3 Bevans 1153 (*entered into force* 24 Oct. 1945).

the Charter these obligations prevail over any other treaty obligations that states may have, including those of IHL.[90] Moreover, it is questionable whether the Security Council itself is bound by any limitations derived from IHL.[91]

IV. THE WAY FORWARD

Improvements in the protection offered to women by IHL should be based on evidence of the effects of armed conflict on women in a wide variety of situations and conflicts, both civil and international.[92] Considerable differences of opinion exist as to what law has to offer in ameliorating the impact of armed conflict.[93] Doubts also exist as to the ability of law to achieve fundamental change for women. Maybe all that will be achieved, as Christine Chinkin puts it, is "a triumph of form over substance."[94] On the other hand, law generally serves to reinforce existing societal structures, in this case, discrimination against women.[95] It therefore, at the very least, has a significant symbolic role to play in any improvements for the position of women in armed conflict.

One option is to reform the rules of IHL to adequately address the inherent discriminatory operation of the provisions. However, in the current international political climate a fear exists that to open up reform of IHL may threaten the maintenance of useful existing rules. Another possible approach is to encourage a reinterpretation of the existing provisions of IHL to take account of gender perspectives and changing interpretations of the rules. The Special Rapporteur on Violence Against Women, in her report on armed conflict, recommends that the Geneva Conventions should be re-examined and reevaluated so as to "incorporate developing norms on violence against women during armed conflict."[96] Of particular relevance in

---

90. *See id.* art. 103.
91. As things stand at the moment, the United Nations is not bound by the treaty rules of IHL. The extent to which it is bound by customary principles remains unresolved. *Cf.* Reisman & Stevick, *supra* note 81, at 95, 127. *See also* Theodor Meron, *Prisoners of War, Civilians and Diplomats in the Gulf Crisis,* 85 Am. J. Int'l L. 104 (1991) (expressing concern about the differences in standards between the requirements of the Fourth Geneva Convention and those put in place by Security Council Resolution 661 of 6 Aug. 1990).
92. The study by Graça Machel on the effect of armed conflict on children is a precedent. *See Machel, supra* note 18.
93. *See, e.g., Beijing Platform for Action, supra* note 1, ¶ 132 (acknowledging that international humanitarian law is at times systematically ignored).
94. Chinkin, *supra* note 6, at 18.
95. *See* Judith Gail Gardam, *A Feminist Analysis of Certain Aspects of International Humanitarian Law,* 12 Austl. Y.B. Int'l L. 265 (1992).
96. *See* Coomaraswamy, *supra* note 2, ¶ 95.

this context, in light of the work of the International Criminal Tribunals for the Former Yugoslavia and Rwanda, is the question of the place of rape in the system of grave breaches.

A focus on a reconceptualization of the existing rules is consistent with the idea of mainstreaming gender issues that was reiterated in the Beijing Platform for Action.[97] Paragraph 143 reads: "[i]n addressing armed or other conflicts, an active and visible policy of mainstreaming a gender perspective into all policies and programs should be promoted so that before decisions are taken an analysis is made of the effects on women and men, respectively."[98] This process, already under way in the field of human rights,[99] can be extrapolated to the provisions of IHL in a number of ways. For instance, a revision of the ICRC commentaries on the Geneva Conventions and Protocols could be undertaken to provide a gender perspective on their provisions and to take into account the changing interpretations of the rules. These documents are regarded as an important source for interpreting the Conventions and the Protocols. The commentaries on the Conventions, however, were written some forty years ago and incorporate ideas and concepts that are now outdated. An illustration is the commentary on Article 12 of the Second Geneva Convention—"[w]omen shall be treated with all consideration due to their sex"[100]—which states: "[w]hat special consideration? No doubt that accorded in every civilised country to beings who are weaker than oneself and whose honor and modesty call for respect."[101] The commentaries, moreover, in some cases, no longer accurately reflect the interpretations of the provisions as adopted by states.[102]

Another method of mainstreaming gender perspectives into IHL is the adoption of an initiative for the better dissemination of the rules relating to women, to be undertaken by the state parties to the Geneva Conventions and Protocols in consultation with the ICRC. Dissemination is a treaty

---

97. *See Beijing Platform for Action, supra* note 1, ¶ ¶ 222, 231. This process commenced with the demand expressed in the Vienna Declaration that "the equal status of women and the human rights of women . . . . be integrated into the mainstream of United Nations system-wide activity" and "form an integral part of United Nations human rights activities." *See also* Gallagher, *supra* note 38, at 292 n.31.

98. *Id.*

99. *See* Jane Connors, Mainstreaming Gender Within the International Framework (1996) (unpublished paper delivered to the Law and the Social Inclusion of Women Conference, University of Warwick) (on file with authors); Gallagher, *supra* note 38, at 292 n.31; Christine Ainetter Brautigam, *Mainstreaming a Gender Perspective in the Work of the United Nations Human Rights Treaty Bodies,* ASIL Proc., Apr. 1997, at 389–94.

100. Geneva II, *supra* note 14, art. 12.

101. Commentary on Geneva Convention II for the Amelioration of the Condition of Wounded, Sick and Shipwrecked Members of Armed Forces at Sea 92 (Jean S. Pictet ed., 1960).

102. An example is the interpretation of the phrases "wilfully causing great suffering or serious injury to body and health" and "torture and inhumane treatment," both of which currently constitute grave breaches of the Conventions.

obligation of these States.[103] The training of peacekeepers in IHL and the treatment of women in armed conflict is a topic that requires attention both from the United Nations itself and from States supplying peacekeeping forces.[104] Such undertakings in relation to dissemination, moreover, are consistent with paragraph 33 of the Beijing Platform for Action which refers to the need to "[e]nsure respect for international law, including humanitarian law, in order to protect women and girls in particular."[105]

Some progress is being made in the context of reconstruction and peacebuilding initiatives after the cessation of hostilities. Paragraph 135 of the Beijing Platform for Action refers to the need to ensure:

> [t]he equal access and full participation of women in power structures and their full involvement in all efforts for the prevention and resolution of conflicts. . . . If women are to play an equal part in securing and maintaining peace, they must be empowered politically and economically and represented adequately at all levels of decision-making.[106]

Several States and Agencies are pursuing these initiatives—for example, the Canadian Government,[107] the UN Division for the Advancement of Women,[108] and the UNHCR.[109]

Simply including women in post-conflict resolution or peacebuilding initiatives can be perceived as an "add women and mix" approach that has been unsuccessful in achieving any transformation in the existing structures.[110] Anne Gallagher writes that the new approach to mainstreaming gender perspectives in the human rights field is so-called "transformative mainstreaming," a process that is designed to achieve fundamental change.[111] One of the assumptions that frequently underlies initiatives designed to include women in public roles is that women are intrinsically more peaceful and cooperative than men. This assumption is problematic because it reinforces stereotypes of women that limit their options and fail to take account of their diverse potentials. A less contentious justification for the inclusion of women in these activities is one of simple justice. Their lives are what is being dealt with; thus they should have a say in any decisions that are made.

---

103. *See, e.g.,* Protocol I, *supra* note 14, art. 83.
104. For signs of progress in this area, see Annan, *supra* note 55.
105. *See Beijing Platform for Action, supra* note 1, ¶ 33.
106. *Id.* ¶ 135.
107. *See generally* Canadian Centre For Foriegn Policy and Development, *supra* note 20.
108. *See id.*
109. *See* UNHCR, *Rebuilding a Future Together,* UNHCR Refugee Women (1997); UNHCR, Implementing the Beijing Platform for Action 17–19 (1998).
110. *See* Chinkin *supra* note 6, at 23.
111. Gallagher, *supra* note 38 at 288.

It may be advantageous to continue the process of focusing attention specifically on women but in a way that takes account of the various roles they perform in societies and not merely as mothers and sexual objects. Thus, comprehensive guidelines on the treatment of women in armed conflict could be adopted under the auspices of the ICRC.[112]

Finally, a forum is needed to discuss the way forward for the better protection of women in armed conflict. Increasingly, the topic is on the agenda of a widespread variety of bodies, both governmental and non-governmental. However, their activities are fragmented and need to be drawn together.

V. CONCLUSION

IHL is an ancient, conservative, and relatively inflexible area of international law. The number of challenges posed to its relevance and effectiveness in the last half century has been bewildering.[113] It now must meet the demands of women to truly reflect their life experiences. The ICRC, a deeply conservative organization, has special responsibility for the development of IHL and is in danger of losing the initiative in many areas where it should be at the forefront of developments. The ICRC is finally recognizing the need to address the specific needs of women in armed conflict. However, a serious commitment to real change is needed. As the traditional guardian of IHL, the ICRC must take concrete steps to make the law relevant to the lives of the majority of the world's population.

---

112. In Oct. 1999, the ICRC decided to develop and implement guidelines regarding the protection and assistance of women in conflict situations. *See Update on ICRC's Initiative to Better Respond to the Needs and Resources of Women Affected by Armed Conflicts,* 29 Oct. 1999, *available on* <http://www.icrc.org/icrceng.nsf/5cacfdf48ca 698b641256242003b3295/7d20b9263cab7582412568190042e673 ?OpenDocument> (visited 18 Nov. 1999).

113. Two examples of such challenges are the development of weapons of mass destruction and the vast increase in non-international conflicts.

Part III
Objects

[13]

CAPTURED ENEMY PROPERTY: BOOTY OF WAR AND SEIZED ENEMY PROPERTY

By WILLIAM GERALD DOWNEY, JR.*

Chief, International Law Branch, Judge Advocate General's Office, Department of the Army

In an address before the 1949 annual meeting of the American Society of International Law this writer remarked that the laws governing captured enemy property have never been codified or collected in one place and are very difficult to find and apply.[1] The lack of a handy tool in the field of captured property has been noted at times by others, including Professor H. A. Smith, formerly a colonel with the British 21st Army Group, who observed that the "law of booty is almost unwritten"[2] and Judge Manley O. Hudson, who wrote some years ago in an editorial in this JOURNAL that the "literature on captured property and war booty seemed inadequate."[3]

In the fall of 1947 the now famous case of the captured Hungarian horses focused the attention of the Congress as well as that of the various interested executive departments of this Government on the difficulties arising in the application of the legal principles governing captured property when faced with the political concept of restitution, and the various considerations inherent therein.[4]

I—DEFINITIONS

The first question to be determined is: What is captured enemy property?

Generally speaking, any property which is useful in war or is taken or seized on the ground of military necessity for the purpose of depriving the enemy of its use or of turning it to the captor's advantage is considered

---

* Major, JAGC, U. S. Army. The views expressed herein are those of the author and do not necessarily reflect the opinions of the Secretary of Defense, the Secretary of the Army or of the Judge Advocate General of the Army. This article has been cleared for publication by the Office of the Secretary of Defense.

[1] Proceedings, 1949, p. 104.

[2] Col. H. A. Smith, "Booty of War," XXIII British Yearbook of International Law (1946), p. 227.

[3] Manley O. Hudson, "A Soldier's Property in War," this JOURNAL, Vol. 26 (1932), pp. 340, 342.

[4] See 80th Cong., 2d Sess., Report of a Subcommittee of the Committee on Armed Services, United States Senate, Questions of Ownership of Captured Horses (Washington, D. C.: Government Printing Office, 1948).

captured enemy property.[5]   However, international law restricts the taking or seizing of enemy property to that property having the nature of personal as distinguished from real property.   Enemy public property and enemy private property are the two classes of enemy personal property, *i.e.*, enemy chattels, susceptible of becoming captured enemy property.[6]

Enemy *public* property is defined as chattels, the title to which is vested in a state or in any agency of such state.   Enemy *private* property is defined as chattels, the title to which is vested in an individual, a private corporation or a public corporation not owned by the state or by an agency of the state.

Each of the three words in the term "captured enemy property," has a special significance of its own.   John Bassett Moore has ably stated that "The word 'capture' is in law a technical term, denoting the hostile seizure of persons, places and things. . . ."[7]   The Supreme Court of the United States has defined the word "enemy" as meaning a "State which is at war with another State."[8]   The word "property" as herein used is restricted to personal property or chattels, and has been defined "in the strict legal sense as the aggregate of rights which are guaranteed and protected by law; more specifically . . . ownership, the unrestricted and exclusive right to a thing."[9]

It would appear therefore that the term "captured enemy property" may be legally defined as "*Chattels, the aggregate of unrestricted and exclusive rights in which has been acquired through hostile seizure on land, in conformity with the international law of war, by a belligerent state from an enemy state or from the inhabitants thereof.*"

Captured enemy property is a fairly modern term which has often been used synonymously with the older term "war booty," recently discussed in this JOURNAL as follows:

> "War booty," strictly defined, is limited to movable articles on the battlefield and in besieged towns.   Private property which may be taken as booty is restricted to arms, munitions, pieces of equipment, horses, military papers, and the like.   Public enemy property which may be seized as war booty is limited to movables on the battlefield, and these need not be for military operations or necessity.[10]

It will be readily understood, then, that the term "captured enemy property" defined above embraces much more than the term "war booty,"

[5] See Oppenheim, International Law, Vol. II, §§ 133–145; Feilchenfeld, The International Economic Law of Belligerent Occupation, pp. 51–61, 93–107; Spaight, War Rights on Land, pp. 410–418.

[6] *Ibid.*

[7] John Bassett Moore, International Law and Some Current Illusions, p. 21.

[8] Swiss National Insurance Co. *v.* Miller, 267 U. S. 42 (1924).

[9] Black's Law Dictionary (3d ed.), p. 1447.

[10] Daniel H. Lew, "Manchurian Booty and International Law," this JOURNAL, Vol. 40 (1946), p. 584, at 586.

in that the former includes not only personal property captured on the field of battle, but also personal property seized or requisitioned by an army of occupation.

The concept of war booty is as old as recorded history. It has developed over a period of many centuries from the ancient practice by which the individual soldier was considered to be entitled to take whatever he could find and carry away, to the modern rule under which only the state is entitled to seize property as war booty. The ancient writers, Belli, Grotius and Vattel, were in agreement that the taking of war booty by individual soldiers for their own use was within the legal rights of such soldiers.[11] Recently and concurrently with the development of the theory of the inviolability of private property, the practice of warring nations has tended to restrict the taking of war booty by individual soldiers for their own use. Nearly all of the modern writers, particularly Calvo, Fiore, Davis, Hyde and Oppenheim, have condemned the ancient practice and have thrown the weight of their authority behind the idea that the taking of war booty is a right belonging only to a belligerent state.[12] Heffter, however, standing alone among the moderns, believes that international law permits individual soldiers to take war booty for their own use in exceptional cases as a special reward for their efforts.[13]

Opposed to the concept of war booty is the concept of requisitions which, according to Oppenheim, is the outgrowth of the eternal principle that war must support war. Around the beginning of the eighteenth century the armies of civilized nations began to requisition from the inhabitants of the invaded country such property as was needed by the army in lieu of the former practice of appropriating all public or private property obtainable.[14] For centuries the generals of invading armies never gave any thought to paying for requisitioned property, but during the nineteenth century a practice of paying cash for requisitioned property grew up.[15] With the coming into force of the Hague Regulations it became a legal requirement that payments for requisitions must be made in cash, or if payment in cash is impossible, acknowledged by receipt.[16]

[11] Belli, *De Re Militari et Bello Tractatus* (Translation, Vol. II, Carnegie Endowment for International Peace, 1936), p. 106; Grotius, On the Law of War and Peace (Translation, Vol. III, Carnegie Endowment for International Peace, 1925), p. 672; Vattel, The Law of Nations (Translation, Vol. III, Carnegie Endowment for International Peace, 1916), p. 292.

[12] Calvo, *Le Droit International Théoretique et Pratique*, Vol. IV, p. 240; Fiore, *Nouveau Droit International Public*, Vol. III, pp. 1381–1382; Davis, The Elements of International Law, p. 310; Hyde, International Law, Vol. III, pp. 806–809; Oppenheim's International Law (Lauterpacht, 6th ed.), Vol. II, p. 310.

[13] Heffter, *Das Europäische Völkerrecht der Gegenwart* (8th ed.), § 135.

[14] Oppenheim, *op. cit.*, p. 316.

[15] Keller, *Requisition und Kontribution*, pp. 5–26.

[16] Art. 52, Regulations respecting the Laws and Customs of War on Land, annexed to Hague Convention IV of Oct. 18, 1907, 36 Stat. 2277; Department of State, Treaty Series, No. 539; 2 Malloy's Treaties 2269.

II—BOOTY OF WAR

It has long been a basic principle of the international law of war that enemy *public* property captured on a battlefield becomes the property of the capturing Power.[17]

A recent example of the application of this principle is contained in the case of one *X*, who during the fighting in France in 1944 investigated a hastily evacuated enemy regimental headquarters and found therein a box of French francs. He kept the box of francs and later used them to buy U. S. money orders which he sent to his wife. *X* was tried and convicted by court martial for violation of Article of War 80.[18] In its holding the Board of Review stated that Article of War 80 was in accordance with the principle of the international law of war that enemy public property captured in war becomes the property of the government or Power by whose force it is taken, and does not become the property of the individual who takes it.[19]

A similar case involving currency, reported by Colonel H. A. Smith,[20] concerned three Belgians who on September 3, 1944, were walking along a country road and found in an abandoned German truck two boxes of currency containing 269,940 Belgian and 309,165 French francs. This money, less a certain amount alleged to have been spent by or on their respective wives, was subsequently discovered by the Belgian police in the men's homes. The men were tried and sentenced by the Belgian courts. In this case the physical identity of the currency which had been stolen was clearly established, so there was no difficulty in treating it as booty of war. The crime against Belgian law which had been committed consisted in the unlawful possession of Allied property.

Another case involving currency arose from a claim submitted by an American soldier who was wounded in action against the Germans during the summer of 1944 and took cover in a shell hole where he found a wounded German officer. The German is reported to have said: "Here's something for you, there's plenty more where I got that," and to have given the soldier French currency in the value of $4,942.87. At the time that he was evacuated to a hospital, the soldier turned over the currency to an American finance officer. Later he submitted a claim for the amount of the money. His claim was denied on the grounds that the circumstances

[17] Oakes *v.* U. S. (1898), 174 U. S. 778, 786; Brown *v.* U. S. (1814), 8 Cranch 110; Oppenheim, *op. cit.*, Vol. II, p. 307; Spaight, War Rights on Land, p. 198; Wheaton's International Law (7th ed.), p. 307; Ware *v.* Hylton (1814), 3 Dall. 199, 226; Field Manual 27–10, par. 327; Davis, *op. cit.*, p. 310; Hague Convention IV, 36 Stat. 2277; Geneva (Prisoners of War) Convention, 47 Stat. 202; Geneva (Red Cross) Convention, 47 Stat. 2074.

[18] For text of Article of War 80, see below, p. 499.

[19] 4 Bulletin of the Judge Advocate General of the Army (hereafter referred to as Bull. JAG) (1945) 338.

[20] Smith, *loc. cit.*, p. 235.

of the gift indicated that the money did not belong to the German officer and that unexplained possession by soldiers in the field of unusually large sums of money would justify the conclusion that the money belonged to the enemy government. If so, upon capture it became the property, not of the individual captor, but of the nation in whose army he served.[21]

It is generally held that title to captured enemy public property susceptible of becoming war booty passes from the losing Power to the capturing Power immediately upon the effective seizure, that is, as soon as the property is placed under substantial guard and is in the "firm possession" of the captor, or at the latest, within 24 hours after the seizure,[22] without the necessity of an adjudication by a court as is required in the case of prizes captured at sea.[23]

It is further generally held that when such a capture becomes perfect, *i.e.*, when title to the property is vested, a subsequent sale is good even against the former owner. The principle is thus established that whatever divests the possession of the original owner and substitutes the military in his place is good capture.[24]

An interesting and enlightening illustration of these principles is the case of the captured Iranian pistol. During the war certain pistols of American manufacture were shipped to the Soviet Union under Lend-Lease authority. Among these pistols was No. 943481. The history of this pistol from the time of its arrival in Russia until the day it was captured by the Iranian Army in operations against the Iranian rebels in Azerbaidjan is unknown. However, the facts are clear that this pistol was part of a caché of arms which was captured by the Iranian forces during the Iranian civil war. Later the Chief of Staff of the Iranian Army presented the pistol as a trophy of war to a United States Army officer serving as an observer with the Iranian forces. The question of title to the pistol was raised and it was held that legal title had been vested in the Iranian Government by reason of capture. Assuming that the Iranian Government authorized the gift to the United States observer, it would appear that title to Pistol No. 943481 was vested in the United States observer. However, the attention of the interested officer was called to the clause of the United States Constitution which provides that no person holding an office of trust under the United States, shall, without the consent of Congress, accept any present from a foreign state.[25]

[21] 4 Bull. JAG (1945) 390.

[22] Oakes *v.* U. S., *supra;* Porte *v.* U. S., Devereaus' Reports (Ct. Cls., 1856), p. 109, § 433; Wheaton's International Law, p. 307; Halleck, International Law, p. 366; Lawrence, Principles of International Law (6th ed.), p. 430.

[23] Lamar *v.* Browne (1875), 92 U. S. 187, 195; Young *v.* U. S. (1877), 97 U. S. 39, 60; Wheaton, *supra;* Davis, *supra*, p. 211; 3 Phillimore, International Law, p. 213.

[24] Hannis Taylor, A Treatise on International Public Law, p. 540.

[25] CSJAGA 1949/1355, March 2, 1949. Mss. opinion.

An examination of the origin of the rule of reduction to firm possession indicates that it was during the 16th century that the rule of "possession for 24 hours" was first applied. Later the rule was established that in respect of movable property title went with the seizing and that the mere act of seizing determined the right of property therein, provided that no property was seized the very nature of which had placed it beyond capture.[26]

C. H. Calvo, writing in 1896, stated the general proposition that:

> In order that the belligerent who comes into possession of movable property of the enemy may be able to acquire the serious and real title to these goods, it is absolutely necessary that he retain them in his power for more than 24 hours, the time generally considered as sufficient to place this booty in safety.
>
> Such is the theory, but grave difficulties present themselves when we examine the basis on which rest the rights which war confers concerning private property and the exact moment at which it can be admitted that there is a legitimate transfer of property.[27]

In our day, Calvo stated, the transfer of title is considered as taking place instantaneously from the moment of capture and the principle of 24 hours is no longer used except in maritime war.[28]

The Legal Adviser of the Office of Military Government for Germany (OMGUS), in an opinion dated August 5, 1947, considered the question of the applicability of the term "reduction to firm possession" to certain items of captured enemy property which had not been seized but were located in the area of operations. He stated that:

> . . . a belligerent does not acquire title to enemy public movable property until he has reduced it to firm possession. It appears that "firm possession" requires some manifestation of intention to seize and retain the property involved and some affirmative act or declaration of a possessory or custodial nature with respect to the property. The circumstances which will satisfy these two elements of firm possession will, of course, vary in each case. It is, however, our conclusion that the general occupation of an area by a belligerent is not of itself sufficient to satisfy either of the two elements of the doctrine of firm possession.[29]

An interesting case involving the necessity for reduction to firm possession arose in connection with certain Confederate cannon which were found during World War II lying on the bottom of a certain river in Arkansas where they had been placed by the Confederate forces during the Civil War. It was held in 1947 that such cannon "became the property of the United States when the area where the cannon was located

---

[26] Calvo, *op. cit.*, Vol. IV, § 2210, translation supplied.

[27] *Ibid.*, § 2208.

[28] *Ibid.*, § 2210.

[29] IX Selected Opinions, OMGUS, 57, 60.

was captured by the Federal forces and continued to remain the property of the United States to this time." [30]

It is necessary to note that these two cases are not in agreement as to what is needed in order to achieve reduction to firm possession. In the Confederate cannon case it was held that mere seizure and occupation of the territory by the Federal forces was sufficient to reduce the property to firm possession and thus to transfer title to the United States Government. In the OMGUS case, on the other hand, it was held that some indication of an intention to seize and reduce to firm possession must be shown in order to transfer title. It is the opinion of this writer that the OMGUS view is preferable and that some manifestation of intention is necessary. It would furthermore appear that the case of the Confederate cannon could have been decided on much stronger ground, such as that of abandoned property, rather than on the ground of captured enemy property.

There are several classes of property exempted from the rule that captured enemy *public* property becomes the property of the captor state.[31] The Geneva (Sick and Wounded) Convention of 1929 [32] provides that the *matériel* and means of transportation of mobile sanitary formations are not generally subject to seizure, but that in case of urgent necessity, after the wounded and sick have been provided for, such material and transportation may be requisitioned. The same convention provides that aircraft used as sanitary transportation, provided it meets the other requirements of the convention, is not generally subject to seizure. The Hague Regulations [33] provide that works of art and science and historical monuments may not be seized, and the Geneva (Prisoners of War) Convention of 1929 [34] provides that all effects and objects of personal use, except arms, horses, military equipment and military papers, shall remain in the possession of prisoners of war, as well as metal helmets and gas masks.

It is now generally recognized that *private* enemy property is immune from capture on the battlefield.[35] There are, however, several exceptions to this rule. Military papers, arms, horses and the like can be seized as

[30] 6 Bull. JAG (1947) 238–239.

[31] See Field Manual 27–10, pars. 188–190.

[32] See Arts. 14–18. Arts. 33–37 of the Geneva (Sick and Wounded) Convention of August 12, 1949, have similar provisions pertaining to mobile and fixed sanitary installations as well as aircraft used as hospital transports.

[33] See Art. 56. In respect of the present immunity from capture of works of art and science and historical monuments, it is interesting to note that Richard R. Baxter in General Orders 100, The Code and its Origin (still in MSS), has pointed out that Francis Lieber was of the belief that works of art and science should be seized ''for the sake of chastisement.'' Fortunately such views did not prevail.

[34] See Art. 6. Art. 18 of the Geneva (Prisoners of War) Convention of August 12, 1949, contains similar provisions. None of the Geneva Conventions of 1949 have been ratified by the United States.

[35] See note 5 above and sources cited therein.

war booty whether they can be used for military operations or not, and the mere fact that enemy private property has been found on a battlefield entitles a belligerent to seize it Thus, in two cases involving the diaries of former high-ranking German officers, it was held in one case that if the diary was so related to the official duties of the writer that it might be considered as properly a part of the official papers pertaining to the German war effort, it may properly be considered to be "military papers," but in the second case it was held that if a similar diary reflected merely the personal observation of the writer, it would not constitute "military papers" and therefore must be considered as private property protected by the Convention.[36]

It has been held in a recent case involving private property that if enemy private property was unlawfully taken by an individual member of the occupying forces from the original enemy owner or possessor, such misappropriation or taking would constitute a compensable claim, provided the seizure did not occur as an act of any of the armed forces engaged in combat, and further provided that the claim were asserted within four months or sufficient cause for delay in presenting the claim were shown.[37]

The general rule, as expressed in Field Manual 27–10, *Rules of Land Warfare,* is that private property cannot be confiscated.[38] Here too, however, there is an exception which provides that private property can be seized only by way of military necessity for the support of the army.[39]

The rule concerning property of unknown ownership is that if the ownership of property is unknown, or if, as frequently happens, there is any doubt as to whether it is public or private, it should be treated as public property until such time as the ownership is definitely settled.[40] Thus, in a case involving French currency of unknown origin captured by an American soldier, it was held that as it was possible that the money had been taken from the French Government, and because the ownership of the money was not known with certainty, it should be treated as public property in accordance with paragraph 322 of Field Manual 27–10. Therefore, in the absence of further proof of the origin and ownership of the money, the soldier concerned had no valid legal claim thereto.[41]

Joint captors are those who have assisted the actual captors to make the capture. In order that title to the captured property may vest in each of the joint captors it is necessary that there be a union of both forces and that both forces be under the command of the same officer at the

---

[36] CSJAGA 1949/2472, March 25, 1949. Mss. opinion.
[37] X Selected Opinions, OMGUS, 50.
[38] Field Manual 27–10, par. 326.
[39] *Ibid.*, par. 330.
[40] *Ibid.*, par. 322.
[41] 4 Bull. JAG (1945) 390.

time of the capture. Community enterprise does not constitute a sufficient bond of association to justify joint sharing.[42] Therefore it is the opinion of this writer that German property captured by the United States Fifth Army in Italy would not be considered as a joint capture even though the British and United States forces were fighting in Italy under a supreme commander. However, German property captured by a United States infantry regiment, aided in such capture by a British infantry brigade on the right flank, both units being part of a task force under the command of a United States officer, should be considered a joint capture and title to such captured property should be considered as equally vested in the United States and United Kingdom as joint captors.

III—SEIZED OR REQUISITIONED ENEMY PROPERTY

The laws governing enemy property seized or requisitioned by an army of occupation are more complete than those concerning property captured on the battlefield. The rules governing the seizing or requisitioning of such property are well fixed.

It has long been a general principle of the law of war that enemy *public* property may be seized by an army of occupation.[43] In addition, Article 53 of the Hague Regulations[44] provides that:

> An army of occupation can only take possession of cash, funds, and realizable securities which are strictly the property of the State, depots of arms, means of transport, stores and supplies, and, generally, all movable property belonging to the State which may be used for military operations.
>
> All appliances, whether on land, at sea, or in the air, adapted for the transmission of news, or for the transport of persons or things, exclusive of cases governed by naval law, depots of arms, and, generally, all kinds of ammunition of war, may be seized even if they belong to private individuals, but must be restored and compensation fixed when peace is made.

Paragraph 332 of Field Manual 27–10, *Rules of Land Warfare,* in discussing what items are included in the second paragraph of Article 53, states:

> The foregoing rule includes everything susceptible of direct military use, such as cables, telephone and telegraph plants, horses and other draft and riding animals, motors, bicycles, motorcycles, carts, wagons, carriages, railways, railway plants, tramways, ships in port, all manner of craft in canals and rivers, balloons, airships, airplanes, depots of arms, whether military or sporting, and in general all kinds of war material.

[42] Wheaton, *op. cit.,* pp. 313–314; Risley, Law of War, pp. 141–142.
[43] See authorities cited in notes 17, 22, 23, *supra.*
[44] 36 Stat. 2277.

Thus it has been recently held that horses, raised by the German Army and seized by the United States Army on a German Army breeding farm, became the property of the United States; [45] that a German commercial cable owned by a private corporation and seized by the United States forces, need not be restored to its private owners prior to the making of a treaty of peace, at which time the question of compensation therefor would also be determined; [46] and that certain wine vats originally owned by the French Government and used in the supply of the French Army, which were seized by the occupying German forces under Article 53 of the Hague Regulations and sold to defendant, had become the property of the German Reich and, through sale, the property of the defendant.[47]

It is a generally recognized principle of the international law of war that enemy private property may not be seized unless it is susceptible of direct military use, but that it may be requisitioned.[48] In addition to the general rule, Articles 46 and 47 of the Hague Regulations enacted that private property cannot be confiscated and that pillage is formally forbidden. Article 52 of the Hague Regulations provides that requisitions in kind and services shall not be demanded from municipalities or inhabitants except for the "needs of the Army of occupation" and that such requisitioning shall be in proportion to the resources of the country. They shall only be demanded on the authority of the commander in the locality occupied. Contributions in kind shall be paid for as far as possible in cash. If not, a receipt shall be given and the payment of the amount due shall be made as soon as possible.[49]

Field Manual 27–10, *Rules of Land Warfare*, states that under Article 52, practically everything necessary for the maintenance of the Army may be requisitioned, *e.g.*, fuel, food, forage, clothing, tobacco, printing presses, type, leather, cloth, etc. It also authorizes the billeting of troops for quarters and subsistence.

Oppenheim wrote in a similar view that: "Requisition is the name for the demand for the supply of all kinds of articles necessary for an army, such as provisions for men and horses, clothing, or means of transport. . . ."; and that "all requisitions must be paid for in cash, and if this is impossible they must be acknowledged by receipt, and the payment of the amount must be made as soon as possible." [50]

Field Manual 27–10 states the rules concerning requisitions to be applied by United States forces. It provides that requisitions must be made under

---

[45] JAGA 1947/4808, May 23, 1947. Mss. opinion.

[46] JAGR 1946/3392, Aug. 30, 1946. Mss. opinion.

[47] *État Français c. Établissements Monmousseau*, Cour d'Appel d'Orléans, this JOURNAL, Vol. 43 (1949), p. 819.

[48] See authorities cited in note 5, *supra*.

[49] 36 Stat. 2277, Department of State, Treaty Series, No. 539.

[50] 2 Oppenheim 317–318.

the authority of the commander in the locality. It fixes no prescribed method of requisitioning but states that, if practicable, requisitions should be accomplished through the local authorities by systematic collection in bulk. If, for any reason, local authorities fail to make the required collections, they may be made by military detachments. Explaining the meaning of the expression "needs of the army" it states that such expression was adopted rather than "necessities of the war" as being more favorable to the inhabitants, but that the commander is not thereby limited to the absolute needs of the troops actually present. The prices of articles requisitioned will be fixed by agreement if possible, otherwise by military authority. It provides that cash will be paid, if possible, and receipts will be taken up as soon as possible. If cash is paid, coercion will seldom be necessary. The coercive measures adopted will be limited to the amount and kind necessary to secure the articles requisitioned.[51]

In the case of *Karmatzucas* v. *Germany*, the Germano-Greek Mixed Arbitral Tribunal held that only those requisitions were lawful that complied with the provisions of Article 52 of the Hague Regulations, namely, that payment of the amount due should be made as soon as possible after the requisition. As nearly nine years had elapsed since the requisition was made and as full payment therefor had not been made, such requisition was contrary to international law and afforded a good ground for the recognition of the competence of the Tribunal and for an award of compensation.[52]

There appears to be considerable doubt about the reasoning of the Tribunal concerning the invalidity of the requisition in the Karmatzucas pronouncement. As Sir Arnold McNair and H. Lauterpacht, the editors of the *Annual Digest of Public International Law Cases*, have stated, "it is difficult to see how subsequent failure to pay rendered the requisition unlawful *ab initio*. It would have sufficed to hold that the subsequent failure to pay was illegal."[53]

Oppenheim remarked that "There is little room for doubt that acts of deprivation of property in disregard of international law are incapable of creating or transferring title."[54] The Belgian Court of Cassation held that a requisition unaccompanied by a receipt or payment was no more capable of transferring property than theft,[55] and this view was also that of the Hungarian Supreme Court.[56] It would follow, therefore, that acts of deprivation of property, *i.e.*, requisitions, properly made and for which receipts have been issued or payment made, are valid and transfer title to the requisitioner upon issuance of such receipt. This view was upheld by

---

[51] Field Manual 27–10, pars. 337, 338, 339, 340.

[52] Annual Digest of Public International Law Cases, 1925–1926, Case No. 365.

[53] *Ibid.*, p. 479.   [54] 2 Oppenheim, note, p. 319.

[55] *Laurent* v. *Le Jeune*, Annual Digest, 1919–1922, Case No. 343.

[56] *Ibid.*, p. 482.

the Anglo-German Mixed Arbitral Tribunal which declared that although some coffee requisitioned in Belgium was, contrary to the provisions of Article 52, sent to Germany for the use of the army there, the requisition was not void in international law and that it therefore deprived the plaintiffs of their property there and then.[57]

An illustrative recent case involving the application of the above rules arose as a result of a claim by *B*, a national and resident of Strasbourg, France, for restitution of a motor vehicle in the possession of one *C*, a United States national employed by the Army in Germany. The record indicated that *B*'s motor vehicle had been requisitioned by the German Army from *B* in January, 1944. The notice of requisition stated that the owner would receive payment for the vehicle upon presentation of the receipt which would be given for the property. The vehicle was turned over to the German military authorities, as directed, in June, 1944. *B* was given a receipt therefor by the proper German Army authorities but did not attempt to secure payment from the German Army, although he had ample time (five months) in which to do so before the German forces were driven out of Strasbourg. In April, 1945, the vehicle was captured by the United States forces in a German Army motor pool at Stuttgart, Germany. It was later transferred on a quantitative receipt as captured enemy property to the German traffic authorities, from whom *C* claimed to have derived his title thereto. It was held that title to the motor vehicle was vested in *C* and *B*'s claim for restitution thereof should be denied. Title to the vehicle passed from *B* to the Government of Germany upon requisition and issuance of the receipt, although *B*, who had sufficient time to do so, did not present the receipt for payment. Upon capture by the United States forces title to the vehicle passed from the Government of Germany to the Government of the United States. The transfer of the vehicle by the United States Army to the German traffic authorities passed title to them. Thereafter, through valid sales effected under the pertinent provisions of the German Civil Code, title passed to *C*.[58]

IV—DISPOSITION OF CAPTURED ENEMY PROPERTY

The ultimate disposition of captured enemy property is not a question for international but for domestic law. The United States Constitution provides that the Congress shall make rules concerning captures on land and water.[59] Under this authority the Congress enacted Articles of War 79 and 80 [60] which provide in pertinent part:

> All public property taken from the enemy is the property of the United States and shall be secured for the service of the United States. . . .

[57] Tesdorpf *v.* German State, Annual Digest, 1923–1924, Case No. 340.
[58] 8 Bull. JAG (1949) 109.   [59] Article I, sec. 8, cl. 11.
[60] Public Law 759, 80th Cong.; 10 U.S.C. 1551.

Any person subject to military law who buys, sells, trades, or in any way deals in or disposes of captured or abandoned property, whereby he shall receive or expect any profit, benefit, or advantage to himself or to any other person directly or indirectly connected with himself, or who fails whenever such property comes into his possession or custody or within his control to give notice thereof to the proper authority and to turn over such property to the proper authority without delay, shall, on conviction thereof, be punished by fine or imprisonment, or by such other punishment as a court-martial, military commission, or other military tribunal may adjudge, or by any or all of said penalties.

The English rule is that "all booty captured from a hostile nation, whether on sea or land, belongs to the Crown. . . ." [61] Whenever booty is still admissible and therefore taken, it becomes the property of the state and not of the individual who captures it. The former practice by which booty was sold and the proceeds divided amongst the captors has vanished. [62]

Thus in an older case the Judge Advocate General held that the captor government, after capture, had "as full and complete title to captured property as to any of its property otherwise acquired. . . ." [63]

In a recent case where a Division Memorial Commission requested that certain enemy property captured by the Division be transferred to the Commission for permanent display in a museum to be built upon the termination of the war, it was held that there was no existing authority under which the War Department could comply with the request, as property captured from the enemy became the property of the United States and could only be disposed of in accordance with Congressional direction. It was further held that the Act of June 7, 1924, [64] which authorized and directed the Secretary of War to apportion and distribute pro rata "among the several States and Territories and possessions of the United States and the District of Columbia" certain war trophies captured from the armed forces of Germany, was applicable only to property captured during the period of the first World War, April 7, 1917, to November 11, 1918, and furnished no authority for the distribution of property captured in World War II. [65]

By virtue of the authority of the war powers of the President and in order to improve the morale of United States forces in theaters of operations, the War Department published Circular 353 on August 31, 1944, which authorized:

. . . the retention of war trophies by military personnel and merchant seamen and other civilians serving with the United States

[61] 6 Halsbury's Laws of England (2d ed.), p. 528.
[62] War Office, Manual of Military Law, 1929, p. 333.
[63] Digest of Opinions of the Judge Advocate General, 1912, p. 1060.
[64] 43 Stat. 597.   [65] 3 Bull. JAG (1944) 381.

Army overseas . . . under the conditions set forth in the following instructions. Retention by individuals of captured equipment as war trophies in accordance with the instructions contained herein is considered to be for the service of the United States and not in violation of the 79th Article of War.

2. War trophies will be taken only in a manner strictly consistent with the following principles of international law:

a. Article 6 of the Geneva (Prisoners of War) Convention of 1929 (par. 79, FM 27–10; Ch. 6, TM 27–251 (p. 69)) provides:

All effects and objects of personal use—except arms, horses, military equipment, and military papers—shall remain in the possession of prisoners of war, as well as metal helmets and gas masks.

Money in the possession of prisoners may not be taken away from them except by order of an officer and after the amount is determined. A receipt shall be given. Money thus taken away shall be entered to the account of each prisoner.

Identification documents, insignia of rank, decorations, and objects of value may not be taken from prisoners.

b. Metal helmets and gas masks may be taken from prisoners by the proper authorities when prisoners have reached a place where they are no longer needed for protection.

c. Article 3 of the Geneva (Red Cross) Convention of 1929 (par. 176, FM 27–10; Ch. 7, TM 27–251 (p. 131)) provides:

After every engagement, the belligerent who remains in possession of the field of battle shall take measures to search for the wounded and the dead and to protect them from robbery and ill treatment.

d. The taking of decorations, insignia of rank, or objects of value either from prisoners of war or from the wounded or dead (otherwise than officially for examination and safe keeping) is a violation of international law. There is nothing unlawful, however, in a soldier of our Army picking up and retaining small objects found on the battlefield, or buying articles from prisoners of war, of the sort, which, under the articles quoted, it is unlawful for him to take from a prisoner, the wounded, or the dead. In view of the practical difficulty of determining in a particular case whether an object has been acquired from a prisoner by coercion or otherwise obtained in a manner contrary to international law, commanding officers will take appropriate measures to prevent violation or evasion of either the letter or spirit of the conventions. Under no circumstances may war trophies include any item which in itself is evidence of disrespectful treatment of enemy dead.

3. *a.* With the exceptions noted in *b* below, military personnel returning to the United States from theaters of operations may be permitted to bring back small items of enemy equipment which have not been obtained in violation of the articles of the Geneva Convention as quoted in paragraph 2.

b. The following items are prohibited:

    (1) Nameplates. (These will not be removed from captured equipment except by authorized military personnel.)

    (2) Items which contain any explosives.

(3) Items of which the value as trophies, as determined by the theater commander, is outweighed by their usefulness in the service or for research or training purposes in the theaters of operations or elsewhere, or by their value as critical scrap material.

In connection with the above-authorized retention of captured enemy property as war trophies it is sufficient to point out that such retention was authorized under the pertinent provisions of domestic law, not international law, and that such authorization was in no way a reversion to the older practice approved by Heffter [66] which looked upon the taking of booty as a right of the individual soldier under international law.

In any attempt to solve the many knotty problems relating to the disposition of captured enemy property, the London Declaration of 1943 cannot be overlooked, for it added substantial difficulties to legal solutions by bringing into the picture the political concept of restitution. By the London Declaration the United States and certain others of the United Nations issued

> . . . formal warning to all concerned, and in particular to persons in neutral countries, that they intend to do their utmost to defeat the methods of dispossession practiced by the governments with which they are at war against the countries and peoples who have been so wantonly assaulted and despoiled.
>
> Accordingly the governments making this declaration and the French National Committee reserve all their rights to declare invalid any transfers of, or dealings with, property, rights and interests of any description whatsoever which are, or have been, situated in the territories which have come under the occupation or control, direct or indirect, of the governments with which they are at war or which belong or have belonged, to persons, including juridical persons, resident in such territories. This warning applies whether such transfers or dealings have taken the form of open looting or plunder, or of transactions apparently legal in form, even when they purport to be voluntarily effected.[67]

The concept of restitution as contained in the Declaration of London would appear to imply that the capture, seizure or requisition of property by an invading army is illegal, that after the fact of such capture, seizure or requisition, title to such property remains vested in the original owner, and that the laws of war by which title to such property is transferred by capture, seizure or requisition are inoperative. While the language of the Declaration would appear to render it easy to make such an inference and while such inferences were made by nations whose property was seized, it is obvious that such inferences had no basis in law. Certainly it would not be maintained on any legal ground that the Declaration of London invalidated or rendered inoperative the unwritten rules

[66] See note 13, *supra.*
[67] Department of State Bulletin, Vol. 8, No. 184 (January 2, 1943), p. 21.

of the international law of war or the written rules contained in the Hague and Geneva Conventions.

Based upon the Declaration of London, claims against the United States for the restitution of items of military equipment were made by several foreign governments, including Hungary, Poland, Yugoslavia, Belgium and Norway. Each of these governments assumed that whatever property was seized by the German armed forces was to be considered as "looted" under the terms of the Declaration of London. As much of this equipment was later captured or seized by the United States, it was necessary, in attempting to determine the United States' interest in such equipment, to investigate as fully as possible the facts surrounding the German acquisition of such equipment, and to distinguish between property which could be legally captured or seized or requisitioned under the Hague Regulations by the German armed forces, and property which appeared in fact to have been "looted." As stated above, property captured on the battlefield or legally seized and requisitioned by an army of occupation became the property of the captor government. Under appropriate restitution directives property which was *illegally* seized was considered as "loot" and, if recovered, was restitutable.

Great difficulties, however, arose in the application of these apparently simple principles. In cases wherein it was found that Germany acquired such property as a result of capture on the battlefield or through seizure or requisition under the general rules of international law, applicable as well to Germany and its allies as to the United States and its allies, the determination was made that Germany's title thereto was valid. Under the ordinary rules governing captured property, *supra,* it is usually not necessary for the capturing Power to go behind the fact of seizure or capture by its own forces in order to determine the validity of its own title. However, in these and similar cases, because of the Declaration of London, it was necessary to establish that such captured enemy property had not been "looted" by the German forces.

The case of the captured Hungarian horses is a fair illustration of the difficulties encountered. Certain Hungarian horses, belonging to private and public owners, were taken from Hungary by the retreating German Army early in 1945. Later they were captured in combat by the United States Army on German army farms and were reduced to firm possession. The best of them were brought to the United States for use at the United States Army breeding farms. In 1947 the Hungarian Government requested their return under the provisions of the Declaration of London. The United States Army, believing the horses to be captured enemy property, desired to retain them, while the Department of State, anxious to prove the international good faith of the United States, desired to return the horses to Hungary. After extended hearings before a subcommittee of the Armed Services Committee of the United States Senate, where all the relevant facts were brought to light, it was finally decided by the Departments of State and Army that the horses were captured enemy property, title to which was vested in the United States, and that such horses could not be sent to Hungary, or otherwise disposed of, without the specific authorization of an Act of Congress.

In conclusion, it is hoped that the material here presented will contribute to an understanding of the legal principles and problems inherent in the expression "captured enemy property." Colonel H. A. Smith stated that it would be for the jurists of tomorrow to determine how successfully we of today have solved in our small part such problems as have been presented for decision.[68] If this writer, by setting forth the general principles which have been illustrated by recently decided cases, has rendered this subject more understandable and the sources more available, he will have achieved his purpose and will have given the jurists of tomorrow some material upon which their judgment concerning the success of our efforts can be based.

[68] See note 2, *supra*.

[14]

Green War: An Assessment of the Environmental Law of International Armed Conflict

Michael N. Schmitt[†]

      † Advanced Research Fellow, United States Naval War College; Lieutenant Colonel, United States Air Force. LL.M 1991, Yale Law School; J.D. 1984, University of Texas; M.A. 1996, Naval War College; M.A. (1983) and B.A. (1978), Southwest Texas State University. The views expressed in this Article are those of the author in his personal capacity and should not be construed as representing those of the Department of Defense, United States Air Force, or Naval War College.

Victory smiles upon those who anticipate the changes in the character of war, not upon those who wait to adapt themselves after they occur.[1]

I. FRAMING THE ISSUES

As the twenty-first century approaches, the methods, means, and effects of warfare are in the midst of a profound revolution.[2] This revolution is evident, for instance, in the new focus of the U.S. armed forces on military operations other than war (MOOTW),[3] in revised tactics designed to exploit stealth technology, and in a probably healthy obsession with the potential for information warfare.[4] One of the most visible aspects of this revolution is a growing interrelationship between war and the environment, reflected both in armed conflict's impact on nature and in the use of the environment as a tool of warfare. While these are not novel phenomena in war, the potential scope of damage and the next generation of environmental weapons that science is making possible *are* unprecedented. There is little question that this quantitative and qualitative evolution merits characterization as "revolutionary."

This Article identifies and assesses the law that *might* govern activities bearing on the environment during hostilities.[5] Lack of consensus on the content of the relevant law highlights the importance of this task. Prior to considering the prescriptive environment proper, it is necessary to explore the genesis and evolution of the current norms. Therefore, Part II examines the history of environmental damage during warfare, as well as the legal responses thereto. A historical survey is an essential first step in any comprehensive legal analysis, for law is both contextual and directional. It is contextual in that it is understood and applied based upon the social, political, and economic environment in which it operates.[6] This is certainly the case

---

1. THE COMMAND OF THE AIR 338 (Office of Air Force History ed., 1983) (quotation attributed to Air Marshall Guilio Douhet).

2. For an interesting discussion of what constitutes a "revolution in military affairs," see Andrew F. Krepinievich, *Cavalry to Computer: The Pattern of Military Revolutions, in* STRATEGY AND FORCE PLANNING 58 (Naval War College ed., 1995). Throughout this Article, the terms "armed conflict" and "war" will be used interchangeably. Some scholars draw a distinction between the two, reserving the term "war" for those situations in which a formal declaration has been made. This distinction serves little purpose given the scope and scale of post-World War II conflicts and the lack of a declaration of war in the vast majority of them.

3. For a basic description of MOOTW, see JOINT CHIEFS OF STAFF, DOCTRINE FOR JOINT OPERATIONS ch. V (Joint Publication 3-0, 1995).

4. Information warfare has generated a flurry of activity in the Department of Defense. For an introduction to the subject, see Martin C. Libicki, *What Is Information Warfare?*, STRATEGIC F., May 1995, at 1; *see also* JOINT CHIEFS OF STAFF, INFORMATION WARFARE: LEGAL, REGULATORY, POLICY AND ORGANIZATIONAL CONSIDERATIONS FOR ASSURANCE (Research Report for the Chief, Information Warfare Division-J6K, July 4, 1995).

5. I first addressed this topic in tentative form in a comment. *See* Michael N. Schmitt, *The Environmental Law of War: An Invitation to Critical Reexamination*, 7 U.S.A.F.A. J. LEGAL STUD. 237 (1996). Though parts of this Article draw directly on the previous piece, it builds on my initial thoughts and expands the focus of consideration beyond core *jus in bello* substantive prescriptions.

6. This contextuality is apparent in the growing willingness of the international community to subordinate sovereignty to humanitarian interests in the post-Cold War, post-bipolar environment. The humanitarian operations in Somalia, Iraq, or Bosnia would not have been possible had the Cold War continued. On contextuality and the use of force, see Michael N. Schmitt, *The Resort to Force in International Law: Reflections on Positivist and Contextual Approaches*, 37 A.F. L. REV. 105, 110-15

with the environmental law of war, which is primarily the product of two historic events—Vietnam and the Gulf War. At the same time, law tends to be directional; it evolves over time in distinct directions.[7] Seldom spontaneous or random, these trends are often identifiable and occasionally predictable. The environmental law of war demonstrates several trends, one of which—a growing tendency to value the environment for more than merely what it offers us—has enormous potential to complicate and transform the law.

Once context and direction are established, Part III proceeds to catalogue and analyze the current law pertaining to the environment. For analytical clarity, it is grouped into three categories: peacetime prescriptions, customary law, and treaties. The part begins by exploring whether peacetime environmental prescriptions remain intact during armed conflict, and, if so, between whom and in what circumstances. Since peacetime environmental law continues to evolve, it is less useful to catalogue substantive norms than to ascertain the criteria for their applicability during hostilities. Analysis of the law of war follows. Customary law, which lies at its core, is examined to determine when traditional norms can be interpreted as providing environmental safeguards. An evaluation of treaty law—not only the sparse collection of environment-specific provisions, but also its broader nonspecific components—completes the review of prescriptive norms.

Throughout Part III, one should bear in mind that the assorted relevant prescriptions do not operate autonomously; jurisprudential vacuums exist only in theory. Instead, the various components of the law, whether customary or treaty-based, operate together to create a prescriptive environment. It is that environment that bounds warfare. Thus, treaty provisions may be interpreted by resort to customary law principles; treaty law may be deemed declarative of customary law and thereby clarify it; customary law may fill voids in applicable conventions; or custom and treaty law may operate synergistically to create tiers of protection for the environment.[8] Even when the law has been sorted out, it remains necessary to determine who has consented to be bound by what law in relation to whom. It is also necessary to ask how the

---

(1994).

7. An excellent example of this evolution of law is the erosion of neutral (as opposed to belligerent) interests in the law of naval warfare. The erosion has resulted from both technological advances in the means of warfare and the increasing interdependency of the international economy.

8. *See infra* Subsection III.C.3 (discussing Protocol I). For example, proportionality is a classic law of war principle intended to be codified in Protocol I. *See* Protocol Additional to the Geneva Conventions Relating to the Protection of Victims of International Armed Conflicts, June 8, 1977, U.N. Doc. A/32/144, 16 I.L.M. 1391 [hereinafter Protocol I]. Thus, its customary law meaning can be invoked in exploring the Protocol I restatement of the concept. On the other hand, the United States has not ratified Protocol I, but considers many of its provisions to be declarative of customary international law. *See infra* note 318 and accompanying text. Therefore, it remains a useful source for clarification of customary law principles. Furthermore, conventions are often drafted narrowly. Consider the Protocol I prohibitions on attacking dams, dikes, and nuclear power generating stations. *See* Protocol I, *supra*, art. 56. Its drafters debated whether this list is illustrative or exhaustive, ultimately deciding on the latter. However, this does not mean that other types of targets are fair game in article 56 situations. Customary principles such as proportionality and necessity will continue to govern such attacks. Moreover, the various types of law may intersect in terms of quantum of damage or nature of the target. This is particularly true in the environmental context, for some of the relevant conventional law has been criticized as setting an excessively high threshold for damage before a proscription applies. Protocol I is an excellent example. *See infra* note 353 and accompanying text.

affected international actors understand the law and how they intend to implement its standards. In this regard, the law of war manuals that the world's militaries employ are particularly useful. Part III, therefore, discusses not only which norms govern damage to the environment during armed conflict, but also how they interact in theory and practice. It is in this dynamic that the drama of the law is to be found.

While Part III highlights various strengths and weaknesses of the prescriptive regime's individual components, Part IV assesses the current state of the law. As will be seen, most commentators judge the law to be adequate but fault lax enforcement and weak dissemination for the impunity with which rogue leaders have abused the environment in this decade. This Article tests their characterization both from the perspective of adequate environmental protection and from that of usable normative guidance for policymakers and warfighters. Ultimately, it concludes that, despite assertions to the contrary, the emperor is rather scantily clad. The relevant law is difficult to apply in practice, is definitionally flawed, and lacks internal coherence. Equally distressing is a growing tendency to view the environment as wholly distinct from human existence. This trend may lead us to sacrifice compelling human values on the altar of formalistic environmentalism.

Lest this criticism be labeled gratuitous, Part IV also suggests how the international community, and particularly the U.S. armed forces, should safeguard the environment during armed conflict. There could not be a more propitious time to consider the options, as the U.S. military is currently drafting a new multi-service law of war manual. Since many of the world's armed forces look to the United States in military affairs, this manual is destined to be enormously influential on an international scale. Therefore, to help translate theory into reality, Part IV outlines the environmental factors that the drafters of the new U.S. law of war manual should consider.

Before setting off on these endeavors, however, it is perhaps useful to delineate the boundaries of my inquiry. First, this Article does not analyze arms limitation, arms proliferation, and test ban treaty regimes.[9] The issue at hand is one of use, not possession. An assessment of environmental prescriptions operative during noninternational armed conflict is likewise absent.[10] My goal is to consider only those hostilities that are truly

---

9. Many of these treaties bear on the relationship between war and the environment because they limit or prohibit environmentally destructive weapons. *See, e.g.*, Treaty on the Principles Governing the Activities of States in the Exploration and Use of Outer Space, Including the Moon and Other Celestial Bodies, Jan. 27, 1967, art. IV, 18 U.S.T. 2410, 610 U.N.T.S. 205 (banning placement in orbit of nuclear weapons or weapons of mass destruction); Treaty Banning Nuclear Weapons Tests in the Atmosphere, in Outer Space and Under Water, Aug. 5, 1963, art. 1, 14 U.S.T. 1313, 480 U.N.T.S. 43; Antarctic Treaty, June 23, 1961, art. I, para. 1, 12 U.S.T. 794, 402 U.N.T.S. 71 (prohibiting any weapons testing in Antarctica).

10. The distinction between international and noninternational armed conflicts is not always clear. Protocol II Additional to the Geneva Conventions defines noninternational armed conflict as

> armed conflicts . . . which take place in the territory of a [party to the Convention] between its armed forces and dissident armed forces or other organized armed groups which, under responsible command, exercise such control over a part of its territory as to enable them to carry out sustained and concerted military operations.

Addition to Protocol II, art. 1, para. 1, U.N. Doc. A/32/144, Annex II (1977), *reprinted in* 16 I.L.M. 1442, 1443 [hereinafter Protocol II]. International armed conflict is that which arises between states (or

international in scope. Furthermore, this Article does not address the *jus ad bellum* issue of when an "attack" on, or use of, the environment constitutes a resort to force in violation of the U.N. Charter.[11] Instead, analysis of the *jus in bello* (i.e., *how*, not *when*, force may be employed) dominates the study. Finally, this Article makes no attempt to evaluate comprehensively the legality of individual environmentally harmful episodes of warfare; analysis and commentary focus instead on the law itself.[12]

Clarifying definitions, particularly that of the term "environment," is equally important. As used here, "environment" indicates those conditions, circumstances, substances, and organisms that affect the global ecosystem. Physical phenomena such as weather and the permeability of the ozone layer are examples of "conditions," whereas the course of a river and the existence of a lake illustrate the term "circumstances." Food, timber, soil, water, and oil exemplify "substances," and "organisms" include both plant and animal life. The concept of the "environment" also extends to usability. For example, spreading mines or bomblets through an area can render it unusable; such denial of use is the functional equivalent of damage.

While the need to define the environment before evaluating prescriptions governing harm to it is self-evident, far less obvious is the importance of identifying the motivations underlying environmental protection. The issue has been addressed only sparingly in the literature, primarily within governmental fora and at conferences. Interestingly, those who consider it tend to arrive at very different conclusions regarding the law's adequacy than from most of their colleagues.[13] Therefore, it is useful to alert the reader early on to the

---

other subjects of international law). *See, e.g.*, Geneva Convention for the Amelioration of the Condition of the Wounded and Sick in Armed Forces in the Field, Aug. 12, 1949, art. 2, 6 U.S.T. 3114, 75 U.N.T.S. 31 ("[T]he present Convention shall apply to all cases of declared war or of any other armed conflict which may arise between two or more of the High Contracting Parties, even if a state of war is not recognized by one of them."); Geneva Convention for the Amelioration of the Condition of the Wounded, Sick and Shipwrecked Members of the Armed Forces at Sea, Aug. 12, 1949, art. 2, 6 U.S.T. 3217, 75 U.N.T.S. 85 (same); Geneva Convention Relative to the Treatment of Prisoners of War, Aug. 12, 1949, art. 2, 6 U.S.T. 3316, 75 U.N.T.S. 135 (same); Geneva Convention Relative to the Protection of Civilian Persons in Time of War, Aug. 12, 1949, art. 2, 6 U.S.T. 3516, 75 U.N.T.S. 287 (same) [hereinafter Geneva Convention IV]. Additional Protocol I, which supplements the Geneva Conventions with regard to international armed conflict, simply refers back to the common article 2 of the Geneva Conventions. *See* Protocol I, *supra* note 8, art. 1, para. 3. In a somewhat controversial provision, Protocol I includes as *international* armed conflicts "armed conflicts in which peoples are fighting against colonial domination and alien occupation and against racist regimes in the exercise of their right of self-determination." *Id.* art. 1, para. 4. Note that "internal disturbances and tensions, such as riots, isolated and sporadic acts of violence and other acts of a similar nature" are not armed conflict—either international or noninternational. *See* Protocol II, *supra*, art. 1, para. 2.

.11. Article 2(4) of the U.N. Charter provides that "[a]ll Members shall refrain in their international relations from the threat or use of force against the territorial integrity or political independence of any state, or in any other manner inconsistent with the Purposes of the United Nations." U.N. CHARTER art. 2, para. 4. The Charter does authorize the use of force when pursuant to a Security Council determination that it is "necessary to maintain or restore international peace and security," *id.* art. 42, or required in individual or collective self-defense, *see id.* art. 51.

12. For instance, the question is not whether the Iraqis violated the law of armed conflict, but rather what law governs the types of activities in which they engaged.

13. The most notable example is Wil Verwey, Chairman of the National University of Gronigen (Netherlands) Department of International and Constitutional Law. *See, e.g.*, Wil D. Verwey, *Observations on the Legal Protection of the Environment in Times of International Armed Conflict, in* 1994 HAGUE Y.B. INT'L L. 35, 49 [hereinafter Verwey, *Observations*]; Wil D. Verwey, *Protection of the*

6   YALE JOURNAL OF INTERNATIONAL LAW   [Vol. 22: 1

effects of this distinction.

There are basically two approaches: "utilitarian" and "intrinsic worth."[14] The prevailing one values the environment for what it offers humankind—food, shelter, fuel, and clothing, for example. This anthropocentric approach focuses on the environment's ability to make life possible—and to take it away. Beyond providing survival benefits, the environment merits protection because of its impact on the quality of human life. For instance, natural preserves or endangered species must be safeguarded lest we be deprived of their aesthetic value. Reduced to basics, anthropocentrism displays a strong utilitarian flavor.

On the other hand, the environment can be viewed as possessing *intrinsic* value, that is, value that is independent of the uses for which human beings may exploit it. This value is not in lieu of anthropocentric value but in addition to it. For intrinsic valuation advocates, determining the environment's contribution to human existence is only half the story when assessing whether its destruction is justifiable and lawful. Calculating the intrinsic value of the environment's damaged component is equally necessary. Of course, intrinsic value measurements are inherently difficult since the point of departure is not the human self. Proponents, however, might argue that through consideration of such factors as ecosystem function or species regeneration capacity, intrinsic value is sufficiently discernible to merit inclusion in legal formulae.

The distinction between anthropocentric and intrinsic value is, borrowing from the law of evidence, both an issue of weight and one of admissibility. At heart, laws of war are often about balancing competing interests. Whether one operates from within an anthropocentric or intrinsic value cognitive prism determines the relative weight accorded competing interests. An even more basic question is whether intrinsic valuation has a place in the law of war at all—whether it is admissible, if you will. Thus, this study searches for evidence of the distinction and, if one exists, its implications. It concludes by evaluating the appropriateness of any trends identified.

It might be assumed that the anthropocentric/intrinsic divide, or the environment and warfare issue more generally, is highly politicized.[15] In fact, there are some predictable distinctions among those who have taken positions on the matter. For instance, organizations such as Greenpeace tend to advocate a higher standard of environmental protection than do others. However, all concerned basically agree that there must be heightened

---

Environment in Times of Armed Conflict: In Search of a New Legal Perspective, 8 LEIDEN J. INT'L L. 7, 39–40 (1995) [hereinafter Verwey, *Protection*]; Wil D. Verwey, Protection of the Environment in Times of Armed Conflict: Do We Need Additional Rules?, Paper Presented at the Symposium on the Protection of the Environment During Armed Conflict and Operations Other Than War (Sept. 1995) [hereinafter Verwey, Additional Rules]. The last paper and all others presented at the Symposium are forthcoming in PROTECTION OF THE ENVIRONMENT DURING ARMED CONFLICT & OTHER MILITARY OPERATIONS (Naval War College International Law Studies No. 69) (Richard Grunawalt et al. eds., forthcoming 199_) [hereinafter NWC SYMPOSIUM PAPERS].

14. For an interesting discussion of these two approaches, see Merrit P. Drucker, *The Military Commander's Responsibility for the Environment*, 11 ENVTL. ETHICS 135, 136–40 (1989).

15. Peacetime international environmental law is much more politicized. For instance, lesser developed states often oppose constraints on industrialization that might retard development. *See infra* note 215 and accompanying text.

environmental safeguards during armed conflict. Given this agreement, one aspect of the debate centers on how best to effect those safeguards—through new law or through improved enforcement mechanisms. The debate over the anthropocentric/intrinsic division is much more fundamental; it centers on how to balance worthy values that sometimes conflict.

This debate cuts across traditional political lines and international boundaries. For example, the International Committee of the Red Cross (ICRC), an organization dedicated to mitigating the impact of warfare on humanity, finds itself allied with hard-core warfighters in opposing any movement away from anthropocentrism. The ICRC fears that applying the intrinsic value approach may decrease human protection, whereas warfighters tend to be concerned that it may distort proportionality calculations and thereby immunize valid military objectives. Nevertheless, that the ICRC and warfighters arrive at similar conclusions indicates that political dimensions to the issue have minimal practical effect. Paradoxically, the politicization that does occur is often the result of ideological prejudices. Thus an organization like Greenpeace evokes an almost visceral response from some parties that is entirely disproportionate to the actual difference in their respective views on the subject. Given the identity of the participants, observers expect politicization of the issues. In fact, the issues here are often less politicized than the participants.

With the boundaries of inquiry set, and with the reader sensitized to the role of cognitive perspectives, analysis may proceed. As it does, reflect on the following pervasive questions: Does the law adequately protect the environment during international armed conflict? If so, does the law sufficiently preserve and foster important human interests? Does the present law facilitate the balancing of environmental interests with other interests during warfare? Does it adequately deter unacceptable environmental damage during warfare, and, if not, why not? To what extent are the prescriptions sufficiently precise to guide policymakers and warfighters? Finally, if the law falls short, how should its shortfalls be remedied? Bearing these questions in mind, I now turn to the historical context that informs the environmental law of war.

II.   HOW DID WE GET HERE?

A.   *The Environment and Warfare Before Vietnam*

That war damages the environment is a truism. So, too, can the forces of nature serve as a powerful weapon during war.[16] In the seventeenth century, for example, the Dutch destroyed dikes to flood their lowlands and stem the advance of their enemies, thereby devastating vast tracts of farmland. In 1938, during the second Sino-Japanese War, the Chinese adopted an identical tactic

---

16.   An extensive discussion of the history of the environmental effects of warfare can be found in ARTHUR H. WESTING, WARFARE IN A FRAGILE WORLD: THE MILITARY IMPACT ON THE HUMAN ENVIRONMENT (1980). In particular, refer to table 1.2, which gives a selection of "ecologically disruptive wars." *Id.* at 14–19 tbl.1.2.

when they destroyed the Huayuankow dike on the Yellow River to halt the Japanese invaders. Although a short–term military success, the operation killed thousands of civilians and flooded millions of acres of cultivated land. In the next decade, the Germans employed a similar technique by flooding a number of areas in the Netherlands to slow the Allied advance eastward. The European theater also witnessed repeated attacks on hydroelectric dams. To cite only one example, raids on the Möhne and Eder dams in May 1943, although effectively depriving the Ruhr industrial complex of water and power, killed more than 1300 civilians and shut off drinking water and energy to the four million Germans in the region. Dam attacks continued during the Korean and Vietnam conflicts.[17]

This century witnessed the first major environmental damage caused by the destruction of oil facilities. In a notable chapter of the First World War, British Colonel Norton Griffiths destroyed Romanian oil fields, the richest in Europe, to prevent them from falling into enemy hands when the Central Powers invaded.[18] Romanian oil was again a target in the Second World War. Most noteworthy were the 1943 air raids on the oil producing center at Ploesti. Memorable for the feats of airmanship involved in the fifteen-hundred mile flight, much of it through enemy fighter cover, the raids significantly damaged refineries and oil tanks fueling the Reich's war machine. As might be imagined, all such attacks wrought extensive environmental damage.

Of course, it was in the Second World War that the only instances in history of wartime environmental destruction by nuclear weapons took place when U.S. aircraft bombed Hiroshima and Nagasaki in August 1945. Tens of thousands died immediately, with thousands of others doomed to suffer the effects of radiation for decades to come. The target area was reduced to a virtual wasteland.[19] That those weapons are dwarfed by modern nuclear

---

17. The foregoing events are described in many sources. Of particular note is their inclusion in the ICRC Commentary to article 56 of Protocol I. *See* INTERNATIONAL COMM. OF THE RED CROSS, COMMENTARY ON THE ADDITIONAL PROTOCOLS OF 8 JUNE 1977 TO THE GENEVA CONVENTIONS OF 12 AUGUST 1949, at 667 (Yves Sandoz et al. eds., 1987) [hereinafter ICRC COMMENTARY]. The raid on the Möhne dam was poignantly described by Wing Commander Guy Penrose Gibson of the RAF:

As Gibson flew his Lancaster up and down the dam, he saw the water of the dammed lake rising "like stirred porridge in the moonlight, rushing through a great breach." A few minutes later, he reported: "The valley was beginning to fill with fog and . . . we saw cars speeding along the roads in front of this great wave of water which was chasing them. . . . I saw their headlights burning and I saw water overtake them, wave by wave, and then the color of the headlights underneath the water changing from light blue to green, from green to dark purple until there was no longer anything except the water bouncing up and down."

THE AMERICAN HERITAGE HISTORY OF WORLD WAR II, at 418 (David G. McCullough ed., 1966).

18. *See* Adam Roberts, Environmental Issues in International Armed Conflict: The Experience of the 1991 Gulf War, Paper Presented at the Symposium on the Protection of the Environment During Armed Conflict and Operations Other Than War *in* NWC SYMPOSIUM PAPERS, *supra* note 13 (manuscript at 5, on file with *The Yale Journal of International Law*) (citing C.R.M.F. CRUTTWELL, A HISTORY OF THE GREAT WAR, 1914–1918, at 297–98 (1934)).

19. One eyewitness of the explosion in Hiroshima described the destruction:

Within a few seconds the thousands of people in the streets and the gardens in the center of the town were scorched by a wave of searing heat. Many were killed instantly, others lay writhing on the ground, screaming in agony from the intolerable pain of their burns. Everything standing upright in the way of the blast, walls, houses, factories, and other buildings, was annihilated. . . . Horses, dogs, and cattle suffered the same fate as human beings. Every living thing was petrified in an attitude of indescribable suffering. Even the

capabilities emphasizes the environmental apocalypse that their widespread use would ensure today.

Despite the destructiveness of such events, the international community paid scant attention to their environmental consequences. The limited expressions of concern were from a purely anthropocentric perspective, as demonstrated by the failure to mention the environment in the four Geneva Conventions promulgated in the immediate aftermath of World War II. In part, this may have been because, as Geoffrey Best has perceptively noted, until the Second World War, man's destructive capabilities primarily threatened the anthropogenic environment.[20] It was also surely the result of a failure to understand the complex interrelationships between human activities and the environment, the fragility of the environment, or even its finite nature. Until the war in Vietnam, whatever protection the environment enjoyed under international law was purely coincidental.

B. *Vietnam and Its Aftermath*

During the Vietnam conflict, the environment began to play a prominent role in considerations of warfare's means and methods.[21] For military planners, Vietnam presented unique challenges. United States and South Vietnamese forces faced both regular North Vietnamese Army troops who had infiltrated the South and indigenous guerrilla units—the Viet Cong—supplied via a complex network of trails from the North and from Cambodian and Laotian sanctuaries. Among the factors that contributed to the Communist forces' ultimate success was an ability to blend into the surrounding vegetation and forests whenever threatened. Operating from these areas, they effectively employed small unit tactics to wear down the U.S. and South Vietnamese forces. While this did little to "win the war" militarily, it drove the political cost up measurably, especially in the United States.

Understandably, U.S. forces worked hard to defeat these tactics.[22] One approach was to destroy forests and dense vegetation to deny the enemy cover, mobility, logistic support, and, in some cases, sustenance. U.S. forces utilized two techniques—beyond merely bombing the targeted zones with conventional munitions (an especially ineffective and inefficient method)—to accomplish this end. First, they dropped herbicides over enormous areas of

---

vegetation did not escape. Trees went up in flames, the rice plants lost their greenness, the grass burned on the ground.
THE AMERICAN HERITAGE HISTORY OF WORLD WAR II, *supra* note 17, at 616.

20. *See* Geoffrey Best, *The Historical Evolution of Cultural Norms Relating to War and the Environment*, *in* CULTURAL NORMS, WAR AND ENVIRONMENT 18, 18–20 (Arthur H. Westing ed., 1988).

21. Probably the best account of the war's environmental impact is in ARTHUR H. WESTING, ECOLOGICAL CONSEQUENCES OF THE SECOND INDOCHINA WAR (1976).

22. Perhaps the best known of the attempted remedies was the failed Strategic Hamlet Program, an effort to deny the enemy sanctuary in villages throughout the South by securing the allegiance of the local villagers. Ultimately, this effort failed, in no small part due to the corruption and lack of commitment of the United States's South Vietnamese allies. An interesting description of the counterinsurgency effort in South Vietnam from the perspective of senior South Vietnamese officers can be found in CAO VAN VIEN & DONG VAN KHUYEN, REFLECTIONS ON THE VIETNAM WAR 1–84 (U.S. Army Center of Military History Indochina Monographs, 1980).

South Vietnam, both in wooded areas (86%) and on crop lands (14%).[23] By one estimate, approximately one-tenth of South Vietnam was sprayed during the war.[24] At the same time, U.S. troops used heavy tractors with large blades attached—Rome plows—to cut through vegetation and trees. Initially, the effort concentrated on clearing land alongside roads to minimize the risk of ambushes. However, in 1967 large tracts began to be leveled; by the end of the war, Rome plows had cleared nearly three-quarters of a million acres. Though more labor intensive than spraying, plowing was more effective in rendering an area unusable. As might be expected, both techniques caused extensive damage to the flora (the military objective) and fauna of the region. In particular, the operations led to massive soil erosion in Vietnam's hilly terrain. The effect on animal habitats was especially severe, for the vegetation that regenerated proved less capable of supporting animal life than in the past.[25]

Between 1963 and 1972, the Air Force also seeded clouds in operations designed to lengthen the rainy season.[26] Since the roadways were unpaved, U.S. forces hoped that extended rainfall would soften the road surfaces and cause them to collapse, thereby slowing movement along the Ho Chi Minh trail.[27] Reportedly, a secondary goal was to degrade enemy surface-to-air missile radar capabilities.[28] Disagreement exists over the success of these operations.[29] Nevertheless, there is little doubt that increasing rainfall can

---

23. *See* WESTING, *supra* note 21, at 27. Three types of herbicides were used: Agents Orange and White operated to interfere with plant metabolism, while Agent Blue dehydrated plants. The agents were generally dispersed from the air by C-123 aircraft. However, helicopters and even truck- and boat-mounted sprayers were also used. *See id.* at 24–27.

24. Approximately 2% of Indochina was sprayed, though most such operations were limited to South Vietnam. In the South, the bulk of the defoliation efforts were centered in Military Region III, which surrounded Saigon. Some 30% of this area was sprayed at least once. *See id.* at 28.

25. *See* Richard Carruthers, *International Controls on the Impact on the Environment of Wartime Operations*, 10 ENVTL. & PLAN. L.J. 38, 40 (1993). Arthur Westing points out that the spraying affected not only the autotrophic aspect of the ecosystem, but also the heterotrophic links (i.e., those beyond the first link in the food chain). In great part, this occurred because much animal activity takes place in the upper reaches of vegetation, which were most severely affected by the spraying. *See* WESTING, *supra* note 21, at 32. Westing describes the destruction resulting from the spraying, *see id.* at 28–40, and from the plowing, *see id.* at 47–49. He also gives a general discussion of the overall damage. *See id.* at 63–82.

26. On March 20, 1974, the Department of Defense conducted a top secret briefing before a Senate Subcommittee in which the Department described the program. This briefing, since declassified, is reprinted in *Environmental Modification Treaty: Hearings on the Convention on the Prohibition of Military or Any Other Hostile Use of Environmental Modification Techniques Before the Senate Comm. on Foreign Relations*, 95th Cong. 101 (1978) [hereinafter *TS Brief*].

27. *See id.* at 102.

28. Although this intent was not described in the TS Brief, it was noted by Seymour Hersch. He cited an unidentified U.S. government source as stating that a method of treating clouds with an acid chemical that would foil the operation of North Vietnamese radars had been developed. Other purposes of the rainmaking included, according to the Hersch report, providing "cover for infiltration of South Vietnamese commando and intelligence teams"; "serving as a 'spoiler' for North Vietnamese attacks and raids"; "altering or tailoring the rain patterns over North Vietnam and Laos to aid United States bombing missions"; and "diverting North Vietnamese men and material from military operations to keep muddied roads and lines of communication in operation." Seymour M. Hersch, *Rainmaking Is Used as a Weapon by U.S.*, N.Y. TIMES, July 3, 1972, at A1.

29. The Air Force asserted that rainfall increased by 30% in some locations, *see TS Brief*, *supra* note 26, at 115, but admitted that "[w]hile this program had an effect on the primitive road conditions in these areas, the results were certainly limited and unverifiable." *Id.* at 120. Arthur Westing noted that "[a]lthough the military seemed satisfied with the level of success of its weather-modification operations

cause negative environmental consequences, including increased soil erosion, destruction of vegetation, and disease among animals.

For the first time, the environmental impact of military operations drew domestic and international attention. Multiple factors contributed to this new phenomenon. A general increase in environmental awareness coincided with the Vietnam War to help focus public attention on the environmental effects of the war. So, too, did antiwar sentiment. In a sense, the environmental damage provided a rallying point—one that did not smack of purely political motivation—for opposition to the conflict. These factors came together as war began to be brought into the living room nightly through television. For the first time in history, the general public witnessed the consequences of a war fought halfway around the globe.

Not only did the conflict spotlight the fact of environmental damage, but it also raised questions of its legality. Indeed, the State Department's legal staff recommended that the defoliation operations be limited to the territory of South Vietnam and Laos, lest they be interpreted as precedent for use by others elsewhere.[30] In South Vietnam, the operations would have negligible precedential effect because the South Vietnamese consented to application of the chemicals.

Despite official sensitivity, environmental legal norms were still in a nascent stage.[31] Even at this late stage, no law of war treaty mentioned the word "environment." Predictably, calls for new law were soon heard. For example, Senator Claiborne Pell proposed a draft treaty to "prohibit and prevent, at any place, any environmental or geophysical modification activity as a weapon of war."[32] He also recommended the prohibition of research aimed at the development of such weapons. In July 1973, his document was deemed a "sense of the Senate,"[33] an important first step towards the Environmental Modification Convention (ENMOD) that came into force a mere five years later.[34]

Particularly interesting was a proposal, this time emanating from the halls of academia, by Princeton's Richard Falk. Adopted at the Emergency Conference Against Environmental Warfare in Indochina, held in Stockholm in June 1972 it included a Convention on Ecocide that criminalized many of the activities in which the United States had engaged during the war.[35] For instance, the Convention defined ecocide as, inter alia,

---

in Indochina, a dispassionate arbiter would be hard put to recognize a basis for this optimism." WESTING, *supra* note 21, at 56 (citation omitted).

30. *See* George H. Aldrich, *Prospects for the United States Ratification of Additional Protocol I to the 1949 Geneva Conventions*, 85 AM. J. INT'L L. 1, 14 (1991).

31. For instance, the use of Agent Orange continued to be characterized as an issue of primarily tort, rather than environmental, law. This point was noted in the U.S. Army's post–Desert Storm/Shield legal report. *See* LEGAL SERV. AGENCY, U.S. ARMY, THE DESERT STORM ASSESSMENT TEAM'S REPORT TO THE JUDGE ADVOCATE GENERAL OF THE ARMY pt. G, at 1 (1992) [hereinafter ARMY ASSESSMENT].

32. S. Res. 71, 93d Cong. (1973).

33. *Id.*

34. *See* Convention on the Prohibition of Military or Any Other Hostile Use of Environmental Modification Techniques, Dec. 10, 1976, 31 U.S.T. 333, 1108 U.N.T.S. 152 [hereinafter ENMOD].

35. *See* Proposed International Convention on the Crime of Ecocide, *reprinted in* Richard A. Falk, *Environmental Warfare and Ecocide—Facts, Appraisal, and Proposals*, 4 BULL. PEACE PROPOSALS 80 app. I at 93–95 (1973) [hereinafter Proposed International Convention on the Crime of Ecocide].

(b) The use of chemical herbicides to defoliate and deforest natural forests; (c) The use of bombs and artillery in such quantity, density, or size as to impair the quality of the soil or to enhance the prospect of diseases dangerous to human beings, animals, or crops; (d) The use of bulldozing . . . to destroy large tracts of forest or cropland for military purposes; (e) The use of techniques designed to increase or decrease rainfall or otherwise modify weather as a weapon of war.[36]

The Convention also forbade the forcible removal of human beings or animals from their habitats and the employment of weapons of mass destruction (WMD).[37] Those who committed such acts, or were otherwise culpable for their commission, would, at minimum, be removed from any position of public trust.[38] Professor Falk also recommended the passage of national implementing legislation, as well as the establishment of a Commission for the Investigation of Ecocide.[39] In certain cases, the United Nations would be called upon to take "appropriate" action under the U.N. Charter to prevent and suppress ecocide.[40] This implied that ecocide could amount to a breach of peace or act of aggression that might warrant a forceful response under article 42 of the Charter.[41]

The conference also adopted the Draft Protocol on Environmental Warfare.[42] It began by claiming that "environmental warfare has been condemned by public opinion throughout the world."[43] Signatories therefore agreed "as a matter of conscience and of law to refrain from the use of tactics and weapons of war that inflict irreparable harm to the environment or disrupt fundamental ecological relationships."[44] In addition to outlawing weapons of mass destruction, the document specifically prohibited spreading chemical defoliants, bulldozing, and employing conventional munitions that cause extensive cratering. The Protocol deemed such violations a crime under international law, thus allowing for individual responsibility.[45]

Though the community of nations never formally adopted either proposal, it was clear that laws to protect the environment—the newest "victim" of war—were on the horizon. A two-track approach was taken. First, negotiations to limit the use of the environment as a weapon led to the

---

36. *Id.* art. 1, at 93.
37. *See id.* art. 2, at 93.
38. *See id.* art. 4, at 93.
39. *See id.* art. 6, at 93–94.
40. *See id.* art. 9, at 94.
41. "The Security Council shall determine the existence of any threat to the peace, breach of peace, or act of aggression and shall make recommendations, or decide what measures shall be taken in accordance with Articles 41 and 42, to maintain or restore international peace and security." U.N. CHARTER art. 39. "The Security Council may decide what measures not involving the use of force are to be employed to give effect to its decisions . . . ." *Id.* art. 41. "Should the Security Council consider that measures provided for in Article 41 would be inadequate or have proven to be inadequate, it may take such action by air, sea, or land forces as may be necessary to maintain or restore international peace and security." *Id.* art. 42.
42. Draft Protocol on Environmental Warfare, *reprinted in* Falk, *supra* note 35, app. II at 95–96 [hereinafter Draft Protocol on Environmental Warfare].
43. *Id.* at 95.
44. *Id.*
45. *See id.* For Professor Falk's views on ecocide and environmental warfare (as well as reprints of both proposed documents), see Richard A. Falk, *Environmental Warfare and Ecocide, in* 4 THE VIETNAM WAR AND INTERNATIONAL LAW 287 (Richard A. Falk ed., 1976); *see also* Falk, *supra* note 35.

Convention on the Prohibition of Military or Any Other Hostile Use of Environmental Modification Techniques Convention (ENMOD). Opened for signature in 1977, this convention came into force for the United States in January 1980. By the terms of ENMOD, states agree not to "engage in military or any other hostile use of environmental modification techniques having wide-spread, long-lasting or severe effects as the means of destruction, damage or injury" to other parties.[46] Reminiscent of the treaty called for by Senator Pell in 1972, ENMOD was the first environment-specific law of armed conflict. However, it does not necessarily protect the environment proper. Instead, ENMOD proscribes environment-modifying processes as a method of warfare only if significant destruction, damage, or injury would result. Whether that damage is to the environment is irrelevant, though in most cases it would be.

Contemporaneously, the second track was taken. The Vietnam experience had highlighted the need to account in the law of war for the new methods, means, and characteristics of armed conflict. Existing international conventions, notably the Hague and Geneva Conventions, had been designed to apply to a genre of warfare very different from that prevalent in Vietnam. In response, the international community gathered between 1974 and 1977 under the auspices of the ICRC to bring the law of war up to date. This Diplomatic Conference on the Reaffirmation and Development of International Humanitarian Law Applicable in Armed Conflicts met on four occasions to draft Protocols Additional I and II to the Geneva Conventions.[47]

Protocol I, governing international armed conflict, is central to the environmental law of war, for it contains the only specific prohibitions on damaging (as opposed to using) the environment. Article 35(3) provides that "[i]t is prohibited to employ methods or means of warfare which are intended, or may be expected, to cause widespread, long-term and severe damage to the environment."[48] The protocol devotes article 55 to the subject:

> 1. Care shall be taken in warfare to protect the natural environment against widespread, long-term and severe damage. This protection includes a prohibition of the use of methods or means of warfare which are intended or may be expected to cause such damage to the natural environment and thereby to prejudice the health or survival of the population.
> 2. Attacks against the natural environment by way of reprisals are prohibited.[49]

ENMOD and Protocol I reveal a directional trend in the environmental law of war. Prior to the Vietnam experience, attitudes towards the environment were purely anthropocentric. The lack of any mention of the environment in the law of war suggests that it was understood solely in its utilitarian context. Indeed, it would be difficult to assert that the international community viewed the environment as a distinct entity at all. However, by the end of the Vietnam War the concept of an "environment" had been grasped, albeit primarily anthropocentrically. This perspective is evident in ENMOD's prohibition on the use of (but not damage to) the environment and in the

---

46. ENMOD, *supra* note 34, art. I, para. 1.
47. Protocol I, *supra* note 8; Protocol II, *supra* note 10.
48. Protocol I, *supra* note 8, art. 35, para. 3.
49. *Id.* art. 55.

14   YALE JOURNAL OF INTERNATIONAL LAW   [Vol. 22: 1

requirement of article 55 that the threshold environmental damage prejudice the population's health or survival. Only in article 35(3) does a prescription appear that is divorced from impact on the human population. By its formula, the question is the *degree* of damage to the environment, rather than its *effect* in human terms. As shall be discussed below, the drafters included article 35(3) to appease intrinsic value advocates who urged protection of the environment per se. Thus, while the cognitive perspective was primarily anthropocentric in the immediate post-Vietnam period, it was an anthropocentrism increasingly sensitized to the existence of the environment *qua* environment. Moreover, the first glimpses of an evolutionary trend in the direction of intrinsic valuation were apparent. It should be noted that the United States, although a participant in the negotiations, has elected not to ratify Protocol I, a decision motivated in part by opposition to its environmental provisions.[50]

In the 1980s, efforts to strengthen the environmental law of war faded. This was true despite significant environmental damage during the Iran-Iraq War—particularly oil spills caused by the tanker war. Between May 1980 and December 1987, some 447 tankers were attacked in the Persian Gulf.[51] Also attacked were oil facilities, both ashore and offshore. These operations caused substantial damage. For example, raids against Iran's Nowruz oil drilling facility in 1983 led to the release of two million barrels of oil into the Persian Gulf. Iraq's refusal to agree to a temporary truce that would allow the wells to be capped compounded the situation.[52]

Yet despite the pervasive environmental destruction, the international legal community focused far more attention on neutrality issues. Perhaps this was because the leading nations of the world were nonbelligerents during the Iran-Iraq War. By framing tanker destruction in neutrality terms, neutrals could concentrate on maintaining a free flow of oil, an emphasis that had the

---

50. For articles bearing on the debate over ratification, see George H. Aldrich, *Progressive Development of the Laws of War: A Reply to Criticisms of the 1977 Geneva Protocol I*, 26 VA. J. INT'L L. 693 (1986); Aldrich, *supra* note 30; David A. Bagley, *Ratification of Protocol I to the Geneva Conventions of 1949 by the United States: Discussion and Suggestions for the American Lawyer-Citizen*, 11 LOY. L.A. INT'L & COMP. L.J. 439 (1989); Hans-Peter Gasser, *AGORA: The U.S. Decision Not to Ratify Protocol I to the Geneva Conventions on the Protection of War Victims*, 81 AM. J. INT'L L. 910 (1987); Michael J. Matheson, *Session One: The United States Position on the Relation of Customary International Law to the 1977 Protocols Additional to the 1949 Geneva Conventions*, 2 AM. U. J. INT'L L. & POL'Y 419 (1987); Guy B. Roberts, *The New Rules for Waging War: The Case Against Ratification of Additional Protocol I*, 26 VA. J. INT'L L. 109 (1985); William G. Schmidt, *The Protection of Victims of International Armed Conflicts: Protocol I Additional to the Geneva Conventions*, 24 A.F. L. REV. 189 (1984); Abraham D. Sofaer, *AGORA: The U.S. Decisions Not to Ratify Protocol I to the Geneva Conventions on the Protection of War Victims*, 82 AM. J. INT'L L. 784 (1988).

51. In 1984 alone, over two million tons of oil were spilled into the Gulf. *See* Phillipe Antoine, *International Humanitarian Law and the Protection of the Environment in Time of Armed Conflict*, INT'L REV. RED CROSS, Nov.-Dec. 1992, at 517, 530. Mr. Antoine asserts that the damage caused during the tanker war rose to the level of "widespread, long-term and severe," though neither Iran nor Iraq was party to Protocol I. *See id.*

52. *See* 29 KESSING'S CONTEMP. ARCHIVES 32, 594-95 (1983); *see also* Margaret T. Okorodudu-Fubara, *Oil in the Persian Gulf War: Legal Appraisal of an Environmental Warfare*, 23 ST. MARY'S L.J. 123, 129-31 (1991); George K. Walker, Oceans Law, the Maritime Environment, and the Law of Naval Warfare, Paper Presented at the Symposium on the Protection of the Environment During Armed Conflict and Operations Other Than War, *in* NWC SYMPOSIUM PAPERS, *supra* note 13 (manuscript at 2-3, on file with *The Yale Journal of International Law*).

practical effect of indirectly fostering broader environmental interests. The prevailing paradigm of the Iran-Iraq War would shift dramatically with the Iraqi invasion of Kuwait in 1990.

C. *The Gulf War*

The Gulf War brought warfare's environmental destructiveness to the forefront of international attention. Even before the air campaign commenced on January 17, 1991, there were clear indications that, environmentally speaking, this conflict would represent a new model. As early as September 1990, Saddam Hussein threatened to destroy oil fields if Coalition forces attempted to expel him from Kuwait.[53] Other senior Iraqi leaders made similar pronouncements. Two days before Christmas, for example, the Iraqi Defense Minister, Said Tuma Abbas, responded to Secretary of Defense Cheney's statement that the "clock is ticking" by boasting that "Cheney will see how land burns under the feet of his troops and stooges."[54] That very month the Iraqis detonated six Kuwaiti oil wells to practice for later operations.[55]

Those beyond Iraqi borders viewed these bellicose statements as more than mere puffery. Among the most vocal in singling out the environmental threat was King Hussein of Jordan. Speaking in November at the Second World Climate Conference in Geneva, he pointed to the possibility of widespread environmental destruction in an attempt to prevent war.[56] The Secretary General of Jordan's Higher Council for Science and Technology, Dr. Abdullah Toukan, echoed the theme at a scientific symposium held in London in January. He warned that the destruction of the Gulf's oil installations could lead to the spillage of up to two million barrels of oil per day. At the same meeting, John Cox, a chemical engineer experienced in the field, suggested that igniting the oil installations could generate smoke equal to that produced by a nuclear explosion, thereby blotting out sunlight and

---

53. On September 23, 1990, the Iraqis released a statement following the joint meeting of the Iraqi Revolution Command Council and the regional command of the Arab Socialist Baath Party, chaired by Saddam Hussein. It proclaimed:

> The oil, its areas, and Israel will be transformed into something different from what they are now. Thus will be the deluge. . . . The oil areas in Saudi Arabia and in other parts of the states of the region and all the oil installations will be rendered incapable of responding to the needs of those who came to us as occupiers in order to usurp our sovereignty, dignity and wealth.

Partial Text of Statement by Iraq's Revolution Command Council, REUTERS, Sept. 23, 1990, *available in* LEXIS, News Library, Allnws File; *see also* Nora Boustany, *Saddam Threatens Mideast's Oil Fields: "Choking" Embargo Cited as Justification*, WASH. POST, Sept. 24, 1990, at A1.

54. Gayle Young, *Cheney: "Clock is Ticking" for War*, UPI, Dec. 23, 1990, *available in* LEXIS, News Library, Allnws File.

55. William M. Arkin, The Environmental Threat of Military Operations, Paper Presented at the Symposium on the Protection of the Environment During Armed Conflict and Operations Other Than War, *in* NWC SYMPOSIUM PAPERS, *supra* note 13 (manuscript at 6, on file with *The Yale Journal of International Law*).

56. King Hussein warned of an "environmental catastrophe." *Gulf War Threatens Environment, Jordan King Warns*, L.A. TIMES, Nov. 6, 1990, at A2.

causing a drop in temperatures by as much as sixty-eight degrees.[57]

Oxford's Adam Roberts has noted astutely that the environmental issue soon took on political overtones. Those concerned with the environmental impact of hostilities generally opposed the war, whereas supporters of Iraqi expulsion by force of arms devoted little attention to environmental matters. For Professor Roberts, this "polarization" had an important consequence: "There was little if any public discussion of the means which might be used, if there was a war, to dissuade Iraq from engaging in environmentally destructive acts; and little if any reference to the laws of war as one possible basis for seeking limitations of this kind."[58] As one possible remedy, he suggested an unequivocal pre–Desert Storm pronouncement by the United Nations that the laws of war were applicable to environmental damage.[59]

At that late date, it is doubtful that putting Iraqi leaders on notice would have yielded significant deterrent returns. After all, the Iraqis already had violated international law with impunity on multiple occasions. For example, the seizure of foreign civilians and the use of them as human shields were breaches beyond even theoretical doubt. Their subsequent release can be attributed more to "rational" decisionmaking than to any last-minute epiphany that the acts were unlawful. The same can be said with regard to chemical weapons. Was it law or the thinly veiled threat of retaliation with weapons of mass destruction that deterred Saddam Hussein?

To complicate matters, the law in this area was (and still is) unsettled—a point Iraq probably grasped better than most, given its experiences during the war with Iran. An eleventh-hour proclamation on the environmental law of war by the United Nations, which had proven impotent during the Cold War and was now being informally led by a Protocol I nonsignatory, would hardly have proven a panacea. Furthermore, the last international war crimes trials had been held over forty years earlier in the aftermath of the Second World War. Therefore, not only was the law uncertain (a point discussed more fully below), but there was also evidence of the international community's unwillingness to impose state or individual responsibility following armed conflict. That said, Professor Roberts's suggestion is well taken. Emphasizing the law of war would have hurt nothing, was the right thing to do,

---

57. *Scientists Warn of Environmental Disaster from a Gulf War*, REUTERS, Jan. 2, 1991, *available in* LEXIS, News Library, Allnws File; *see also Experts Warn of Global Fallout from Warfare: Environment; Scientists Say that Smoke from Blazing Kuwait Oil Fields Could Affect the Climate*, L.A. TIMES, Jan. 3, 1991, at A8.

58. Roberts, *supra* note 18, at 31.

59. In his words, "[n]ew environmental threats and public environmental concerns strengthened the case for having a clear statement about how environmental destruction ran counter to older as well as newer agreements on the laws of war." *Id.* at 33. Along these lines, Professor Roberts made a very good point:

> The failure to prevent damage to the environment in the 1991 Gulf War was in marked contrast to a degree of success in preventing the conflict from getting out of hand in some other respects: many hostages, seized in the early weeks of the Iraqi occupation of Kuwait, were released before war broke out; Iraq was kept isolated; the war was kept within geographical limits and was brought to a swift conclusion; and gas, bacteriological and nuclear weapons were not used. Why was there so conspicuous a failure over matters relating to the environment?

Id. at 4.

and—considering the minimal military value of his actions—might have given Saddam Hussein pause. It certainly would have strengthened the basis for condemnation by the international community after the hostilities.

Just prior to the commencement of the air campaign, President Bush did specifically address destruction of oil fields and installations. In the now-famous letter from President Bush to Saddam Hussein, which Iraqi Foreign Minister Tariq Aziz refused to accept from Secretary of State James Baker in Geneva on January 9, the President warned that "[y]ou and your country will pay a terrible price if you order unconscionable acts of this sort."[60] The ICRC also endeavored to focus attention on the potential belligerents' international legal obligations. It issued its most comprehensive reminder in the form of a note verbale (with attached memorandum of law) on December 14,[61] not long after the Security Council passed Resolution 678.[62] The resolution authorized the use of "all necessary means" to implement Resolution 660 (the demand for Iraqi withdrawal)[63] and to restore peace and security.[64] Each of the 164 parties to the 1949 Geneva Conventions received the note verbale.

In it, the ICRC reiterated numerous customary and conventional laws of armed conflict. The memorandum of law specifically cited article 55 of Protocol I, and invited states that were not parties to the Protocol (for example, Iraq, France, the United Kingdom, and the United States) to respect that article. It also urged compliance with article 56, a provision that extends protection to works and installations containing dangerous forces, such as dams and nuclear generating stations.[65] This protection, as shall be seen, has important environmental implications. When the air campaign was launched in January, the ICRC issued yet another appeal to respect the law of war.[66] On February 1, with oil now pouring into the Persian Gulf, the ICRC issued its strongest pronouncement. Warning that the law of war "might be swept aside by the political, military or propaganda demands of the moment," it emphasized that "[t]he right to choose methods or means of warfare is not unlimited. Weapons having indiscriminate effects and those likely to cause disproportionate suffering and damage to the environment are prohibited."[67]

The ICRC's warnings and pleas had little effect. Two days after the air

---

60. *Text of Bush Letter to Saddam Hussein*, UPI, Jan. 12, 1991, *available in* LEXIS, News Library, UPI File. Additionally, destruction of the Kuwaiti oil resources was one of the three "unconscionable acts" for which the Iraqi leadership would be held personally responsible—the others being use of chemical/biological weapons and terrorism. *See* Arkin, *supra* note 55, at 2-3 (citing National Security Directive (NSD) 54, Jan. 15, 1991). NSD 54 remains classified, but is described generally in CHRISTOPHER SIMPSON, NATIONAL SECURITY DIRECTIVES OF THE REAGAN AND BUSH ADMINISTRATIONS 947 (1995). NSD 54 authorized offensive operations against Iraqi forces. *Id.*

61. ICRC, Note Verbale and Memorandum (Dec. 14, 1990), *reprinted in* INT'L REV. RED CROSS, Jan.-Feb. 1991 [hereinafter ICRC Note Verbale].

62. S.C. Res. 678, U.N. SCOR, 45th Sess., 2963d mtg., U.N. Doc. S/RES/678 (1990). On this resolution, see Burns H. Weston, *Security Council Resolution 678 and Persian Gulf Decision Making: Precarious Legitimacy*, 85 AM. J. INT'L L. 516 (1991).

63. S.C. Res. 660, U.N. SCOR, 45th Sess., 2932d mtg., U.N. Doc. S/RES/660 (1990).

64. *See* S.C. Res. 678, *supra* note 62, para. 2.

65. *See* ICRC Note Verbale, *supra* note 61, at 22-26.

66. ICRC, Appeal (Jan. 17, 1991), *reprinted in* INT'L REV. RED CROSS, Jan.-Feb. 1991, at 26.

67. ICRC, Appeal (Feb. 1, 1991), *reprinted in* INT'L REV. RED CROSS, Jan.-Feb. 1991, at 27.

war commenced, the Iraqis began pumping oil into the Persian Gulf from Sea Island Terminal, an offshore oil loading dock. The flow was stemmed only after Coalition air forces bombed the terminal.[68] Not to be deterred, the Iraqis exacerbated the pollution by dumping oil into the Gulf from five tankers moored at Mina al-Ahmadi. The Defense Department estimates that by the end of the conflict, the Iraqis had intentionally spilled between seven and nine million barrels of oil.[69] It eventually covered approximately 600 square miles of water and spread along 300 miles of shoreline.[70] To place the Iraqi actions in context, the spill was the largest, intentional or accidental, in history.

Not all of the oil that found its way into the Persian Gulf derived from Iraqi actions. In fact, the first oil spill of the war may have come on the morning of the seventeenth when U.S. Navy aircraft bombed an Iraqi oil platform at Mina al-Bakr. A week later, Navy planes hit the *Amuriyah*, an Iraqi tanker that was refueling an air-cushioned landing craft. French aircraft struck a tanker of their own that same day. Other air attacks may also have contributed to the spills.[71] These operations are, however, easily distinguishable from the Iraqi actions. Not only were Coalition-caused releases dwarfed by those of the Iraqis, but there is no evidence to suggest purposeful environmental damage by Coalition forces. From a legal perspective, these are critical facts, for there is a clear difference in the law between incidental (collateral, in law of war terminology) and intentional damage.

Soon after Desert Storm began, the Iraqis started destroying oil wells to complement their maritime misconduct. For instance, on January 21, they detonated sixty wells in the vicinity of Al Wafra in Kuwait. They also set fire to the Mina ash Shuaybah and Mina Abd Allah oil installations on the coast.[72] Nevertheless, it was not until just prior to the start of the ground war on February 23–24 that systematic destruction began in earnest, with the Al Burgan oil fields suffering the heaviest toll. By the end of hostilities, the Iraqis had damaged or destroyed 590 oil well heads. Of these, 508 were set afire, and eighty-two were damaged in a manner that caused oil to flow from

---

68. *See* Peter Ford, *Vital Saudi Water Plant Prepares for Oil Slick*, CHRISTIAN SCI. MONITOR, Feb. 1, 1991, at 1.

69. *See* U.S. DEP'T OF DEFENSE, CONDUCT OF THE PERSIAN GULF WAR: FINAL REPORT TO CONGRESS, at O-26 (1992) [hereinafter DOD REPORT]. A Greenpeace study cites similar figures, but notes that smaller quantities of oil continued to leak into the Gulf until May or early June of 1991. *See* WILLIAM M. ARKIN ET AL., ON IMPACT: MODERN WARFARE AND THE ENVIRONMENT: A CASE STUDY OF THE GULF WAR 63–64 (1991) [hereinafter GREENPEACE STUDY]. The size of the spill also is discussed in KUWAIT ENV'T PROTECTION COUNCIL, STATE OF THE ENVIRONMENT REPORT: A CASE STUDY OF IRAQI REGIME CRIMES AGAINST THE ENVIRONMENT 29–33 (1991). .

70. *See* Walter G. Sharp, Sr., *The Effective Deterrence of Environmental Damage During Armed Conflict: A Case Analysis of the Persian Gulf War*, 137 MIL. L. REV. 1, 41 (1992).

71. *See* Arkin, *supra* note 55, at 7–8. Mr. Arkin has noted: "What the public heard during the war was that around 19 January, Iraq opened valves at the Sea Island terminal, pumping oil directly into the Gulf." *Id.* at 8. In fact, the Coalition contribution to the spill *was* reported. For instance, on February 21, 1991, the Associated Press reported that Coalition bombing missions may have been responsible for 30% of the oil spilled. *See* Martin Marris, *Sophisticated Radar to Gauge Size of Oil Spill*, AP, Feb. 21, 1991, at 2.

72. *See* Arkin, *supra* note 55, at 6–7.

them.[73] The blazes reached their destructive peak during May and June, when 4.5 million barrels of oil per day were lost to the fires. Several comparisons illustrate the gravity of this situation. The oil fires generated eighty-six billion watts of heat, roughly equal to that of 500 forest fires. Daily soot release into the atmosphere, which drifted as far away as the Himalayas, was the equivalent of 10% of global biomass burning, while sulfur dioxide output approximated 57% of the emissions from electrical utilities. Carbon dioxide production was at the level of 2% of the fossil fuel and biomass burning that occurs worldwide on a daily basis.[74]

The international community mounted an aggressive campaign to contain the spills and put out the fires. Many U.S. government agencies, with the U.S. Coast Guard at the forefront, took part in the valiant recovery operation. Foreign and international organizations that were active in the effort included the Saudi Meteorology and Environmental Protection Administration and the International Maritime Organization. Ultimately, two million barrels of oil were recovered from the Gulf.[75] The battle against the burning oil wells also went well. Nearly thirty firefighting teams from ten countries attacked the blazes, extinguishing them much more quickly than had been expected.[76]

Despite predictions of doom such as those offered at the scientific symposium in London, the environmental damage was not catastrophic. Warnings of drastic drops in temperature, and the effect this might have on wind currents, proved very much overblown. Similarly, early fears of severe human health problems and wholesale destruction of animal habitats were not borne out.[77] Nevertheless, the pooling oil, oil mist, and settling soot did damage the terrestrial environment, particularly the fragile desert ecosystem. In many areas. the annual seed flora failed to set, and perennial vegetation, critically important because its roots are a food source for many animals, incurred damage or died. Additionally, oil harmed intertidal habitats such as mangroves, beaches, and mud flats. Though no major threat to individual human health surfaced, the increase in inhalable particulants that the fires caused was significant when considered in terms of exposure of a large population. This exposure could potentially increase the prevalence and severity of disease, both chronic and acute.[78] Of course, the overall

---

73. *See* DOD REPORT, *supra* note 69, at O-26. Estimates of the number of wells damaged or destroyed by the Iraqis differ. Walter Sharp reports the figure as 732, with 650 catching fire. *See* Sharp, *supra* note 70, at 40–41. The Kuwaiti government reported that, after February 28, 1991, 613 wells were set on fire, 76 were gushing, and 99 were damaged. *See* KUWAIT ENV'T PROTECTION COUNCIL, *supra* note 69, at 1 & fig.2.

74. *See* Sylvia A. Earle, *Persian Gulf Pollution: Assessing the Damage One Year Later*, NAT'L GEOGRAPHIC, Feb. 1992, at 122.

75. *See* Adam Roberts, *Environmental Destruction in the 1991 Gulf War*, INT'L REV. RED CROSS, Nov.-Dec. 1992, at 538, 549.

76. *See* JOHN NORTON MOORE, CRISIS IN THE GULF: ENFORCING THE RULE OF LAW 80 (1992).

77. The United Nations Environment Programme (UNEP) reported in May 1992 that the oil well fires did not affect the global climate and that the pollution they caused was not severe enough to result in major human health problems. *See State of the Environment: Updated Scientific Report on the Environmental Effects of the Conflict Between Iraq and Kuwait*, Governing Council of the U.N. Environment Programme, 17th Sess., at 12–13, U.N. Doc. UNEP/GC.17/Inf.9 (1993).

78. On the impact of the spills generally, see *Report on the UN Inter-Agency Plan of Action for the ROPME Region*, U.N. Environment Programme, Oct. 12, 1991 [hereinafter UNEP REPORT], *reprinted*

assessment may change as unexplained health problems begin to develop among those who were present during the conflict.

Why the Iraqis committed the misdeeds remains unanswered. As will be discussed later, the degree of military advantage obtained from an act during war is a critical data point in assessing its lawfulness. The Department of Defense (DOD) has concluded that the Iraqi actions were of little military utility. In arriving at this conclusion, Pentagon analysts explored possible military benefits of the oil spills. One was to foil Coalition amphibious operations. A secondary purpose may have been to foul desalinization plants in Saudi Arabia either to disrupt military activities ashore or to cause unrest among the Saudi population by depriving it of fresh water.[79] The fires arguably could have been intended to obscure Iraqi forces, shielding them from air and ground attack.[80]

The DOD concluded, however, that Iraq's actions were probably purely punitive in nature—"environmental terrorism," to use President Bush's characterization.[81] Addressing the issue in its official Gulf War Report, the DOD points out that the oil spills had negligible effect on Coalition naval operations. If the goal was to frustrate a Coalition landing force, then the operation was very poorly conceived. The oil well fires present even more compelling circumstantial evidence of malevolent intent. If the purpose was to create obscurants, why did the Iraqis not just open the valves of the wells, allow the oil to pool, and then set it on fire? Instead, the Iraqis destroyed the wells in a manner that made it difficult to extinguish the resulting fires; this suggests a broader, longer-term purpose than merely to complicate immediate Coalition intelligence gathering, maneuvers, and attacks.[82]

A counterargument is that since the wells were previously wired with explosives, blowing them up may have been the most expedient method of destruction in the face of the Coalition onslaught. Interestingly, the DOD Report queries why the Iraqis did not set ablaze their own Ar-Rumaylah oil fields, which lay just across the border, if the goal was to obscure their troops from Coalition attack. This, the report contends, further demonstrates Iraq's punitive motivation.[83] From the perspective of rational decisionmaking, the DOD Report falters here. Not knowing the course that the war and post-war settlement would take, it would have made very little sense for Iraq to destroy its own primary resource merely for short-term tactical and operational gain.

---

in IRAQ AND KUWAIT: THE HOSTILITIES AND THEIR AFTERMATH 339 (M. Weller ed., 1991).

79. *See* DOD REPORT, *supra* note 69, at O-27.

80. *See id.*

81. Address Before a Joint Session of the Congress on the State of the Union, 1 PUB. PAPERS 74, 79 (1991). Some have suggested that a possible motive was "ecological terrorism in retaliation for the bombing." *See, e.g.*, Robert McFadden, *Oil Threatens Fishing and Water Supply*, N.Y. TIMES, Jan. 26, 1991, at 4. A more remote possibility is that the motive was economic: Iraq hoped to devastate a competitor, drive up the price of oil, or create an incentive for the removal of sanctions on its own oil exports.

82. *See* DOD REPORT, *supra* note 69, at O-27.

83. *See id.* Iraq also damaged all twenty-six gathering centers used to separate oil, gas, and water. This process is integral to oil production. Additionally, the Iraqis destroyed the wells' technical specifications. *See* Sharp, *supra* note 70, at 45. If the purpose was military, what would have justified such acts? One possibility is that the Iraqis wanted to prevent the use of the oil wells by the Coalition forces and Kuwait. However, the DOD Report has the better argument.

Doing so would have been very different from destroying resources in an occupied territory from which it was about to be ejected. The respective cost-benefit calculations hardly yield comparable results.

Greenpeace has cited various sources to suggest that the Iraqi actions may have had military ends. For example, a Navy spokesman on the U.S.S. Midway reportedly admitted that the smoke from oil fires precluded target acquisition in some cases.[84] An F-15 pilot interviewed by the Associated Press reported the same effect.[85] On one occasion the Iraqis supposedly even used the smoke from a burning oil field to mask an attack.[86] It is not difficult to imagine the problems that Iraq might have hoped the fires would create for the Coalition. It could even be argued that the fires were intended to take advantage of "weaknesses" in high-tech Coalition weapons. Blocking ambient light, for example, diminishes the effectiveness of night vision goggles. Brightness also blinds them.[87] Smoke has the former effect, fire the latter. Similarly, smoke can foil guided munitions. Consider the difficulty, for instance, of using an electro-optical guided weapon on a smoke-covered target.

Ultimately, there is little question that on various occasions Iraqi actions did affect Coalition military operations. There is also little question that they had minimal impact on the overall campaign. Given the difficulty of determining the intent of a dictator who remains in control of a closed society, probably the most objective interpretation of the oil spills and fires is that they *may* have been intended to achieve military advantages. Despite this possibility, the damage inflicted so outweighed possible gains that the acts were wrongful under international law.[88]

As a final note, it is important to remember that although the oil spills and fires stole the headlines, the war caused a great deal of additional environmental damage. Mines presented a particular problem. On many occasions, the Iraqis indiscriminately laid mine fields without adequately marking them or accurately recording their locations. This made large areas of land impassable and posed a significant danger to humans and animals alike. Massive mine-clearing efforts had to be mounted to make the land usable again. In areas controlled by Coalition forces after the war, such as the U.N. security zone in the north and Kuwait in the south, mine operations became an integral part of the international relief efforts. To a lesser extent, the same is true of unexploded ordnance (UXO), i.e., the remnants of munitions that failed to explode.[89]

The war also had less sensational, though still significant, effects on the environment. For instance, explosions and vehicle movement disrupted the

---

84. *See* GREENPEACE STUDY, *supra* note 69, at 141.

85. *See id.*

86. *See id.*

87. *See* Joel P. Kane, *Night Vision Goggles and Desert Storm*, MARINE CORPS GAZETTE, Feb. 1992, at 42.

88. For discussion of the customary international law concepts of military necessity and proportionality, see *infra* Section III.B.

89. *See* Tony Horowitz, *These Men Dance Through Minefields, Cleaning Up Kuwait*, WALL ST. J. EUR., Jan. 21, 1992, at 1. The report noted that in the year following the war, more than 1250 civilians were killed or wounded by explosive ordnance and 5 demolition specialists had died. *See id.*

desert ecosystem by loosening its surface, rendering it susceptible to wind and water erosion. Enormous quantities of hazardous materials were also generated, ranging from dishwater and human waste to antifreeze and engine oil. Despite minor problems, U.S. military forces successfully handled these substances in an environmentally responsible manner.[90] In retrospect, the military campaign fielded by the United States was the most environmentally conscious in its history. Moreover, it has improved its performance since then.[91] Unfortunately, not all of the world's military forces are fully sensitized to the environmental consequences of their operations. Many U.S. allies, in addition to the Iraqis, caused significant environmental damage merely by their presence.

D. *The Post–Gulf War Period*

Serious attention to the Gulf War's environmental impact was apparent as early as March 1991, when Japan proposed that the Governing Council of the United Nations Environment Programme (UNEP) adopt a declaration of principles proscribing the environmentally destructive techniques witnessed during the war. Simultaneously, France recommended a prohibition against targeting ecological areas and "world heritage monuments."[92] Both proposals were raised two months later during UNEP's sixteenth Session, at which Canada and Greenpeace announced their sponsorship of conferences on the environmental law of war. Additionally, UNEP's Governing Council endorsed a prohibition against weapons that could "cause particularly serious effects on the environment."[93]

In June 1991, Greenpeace, in conjunction with the London School of Economics and the British Center for Defence Studies, convened its

---

90. For instance, in one case, a unit collected hazardous waste in barrels so as not to dump it improperly, but failed to mark the barrels. As a result, the contents had to be tested prior to disposal, an extremely costly and time-consuming process. *See* ARMY ASSESSMENT, *supra* note 31, pt. G, para. 1, at 2.

91. The Army Assessment noted that
> [i]n general, there was an environmental awareness in the U.S. Army that caused us to consider the environmental consequences of military actions and kept us in concert with the law. . . . This environmental awareness was carefully balanced against the often conflicting needs of waging war. In SWA [Southwest Asia], this translated to: Army policy is to adhere to United States environmental requirements if possible. As a result, environmental law issues were a SJA [Staff Judge Advocate] concern in theater as well as in the United States.

Id. pt. G, at 1–2. There were problems, however, with environmental issues during deployment. The Army Assessment noted that "[c]ommanders [wanted] to do the right thing, but [had] a low tolerance for the impractical." *Id.* pt. G, para. 3, at 3. Quoting an attorney from the Army's Operations and Law Division, the Assessment provides a clear indication of the mindset:
> Our attitude at the time was that, you know, we've got a deployment going on. To the extent that we can respect the environment, that's fine, but it's not our job . . . . We've got other things to do and essentially, I don't know if you call it what we did, "stonewalling," but essentially, the environmental issues, as far as we saw, went away for the long term.

Id. The Assessment characterized this statement not as "callousness to environmental concerns," but instead as "the frustration of trying to deal with environmental laws drafted without regard for military necessity." *Id.*

92. *See* James P. Terry, *The Environment and the Laws of War: The Impact of Desert Storm*, 15 NAVAL WAR C. REV. 61, 65 (1992).

93. G.A. Res. 16/11, U.N. GAOR, 16th Sess., Supp. No. 25, at 48, U.N. Doc. A/46/25 (1992).

conference in London. For the conference, Professor Glen Plant of the London School of Economics developed a straw man outline of what the elements of a Fifth Geneva Convention on the Environment might look like.[94] Its most significant provision dealt with methods and means of warfare, setting forth four options for a threshold at which environmentally destructive methods and means should be prohibited:

> Option (a): prohibiting the employment of methods or means of warfare which are intended, or may be expected, to cause *any* (except *de minimis*) damage to the environment;
> Option (b): prohibiting it at least where the damage is widespread, long-lasting *or* severe;
> Option (c): prohibiting it as under alternative (b), but adding a fourth alternative criterion, "significant" (or "appreciable") and irreversible;
> Option (d): choosing some midway position between alternative (b) and the existing excessively high threshold as it appears in Article 35(3) of Protocol I.[95]

Despite generating a great deal of attention and Greenpeace support,[96] Professor Plant's proposal has not led to a serious international effort to produce an agreement along the lines suggested.[97]

In July 1991, the Canadian Ministry of External Affairs convened its own conference. The prevailing view of those who gathered in Ottawa was that the existing law adequately addressed the environmental effects of war. However, they recognized the need to consider the evolutionary nature of environmental concerns when applying existing prescriptions. In other words, the "value" of the environment would shift over time, an important factor in performing the balancing tests that dominate the law of war. The conference also took the position that peacetime norms generally remain applicable during hostilities.[98]

Of particular interest was the position of the U.S. participants. According to one account of the proceedings, they

> carefully underscored the merits of the existing regime, which is based on the principles of military necessity and proportionality under the law of armed conflict. The U.S. concern regarding more restrictive environmental provisions is that they could be implemented only at the expense of otherwise lawful military operations—such as attacking targets which require fuel-air explosives (FAE) for their destruction.[99]

This is a revealing statement because almost all treaty law of war, except that which merely codifies customary law, limits otherwise legal activities. That is its purpose: to render illegal those legal activities that become contrary to current normative values. The U.S. participants clearly were taking the stance

---

94. Glen Plant, *Elements of a 'Fifth Geneva' Convention on the Protection of the Environment in Time of Armed Conflict*, *in* ENVIRONMENTAL PROTECTION AND THE LAW OF WAR 37, 43–61 (Glen Plant ed., 1992).

95. *Id.* at 46.

96. *See The Gulf War: Environment as a Weapon*, 85 AM. SOC'Y INT'L L. PROC. 214, 220 (1991) (remarks of Sebia Hawkins).

97. The proceedings of the conference are published in ENVIRONMENTAL PROTECTION AND THE LAW OF WAR, *supra* note 94, at 65–150.

98. *See* Hans-Peter Gasser, *For Better Protection of the Natural Environment in Armed Conflict: A Proposal for Action*, 89 AM. J. INT'L L. 637, 639 (1995); *see also infra* Subsection III.A.1.

99. Terry, *supra* note 92, at 65.

that the present law suffices, that is, it reflects the global community's values and serves its aspirations.

Arguments of this nature represent a failure to see the forest for the trees. That a regime might restrict useful means does not necessarily lead to the conclusion that it deserves rejection. Instead, the question is whether the new regime represents an *overall* step forward (however one defines "forward"). Furthermore, to argue for rejection of a legal regime because it would limit currently legal techniques is, in a sense, meaningless. The relevant factor is not the weapon used, but its target. Simply put, what are the consequences if a target cannot be struck, or be struck as effectively, as otherwise would be the case?

Opposition to additional prescriptions on the grounds that they might limit the ability to employ otherwise lawful techniques is classically anthropocentric. By the Ottawa Conference, the lines of demarcation between two opposing camps were becoming clear. One side, exemplified by Greenpeace, had adopted an intrinsic worth approach and took the stance that more law was needed. The anthropocentrics, on the other hand, hesitated to extend the law further out of concern that the hands of the decisionmakers might be tied. In their view, the law should be left alone to evolve within the existing framework.

In December 1991, a third major international conference convened in Munich. Co-sponsored by the International Council of Environmental Law (ICEL) and the Commission on Environmental Law of the International Union for the Conservation of Nature and Natural Resources, and financed in part by the Dutch government, it brought together a distinguished group of scholars and practitioners. The conference broke into two working groups: the first to consider how the effectiveness and implementation of existing legal instruments might be improved, the second to reflect on possible directions for further development of the legal regime governing the environmental law of war.[100] They produced a series of innovative recommendations that are particularly useful in focusing attention on alternatives to the current state of affairs.

As to the present law, the conference recommended that Protocol I, and other relevant legal instruments, be universally accepted. It stressed the importance of customary international law norms (e.g., military necessity) to environmental protection, as well as the need to disseminate effectively the law of armed conflict. In an interesting comment, the final report also "observed that the current recognition that the environment itself is an object of legal protection in times of armed conflict implies that traditional perceptions of proportionality and military necessity have become obsolete."[101] This assertion is a bit inartfully stated, for it would have been more accurate to note that the traditional perceptions are *evolving*. Nevertheless, the statement demonstrates movement along the continuum

---

100. *See* International Council of Envtl. Law, Law Concerning the Protection of the Environment in Times of Armed Conflict, Final Report of Consultation of Dec. 13–15, 1991, at 1 (unpublished memorandum, on file with author) [hereinafter Munich Report].

101. *Id.* para. 2.

between the anthropocentric and intrinsic value cognitive perspectives because it is based on the proposition that the environment per se should be protected. However, the recommendation does not go so far as to suggest that the environment should be safeguarded absolutely without regard to human-related considerations.

With respect to the further development of the law, a number of innovative recommendations were proffered. The conference report proposed that any new law be based on protection of the environment per se.[102] Again, while this is not necessarily an intrinsic value perspective, it does lean in that direction. Although it did not recommend a new convention, the report did suggest the compilation of two lists. The first would consist of activities during hostilities that could harm the environment, some of which would be absolutely forbidden, with others allowed only conditionally. Reflecting the desire to protect the environment per se, the law would prohibit: "(i) intentional attacks on the environment; (ii) the manipulation of natural processes causing environmental damage; and (iii) significant collateral damage to the environment."[103] Violations would constitute grave breaches under international law, thereby imbuing all states with the jurisdictional competence to seize and try alleged offenders.

The second list would consist of a registry of protected areas. Though criteria for inclusion would have to be developed, inventories such as the U.N. List of National Parks and Equivalent Reserves, the Ramsar Wetlands of International Importance, the UNESCO Biosphere Reserves, and the Council of Europe's Biogenic Reserves could be adopted immediately. As to areas not on one of these preexisting lists, studies would have to be conducted to determine their vulnerability to military activities. Ultimately, areas selected for protection would be noted on maps and marked with distinctive symbols.[104]

The report also urged states to rethink and revise targeting practices in light of technological advances. As an example, it pointed to the sinking of oil tankers. Noting the myriad of methods for preventing the delivery of oil to an adversary, the group argued that actual destruction of vessels should be avoided. Specifically proscribed as targets were sites that contained dangerous forces or in which ultrahazardous activities were carried out.[105] This restriction harkens back to article 56 of Protocol I, which limits how and when works containing "dangerous forces" can be attacked.[106] However, whereas article 56's interpretation usually is limited to dams, dikes, and nuclear electrical generating stations,[107] the Munich proposal would extend protection beyond these categories. For instance, oil reserves were cited as protected targets, an illustration clearly selected with the Gulf War experience in mind. The group also addressed practices from that war when it recommended prohibiting the targeting of "potentially dangerous" sites, i.e.,

---

102. *See id.* para. 10.
103. *Id.* para. 13(a).
104. *See id.* para. 13(b).
105. *See id.* para. 16.
106. Protocol I, *supra* note 8, art. 56, para. 1.
107. *See infra* Subsection III.C.3.

26   YALE JOURNAL OF INTERNATIONAL LAW   [Vol. 22: 1

those essential either to human health or to the environment. Examples are water purification facilities and sewage treatment plants.[108]

To enforce the prohibitions, the conference recommended the imposition of state responsibility for either actual or potential damage. Potential damage would be measured by the likelihood of occurrence and the magnitude of harm.[109] Characterizing potential damage as actionable represents a novel approach to the issue of state responsibility, because under international law states are seldom responsible for speculative future damage. As the report noted, the concept of responsibility would have to be refined by states, as well as by various national and international governmental and nongovernmental organizations, "in order to make it fully operational."[110] Certainly, refinement would include clarifying what is meant by potential damage; it would also require crafting remedies. The group recommended a scheme whereby damaged or destroyed aspects of the environment would be replaced or restored to a pre-war level. When restoration was not possible, "compensation in kind would be required."[111]

Finally, the Munich Conference took on the *jus ad bellum* issue of when environmental damage amounts to a threat to, or breach of, peace—a characterization that permits response under the U.N. Charter.[112] In particular, it included threatened or actual damage to "the commons" in the category of threat/breach.[113] The term extends to areas such as the high seas, which are *res communes*. Beyond singling out the matter as an issue of importance, and blandly stating the obvious proposition that in the event of a threat or breach "appropriate measures" should be taken, the conference accomplished little else regarding the *jus ad bellum*. Nevertheless, the Munich Conference was significant in that it generated a consensus product consisting of substantive recommendations. Though the international community is not likely to adopt these without modification any time soon, the conference's recommendations provide a useful point of departure in discussions of how new law might be shaped.

A fourth conference of significance, although dedicated to environmental law issues extending well beyond armed conflict, was the June 1992 United Nations Conference on the Environment and Development (UNCED) in Rio de Janeiro. It issued the Rio Declaration, principle 24 of which specifically addressed environmental concerns in warfare: "Warfare is inherently destructive of sustainable development. States shall therefore respect international law providing protection for the environment in times of armed conflict and cooperate in its further development, as necessary."[114] The compromise character of the declaration is apparent. It responds to claims of the law's adequacy when it urges respect, but displays a revisionist flavor by

---

108. *See* Munich Report, *supra* note 100, para. 16.
109. *See id.*
110. *Id.*
111. *Id.* para. 18.
112. *See* U.N. CHARTER art. 39.
113. *See* Munich Report, *supra* note 100, para. 17.
114. Rio Declaration on Environment and Development, princ. 24, U.N. Doc. A/CONF.151/Rev. 1 (1992) [hereinafter Rio Declaration], *reprinted in* 31 I.L.M. 874.

encouraging cooperation in the law's continued development.

As the various conferences were being held, the United Nations proper was addressing the matter. The effort began in earnest in July 1991 when the Jordanian representative forwarded a note verbale to the Secretary General faulting the ENMOD Convention for its ineffectiveness in preventing Gulf War environmental damage. Claiming that the Convention was so vague and broad as to be unenforceable, Jordan also criticized the lack of any dispute resolution mechanism in the ENMOD regime.[115] To remedy these shortcomings, Jordan urged the creation of a committee to examine the environmental law of war and make recommendations for its improvement. In doing so, Jordan held out the drafting of a new treaty as one remedial option.[116]

The General Assembly referred the matter to the Sixth (Legal) Committee, which placed the item on its 1991 agenda under the title "Exploitation of the Environment as a Weapon in Time of War." Jordan, emphasizing that the issue was broader than use of the environment as a weapon, argued for expanding consideration to encompass environmental damage generally.[117] The title was changed accordingly to "Protection of the Environment in Times of Armed Conflict."[118]

During the multiple meetings of the Sixth Committee, there was general consensus that Iraq's intentional dumping of oil into the Persian Gulf and setting ablaze of oil wells constituted violations of international law.[119] As evidence, several states referred to Security Council Resolution 687, which held Iraq liable for "any direct loss, damage, including environmental damage, and the depletion of natural resources" caused by the Iraqi invasion.[120] In fact, Resolution 687 liability derived not from the environmental law of war, but instead from the *ab initio* unlawfulness of the Iraqi use of force. Resolution 687 reflected the *jus ad bellum*, not the *jus in bello*.[121]

Unfortunately, there was no consensus on the legal basis for characterizing the environmental destruction as wrongful. The United States, for example, labeled the actions militarily unnecessary and, therefore, a violation of the Fourth Geneva Convention.[122] It also cited them as violations of the customary international law rules of proportionality and necessity. Other states referred to Protocol I and ENMOD, while a third group suggested that peacetime environmental law carried forward into

---

115. *See Note Verbale Dated 5 July 1991 from the Charge D'affaires of the Permanent Mission to Jordan to the United Nations Secretary General*, U.N. GAOR, 46th Sess., Annex, para. 2, U.N. Doc. A/46/141 (1991).

116. *See id.* para. 3.

117. *See Summary Record of the 18th Meeting*, U.N. GAOR 6th Comm., 46th Sess., 18th mtg., at 3, U.N. Doc. A/C.6/46/SR.18 (1991).

118. *See Summary Record of the 19th Meeting*, U.N. GAOR 6th Comm., 47th Sess., 19th mtg., at 5, U.N. Doc. A/C.6/47/SR.19 (1992).

119. *See id.* at 8–9.

120. S.C. Res. 687, U.N. SCOR, 45th Sess., 2981st mtg., para. 16, U.N. Doc. S/RES/687 (1991).

121. *See infra* Section III.D.

122. For discussion of the relevant sections of the Geneva Convention IV, see *infra* Subsection III.C.2.

periods of hostilities and applied in the case of the Gulf War.[123]

Further disagreement arose in the Sixth Committee over whether new law was needed. The United States vocally opposed a new convention on the grounds that none of the proposals made to date adequately balanced the desire for environmental protection with the need to ensure against an erosion of self-defense rights under article 51 of the U.N. Charter.[124] The opposing view emphasized that the Gulf War had demonstrated convincingly the need for further development of the legal regime. Additional unresolved issues included dispute resolution, the applicability of peacetime norms during armed conflict, damage assessment processes, and the imposition of liability.[125]

As this debate unfolded, the ICRC was planning its twenty-sixth International Conference, at which one topic was to be environmental damage during warfare. When the conference was later canceled, the ICRC decided to convene a meeting of experts in April 1992 to consider the issue.[126] The United Nations took advantage of this opportunity by asking the ICRC to study and report back on current activities in the field.[127]

In its 1992 report to the Secretary General, the ICRC noted that experts generally had concluded that, despite a "number of gaps in the rules currently applicable," the best approach was not a new body of law.[128] Concurring with the experts, the ICRC recommended efforts to convince more states to accede to existing instruments (an obvious reference to Protocol I), enact implementing legislation at the domestic level, and observe their international obligations.[129] It also set forth what it believed to be the current law in the area: Hague IV,[130] the Fourth Geneva Convention,[131] Protocol I, ENMOD, the Gas Protocol of 1925,[132] the Biological Weapons Convention of 1972,[133] the Conventional Weapons Convention,[134] and the draft

---

123. *See Summary Record of the 18th Meeting, supra* note 117, at 2–12.

124. *See id.* at 9.

125. *See id.* at 2–12. On this and the issue of the basis for unlawfulness of the Iraqi actions, see Virginia Morris, *Protection of the Environment in Wartime: The United Nations General Assembly Considers the Need for a New Convention,* 27 INT'L LAW. 775, 777–79 (1993).

126. The cancellation was required due to a dispute over the attendance of a Palestinian representative. *See* Verwey, *Protection, supra* note 13, at 12.

127. *See* G.A. Res. 417, U.N. GAOR, 46th Sess., Supp. No. 49, at 319, U.N. Doc. A/46/49 (1991).

128. *See Protection of the Environment in Times of Armed Conflict: Report of the Secretary General,* U.N. GAOR, 47th Sess., para. 40, U.N. Doc. A/47/328 (1992) [hereinafter *1992 Secretary General Report*].

129. *See id.*

130. Convention Respecting the Laws and Customs of War on Land, Oct. 18, 1907, 36 Stat. 2277, 205 Consol. T.S. 277 [hereinafter Hague IV].

131. Geneva Convention IV, *supra* note 10.

132. Protocol for the Prohibition of the Use in War of Asphyxiating, Poisonous or Other Gases, and of Bacteriological Methods of Warfare, June 17, 1925, 26 U.S.T. 571, 14 I.L.M. 49 (1975) [hereinafter Gas Protocol]. The Gas Protocol entered into force for the United States in 1975.

133. Convention on the Prohibition of the Development, Production and Stockpiling of Bacteriological (Biological) and Toxin Weapons and on Their Destruction, Apr. 10, 1972, 26 U.S.T. 583, 11 I.L.M. 310 [hereinafter Biological Weapons Convention].

134. Convention on Prohibitions or Restrictions on the Use of Certain Conventional Weapons Which May Be Deemed To Be Excessively Injurious or To Have Indiscriminate Effects, Oct. 10, 1980, 19 I.L.M. 1524 [hereinafter Conventional Weapons Convention]. The United States ratified this convention in March 1995. Interestingly, there has been relatively little attention paid to the Convention's preamble:

Chemical Weapons Convention.[135] The customary international law of war principles of military necessity and proportionality, as well as the general principle that methods and means of warfare are not unlimited, were said to be applicable, and peacetime environmental law was said to remain in force during armed conflict, particularly between belligerents and neutrals.[136]

Though the ICRC recommended against further codification, it did highlight four topics that it felt required further clarification. First, it recommended harmonizing the understanding of terms common to Protocol I and ENMOD. Both use the terms "widespread," "long-term," and "severe," but the terms are subject to varying interpretations—a situation that invites confusion in their application. The ICRC also recommended inquiry into the relationship between international environmental law (primarily peacetime law) and the law of armed conflict (labeled "humanitarian law" by the ICRC). Associated with that inquiry was the need to determine the obligations of belligerents toward nonbelligerents with regard to environmental damage occurring in the territory of the latter. Finally, the ICRC called for a study of how the natural environment per se might be better protected.[137]

The Sixth Committee reviewed this report. Interestingly, the United States and Jordan submitted a joint memorandum of law to the Chairman of the Sixth Committee for use during the Committee's consideration.[138] Though not as comprehensive as the ICRC's report, the memorandum set forth an identical set of core prescriptions: Hague IV, Geneva Convention IV, and customary law principles such as military necessity, proportionality, and discrimination. Additionally, the memorandum mentioned Protocol I and the ENMOD as binding on parties to those agreements.[139]

Not long after the Sixth Committee's proceedings began, it became clear that the disputes over the law's sufficiency remained:

"[I]t is prohibited to employ methods or means of warfare which are intended, or may be expected, to cause widespread, long-term and severe damage to the natural environment." *Id.* pmbl. In a reservation, France noted that the provision only applies to countries that have ratified Protocol I Additional, which contains identical language. Protocol III of the Conventional Weapons Convention governs incendiary weapons. *See* Protocol on Prohibitions or Restrictions on the Use of Incendiary Weapons (Protocol III), 19 I.L.M. 1534 (1980) [hereinafter Protocol III]. Its restrictions cover attacks on "forests or other kinds of plant cover . . . except when such natural elements are used to cover, conceal or camouflage combatants or other military objectives or are themselves military objectives." *Id.* art. 2, para. 4. The United States did not ratify Protocol III. *See* discussion *infra* Subsection III.C.3.

135. Convention on the Prohibition of the Development, Production, Stockpiling and Use of Chemical Weapons and on Their Destruction, Jan. 13, 1993, 32 I.L.M. 800 [hereinafter Chemical Weapons Convention]. This convention was transmitted to the Senate in November 1993, but at the time this Article was written, had not yet been ratified. *See* < http://www.un.org/Depts/Treaty > .

136. *See 1992 Secretary General Report, supra* note 128, para. 56. The experts compared international environmental law with human rights law. As in the latter, certain provisions of the former were to be inapplicable during armed conflict. Nevertheless, the core provisions, analogized to "hard core" provisions in human rights law, remain in effect. *See id.* The participants recommended that any new treaty dealing with international environmental law specifically address the issue of applicability during armed conflict. *See id.*

137. *See id.* para. 43.

138. *Protection of the Environment in Times of Armed Conflict, Letter from the Permanent Missions of the Hashemite Kingdom of Jordan and of the United States of America to the Chairman of the Sixth Committee* (Sept. 28, 1992), U.N. GAOR 6th Comm., 47th Sess., Agenda Item 136, U.N. Doc. A/C.6/47/3 (1992).

139. *See id.* at 2-3.

[S]ome States felt that the existing rules were sufficient and that what was needed was ensuring greater compliance with them. However, most of the States represented thought it also necessary to clarify and interpret the scope and content of some of those rules, and even to develop other aspects of the law relating to the protection of the environment in times of armed conflict. These include the need for better protection of the environment as such; the need for stricter application of the principle of proportionality (and, to this end, for a more precise definition of its scope in specific situations), the importance of defining more precisely the threshold of application of the rules; the need for a clear decision regarding the applicability in wartime of provisions of international environmental law; and the advisability of setting up a mechanism to sanction breaches thereof.[140]

All suggestions for a "complete overhaul of existing law" were rejected.[141]

Based on its review of the initial ICRC report, the Sixth Committee recommended that the ICRC continue its work in the field and again report its conclusions. By resolution, the General Assembly agreed.[142] General Assembly Resolution 47/37 also called for states to become party to the relevant international agreements, a clear reference to Protocol I and its "rejection" by most of the key players in the international arena. Moreover, it contained a plea for compliance with the environmental law of armed conflict and urged states to incorporate its provisions into their law of war manuals. The resolution expressed concern about the environmentally destructive Iraqi actions during the Gulf War, and noted "that existing provisions of international law prohibit such acts."[143]

The General Assembly resolution also stressed the illegality of environmental destruction unjustified by military necessity.[144] This condemnation, unanimously adopted by the General Assembly, has been proffered as "of special interest" to those who expressed concern in the Gulf War's aftermath that "the international legal structure was not sufficiently developed to deal with problems such as these."[145] Despite this assertion, at the time there was great difference of opinion regarding which law was applicable and how to remedy the applicable law's purported shortcomings. The fact that all could agree that the acts violated *some* international legal norm hardly demonstrates that the relevant law is sufficiently developed.

Retasked, the ICRC began a second round of consultations. It first considered whether to draft new law or look for ways to improve compliance with existing legal norms. Upon the advice of the experts it had gathered to

---

140. *United Nations Decade of International Law: Report of the Secretary-General on the Protection of the Environment in Times of Armed Conflict*, U.N. GAOR, 48th Sess., Provisional Agenda Item 144, paras. 14–15, U.N. Doc. A/48/269 (1993) [hereinafter *1993 Secretary General Report*]. The Sixth Committee debates produced many suggestions for improving the legal regime. They addressed the need for harmonization of interpretation and clarification of the norms, the possibility of new law in the field, and potential improvements to the implementation and enforcement regimes, such as fact-finding committees or an international criminal court. *See Summary Record of the 19th Meeting, supra* note 118; *Summary Record of the 9th Meeting*, U.N. GAOR 6th Comm. 47th Sess., 9th mtg., U.N. Doc. A/C.6/47/SR.9 (1992); *Summary Record of the 8th Meeting*, U.N. GAOR 6th Comm., 47th Sess., 8th mtg., U.N. Doc. A/C.6/47/SR.8 (1992).

141. *See 1993 Secretary General Report, supra* note 140, para. 15.

142. *See* G.A. Res. 47/37, U.N. GAOR 6th Comm., 47th Sess., Agenda Item 136, U.N. Doc. A/RES/47/37 (1993).

143. *Id.* at 2.

144. *See id.* On the issues of military necessity and wantonness, see *infra* Subsection III.B.1.

145. John H. McNeill, *Protection of the Environment in Times of Armed Conflict: Environmental Protection in Military Practice*, 1993 HAGUE Y.B. INT'L L. 75, 77.

consider the issue, the ICRC chose the latter course of action. In particular, it decided to develop guidelines for wartime environmental protection that could be adopted into instructions that individual countries would issue to their armed forces.[146] By its third meeting, the ICRC completed a draft, the ICRC Guidelines, which it forwarded to the United Nations.[147] The General Assembly, in turn, invited member states to review and comment upon the ICRC Guidelines. It also welcomed the intention of the ICRC to consider member states' comments about the Guidelines, make appropriate changes, and resubmit them.[148] These steps were completed by 1994, at which time the General Assembly, without formally approving the Guidelines, urged all states to consider incorporating them into their law of armed conflict directives.[149]

Essentially a restatement of the law of war provisions that the ICRC had cited in its report to the Secretary General two years earlier, the Guidelines begin with the assertion that "existing international legal obligations and . . . State practice"[150] make up their foundation. In fact, however, they rely heavily on the Protocol I environmental articles that many countries, in particular the United States, oppose. Nevertheless, given the growing number of states that are Protocol I parties, it would be fair to cite its prescriptions as the direction in which the environmental law of war is heading.[151] As for state practice, the ICRC position is on firm ground. Whether or not Protocol I is binding on nonsignatories, the only country that arguably has violated articles 35(3) and 55 in a major conflict during the last decade is Iraq, and it suffered nearly unanimous condemnation for its conduct.

In addition to Protocol I, the Guidelines refer to a number of other familiar sources of law: Hague VIII (submarine mines),[152] Hague IV, Geneva IV, the Conventional Weapons Convention, the Convention for the Protection of Cultural Property,[153] and ENMOD. They also emphasize the centrality of classic law of war principles such as the rule of proportionality;[154] note that peacetime environmental law remains applicable

---

146. *See* Gasser, *supra* note 98, at 640.

147. *See 1993 Secretary General Report*, *supra* note 140.

148. *See* G.A. Res. 48/30, U.N. GAOR, 48th Sess., at 2, U.N. Doc. A/RES/48/30 (1993). The draft resolutions are U.N. GAOR, 47th Sess., U.N. Doc. A/C.6/47/L.2 (1992); U.N. GAOR, 47th Sess., U.N. Doc. A/C.6/47/L.2/Rev. 1 (1992).

149. *See* G.A. Res. 49/50, U.N. GAOR, 49th Sess., U.N. Doc. A/RES/49/50 (1995). The Guidelines are reprinted in U.N. GAOR, 49th Sess., Annex, Agenda Item 139, at 49–53, U.N. Doc. A/49/323 (1994) [hereinafter ICRC Guidelines]; Gasser, *supra* note 98, at 641–43.

150. ICRC Guidelines, *supra* note 149, para. 1.

151. As of November 30, 1996, there were 145 parties to Protocol I. *See* <http://gvalnex1.icrc.org>. Among the parties with whom the United States has close military ties are Australia, Canada, Egypt, Germany, Greece, Korea, and the Netherlands. The Russian Federation is also a party. *See id.*

152. Convention Relative to the Laying of Automatic Submarine Contact Mines, 36 Stat. 2332 (1907) [hereinafter Hague VIII].

153. Convention for the Protection of Cultural Property in the Event of Armed Conflict, May 14, 1954, 249 U.N.T.S. 240 [hereinafter Convention for the Protection of Cultural Property], *reprinted in* THE LAWS OF ARMED CONFLICTS 745 (Dietrich Schindler & Jiri Toman eds., 1988).

154. For example:

[T]he general principles of international law applicable in armed conflict—such as the principle of distinction and the principle of proportionality—provide protection to the environment. In

32   YALE JOURNAL OF INTERNATIONAL LAW   [Vol. 22: 1

during armed conflict to the extent that it is consistent with the law of armed conflict;[155] and include what has become known as a "Martens clause."[156] Considered a general principle of international law, this latter provision provides that "[i]n cases not covered by rules of international agreements, the environment remains under the protection and authority of principles of international law derived from established custom, from the principles of humanity and from the dictates of public conscience."[157] In other words, when its criteria are met, the clause denies offenders the argument that their conduct is not actionable because it falls outside applicable international agreements.

Specific prohibitions in the ICRC guidelines include those against destroying the environment when not justified by military necessity;[158] attacking forests with incendiary weapons unless the area is being used for cover, concealment, or camouflage, or unless the forests or plant cover are legitimate targets in themselves;[159] and attacking objects on which the civilian population depends for survival (when carried out to deny civilians those objects).[160] Particular types of historic monuments and places of worship are forbidden targets,[161] as are installations or works containing dangerous forces.[162] In a novel provision, the experts recognized the environmental dangers of mines by prohibiting their indiscriminate laying.[163] As might be expected, the "widespread," "long-term," and "severe" formula of Protocol I and ENMOD makes another appearance,[164] and reprisals

---

particular, only military objectives may be attacked and no methods or means of warfare which cause excessive damage shall be employed.
ICRC Guidelines, *supra* note 149, para. 4.

155. *See id.* para. 5.

156. The clause is named after the Russian representative who proposed it at the Hague Conference of 1899.

157. ICRC Guidelines, *supra* note 149, para. 7.

158. *See id.* para. 8 (citing Hague IV, *supra* note 130, art. 23(g); Geneva Convention IV, *supra* note 10, arts. 53, 147; Protocol I, *supra* note 8, arts. 35, para. 3, 55); *see also infra* Subsection III.C.3.

159. *See* ICRC Guidelines, *supra* note 149, para. 9(a) (citing Conventional Weapons Convention, *supra* note 134; Protocol III, *supra* note 134).

160. *See id.* para. 9(b) (citing Protocol I, *supra* note 8, art. 54).

161. *See id.* para. 9(d) (citing Convention for the Protection of Cultural Property, *supra* note 153; Protocol I, *supra* note 8, art. 53).

162. *See id.* para. 9(c) (citing Protocol I, *supra* note 8, art. 56). Note that the United States is opposed to this provision in Protocol I. *See infra* Subsection III.C.3.

163. The Guidelines state:
The indiscriminate laying of landmines is prohibited. The location of all pre-planned minefields must be recorded. Any unrecorded laying of remotely delivered, non-self neutralizing land mines is prohibited. Special rules limit the emplacement and use of naval mines.
ICRC Guidelines, *supra* note 149, para. 10 (citing Conventional Weapons Convention, *supra* note 134, art. 3; Protocol I, *supra* note 8, art. 51, paras. 4–5; Hague VIII, *supra* note 152).

164. The ICRC Guidelines provide:
Care shall be taken in warfare to protect and preserve the natural environment. It is prohibited to employ methods or means of warfare which are intended, or may be expected, to cause widespread, long-term and severe damage to the natural environment and thereby prejudice the health or survival of the population.
ICRC Guidelines, *supra* note 149, para. 11. Note that the ICRC has elected to include the anthropocentrically based prescription found in article 55 of Protocol I, rather than the more heavily intrinsic value prohibition of article 35(3). For discussion of this distinction, see *infra* Subsection III.C.3.

against the environment are proscribed.[165] These latter provisions are certain to hinder universal adoption, for both are derived from controversial Protocol I articles. Finally, the responsibility to "prevent and, where necessary, to suppress and to report to competent authorities" breaches of the rules is imposed on military commanders.[166] Using nondiscretionary language, the Guidelines provide that "[i]n serious cases, offenders shall be brought to justice."[167] It will be instructive to watch the progress of adoption, if only because of the relationship between the Guidelines and controversial Protocol I prescriptions.

In fact, increased awareness of warfare's environmental implications slowly is beginning to be reflected where it will have its greatest practical effect—in guides for planners, warfighters, and operational lawyers. The German law of war manual is among the most progressive.[168] Not only does this 1992 document provide for basic protections based on such principles as military necessity, unnecessary suffering, and distinction, but it also includes prohibitions that track those found in Protocol I and ENMOD. Specifically, article 401 provides that "[i]t is particularly prohibited to employ means or methods of warfare which are intended or of a nature . . . to cause widespread, long-term and severe damage to the natural environment."[169] The manual contains a similar provision with regard to naval warfare. What is most noteworthy about the German manual is that it clarifies the ENMOD and Protocol I terminology that is the source of much controversy. In article 403, the manual states that

> "widespread", "long-term" and "severe" damage to the natural environment is a major interference with human life or natural resources which considerably exceeds the battlefield damage to be regularly expected in war. Damage to the natural environment by means of warfare and severe manipulation of the environment as a weapon are likewise prohibited.[170]

The extent to which this attempt to square the terminological circle of these two agreements will prove successful remains to be seen.

Another example of a law of war guide that addresses the environment is the San Remo Manual.[171] Drafted for the International Institute of Humanitarian Law by a group of distinguished experts between 1988 and 1994 as a "restatement" of the international law of armed conflict at sea, this influential guide takes a different approach than its German counterpart. Whereas the German Manual adopts the phraseology of Protocol I and

---

165. *See id.* para. 13 (citing Protocol I, *supra* note 8, art. 55, para. 2).

166. *Id.* para. 20.

167. *Id.* para. 20 (citing Geneva Convention IV, *supra* note 10, arts. 146–147; Protocol I, *supra* note 8, arts. 86–87).

168. FEDERAL MINISTRY OF DEFENCE OF THE F.R.G., HUMANITARIAN LAW IN ARMED CONFLICTS: MANUAL (1992) [hereinafter GERMAN MANUAL].

169. *Id.* para. 401.

170. *Id.* para. 403.

171. INTERNATIONAL INST. OF HUMANITARIAN LAW, SAN REMO MANUAL ON INTERNATIONAL LAW APPLICABLE TO ARMED CONFLICTS AT SEA (Louise Doswald-Beck ed., 1995) [hereinafter SAN REMO]. The group assembled to draft the manual included Professor Salah El-Din Amer, Louise Doswald-Beck, Vice Admiral (ret.) James H. Doyle, Jr., Commander William J. Fenrick, Christopher Greenwood, Professor Horace B. Robertson, Jr., Gert-Jan F. Van Hegelsom, and Dr. Wolff Heintschel von Heinegg.

ENMOD, the San Remo Manual employs the "due regard" standard of care found in the Law of the Sea Convention.[172] Paragraph 44 of the manual provides that "methods and means of warfare should be employed with due regard for the natural environment taking into account the relevant rules of international law. Damage to or destruction of the natural environment not justified by military necessity and carried out wantonly is prohibited."[173] Although this provision is less stringent than those found in Protocol I and ENMOD, it may be more appropriate in the naval context because "due regard" is a familiar concept in maritime law and practice. Additionally, Protocol I was never intended to encompass naval warfare.[174]

None of the primary U.S. law of war manuals highlights environmental concerns to any significant degree. Current Army and Air Force versions are simply too dated to have focused on the issue.[175] However, while the Navy's old manual was also silent on this issue,[176] the newly published Navy manual does mention the topic.[177] Since it represents the most current expression of U.S. policy on the subject, the manual's sole environmental provision merits quotation in its entirety:

> It is not unlawful to cause collateral damage to the natural environment during an attack upon a legitimate military objective. However, the commander has an affirmative obligation to avoid unnecessary damage to the environment to the extent that it is practicable to do so consistent with mission accomplishment. To that end, and as far as military requirements permit, methods or means of warfare should be employed with due regard to the protection and preservation of the natural environment. Destruction of the natural environment not necessitated by mission accomplishment and carried out wantonly is prohibited. Therefore, a commander should consider the environmental damage which will result from an attack on a legitimate military objective as one of the factors during targeting analysis.[178]

It will be particularly interesting to see how the new U.S. multiservice law of war manual, on which the Army has taken the lead, handles environmental matters. If the most recent edition of the Army's excellent *Operational Law Handbook* is any indication, the manual will display a

---

172. *See* United Nations Convention on the Law of the Sea, Dec. 10, 1982, U.N. Doc. A/CONF.62/122, 21 I.L.M. 1261 [hereinafter LOS Convention]. For instance, article 58(3) provides that "[i]n exercising their rights and performing their duties under this Convention in the exclusive economic zone, States shall have due regard to the rights and duties of the coastal State." *Id.* art. 58, para. 3.

173. SAN REMO, *supra* note 171, para. 44.

174. On the applicability of Protocol I to naval warfare, see *infra* Subsection III.C.3. At the meeting there was significant debate over whether to use a "due regard" or "respect for" standard. According to the Rapporteur, some of the participants wanted to use the latter to maximize protection of the environment. *See* SAN REMO, *supra* note 171, para. 44.9. However, the "due regard" standard was eventually agreed upon because it was already in use in the LOS Convention and because it "more appropriately expressed the balance that must exist between the right of the States involved in naval conflict at sea to use lawful methods and means of warfare on the one hand, and the duty of such States to protect the marine environment on the other." *Id.*

175. *See* DEPARTMENT OF THE AIR FORCE, INTERNATIONAL LAW—THE CONDUCT OF ARMED CONFLICT AND AIR OPERATIONS (Pamphlet No. 110-31, 1976) [hereinafter AFP 110-31]; DEPARTMENT OF THE ARMY, THE LAW OF LAND WARFARE (Field Manual 27-10, 1956) [hereinafter AFM 27-10].

176. DEPARTMENT OF THE NAVY, THE COMMANDER'S HANDBOOK ON THE LAW OF NAVAL OPERATIONS (Navy Warfare Publication 9-Rev. A, 1989).

177. Note that both the Marine Corps and the Coast Guard have agreed to the new manual's use in a multiservice format.

178. DEPARTMENT OF THE NAVY, COMMANDER'S HANDBOOK ON THE LAW OF NAVAL OPERATIONS para. 8.13 (Naval Warfare Publication 1-14M, 1996) [hereinafter NWP 1-14M].

growing awareness of, and commitment to, environmental protection during warfare.[179] The handbook devotes an entire chapter to the subject of the environmental law of war, citing to sources that were referenced in the Secretary General's Report and the Jordanian-U.S. memorandum discussed previously. However, what is noteworthy about the handbook is that in discussing military necessity, it directs judge advocates to "pay particular attention to (1) the geographical extent (how widespread the damage will be), (2) the longevity, and the (3) severity of the damage upon the target area's environment."[180] Significantly, these three factors mirror those found in the Protocol I provisions to which the United States objects. The handbook also notes that while the United States is not a party to the protocol, U.S. forces need to be sensitive to the implications of combined operations with the military forces of states that are parties to the protocol. This is superb advice of very practical warfighting import.

Finally, mention should be made of a NATO initiative in the environmental field that has borne little fruit thus far. In January 1994, Norwegian, German, and Canadian representatives recommended that NATO's Committee on the Challenges of Modern Society conduct a pilot study on environmental protection. Though most delegations received the proposal favorably, two expressed a concern that the study might have negative consequences for military effectiveness. At present, the proposal has been placed on hold pending further assessment of its merits.[181] Whether it resurfaces will be an excellent indicator of shifts in attitudes toward the place of environmental concerns in combat.

Do these various steps forward portend an emergent military sensitivity to the environmental law of war? That the Office of the Secretary of Defense (OSD) sponsored *The Symposium on the Protection of the Environment During Armed Conflict and Operations Other Than War* at the Naval War College in September 1995 suggests that the answer is yes. Despite heightened interest in such protection, the prevailing view—that no effort to fashion new law, or to codify existing law, is needed—remains firmly entrenched. It was certainly the general consensus of the scholars, warfighters, and policymakers who gathered in Newport.[182] That the dominant cognitive perspective remains

---

179. *See* INTERNATIONAL & OPERATIONAL LAW DEP'T, U.S. ARMY, OPERATIONAL LAW HANDBOOK (1995) [hereinafter OPERATIONAL LAW HANDBOOK]. The Handbook provides:

> Protecting the environment has become steadily more important during the past several decades. The international community is increasingly vigilant in its oversight of the environmental consequences of military operations. . . . Failure to comply with environmental law can jeopardize current and future operations, generate domestic and international criticism, produce costly litigation, and even result in personal liability of both the leader and the individual soldier.

Id. at 5-1.

180.   *Id.* at 5-4.

181.   This initiative is described in Dieter Fleck, Protection of the Environment During Armed Conflict and Other Military Operations: The Way Ahead, Paper Presented at the Symposium on the Protection of the Environment During Armed Conflict and Operations Other Than War, *in* NWC SYMPOSIUM PAPERS, *supra* note 13 (manuscript at 7-8, on file with *The Yale Journal of International Law*).

182.   However, it was not the unanimous consensus; some participants called for new law. *See id.* at 5.

overwhelmingly anthropocentric is also clear. The comments of the ICRC's Hans-Peter Gasser may reflect the prevailing attitude. Speaking at the 1991 London Conference in his personal capacity, he noted that

> the ICRC does not look so much at the environment as such but more at the environment in the context of and around human beings. As you know the Geneva Conventions are geared essentially to the protection and safeguarding of human beings in times of armed conflict . . . . [The environmental provisions of Geneva law] protect the environment for human beings—when both civilians and combatants are affected.[183]

This perspective could apply equally to the law beyond the Geneva Conventions (and Protocol I) and to international attitudes other than those of the ICRC. Having set the law within its proper historical context, it is appropriate to turn to an analysis of the law and the effect of the various perspectives on it.

III. WHERE ARE WE?

A. *Peacetime Prescriptions*

Since the Gulf War, there has been widespread recognition that the role of peacetime environmental prescriptions during armed conflict merits further study.[184] Part of the uncertainty in deciding which prescriptions apply derives from the context within which this body of law was intended to operate. As one commentator has perceptively noted, environmental law emerged primarily in response to major accidents such as the Torrey Canyon disaster and Chernobyl.[185] It was never intended to govern the intentional infliction of damage to another's territory; in several cases, the issue has been resolved explicitly through treaty provisions excluding applicability during armed conflict.[186] Yet to the extent that international actors are liable for negligent actions (or even nonnegligent actions, in cases of strict liability) that damage the environment, should they not also be held liable when they intentionally set out to realize the forbidden end? From a moral perspective,

---

183. Awn Al-Khasaweh, *Round-Table Session I, General Principles and Methods for Executing a New Convention*, in ENVIRONMENTAL PROTECTION AND THE LAW OF WAR, *supra* note 94, at 111 (statement of Hans-Peter Gasser).

184. The matter was addressed in both the ICRC and Munich Conference reports, whose specific conclusions are nearly interchangeable. The ICRC experts opined that environmental law remained largely applicable during hostilities and that core environmental treaties needed to be analyzed to assess applicability. *See 1992 Secretary General Report*, *supra* note 128, para. 56. The Munich Conference went slightly further by noting that environmental law remained in force as between belligerents and nonbelligerents, but that the rules concerning its effect vis-à-vis opposing belligerents needed to be clarified. *See* Munich Report, *supra* note 100, para. 6. The consensus view is that while some peacetime environmental law may certainly remain in effect during hostilities, no ready-made catalogue of applicable law exists, nor are the rules for applicability well defined.

185. *See* Anthony Leibler, *Deliberate Wartime Environmental Damage: New Challenges for International Law*, 23 CAL. W. INT'L L.J. 67, 69–70 (1992).

186. *See, e.g.*, International Convention for the Prevention of Pollution of the Sea by Oil, May 12, 1954, art. 19, 12 U.S.T. 2989, 327 U.N.T.S. 3 ("In case of war or other hostilities [a party may] suspend the operation of the whole or any part of the present convention . . . .").

the response may well be that they should; legally, things look much hazier.[187]

The uncertainty is of consequence, for the bulk of international environmental law is found in sources outside the law of armed conflict. Selected elements of the former will be surveyed in the following sections. However, much more important than the issue of *what* law applies is the issue of *when* it applies. What are the "rules" for applying peacetime norms during armed conflict? Without understanding these rules, any consideration of specific scenarios that might involve peacetime norms will prove futile because most environmental agreements fail to address the issue directly. Therefore, the inquiry into peacetime prescriptions must begin with the issue of applicability.

1. *Applicability*

In the classic understanding, treaties did not survive the initiation of hostilities. War was a state of affairs that existed beyond the realm of international law and relations. Indeed, it represented the breakdown of those entities. However, the more modern view is that war is a continuation of interstate relations and, thus, subject to legal limits. This was the position that Justice Benjamin Cardozo expressed in the landmark case of *Techt v. Hughes*.[188] According to Justice Cardozo, "international law to-day does not preserve treaties or annul them, regardless of the effects produced. It deals with such problems pragmatically, preserving or annulling as the necessities of war exact. It establishes standards, but it does not fetter itself with rules."[189]

Within this contemporary approach, three camps may be discerned.[190] The oldest school suggests that whereas certain relations animated by legal content might survive the outbreak of hostilities, treaties do not; a treaty relationship is inconsistent with a state of armed conflict.[191] Its advocates point to the fact that no peacetime environmental convention specifically provides for applicability during hostilities as further support.[192] On the

---

187. In his excellent article, Anthony Leibler notes that "to the extent that these laws apply to the negligent or careless pollution, it is logical to assume that they must certainly apply to deliberate pollution." Leibler, *supra* note 185, at 70. While it may in fact be logical, such a conclusion does not hold as a matter of international law. As will be discussed below, the existence of a state of armed conflict has much play on the issue.

188. 128 N.E. 185 (N.Y.), *cert. denied*, 254 U.S. 643 (1920).

189. *Id.* at 191.

190. For an excellent discussion on which much of this analysis builds, see Jost Delbrück, *War, Effect on Treaties*, *in* 4 ENCYCLOPEDIA OF PUBLIC INTERNATIONAL LAW 311 (1982).

191. For example, one prominent scholar has noted that "[a]s a rule, bilateral treaties are terminated or suspended by the outbreak of a war unless they were concluded with the war in mind. The effects of multilateral treaties are also suspended between the adversaries unless they were concluded specifically with a view to the state of war." Michael Bothe, *The Protection of the Environment in Times of Armed Conflict: Legal Rules, Uncertainty, Deficiencies and Possible Developments*, 34 GERM. Y.B. INT'L L. 54, 59 (1991). He goes on to acknowledge, however, that "modern opinion . . . favors the non-suspension of certain types of obligations even between belligerents. It would appear that some basic rules relating to the environment might be counted among the latter obligations." *Id.*

192. *See, e.g.*, Verwey, Additional Rules, *supra* note 13, at 11.

other extreme are those who maintain that treaties do survive, except to the extent that they are by their specific nature inconsistent with hostilities. Examples of inconsistent agreements between opposing belligerents are status of forces agreements, alliance arrangements, and military aid treaties. A third approach takes the middle ground. Labeled the "theory of differentiation," it is contextual in nature and reflects an effort to balance the stability that international agreements offer with a realization that armed conflict may be at odds with the fulfillment of treaty obligations and rights. Notably, it acknowledges that treaties may concern parties other than belligerents. Thus, in determining whether an agreement survives, it is necessary to ask whether continued vitality is consistent with the larger context in which the agreement will operate.

The Vienna Convention on the Law of Treaties does little to resolve the matter. In article 73, it simply states that "[t]he provisions of the present Convention shall not prejudge any question that may arise in regard to a treaty . . . from the outbreak of hostilities."[193] In the absence of a definitive statement of law, and in the face of disagreement over the effect of war on treaties, one must turn to logic and context to select from among the three approaches.

To argue *sans plus* that treaties become inoperative upon the start of hostilities is to suggest that war is really all that matters once it breaks out. However, many treaties are the expression of mutual interests wholly unrelated to the causes or effects of conflict. The first approach would, therefore, forfeit the mutual benefits that treaties might continue to provide to both parties.[194] On the other hand, the second approach's claim of near-universal continued validity is unrealistic. States become involved in armed conflict for many different reasons. Some conflicts are the product of rational decisionmaking; some are not. Yet all wars are laden with emotion. Even aspects of ante bellum relations unrelated to the conflict are bound to be affected, a reality for which the law should account. The aim should be to preserve treaty regimes that can survive; to perpetuate artificially those that are destined to splinter will dilute the effect of those that might not.

Best fostering this aim and upholding international interests in global order is the third conceptual approach. It suggests certain conclusions about continued vitality that derive from the nature of the treaty at hand and the type of conflict underway. On the one hand, there are those agreements intended for armed conflict, such as the Geneva Conventions. Obviously, all such treaties survive; indeed, they may not even become operative until hostilities occur. Also surviving are treaties that expressly provide for continuance

---

193. Vienna Convention on the Law of Treaties, May 23, 1969, art. 73, 1155 U.N.T.S. 331, 8 I.L.M. 679 [hereinafter Vienna Convention]. The Vienna Convention came into force in 1980, but, as of the date of this Article, has not been ratified by the United States. Nevertheless, most of its provisions are declaratory of customary international law.

194. For example, mutual safeguarding of straddling stocks of fish pursuant to article 63 of the Law of the Sea Convention benefits both sides by preserving a mutually important natural resource. *See* LOS Convention, *supra* note 172, art. 63.

during war.[195] At the other end of the spectrum lie those treaties that either become inoperative by their own terms once armed conflict breaks out[196] or are so obviously inconsistent with hostilities that they are *a priori* deemed to terminate when hostilities commence. Military aid agreements are a good example.

The issue becomes much more difficult between the two extremes. However, given the goals underlying the theory of differentiation, it is possible to pose a series of questions that can help identify where along the continuum a treaty is likely to fall. Consider the following indicators of survivability. Bear in mind that these indicators apply contextually; it would be foolhardy to assess survivability apart from the actual situation in which the applicability issue arises.

(1) Does the treaty regulate private or public interests? Treaties governing purely private interests are more likely to survive, for citizens may continue to reap their benefits even after the outbreak of hostilities without damaging the state's interests. Since environmental treaty law performs both functions, a case-by-case analysis is required.

(2) Is the treaty multilateral or bilateral? Bilateral treaties are much more likely to be suspended or terminated. In contrast, multilateral treaties will generally remain operative between belligerent and nonbelligerent signatories. As between opposing belligerents, if the obligation or right involved has ramifications (collateral damage, if you will) that extend beyond the belligerents, then it is less likely to be suspended or terminated. This often will be the case with treaties that create international regimes for a shared good.[197] Given the interconnectedness of the global environment, the survival of environmental obligations and rights is especially likely.[198]

(3) If a bilateral treaty is at issue, who is party to the treaty? If it is between belligerents, then it will almost surely be suspended or terminated. Conversely, bilateral treaties between a belligerent and nonbelligerent usually will remain in force. There are certain exceptions to this generalization; the most common is the legal principle of "fundamental changed circumstances"—*rebus sic stantibus*. This customary principle, codified in article 62(1) of the Vienna Convention on the Law of Treaties, holds that an unforeseen fundamental change of circumstances may justify termination or withdrawal when the anticipated circumstances constituted an "essential basis

---

195. *See, e.g.*, General Act of the Berlin Conference Respecting the Congo, Feb. 26, 1885, 165 Consol. T.S. 485 (providing for freedom of navigation on Congo and Niger rivers); Convention Relating to the Non-fortification and Neutralization of the Aaland Islands, Oct. 20, 1921, 9 L.N.T.S. 211.

196. *See, e.g.*, International Convention for the Prevention of Pollution of the Sea by Oil, *supra* note 186 (permitting parties to suspend operation of treaty either in whole or in part in event of war or other hostilities).

197. *See, e.g.*, Convention on International Civil Aviation, Dec. 7, 1944, 61 Stat. 1180, 15 U.N.T.S. 295 (setting forth rules of air for nongovernmental aircraft).

198. Consider the case of the Kuwait Regional Convention for Cooperation on the Protection of the Marine Environment from Pollution, Apr. 24, 1978, 17 I.L.M. 511. This treaty, to which Bahrain, Iran, Iraq, Kuwait, Oman, Qatar, Saudi Arabia, and the United Arab Emirates are parties, provided for the establishment of the Regional Organization for the Protection of the Marine Environment (ROPME), headquartered in Kuwait. ROPME continued to operate during the Gulf War, with the participation of both Kuwait and Iraq, even though its staff elements did leave Kuwait during the Iraqi occupation. Furthermore, the organization was instrumental in the post-hostilities cleanup effort.

of the consent" of the parties at the time of agreement *and* the effect of enforcing the treaty in the new circumstances would be to "radically transform" the unperformed obligations of one of the parties.[199] There can be little debate about whether the outbreak of armed conflict constitutes a fundamental change of circumstances. In the environmental arena, though, a state of peace would probably not have been an essential basis of agreement, unless compliance with the environmental restrictions would hinder effective combat operations. If so, such restrictions would fall into the category of radically transformed unperformed obligations. This analysis is equally applicable to multilateral treaties. Note that an "aggressor" may not invoke fundamentally changed circumstances to excuse itself from treaty obligations, because the change in question cannot result from the breach of international obligations owed to other treaty parties.[200] Thus, if the invoking party is in violation of article 2(4) of the U.N. Charter, it may not rely on article 62 of the Vienna Convention.

(4) Are treaty obligations and/or rights executed or executory? The finality of a treaty is a powerful indication that it should remain in effect.[201] Only in extraordinary circumstances would it be disturbed, and such circumstances would generally involve issues of fraud, coercion, and the like—not the existence of armed conflict.[202] Most environmental treaties, in contrast, are executory because they impose continuing obligations.

(5) What type of conflict is involved? Current legal perspectives on treaty survival were conceived of as operating in the context of robust warfare, that is, hostilities of relatively significant intensity and extended duration. Furthermore, they responded to a classic aggression/self-defense paradigm. Today, however, the United States and other major powers are most likely to find themselves involved in low-intensity, limited-duration military operations other than war (MOOTW) motivated by nondefensive considerations.

MOOTW—peacekeeping, peace enforcement, peacemaking, humanitarian intervention, humanitarian relief, etc.—should not be deemed to have the same effect on treaties as more traditional forms of combat. Warfare in the familiar sense is a breakdown in relations, followed by an aggressive act. In response, the "victim" state acts in self-defense. Normal relations have been supplanted by the desire to harm an opponent. Though the intent may not be malicious (for example, to force an enemy to come to his senses regarding the costs of aggression), harm nevertheless remains the objective. In MOOTW, on the other hand, the goal usually is to avoid having to harm an opponent, assuming

---

199. Vienna Convention, *supra* note 193, art. 62, para. 1. It is a contextual standard. Consider the Convention on International Trade in Endangered Species of Wild Fauna and Flora, July 1, 1975, 27 U.S.T. 1087, 12 I.L.M. 1085, an agreement which appears to have little relationship to armed conflict. of the case of an extremely poor (failing) state engaged in an armed struggle for survival? If endangered species were one of the state's few sources of funds, would that state be required to comply with the denunciation provisions set forth in the treaty, or would the conflict represent changed circumstances radically transforming the state's obligations?

200. *See* Vienna Convention, *supra* note 193, art. 62, para. 2.

201. For instance, in the Treaty of Peace Between the United States and Great Britain, the United States is acknowledged to be a free state. The provision binds all the King's successors. Treaty of Peace, Sept. 3, 1783, U.S.-Gr. Brit., art. 2, 8 Stat. 80.

202. On the grounds for invalidity of treaties, see Vienna Convention, *supra* note 193, arts. 46-53.

one can be identified. There should therefore be a presumption in favor of continued legal relations among all parties. When this presumption proves unreasonable or impractical in specific circumstances, the fallback position should logically be a presumption favoring suspension over termination of the treaty. The avoidance of environmental damage fits well within this relatively benign perspective.

To summarize, the approach that best comports with the reality of armed conflict while fostering world order is one in which a presumption of survivability attaches to peacetime environmental treaties, absent either de facto incompatibility with a state of conflict or express treaty provisions providing for termination. That said, the issue is best analyzed on a case-by-case basis. Particularly important is an awareness that urging the continued validity of treaties that, for practical purposes, are inconsistent with the existence of belligerent relations may be counterproductive to maintaining survivable treaty regimes. Finally, in assessing whether war has rendered treaty obligations void, voidable, suspended, or suspendable, it is essential to ask to whom the treaty obligations apply, for a key criterion is whether the treaty is between belligerents or between a belligerent and a nonbelligerent.

2. *Substantive Norms*

Those hoping to find comprehensive peacetime limits on environmental damage either in customary law or in the decisions of international adjudicative bodies will be disappointed. Instead, the prolific output of various international bodies, particularly the United Nations, has been primarily hortatory and aspirational in nature. As will become clear, it is only with great reluctance that states surrender sovereign prerogatives over the use of, and activities within, their territory. Thus, international instruments that have been agreed upon tend to be either nonbinding or narrowly crafted.

The beginning of the modern international environmental effort can be traced to the Stockholm Conference of 1972. Attended by representatives of over 100 countries, the U.N.-sponsored gathering produced two hortatory documents: a Declaration on the Human Environment[203] and an Action Plan.[204] Principle 21 serves as the Declaration's capstone. Reiterating the most basic premise of international environmental law, it provides:

> States have, in accordance with the Charter of the United Nations and the principle of international law, the sovereign right to exploit their own resources pursuant to their own

---

203. *United Nations Conference on the Human Environment, Stockholm Declaration on the Human Environment*, June 16, 1972, U.N. Doc. A/CONF.48/14 (1972), *revised by* U.N. Doc. A/CONF.48/14/Corr.1 (1972), *reprinted in* 11 I.L.M. 1416 [hereinafter *Stockholm Declaration*]. The Declaration sets forth 26 guiding principles for crafting international environmental prescriptions. It asserts that there is a "fundamental right to freedom, equality and adequate conditions of life, in an environment of a quality that permits a life of dignity and well-being." *Id.* princ. 1. This right contains the corollary duty to "protect and preserve the environment for present and future generations." *Id.* Other principles address such matters as the relationship between underdevelopment and the environment, and liability and compensation. *See id.* princs. 9, 22.

204. *United Nations Conference on the Human Environment, Action Plan for the Human Environment*, U.N. Doc. A/CONF.48/14 (1972), *reprinted in* 11 I.L.M. 1421 (adopting 109 recommendations on such matters as management of global environment and environmental assessment).

42   YALE JOURNAL OF INTERNATIONAL LAW   [Vol. 22: 1

environmental policies, and the responsibility to ensure that activities within their jurisdiction or control do not cause damage to the environment of other States or of areas beyond the limits of national jurisdiction.[205]

The principle thereby recognizes the tension between sovereignty and international environmental law, and attempts to balance the two. The final clause of the principle also suggests extending state responsibility to acts that cause environmental damage in the global commons, such as the high seas.[206] Finally, though the Declaration does not address war per se,[207] principle 26 emphasizes that "[m]an and his environment must be spared the effects of nuclear weapons and all other means of mass destruction."[208] Thus, at this early point, consideration of the effect of warfare on the environment centered less on the fact of an impact than it did on the quantum of damage that could be caused—a very anthropocentric approach.

Although it did not generate new law, the Stockholm Declaration certainly indicated where international attitudes were headed in 1972. The environment was now acknowledged as a separate entity, but legal norms affording it protection continued to employ balancing tests. The next major environmental effort came ten years later when the World Conservation Union issued the World Charter for Nature, a document promptly adopted by the U.N. General Assembly, albeit with minor modifications.[209] Of course, a General Assembly resolution, like the Stockholm Declaration, is only hortatory and aspirational. Nevertheless, it broadly articulates the standards influencing assessments of environmentally destructive conduct.[210]

With regard to extending peacetime norms to armed conflict, the Charter presents five key principles.[211] The most important, principle 5, states that "[n]ature shall be secured against degradation caused by warfare or other hostile activities."[212] Building on this aspiration in the section on implementation is principle 20, a provision that could apply equally to times of peace and war: "Military activity damaging to nature shall be

---

205. *Stockholm Declaration, supra* note 203, princ. 21.

206. The conference sped establishment of the United Nations Environment Programme (UNEP). Created in 1973, UNEP is responsible for coordinating U.N. activities involving the environment. It is also charged with pursuing agreement on international environmental treaties such as the Vienna Convention for the Protection of the Ozone Layer, Mar. 22, 1985, T.I.A.S. No. 11,097, 26 I.L.M. 1529 [hereinafter Ozone Convention].

207. Stephanie Simonds argues that principle 21 does not apply during warfare. *See* Stephanie N. Simonds, *Conventional Warfare and Environmental Protection: A Proposal for International Legal Reform*, 29 STAN. J. INT'L L. 165, 192 (1992).

208. *Stockholm Declaration, supra* note 203, princ. 26.

209. *See* G.A. Res. 37/7, U.N. GAOR, 37th Sess., Supp. No. 51, at 21, U.N. Doc. A/RES/37/7; World Charter for Nature, U.N. Doc. A/37/L.4 & Add.1 (1982). In the General Assembly vote, 17 nations abstained, while one, the United States, voted against the resolution. The U.S. vote was not based on the provisions concerning warfare. *See* 1981 U.N.Y.B. 1026.

210. In the General Assembly resolution, those principles of conservation intended to serve as "the common standard by which all human conduct affecting nature is to be guided and judged" are set forth. World Charter for Nature, *supra* note 209, pmbl.

211. The first four of these principles urge against disruption of the "essential processes" of nature, assert the need to safeguard habitats to prevent extinction, encourage protective regimes for unique areas, and argue for an ecosystem approach to maintenance of environmental well-being. *Id.* princs. 1–4.

212. *Id.* princ. 5.

avoided."[213] Coming on the heels of Protocol I and ENMOD, the World Charter reflected the broadest statement on war and the environment to date by an intergovernmental organization.[214]

A decade after adoption of the World Charter, the United Nations sponsored the "Earth Summit" in Rio de Janeiro to commemorate the twentieth anniversary of the Stockholm Conference. At the summit, five documents were produced: the Climate Change Convention, the Declaration of Principles on Forest Conservation, the Convention on Biological Diversity, Agenda 21, and the Rio Declaration. It is the last of these that is relevant to this study.

The Rio Declaration is an effort to update the Stockholm Declaration. Of particular importance is principle 2, which revises Stockholm principle 21 by placing greater emphasis on the sovereign prerogative to develop one's own resources.[215] This was done to satisfy the developing states' desire to ensure that environmental "restrictions" (the Declaration is technically nonbinding) would not hinder their growth. Unfortunately, the concession actually decreases environmental protection, for development will assume greater weight in the balancing process. Additionally, the emphasis on development highlights the Declaration's relatively anthropocentric nature. Indeed, it exemplifies the fact that evolution toward an intrinsic value approach is most likely to come in presently developed countries. After all, it is only logical that basic human needs must be satisfied before a cognitive prism other than an anthropocentric one can be internalized.

Despite this rather restrictive view, the Rio Declaration, unlike its predecessors, directly addresses the effect of warfare on the environment. In principle 24, it characterizes warfare as "inherently destructive of sustainable development" and notes that states must, therefore, "respect international law providing protection for the environment in times of armed conflict and cooperate in its further development, as necessary."[216] It is not surprising

---

213. *Id.* princ. 20.

214. As might be expected, the Charter was a predominantly anthropocentric product. This is particularly apparent in the seven principles related to "responsibilities" of parties. For instance, the section begins with the statement that "[i]n the decision-making process it shall be recognized that man's needs can be met only by ensuring the proper functioning of the natural systems." *Id.* princ. 6. Similarly, in assessing whether to proceed with activities that pose a significant risk to nature, proponents are required to "demonstrate that expected benefits outweigh potential damage to nature." *Id.* princ. 11(b). While not purely anthropocentric (because the risk calculation need not be measured in terms of the contribution nature's damaged aspect makes to man), the mere fact that balancing occurs suggests an anthropocentric perspective.

215. Principle 2 of the Rio Declaration provides:

States have, in accordance with the Charter of the United Nations and the principles of international law, the sovereign right to exploit their own resources pursuant to their own environmental *and developmental* policies, and the responsibility to ensure that activities within their jurisdiction or control do not cause damage to the environment of other States or of areas beyond the limits of national jurisdiction.

Rio Declaration, *supra* note 114, princ. 2 (emphasis added). The next two principles cement the theme: "The right to development must be fulfilled so as to equitably meet developmental and environmental needs of present and future generations." *Id.* princ. 3. "In order to achieve sustainable development, environmental protection shall constitute an integral part of the development process and cannot be considered in isolation from it." *Id.* princ. 4.

216. *Id.* princ. 24.

44   YALE JOURNAL OF INTERNATIONAL LAW   [Vol. 22: 1

that the Declaration included this principle, coming as it did on the heels of the Gulf War. Though an exhortation to comply with existing law is purely hortatory, and the admonition to cooperate merely aspirational, the Rio Declaration provides additional evidence that environmental damage during combat remains in the international spotlight.

Finally, the Rio Declaration handles the issue of state responsibility for environmental damage by urging further development in that area of the law. It encourages states to address liability and compensation issues through national legislation. Recognizing, however, that the problem is one of international scope that requires an international remedy, the Declaration also exhorts states to "cooperate in an expeditious and more determined manner to develop further international law regarding liability and compensation for adverse effects of environmental damage caused by their activities within their jurisdiction or control to areas beyond their jurisdiction."[217]

A last document of importance among nonbinding instruments is the Draft Articles on State Responsibility of the International Law Commission (ILC).[218] In article 19(3)(d), the ILC recommends that "a serious breach of an international obligation of essential importance for the safeguarding and preservation of the human environment, such as those prohibiting massive pollution of the atmosphere or of the seas," should be regarded as an international crime.[219] To date, the article remains purely aspirational. Nevertheless, it is another indication that the environment per se is increasingly deemed deserving of protection.[220]

In terms of binding international environmental law, the most basic and widely accepted traditional principle is expressed in the maxim *sic utere tuo ut alienum non laedas*—use your property in such a manner so as not to injure another. This principle was the basis for the holding in *Trail Smelter*.[221] The case involved a smelter that was discharging sulfur dioxide near the town of Trail in British Columbia. According to the United States, the sulfur dioxide drifted over parts of the state of Washington, thereby damaging commercial forests. The United States and Canada referred the case to an arbitration

---

217. *Id.* princ. 13.
218. *International Law Commission Draft Articles on State Responsibility*, [1980] 2 Y.B. INT'L L. COMM'N 26, U.N. Doc. A/35/10. In 1947 the U.N. General Assembly established the ILC for the purpose of conducting international law research and drafting conventions. Its membership includes internationally recognized scholars and practitioners of international law.
219. *Id.* art. 19, para. 3(d).
220. Note that this article is referring to *state* crimes, not individual crimes under international law. Professor Greenwood has placed this in appropriate perspective:

> Whether the Commission's attempt to create a concept of State crimes separate from other breaches by states of their international obligations will prove acceptable and whether it will actually make any difference to the substantive law (as opposed to such issues as the standing to bring a claim) is debatable. What matters for present purposes is the clear recognition that a State incurs responsibility under international law for the breach of its environmental obligations.

Christopher Greenwood, State Responsibility and Civil Liability for Environmental Damage Caused by Military Operations, Paper Presented at the Symposium on the Protection of the Environment During Armed Conflict and Operations Other Than War, *in* NWC SYMPOSIUM PAPERS, *supra* note 13 (manuscript at 2, on file with *The Yale Journal of International Law*).
221. Trail Smelter (U.S. v. Can.), 3 R.I.A.A. 1911 (1941). For an interesting revisionist view of the case, see Karin Mickelson, *Rereading* Trail Smelter, 31 CAN. Y.B. INT'L L. 219 (1993).

tribunal, which held for the United States on the grounds that countries have a duty not to use, or allow the use of, their territory for activities harmful to another state.[222] Since then, the principle has been reiterated in international agreements and domestic tribunals.[223] Drawing on tort law, the arbitration award emphasized that the plaintiff has to show both material damage and causation. Purely speculative damage is not actionable.[224]

Little additional case law specifically addresses environmental damage. Two interesting cases that might have moved the law forward, had they been decided on the merits, are the *Nuclear Test Cases*.[225] Resorting to the ICJ, New Zealand and Australia charged that French atmospheric nuclear testing in the South Pacific harmed them. The case was never heard on the merits because France voluntarily ceased testing. When it did so, the ICJ dismissed the case as moot.[226] Interestingly, prior to the French agreement to halt the tests, the court issued interim relief that directed France to stop testing.[227] While this might be characterized as suggesting sympathy for Australia and New Zealand's position, a better reading is that it was merely standard injunctive relief designed to foreclose the possibility of irreparable harm.

General acceptance of the *Trail Smelter* principle was signaled most clearly when the American Law Institute included a section addressing the concept in its *Restatement (Third) of Foreign Relations Law of the United*

---

222. *See Trail Smelter*, 3 R.I.A.A. at 1965.The arbitral tribunal stated:
   [U]nder the principles of international law, as well as of the law of the United States, no State has the right to use or permit the use of its territory in such a manner as to cause injury by fumes in or to the territory of another or the properties or persons therein, when the case is of serious consequence and the injury is established by clear and convincing evidence.
Id. Interestingly, in addition to international law, the arbitral tribunal looked to domestic law, including such U.S. Supreme Court cases as *Missouri v. Illinois*, 200 U.S. 496 (1906) (water pollution) and *Georgia v. Tennessee Copper Co.*, 206 U.S. 230 (1907) (air pollution). *See Trail Smelter*, 3 R.I.A.A. at 1964–65.
223. *See, e.g.*, LOS Convention, *supra* note 172, art. 194, para. 2 ("States shall take all measures necessary to ensure that activities under their jurisdiction or control are so conducted as not to cause damage by pollution to other States and their environment, and that pollution arising from incidents or activities under their jurisdiction or control does not spread beyond the areas where they exercise sovereign rights . . . ."); *see also* Convention on Long-Range Transboundary Air Pollution, Nov. 13, 1979, pmbl., 18 I.L.M. 1442 [hereinafter Air Pollution Convention]. For examples of national cases, see Antoine, *supra* note 51, at 519 n.4 (citing cases decided in Strasbourg and Rotterdam).
224. Though no other international cases involve environmental damage as a core issue, others bear more generally upon uses of a state's territory that cause damage beyond its borders. *See, e.g.*, Corfu Channel (U.K. v. Alb.), 1949 I.C.J. 4 (Apr. 9). *Corfu Channel* involved two British warships that were damaged in 1946 when the vessels hit German mines in Albanian waters in the Straits of Corfu. Several sailors were killed. On the issue of state responsibility, the ICJ ruled in the United Kingdom's favor, finding that Albania must have known of the mines' presence, and did nothing to warn the ships despite its duty to do so. As it bears on the environment, *Corfu Channel* stands for the principle that a state is obligated to refrain from allowing its territory to be used in a fashion that causes harm to others. *See id.* at 22; *see also* Lake Lanoux Arbitration (Fr. v. Spain), 12 R.I.A.A. 281 (1957) (holding that although Spain cannot preclude France from using upstream water as it sees fit, as matter of equity, France should consider Spain's counterproposals for use).
225. Nuclear Tests (Austl. v. Fr.), 1974 I.C.J. 253 (Dec. 20); Nuclear Tests (N.Z. v. Fr.), 1974 I.C.J. 457 (Dec. 20).
226. *See* Nuclear Tests (Austl. v. Fr.), 1974 I.C.J. at 271–72; Nuclear Tests (N.Z. v. Fr.), 1974 I.C.J. at 477–78.
227. *See* Nuclear Tests (Austl. v. Fr.), 1973 I.C.J. 99 (Interim Protection Order of June 22); Nuclear Tests (N.Z. v. Fr.), 1973 I.C.J. 135 (Interim Protection Order of June 22).

States.[228] Since it succinctly sets forth not only the substantive law, but also the concept of state responsibility, it merits quotation in full:

> (1) A state is obligated to take such measures as may be necessary, to the extent practicable under the circumstances, to ensure that activities within its jurisdiction or control
>
>   (a) conform to generally accepted international rules and standards for the prevention, reduction and control of injury to the environment of another state or of areas beyond the limits of national jurisdiction; and
>
>   (b) are conducted so as not to cause significant injury to the environment of another state or of areas beyond the limits of national jurisdiction.
>
> (2) A state is responsible to all other states
>
>   (a) for any violation of its obligations under Subsection (1)(a), and
>
>   (b) for any significant injury, resulting from such violation, to the environment of areas beyond the limit of national jurisdiction or control.
>
> (3) A state is responsible for any significant injury, resulting from a violation of its obligations under Subsection (1), to the environment of another or to its property, or to persons or property within that state's territory or under its jurisdiction or control.[229]

Would this principle apply in times of armed conflict? That would depend on the context. The principle is less about the environment than about state responsibility for the use of its territory. In *Trail Smelter*, for example, the importance of the environmental element is subsumed in the broader principle imposing an obligation to protect other states from injurious acts emanating from within one's own borders. Characterized this way, it would be illogical for such a principle to apply between belligerents, for the use of one's territory to damage an enemy is the essence of warfare.

But what about harm caused to nonbelligerents? There is nothing necessarily inconsistent between an obligation to avoid causing harm to the territory of a nonbelligerent and engaging in hostilities with a third state. Nevertheless, this is a more complex question. The most basic principle of neutrality law is that the territory of neutral powers is generally inviolable.[230] Would the passage of pollutants into a nonbelligerent's territory constitute a violation of territorial integrity? It might not; Canada's breach in *Trail Smelter* was that it caused damage from within its territory, not that substances originated there and passed into the United States. The key is effect, not movement. Furthermore, the neutrality principle was traditionally based on physical intrusions, usually by military assets of the belligerents.[231]

A better approach is to recognize that neutrality law is premised on the need to balance the rights of neutrals and those of belligerents during armed

---

228. RESTATEMENT (THIRD) OF FOREIGN RELATIONS LAW OF THE UNITED STATES § 601 (1987) [hereinafter RESTATEMENT (THIRD)].

229. *Id.* Professor Walker has argued that the *Restatement* may not be very helpful when law of armed conflict issues interact with the law of the sea and environmental law. *See* Walker, *supra* note 52, at 192.

230. *See* Convention Respecting the Rights and Duties of Neutral Powers and Persons in Case of War on Land, Oct. 18, 1907, art. 1, 36 Stat. 2310; *see also* AFM 27-10, *supra* note 175, ch. 9 (land warfare); Convention Concerning the Rights and Duties of Neutral Powers in Naval War, Oct. 18, 1907, 36 Stat. 2415.

231. On the purposes underlying the law of neutrality, see Patrick M. Norton, *Between Ideology and the Reality: The Shadow of the Law of Neutrality*, 17 HARV. INT'L L.J. 249 (1976); Walter L. Williams, *Neutrality in Modern Armed Conflicts: A Survey of the Developing Law*, 90 MIL. L. REV. 9 (1980).

conflict. In other words, *Trail Smelter* should stand for the premise that causing, or allowing to be caused, environmental damage in another country can lead to state responsibility unless belligerent interests served by the action in question outweigh the victim state's interests in avoiding the damage. Relevant factors would include (a) the magnitude of harm caused and (b) the nature of the threat to the "breaching" state that necessitated the harmful actions.[232] This mode of analysis is not unprecedented in international law. Blockade law, for instance, emerged from a need to balance belligerents' interests in effective warfare with neutrals' interests in international commerce.[233] It would be reasonable to conduct an analogous balancing test here. In much the same way that an interest in international commerce arose in the nineteenth century, an interest in being free from environmental damage has surfaced in the latter half of the twentieth century. It is therefore appropriate that sovereignty interests in the use of one's territory, and in effectively conducting combat operations, yield to some extent in the face of growing international concern over the environment.

Environmental treaty law is much narrower than the general principles discussed above, in that it tends to focus on a single component of the environment. In fact, the only rules that are designed to protect the environment in general appear in nonbinding instruments. Of the multitude of environmental provisions scattered throughout international conventions, and the many international, regional, and bilateral agreements addressing specific issues, three have been selected for sake of illustration: the Law of the Sea (LOS) Convention,[234] the Convention for the Protection of the Ozone Layer,[235] and the Convention on Long-Range Transboundary Air Pollution.[236] As mentioned earlier, the essential task when considering the issue of peacetime environmental prescriptions is not to catalogue them, since they constitute a body of law that is constantly evolving, but rather to understand when peacetime instruments and legal principles apply in armed conflict.

The LOS Convention is the first global attempt to limit marine pollution in any comprehensive way.[237] This 1982 instrument, which entered into force in 1994, requires states to take whatever measures are necessary "to prevent, reduce and control pollution of the marine environment from any

---

232. The remedy for a breach is set forth in section 602(1) of the *Third Restatement*: "A state responsible to another state for violation of section 601 is subject to general interstate remedies to prevent, reduce or terminate the activity threatening or causing the violation, and to pay reparations for the injury caused." RESTATEMENT (THIRD), *supra* note 228, § 602(1).

233. *See* Michael N. Schmitt, *Aerial Blockades in Historical, Legal and Practical Perspective*, 2 U.S.A.F.A. J. LEGAL STUD. 21, 24–33 (1991).

234. LOS Convention, *supra* note 172.

235. Ozone Convention, *supra* note 206.

236. Air Pollution Convention, *supra* note 223.

237. *See* LOS Convention, *supra* note 172. One of its precursors, the 1958 Convention on the High Seas, addressed marine pollution in only two provisions. Article 24 required state regulation of marine pollution by oil discharges from vessels, pipelines, or deep seabed activities, and article 25 called upon parties to prevent pollution of the seas from radioactive materials. *See* Convention on the High Seas, Apr. 29, 1958, arts. 24–25, 13 U.S.T. 2312, 450 U.N.T.S. 82. The nonbinding Stockholm Declaration exhorted states to take "all possible steps" to prevent marine pollution. *Stockholm Declaration, supra* note 203, princ. 7.

48   YALE JOURNAL OF INTERNATIONAL LAW   [Vol. 22: 1

source, using for this purpose the best practicable means at their disposal."[238] It also restates the general principle that states must ensure that activities over which they exercise control or jurisdiction do not cause damage to other states or the environments thereof.[239] Interestingly, this standard does not contain the *Third Restatement's* qualifier that only "significant" damage will trigger the protections.

While these statements appear broad, the LOS Convention excludes vessels owned or operated in noncommercial service by a government, including warships, from compliance with its marine protection principles.[240] Does this mean that the Convention is devoid of environmental provisions that might offer protection in wartime?[241] It does not, because a state might cause the spill of pollutants (e.g., oil) from vessels that are not exempted, as the Iraqis did when they began releasing oil from commercial tankers during the Gulf War.[242] More importantly, the agreement encompasses activities other than releases from vessels. For instance, the Convention's general principles specifically apply to minimizing the release of "toxic, harmful or noxious substances, especially those which are persistent, from land-based sources."[243] The release of oil from shore-based facilities during the Gulf War immediately comes to mind. The principles also extend to "installations and devices operating in the marine environment"[244] other than vessels, such as offshore oil platforms. Additionally, parties are obligated to adopt, through domestic legislation and in cooperation with international organizations, laws and measures to preclude marine pollution originating from shore-based or seabed activities, as well as from or through the atmosphere.[245]

The problem with these prescriptions is their inherent imprecision. By

---

238. LOS Convention, *supra* note 172, art. 194, para. 1. The LOS Convention defines pollution of the marine environment as

the introduction by man, directly or indirectly, of substances or energy into the marine environment, including estuaries, which results or is likely to result in such deleterious effects as harm to living resources and marine life, hazards to human health, hindrance to marine activities, including fishing and other legitimate uses of the sea, impairment of quality for use of sea water and reduction of amenities.

Id. art. 1, para. 1(4).

239. *See id.* art. 194, para. 2 ("[s]tates shall take all measures necessary to ensure that activities under their jurisdiction or control are so conducted as not to cause damage by pollution to other states and their environment.").

240. *See id.* art. 236 ("The provisions of this Convention regarding the protection and preservation of the marine environment do not apply to any warship, naval auxiliary, other vessels or aircraft owned or operated by a State and used, for the time being, only on government non-commercial service.").

241. Though not on point at this juncture, the Convention contains two provisions relevant to the issue of the *jus ad bellum.* In article 88, it provides that "[t]he high seas shall be reserved for peaceful purposes," whereas in article 301 it states that

[i]n exercising their rights and performing their duties under this Convention, States Parties shall refrain from any threat or use of force against the territorial integrity or political independence of any State, or in any other manner inconsistent with the principles of international law embodied in the Charter of the United Nations.

Id. art. 301. Of course, neither article would preclude a state's exercise of appropriate collective or individual self-defense under article 51 of the U.N. Charter.

242. Iraq ratified the LOS Convention in 1985.

243. LOS Convention, *supra* note 172, art. 194, para. 3(a).

244. *Id.* art. 194, para. 3(d).

245. *See id.* arts. 207–08, 212.

what standard, for example, should a state's cooperation with international organizations be measured? What steps satisfy the requirement to "minimize" releases? What does the phrase "necessary measures" encompass? There is little question that the LOS Convention will be difficult to apply in practice. That said, law is seldom precise, nor should it always be. It has to be flexible enough to fit a multiplicity of situations—many unforeseen when the law emerges. Moreover, the concerns expressed here are primarily about negligent or reckless conduct; intentional conduct, such as Iraqi conduct during the Gulf War, would be less susceptible to interpretive variation under the Convention. As with all peacetime law, though, applicability of the LOS Convention would have to be tested against the contextual standards suggested during the discussion of the theory of differentiation.

The Convention's enforcement regime is unique in approach. With reference to pollution, it places authority, depending on the specific circumstances, in the hands of the flag, port, or coastal state. Furthermore, it provides for an International Tribunal for the Law of the Sea to resolve Convention-based disputes. At the time of signing, ratifying, or acceding to the Convention, parties are required to accept the jurisdiction of this body (currently being established) or of the International Court of Justice, or to agree to submit disputes to arbitral proceedings. By peacetime enforcement standards, this is a particularly robust system for remedying alleged wrongs.

A second sample treaty with potential prescriptive effect during armed conflict is the 1985 Vienna Convention for the Protection of the Ozone Layer (the Ozone Convention).[246] Its normative component is article 2(1), by which parties agree to "take appropriate measures in accordance with the provisions of [the] Convention and of [related protocols] to protect human health and the environment against adverse effects resulting or likely to result from human activities which modify or are likely to modify the ozone layer."[247] Beyond this, the agreement essentially is designed to foster the exchange of information on potential ozone layer damage. As to enforceability, the Convention has few teeth. It provides for dispute settlement through negotiation or mediation, and encourages parties to agree in advance to the compulsory jurisdiction of the ICJ or to binding arbitration.[248]

The third sample peacetime agreement is the Convention on Long-Range Transboundary Air Pollution of 1979.[249] In this agreement, party states express their determination to "protect man and his environment against air pollution and . . . endeavour to limit and, as far as possible, gradually reduce and prevent air pollution including long-range transboundary air pollution."[250] In the Convention, transboundary air pollution is defined as pollution originating in one state and causing harm in another, but in which

---

246. Ozone Convention, *supra* note 206.

247. *Id.* art. 2, para. 1. Adverse effects are defined as "changes in the physical environment or biota, including changes in climate, which have significant deleterious effects on human health or on the composition, resilience and productivity of natural and managed ecosystems, or on materials useful to mankind." *Id.* art. 1, para. 2.

248. *See id.* art. 11.

249. Air Pollution Convention, *supra* note 223.

250. *Id.* art. 12.

the relative contribution from individual sources cannot be determined.[251] This is an attempt to escape from the classic tort problems of determining causation and harm. In this sense, it certainly represents a step beyond the principle of responsibility expressed in *Trail Smelter*. On the other hand, though the *ambit* of responsibility is stretched beyond the traditional levels, the *standard* of responsibility is *de minimis*. Note the terminology—"endeavour," "as far as possible," and "gradually." It would be difficult to craft a more aspirational norm. To compound matters, the Convention does not impose conditions of responsibility or liability; rather, it encourages "negotiation" or resort to other "method[s] of dispute settlement acceptable to the parties to the dispute."[252]

After a review of the state of peacetime environmental law and its applicability during armed conflict, it should be apparent that reports of its death during armed conflict are greatly exaggerated. Nevertheless, much uncertainty plagues the topic. The most reasonable approach is one in which a treaty's survival during armed conflict depends on a contextual evaluation employing factors such as those suggested above. As to the *Trail Smelter* principle, applicability during hostilities optimally should depend on a balancing of the interests of belligerents and nonbelligerents.

The substantive law presents less of an analytical problem because, at least to date, it offers little normative guidance of direct relevance to warfare beyond the hortatory and aspirational. Peacetime law was not intended to respond to the intent to create environmental destruction or to use the environment as a weapon. What is contemplated, then, is extension of a law designed primarily for reckless, negligent, or intentional acts motivated by a purpose other than harm. This is reflected in the limited remedies available to injured parties. Also apparent is an inherent tension between developing and developed states over how to balance the requirements of development with the desire to protect the environment. Application of peacetime environmental law during armed conflict will be limited by competing interests, much as the *Trail Smelter* principle was limited by belligerents' interests in effective warfighting. The result is that, despite some useful provisions (and even if consensus could be reached on its applicability), peacetime environmental law contributes little to wartime environmental protection.

Finally, mention should be made of legal responsibility, a topic applicable to both war and peace.[253] Whereas the law of armed conflict provides for individual responsibility (e.g., war crimes), peacetime instruments generally do not. For instance, the *Third Restatement* provisions do not mention the possibility that wrongful environmental damage might rise to the level of an international crime. Therefore, to the extent that peacetime prescriptions are carried forward into armed conflict, they alone do not form the basis for

---

251. *See id.* art. 1.
252. *Id.* art. 13.
253. An in-depth analysis is beyond the scope of this Article. For two excellent studies of the topic, see L.C. Green, State Responsibility and Civil Reparation for Environmental Damage, Paper Presented at the Symposium on the Protection of the Environment During Armed Conflict and Operations Other Than War, *in* NWC SYMPOSIUM PAPERS, *supra* note 13; Greenwood, *supra* note 220.

criminal responsibility.

Nevertheless, there is little question about state responsibility. If peacetime prescriptions remain in effect, the associated remedial provisions must logically do so as well. The principle that states are responsible for the wrongful acts of their agents—officials, armed forces, etc.—supports this premise.[254] Yet, some practical and legal uncertainty remains. How does one assess responsibility in multilateral operations? Should liability be joint and several? How does one measure harm, recalling, for instance, the imprecision of initial estimates in the Gulf War? How does one handle potential harm that may not become obvious for years after an event? Who has standing to assert claims for damage caused to the global commons? Are the relevant obligations *erga omnes*, such that they can be enforced by any state?[255] How should the two peacetime principles that relieve a state of responsibility—distress and necessity—apply in a wartime context?[256] These and other gaps remain in this essential component of the legal regime designed to deter environmental destruction.

B. *Customary* Jus in Bello

Custom is at the core of the *jus in bello*. Indeed, as a source of the law of war it predates any of the applicable treaty law currently in force.[257] To achieve the status of customary law, a norm must be evident in widespread state practice over time and the international community has to exhibit *opinio juris sive necessitatis*, a conviction that the rule is obligatory.[258] In other

---

254. Numerous law of war treaties provide for such responsibility. *See, e.g.*, Hague IV, *supra* note 130, art. 3 ("A belligerent party which violates the provisions of the said Regulations shall, if the case demands, be liable to pay compensation. It shall be responsible for all acts committed by persons forming part of its armed forces."). A nearly identical provision is found in Protocol I, *supra* note 8, art. 91.

255. The concept of *erga omnes* appears in the *Barcelona Traction Case*. There, the ICJ held that an essential distinction should be drawn between the obligations of a State towards the international community as a whole, and those arising vis-à-vis another State. . . . By their very nature the former are the concern of all States. In view of the importance of the rights involved, all States can be held to have a legal interest in their protection; they are obligations *erga omnes*. Such obligations derive, for example, in the contemporary international law, from outlawing acts of aggression, and of genocide, as also from the principles and rules concerning the basic rights of the human person, including protection from slavery and racial discrimination.
Barcelona Traction, Light & Power Co. (2d Phase) (Belg. v. Spain), 1970 I.C.J. 3, 32 (Feb. 5). The court did not indicate how obligations *erga omnes* were to be enforced.

256. *See International Law Commission Draft Articles on State Responsibility*, *supra* note 218, arts. 32–33; *see also* Leibler, *supra* note 185, at 76–77.

257. That custom can form the basis for war crimes charges was acknowledged by the International Military Tribunal at Nuremberg. The indictment specifically noted that "[a]ll the defendants committed War Crimes . . . [pursuant to] a Common Plan or Conspiracy . . . . This plan involved . . . the practice of 'total war' including methods of combat and of military occupation in direct conflict with the laws *and customs* of war." Indictment, International Military Tribunal, Nuremberg, 1 T.M.W.C. 27, 42–43 (1947) (emphasis added). Today, this premise is accepted as a principle of customary international law.

258. The Statute of the International Court of Justice provides that the court shall apply custom as "evidence of a general practice accepted as law." STATUTE OF THE INTERNATIONAL COURT OF JUSTICE, June 26, 1977, art. 38, para. 1(b). The *Third Restatement* notes that custom "results from a general and consistent practice of states followed by them from a sense of legal obligation." RESTATEMENT (THIRD), *supra* note 228, § 102(2); *see also* The Paquete Habana, 175 U.S. 677 (1900); Right of Passage Over Indian Territory (Port. v. India), 1960 I.C.J. 6 (Apr. 12); Asylum (Colom. v. Peru), 1950 I.C.J. 266

52   YALE JOURNAL OF INTERNATIONAL LAW   [Vol. 22: 1

words, custom is both a behavioral and a perceptional entity.

The foundational customary principle of the law of war, codified in Hague IV and elsewhere, is that the right of belligerents to adopt means of injuring the enemy is not unlimited.[259] From this principle flow a number of subsidiary principles that underlie much of the remainder of the law of war, whether found in custom or treaties.[260] They are perhaps best understood as grouped into four broad categories: military necessity, proportionality, humanity, and chivalry. Chivalry, which involves such matters as perfidy and ruses, is of only peripheral relevance to this study and will not be discussed.

1. *Military Necessity*

Military necessity prohibits destructive or harmful acts that are unnecessary to secure a military advantage. It is well settled that a violation of the principle can constitute a war crime. Article 6(b) of the Charter of the International Military Tribunal specifically characterizes "the wanton destruction of cities, towns or villages or devastation not justified by military necessity" as a war crime.[261] The offense is further clarified in a frequently cited passage from a well known war crimes trial, *The Hostage Case*:

> [Military necessity] does not permit the killing of innocent inhabitants for purposes of revenge or the satisfaction of a lust to kill. The destruction of property to be lawful must be imperatively demanded by the necessities of war. Destruction as an end in itself is a violation of international law. There must be some reasonable connection between the destruction of property and the overcoming of the enemy forces.[262]

By this standard, an actor must be able to articulate the *imperative* military advantage intended to be gained. In other words, the act must be neither wanton nor of marginal military value, and military motivations must underlie it.

There are three basic challenges in applying the principle of military necessity to environmental damage. First, the standard invites interpretive variance. Most importantly, what do the phrases "imperatively demanded" and "reasonably connected" mean? In other words, how "direct" must an advantage be before an act becomes militarily necessary? A subjective concept, directness can be placed along a continuum, and at some point a

---

(Nov. 20); S.S. Lotus (Fr. v. Turk.), 1927 P.C.I.J. (ser. A) No. 10 (Sept. 7).

259. *See, e.g.*, Hague IV, *supra* note 130, art. 22; Protocol I, *supra* note 8, art. 35, para. 1. The principle was first recognized in the Declaration of St. Petersburg, 1868, *reprinted in* 1 AM. J. INT'L L. 95 (Supp. 1907).

260. Unfortunately, though the substance of these principles is subject to little debate, the form in which they are expressed varies. For instance, the Air Force employs the categories of military necessity, humanity, and chivalry, with proportionality folded into necessity, whereas the Navy uses necessity, proportionality and chivalry. *Compare* AFP 110-31, *supra* note 175, at 1-5 to 1-6, *with* NWP 1-14M, *supra* note 178, at 5-1. In substance and application, though, the principles are identical across the military services.

261. Agreement for the Prosecution and Punishment of the Major War Criminals of the European Axis Powers and Charter of the International Military Tribunal, Aug. 8, 1945, art. 6(b), 59 Stat. 1544, 82 U.N.T.S. 279.

262. Hostage (U.S. v. List), 11 T.W.C. 759, 1253–54 (1950).

"direct" advantage becomes "remote" in nature. The question is where.

The fact that the delineation point is contextually determined renders it difficult to identify. All would agree, for example, that it generally would be permissible to set fire to a field through which a superior enemy force is advancing in order to halt the advance or mask one's own retreat. The advantage is direct and military in nature. But would it be permissible to set fire to the field in order to demoralize the rural population and turn it against continuation of the war? Clearly not. The advantage is military only in a convoluted sense and is obviously remote. In legal terms, the chain of causation is too attenuated. This is an easy case. The tough ones lie in the middle. Using a Gulf War example, did setting oil wells on fire to obscure Coalition targeting offer a direct military advantage? If it did, at what point had enough wells been set ablaze to suffice, so that igniting further wells was "wanton"? The contextual character of military necessity was equally apparent in the post–World War II war crimes trials, in which scorched-earth policies were held to be acceptable when motivated by military need in exceptional circumstances, but were condemned when the resulting destruction was found to be wanton.[263] Thus the difficulty in understanding whether an act is militarily necessary is compounded by the fact that it cannot be assessed in the abstract. Only in extreme cases will violation of the principle be apparent on the face of the action.

A related definitional problem lies in discerning requisite likelihood. Return again to the Gulf War. If the Iraqi oil spill was in fact intended to foil amphibious landings (and did not violate any other legal prescriptions), how likely must those landings have been before the advantage sought was direct? Is there a point at which the low likelihood of occurrence renders an advantage remote? There must be, for surely no one would argue that military necessity is consistent with destructive measures taken to counter *any* theoretical threat. To shift direction slightly, how does the likelihood of *success* figure in? A tactic or operation may very well entail an obvious chain of causation, and the threat posed may have a high likelihood of occurrence, but what degree of certainty of success is required to reach the "direct" advantage threshold? Unless one is willing to conclude that the principle of military necessity is intended to prevent only wanton (as opposed to wildly speculative) acts, the likelihood of occurrence and success must be directly relevant to military necessity calculations.

This latter point leads to the second challenge in determining military necessity, that of ascertaining intent. The essence of the principle is a prohibition on wanton, or largely irrelevant, destruction. Wantonness, in turn, implies the absence of intent to secure a military advantage. Thus, though formal statements of the principle, found in such sources as law of war manuals, often do not include an intent element, in practice one must be read into the prescription. The Gulf War illustrated this point. For instance, the

---

263. *See* INTERNATIONAL COMM. OF THE RED CROSS, COMMENTARY: GENEVA CONVENTION RELATIVE TO THE PROTECTION OF CIVILIAN PERSONS IN TIME OF WAR 302 (Jean S. Pictet ed., 1958) [hereinafter Pictet]. The set of four ICRC Commentaries edited by Jean Pictet is the definitive source on interpretation of the Geneva Conventions of 1949.

DOD Report asserted that had Iraq's goal been to obscure target acquisition by Coalition pilots, it could simply have opened the valves and ignited the oil that spilled. Therefore, the destruction of the oil wells themselves was taken as an indication of Iraq's "punitive" intentions.[264] But had the intent *not* been punitive, the requirements of military necessity would probably have been met. Therein lies the quandary. Given that intent is relevant, how is it to be determined in cases in which the act in question is reasonably subject to differing interpretations?

Acknowledging such interpretative and applicative difficulties hardly represents a jurisprudential epiphany on the subject of military necessity. The question, however, is whether environmental issues will exacerbate these difficulties. Unfortunately, they will, at least until warfighters, military lawyers, and scientists better understand the relationship between the art and science of warfare and the environment. Consider a few theoretical operational possibilities. How might a commander fold the ability to control weather into an offensive air operation? Of what use could obscurants be in defending against airborne assaults? How might flooding be used to protect a flank in an armored advance? These and other issues are only beginning to be explored.

To some extent, most emergent technologies or techniques present this type of dilemma. The more difficult it is to articulate a concept of employment, the harder it will be to justify an action as being of direct military advantage. Paradoxically, this difficulty also will hinder unambiguous characterization of a novel practice as a violation of the military necessity principle. To complicate matters further, the less established the technique or tactic in military practice, the more difficult it will be to impute intent to the actor. Lastly, necessity is harder to calculate because novelty generally lowers the reliability of estimates of the probability of success.

A final criticism of the principle is that it operates at cross purposes with the aims of the law of armed conflict, particularly its environmental component. As one commentator has noted, "[t]he dictates of military necessity, as assessed by opposed leaderships, have taken consistent precedence over the laws of war in almost every critical aspect of belligerent policy."[265] While it is true that commanders and their judge advocates occasionally may argue that military necessity justifies an action, such assertions are really about proportionality, not about necessity. After all, the statement implies that a balancing has occurred. Military necessity, in contrast, is less akin to balancing than it is to placement along a continuum. Thus, the criticism wrongly characterizes the assertion of the relevance of "necessity" analysis.

Much more importantly, the criticism seems to turn military necessity on its head. Recall the international law maxim that what is not forbidden is permitted. Military necessity operates within this paradigm to prohibit acts that are not militarily necessary; it is a principle of limitation, not authorization. In its legal sense, military necessity justifies nothing. The

---

264. DOD REPORT, *supra* note 69, at O-27.
265. RICHARD FALK, REVITALIZING INTERNATIONAL LAW 168 (1989).

criticism also mischaracterizes military necessity as in opposition to the law of war, when it is, in fact, an integral part of that corpus of law. The criticism would be more appropriately directed to the principle of war labeled "objective," rather than to a principle of law. It makes little sense to suggest that the legal principle of necessity runs counter to the law of war itself.

The discussion of challenges presented by the principle of military necessity is not meant to suggest that necessity is becoming passé vis-à-vis environmental issues. Instead, the point is merely that before accepting the premise that existing law is adequate, we must understand how much more complex the task of judging military necessity is made by factoring in environmental considerations.[266]

2. *Proportionality*

The difficulties in assessing military necessity pale beside those surrounding proportionality. Proportionality is a concept complementary to, and often considered a component of, military necessity.[267] It is perhaps best characterized as the principle of customary international law that prohibits injury or damage disproportionate to the military advantage sought by an action. Measured not in terms of immediate advantage, but rather with regard to the operation as a whole, the concept extends both to collateral damage suffered by civilians and civilian objects and to destruction of otherwise legitimate targets.[268]

Being relative, proportionality can be placed along a continuum. At some point on that continuum a proportionate impact becomes disproportionate, and the balance shifts. Because dissimilar value systems—military and humanitarian—are being compared, this point is very difficult to locate. For example, if the target is a command post near a residential area, how many surrounding homes may be destroyed before the effort to disable it becomes disproportionate? Similarly, what is the value of an enemy aircraft in terms of human lives? How do you compare the suffering caused by the destruction of joint civilian-military facilities, such as electrical generating facilities, with the military utility of disrupting the enemy's command and control?[269]

---

266. The difficulty in applying the concept was recognized in the Greenpeace Study, as was the imprecision of definition:

> It is in the interpretation of military action, and specifically the concept of "military necessity" (the anticipated military value of one's own action), that there is significant international disagreement as to proper conduct during war. Military necessity is not defined anywhere in the laws of war, but it is intertwined with proportionality and discrimination, the central principles of the "just war" tradition.

GREENPEACE STUDY, *supra* note 69, at 115.

267. The concept often is confused with a principle of war, economy of force. Economy of force is a common sense warfighter's rule of thumb: It does not make sense to apply more force than is necessary to attain the objective. The legal concept of proportionality, in contrast, measures advantage against damage caused.

268. Generally, though, proportionality regarding legitimate targets is more easily dealt with as a military necessity issue.

269. For a discussion of proportionality in the context of attacks on electrical targets, see WILLIAM ARKIN, TARGET IRAQ: A DOCUMENTARY HISTORY OF THE AIR WAR (forthcoming 199_) (manuscript at ch. 9, on file with author). Mr. Arkin, a human rights activist who specializes in military affairs, puts an

The difficulty of making proportionality calculations has been a key impetus towards codification of the law of war. In theory, codification renders legal concepts more manageable. It also eases the task of disseminating them to those charged with deciding on and executing courses of action. Unfortunately, despite the growing body of codified law of war, in many cases no particular provision exists on point to facilitate a specific proportionality calculation. Faced with this predicament, warfighters sometimes are instructed to use "no more force than necessary" to achieve their objective. However, economy of force is a *principle* of war, not a valid legal prescription under the *law* of war. In fact, there are situations in which the application of minimum necessary force against an otherwise lawful target would produce disproportionate results. Therefore, absent a specific provision in treaty law, we are left to our own value systems for guidance (or, perhaps more accurately, the value system deemed authoritative by the international community). Is the law, therefore, nothing more than an articulation of that fighter pilot adage to "trust your gut"? Or is it imbued with a meaning more distinct and developed, perhaps in the sense of the Martens Clause's dictates of public conscience?

Whatever the answer, any value-based balancing test will have disturbing implications for legal predictability and consistency. Value is a cultural and contextual concept: Different societies may value life, suffering, or objects differently. The play of this contextuality grows exponentially when considering the environment. If it is difficult to agree on proportionality when human life is in the balance, how can we hope to achieve consensus on the import of destroying habitats, harming air quality, or disturbing food chains? The quandary is that proportionality requires the act of value balancing, but the very subjectivity of value renders agreement on specific balances highly elusive. Just imagine, for example, the difference between the values that the United States and a failing state might impute to the environment.

Not only do disparate value paradigms impede objective proportionality estimations, but even within our own society the debate over anthropocentric and intrinsic value is an inevitable source of contention. All reasonable people would agree that the value of the environment should be measured, at least in part, by its direct impact on the state of human existence. Some would go further and argue that the environment should be valued in and of itself, even in the absence of a specific benefit to humankind. In other words, the actual value of the environment is its anthropocentric value *plus* its intrinsic value. This is the moderate intrinsic value approach. Others would take the intrinsic value perspective to its extreme by asserting that the environment merits protection even at human expense. In this radical cognitive perspective, human and environmental values are distinguishable—*and equivalent*—in the abstract. The more moderate intrinsic value approach would urge recognition of the autonomy of environmental value, but, all things being "equal," subordinate it to human values if forced to choose between the two.

The dilemma is that each approach will yield a different value for the environmental loss that military action causes. For instance, the first evaluator

interesting, albeit unconventional, spin on how to make proportionality decisions in difficult cases.

will see in a forest a useful source of raw materials. The second will acknowledge that quality, but also will characterize the forest as an entity demanding respect in its own right. For the third evaluator, securing respect for the forest may even require sacrificing human values. Nevertheless, in each of these cases the military advantage obtained by damaging the forest is fixed. This simple example shows that the operation of the proportionality equation will be skewed not only by the subjectivity of value estimates, but also, and perhaps more importantly, by disagreement over *how and on what basis* to measure value in the first place.

The tension between anthropocentric and intrinsic valuations is evident at the state level as well—a point illustrated at the Rio Conference by the developing states' insistence that environmental protections be balanced by the needs of development. Assuming this represents a trend, does it portend a developed/developing state split in attitude towards the appropriateness of the various cognitive perspectives? Perhaps the best way to characterize the situation is to suggest that while the cognitive direction is very roughly constant across the international community (no one seems to be moving in the other direction), the velocity of the phenomenon is much greater in developed states. This is logical, for there is less economic friction in the developed world. If the assessment is accurate, the cognitive gap between the camps will grow, at least until the economic gulf between developed and developing states narrows. The gap will pose the same obstacles to predictable and uniform application of the proportionality principle as differing cross-cultural valuation does.

This in turn raises another point regarding valuation in the proportionality calculation process: Value can be temporally determined.[270] Valuation paradigms inevitably change as history evolves, a fact aptly demonstrated by the rise of environmental consciousness in the last half-century. As this occurs, proportionality calculations shift accordingly. For example, reflect on the assessment that would be made of the Huayuankow Dam incident if it were to occur today. One scholar has suggested that this temporal feature of proportionality, and of customary law generally, is actually beneficial, for it permits the development of law to parallel the development of societal values, avoiding the difficulties inherent in applying treaty law to novel situations.[271]

The phenomenon of evolving value systems has many potential causes: human experience, understanding of the environment, and even technology. Of particular interest among law of war scholars and practitioners is the enormous attention that has been paid to the use of "smart" weapons during the Gulf War. To the extent that it may be technologically possible to limit collateral damage even further, there will inevitably be a tendency to ratchet

---

270. *See* Bothe, *supra* note 191, at 56.

271. As Wil Verwey has written:

Subjecting principles of customary law to a modern, liberal interpretation, i.e. a time-related interpretation which takes account of changing and emerging values cherished by society, may be less objectionable than it would be in the case of treaty law. In the former case, state parties cannot claim so easily that they have accepted a precise obligation as formulated in text, and that "that's it."

Verwey, Additional Rules, *supra* note 13, at 8-9.

58   YALE JOURNAL OF INTERNATIONAL LAW   [Vol. 22: 1

down the acceptable level of collateral damage, environmental or otherwise.

While the effect of new technologies may be reflected primarily in necessity analysis, there is still a subtle impact on the proportionality decision processes. Though there objectively may be no shift in the value of the damaged environment (anthropocentric or intrinsic), a subjective revaluation is bound to occur once a perception that the damage can be avoided takes hold. This is because valuations are in part the product of emotions, and we are more emotional about entities damaged "unnecessarily." Once decision makers are sensitized, proportionality calculations will be affected even when the necessity threshold has been met. Albeit not in the context of new technology, the Gulf War environmental experience offers a telling example of how this sensitization can work over time to alter existing valuation paradigms. When the Iraqis began spilling oil into the Persian Gulf and setting fire to well heads, actions that many felt were clearly unnecessary, the international community was enraged and became sensitized to the issue. As a result, operations posing environmental risks in the next war are likely to be evaluated very closely before being approved as proportional. What is interesting is that this is so despite the fact that, objectively, the environment is no more valuable than it was six years ago. On the contrary, since predictions of what Gulf War damage would do to the environment were themselves exaggerated, environmental concerns actually should have diminished somewhat. Yet that has not occurred.

Valuation is, therefore, a temporally, contextually, culturally, and conceptually determined process. Thus far, though, the complexity of the comparison between military advantage and the resultant destruction or damage has been explored only in its two-dimensional aspect. Regrettably, it is necessary to complicate matters further by factoring in a third dimension: environmental versus human (as opposed to military advantage) valuation. This dimension is present in two contexts: (1) risk to military personnel, and (2) nonenvironmental collateral damage. Several hypotheticals may help illustrate the point.

Assume shoulder-launched surface-to-air missiles (SAM) are occasionally fired at military aircraft from a residential district along the only feasible route to the target area. Though the risk to the aircraft is *de minimis* in light of the planned flight profile, it remains theoretically possible that a lucky hit might be scored. Can the entire residential area be bombed in hope of killing the lone soldier who launches the SAMs? Obviously not. It is easy to make this calculation for two reasons. First, the *jus in bello* is neutral; there are no "bad guys." In this hypothetical, a remote risk to the life of one combatant is being weighed against certain risk to the lives of scores of civilians. That they are enemy civilians does not shift the balance. Second, the more determinative fact is that the proportionality decision in this case is a human-human calculation.

However, what degree of environmental protection would justify the assumption of risk by our pilots? What if the SAMs were being fired from a dam, the destruction of which would destroy crop lands (anthropocentric valuation)? Harder still, what if destruction of the dam would destroy nonfood source animal habitats (intrinsic worth valuation)? We are back to the apples and oranges problem, albeit writ large. The task is no longer deciding whether to forgo gain, but instead whether to assume risk to protect the environment. Of course, the reflexive response is that environmental values cannot be balanced against human life, or even human suffering. But of course they can, assuming that the very concept of environmental protection in warfare is valid. Whenever a decision is made to forgo or alter an operation that otherwise meets the requirements of military necessity, the benefits of that necessity are lost. Since militarily necessary operations often are intended to lessen risk, either in the short or in the long term, a balance with human values implicitly has been made. The only way to avoid having to balance human and environmental values is to adopt a purely anthropocentric perspective in which protection of the environment is merely a byproduct. What this demonstrates is that treating the environment *qua* environment in making proportionality calculations muddies the waters of an already complicated process.

Yet another iteration of complexity is that in certain circumstances it will be necessary to recognize that nonenvironmental risk to the targeted party, either directly or collaterally, may be increased by extending protection to the environment. For instance, should an avenue of attack that might devastate a fragile amphibian habitat be avoided if the only viable alternative will result in damaged farm land? An even broader scenario can be painted by giving the concept of military necessity wide play. Because military necessity contributes to the success of one of the belligerents, it may also hasten the end of hostilities. Thus putting aside the optimal means of securing a militarily necessary objective in the name of environmental protection may in fact lengthen hostilities, thereby negatively affecting human values.

An obstacle to performing precise proportionality calculations is also apparent in determining what damage to weigh. The preceding discussion of military necessity raised the problem of likelihood of occurrence. Proportionality analysis involves an analogous difficulty in the form of uncertainty as to likelihood of harm. Simply put, when balancing collateral damage against military advantage, should the weight of possible damage be adjusted according to how likely the damage is to occur? Of course it should, but the problem is that whereas fairly reliable data is available on the effect of typical collateral damage (deaths, destruction of property, etc.), it is not available with regard to environmental damage. As the Gulf War demonstrated, estimates of the nature and quantum of environmental destruction can fall far from the mark.

Desert Storm highlighted a related problem. In addition to the difficulties of determining what damage will be caused, there is that of deciding how far down the chain of causation to proceed. During the Gulf War, aerial bombing brought criticism from some about its "reverberating effects." William Arkin, for instance, has written in detail about the unintended effects on civilians of the bombing of electrical targets.[272] How should proportionality analysis be conducted when efforts to take down obvious military objectives, such as command and control nets, result in hospitals losing electricity or in similar

---

272. *See* ARKIN, *supra* note 269, at ch. 9.

60   YALE JOURNAL OF INTERNATIONAL LAW   [Vol. 22: 1

harms to noncombatants? What responsibility do commanders have to consider reverberating effects in their legitimacy analysis?

The environment can only exacerbate such quandaries. Recall the flap over the purported "Lorenz Effect," in which a butterfly beating its wings in Tokyo causes a thunderstorm in New York.[273] The point is that when dealing with the environment, one is making calculations based on incredibly intertwined global relationships among the environment's seemingly infinite components. Unfortunately, despite the advances of science, we are only beginning to unravel this complexity. How, then, does one identify and take into account environmental reverberating effects? What level of environmental knowledge should be required of the commander making such assessments? To what degree must the commander attempt to ascertain potentially reverberating environmental effects? Do environmental engineers need to join judge advocates in command posts to ensure that commanders stay within the somewhat fuzzy confines of the law? These questions will prove particularly problematic because the valuation dynamics noted earlier in this section will influence each of the reverberating effects, which themselves may or may not be incorporated into the balancing process.

Ultimately, it might even be asked whether it is appropriate to apply the customary law of proportionality to environmental concerns at all, for there is certainly no longstanding practice of safeguarding the environment per se during armed conflict. Arguably, environmental benefits should be solely derivative, i.e., resulting from traditional customary law protections. For example, destruction of fish on a trout farm can be seen in terms of the customary law category of civilian objects. However, what would be the significance of an act that rendered the fish stock infertile? Is that the kind of damage to civilian objects contemplated in our customary law? This matter becomes more complicated still as we move beyond anthropocentric protections. Assume that the fish are swimming free and not used as a food source. To what extent would the international community demonstrate *opinio juris sive necessitatis* in such a case? It is one thing to argue that the customary law of proportionality must be flexible enough to provide protection to new objects that fall into traditionally protected categories. It is quite another to argue in the absence of state practice that protections should apply to newly recognized categories.

Hopefully, this discussion will have served to display again the complexity of factoring environmental considerations into the application of traditional law of war principles, in this case proportionality. Though some scholars might herald the demise of proportionality analysis,[274] it remains a useful tool for securing humanitarian—and environmental—values during armed conflict. But it is no panacea; environmental considerations will

273. *See generally* JAMES GLEICK, CHAOS: MAKING A NEW SCIENCE 9–31 (1987) (discussing use of Lorenz (or Butterfly) Effect in chaos theory).

274. One distinguished international law scholar suggested during the Gulf War that "[t]he enormous devastation that did result from the massive aerial attacks suggests that the legal standards of distinction and proportionality did not have much practical effect." Oscar Schachter, *United Nations Law in the Gulf Conflict*, 85 AM. J. INT'L L. 452, 466 (1991). This is a minority opinion. Most commentators characterize the air campaign as well within the bounds of legality. *See, e.g.*, Roberts, *supra* note 18, at 41.

complicate reliance on the principle, if only because it will be difficult to achieve consensus on what is and is not proportional. Thus, proportionality is likely to serve as a completely predictable constraint in only the most aggravated cases of environmental damage during armed conflict.

3. *Humanity*

The principle of humanity prohibits methods and means of warfare that are inhumane.[275] It is theoretically implicit in both military necessity and proportionality, but merits separate characterization in order to highlight particular prohibitions, such as those forbidding indiscriminate techniques[276] and unnecessary suffering. That environmental destruction can easily violate the principle of humanity should be obvious. Water supplies can be poisoned, destruction of food sources can result in the starvation of innocents, or air quality can be so lowered that respiratory distress results. Of particular concern is the environment's susceptibility to indiscriminate use or damage. Destruction of the Huayuankow Dam is a classic example of an indiscriminate act with disastrous environmental consequences.[277] Other theoretical uses of the environment, such as generating tidal waves or earthquakes, changing climate, or creating wetlands, are also inherently indiscriminate; once they are set in motion, their effects cannot be easily controlled. Given current technologies, it is difficult to envision an attack employing the environment that permits much discrimination at all.

Conceptually, the principle of humanity is overwhelmingly anthropocentric in nature. After all, it is labeled humanity. Nevertheless, the humanity principle is less utilitarian than the other customary principles, for it is not necessary to conduct a balancing test when applying it. In fact, any balancing that is required to assess humanity (e.g., in determining whether the suffering was "necessary") will probably be accounted for during the military necessity and proportionality analyses. If we put this cumulative component of humanity aside, the bulk of what remains are *ab initio* prohibitions on activities that are not so much inhumane as *inhuman*. They are acts we intuitively recognize as inherently wrongful regardless of the context in which they occur. In a sense, they are violative of the "dictates of public conscience."

---

275. Among the first formal expressions of the principle was the St. Petersburg Declaration of 1868. The Declaration provided:

> Considering that the progress of civilization should have the effect of alleviating, as much as possible the calamities of war;
>
> That the only legitimate object which states should endeavor to accomplish during war is to weaken the military force of the enemy;
>
> That for this purpose, it is sufficient to disable the greatest possible number of men;
>
> That this object would be exceeded by the employment of arms which uselessly aggravate the sufferings of disabled men, or render their death inevitable;
>
> That the employment of such arms would, therefore, be contrary to the laws of humanity.

Declaration of St. Petersburg, 1868, *supra* note 259, at 95.

276. An indiscriminate technique insufficiently distinguishes protected persons (e.g., civilians) and objects from legitimate military objectives.

277. *See supra* text accompanying note 17.

The concept of an inherently wrongful act may offer an avenue for expanding protection of the environment. As was noted, the central difficulty with military necessity and proportionality is comparative valuation. What the principle of humanity offers is an opportunity to move beyond that conundrum to the relatively simpler prospect of forging agreement on those things that civilized people *just don't do*. The immediate obstacle to doing this in the environmental context is that the principle of humanity generally is not thought of as applicable to anything other than immediate human suffering. Thus, when environmental violence such as that which occurred during the Gulf War is considered, the analysis tends to be in terms of proportionality or necessity, not in terms of humanity. Legalistic minutiae aside, though, the global community viewed the acts as "just don't do that" violations, a cognitive perspective that best comports with humanity analysis. Arguably, the world's reaction may portend the beginning of a subtle expansion of the principle. The shift would be from a prescription understood within the "there are certain things that you do not do to human beings" paradigm to that of "there are certain things that human beings do not do." This would temper disputes and avoid confusion about the relative value of dissimilar objects and goals.

Despite the appeal of a process that eases the inherent difficulties of balancing tests, the risk of this tack is great. It presumes that in some cases environmental damage should be avoided regardless of the cost to humanity. Perhaps in truly extreme cases of environmental damage in which a correspondingly high level of human suffering is inevitable, or in which the likelihood of accruing military advantage is very low, this technique could be used as prescriptive shorthand for humanitarian concerns. In other words, human suffering would not be ignored, but instead would simply be evaluated by a measure that offers ease of application. Such prescriptions could be crafted in terms of type of technique (e.g., oil spills), quantum of damage (e.g., long-term, widespread, and severe), target (e.g., the atmosphere), or any combination thereof. The defining characteristic, however, must be that it is not necessary to conduct a complex analysis of human suffering because the latter is presumed based on the level of environmental damage. Thus, while the approach may offer some benefits, any movement in this direction should proceed very cautiously.

C. *Treaty Based* Jus in Bello

1. *Hague IV*

The Hague Conventions reflected changes in the nature of warfare that occurred with the Napoleonic Wars. They marked the evolution of war into a national endeavor, fought on a grand scale by armies sometimes numbering in the hundreds of thousands, and resulting in previously unimaginable carnage. This transformation led to efforts to limit the effects of armed conflict. One of the earliest was the First Hague Peace Conference, convened at the urging of Czar Nicholas II in 1899. The Conference produced three instruments designed to limit armaments and their effects.[278] In 1907, a Second Hague Peace Conference was assembled on the initiative of Theodore Roosevelt. Of the thirteen conventions that issued, Hague IV, which governs the conduct of land warfare, is environmentally relevant today.[279] It remains in effect for its signatories, though party status is relatively unimportant because most of the treaty is now considered customary international law.[280] In fact, "Hague Law" has become a general term of reference for laws of armed conflict designed to limit the methods and means of warfare.

Article 22 of Hague IV codifies the foundational customary law of war principle mentioned earlier, that the "right of belligerents to adopt means of injuring the enemy is not unlimited."[281] This principle is consistently cited as a conceptual basis for environmental prescriptions.[282] Also directly relevant is article 23(e), which forbids the employment of "arms, projectiles or material calculated to cause unnecessary suffering."[283] It applies to the environment in a manner analogous to the unnecessary suffering component of the humanity principle. As it is treaty rather than customary law, significant expansion of article 23(e) beyond its intended anthropocentric application is unlikely. Instead, evolution in that direction will probably emanate first from its customary law counterpart.[284]

The most important Hague IV provision applicable to environmental damage is article 23(g). It codifies the classic military necessity principle by prohibiting acts that "destroy or seize the enemy's property, unless such destruction or seizure be imperatively demanded by the necessities of war."[285] Though there is occasional discussion over whether the article is intended to protect all property or only state property, the better view as a matter of law, and that adopted by both the U.S. Army and the ICRC, is that it covers any property, wherever situated and however owned.[286]

Since article 23(g) is the codification of the military necessity principle, the earlier discussion of that principle also applies here.[287] One further issue

---

278. These Declarations included a ban on launching projectiles or explosives from the air, a prohibition on the use of projectiles containing asphyxiating or deleterious gases, and a ban on bullets that expand or flatten in the body (Dum Dum bullets). *See* Final Act of the International Peace Conference, July 29, 1899, *reprinted in* 1 AM. J. INT'L L. 103 (Supp. 1907); Declaration Concerning Asphyxiating Gases, July 29, 1899, *reprinted in* 1 AM. J. INT'L L. 157 (Supp. 1907).

279. *See* Hague IV, *supra* note 130.

280. This status was recognized by the International Military Tribunal in 1939. *See* International Military Tribunal (Nuremberg), Judgment and Sentences, Oct. 1, 1946, *excerpted in* MYRES MCDOUGAL & W. MICHAEL REISMAN, INTERNATIONAL LAW IN CONTEMPORARY PERSPECTIVE 1043, 1050 (1981).

281. Hague IV, *supra* note 130, art. 22.

282. For a pre–Gulf War argument along these lines, see Best, *supra* note 20.

283. Hague IV, *supra* note 130, art. 23(e).

284. This contention is not universally accepted. One commentator has argued by reference to the French text that article 23(e) "suffering" includes "property damage, environmental damage, or damage to anything." Leibler, *supra* note 185, at 100. This is an accurate characterization if the damage causes direct human suffering. However, an extension to property or environmental damage per se is not supportable. At any rate, such damage would likely be prohibited under article 23(g).

285. Hague IV, *supra* note 130, art. 23(g).

286. *See* 2 DEPARTMENT OF THE ARMY, INTERNATIONAL LAW 174 (Pamphlet No. 27-161-2, 1962) [hereinafter ARP 27-161-2]; Pictet, *supra* note 263, at 301.

287. Treaty law may, of course, apply with different force than does customary law. As the ICJ has noted, "even if a treaty norm and a customary norm . . . were to have exactly the same content, this would not be a reason for the Court to take the view that the operation of the treaty process must

64   YALE JOURNAL OF INTERNATIONAL LAW   [Vol. 22: 1

bearing on environmental damage revolves around the definition of "property." There is little question that article 23(g) applies to tangible property such as land, cattle, crops, or water supplies. In fact, the War Crimes Commission cited article 23(g) in charges against ten German administrators of Polish forests for the unnecessary destruction of timber resources.[288] Its applicability in other environmental contexts is not as clear-cut. For instance, is the atmosphere "property"? What about climate or the ozone layer? How would destruction of a straddling stock of fish or a migratory bird species be handled? These examples illustrate the determinative importance of ·evolving property concepts to contemporary and future understandings of article 23(g).

A second key Hague IV provision relevant to environmental protection is article 55. It provides that a belligerent occupying enemy territory "shall be regarded only as administrator and usufructuary of public buildings, real estate, forests, and agricultural estates belonging to the hostile State, and situated in the occupied country. [The occupier] must safeguard the capital of these properties, and administer them in accordance with the rules of usufruct."[289] As an usufructuary, the occupying power has the right to enjoy public property, including the right reasonably to exploit it for its natural resources. However, it may not permanently alter or destroy the property. By its own terms, the article does not become effective until open hostilities have ended in an area and a state of occupation has been declared, and it is limited to abuse or destruction of the four categories delineated. If hostilities in the area recommence, then Hague protection reverts to article 23(g) military necessity.

Note should also be taken of the Martens Clause found in the preamble to each of the Hague Conventions. Given the novelty of environmental considerations in warfare, it could prove to be a key protection afforded by Hague IV:

> Until a more complete code of laws has been issued, the high Contracting Parties deem it expedient to declare that, in cases not included in the Regulations adopted by them, the inhabitants and the belligerents remain under the protection and the rule of the principles of the laws of nations, as they result from the usages established among civilized peoples, from the laws of humanity, and from the dictates of the public conscience.[290]

A Martens Clause is also found in Protocol I[291] and, as discussed earlier, generally is considered to be a principle of customary international law.

The major benefit of such a principle is that it operates during the evolution of prescriptive norms. As the law proper grapples with how to handle environmental issues, the "laws of humanity" and the "dictates of public conscience" theoretically will ensure a modicum of protection. Of

---

necessarily deprive the customary norm of its separate applicability." Military and Paramilitary Activities (Nicar. v. U.S.), 1986 I.C.J. 4, 84 (June 27).

288.   *See* Leibler, *supra* note 185, at 106 (citing U.N. War Crimes Commission, Case No. 7150-469 (1948)).

289.   Hague IV, *supra* note 130, art. 55.

290.   *Id.* pmbl.

291.   Protocol I, *supra* note 8, art. 1, para. 2.

course, the problem is that it is often difficult to extract specific prohibitions from "moral law and public opinion." As has been noted, for example, saturation bombing of cities and the practice of "dumping" bomb loads prior to returning to base during World War II "left the public conscience relatively undisturbed."[292] Much of the difficulty in determining whether a Martens situation has presented itself will result from the surfacing of crosscultural and intersocietal differences. There will certainly be differences of perception as to the content of "the laws of humanity" and "the dictates of public conscience." Nonetheless, the provision at least offers a final line of defense to those facing legalistic explanations of why the traditional law of war does not apply in a particular situation.

How useful is Hague IV in limiting environmental damage during warfare? In the view of some, very much so. One distinguished commentator argued in 1992, for example, that had the Hague IV principles "been observed by Iraq, there would have been no significant violation of the Kuwaiti environment."[293] Similarly, the DOD Report on the Gulf War stated that the oil spills and sabotage of the oil wells were violations of article 23.[294] While probably accurate, such characterizations are fact-specific; they fail to demonstrate that the Hague IV prescriptions are sufficiently comprehensive or that they can be applied successfully in other scenarios. What if an amphibious operation actually had been imminent when the oil was spilled? What if the Iraqis merely had opened the valves on the oil wells and then set the pools ablaze as the DOD report noted they had not? Possibly more revealing still, what if the opponent had not been as universally ostracized as Saddam Hussein? Finally, what would have been the international reaction to the environmental destruction if the victim had been Israel or Iran instead of Kuwait? While it is certainly correct that Hague IV provides significant protection to the environment, these hypotheticals aptly illustrate potential fault lines.[295]

2. *Geneva Convention IV*

"Geneva law" is that component of the law of war, often labeled "humanitarian law," that protects certain categories of individuals and objects. Whereas Hague law governs what methods and means are appropriate in warfare, Geneva law delineates against what and whom those methods can be

---

292. *See* ARP 27-161-2, *supra* note 286, at 15.

293. Terry, *supra* note 92, at 63; *see also* Michael Bothe, *Environmental Destruction as a Method of Warfare: Do We Need More Law?*, 15 DISARMAMENT 101, 104 (1992) (asserting that Iraqi actions violated unnecessary suffering provision of article 23(e)).

294. *See* DOD REPORT, *supra* note 69, at O-22. Note that the Convention contains a general participation clause, i.e., a provision to the effect that the treaty applies only between parties, and then only if all belligerents are parties. *See* Hague IV, *supra* note 130, art. 2. Iraq was not a party to Hague IV. In 1907 it was still a part of the Ottoman Empire. Twelve years later Iraq became a British mandate, but Great Britain never acceded to Hague IV on its behalf. Therefore, when Iraq gained its independence in 1932 it did not have to acknowledge party status. Of course, the fact that the treaty is recognized as customary international law makes this point somewhat irrelevant.

295. Other Hague IV provisions that might bear on environmental damage in individual cases include the requirement to respect private property, *see* Hague IV, *supra* note 130, art. 46, and the prohibition of pillage, *see id.* art. 47.

used. Thus, the two bodies of law are complementary. There is a long line of Geneva Conventions stretching back to 1864. Today, the four 1949 Geneva Conventions are the most universally recognized instruments in the law of armed conflict and are considered to have become in great part customary international law. For the purposes of this study, the most relevant is Geneva Convention IV, which governs the protection of civilians and civilian objects in war.[296]

With regard to environmental destruction, article 53 is the highlight of Geneva Convention IV. It provides that "[a]ny destruction by the Occupying Power of real or personal property belonging individually or collectively to private persons, or to the State, or to other public authorities, or to social or cooperative organizations, is prohibited, except where such destruction is rendered absolutely necessary by military operations."[297] Several characteristics of this prohibition are worthy of comment. First, though many objects are granted protection, it is limited, as in article 55 of Hague IV, to occupied territory. Extending protection beyond occupied territories was felt to be unnecessary on the basis that article 23(g) of Hague IV sufficed.[298] Of course, also filling in the gap is the customary international law principle of military necessity. Thus, the criticism that has been leveled against the limited scope of article 53 may be valid if the provision is viewed in isolation, but in terms of practical impact during armed conflict, it is inconsequential.[299]

Although applying only to occupied territories, the provision does offer meaningful protection because environmental damage often occurs in such situations. Historically, this is particularly likely as an occupying force is being ejected. For instance, scorched-earth policies in occupied territory during World War II formed the basis for multiple war crimes prosecutions.[300] More recently, much of the environmental damage that occurred in the Gulf War took place as a result of property destruction in occupied Kuwait, most notably destruction of the oil wells. In fact, when the Commission for International Due Process of Law prepared a draft indictment of Saddam Hussein and his key advisers for submission to the U.N. Secretary General, a violation of article 53 was specifically alleged.[301] Most scholars and practitioners agree with this characterization of the actions of Iraq,[302]

---

296. Geneva Convention IV, *supra* note 10.

297. *Id.* art. 53.

298. *See* Pictet, *supra* note 263, at 301.

299. *See* Richard A. Falk, *The Environmental Law of War: An Introduction*, *in* ENVIRONMENTAL PROTECTION AND THE LAW OF WAR, *supra* note 94, at 78, 88.

300. *See, e.g.*, Hostage (U.S. v. List), 11 T.W.C. 759 (1950) (acquitting general who had ordered destruction during German evacuation of Norway on basis that destruction was necessary due to general's (mistaken) belief that Russians were pursuing his forces); *see also* High Command Case (U.S. v. Von Leeb), 11 T.W.C. 462 (1950) (involving destruction in Soviet Union).

301. *See* Luis Kutner & Ved P. Nanda, *Draft Indictment of Saddam Hussein*, 20 DENV. J. INT'L L. & POL'Y 91, 93 (1991). In specification 10 of charge I, the Iraqis were charged with having "destroyed the real and personal property of protected persons and the State of Kuwait; this destruction was not absolutely necessary to military operations and occurred for the most part after military operations had ceased." *Id.*

302. *See, e.g.*, DOD REPORT, *supra* note 69, at O-22; McNeill, *supra* note 145, at 80; Roberts, *supra* note 18, at 39. Additionally, Professor Roberts and Mr. McNeill would concur with Michael Bothe that the actions constituted grave breaches under article 147. *See* Bothe, *supra* note 293, at 104.

a state which had acceded to the Convention in 1956.

Article 53 is caveated with the proviso that the prohibition does not apply when destruction is "rendered absolutely necessary by military operations."[303] This leads us back into the interpretive maze of the customary law principle's directness requirement. Although "absolutely" would seem to set a high standard—an extreme on the continuum of necessity, if you will—it is still subject to interpretation. As Jean Pictet has noted in his authoritative ICRC-sponsored commentary on the Convention, "[i]t is therefore to be feared that bad faith in the application of the reservation may render the proposed safeguards valueless; for unscrupulous recourse to the clause concerning military necessity would allow the Occupying Power to circumvent the prohibition set forth in the Convention."[304] To address this weakness, he urges occupying powers to interpret the provision reasonably and with a "sense of proportion in comparing the military advantages to be gained with the damage done."[305] The catch-22 is that those states likely to follow Pictet's admonition are the ones that least need to be deterred from "unscrupulous recourse to the clause." At the same time, an unscrupulous belligerent is most likely to take advantage of the additional uncertainty that environmental concerns bring to necessity calculations.

Despite the difficulty in interpretation and application, one positive note is that article 147 of the Convention includes as grave breaches "extensive destruction . . . of property, not justified by military necessity and carried out unlawfully and wantonly."[306] As a result, a violation of article 53 is a grave breach whenever the destruction involved is "extensive." Characterization as a grave breach is crucial because parties to the Convention are required to pass domestic legislation providing for the punishment of those who commit or order grave breaches.[307] More significantly, a party is obligated to search for offenders and to bring them before its courts, regardless of their nationalities.[308] Offenders may also, consistent with extradition agreements, be turned over to other states for prosecution.[309] Therefore, while the prescription itself admits of imprecision, the sanctions mechanism should operate to heighten deterrence. Sadly, the Gulf War illustrated that it may not always have this effect, assuming that the DOD Report's characterization of the Iraqi actions as violations of articles 53 and 147 is accurate as a matter of law.[310]

Finally, some additional indirect protection for the environment is found in article 147's inclusion of "willful killing [and] willfully causing great suffering or serious injury to body or health" in the universe of grave breaches.[311] Although this applies only to "protected persons" under the

303. Geneva Convention IV, *supra* note 10, art. 53.
304. Pictet, *supra* note 263, at 302.
305. *Id.*
306. Geneva Convention IV, *supra* note 10, art. 147.
307. *See id.* art. 146.
308. *See id.*
309. *See id.*
310. *See* DOD REPORT, *supra* note 69, at O-22.
311. Geneva Convention IV, *supra* note 10, art. 147.

convention, i.e., those who are "in the hands of a Party to the conflict or Occupying Power of which they are not nationals,"[312] there are certainly many situations involving environmental damage that could have these results. The acts do have to be willful, an intent requirement that appears to exclude purely collateral injuries.[313]

Have the relevant Geneva Convention IV principles become recognized as customary international law in the fashion of their Hague counterparts? While there is no international judicial decision on point, the extensive dissemination of the principles through teaching, scholarship, and publication in law of war manuals would suggest they have been. Indeed, no law of war class or manual would be complete without a discussion of Geneva Convention IV. All significant players in the international arena are parties to this Convention, and state practice demonstrates a consensus that the norms expressed are obligatory. The fact that Geneva Convention IV exists as a treaty does not preclude it from evolving over time into customary law, despite the concerns that some have expressed.[314] As a result, the normative Geneva prescriptions discussed above are almost certainly binding on parties and nonparties alike.[315]

3. *Protocol I*

In 1965 the Twentieth Conference of the Red Cross directed the ICRC to begin work on proposals for updating the law of war. This was in great part a response to an emerging belief that the nature of warfare had begun to experience a qualitative transformation that merited revision of the prescriptive norms governing its conduct. Accordingly, the ICRC convened the Diplomatic Conference on the Reaffirmation and Development of International Humanitarian Law Applicable in Armed Conflicts. The Conference, which met over four sessions between 1974 and 1977, was attended by representatives of well over one hundred nations and fifty intergovernmental

---

312. *Id.* art. 4.
313. *See* Pictet, *supra* note 263, at 597.
314. The reasoning behind such concerns is as follows:

>   The large number of nations which accept the Geneva Conventions, rather than evidencing a development of well-accepted custom, may actually *obscure* the degree to which the treaties have become customary law. As parties to the treaties, nations may be simply following their *conventional* obligations rather than forging new *customary* practices. Because of this possibility, the Geneva Conventions paradoxically may remain conventional law rather than having evolved into customary law. Presumably, customs cannot develop when widely subscribed to conventions already exist.

Mark J. T. Caggiano, *The Legitimacy of Environmental Destruction in Modern Warfare: Customary Substance Over Conventional Form*, 20 B.C. ENVTL. AFF. L. REV. 479, 493 (1993) (footnotes omitted). However, recall that the International Military Tribunal found Hague IV to be customary law, *see supra* note 280, even though by its own terms, it is limited in application to parties, *see* Hague IV, *supra* note 130, art. 2. I doubt whether there is an inverse relationship between accession to a treaty and the customary character of its provisions. *See* Theodor Meron, *The Geneva Conventions as Customary Law*, 81 AM. J. INT'L L. 348 (1987).

315. *See* Vienna Convention, *supra* note 193, art. 38 ("Nothing . . . precludes a rule set forth in a treaty from becoming binding upon a third State as a customary rule of international law, recognized as such."); *see also* North Sea Continental Shelf (F.R.G. v. Den.) (F.R.G. v. Neth.), 1969 I.C.J. 4 (Feb. 20).

or nongovernmental organizations. Additionally, eleven national liberation movements sent observers. In 1977 this conference adopted two "Protocols Additional" to the Geneva Conventions of 1949. Protocol I addressed international armed conflict. It is a particularly interesting product in that it combines elements of both Hague and Geneva law. The other, Protocol II, was designed to protect victims of noninternational armed conflict; it will not be discussed here.

The United States signed the protocols in 1978, and some six years later the Joint Chiefs of Staff were directed to develop a final position on ratification.[316] Their conclusions, in which the Office of the Secretary of Defense and the Department of State concurred, recommended against ratification of Protocol I, and President Reagan accepted that advice, calling the Protocol "fundamentally and irreconcilably flawed,"[317] a position which is under review by officials of the current administration. Despite its rejection of the treaty, the United States does acknowledge that much of Protocol I is customary law and, therefore, binding on its armed forces.[318] This position has important implications for applicability of the treaty. For example, if the position is accurate, the customary provisions were applicable during the Gulf War, even though at the time the United States, France, the United Kingdom, and Iraq were nonparties.[319]

The bulk of the relevant prescriptions found in the Protocol safeguard the environment "indirectly," either through anthropocentrically based protections or through the extension of traditional concepts designed for purposes other than environmental protection.[320] However, Protocol I was the first instrument intended exclusively for armed conflict to provide *direct* environmental protection. The idea of doing so initially surfaced at the Conference of Government Experts in 1972.[321] This ICRC-sponsored body was tasked with laying the groundwork for the effort to update the law of armed conflict. Interestingly, despite a suggestion that the environment per se be granted protection, the preliminary ICRC draft did not contain any

---

316. *See Agora: The U.S. Decision Not to Ratify Protocol I to the Geneva Conventions on the Protection of War Victims*, 81 AM. J. INT'L L. 910, 916 (1987) [hereinafter *Agora*].

317. Letter of Transmittal from President Ronald Reagan, Protocol II Additional to the 1949 Geneva Conventions, and Relating to the Protection of Victims of Non-International Armed Conflicts, S. TREATY DOC. NO. 2, 100th Cong. (1987), *reprinted in Agora, supra* note 316, at 911.

318. *See* INTERNATIONAL AND OPERATIONS LAW DIV., OFFICE OF THE JUDGE ADVOCATE GEN., DEP'T OF THE AIR FORCE, OPERATIONS LAW DEPLOYMENT DESKBOOK tab 12 [hereinafter DEPLOYMENT DESKBOOK] (summarizing Protocol I and stating U.S. position on key articles).

319. The interesting question is whether all the parties can agree on which provisions are customary. For an analysis of the Protocol as customary law in the Gulf War, see Christopher Greenwood, *Customary International Law and the First Geneva Protocol of 1977 in the Gulf Conflict, in* THE GULF WAR 1990-91 IN INTERNATIONAL AND ENGLISH LAW (Peter Rowe ed., 1993).

320. *See* ICRC COMMENTARY, *supra* note 17, at 661.

321. The proposal submitted by the experts of Czechoslovakia, the German Democratic Republic, and Hungary read: "It is forbidden to use weapons, projectiles or other means and methods which upset the balance of the natural living and environmental conditions." 2 INTERNATIONAL COMM. OF THE RED CROSS, REPORT ON THE WORK OF THE CONFERENCE OF GOVERNMENT EXPERTS ON THE REAFFIRMATION AND DEVELOPMENT OF INTERNATIONAL HUMANITARIAN LAW APPLICABLE IN ARMED CONFLICTS 51 (1972). The proposal submitted by the experts of Poland forbade the use of "methods and means which destroy the natural human environment." *Id.* at 52.

provisions expressly addressing the topic.[322] After several of the delegations pressed the issue, an informal working group, known as "Biotope," was established within Conference Committee III to consider proposals for environmental provisions.[323] The working group recommended two types of articles. First, it recommended articles that tended to treat the environment anthropocentrically—that is, as meriting protection because environmental damage can lead to human suffering.[324] Efforts in this direction led to the adoption of article 55.[325] On the other hand, some members, recalling the environmental destruction of the Vietnam War, urged adoption of a standard unqualified by the human factor—an intrinsic value approach.[326] This led to adoption of the article 35(3) restriction on means and methods of warfare that damage the environment.[327]

Articles 35(3) and 55 represented the furthest steps toward safeguarding the environment in any international law instrument. The two provisions are complementary: The former is basically a Hague law variant (limits on methods and means of warfare), while the latter is a Geneva law protection (protection of civilians and civilian objects). To foster this relationship, they employ analogous standards.[328]

As mentioned earlier, inclusion of both provisions was in part an effort to respond equally to the anthropocentric and intrinsic value camps.[329] Note the absence in article 35(3) of any connection to, or balancing with, human values. This is particularly interesting because it is an "intrinsic value plus" standard. Basic intrinsic valuation requires assessing more than human worth; it does not preclude balancing environmental and human values once the weighing process is complete. Article 35(3), however, operates independently of human variables. In contrast, article 55(1) focuses on the damage's "prejudice [to] the health or survival of the population," a classically anthropocentric formulation.[330]

The express Biotope rationale for retaining the two approaches was that

---

322. See ICRC COMMENTARY, *supra* note 17, para. 2129, at 662.

323. See *id.*, para. 2130, at 663; 15 OFFICIAL RECORDS OF THE DIPLOMATIC CONFERENCE ON THE REAFFIRMATION AND DEVELOPMENT OF INTERNATIONAL HUMANITARIAN LAW APPLICABLE IN ARMED CONFLICTS 220 [hereinafter O.R.].

324. See 15 O.R., *supra* note 323, at 358–59.

325. See 14 *id.* at 405–06.

326. See 15 *id.* at 358–59.

327. See 14 *id.* at 404.

328. See *supra* text accompanying notes 48–49 (quoting articles 35(3) and 55).

329. Inclusion of both raised a few hackles. The United Kingdom, for example, went on record disapproving inclusion of article 35(3) in this section, and interpreted it as a mere repetition of article 55. It is particularly important that the United Kingdom viewed the provisions as protecting the environment in order to protect civilians living in it. See 6 O.R., *supra* note 323, at 118.

330. See Protocol I, *supra* note 8, art. 55, para. 1. For purposes of clarity, it should be noted that article 55 falls under part IV, chapter III, entitled "Civilian Objects." Therefore, it does not protect military objectives. In contrast, there is no such structural limitation with regard to article 35(3). Additionally, note that article 55 refers to the "population" without the adjective "civilian." The official record makes clear that this omission was intentional—the goal was to extend the protection to the whole population, since the damage was to be long-term. See 15 O.R., *supra* note 323, at 360. Finally, "health" is used in the provision to provide protection beyond that needed for bare survival. Effects that would pose a serious blow to health—such as congenital defects or deformities—would, therefore, be encompassed within the meaning of the provision. See 15 *id.* at 281.

whereas article 55 provides for the protection of the civilian population, article 35(3) is an unnecessary suffering standard. That may explain the methods/means versus civilian population distinction, but it does not explain the absence of reference either to humans or to balancing. In fact, the ICRC commentary on the issue is fairly clear. It states that article 35(3)

> is a matter not only of protecting the natural environment against the use of weapons or techniques deliberately directed against it, nor merely of protecting the population and the combatants of the countries at war against any of these effects, but also one of protecting the natural environment itself.[331]

If article 35(3) is about unnecessary suffering, then that suffering extends beyond humans to the "suffering" of the environment.

Most opposition to these provisions has centered on the definition of "widespread, long-term, and severe." Use of the conjunctive "and" is particularly problematic, for so interpreted the articles mandate a three-part test which is nearly impossible to meet except in the most egregious cases. Unfortunately, there is very little indication in the negotiating history of what the delegates intended by the phrase. Some referred to "long-term" as a period measured in decades.[332] In fact, other than a passing mention that the battlefield damage in France during the First World War was not of the type contemplated,[333] little emanated from the conferences to clarify matters.[334] This lack of clarity is one basis for the objections of the United States and other countries.[335]

Attempts have been made to remedy this flaw, though they have not been international in scope. For instance, the German law of war manual defines the quantum of damage necessary as "a major interference with human life or natural resources which considerably exceeds the battlefield damage to be regularly expected in a war."[336] Surprisingly, some of the best guidance has come from the military of the key state that has not ratified Protocol I—the United States. In its *Operational Law Handbook*, the Army Judge Advocate General School asserts that "long-standing" should be understood as decades; "widespread" probably means "several hundred square kilometers . . . [and] 'severe' can be explained by Article 55's reference to any act that 'prejudices the health or survival of the population.'"[337] The "widespread" definition is taken from ENMOD. This is an interesting approach given the fact that an Understanding was appended to ENMOD disclaiming any intention for its definitions to apply to other instruments—an unstated but obvious reference

---

331. ICRC COMMENTARY, *supra* note 17, para. 1441, at 410.

332. *See* 15 O.R., *supra* note 323, at 268.

333. *See id.* at 269.

334. According to the ICRC Commentary, "[i]t appeared to be a widely shared assumption that battlefield damage incidental to conventional warfare would not normally be proscribed by this provision." ICRC COMMENTARY, *supra* note 17, para. 1454, at 417 (citations omitted).

335. *See* DOCUMENTS ON THE LAW OF WAR 461–63 (Adam Roberts & Richard Guelff eds., 1982) (reporting reservations to Protocol).

336. GERMAN MANUAL, *supra* note 168, para. 403. However, note that this definition complements a provision in the manual that was developed from *both* Protocol I and ENMOD.

337. OPERATIONAL LAW HANDBOOK, *supra* note 179, at 5-8. According to the handbook, most of the damage that occurred during World War II would not have met this threshold. *See id.*

to Protocol I. From the perspective of the overall development of the environmental law of war, the Army's reference to human "health and survival" is more important. To use this standard in setting an article 35(3) threshold is to come down firmly in the anthropocentric camp, thereby neglecting the drafters' rationale for including two distinct environmental provisions.

Articles 35(3) and 55 present other interpretive challenges. Some commentators are concerned that the "may be expected" language creates a subjective "should have known" standard that will be used to judge commanders.[338] If that is so, they argue, war crimes charges could be based on incidental environmental damage caused in the course of otherwise valid military operations.[339] These concerns are overstated. The "expected" verbiage is obviously designed to preclude any argument that since collateral damage is not "intended," it is not encompassed in the prohibition. Isn't that as it should be? A prohibition on excessive collateral damage is hardly novel in the law of war. More to the point, the commentators are entirely accurate—commanders could be made subject to a "should have known standard." But that is the standard of criminal responsibility imposed in the domestic law of many states. Under the Uniform Code of Military Justice, for instance, commanders are already held criminally responsible for operational consequences about which they *should have* known.[340] Lack of actual knowledge is a mitigating factor, not a defense based on the absence of an element of the offense.

What should be of far greater concern to the operational commander than definitional legerdemain or questionable scienter standards is that the provisions are devoid of reference to military necessity or proportionality. Any action taken by a commander that reaches the "long-term, widespread, and severe" threshold will violate the prescriptions even if it is militarily necessary and clearly proportional. No balancing occurs beyond this point. Especially troubling is the possibility that there may be *human* values, military advantages aside, that outweigh the environmental protection being afforded.[341]

---

338. In fact, that appears to have been the intent. The ICRC Commentary explains that the English text originally read "calculated to cause," whereas the French text used the phrase "de nature à." The English iteration suggested that the mental state required was one of intent or deliberation, whereas the French was more restrictive. Therefore, the Conference discarded the "calculated to cause" phraseology, replacing it with "intended, or may be expected." *See* ICRC COMMENTARY, *supra* note 17, para. 1458, at 418.

339. *See* Roberts, *supra* note 50, at 146–48. He argues that the "standards set forth in articles 35(3) and 55 are too ambiguous and subject to diverging interpretation to be workable. They could conceivably make military commanders and political leaders subject to prosecution for committing war crimes if they 'should have known' their actions would result in proscribed damage to the environment." *Id.* at 148. This assertion confuses possibly valid criticism of substantive legal standards with issues of mens rea.

340. *See* JOINT SERV. COMM. ON MILITARY JUSTICE, MANUAL FOR COURTS-MARTIAL, UNITED STATES § 16a(3)(b) (pt. IV 1995). The explanation to article 92 of the code indicates that dereliction of duty may be charged using this standard: "[a]ctual knowledge need not be shown if the individual reasonably should have known of the duties." *Id.* § 16c(3)(b).

341. The issue is not an "either-or" proposition—it is a question of balance. Even intrinsic value advocates would agree that environmental values can be outweighed by human ones. The precise balance depends on the circumstances.

Imagine, for instance, a large population center at risk of falling to enemy forces operating from forested terrain surrounding it. The forest effectively serves as a sanctuary for the attackers. To complicate matters, prior instances of occupation by the enemy have revealed a callous, wanton occupier with little regard for the civilian population. The only option available to the defending commander is to destroy the forest surrounding the city, but the sole method available for doing so quickly will result in long-term, widespread, and severe destruction of the forest's flora and fauna. On the other hand, denial of sanctuary will force the enemy to withdraw. Under article 35(3), the commander seemingly would be precluded from taking the action despite the potential for tragic human suffering should the enemy occupy the city. Yet absent article 35(3), the commander's proposed course of action would clearly meet the requirements of military necessity and proportionality.

That is one side of the coin, namely, whether the articles raise the standard of protection too high by excluding from the process important considerations that safeguard human values. On the other side is the debate about whether the standard of protection is lowered by the articles. Professor Wil Verwey has argued that it very well *might*, by pointing to the general principle of law that *lex specialis* applies over *lex generalis*. According to this argument, an action that does not cause widespread, long-term, or severe damage will not be prohibited because it is otherwise disproportionate or causes unnecessary suffering.[342] The better view, however, is that neither provision has such an effect. First, the *lex specialis* principle applies in situations in which norms appear to conflict. It is a principle of resolution. Here it can be argued that proportionality and unnecessary suffering are complemented by the Protocol provisions and vice versa; they are each designed to further humanitarian concerns.[343] Much more importantly, the inclusion of environment-specific prescriptions was not intended to forgo protection already in place. Nor did the Diplomatic Conference use articles 35(3) and 55 merely to clarify existing norms, a fact illustrated by the differing perspectives reflected in the two. Instead, the purpose was obvious—to enhance protection of the environment. Arguments to the contrary ignore the historical, political, and social milieu from which Protocol I emerged, as well as the principle of international law that treaties are to be interpreted in accordance with their context, object, and purpose.[344]

Another interpretive challenge is determining what to make of the "care shall be taken" language in the first sentence of article 55. No such exhortation appears in article 35(3). Though reference to "taking care" might at first glance appear to set a low standard, article 55 continues by prohibiting methods or means that would result in the requisite damage. Thus, the phrase is actually a hortatory provision that encourages greater protection of the environment than the minimum standard set forth in the next sentence. This

---

342. *See* Verwey, Additional Rules, *supra* note 13, at 2.

343. Bear in mind that proportionality and unnecessary suffering are principles of law, not war.

344. *See* Vienna Convention, *supra* note 193, art. 31, para. 1 ("A treaty shall be interpreted in good faith in accordance with the ordinary meaning to be given to the terms of the treaty in their context and in the light of its object and purpose.").

makes particular sense in the context of an anthropocentrically based article: One should always strive to improve the protection of humans from the dangers of war. Perhaps, then, the provision is intended to address situations involving methods or means not designed to damage the environment.[345] By this interpretation, the care standard is a collateral damage provision. Alternatively, it might be simply hortatory, and merit no formal prescriptive valance beyond that.[346]

In a sense, these articles, particularly article 35(3), are analogous to the "just don't do that" prohibitions discussed in conjunction with the humanity principle.[347] Here we see the flip side of the benefits provided by such prohibitions. While they may obviate the necessity of engaging in complex balancing analysis, in certain unique circumstances they may also operate to bypass human values that could be fostered by the prohibited actions. Of course, any appraisal of the prescriptions must be based on an analysis of costs and benefits. Do the clear benefits offered by environment-specific provisions outweigh the costs generated, in the unlikely event that actions forbidden by Protocol I foster human values? The answer depends, as it did with the customary international law balancing tests, on the relative assessment of human and environmental values. This returns us to the anthropocentric versus intrinsic value debate.

In the search for the meaning of the prescriptions, a distracting twist is the assertion that the use of nuclear weapons might be prohibited by the Protocol. After all, while no weapon is more destructive, many strategists have argued that the very destructiveness of nuclear weapons is what provides the greatest protection to human values—a protection that takes the form of deterrence. Concerns have been expressed that if Protocol I were held applicable to nuclear weapons, "the careful balance fashioned with the other nuclear powers in existing agreements affecting those weapons could be adversely impacted."[348] However, although the legality of nuclear weapons is a valid topic for discussion in international law circles, the applicability of articles 35(3) and 55 is not. From the very beginning, it was clear that the Protocol provisions were not meant to reach nuclear weapons. When the ICRC first provided draft protocols to the Diplomatic Conference for consideration, it specifically noted that they were not intended to encompass atomic, chemical, or bacteriological weapons because those weapons were already the subject of other international instruments. Later, the United States, France, and the United Kingdom, among other states, reiterated the exclusion of nuclear weapons from the reach of the Protocol provisions. In fact, the only country that appeared to adopt the position that nuclear weapons were covered was India.[349]

---

345. See MICHAEL BOTHE ET AL., NEW RULES FOR VICTIMS OF ARMED CONFLICTS 345–46 (1982).

346. Professor Verwey has observed that the ICRC has never claimed that the care standard of the first sentence was intended to extend the level of protection. See Verwey, Additional Rules, supra note 13, at 3.

347. See supra Subsection III.B.3.

348. Terry, supra note 92, at 64–65.

349. For discussions of this issue, see DEPLOYMENT DESKBOOK, supra note 318, tab 12, para. 1.7.1.4; Aldrich, supra note 50, at 718–19; Frits Kalshoven, Reaffirmation and Development of

After all is said and done, how much protection do Protocol I's environmental provisions actually provide? The answer remains clouded, but the best estimate is that it is measurable. For instance, even in advance of the Gulf War, the ICRC Commentary noted that "[t]here is no doubt that article 55 will apply to the destruction of oil rigs resulting in oil gushing into the sea and leading to extensive damage such as that described in that article."[350] With impressive foresight, it also addressed the tactic of setting oil facilities ablaze, noting that "it is hardly necessary to stress the grave danger that may ensue for the civilian population."[351]

Yet some would counter that the standards are "too broad and too ambiguous for effective use in military operations."[352] This criticism is basically irrelevant because any action that might rise to the Protocol levels of harm would probably already be precluded by general principles such as proportionality. Still others suggest that the standard is too high to have any real effect.[353] The position taken by the DOD's Gulf War Report falls squarely within the naysayer camp:

> [T]here were questions as to whether the Iraqi actions would have violated its environmental provisions. During [the] treaty's negotiation, there was general agreement that one of its criteria for determining whether a violation had taken place ("longterm") was measured in decades. It is not clear [whether] the damage Iraq caused, while severe in a layman's sense of the term, would meet the technical-legal use of the term in Protocol I. The prohibitions on the damage to the environment contained in Protocol I were not intended to prohibit battlefield damage caused by conventional operations and, in all likelihood, would not apply to Iraq's actions in the Persian Gulf War.[354]

While it may or may not be accurate to deny that the damage technically reached the Protocol I threshold, it certainly is quite a stretch to suggest that either the intentional spilling of nine million barrels of oil into the sea or the setting of over five hundred oil well fires is analogous to "battlefield damage caused by conventional operations." The ICRC's Hans-Peter Gasser has succinctly noted that "[a]s a legal statement this is questionable."[355] He is quite right. Though the level of damage caused by the Iraqi actions was overestimated, it would appear clear from the commentary that this was precisely the type of action that the drafters had in mind.

As noted earlier, the United States has chosen not to ratify Protocol I

International Humanitarian Law Applicable in Armed Conflicts: The Diplomatic Conference, Geneva, 1974–1977, 9 NETH. Y.B. INT'L L. 107, 108–09 (1978).

350. ICRC COMMENTARY, *supra* note 17, at 668–69.

351. *Id.* at 669.

352. Matheson, *supra* note 50, at 436. This contention is insupportable. Imagine a small state facing a large invasion force from the sea. Furthermore, assume that the human rights record of the aggressor force during occupation is dismal.he small state could foil amphibious operations by dumping oil into the path of the oncoming fleet, would not such an action be both proportionate and militarily necessary even though the damage caused would reach Protocol I levels?

353. *See, e.g.*, Betsy Baker, *Legal Protections for the Environment in Times of Armed Conflict*, 33 VA. J. INT'L L. 352, 368 (1993).

354. DOD REPORT, *supra* note 69, at O-27.

355. Hans-Peter Gasser, The Protection of the Environment During Armed Conflict and Other Military Operations, Paper Presented at the Symposium on the Protection of the Environment During Armed Conflict and Operations Other Than War, *in* NWC SYMPOSIUM PAPERS, *supra* note 13 (manuscript at 10 n.4, on file with *The Yale Journal of International Law*).

(though over 130 other states have),[356] and has objected specifically to those provisions that are directed to environmental protection. Are they nevertheless declaratory of customary international law? A number of commentators have argued that articles 35(3) and 55 may be.[357] The better argument is that while there may be an emergent "operational code" regarding environmental damage during warfare, it is premature to assert that customary law in the classic sense has solidified.[358] Lack of international unanimity among the relevant actors, most notably the United States, is ample evidence of this fact. The ICRC also takes the position that articles 35(3) and 55 have not attained the status of customary law,[359] which explains its aggressive dissemination efforts, particularly vis-à-vis its new environmental law of war guidelines.

While articles 35(3) and 55 are the only environment-specific prescriptions found in Protocol I, many of its other provisions also bear on issues of warfare and the environment. Some simply further codify elements of the law of war that already have been addressed. For instance, article 35(1) notes that the right of the parties to choose methods or means of warfare is not unlimited;[360] article 35(2) expresses the customary unnecessary suffering prohibition;[361] article 51 proscribes indiscriminate attacks;[362] and both articles 51[363] and 57[364] mandate proportionality analysis. General concepts relevant to the environment are implicit in several other provisions. The requirement to distinguish civilian from military objects in articles 48[365] and

---

356. A current listing of the parties is maintained by the ICRC at the net site (visited Oct. 23, 1996) <http://www.icrc.ch/icrcnews>.

357. *See, e.g.*, MOORE, *supra* note 76, at 78 (noting that articles 35(3) and 55 "may be declaratory of a rapidly developing customary international law").

358. For a discussion of operational codes and myth systems, see W. MICHAEL REISMAN, JURISPRUDENCE: UNDERSTANDING AND SHAPING LAW 23–25 (1987); W. MICHAEL REISMAN & JAMES E. BAKER, REGULATING COVERT ACTION 23–24 (1992).

359. *See 1993 Secretary General Report, supra* note 140, at 5.

360. *See* Protocol I, *supra* note 8, art. 35, para. 1 ("In any armed conflict, the right of the Parties to the conflict to choose methods or means of warfare is not unlimited.").

361. *See id.* art. 35, para. 2 ("It is prohibited to employ weapons, projectiles and material and methods of warfare of a nature to cause superfluous injury or unnecessary suffering.").

362. *See id.* art. 51, para. 4. The article states that
indiscriminate attacks are prohibited. Indiscriminate attacks are:
      (a) those which are not directed at a specific military objective;
      (b) those which employ a method or means of combat which cannot be directed at a specific military objective; or
      (c) those which employ a method or means of combat which cannot be limited as required by this Protocol; and consequently, in each case, are of a nature to strike military objectives and civilians or civilian objects without distinction.
Id.

363. *See id.* art. 51, para. 5 ("[A]n attack which may be expected to cause incidental loss of civilian life, injury to civilians, damage to civilian objects, or a combination thereof, which would be excessive in relation to the concrete and direct military advantage anticipated" is one type of indiscriminate attack).

364. *See id.* art. 57, para. 2(b) ("[A]n attack shall be canceled or suspended if it becomes apparent that the objective is not a military one or is subject to special protection or that the attack may be expected to cause incidental loss of civilian life, injury to civilians, damage to civilian objects, or a combination thereof, which would be excessive in relation to the concrete and direct military advantage anticipated.").

365. *See id.* art. 48 ("In order to ensure respect for and protection of the civilian population and civilian objects, the Parties to the conflict shall at all times distinguish between the civilian population and combatants and between civilian objects and military objectives and accordingly shall direct their operations only against military objectives.").

52,[366] for example, is a basic step both in military necessity or proportionality analysis and in assessing discrimination (humanity) requirements. Of course, the Martens Clause of article 1 provides protection even beyond the specific safeguards enunciated in the Protocol.[367]

However, Protocol I stretches the envelope of environmental protection much further than mere codification of preexisting norms. Under article 54(2), for example,

> [i]t is prohibited to attack, destroy, remove or render useless objects indispensable to the survival of the civilian population, such as food-stuffs, agricultural areas for the production of food-stuffs, crops, livestock, drinking water installations and supplies and irrigation works, for the specific purpose of denying them for their sustenance value to the civilian population or to the adverse Party, whatever the motive, whether in order to starve out civilians, to cause them to move away, or for any other motive.[368]

As the provision's examples illustrate, in many cases it is the environment itself that provides the objects necessary for survival. It must also be noted that the list is not exhaustive. Other items such as fuel oil, electricity, or lines of communication could, depending on circumstances, also merit protection, as long as the attack on them is for the purpose of denying sustenance. Their destruction (absent the article 54(2) safeguards) certainly could have environmental consequences. Under paragraph (2), protected objects are immune from targeting even if the reason for denying sustenance is to secure a military advantage. This is so regardless of whether the intent is to deny sustenance to the civilian population *or* to the "adverse party," i.e., enemy forces. Exceptions arise only when the protected objects are (1) used *solely* for the armed forces; (2) not used as sustenance, and destruction will not deprive the civilian population of food or water; or (3) required in the defense of, and executed on, one's own territory.[369] This essentially outlaws the scorched-earth tactics used during the Second World War with such tragic consequences for both humans and their environment. Of particular importance is the fact that military necessity has been completely removed from the equation, although the requirement of intent to deny sustenance will limit the reach of article 54(2) somewhat. Finally, the article would preclude

---

366. *See id.* art. 52, para. 2. Article 52(2) provides:
Attacks shall be limited strictly to military objectives. In so far as objects are concerned, military objectives are limited to those objects which by their nature, location, purpose or use make an effective contribution to military action and whose total or partial destruction, capture or neutralization, in the circumstances ruling at the time, offers a definite military advantage.
Id.

367. *See id.* art. 1, para. 2 ("In cases not covered by this Protocol or by other international agreements, civilians and combatants remain under the protection and authority of the principles of international law derived from established custom, from the principles of humanity and from the dictates of public conscience.").

368. *See id.* art. 54, para. 2.

369. *See id.* art. 54, paras. 3, 5. Anthony Leibler has suggested that since the provision is limited to destruction intended to deny civilians sustenance, and other actions are not treated as prohibited, "at least from the perspective of environmental protection Article 54 is of negligible utility." Leibler, *supra* note 185, at 107. On the contrary, article 54 may limit efforts to foment unrest among a population, destroy sustenance available to an advancing force that lives largely off the land, or even foul desalination plants on which both civilians and the military rely.

use of the environment as a weapon if the prohibited effect might result.[370]

While article 54(2) has not proven controversial, another provision with significant environmental consequences, article 56, has. It prohibits attacking dams, dikes, and nuclear electrical power generating stations if the release of "dangerous forces and consequent severe losses among the civilian population" might result.[371] This clearly anthropocentric prohibition applies even if the facility is a valid military objective. It also includes attacks on any surrounding military objective that might result in the release of dangerous forces. For dams and dikes, the protection is forfeited if they are used for purposes other than their normal functions and "in regular, significant and direct support of military operations and such attack is the only feasible way to terminate such support."[372] As to nuclear electrical generating stations, attack is permissible only when the facility provides power "in regular, significant and direct support of military operations" *and* the only way to cut off that support is through attack.[373] Parties are permitted to arm the facilities, though any armament is limited to defensive use and cannot exceed that necessary to repel hostile action.[374]

Assertions have been made that the article, if given a liberal interpretation, would extend protection to any facility containing "dangerous forces," in particular oil wells or tanks. These assertions are unconvincing. The question whether the list provided should be exhaustive or illustrative surfaced during the drafting process. It was decided that to permit specificity regarding those facilities about which the drafters were most concerned (dams, dikes, and nuclear power facilities), the list would be exhaustive.[375]

Despite limitation in scope, the degree of protection is consequential. First, though the term "severe" appears to mandate a high degree of loss before protections come into effect, that is not the case, for in the official ICRC Commentary the term is clarified as meaning "important" or "heavy."[376] Conceptually, then, it may be easier to think of the provision as excluding losses that are "unimportant" or "light." Assuming this is a fair characterization rather than merely semantic gymnastics, the quantum of damage necessary to activate article 56 would not be difficult to reach. Furthermore, an attack need not even be certain to result in a release; instead, the criterion is "may cause." Whether an attack *may* result in a release is a much less subjective determination than whether it *will* do so.

The robustness of the protection is also apparent in the hurdles to be

---

370. *See* Protocol I, *supra* note 8, art. 54, para. 2. For instance, altering weather or climate could severely affect food production.

371. Protocol I, *supra* note 8, art. 56, para. 1.

372. *Id.* art. 56, para. 2(a).

373. *Id.* art. 56, para. 2(b).

374. *See id.* art. 56, para. 5.

375. *See* 15 O.R., *supra* note 323, para. 326. *See also* BOTHE ET AL., *supra* note 345, at 352. The Greenpeace Study's statement that "[i]t is unclear whether oil wells constitute installations containing 'dangerous forces.' The examples given in Protocol I . . . are not meant to be exhaustive, and a liberal construction could say that the release of the force of the oil fires and spills is covered," GREENPEACE STUDY, *supra* note 69, at 140, is thus incorrect.

376. ICRC COMMENTARY, *supra* note 17, para. 2154 ("[A]s so often in this Chapter, this concept is a matter of common sense and it must be applied in good faith on the basis of objective elements such as proximity of inhabited areas, the density of population, the lie of the land, etc.").

overcome before attack is permitted. Dams and dikes must be used for other than their intended purposes *and* their support of the enemy effort must be regular, significant, and direct *and* attacking them must be the only option. Nuclear generating stations enjoy similar safeguards, though they need not be used for other than their normal function.[377] Notice that virtually all the criteria are stated in the conjunctive. Therefore, even when support is direct and substantial and attack is the only option, if the support is irregular the facility enjoys immunity. The requirement to eliminate feasible alternatives further complicates matters. Once it is determined that there is no other choice, must the weapon that best avoids damage be selected? Normally, the law of armed conflict does not dictate the use of specific tactics, e.g., the use of smart weapons. However, given the heightened protection afforded to these facilities, as well as the requirement to select alternative courses, it would make sense that weapons choice criteria would apply. The Rapporteur acknowledged as much by suggesting that the capabilities of modern weapons heightened the protection afforded under the provision.[378]

Other indications of stringency are found in the intent underlying the relevant verbiage, intent that may suggest, as was the case with "severe," a meaning that differs from common usage. Resort to the ICRC Commentary again illustrates the extent of the protection afforded. It offers two examples: a dike forming *part of a system of fortifications* and a road across a dam that can be used as an *essential route for the movement of armed forces.* Even in these circumstances, the regular, significant, and direct criteria apply, thereby indicating that there are times when they might *not* be met.[379] The ICRC Commentary then goes on to dismiss criticisms of the standard's apparent subjectivity by noting that the "terms merely express common sense, i.e., their meaning is fairly clear to everyone"; therefore, they simply "need to be interpreted in good faith on the basis of objective elements."[380]

At this point, it might seem a daunting task to identify examples of support for military operations that would allow exclusion from the broader protection. In fact, it may be easier than it seems at first glance. Lest those who apply the standard not possess the perceptive abilities to discern what is "fairly clear to everyone," the commentary defines the terms, using the technique of semantic inversion employed above to illustrate "severe." "Regular" implies a time standard and is said not to be "accidental or sporadic." "Significant," according to the commentary, is less precise than regular, but implies support that is more than "negligible" or "merely an incidental circumstance." "Direct" means "not in an intermediate or roundabout way."[381] These definitions actually appear to set a *lower*

---

377. *See* Protocol I, *supra* note 8, art. 56, para. 2(b). The issue of targeting nuclear facilities was raised at the 1990 Review Conference for the Nuclear Non-Proliferation Treaty. The Hungarian and Dutch delegates, with support from several other delegations, suggested an international agreement to address the topic. The U.S. delegation did not respond to the proposal. *See* David Fischer & Harald Müller, *The Fourth Review of the Non-Proliferation Treaty*, 1991 STOCKHOLM INT'L PEACE RES. INST. Y.B. 555, 566.

378. *See* 15 O.R., *supra* note 323, at 284.

379. *See* ICRC COMMENTARY, *supra* note 17, para. 2162, at 671.

380. *Id.*

381. *Id.*

standard of protection than would result from reference to common American usage of the terms.

The United States opposes article 56 as excessively restrictive, pointing to the protections already provided to the civilian population by the principle of proportionality. From the U.S. perspective, setting the threshold for attack so high invites the enemy to use protected facilities for military purposes. If the attacker decides that the criteria are not met, he will refrain from attack. On the other hand, if he decides that the criteria have been met, he opens himself up to condemnation by those who would disagree with his assessment. Given the multiplicity of criteria and their inherent subjectivity, it would be very difficult to cite an action that would be objectively permissible. Finally, critics argue that the protection for nuclear electrical power generation facilities ignores the existence of integrated power grids, an argument contradicted by the ICRC Commentary.[382]

Advocates of the prohibition would reply by pointing to the requirement that the resultant losses among the civilian population be "severe."[383] Therefore, only attacks with dramatic consequences are forbidden. Furthermore, since severity of loss is a prerequisite to protection, in most cases simple proportionality analysis will preclude those attacks that the article's opponents might complain of being prohibited from conducting. It is hard to imagine an attack with severe civilian losses that would be proportional if its contribution to the enemy's military effort were not regular, significant, and direct. From this perspective, article 56 essentially operates to resolve gray area situations in favor of the civilian population.

There is little doubt that adherence to article 56 would heighten protection of the environment during warfare. Though proportionality analysis would provide similar levels of protection in most cases, article 56's greater specificity serves as a restraint on self-serving interpretations of proportionality by the malevolent. This does not answer the question whether Protocol I is worthy of ratification, or even whether article 56 is an overall step forward in the law of war. Yet because it is less susceptible to avoidance through interpretation, *from an environmental perspective* it represents progress.

As a final aside, it bears mentioning that U.S. aircraft attacked nuclear facilities during the Gulf War. However, article 56 was not applicable because the United States was not a Protocol I party and because it would be difficult to make a case that the provision represented customary international law. Furthermore, the targets were not nuclear electrical generating stations. Some may argue about whether the attacks "may" have resulted in a release, or even whether the United States took all "practical precautions" to avoid causing one, but ultimately the missions did not implicate Protocol I.[384]

---

382. *See* DEPLOYMENT DESKBOOK, *supra* note 318, tab 12, para. 1.8.7.1; ICRC COMMENTARY, *supra* note 17, paras. 2164-66, at 671-72.

383. Ambassador Aldrich, who negotiated Protocol I for the U.S., provides the core analysis supporting ratification. *See* Aldrich, *supra* note 50, at 714-16.

384. *See* Jozef Goldblat, *Legal Protection of the Environment Against the Effects of Military Activities*, 22 BULL. PEACE PROPOSALS 399, 400-01 (1991). Professor Goldblat takes a fairly critical approach to the topic, using as an example the 1981 bombing of the Iraqi nuclear reactor by the Israelis.

Like Geneva Convention IV, Protocol I provides for grave breaches. Neither of the environmental provisions to be discussed in greater detail below, articles 35(3) and 55, is included in the category. Nevertheless, the causation of environmental damage could, under specific circumstances, constitute a grave breach (war crime) if the act in question were willful and death or serious bodily injury would result. These include making the civilian population the object of attack, launching an indiscriminate attack against civilians or civilian objects, and striking works or installations containing dangerous forces knowing that the harm caused will be excessive.[385] In such cases, damage to the environment may be collateral *or* the environment might be attacked for the purpose of causing the requisite result. As war crimes constituting grave breaches, such acts would require the state in which the offender is found to prosecute him or cooperate in his extradition.[386] The mere fact that an offense is not a grave breach, however, does not preclude prosecution; it only means that the heightened enforcement regime set forth for grave breaches does not apply.

Finally, one notable limitation of the Protocol is that its articles regarding protection of the civilian population and civilian objects (arts. 48–67) are not generally applicable to naval warfare or aerial combat.[387] What is interesting is that this restriction affects all of the significant provisions relevant to the environment that will be discussed *except* article 35(3). This is due to the placement of article 35(3) in an earlier section on methods and means of warfare. As a result, the scope of article 35(3) will be broader than that of its counterpart, article 55, even though their text is nearly identical. This is especially significant in light of the fact that the former adopts an intrinsic value approach,[388] whereas the latter is anthropocentric in nature.

---

385. *See* Protocol I, *supra* note 8, art. 85, para. 3(a)–(c).
386. *See id.* art. 88.
387. *See id.* art. 49, para. 3. Article 49(3) provides:

> The provisions of this Section [Civilian Population] apply to any land, air, or sea warfare which may affect the civilian population, individual civilians or civilian objects on land. They further apply to all attacks from the sea or from the air against objectives on land but do not otherwise affect the rules of international law applicable in armed conflict at sea or in the air.

Id. The exclusion resulted from a conscious effort by the delegates of the Diplomatic Conference to secure agreement where it was most likely to come—in the "well-established" body of law governing land warfare. Their concern was that naval warfare had fundamentally changed, thereby becoming unsettled, during and after the Second World War. In particular, differences of opinion over the state of the law governing issues such as visit and search, the legality of attacks on merchant vessels, and submarine warfare were felt likely to impede the process of updating the existing Geneva Conventions. *See* BOTHE ET AL., *supra* note 345, at 290; ICRC COMMENTARY, *supra* note 17, at 606. The Bothe commentary notes that this approach was ICRC-proposed and had the support of the states with the largest navies. These parties believed it would be counterproductive to pursue revision of the law of naval warfare at the time, particularly as the preparatory work of the experts had not focused on the subject. *See* BOTHE ET AL., *supra* note 345, at 290.

Similarly, the laws of aerial warfare are not formally codified, and the customary law that addresses the topic is ambiguous. Therefore, the delegates decided to make Protocol I inapplicable at sea or in the air *unless* the attack in question targeted land objectives. *See* Protocol I, *supra* note 8, art. 49, para. 3. It has been suggested that one additional exception is the extension of applicability to attacks from the sea or air against targets in the territorial sea. *See* Walker, *supra* note 52, at 122. This reasonable approach is based on the Protocol's use of "territory" and "national territory," terms which in their legal context include the territorial sea.

388. *See supra* notes 323–31 and accompanying text.

4. *ENMOD*

The final core prescriptive instrument relevant to the environment in the *jus in bello* is ENMOD. Negotiated contemporaneously with Protocol I and ratified by the United States in 1980, it was in part a reaction to the environmental modification techniques practiced during the Vietnam War, such as attempts to alter weather.[389] Though the Soviet Union was the first to propose a limitation on environmental modification, the United States quickly became a prime mover behind the Convention.[390] In fact, the United States already had renounced the use of climate modification techniques in 1972 as a matter of policy.[391] As of April 1996, there were sixty-four parties to the Convention, including most major states (e.g., the United States, Russia, Germany, and Japan). Countries that have signed but not ratified it include Iraq, Iran, and Syria, whereas two significant holdouts are France and China.[392]

ENMOD is "Hague Law" in that it limits methods and means of warfare. It is not necessary that those methods and means actually affect the environment, for the only prohibition is on *use* of the environment as a weapon.[393] Article I provides:

> (1) Each State Party to this Convention undertakes not to engage in military or any other hostile use of environmental modification techniques having widespread, long-lasting or severe effects as the means of destruction, damage or injury to any other State Party.
> (2) Each State Party to this Convention undertakes not to assist, encourage or induce any State, group of States or international organization to engage in activities contrary to the provisions of paragraph 1 of this article.[394]

Though the "widespread, long-lasting or severe" formula resembles that found in Protocol I, here it is stated in the alternative, using "or." Since a technique meeting any of the threshold criteria will be prohibited, the result is a much more stringent standard of protection than that found in Protocol I.

An effort was made during the ENMOD drafting process to clarify

---

389. *See Hearings to Hear Testimony on the Convention on the Prohibition of Military or Any Other Hostile Use of Environmental Modification Techniques Before the Senate Comm. on Foreign Relations,* 96th Cong. (1979); *Environmental Modification Treaty: Hearings on the Convention on the Prohibition of Military or Any Other Hostile Use of Environmental Modification Techniques Before the Senate Comm. on Foreign Relations,* 95th Cong. (1978).

390. *See* THE LAWS OF ARMED CONFLICTS, *supra* note 153, at 163. In 1974 the Soviet Union submitted a draft convention to the General Assembly, which in turn referred it to the Conference of the Committee on Disarmament. At that point the United States and the Soviet Union provided the Conference with identical drafts of a proposed convention. The text was revised in committee and submitted to the General Assembly, which approved it on December 10, 1976. The Convention was then opened for signature. It entered into force on October 5, 1978. *See id.*

391. *See* Terry, *supra* note 92, at 64. Also recall the sense of the Senate Resolution. *See supra* notes 32–33 and accompanying text.

392. A list of current parties is maintained at net site: <http://www.un.org/Depts/Treaty>. Note that a state that has signed but not ratified a convention is obligated not to take actions contrary to the object and purpose of the agreement, at least until it has made clear its intent not to become a party. *See* Vienna Convention, *supra* note 193, art. 18.

393. This distinction motivated the name change in the Jordanian Note Verbale. *See supra* notes 115–16 and accompanying text.

394. ENMOD, *supra* note 34, art. I.

terminology. In the Understanding Relating to Article I, "widespread" was defined as "encompassing an area on the scale of several hundred kilometres"; "long-lasting" as "lasting for a period of months, or approximately a season"; and "severe" as "involving serious or significant disruption or harm to human life, natural and economic resources or other assets."[395] Again, this constitutes a higher standard than that found in Protocol I, particularly when comparing the definition of "long-lasting" as seasonal with the commonly accepted understanding of the Protocol I limit as being measured in decades. Similarly, describing "severe" as "serious or significant" also serves to heighten protection, as does the use of "disruption" instead of "damage" in setting forth the requisite violative effect. This attempt to define the core verbiage of the prescription was not universally accepted, though the vast majority of the parties have effectively accepted it by not filing reservations (interpretive statements) related to the definitional issues.[396]

One source of confusion may be differences in opinion regarding whether to use individual or cumulative effect in assessing the damage. This is an important issue in the Protocol I context as well. For instance, the United States has reportedly stated that the use of herbicides to modify the environment would not be forbidden unless the end result of an individual use were widespread, long-lasting, or severe destruction.[397] As one commentator notes, "[i]t follows that, as the consequences of an individual mission would probably fall below these thresholds, such missions would not be prohibited, despite the fact that overall the damage would clearly fall well outside allowed limits."[398]

This assertion is certainly incorrect in the context of current understandings. Consider the most vivid example of environmental damage during hostilities in recent times, the intentional Gulf War oil spills. Virtually no one asserted that each Iraqi spill should be considered individually in assessing legality. On the contrary, commentators were unanimous in citing the releases as a single operation despite the fact that the spills were separated in time and executed in differing ways (release from oil terminals, ships, etc.). Though this example is not an ENMOD scenario, it illustrates the international community's attitude towards severability. What it did distinguish were the spills from the fires.

The best approach acknowledges, on the one hand, the inappropriateness

---

395. *Understanding Relating to Article I, Report of the Conference of the Committee on Disarmament*, U.N.GAOR, 31st Sess., Supp. No. 27, at 91–92, U.N. Doc. A/31/27 (1976), *reprinted in* THE LAWS OF ARMED CONFLICTS, *supra* note 153, at 168. There were four Understandings which, though not part of the Convention, were included in the report transmitted by the Conference of the Committee on Disarmament to the United Nations General Assembly.

396. Turkey, however, filed an interpretive understanding stating that in its opinion the "terms 'widespread,' 'long-lasting' and 'severe effects' . . . need to be clarified. So long as this clarification is not made the Government of Turkey will be compelled to interpret itself the terms in question and consequently it reserves the right to do so as and when required." Turkish Interpretive Statement Filed at Time of Signature, May 18, 1977, *reprinted in Multilateral Treaties Deposited with the Secretary General* (visited Oct. 23, 1996) <http://www.un.org/Depts/Treaty>.

397. *See* Jozef Goldblat, *The Environmental Modification Convention of 1977: An Analysis, in* ENVIRONMENTAL WARFARE: A TECHNICAL, LEGAL AND POLICY APPRAISAL 53, 55 (Arthur Westing ed., 1984).

398. Carruthers, *supra* note 25, at 47.

of simply lumping all wartime environmental damage together to determine whether the article I thresholds are met. This is so if only because an actor is unlikely to have been able to anticipate reasonably what the net results of his many environmentally destructive actions would be; it would be difficult to demonstrate even a "should have known," let alone a "knew," level of scienter. On the other hand, it would be even more absurd to excuse conduct because the ultimate damage resulted from multiple actions, such as aerial flights, none of which alone caused the requisite level of destruction. Instead, it should be asked whether the actions are part of a single integrated plan or operation designed to achieve a common, or closely related, result. By using an intent element as the connective variable, scienter problems (at least those involving scope of the relationship) are rendered *de minimis*.

Definitional issues also pervade article II's use of the phrase "environmental modification technique" as "any technique for changing—through deliberate manipulation of natural processes—the dynamics, composition or structure of the earth, including its biota, lithosphere, hydrosphere and atmosphere, or of outer space."[399] Illustrative examples cited in the Understanding relating to article II include earthquakes, tsunamis, an upset in the ecological balance of a region, changes in weather patterns, changes in climate patterns, changes in the state of the ozone layer, and changes in the state of the ionosphere.[400] The Understanding indicates that while these are only examples, their use would create the presumption of a violation.

What stands out in the definition is its limitation to techniques that involve manipulation of natural processes. There is relative consensus, for instance, that the techniques employed by Iraq during the Gulf War did not implicate ENMOD prohibitions, and would not have done so even had Iraq been a party.[401] While the environment may have been the target, it was not the weapon. Therefore, despite a very restrictive standard, the narrow range of techniques contemplated in ENMOD suggests that, given current technologies, the Convention will be of limited value. Probably its greatest impact will be

---

399. ENMOD, *supra* note 34, art. II.

400. *See Understanding Relating to Article II, Report of the Conference of the Committee on Disarmament*, U.N.GAOR, 31st Sess., Supp. No. 27, at 91–92, U.N. Doc. A/31/27 (1976), *reprinted in* THE LAWS OF ARMED CONFLICTS, *supra* note 153, at 168. The Understanding reads as follows:

It is further understood that all the phenomena listed above, when produced by military or any other hostile use of environmental modification techniques, would result, or could reasonably be expected to result, in widespread, longlasting or severe destruction, damage or injury. Thus, military or any other hostile use of environmental modification techniques as defined in article II, so as to cause those phenomena as a means of destruction, damage or injury to another State Party, would be prohibited.

It is recognized, moreover, that the list of examples set out above is not exhaustive. Other phenomena which could result from the use of environmental modification techniques as defined in article II could also be appropriately included. The absence of such phenomena from the list does not in any way imply that the undertaking contained in article I would not be applicable to those phenomena, provided the criteria set out in that article were met.

Id.

401. The DOD report cited with approval the conclusions of the Ottawa Conference on this point. *See* DOD REPORT, *supra* note 69, at O-26 to O-27. However, the Commission for International Due Process of Law, in its draft indictment of Saddam Hussein and his advisers, did allege an ENMOD violation. *See* Kutner & Nanda, *supra* note 301, at 95.

directional, by foreclosing weapons development along the prohibited lines.

The future effectiveness of ENMOD may be further limited by its enforcement regime. It is a regime based exclusively on state responsibility, possibly because the greater part of the Convention is focused on peacetime activities. The result is an essentially political system for assuring compliance.[402] In situations preliminary to armed conflict, or in armed conflict itself, the primary remedy is referral to the Security Council for enforcement action. However, the Security Council already is empowered under the Charter to take appropriate actions in response to most potential breaches of ENMOD; the Convention's enforcement provisions add little new power. Further limiting the enforcement regime's effectiveness is the fact that the Convention's scope is limited to damage caused to parties.[403]

How should ENMOD be assessed overall?[404] Most importantly, ENMOD affects only a very narrow band of possible operations, many of which have not advanced beyond the concept stage.[405] Furthermore, it has not attained the wide acceptance that Protocol I enjoys, a particularly unfortunate state of affairs given its limitation to the territory of parties. Finally, ENMOD is another example of an absolute prohibition in that no military necessity or proportionality balancing is required prior to its taking effect. This poses the same risk discussed with regard to Protocol I—that human values might suffer for environmental ends. Of course, the fact that the requisite damage need not be to the *environment* of another party suggests that the prohibition is framed in essentially anthropocentric terms. To some extent, this will mitigate the danger of not factoring in proportionality and necessity. Whether the gains represented by ENMOD merit this risk is a fair matter for debate. Regardless of the answer, ENMOD is finding its way into the documents that underlie development of the operational code—law of war manuals.[406]

5. *Miscellaneous Prescriptions*

Though the four conventions addressed above represent the core environmental prescriptions in the *jus in bello*, others also contain provisions that enhance protection of the environment during hostilities. Among the most

---

402. *See* ENMOD, *supra* note 34, art. V.

403. *See id.* art. I, para. 1 ("Each State Party to this Convention undertakes not to engage in military or any other hostile use of environmental modification techniques having widespread, long-lasting or severe effects as the means of destruction, damage or injury to *any other State Party*.") (emphasis added).

404. The ENMOD Convention provided for review conferences to assess the provisions and compliance therewith. *See* ENMOD, *supra* note 34, art. VIII. Neither the first conference in 1984 nor the second in 1992 was able to arrive at a consensus on anything significant. The second, however, did reaffirm the need to conduct further reviews. *See* Dieter Fleck, *Legal and Policy Perspectives, in* EFFECTING COMPLIANCE 155–56 (Hazel Fox & Michael A. Meyer eds., 1993).

405. One such concept involves melting the Arctic ice cover in order to raise the level of the sea and thereby flood coastal areas. *See* Hans Blix, *Arms Control Treaties Aimed at Reducing the Military Impact on the Environment, in* ESSAYS IN INTERNATIONAL LAW IN HONOUR OF JUDGE MANFRED LACHS 703, 709 (Jerzy Makarczyk ed., 1984).

406. *See, e.g.,* GERMAN MANUAL, *supra* note 168, para. 403 (distinguishing Protocol I from ENMOD damage).

important are the 1925 Gas Protocol,[407] the 1993 Chemical Weapons Convention,[408] and the United Nations Conventional Weapons Convention.[409] It is instructive to mention each briefly.[410]

The United States ratified the first of these, the 1925 Gas Protocol, in 1972. The Protocol prohibits the use of "asphyxiating, poisonous, or other gases, and of analogous liquids, materials, and devices."[411] Extending to both chemical and biological agents, the treaty is widely held to be declaratory of customary international law. In terms of environmental protection, the prohibitions are significant, especially in light of the fact that chemicals can be transferred through the food chain.

Unfortunately, there is significant controversy over the scope of the Convention, a point that should be obvious from the half-century that it took the United States to become a party. Even when it did ratify, the United States included a first-use reservation—a statement that it would not be bound by the prohibitions if the other side in a conflict violated the agreement first.[412] Executive Order 11,850 implements the agreement with respect to the wartime use of chemical herbicides and riot control agents.[413] Setting forth U.S. policy, it retains the option of retaliation, but renounces the use of herbicides. Executive Order 11,850 goes on to cite explicitly two circumstances in which the use of herbicides is authorized even absent formal authorization—domestic employment and use to clear vegetation around the "immediate defensive perimeter" surrounding U.S. bases.[414]

Other states also have adopted first-use reservations,[415] thereby creating two distinct treaty regimes. The exclusion of herbicides, however, is not widespread; a number of close allies have interpreted the prohibition as extending to all gases.[416] In fact, during the Vietnam War, the U.N. General Assembly issued a resolution in response to U.S. use of herbicides that purported to clarify the scope of the Protocol. The resolution stated that the Protocol prohibited use of:

(a) [a]ny chemical agents of warfare—chemical substances, whether gaseous, liquid or

---

407.   Gas Protocol, *supra* note 132.

408.   Chemical Weapons Convention, *supra* note 135.

409.   Conventional Weapons Convention, *supra* note 134.

410.   Three other conventions cited in the 1993 Secretary General Report that also have some marginal environmental effect are the Biological Weapons Convention, *supra* note 133; the Convention for the Protection of Cultural Property, *supra* note 153; and the Convention for the Protection of the World Cultural and Natural Heritage, Nov. 16, 1972, 1037 U.N.T.S. 151.

411.   Gas Protocol, *supra* note 132, pmbl.

412.   The "Protocol shall cease to be binding on the government of the United States with respect to the use in war of asphyxiating, poisonous or other gases, and of all analogous liquids, materials, or devices, in regard to an enemy State if such State or any of its allies fails to respect the prohibitions laid down in the Protocol." Reservation Made on Ratification, *reprinted in* THE LAWS OF ARMED CONFLICTS, *supra* note 153, at 126.

413.   *See* Exec. Order No. 11,850, 40 Fed. Reg. 16,187 (1975).

414.   *See id.*

415.   These include France, Iraq, Israel, Libya, the former Soviet Union, and the United Kingdom. For the text of the reservations, see THE LAWS OF ARMED CONFLICTS, *supra* note 153, at 121–27.

416.   *See* THE LAWS OF WAR: A COMPREHENSIVE COLLECTION OF PRIMARY DOCUMENTS ON INTERNATIONAL LAWS GOVERNING ARMED CONFLICT 58 (W. Michael Reisman & Chris Antoniou eds., 1994).

solid—which might be employed because of their direct toxic effect on man, animals or plants;

(b) [a]ny biological agents of warfare—living organisms, whatever their nature, or infective material derived from them—which are intended to cause disease or death in man, animals, or plants, and which depend for their effect on their ability to multiply in the person, animal or plant attacked.[417]

Nevertheless, the issue of scope remains alive today, with lack of unanimity continuing to weaken the overall regime.[418]

A related convention is the Chemical Weapons Convention of 1993. The war between Iran and Iraq, in a fashion reminiscent of the First World War, drew attention to the horrors of chemical weapons when they were used both during military campaigns and against the Iraqi Kurds. As a result of these tragedies, the Conference on the Prohibition of Chemical Weapons adopted the Declaration on the Prohibition of Chemical Weapons in January 1989.[419] Signatories of the Declaration condemned the states that had employed chemical weapons and renounced their use. They also reaffirmed their commitment to the 1925 Gas Protocol prohibitions and urged nonparties to accede to the agreement.[420]

Concerted efforts to secure a robust chemical weapons convention followed the Conference. Those efforts came to fruition in 1993. As of April 1996, the Chemical Weapons Convention has 160 signatories, including the United States. Of the 160 signatories, forty-nine have become parties.[421] It was transmitted to the Senate for ratification in November 1993. The treaty remains open for signature and will come into force in accordance with its terms 180 days after deposit of the sixty-fifth instrument of ratification.[422]

Under the Convention, parties bind themselves not to use, under any circumstances, chemical weapons, or to "develop, produce, otherwise acquire, stockpile or retain chemical weapons, or transfer, directly or indirectly, chemical weapons to anyone."[423] The preamble emphasizes that this

---

417. G.A. Res. 2603, U.N. GAOR, 24th Sess., Supp. No. 30, at 16, U.N. Doc. A/7630 (1969).

418. For example, Professor Verwey has noted:

The better view appears to be . . . that this Protocol was never intended to protect the environment, and that even the employment of herbicides and defoliant agents of the types used during the Vietnam War would only be prohibited to the extent that they can be proven to be toxic to *human beings* and to actually cause *human* casualties.

Verwey, Additional Rules, *supra* note 13, at 5. On the other hand, Professor Goldblat states that the Protocol "is widely interpreted as applying not only to humans and animals, but also to plants. This is now recognized also by the United States, which made extensive use of herbicides during the war in Vietnam." Goldblat, *supra* note 384, at 403. In fact, most states do see the Protocol as extending to plants, and though the United States does not, it has renounced the use of herbicides as a matter of policy except in certain circumstances. *See supra* notes 413–14 and accompanying text.

419. Final Declaration of the Conference of the States Parties to the 1925 Geneva Protocol and Other Interested States on the Prohibition of Chemical Weapons, Jan. 11, 1989, 28 I.L.M. 1020.

420. *See id.*

421. *See Multilateral Treaties Deposited with the Secretary General* (visited Oct. 23, 1996) <http://www.un.org/Depts/Treaty>.

422. *See* Chemical Weapons Convention, *supra* note 135, art. XXI. For an excellent summary of the Convention, as well as the history leading up to its completion, see *The Chemical Weapons Convention* (visited Oct. 23, 1996) <http://www.opcw.nl/guide.htm>.

423. Chemical Weapons Convention, *supra* note 135, art. I, para. 1(a). The Convention is not subject to reservation. *See id.* art. XXII.

88   YALE JOURNAL OF INTERNATIONAL LAW   [Vol. 22: 1

prohibition is complementary to, not in lieu of, the 1925 Gas Protocol.[424] It also addresses several issues that have generated controversy regarding the latter agreement. For instance, it rules out retaliation with chemicals and, by characterizing them as such, settles much of the debate over whether herbicides are chemicals.[425]

An important feature of the Convention is its description of its prohibitions in terms of means or methods of warfare.[426] This raises the question whether use in situations such as *in extremis* hostage rescue or riot control during civil affairs operations is permissible. The position of the Army is that the Convention is inapplicable in MOOTW because they are operations "conducted for peaceful purposes and do not constitute armed conflict."[427] Lest this position be characterized as an excessively liberal interpretation, it must be remembered that Executive Order 11,850 restrictions remain intact during MOOTW.[428]

The last of the three agreements is the United Nations Conventional Weapons Convention. Like Protocol I and ENMOD, this agreement specifically addresses the environment, but does so in a slightly different fashion. Protocol I discusses use of weapons, but not weapons themselves. ENMOD also fails to discuss weapons themselves, for it is concerned with the use of the environment as a weapon through the manipulation of natural processes. The Conventional Weapons Convention begins to fill the gap by focusing on specific conventional weapons, some of which are capable of harming the environment.

The agreement begins somewhat controversially. After reiterating the customary international law principle of humanity,[429] it restates the provisions of article 35(3) of Protocol I.[430] This led France and the United States to attach reservations (the United States referred to its reservations as understandings) to their instruments of ratification indicating that the preamble

---

424. *See id.* pmbl.

425. *See id.* art. II, para. 2. The Convention defines "toxic chemical" as

> any chemical which through its chemical action on life processes can cause death, temporary incapacitation or permanent harm to humans or animals. This includes all such chemicals, regardless of their origin or of their method of production, and regardless of whether they are produced in facilities, in munitions or elsewhere.

Id.

426. For example, in setting forth uses of chemicals that are not prohibited, the Convention includes "[m]ilitary purposes not connected with the use of chemical weapons and not dependent on the use of the toxic properties of chemicals as a method of warfare." *Id.* art. II, para. 9(c).

427. OPERATIONAL LAW HANDBOOK, *supra* note 179, at 5-5.

428. While the Army's approach makes sense, where does its outer limit lie? For instance, would Saddam Hussein's actions against Iraqi Kurds be covered? That would depend on whether the operations were characterized as "armed conflict." The best interpretation is that use is forbidden in situations amounting either to international (Protocol I) or noninternational (Protocol II) "armed conflict." *See supra* note 10 (distinguishing between international and noninternational armed conflict).

429. *See* Conventional Weapons Convention, *supra* note 134, pmbl. ("Basing themselves on the principle of international law that the right of the parties to an armed conflict to choose methods or means of warfare is not unlimited, and on the principle that prohibits the employment in armed conflicts of weapons, projectiles and material and methods of warfare of a nature to cause superfluous injury or unnecessary suffering . . . .").

430. *See id.* ("Also recalling that it is prohibited to employ methods or means of warfare which are intended, or may be expected, to cause widespread, long-term and severe damage to the natural environment . . . .").

applies only to Protocol I parties.[431] Issues of applicability aside, the heart of the Convention is found in three attached protocols.[432] The first, which addresses nondetectable fragments, is not applicable to this study and will not be addressed.[433] Protocol II covers mines, booby traps, and similar devices.[434] While mines would be unlikely to cause extensive damage to the environment, they certainly could harm humans and animals, and render areas of land unusable. Protocol II provides environmental protection in two ways. First, a proportionality standard balances damage to civilian objects against direct military advantage.[435] The Protocol then imposes humanity-based standards by forbidding indiscriminate use, requiring mine locations to be recorded, and permitting the remote delivery of only self-neutralizing mines.[436] These are classic anthropocentric provisions providing indirect environmental protection.

Direct protection of the environment is found in article 2(4) of the agreement on incendiary weapons, Protocol III, which provides that "[i]t is prohibited to make forests or other kinds of plant cover the object of attack by incendiary weapons except when such natural elements are used to cover, conceal or camouflage combatants or other military objectives, or are themselves military objectives."[437] The United States has elected not to ratify this Protocol, although its objections are broadly based on the overall utility of incendiaries in situations in which an enemy is dug in well, rather than on the Protocol's environmental protection component.

There is little question that article 2(4) would enhance environmental protection, for incendiary weapons, like forest fires, can have devastating environmental impact.[438] Animal and plant life is destroyed and habitats

---

431. The understandings and reservations appear at *Multilateral Treaties Deposited with the Secretary General, supra* note 421. The U.S. Understanding is as follows: "The United States considers that the fourth paragraph of the preamble to the convention, which refers to the substance of the provisos of article 35(3) and article 55(1) of Additional Protocol I to the Geneva Conventions for the Protection of War Victims of August 12, 1949, applies only to States which have accepted those provisions." *Id.*

432. Addition of a fourth protocol on blinding lasers was approved by the October 1995 Review Conference. *See* Additional Protocol on Blinding Laser Weapons (Protocol IV) to the Convention on Prohibitions or Restrictions on the Use of Certain Conventional Weapons Which May be Deemed to be Excessively Injurious or to Have Indiscriminate Effects, Oct. 12, 1995, U.N. Doc. CCW/CONF.I/7 (1995).

433. *See* Protocol on Non-Detectable Fragments (Protocol I), Conventional Weapons Convention, *supra* note 134.

434. *See* Protocol on Prohibitions or Restrictions on the Use of Mines, Booby-Traps and Other Devices (Protocol II), Conventional Weapons Convention, *supra* note 134.

435. *See id.* art. 3, para. 3(c) (prohibiting states from placing weapons "which may be expected to cause incidental loss of civilian life, injury to civilians, damage to civilian objects, or a combination thereof, which would be excessive in relation to the concrete and direct military advantage anticipated").

436. *See id.* arts. 3, 5, 7.

437. Protocol III, *supra* note 134, art. 2, para. 4.

438. In 1973, the Secretary General of the United Nations noted that

[a]lthough there is a lack of knowledge of the effects of widespread fire in these circumstances, such attempts may lead to irreversible ecological changes having grave long-term consequences out of all proportion to the effects originally sought. This menace, though largely unpredictable in its gravity, is reason for expressing alarm concerning the massive employment of incendiaries against the rural environment.

UNITED NATIONS DEP'T OF POLITICAL AND SEC. COUNCIL AFFAIRS, NAPALM AND OTHER INCENDIARY WEAPONS AND ALL ASPECTS OF THEIR POSSIBLE USE, U.N. Doc. A/8803/Rev.1, U.N. Sales No. E.73.I.3 (1973).

often are irreparably damaged by fire and smoke. At the same time, though, the article allows for necessity by excluding the three most likely military uses of such areas; it acts as a toggle switch for the protections provided. Of course, once the prohibition is "turned off," proportionality analysis is still necessary to determine if the target is indeed legitimate.

Issues of the overall utility of incendiary weapons aside, this general approach may serve as a useful model for future environmental prescriptions. Absolute prohibitions, such as that in article 35(3), risk the possibility of actually increasing the harm caused by not accounting for proportionality or military necessity. On the other hand, simply to cite the principles is to create an exception that swallows the rule. Protocol III mitigates these problems by outlining the actions to which a response is militarily necessary,[439] thereby opening the door for a subsequent proportionality analysis. Admittedly, any time applicable scenarios are catalogued in law of war instruments, some either slip through the cracks or surface later as warfare evolves. However, it is preferable to address them supplementally than to craft a prescription devoid of substantive effect. Therefore, albeit limited in scope, Protocol III's environmental provision does offer a workable means for protecting one aspect of the environment, and contains the seeds for future environmental law of war efforts.

D. *Responsibility Under the* Jus in Bello

Wartime responsibility is a relatively well settled topic. Generally, a wrong committed during wartime results in liability for consequences arising therefrom. Payment of reparations is the usual remedy. The basic principle was expressed more than half a century ago by the Permanent Court of International Justice in the well known case of *The Factory at Chorzów*.[440] There, the court held that "reparation must, as far as possible, wipe out all the consequences of the illegal act and reestablish the situation which would, in all probability, have existed if that act had not been committed."[441] The compensation requirement, including compensation for all wrongful "acts committed by persons forming part of a Party State's armed forces," also is found in Hague IV and Protocol I.[442] ENMOD contains no liability provision.[443]

Interestingly, under Hague IV and Protocol I, responsibility lies for acts by a state's "organs"—including members of its armed forces—even if those acts are *ultra vires*.[444] This is not the case under general principles of international law, such as those set forth in the International Law Commission's Draft Articles of State Responsibility. Thus, on the one hand, Hague IV and Protocol I would appear to establish a higher standard of

---

439. *See* Protocol III, *supra* note 134, art. 2, para. 4.
440. Factory at Chorzów (Germ. v. Pol.), 1928 P.C.I.J. (ser. A) No. 17 (Sept. 13).
441. *Id.* at 47.
442. *See* Hague IV, *supra* note 130, art. 3; Protocol I, *supra* note 8, art. 91.
443. *See* ENMOD, *supra* note 34.
444. *See* Greenwood, *supra* note 220, at 5 (citing decision of arbitral tribunal in United States-Mexican Mixed Claims Commission, Youmans, 4 R.I.A.A. 110 (1926)).

responsibility for violations of their rules than would otherwise be the case. On the other hand, one might argue that the two instruments merely codify what has become a generally accepted principle of state responsibility during armed conflict. This determination is difficult to make because of international law's limited experience with reparations. Consequently, as Professor Christopher Greenwood has noted, "[o]n the whole . . . State responsibility has not proved a particularly effective means of enforcing the law."[445]

Even if reparations were widely imposed, it is unlikely that they would be an effective deterrent to environmental destruction. States that resort to armed force are unlikely to decide to forgo an act because of the pecuniary risk, for the risk only becomes a reality if the state suffers a military defeat. The desire to avoid possible defeat would certainly outweigh any deterrent effect generated by the possibility that the loser might have to make reparations. After all, in the vast majority of cases, the likelihood of defeat will exceed the likelihood of having to pay reparations; states sometimes lose without having to pay reparations, but they almost never make reparations without having lost. This is certain to remain the case, at least until the emergence of a supranational authority with true adjudicative and enforcement powers sufficient to compel a wrongdoing *victor* to pay.

What the logic demonstrates is that two purposes, retribution and restitution—punishing wrongdoers and making victims whole—are at the core of reparations. If deterrence were the goal, then the imposition of reparations would have to make wrongdoers believe that their misdeeds almost certainly would result in punishment. Reparations, however, are too infrequent to induce this belief. In contrast, both restitution and retribution are more easily balanced by competing interests (e.g., post-hostilities political stability) because they are not generally intended to alter the violator's behavior. Instead, they are victim focused.

It is not the intent here to downplay the role of state responsibility, or the reparations that flow therefrom. That retribution is a valid aim of punishment in the international arena, much as it is in domestic judicial systems, can be argued convincingly. More importantly, reparations contribute to the rebuilding of a global community that has been harmed by a breach of its norms. This perspective makes particular sense in the environmental context because restoration is a costly proposition.

The Gulf War is an excellent case in point. In October 1990, the Security Council passed Resolution 674, which stated that "under international law [Iraq] is liable for any loss, damage or injury arising in regard to Kuwait and third States, and their nationals and corporations, as a result of the invasion and illegal occupation of Kuwait by Iraq."[446] This was followed in March by Resolution 686, which insisted that Iraq "accept in principle its liability under international law for any loss, damage, or injury" that resulted from its occupation of Kuwait.[447] As the Gulf War drew to a close, Resolution 687,

---

445. *Id.* at 8.
446. S.C. Res. 674, U.N. SCOR, 45th Sess., 2951st mtg. para. 8, U.N. Doc. S/RES/674 (1990), *reprinted in* 29 I.L.M. 1561, 1563.
447. S.C. Res. 686, U.N. SCOR, 46th Sess., 2978th mtg. para. 2(b), U.N. Doc. S/RES/686 (1991), *reprinted in* 30 I.L.M. 568, 569.

the ceasefire resolution passed by the Security Council, plainly stated that Iraq was responsible for the damage caused by its invasion and occupation of Kuwait and called for the establishment of a body to handle claims against Iraq from a fund capitalized by a levy on Iraqi oil exports.[448] The United Nations Compensation Commission was established by Resolution 692 and is currently involved in the process of receiving claims.[449] The only money in the fund, however, consists of contributions by several states drawn primarily from frozen Iraqi assets.

By basing liability on Iraq's invasion and illegal occupation of Kuwait rather than an on environment-specific prescription, the Security Council neatly sidestepped the issue of responsibility for violation of the environmental law of war. Specifically, the basis of liability was a violation of article 2(4) of the U.N. Charter, a wrongful resort to force under the *jus ad bellum*. This facilitates the making of claims because framing them in this fashion avoids various technical legal issues involving party status, interpretation of treaty text, the content of customary international law, etc. Essentially, the inquiry is reduced to two issues of fact: causation and damage. Environmental damage is merely one of many forms of compensable damage.[450] This approach

---

448. *See* S.C. Res. 687, U.N. SCOR, 46th Sess., 2981st mtg. paras. 16-19, U.N. Doc. S/RES/687 (1991), *reprinted in* 30 I.L.M. 847, 852.

449. *See* S.C. Res. 692, U.N. SCOR, 46th Sess., 2987th mtg., U.N. Doc. S/RES/692 (1991), *reprinted in* 30 I.L.M. 864. On the work of the Commission, see Ronald J. Bettauer, *The United Nations Compensation Commission—Developments Since October 1992*, 89 AM. J. INT'L L. 416 (1995); John R. Crook, *The United Nations Compensation Commission—A New Structure to Enforce State Responsibility*, 87 AM. J. INT'L L. 144 (1993); Hazel M. Fox, *Reparations and State Responsibility*, *in* THE GULF WAR 1990-91 IN INTERNATIONAL AND ENGLISH LAW, *supra* note 319, at 261; Conrad K. Harper, Protecting the Environment During Armed Conflict: The International Community's Effort to Enforce Norms, Remedy Harms, and Impose Accountability, Paper Presented at the Symposium on the Protection of the Environment During Armed Conflict and Operations Other Than War, *in* NWC SYMPOSIUM PAPERS, *supra* note 13 (manuscript at 7-9, on file with *The Yale Journal of International Law*). The current deadline for claims submission is February 1, 1997. *See* Compensation Commission, Governing Council Decision No. 12, U.N. Doc. S/AC.26/1992/12. The State Department ultimately expects approximately 200 billion dollars in claims to be filed. *See* Harper, *supra* at 7.

450. Included within the damage for which Iraq is responsible is that caused as a result of Coalition operations. This approach is premised on the theory that "but for" Iraq's wrongful acts, Coalition operations would never have occurred. The relevant provision provides:

This [responsibility] will include any loss suffered as a result of: (a) Military operations or threat of military action by either side during the period 2 August 1990 to 2 March 1991 . . . [and] (c) Actions by officials, employees or agents of the Government of Iraq or its controlled entities during that period in connection with the invasion or occupation.

Compensation Commission, Governing Council Decision No. 7, para. 34, U.N. Doc. S/AC.26/1991/7/Rev. 1, *reprinted in* UNITED NATIONS, THE UNITED NATIONS AND THE IRAQ-KUWAIT CONFLICT, 1990-1996, at 429, 429 (1996). The actual damage for which the Iraqis will pay includes: direct environmental damage and the depletion of natural resources as a result of Iraq's unlawful invasion and occupation of Kuwait. This will include losses or expenses resulting from: (a) Abatement and prevention of environmental damage, including expenses directly relating to fighting oil fires and stemming the flow of oil in coastal and international waters; (b) Reasonable measures already taken to clean and restore the environment or future measures which can be documented as reasonably necessary to clean and restore the environment; (c) Reasonable monitoring and assessment of the environmental damage for the purposes of evaluating and abating the harm and restoring the environment; (d) Reasonable monitoring of public health and performing medical screenings for the purposes of investigation and combating increased health risks as a result of the environmental damage; and (e) Depletion of or damage to natural resources.

Id.

casts the net of liability much more broadly than would have been the case if damages for environmental damage had been based on the law of armed conflict's environmental provisions. The disadvantage of this approach is that an opportunity to clarify the substantive law may have been missed.

Finally, mention should be made of individual responsibility. There is little doubt that environmental damage during armed conflict can form the basis for criminal culpability under the laws of war. In addition, the ILC's Draft Code of Crimes Against the Peace and Security of Mankind provides for trial of "an individual who willfully causes or orders the causing of widespread, long-term and severe damage to the natural environment."[451] This applies during both peace and war but, as indicated in the text, is limited to intentional acts (as opposed to negligent or reckless acts). Though the Draft Code is nonbinding, it certainly enhances the argument that individual responsibility should lie in cases of environmental destruction.

In the Gulf War, however, there was no attempt to impose individual responsibility on Iraqi war criminals. The U.S. Army's War Crimes Documentation Center, given the task of assessing Iraqi actions and gathering evidence of violations, specifically found that individual war crimes had been committed.[452] In its final report, the Center characterized the Iraqis as having violated both article 23(g) of Hague IV and article 147 of Geneva Convention IV, even though it described the rationale behind the Iraqi destructive acts as "unclear."[453] Noting that criminal responsibility rests with the commander when he orders, permits, or fails to stop offenses of which he knew or should have known, the report was unambiguous when referring to Saddam Hussein:

> The evidence collected during this investigation establishes a *prima facie* case that the violations of the law of war committed against Kuwaiti civilians and property, and against third party nationals, were so widespread and methodical that they could not have occurred without the authority or knowledge of Saddam Husayn. They are war crimes for which Saddam Husayn, officials of the Ba'ath Party, and his subordinates bear responsibility. However, principal responsibility rests with Saddam Husayn.[454]

Submitted to the President of the Security Council in March 1993, the report was subsequently circulated throughout the United Nations.[455]

Why were no charges ever brought if the evidence was so clear? The reasons are primarily practical, not legal. First, it would have been nearly impossible to bring Saddam Hussein and his cohorts to trial. As a result, any proceedings would have to have been held in absentia. Furthermore, the

---

451. Draft Code of Crimes Against the Peace and Security of Mankind, art. 26, *in Report of the International Law Commission on the Work of Its 43d Session*, U.N. GAOR, 46th Sess., U.N. Doc. A/46/405, *reprinted in* 30 I.L.M. 1563, 1593 (1991).

452. *See* WAR CRIMES DOCUMENTATION CTR., OFFICE OF THE JUDGE ADVOCATE GEN., U.S. ARMY, REPORT ON IRAQI WAR CRIMES (DESERT SHIELD/DESERT STORM) 45–48 (1992) (unclassified version on file at Naval War College Library, Newport, Rhode Island).

453. *See id.* at 10–11.

454. *Id.* at 13.

455. *See Letter Dated 19 March 1993 from the Deputy Permanent Representative of the United States of America to the United Nations Addressed to the President of the Security Council*, U.N. Doc. S/25441 (1993).

possibility of individual criminal punishment would have made it difficult to negotiate war termination with the Iraqis. Those likely to face criminal proceedings were still in firm control of the country and would not have agreed to truce terms that included their arrest. Finally, the political context at the time was important. That a coalition with membership ranging from Syria to Canada held together at all is surprising. Since the attitude toward legal proceedings varied widely, particularly in the Arab world, convening trials in this postwar environment, which was laden with politics and emotion, might well have ruptured the fragile relations that had been forged. War aims had been deliberately delimited to make possible the coalition's creation. To bring Saddam Hussein to trial would have represented a clear expansion beyond those aims.

Did the absence of trials negatively affect the law of war? In the view of the State Department's Legal Adviser, Conrad Harper, trials would have been untimely:

> Whether the international community will one day elect to bring to bear the force of criminal sanctions against those who perpetrate gross and unjustified environmental damage in warfare remains to be seen. In my view, we have not yet arrived at the point where the international community is willing to put its credibility, commitment, and the full force of its conscience behind environmental crimes prosecutions in much the same way that it has demanded accountability in the context of Rwanda and Bosnia.[456]

If his assessment is correct, and there is no reason to believe it is not, then trials would actually have been a step backward; they would have revealed divisiveness within the international legal community over what the prescriptions actually are. While this might have been a useful exercise from a pedagogical perspective, the environmental protection regime would have been weakened by highlighting the legal fault lines in a politically charged matter.

IV. WHERE TO FROM HERE?

A. *Appraising the Present Law*

By now, there should be little question that the prevailing assessment of the environmental law of war is that it is adequate. In response to those who would argue the contrary by pointing to Iraqi actions in the Gulf, adequacy advocates urge that the problem is enforcement, not law. If only Iraq had complied with the existing law of war, all would have been well. They cite the nearly unanimous condemnation of Saddam Hussein's actions as evidence of universal acceptance of the relevant prescriptive norms.

This school of thought may perhaps reflect a bit of goal orientation. Guided by our justifiable indignation over Hussein's appalling actions, we wanted him to be guilty of war crimes. As members of a predominantly positivist legal culture, we also wanted to be able to point to specific provisions of international law that had been violated. Thus, we looked to the

---

456. Harper, *supra* note 449, at 10.

classic workhorses of the law of war—customary law, Hague law, and Geneva law—and predictably found what we needed. Having embraced this position, logically we have to attribute shortcomings in the application of the environmental law of war to something else. Usually one of two culprits is cited, poor enforcement mechanisms or failure to understand what the prescriptions "really mean."

Based on the analysis set forth above, this position proves less than convincing. The existing environmental law of war neither adequately echoes community values nor serves to foster its aspirations. This body of law poses numerous obstacles to effective legal deterrence of environmental damage during armed conflict, obstacles that have been described at length. They may be grouped into several broadly expressed failings.

First and foremost, if law is to serve the aspirations of the global community, it must be of practical application. Unfortunately, the lack of environmental specificity forces us to fall back upon traditional law of war principles such as necessity and proportionality, even when applying treaty law provisions. These customary prescriptions employ continuums and balancing tests, the manipulation of which is rendered more complex by the inclusion of environmental concerns. Additionally, consider the plethora of uncertainties that stand in the way of practical and consistent application. Is peacetime environmental law applicable in armed conflict? Is the environment a separate value category? If so, should it be measured in an anthropocentric or inherent value context? What weight should be accorded to environmental values? How far should chains of causation stretch? How should the great uncertainty of environmental impact be handled? These and other issues raised throughout this Article are difficult to contemplate in the sterile environment of academia, let alone in the fog of wartime friction. This would be so even in a monocultural context; to expect consistent results across cultures is ambitious, to say the least.

The second problem is that of definitions. Environment-specific treaty law employs the terms "widespread," "long-term," and "severe" in its key provisions. Since these appear to have become the agreed-upon terms of art to be used, one would imagine that they would enjoy a common understanding. However, their meaning has been variously interpreted, for instance, by the U.S. Army, the German Government, the drafters of Protocol I, and ENMOD signatories. This variation complicates application of the environmental law of war.

Finally, the law that does serve to protect the environment lacks internal coherence. Each facet was developed in response to very different problems, in varying contexts, and at different times. No effort has been made to reconcile its various components, or to seek the protective synergism that complementary humanitarian law offers.[457] In some cases, most notably the definitional quandary just mentioned, this lack of coherence operates to weaken existing prescriptions by muddying the waters. What remains is a body of law that offers only haphazard protection to the environment,

---

457. As was the intent, for example, in the drafting of Protocol I vis-à-vis the Geneva Convention of 1949. *See supra* Subsection III.C.3.

protection characterized by significant gaps.

That the law proper presents problems is clear. But what about the direction in which it is headed? At the outset of this Article, the directional nature of law was highlighted. Is the law on course? Is it moving towards enhancement of world order, or are the trends that have been identified ultimately counterproductive?

While the general vector of the environmental law of armed conflict is correct, it risks going too far. It is absolutely essential that the environment be considered *qua* environment, not simply as yet another civilian object. This is so because of the unique characteristics that the environment exhibits. In particular, warfare affects nonbelligerents environmentally, either in their own territory or in the global commons. To diminish the water quality of a river, for example, is to harm all of the riparian states, not simply the target state. To spew pollutants into the atmosphere is to render damage elsewhere dependent on the whims of the wind. Environmental damage is often difficult to circumscribe, regardless of the intent of the actor.

The qualitative distinction between environmental and more traditional damage is also demonstrated by the difference in the scope of reverberating effects. Traditional warfare is replete with instances of reverberation, some intentional, some not. Scholars and practitioners may quibble about the severity and proportionality of bombing electrical targets during the Gulf War, for example, but no one would suggest either that its consequences were limited to destruction of the target, or that reverberations were irrelevant to proportionality calculations. Even so, the environment is different, for its very essence is interconnectedness. While it is true that warfare may cause harm beyond the direct application of force, it is difficult for acts of war *not* to cause such harm to the environment. Moreover, in nonenvironmental damage, the chain of reverberation is usually much shorter; a building is blown up, only to be rebuilt or have its occupants or function move elsewhere. The impact of environmental damage, in contrast, often will play out through many iterations; an effect on one species influences many, a phenomenon which, in turn, repeats itself at each higher level. It is much more pervasive than the traditional damage to which we are accustomed in armed conflict.

Not only is the impact more likely to be cast broadly, but it is also more likely to prove irreversible. There is no way, for example, to recreate a species that has been destroyed. If that species constitutes the primary food source for others, the reverberating effect will be no less harmful to them. The same is true of the many natural resources on which life, human or otherwise, relies. Some means of warfare may have mutagenic effects, and, unfortunately, science is incapable of returning genetic structures to their original states. Finally, and perhaps most importantly, many species that have suffered harm, including humans, can survive if provided sufficient time, space, and resources to do so. Destruction or contamination of an area, however, denies all species both space and resources. Thus, unlike most other damage in warfare, environmental devastation truly may represent crossing the Rubicon of survival.

There is little doubt that the law has moved, albeit slowly and in a very limited way, toward recognizing the uniqueness of the environment and its need for special protection. This is apparent in Protocol I and ENMOD's environment-specific provisions, the first such provisions in conventions dealing with armed conflict. It is also evident in the various peacetime instruments that have come into effect over the past several decades and in hortatory and aspirational language found in various nonbinding sources, such as the Stockholm and Rio Declarations. Indeed, even though the Security Council resolutions demanding compensation from Iraq were based on nonenvironmentally related *jus ad bellum* grounds, the environment was specifically singled out, in and of itself, as a damaged entity generating Iraqi liability.

There is every indication that the law is moving in the right direction. The problem is that it is moving too far. What law is, and how it operates, really depends on the cognitive prism through which it (and the context in which it will be applied) is viewed. These prisms can be thought of as placed along a continuum. Until Vietnam, the environment was not seen as having any independent existence, a view representing one extreme of the continuum. Following that conflict, the environment began to be recognized as a distinct entity, albeit primarily in anthropocentric terms.

Conceptually, anthropocentrism is not a point on the continuum, but rather an area along it within which there are varying degrees and styles of the perspective. For instance, article 55 of Protocol I is framed in terms of "health or survival," whereas the Rio Declaration placed great weight on the interests of developing states. At the limit of anthropocentric environmentalism are those who would weight the environment using measures such as its aesthetic contribution, or perhaps even the sense of placement in the greater scheme of things that it offers humanity. Yet in all of these cases, the human variable is a factor. One may disagree with the precise value that is posited, but at least all valuations are operating from within the same broad context.

The problem is that some would move beyond the limits of anthropocentrism into valuation based on intrinsic worth. An excellent example of this approach is found in Professor Verwey's thoughtful work. A pioneer in identifying the perspectives that have been developed in this Article, Professor Verwey argues for "common recognition" of three principles:

> 1. the indivisibility of a healthy environment as an indispensable condition for the survival of present and future human generations;
> 2. the necessity to disconnect the legal protection of the environment in times of armed conflict from its anthropocentric legal enclosure; [and]
> 3. the need to expand the protective scope of the relevant rules beyond the current level of merely prohibiting known or expectable and directly demonstrable environmental damage.[458]

Devotion to the first principle is shared by many anthropocentrics; after all, it is couched in anthropocentric terms. Similarly, the third is a principle of causation more likely to be embraced by intrinsic value advocates, but not

---

458. Verwey, *Protection, supra* note 13, at 33.

exclusively by them. After all, one might want to prohibit environmental damage that "may"[459] occur because if it does it will affect humans negatively. In contrast, the second principle, at least as stated,[460] is classic intrinsic valuation. It essentially urges protection of the environment regardless of what it does for humanity. This does not mean that the contribution that the environment makes to humans will be ignored, but that the value of the environment in and of itself will also be considered.

Although it is absolutely clear that anthropocentric approaches of one sort or the other dominate thinking about the impact of war on the environment, there are indications that the law is moving in the intrinsic value direction. The fact that it proved necessary to satisfy both camps by including two environmental provisions in Protocol I demonstrates the degree of support for the approach. Other examples of the degree of support for intrinsic valuation include the menu of options in the proposal offered at the London Conference by Professor Plant, as well as the general tenor of recommendations by organizations such as Greenpeace.[461]

This trend has troubling implications. First, it is one thing to recognize that the environment per se must be protected, and quite another to urge that the environment should be evaluated apart from anthropocentric considerations. In the former case, the uniqueness of the environment is recognized, but the processes of valuation remain relatively intact. Though valuation is more complex when the environment is factored in, anthropocentric valuation not only provides a familiar frame of reference, but it also keeps balancing tests two-dimensional. In purely intrinsic value analysis, in contrast, process and substance are thrown askew. As illustrated in the discussion of customary international law principles, introduction of a third variable necessitates a three-way balancing test among the environment, human values, and military advantage. Furthermore, if human terms are not used to value the environment, what standard should be used? The difficulties of cross-cultural anthropocentric value paradigms pale beside those presented by intrinsic valuation.

In the end, intrinsic valuation leaves us with an incredibly complex process that defies practical application and encourages divisiveness within the community of those who wish to ensure environmental protection during warfare. Well-meaning efforts to enhance protection by recognizing the intrinsic value of the environment will have exactly the opposite result. The flawed prescriptions currently in place will collapse under the weight of attempts to sort through the approach in practice.

There is an even more basic problem with the intrinsic value perspective

---

459. *See id.* at 38–40.
460. Professor Verwey's discussion of the principle includes the concept of per se protection. *See id.* at 36–37. Indeed, he speaks of the possibility of recognizing the environment as the common heritage of mankind, a particularly anthropocentric characterization. The mere fact that the environment is protected per se does not imply that it is not valued for its anthropocentric character. It simply means that it is considered an independent and unique entity. Whether it is valued intrinsically, anthropocentrically, or in both ways is a separate question.
461. *See The Gulf War: Environment as a Weapon, supra* note 96, at 220–23 (remarks of Sebia Hawkins of Greenpeace International).

than determining how to conduct balancing or what weight to attribute to balanced values. Does the international community really want to adopt an approach that would sacrifice human interests to environmental ones? Intrinsic value advocates probably would rush to protest that this is not their intention. But of course it is. Any time one attributes autonomous value to the environment, one risks the possibility that trying to safeguard it will operate at cross purposes with other values. The fact that values conflict is the very raison d'être of balancing tests. Closing territory to military activities may have very real human consequences. Perhaps an attacking force will be forced into an avenue of attack that places the population at greater risk. Maybe environmental restrictions will disallow tactics that would enhance protection of the civilian population. For instance, if smoke that results in extensive collateral damage is the only way to prevent an aerial attack, do we want to deny the tactic to a victimized state with no other means of defending itself?

The issue of sacrificing human values presents itself in two guises. The easier of the two occurs when environmental values are added to the balancing process. Can human values be outweighed by the intrinsic value of the environment? Most reasonable commentators would agree that there are times when humans should be placed at risk to protect the environment. By rejecting intrinsic valuation, the framing of this quite logical assertion in an either/or fashion can be avoided. Viewed anthropocentrically, and very broadly so, the question is not when do human values have to be sacrificed, but rather what are the net human values that will be put into the equation.

A much more disturbing dilemma arises in attempts to determine when the environment should be protected without considering human values at all, that is, without resorting to a balancing test. This is exactly what article 35(3) does; once the level of damage reaches a certain point, the protection kicks in regardless of countervailing human values. Prescriptions crafted in this fashion are extraordinary in that they reject the premise that there are times when human values outweigh environmental ones. For instance, option (a) of the Plant proposal prohibits methods or means of warfare that are intended to, or may, cause any damage to the environment.[462] This is intrinsic value at its extreme. There is no balancing of any sort, only an absolute prohibition. Yet if failure to acknowledge the environment in and of itself is objectionable, why is it any less objectionable to ignore the human factor? Are humans not as much an integral part of the global ecosystem as plants, other animals, or nonliving resources? What is it that makes us less worthy of protection than the environment's other components? Of course, this perspective represents one extreme of the anthropocentric-intrinsic value continuum, and very few responsible individuals who have considered the issue seriously would go so far. Nevertheless, it does constitute a logical and directional conclusion drawn from the premises underlying the intrinsic value approach.

It is important not to read too much into these criticisms of intrinsic value. First, they are not meant to imply that the environment lacks intrinsic value. Instead, the comments are only designed to highlight the pitfalls associated with decisionmaking processes and standards that incorporate an

---

462. *See supra* text accompanying notes 94–95.

intrinsic value component. It is unfortunate that intrinsic value cannot easily be folded into balancing processes without generating inconsistent and divisive results, but that inability is an acceptable cost of maintaining the level of protection that the environment and humanity currently enjoy.

Second, the rejection of intrinsic valuation should not be read as suggesting that it is inappropriate to create "absolute" prohibitions—those in which there is no balancing of interests. On the contrary, they can serve as useful short hand for clear-cut cases, or situations of *res ipsa loquitur*, to borrow from tort law principles. In other words, certain environmental damage (considered anthropocentrically) is so likely to outweigh any potential military advantage that it makes sense to agree upon the prescriptions in advance to facilitate normative clarity and precision. Such prescriptions may be framed in terms of weapons (e.g., persistent chemicals), tactics (e.g., nuclear ground bursts), targets (e.g., nuclear power facilities), or effects (e.g., long-term, widespread, and severe). Furthermore, it is not necessary to establish their prohibitive effect at a damage level above that which traditional legal analysis would yield. This is because the applicative intent of law is designed to foster more than case-specific "right" results. The broader goals of general and specific deterrence require prescriptive systems that are precise and understandable, and that lend themselves to practical enforcement. In isolated cases, right results may have to be sacrificed to secure the overall contributions that absolute prohibitions make to the greater good.

B. *What Is To Be Done?*

The proposition that the law is inadequate raises the question of what to do about its deficiencies. Most of the discussion has centered around the desirability of a new law of armed conflict convention to govern environmental damage during warfare. Notable among the proposals have been Professor Plant's model elements and Greenpeace's call for a "Fifth Geneva Convention." The prevailing view, however, is that a convention actually might prove counterproductive. Not surprisingly, those taking this position also generally assert the adequacy of existing prescriptions. If the law is adequate, why take on the daunting task of drafting a new convention?

However, an assertion that the law is insufficient does not necessarily lead to the conclusion that a new treaty is necessary. Two additional issues must be addressed. First, if the law is insufficient, is an international convention the best remedy, or are alternatives such as domestic legislation or the adoption of common military manuals preferable? Second, even if a treaty is the optimal choice, given the current international political and legal context, is the time ripe for the enormous effort that would have to be mounted to secure an effective convention? This Article concludes that a convention is the answer, but that it might prove counterproductive to pursue one aggressively right now.

With regard to the need for an international agreement, it is useful to consider: (1) what the law needs to do, (2) whether those tasks are being accomplished by the existing law, and, if not, (3) whether a treaty would improve matters. For law to be effective, it must deter wrongful conduct. This purpose requires clearly enunciated practical norms and the support of the community of nations. Otherwise, states would not know the standards by which their conduct would be measured, nor those to which they should hold others; this scenario would be particularly disruptive to a legal regime which, albeit evolving, generally counsels against interference in the affairs of other states.

Does the present environmental law of war meet these requirements? Without reiterating the many points made throughout this Article, it is fair to say that it falls short. The law is internally inconsistent, unclear, subject to varying definitions, haphazardly generated, and lacks the support of all relevant actors. A convention, on the other hand, could address the issue comprehensively, thereby providing the requisite consistency and clarity. Explicating the environmental conduct expected of states would limit destructive activities by those concerned with remaining within the confines of legality. It also would facilitate condemnation and reaction when rogue states violate the agreed-upon and articulated prescriptions. In particular, it would make it harder for states that might be so inclined to look the other way in the face of violations. The net result would be an increase in the deterrent effect of this body of law.

In terms of practical impact, almost as important would be the existence of an agreed-upon set of norms that could be adopted by the world's armed forces in their military manuals and serve as the basis for substantively common training. This is the purpose of the ICRC Guidelines. Regrettably, the ICRC effort has borne little fruit thus far, an unsurprising fact given the hodgepodge of law to which it had to resort in developing its guidelines.[463] A comprehensive international convention on the subject presumably would resolve this obstacle. This, in turn, would advance the emergence of a common operational code among armed forces and policymakers.

Despite the advantages of a treaty, admittedly, there would be downsides. Some critics of the idea contend that a treaty is not the appropriate legal instrument to address the topic. For instance, in order to secure agreement, treaties are often subject to declarations, understandings, and reservations. The result is a complicated web of legal relationships that vary based on the parties involved in a particular issue. Indeed, this phenomenon was illustrated in many of the instruments discussed above, such as Protocol I, ENMOD, and the 1925 Gas Protocol. Given the variety of perspectives on the environmental law of war, declarations, understandings, and reservations are likely; the complexity of an already complex subject would thereby swell. Opponents also note that treaties become outdated, whereas customary law, based as it is in state practice, is more adaptive. The pace of scientific discovery exacerbates this distinction, for when dealing with technologically driven agreements there is always the risk that science will outpace their prescriptive utility.

Such arguments are well taken, but not entirely convincing. Even with reservations, a convention almost certainly would be more comprehensive and

---

463. Another obstacle is the fact that the United States is not a party to one of the ICRC Guidelines' key reference points, Protocol I.

consistent than the current body of law, composed as it is of everything from custom, to turn-of-the-century agreements that are silent on the issue of the environment, to 1970s vintage conventions that still are not universally accepted. Moreover, while international agreements can become outdated, once the ground has been broken with the first iteration of a treaty it is easier to update the regime later.[464] Arguably, then, the risk of becoming dated is outweighed by the benefits that clarity would provide over the life of a treaty. Of course, this assumes that the convention is well done and that it does not create problems such as those raised by Protocol I and ENMOD's terminological schizophrenia. It also assumes that international consensus can be reached on the subject—a major assumption, to say the least.

Despite the usefulness of a convention, is the time right for one? There are very practical reasons to argue that it is not. United States experience with major international treaties has not always been positive. In the cases of both the Law of the Sea Convention and Protocol I, the United States actively participated in negotiations, only to reject what the respective diplomatic conferences produced. Nearly two decades later, the United States is still not a party to either agreement (although this may change with the LOS Convention in the near future). Regardless of the substantive merits of our position, to be the odd man out in these widely accepted treaty regimes certainly is not an enviable position.

Is there any greater likelihood of success in drafting an environmental convention, one with comprehensive norms that are more than hortatory or aspirational, on which all parties can agree? Given the anthropocentric versus intrinsic value and developing versus developed fault lines described earlier, the search for consensus would certainly be challenging. This raises the question of whether it would be preferable to work with the existing prescriptions, accepting their limitations and benefiting from what little common ground does exist. To commence full-fledged negotiations at a point in the development of the law at which normative limits are so unclear and cognitive perspectives so contradictory would be ill advised.

Additionally, the effectiveness of any new convention would be limited by the state of science. As the Gulf War experience made clear, there is much we do not understand about both the effects of war on the environment and its use to harm one's enemies. Is it appropriate to initiate a treaty in an environment of relative ignorance, or would it be better to work with current prescriptions until the quantum and quality of knowledge improve? This is a particularly relevant issue if the goal is to include provisions that address specific means and methods of warfare, rather than abstract descriptions of effect (e.g., widespread, long-term, severe). It will be difficult to reach consensus on weapons, tactics, and targets absent a firmer scientific base than that existing during the Gulf War.

To summarize, we clearly need a convention, and should begin

---

464. This happened with the Law of the Sea Convention. The U.S. objected to the seabed mining provisions of the treaty. *See* LOS Convention, *supra* note 172, pt. XI. Another example is Protocol I, which was designed to update the Geneva Conventions. *See* Protocol I, *supra* note 8. While it has proven somewhat difficult to secure universal agreement on Protocol I, the process of securing consensus probably moves as quickly as the evolution of customary principles.

preparatory work toward formulating a coherent position on its broad parameters. Today we are far enough removed from the emotionalism evoked by the Gulf War environmental destruction to explore rationally the merits and nature of a treaty regime that would respond to contemporary concerns about environmental protection and give warfighters the normative guidance they deserve. Exploratory first steps would force leading states to acknowledge the existing legal shortcomings and begin the process of rectifying them.

That said, *at this point in time*, the benefits of aggressively pursuing an environmental law of war convention are outweighed by the risk that it would further weaken the inadequate regime that currently exists to protect the environment. Weakening could result from the international political machinations that would attend multilateral negotiations, a possibility compounded by the risks associated with negotiating with a less than robust information base. In order to forge the consensus necessary today, an agreement would inevitably end in highly diluted prescriptions; neither law nor science is sufficiently developed to give the effort a fighting chance.

The belief that this is not a propitious time to take on a major new treaty effort is shared by both the ICRC's Hans-Peter Gasser and Conrad Harper of the State Department, though they do not necessarily embrace the approach taken in this Article to arrive at this conclusion. At the Naval War College Conference, Mr. Gasser argued:

> In terms of time, energy and resources, the cost of drafting, negotiating and adopting a new international treaty even on less difficult and controversial issues is today very high indeed. Moreover, failure of a codification attempt may in the end be more harmful to the cause than leaving the law as it is. And there is always the risk that a new treaty may not be ratified by a large number of states.[465]

Speaking at the same conference, Mr. Harper noted:

> To the extent that widespread agreement on new laws and standards could be reached—and I have my doubts—the resulting agreement might likely resemble a lowest, common denominator, decidedly unhelpful in dealing with hard cases. Or, in order to garner consensus, a new agreement might well be a model of ambiguity, the value of which could also be fairly questioned.[466]

Given the current state of affairs, both are correct—for the moment.

This analysis raises the question of what can be done now to alleviate the immediate difficulties posed by the existing law. First, it is self-evident that those with influence on the international lawmaking process need to reconsider the off-the-shelf assessment of the law's adequacy. Problems that have been identified need to be worked through in a measured, reflective, and comprehensive fashion. The dialogue must continue to evolve, and the tough issues—anthropocentric versus intrinsic valuation, the contextuality of law, and law's directional and temporal character—have to be faced head on.

In the interim, states can begin addressing the issue individually. Arguably, the United States should seriously reconsider its refusal to ratify Protocol I. Objections to the agreement that were valid in an era of bipolarity

---

465. Gasser, *supra* note 355, at 5–6.
466. Harper, *supra* note 449, at 9.

104   YALE JOURNAL OF INTERNATIONAL LAW   [Vol. 22: 1

may no longer be as compelling today. As to the environment, it is true that Protocol I's relevant provisions are less than perfect. Yet in the new global paradigm, the United States needs to be much more concerned about becoming the *victim* of environmental destruction than about having its operational hands tied by the Convention's prohibitions. This argument is particularly compelling if our concerns extend to the environments of potential allies and if we reflect upon who our likely adversaries might be. Finally, we should not forget that the United States is better able to adjust to limitations on methods and means of warfare than our enemies because of our overwhelming technological superiority, the redundancy of our capabilities, and the quality of the forces with which we are most likely to be allied. These factors give us some leeway in accepting legal regimes that, though imperfect, represent an overall step forward. Simply put, what is needed is a de novo legal and operational net assessment. We need to look at the big picture, not to become trapped in the minutiae.

Unfortunately, measured reflection and reconsideration of our position on international treaties will not solve the warfighters' immediate dilemma, a daunting void of normative guidance. The problem is very real. How should judge advocates advise their commanders? What decision standards should commanders employ when confronted with the prospect that their militarily necessary actions might damage the environment? What can we do to redress the compelling need for uniform and usable guidance?

Obviously, the armed forces must continue to seek a common understanding of the environmental law of war. Positive steps in this direction are apparent throughout the Department of Defense. Sponsorship of the conference at the Naval War College and publication of its proceedings, addition of the subject to the Environmental Law Advanced Course at the Air Force Judge Advocate General School, and devotion of a chapter to the environment in the Army's *Operational Law Handbook* are all extremely laudable. We need to continue addressing the subject aggressively.

However, the most important and immediate step the United States can take to foster clarity presents itself in the new multiservice law of war manual that is currently being drafted.[467] Once in place, this single source will set a uniform standard for operations by U.S. forces. Perhaps even more significantly, the manual represents a chance to influence the rest of the world in the development of this area of law. Other armed forces inevitably will follow the U.S. lead. As an example of this tendency, consider Naval Warfare Publication 9, *The Commander's Handbook on the Law of Naval Operations*. Widely recognized as the most authoritative official source setting forth the naval law of armed conflict, this handbook is kept within arm's reach of the sailors of many nations and serves as their guide to the law of armed conflict.[468] The new multiservice manual promises to be even more

---

467. For an excellent analysis of the roles of military manuals, see W. Michael Reisman & William K. Leitzau, *Moving International Law from Theory to Practice: The Role of Military Manuals in Effectuating the Law of Armed Conflict, in* THE LAW OF NAVAL OPERATIONS 1 (Naval War College International Law Studies vol. 64, Horace B. Robertson, Jr. ed., 1991).

468. The new Navy manual, NWP 1-14M, *supra* note 178, is certain to be as widely adopted as its predecessor, NWP 9.

influential, particularly in light of the ever-growing leadership role that the United States is playing in international military operations, including MOOTW.

But there is more involved‹ than simply articulating the formal law. Military manuals serve an important function in making law. As Michael Reisman and William Leitzau have noted in their excellent article on the subject, military manuals

> are an essential component in the international lawmaking process, often the litmus test of whether a putative prescriptive exercise has produced effective law. Without adequate dissemination, this putative international lawmaking is an exercise in the elaboration of myth through *lex simulata* rather than the installation of an effective operational code.[469]

In other words, law acquires normative relevance when it becomes internalized, both by the system and by those who are part of it. Systemic internalization is accomplished through acceptance and dissemination of the manual by authoritative military decisionmakers. Individual internalization is fostered by the system's acceptance (military personnel tend to grant the system great deference) and through practice of the norms set forth. Ultimately, an operational code emerges.

Thus, a unique opportunity is at hand, not only to provide our policymakers and warfighters with the legal guidance they require, but also to shape the law itself. Drawing on the analysis presented throughout this Article, and cognizant of the importance of keeping law of war manuals simple (they are designed primarily for warfighters, not lawyers), we can envision the rough outlines of such a manual.

First, the manual's provisions should apply as a matter of policy whenever U.S. forces resort to force, unless the rules of engagement approved by the appropriate authorities (given the political ramifications, most likely the National Command Authorities) indicate otherwise.[470] Avoiding legal dissection of international versus noninternational armed conflict issues in the manual will avoid confusion by troops in the field. A presumption in favor of international armed conflict standards also will help preclude after-the-fact criticism of U.S. actions. Another topic that should be avoided in the manual is the applicability of peacetime law. Its prescriptions are simply too uncertain, and its applicability too complex, for it to be incorporated directly into a usable law of war manual at this time.[471]

The applicability of general customary law principles such as necessity, proportionality, and humanity to environmental damage merits particular

---

469. Reisman & Leitzau, *supra* note 467, at 1.

470. The Army's current position is that the 1993 Chemical Weapons Convention is not generally applicable to MOOTW. However, U.S. policy limiting the uses of chemicals to those set forth in Executive Order 11,850 for riot control agents would apply to MOOTW. *See* OPERATIONAL LAW HANDBOOK, *supra* note 179, at 5-5; *see also supra* notes 427–28 and accompanying text.

471. A caveat that peacetime law may be applicable to the extent it is consistent with the law of armed conflict could be included as a footnote if an annotated version is produced (as is being done with NWP 1-14M, *supra* note 178). The ICRC Guidelines provide an example of how such a provision might read: "International environmental agreements and relevant rules of customary law may continue to be applicable in times of armed conflict to the extent that they are not inconsistent with the applicable law of armed conflict." ICRC Guidelines, *supra* note 149, para. 5.

106   YALE JOURNAL OF INTERNATIONAL LAW   [Vol. 22: 1

emphasis in the manual. Given the confusion it has generated, the concept of military necessity needs to be clarified by pointing out that it is a prerequisite to legality, not a device to excuse deviations from environmental norms.[472] For the sake of clarity, it should also be pointed out that all of the prohibitions extend to the global commons (e.g., the high seas). Similarly, "property" and "civilian objects" are best defined as including *res communes*, such as air.

Also deserving emphasis is the concept of protection of the environment per se. This can be done by including a separate section on the environment or adding qualifiers at appropriate places in the text. Despite the need to address the environment as an independent entity, careful draftsmanship is required to avoid creating the impression that an intrinsic value approach is being adopted. Just because the environment deserves to be singled out for protection does not imply that it should be valued intrinsically instead of anthropocentrically.

Indeed, special care must be taken not to incorporate, even unintentionally, intrinsic value concepts. This is most likely to be done through the inclusion of absolute prohibitions. To minimize this possibility, it is best to articulate prohibitions in terms of weapons, tactics, or targets—not results or effects. All absolute prohibitions present some risk. They are essentially a form of legal shorthand that supplants the need to do proportionality calculations in situations analogous to *res ipsa loquitur*. By their very nature, there will be times when absolute prohibitions preclude an action that would otherwise be acceptable. That is the cost of having them. Depending on how they are written, there is even a risk that their application, by operating outside human concerns, actually would *lower* the level of protection provided to humans. To avoid this unacceptable result, a provision could be included in the manual to the effect that an absolute prohibition does not apply if, using the Protocol I, article 55 language, the prohibition would unacceptably heighten the risk to human health and survival.

Target-based prohibitions should include the Protocol I ban on attacking "objects indispensable to the civilian population" when the purpose is to deny those objects to the civilian population. Since the United States supports this Protocol I prohibition, it is reasonable to state it in the absolute.[473] As a matter of policy, the manual should also include the Convention's prohibition on attacking works containing dangerous forces. This would represent only a minor limitation on U.S. operations, for it would be the exceptional case in which the benefits of attacking them would outweigh the political costs of doing so. Nevertheless, since the prohibition would be policy-based, an exception for NCA-approved strikes is advisable.

Weapons-specific prescriptions found in international law (e.g., the Chemical Weapons Convention when ratified) and U.S. policy pronouncements (e.g., Executive Order 11,850) are equally necessary. In light

---

472. The ICRC Guidelines correctly state the standard: "Destruction of the environment not justified by military necessity violates international humanitarian law. . . .The general prohibition to destroy civilian objects, unless such destruction is justified by military necessity, also protects the environment." ICRC Guidelines, *supra* note 149, paras. 8–9.

473. The technique is considered a form of starvation. *See* DEPLOYMENT DESKBOOK, *supra* note 318, tab 12, paras. 1.8.5–1.8.5.1.

of the political implications deriving from Protocol III to the Conventional Weapons Convention, the use of incendiaries against environmental targets should be prohibited as a matter of policy except when employed against a target that is a military objective clearly separated from concentrations of civilians,[474] or when otherwise authorized in rules of engagement approved by appropriate authorities. Given the political risks, it would be reasonable to designate the NCA as the appropriate authority, though this power could be delegated.

Since not all possible weapons, tactics, and targets could possibly be addressed in the manual, it will be necessary to incorporate some result-based prohibitions. As a general rule, they should contain such caveats as suggested above. Of course, the most compelling dilemma regarding such prescriptions is whether to adopt the "widespread, long-standing, and/or severe" formula. This formula should be adopted. It is clearly the prevailing standard: It is found in both of the binding instruments directly on point, Protocol I and ENMOD, as well as in publications such as the ICRC Guidelines and the German manual. The only potential alternative is the "due regard" criterion offered in NWP 1-14M[475] and the San Remo Manual.[476] While it may make sense to employ this maritime standard of care in the naval context, it is not widely accepted as a standard in land warfare, nor is there any firm basis for its use in existing environmental law of war. Additionally, it is questionable whether due regard adds much beyond traditional customary international law principles; even if it did, it is a standard that invites subjective interpretation. For better or worse, "widespread, long-standing, and/or severe" is the standard of choice in the international community. Therefore, the United States should adopt it as its own and direct its efforts at securing consensus on a suitable definition.

Working towards a common understanding is the key. Since the standard is ill-defined, the fashion in which the manual unravels the definitional maze will prove very influential. How might it do so? To begin with, when speaking of manipulating environmental processes as a weapon, the definitions should be drawn from the ENMOD Understanding. After all, that particular component of the legal regime is relatively settled. However, what of damage to the environment? An excellent approach is that adopted by the Army in defining the Protocol I terms in its *Operational Law Handbook*. "Long-term" is measured in decades (twenty or thirty years), a definition that enjoys the support of most practitioners and scholars because it is viewed as comporting with the original intent of the drafters. Since there is no indication of what was meant by the term "widespread" in the Protocol I drafting process, it makes sense to defer to its sole legal definition, that of ENMOD. Though ENMOD definitions were specifically said not to bind other agreements, this does not negate the logic of using them to minimize confusion if doing so makes sense contextually. Thus, as the Army does, the new manual should

---

474. The Protocol allows use in this circumstance. *See* Protocol III, *supra* note 134, art. 2, para. 3.

475. *See supra* note 178.

476. *See supra* note 171.

describe the term as implying damage that extends to several hundred kilometers. With regard to "severe," the Handbook refers to the "prejudices the health or survival of the population" language of article 55.[477] While it certainly is essential to include damage at this level, ENMOD's definition is more comprehensive. As noted, "severe" was defined in the Understanding related to article I as "involving serious or significant disruption to human life, natural and economic resources or other assets," a definition that encompasses "health and survival," but also has the advantage of extending to "property."[478] Extension of the definition in this manner is consistent with Protocol I protections generally, and with the international law of armed conflict more broadly.

Except when restating the ENMOD prohibition, the phrase "widespread, long-term, and severe" should be cast in the conjunctive. To do otherwise would set an excessively high level of protection. It would be illogical to forbid absolutely an action that caused long-term and widespread environmental damage if that damage were insignificant. Similarly, if the damage were long-term and severe, but isolated, an absolute ban would constitute overreaching. A better result would be achieved through simple proportionality analysis.

Finally, inclusion of a section on responsibility is advisable, though care must be taken not to overstate the case. Individual responsibility could be addressed by noting that breach of the manual's provisions may constitute a violation of the Uniform Code of Military Justice and, in certain cases, amount to a war crime. A provision on state responsibility should point out that states may be held responsible for the acts of their military forces, and that obligations owed under international law to nonbelligerents generally remain in effect during armed conflict.

Hopefully, these suggestions will offer food for thought as the effort to craft the new law of war manual gains momentum. Whatever the outcome, the drafters must understand the great opportunity and responsibility that the task presents. There is probably no endeavor currently underway anywhere having a greater potential for shaping the environmental law of the future.

V. CONCLUSION

After all is said and done, the assertion that the present environmental law of war is adequate does not hold water. It is an imprecise law, full of gaps and competing perspectives. The present standards are simply not sufficiently robust to survive the hostile environment of international relations. Indeed, even after the Gulf War, a case involving near-universal condemnation of the resulting environmental destruction, the basis for state responsibility was found elsewhere. This should be of enormous concern to those who value the environment.

Despite its shortcomings, the time is not ripe for a top-to-bottom reworking of the law. We first have to admit that we have a

---

477. *See supra* note 337 and accompanying text.
478. *See supra* note 395 and accompanying text.

problem—acknowledge that the emperor has no clothes, if you will—and then we must attempt to better our understanding of the problem. To do that, it is necessary to identify legal trends and uncover the law's motivating forces. If we are ever to develop a consensus, we must also grasp the varying cognitive prisms through which the topic is viewed. Hopefully, this Article has contributed to the crucial dialogue that must precede further progress in the field.

Finally, we must understand that this is not an ivory tower exercise for theorists who roam the halls of academia. On the contrary, the environment affects us all in ways that we are only beginning to comprehend. Just as important, the issue has real-world operational implications for commanders in the field. They deserve guidance that is clear, comprehensive, and practical. In the end, this is what the entire discussion has been about—giving warfighters the tools they require to safeguard the values of the global community effectively. If this Article has contributed in any way to that end, then the time and effort expended will have been very well rewarded indeed.

Part IV
Tactics

[15]

RUSES OF WAR AND PROHIBITION OF PERFIDY(*)

Dieter FLECK,

Federal Ministry of Defence, B.R.D.

TABLE OF CONTENTS

(*) Paper presented at the VIth Congress of the International Society for Military
Law and the Law of War, The Hague, 22-25 May 1973 (Committee for the protection of
human life in armed conflicts).

D. FLECK

1. – MILITARY AND LEGAL SIGNIFICANCE

1. Military Aspects.

Current international treaties (1) deal with ruses of war in far too general terms which reflect the minor significance attached to the element of deception by the traditional "strategical" school of thought. According to Clausewitz (2), "sound judgement and perspicacity are more useful and essential qualities in a strategist than ruse, although the latter is no disadvantage, provided that it does not obtain at the expense of other necessary character traits — which, admittedly, happens only far too often"

Even in accordance with this traditional view recourse to ruses of war ought to be subjected to more detailed regulations since they come within the sphere of "tactics" where two reasons require a precise regulation : the diversity of tactical combat situations and the fighting soldier's limited possibilities to asses the overall situation.

In addition, it is held in modern doctrine that ruses of war are not confined to the sphere of tactics. As early as in 1759, Frederick the Great of Prussia held the opinion "that ruses are more essential than force and that wit and imagination should rank higher than mere bravery".

Some armies of the 20th century voiced complaints over the adversary's supposed superiority in the employment of ruses in combat, and it was notably in the period after the first world war that ruse as manifested in mimicry tactics, camouflaging, deception and psychological combat were regarded as an essential feature of modern warfare. True, the significance of ruses in modern war should not be overestimated. Many combat methods characterized by the element of deception were devised at a time where friend and foe used to meet at close range.

These cases are not likely to recur today in any given situation. In addition, the technical precision of modern means and methods of war is unfavourable to the employment of ruses. Exploits formerly decisive for the outcome of a battle are nowadays of merely marginal importance. Hence, many ruses applied successfully in the past have no room in today's warfare. On the other hand, successful ruses may, given the greater measure of mechanization, speed, and vulnerability of modern armed forces, have a much greater effect than in earlier times; I would like to refer in this connection to the example of jet pilots who are led astray by the employment of electronic means of deception. Viewed against this background, the role of deception in modern warfare is by no means insignificant (3).

At the same time, it can be said that the importance of ruse will increase in step with the degree of flexibility required for the operations of armed forces. If mobility, deception, and exploitation of the adversary's errors are

Ruses of War

nowadays required even on the strategic level, a reform of current international law should be aimed not only at confirming the admissibility of specific ruses of war, but also at developing basic rules that permit a distinction between permissible acts and prohibited perfidy (4).

Furthermore, problems relating to the admissibility of ruses of war are basically different from those posed by the use of violence, which, for instance, have thus far dominated the discussions over war crimes. In contrast to the rules prohibiting area bombardments, the killing of hostages, deportations or the ill-treatment of civilians and prisoners of war, the prohibition of perfidious ruses of war presupposes a greater measure of legal understanding. It would be unreasonable to confront the individual soldier with this problem in the absence of unequivocal legal norms covering this subject. On the other hand, the development of practicable rules on the use of ruses of war will be instrumental in enhancing the military's understanding of the significance of international law of war.

2. Basic Legal Aspects.

Anyone desirous of contributing to the rules governing ruses of war must take account of their manifestations in the various types of armed conflicts and must refrain from any undue simplification. The term "ruse of war" covers a vast range of acts of widely differing significance. Surprise and ambush, the passing of false intelligence, the use or imitation of enemy signals, passwords, codes, signs, voices and orders, the removal of landmarks and signposts, bogus troop movement and strength, pretended inactivity, the use of dummy vehicles and positions, the camouflaging of uniforms and vehicles with nets and foliage, blackening faces, the use of cover, the employment of every conceivable decoy, the use of spies, the removal of unit badges from uniforms and escape in civilian clothes — all these are merely examples of individual ruses. Any attempt at exhaustive enumeration is bound to be thwarted by fresh feats of imagination (5).

Many ruses of war involve deception of the enemy, which may be accomplished by optical (dummy positions and dummy airfields), acoustic (engine and track noise), intelligence (bogus radio messages) or operational means and methods (feigned attacks and infiltration manoeuvres). But ruse is also characteristic of some forms of "double playing" which may, for instance, take advantage of psychological constraints on the part of the enemy who is forced to compromise his position in order to prevent even more serious disadvantage. Even acts which forego deception and play-acting from the outset — e.g. the perfidious use of protected persons with the aim of rendering certain points or areas immune from military operations (6), are regarded as (prohibited) ruses of war (7). It should be noted here that a too narrow definition of the term "ruse of war" in international treaties would be neigher feasible nor desirable since a restricted interpretation might be apt to encourage the evasion of general prohibitive clauses. The necessary degree of

271

D. FLECK

legal precision is already attained by the general definition according to which the term "ruse of war" covers "all acts of war aimed at inducing the enemy to compromise his position or to expose himself to danger."

From early times, the belligerents' sense of honour and the idea that a certain basis of mutual confidence must be preserved even on the battlefield have been instrumental in developing internationally acknowledged limits to permissible ruses of war (8).

Honour alone, however, cannot be the legislator since its standards are not the same all over the globe (9). A minimum of confidence between belligerents is, therefore, absolutely necessary in order to draw a valid distinction between ruse and perfidy in international law. The observance of international law in general and the refraining from the commission of perfidious acts in particular are essentially based on that measure of confidence which the parties to an armed conflict place in each other even on the battlefield. Thus, an act of perfidy is only inadequately characterized as "an act of vileness against which there is no defence" (10). Rather, it will be necessary to examine, from case to case, whether a specific act of war is prohibited in view of the protection of confidence granted under the terms of international law. The question of admissibility can therefore be answered only in general terms to the effect that ruses of war are permissible if they do not take improper advantage of the protection afforded by a provision of international law (11).

Yet it must be admitted that these pragmatic efforts, focussed not so much on the belligerents' sense of honour as on the confidence which they place in each other, have by no means succeeded in establishing a firm and stable basis for international doctrine, Mutual confidence can only be established if account is taken of the adversary's sense of honour, and this basis of confidence, too, is affected by customs, sense of justice, and usages of war prevailing at the time. It must also be kept in mind that the standards of confidence applied by the various parties to a conflict are bound to differ. Finally, an erosion of confidence may take place within one and the same armed conflict. This may, "inter alia", be due to the employment of ruses, for instance through the use of a 'double agent" by which one of the parties pretends to agree to betrayal whilst, in fact, the opposite is the case and the enemy who wanted to exploit the treachery involved, is finally enticed into the trap he himself has laid (12).

Since the basis of confidence is affected by so many factors of differing and varying weight, it will be necessary to develop detailed international rule that are both responsive to the requirements of our modern environment and conducive to safeguarding the protection of confidence among belligerents. These rules should be tailored to concrete situations and facts and be

272

expressed in the most precise terms possible. If it appears feasible to reconfirm and develop, in the course of current reformatory efforts, general rules governing the conduct of combatants, the chance of achieving this aim should be exploited to the full — that is to say not only by framing a few specific provisions, but also by drafting a general clause which, in a realistic and circumspect way, assures the recognition of the old legal maxim "fides etiam hosti servanda" in modern armed conflicts.

II. — THE ROLE OF RUSES OF WAR AND PERFIDY IN INTERNATIONAL LAW PRIOR TO THE ENACTMENT OF THE HAGUE REGULATIONS

1. International Doctrine and Practice.

In ancient times. Greeks and Romans devoted careful thought to the significance of ruse in war. The classical example of ruse was the wooden horse with the aid of which the Greeks, after ten years of unsuccessful siege, entered and conquered the city of Troy (13). Odysseus to whom Homer ascribed this "Trojan ruse" won universal praise as the "most artful of strategists"

Ancient literature contains numerous accounts of historical ruses of war; they are in part published in the "exempla", a collection of miscellaneous anecdotes and reminiscenses, whereas another part was compiled in specific anthologies, the so-called "stratagemata" The still existant writings of FRONTINUS (14), a Roman consul and Governor of Britannia (1st century, A.D.) and of the Greek military expert POLYAINOS (15) (2nd century, A.D.) contain such stratagemata, one of the said authors classifying them according to the methods applied and the other according to the generals involved. Characteristically, legal considerations are of only marginal importance in these accounts (16), and many stratagemata reflect an objectionable ethic (17).

Many ruses of war are reported from the Middle Ages (18).
Reference is frequently made here to the battle of Hastings in which the Normans, under William the Conqueror, feigned to retreat in order to entice the Britons to leave their fortifications (19), and then to defeat them in open battle. A Soviet handbook for soldiers offers examples of decoy manoeuvres and sham fights used by Russian forces in their conflicts with the German Knights and the Swedes (20). An account of the Russo-Turkish wars tells how a Russian buglar saved his unit from the Turks by sounding the Turkish retreat (21).

Firm rules prohibiting or permitting specific ruses of war were set up only in recent times. One of the most popular means of deception, the uniform, was not in use in the more remote past. During the time of mercenaries, it

D. FLECK

was often difficult to find out at first sight for which of the parties an individual soldier was fighting, and when coloured sashes and, subsequently, uniforms were introduced in the 16th century, the parties to a conflict had frequently no hesitation in deceiving the enemy by using his uniforms.

The first legal comments on the subject of ruses of war were furnished by HUGO GROTIUS in his famous treatise "De jure belli ac pacis" (22). At a time where the 30 Years' War was in full progress, he discussed the harmless examples set forth in the antique stratagemata and gave a critical review of the opinions held by classical authors. Referring to Vergil's verse, he asks "whether bravery or ruse before the enemy is preferable".

In contrast to Cicero whom he quotes as having repudiated any form of deception. and to Augustinus who considered it permissible "to conceal the truth cautiously beneath a certain amount of distortion ", he arrives at a rather different standpoint of his own : He regards recourse to ruse and deception as permissible unless they involve actions to which custom and tradition have attributed a specific significance (23). In expounding his theory in greater detail, GROTIUS goes rather far in submitting that not only oaths and promises, but also words, gestures, and signals commonly used in a specific sense are illicit means of deceiving the enemy because "they are based on tacit agreement between the parties". In addition, the development of international doctrine has been strongly influenced by GROTIUS' opinion that commitments entered into by two parties who later become involved in an armed conflict must not be used as a means of deceiving the enemy. GROTIUS demands that deception be so chosen "that no harm results, or, at least, only such harm as is admissible irrespective of the deception practised". Referring to a passage in POLYAINOS' stratagemata, he declares that "... the godlessness of those is to be condemned who assert that men can be deceived with oaths just as boys can be deceived with dice".

In addition to GROTIUS' widely disseminated treatise, the influence of the Enlightment played an important role in bringing about a certain humanization of warfare. An outstanding example of such humanisation is the treaty between the United States and Prussia signed by Benjamin Franklin and Frederick the Great in 1785, which includes principles for humanitarian treatment in the event of war. None the less, legal standards set by individual nations were still dominant since multilateral treaties were not concluded until the second half of the 19th century.

BLUNTSCHLI's important textbook of international law first published in 1867 (26), a handbook tailored to the requirements of practice and drafted in the form of a commentary on international law, deals with ruses of war in the context of prohibited means of warfare. BLUNTSCHLI proceeds from the assumption that killing is only allowed in combat and that the killing of an enemy not engaged in combat is a disgraceful and unlawful act, which is tantamount to murder (27). He applies this principles also the deception of the enemy by false flags, uniforms, and insignia. This type of deception, he says, must not go beyond preparations for combat; nobody must be allowed

274

to "attack the enemy masked as a friend and brother-in-arms" (28). Acts constituting a breach of trust towards the enemy are also expressly termed as violations of international law.

2. First National Regulations.

The so-called "Lieber code," a manual drafted by Professor Lieber which Abraham Lincoln put into effect for the US armed forces in 1863 (29), has found wide recognition even beyond the sphere of national legislation. The Code, while reflecting the then most recent views on international law of war, at the same time stimulated a positive development of international doctrine.

The Lieber Code does not expressly refer to the term "ruses in war", but it distinguishes between permissible deception in war on the one hand and clandestine or treacherous attempts to injure the enemy on the other (30). More specifically, the Code prohibits the use of the enemy's uniforms, flags. or emblems of nationality in battle (Art. 63, 65), the abuse of the flag of truce (Art. 114), the violation of armistice conditions (Art. 136, 145), and the outlawing or murder of individuals, no matter whether they are civilians or members of the hostile army (Art. 148) (31).

The "Lieber Code" confirms the classical doctrine enunciated by ROUSSEAU (32) and PORTALIS (33) according to which war is a state of armed hostility between sovereign nations or governments, but not between their peoples or citizens. From this it follows that individuals may be made the subject and object of combat actions only when and in so far as they have a military status. At the same time, it can be concluded from this doctrine that a fighting soldier is not without rights and that he should be granted protection under international law as far as possible.

Manuals for the armed forces of other nations did not attain the status of the "Lieber Code". This applies in particular to the booklet entitled "Kriegsbrauch im Landkriege" (Usages of Land Warfare) which was published by the German General Staff in 1902 (34). This publication was not prepared by a staff of experts, but was drafted by one sole officer, Major (later Lt.General) VON FRIEDERICH, a member of the Supreme General Staff's Historical Research Department who was directed to compile this survey of past and present usages of war within a few weeks. Owing to the time pressure to which he was exposed, VON FRIEDERICH failed to notice that the regulations agreed upon at the first International Peace Conference held at The Hague in 1899 were promulgated in the Reich's Official Gazette in autumn, 1901, when his manual was still in preparation. Unfortunately, VON FRIEDERICH's manuscript was not revised by trained lawyers; it was distributed only in limited numbers and did not attain substantial significance for the German army (36). Rather, the members of the German army (and, in a similar way, those of the other European armies) were indoctrinated on the subject of international law on the basis of the wording of the Hague Regulations which were reproduced as an annex to the service regulations in force (37).

275

None the less, this German study on "usages of land warfare" provides valuable information on the standards of customary law and international practice acknowledged at that time. In particular, the chapter entitled : "Ruse and deception, the non-violent means of warfare; permissible and prohibited ruses of war" is characterized by a well-conceived distinction between permissible courses of action and prohibited acts of perfidy. The author proceeds from the realistic assumption that ruses of war should be valued in the light of their contribution toward achieving the objectives of war without the loss of human lives. Surprise actions, the laying of ambushes, feigned attacks and retreats, pretended inactivity, the dissemination of false intelligence and the use of enemy passwords are quoted as examples of permissible and frequently used ruses of war (38). As regards essential criteria for differentiating between permissible ruses of war and dishonourable acts of perfidy, reference is made to moral and ethical principles that found common recognition at the time, to national standards of education, and to the practical requirements of warfare. Although VON FRIEDERICH does not believe in reliable means of distinguishing ruses of war from perfidy on the spot, he describes perfidious warfare in terms worthy to be noted even in the present day :

VON FRIEDERICH holds the opinion that ruses of war are prohibited if they are "incompatible with honest warfare because they are apt to involve fraud, disloyalty, and breach of a given pledge" In giving examples of perfidious acts, he quotes the violation of an agreed armistice or safe-conduct with the object of winning an advantage over the enemy through surprise action; the feigning of surrender aimed at killing the unsuspecting enemy; the misuse of the Red Cross emblem or the flag of truce in the attack or in preparations for an attack; the wilful violation of formal and solemn pledges, e.g. under a treaty of alliance; the instigation of others to commit crimes, such as murder of enemy generals, arson, robbery, etc., and the use of enemy flags and insignia for the purpose of deception; in the latter case, he refers explicitly. to the fact that the Hague peace conference of 1899 has declared itself against the admissibility of such methods of deception (39).

III. — RUSES OF WAR AND PERFIDY IN CURRENT INTERNATIONAL LAW

1. Permissible Ruses of War.

In view of the long-standing efforts to draw the line between permissible ruses and unlawful acts of perfidy, it is to be regretted that neither the Hague Regulations nor the preparatory drafts contained in the protocols of the

Ruses of War

Brussels Conference (40) provide any policy rules covering this subject. The Oxford Manual of the "Institut de Droit International", too, offers different suggestions in this respect.

The Brussels Conference, following the preliminary draft submitted by the Russian Ambassador, Professor VON MARTENS, merely stated that ruses of war — and even "toute espèce de ruses de guerre" — are permissible (Art. 14 of the Brussels Drafts). This general formule was criticized and discussed in some detail at the 1st International Peace Conference held at The Hague in 1899. In the end, however, experts came to the conclusion that this provision, while recognizing the admissibility of ruse in principle, was not meant to legalize any conceivable ruse of war and that ruses of war would cease to be permissible if they infringed a recognized rule of international law. Since no detailed rules were agreed upon, Article 24 of the Hague Regulations was finally adopted in its present form which does not fully meet the requirement for a clear and workable solution. The article deals with ruses of war and "measures necessary for obtaining information" in one and the same context, gives no definition of the term "ruse of war" and fails to provide any criteria that would permit a distinction between ruses and prohibited acts of perfidy (43).

According to the rules mentioned above, the limits of permissible ruses of war are drawn by the prohibitions listed in Article 23 of the Hague Regulations and by the specific sanctions against the abuse of the status of parlementaire and the violation of the terms of an armistice (Articles 33, 34, 40, and 41 of the Hague Regulations). This solution has the disadvantage that those acts of perfidy which are not clearly covered by a specific prohibitive clause have to be accepted by the persons involved because the Hague Regulations offer no criteria for the interpretation of the expression perfidy. The resultant harmful effects will be discussed later in conjunction with the pertinent provisions of the Hague Regulations. It may suffice here to say that the present version of Article 24 impedes the enforcement of those fundamental restrictions to the belligerent's means of injuring the enemy which have been so impressively postulated in Article 22 of the Hague Regulations. (44) The framers of a forthcoming codification should, therefore, have no hesitation in complementing Article 22 of the Hague Regulations by a general clause drawing the limits between ruses of war and perfidy.

2. Prohibited Acts of Perfidy.

The prohibition of perfidious or treacherous warfare follows from the generally acknowledged legal maxim that the requirements of good faith must be observed in international practice. This fundamental principle repudiates means and methods of combat that are incompatible "with the military's sense of honour and the respect which even enemies owe to each other" (45); at the same time, it proceeds from the assumption that a minimum basis of confidence between belligerents must be legally protected. However, international treaty law has thus far drawn a distinction between permissible ruses and prohibited acts of perfidy only in specific cases :

(a) The prohibition "to kill or wound treacherously" (46) as set forth in Article 23, para (b) of the Hague Regulations implies that it is forbidden to take advantage of the "good faith", that is to say of the trust and confidence of individuals belonging to the hostile army or nation. Such state of mind may be regarded as existing in the case of civilians, the more so since they are undoubtedly protected by international treaties and customs; but there are no indications that the same applies also to combatants in modern armed conflicts. The traditional rule that hostilities must be confined to open combat and must not involve the wilful killing of individuals not engaged in the general confrontation between the parties to the conflict is still valid in principle, but is being increasingly eroded — if not completely thwarted — by the practice of employing sabotage squads and task forces in modern guerilla warfare.

To combatants in modern armed conflicts, a complete lack of suspicion would be tantamount to impardonable recklessness. A soldier may claim protection on account of his good faith only in those exceptional cases where belligerent acts are prohibited in view of a special relationship between him and the adversary.

Such situations exist, for instance, in the case of wounded soldiers, parlementaires, and prisoners of war. Yet it is not entirely certain whether prisoners of war are prohibited from committing hostile acts themselves in view of the protection granted to them.

Prisoners of war have a right to escape. Offenses committed by them with the sole intention of facilitating their escape are normally subject to disciplinary punishment only (Article 93, para 2, 3rd Geneva Convention), and criminal punishment may not be imposed unless such attempts involve resort to violence against life or limb. It remains to be examined whether the aforementioned rules, which legalize the application of disciplinary and penal sanctions, are apt to throw some light on the question of whether hostile acts committed by escaping prisoners of war are permissible under the terms of international law. Is it conceivable that military personnel of the detaining power and, more specifically, guards and sentries on duty in a POW camp are entirely unsuspecting in matters involving prisoners of war?

The Geneva Conventions and the leading commentary published by PICTET (47) provide no information on this point. It should be kept in mind at this juncture that the escape of prisoners — just as espionage and blockade-running at sea — belongs to those "risky acts of war" which, while permissible under international law, are open to sanctions and penalties imposed by the enemy. At any rate, trust and confidence toward prisoners of war does not go so far as to overlook their escape. On the other hand, acts of violence against life or limb are in no way regarded

Ruses of War

as lesser offences if they are committed in connection with the escape of prisoners. Furthermore, prisoners of war who have not made good their escape have no undisputed right to justify belligerent acts with their combatant status; for the protection granted to them by international law in the form of obligations imposed on the detaining power rests on the premise that prisoners of war are not involved in belligerent acts. Hence it appears justified to conclude that international law prohibits prisoners of war from committing belligerent acts involving violence against life or limb as long as they have not made good their escape.

Viewed against this background, the prohibition to kill or wound treacherously is still of concrete significance for the relations between combatants.

(b) Article 23 para (f) of the Hague Regulations with its compilation of various independent prohibitions has given rise to misunderstandings (48). Since Article 23 (f) does not prohibit any use, but only the "improper use" *(d'user indûment)* of the objects enumerated, the question arises under what circumstances the use of such objects may be regarded as permissible.

As regards the use of the flag of truce and the distinctive emblems prescribed by the Geneva Conventions, this question can be easily answered by referring to explicit provisions of international treaties (Article 32 of the Hague Regulations, Articles 38 et seq. of the 1st Geneva Convention). Yet it is still a controversial issue whether the enemy's national flag, military uniforms and insignia may be used for the purpose of deception, at least when such deception is practised by units or individuals not engaged in combat.

Although deception through the "use of false flags" is likely to occur only sporadically in land warfare, this ruse may offer good chances of success in modern guerilla warfare and may, for instance, be employed by infantry units attacked by helicopters. It is therefore still of interest to note that, in the battle of Te-Ling-See which was fought during the Russo-Japanese war on 15 June 1904, Russian troops allegedly advanced under Japanese flags, which prompted the Japanese artillery to discontinue its fire.

The Japanese goverment lodged a protest against this Russian manoeuvre on the ground that it constituted a violation of international custom and, specifically, of Article 23 of the Hague Regulations (49). It is however likely that the Russian troops had taken advantage of the enemy's flags only with the aim of improving their position, that is to say that they resorted to this ruse only "hors de combat". When this incident was dealt with in a legal study published in 1938, the author, basing himself on a narrow interpretation of Article 23 of the Hague Regulations, arrived at the conclusion that this ruse of war was not a perfidious act and that the Japanese protest was therefore unfounded, although "with a view to

D. FLECK

make the situation unmistakably clear to the fighting soldier, and taking account of the unique character of national emblems, it would appear desirable to prohibit the use of the enemy's national flag unconditionally and without qualifications (50).

Examples of the "use of enemy uniforms" are constantly reported in recent times, the cases in point being either parachutists operating in false uniforms behind the enemy's lines in order to avoid getting involved in combat actions, or task forces approaching the enemy in false uniforms with the intention of not removing this camouflage until immediately before opening fire. During the second world war, such ruses of war were repudiated as perfidious because the use of enemy uniforms was regarded as forbidden in all circumstances (51). However, the German brigadier SKORZENY who used false uniforms during the German counter-offensive in the Ardennes was acquitted by US Military Government Tribunal after the second world war (52). Accordingly, the use of enemy uniforms is regarded as permissible by the current US Field Manual on Land Warfare unless such uniforms are used in combat (53). The pertinent British manual shares this opinion although some doubts are voiced (54). By contrast, the service regulations in force in the Federal Republic of Germany prohibit the use of enemy uniforms, national flags and military insignia without any qualification (55).

In interpreting Article 23 (f) of the Hague Regulations, too, much emphasis is placed on the wording of this provision by those who hold that the enemy's flags, uniforms and insignia may be used for the purpose of deception except when in combat. This body of opinion fails to recognize that the catalogue of ruses of war enumerated in Article 23 does not admit of a reliable "argumentum e contrario" because this Article confines itself to quoting typical examples ("notamment"). The admissibility of a specific ruse of war not mentioned in the Hague Regulations could, therefore, only be justified by the argument that neither international custom nor generally accepted principles of international law prohibit the employment of this particular means of injuring the enemy (56). A conclusion to that effect is, however, not supported by current international law.

First of all, the negotiations on the formulation of Article 23 (f) indicate that it was at no time the intention of the states to legalize deception through national emblems, military insignia, or uniforms of the enemy. This ruse of war was regarded as objectionable even prior to the Brussels Conference (57), and was expressly opposed by experts in military literature (58). The Russian preliminary draft prepared for the Brussels Conference envisioned the unrestricted prohibition of the use of enemy national flags, military insignia and uniforms (59). It was merely for

Ruses of War

editorial reasons that, at the suggestion of the Swiss delegate, the last half sentence of Article 13 D was incorporated in Article 12 which corresponds to Article 23 of the Hague Regulations in their present form. Furthermore, Article 12 F prohibited

> "l'emploi du pavillon parlementaire, du pavillon national, des insignes militaires et de l'uniforme de l'ennemi, dans le but de le tromper" (60).

Again for editorial reasons, the passage "l'emploi ... dans le but de le tromper" (to use with the aim of deceiving) was finally replaced by the word "abus" (abuse) on the understanding that this word was no less adequate to the meaning of the paragraph (61). Shortly afterwards, the Oxford Manual suggested the somewhat unprecise version :

> "Il est interdit d'attaquer l'ennemi en dissimulant les signes distinctifs de la force armée; d'user indûment du pavillon national, des insignes militaires ou de l'uniforme de l'ennemi" (62)

to which the Hague Conference of 1899 referred when it replaced the word "abus" by the phrase "user indûment", a differentiation which is so insignificant that it is neither reflected in the English ("improper use") nor in the German translation ("Missbrauch"). For all practical purposes, however, the Conference wished to adhere to the unequivocal regulation set forth in the Declaration of Brussels (63).

Hence, any changes affecting the substance of the provision which might have resulted from the version of the Oxford Manual have been clearly rejected.

In addition, military considerations of topical interest, along with those pertaining to the origin of Article 23 (f) of the Hague Regulations, speak in favour of reconfirming, without any qualification, the prohibition on deceiving the adversary through the use of enemy or neutral national flags, insignia and uniforms. Their use for reconnaissance missions, acts of sabotage or with the aim of "arousing confusion" would, if legalized, permit acts of deception that might have more harmful effects for the enemy than losses sustained in open combat. In addition, a ban on the use of these means of deception which is restricted to combat actions might be of no practical value in specific cases, e.g. if deception fails so that the members of a sabotage squad are detected and attacked by regular troops. The above considerations are not disproved by the outcome of the SKORZENY trial, which lead to the acquittal of the defendant (64). The judgement passed at the time was not published in writing; a subsequent analysis of the case by the UN War Crimes Commission (64) confined itself to brief references to legal theory without giving some deeper thought to the legislatory background of Article 23 (f) of the Hague

D. FLECK

Regulations and to the various aspects of the situation prevailing in modern armed conflicts. The acquittal in the SKORZENY case can, therefore, not be taken as a yardstick.

A few exceptions from the prohibition to employ enemy or neutral uniforms and insignia are, however, conceivable. The escape of prisoners of war wearing enemy or neutral uniforms cannot be regarded as a perfidious act, and it would appear permissible to use enemy uniforms for exercise purposes. Both exceptions apply, however, on the express understanding that these acts of deception are not conducive to facilitating acts of combat (65).

(c) The Convention for the Protection of Cultural Property in the Event of Armed Conflicts of 14 May 1954 (66) has introduced a new distinctive emblem for "cultural property". The use of this distinctive emblem and of the emblems provided for in Article 5 of the Hague Convention No. IX of 1907 (67) and in the so-called Roerich Pact of 1935 (68) are governed by the same principles which prohibit the unlawful use of the Red Cross emblem.

(d) Article 33, para 3 and Article 34 of the Hague Regulations deal with the consequences of an abuse of the "status of parlementaire." The two categories of sanctions imposed ·(temporary detainment in the case of abuse, loss of rights of inviolability in the event of treachery) are adequate and of sufficient clarity.

No difficulties have been encountered in practice.

(e) "Capitulations" agreed upon between parties to a conflict "must take into account the rules of military honour" (Article 35 of the Hague Regulations). A party feigning a capitulation with the aim of winning advantages over an enemy who relies on its terms would commit a dishonourable and, therefore, perfidious act.

(f) Article 40 and 41 of the Hague Regulations deal with the sanctions imposed for the violation of an "armistice." The general rule under which combatants are prohibited from committing perfidious acts applies also to the abuse of a cease-fire agreement.

(g) In addition, any other act is on principle to be regarded as perfidious which, while taking advantage of the protection granted by international law, is aimed at deceiving the enemy in combat or at inducing him to compromise his position. A party feigning to surrender, for instance, acts perfidiously because he claims a right to protection in accordance with Article 23 (c) of the Hague Regulations. The same applies to the feigning of other situations where protection is granted under the terms of international law. No one is allowed to feign death or to claim protection as a

Ruses of War

wounded person, a shipwrecked person, or a crew member of an aircraft in distress with a view to gaining advantages in combat. It is also perfidious to violate, with the same object in mind, agreements entered into between the parties to a conflict, e.g. on the rescue of wounded soldiers or on relief actions for civilians. Finally, it is perfidious to take advantage of the presence of protected persons with the aim of rendering certain points or areas immune from enemy operations (cf. Article 28, 4th Geneva Convention and Article 23, para 1, 3rd Geneva Convention). The problem of whether and in what circumstances the feigning of death constitutes a perfidious act is a rather complex one. Combatants who deceive the enemy by feigning death will not normally commit a perfidious act — even if they rejoin the battle soon after this act of deception — because an enemy who believes a man to be dead does not spare him in observance of a rule of international law, but only because he thinks that there is no need to fight him any longer.

The fact that an act of deception is soon followed by an hostile act is in itself not always indicative of perfidiousness. Rather, both acts must constitute means of achieving one and the same object. A conclusion to that effect appears only to be justified if the deception was practised with the intention of taking advantage of the adversary's loyalty to international law.

3. Current National Regulations on Ruses of War and Perfidy.

A generally accessible survey of pertinent national service manuals and regulations does not exist at the present time. The material so far available varies in scope and quality, and many states have not provided their armed forces with special regulations covering the subject of international law. Although Article 1 of Hague Convention No. IV (69) requires the contracting powers to provide their armed land forces with instructions conforming to the Hague Regulations, many states — among them Germany — confined themselves to communicating the mere text of that Convention to their armies before the first world war. It must be feared that the commitments to disseminate the terms of the Conventions (70) will continue to exist on paper only unless an international exchange of pertinent information is carried on in peacetime.

The International Institute for Humanitarian Law in Sanremo, therefore, deserves full credit for having set about the collection and evaluation of national service regulations (71). Yet a great amount of work remains to be done, and particular attention will have to be devoted to the various methods of instructing members of the armed forces in international law. The work yet to be accomplished in this field will not only add to our knowledge of current international custom and practice but will also furnish concrete information as to how rules of international law not yet agreed upon at the present time can be put to practice in the future. Only a limited number of

283

D. FLECK

national service manuals and regulations could be evaluated for the purposes of the present study (72). They deal, *inter alia,* expressly with the employment of ruses in war and describe a ruse as a lawful means of combat responsive to the conditions obtaining in modern war. In assessing the problem from the legal point of view, reference is generally made to Articles 23 and 24 of the Hague Regulations while attempting to bring the regulations on perfidy in line with the requirements of modern warfare.

As far as the German Federal Armed Forces are concerned, ruses of war are dealt with in the Joint Service Regulation (ZDv) No. 3/11 ("Joint Services Infantry Combat Training") with particular emphasis on the significance of ruses for the individual combatant. In the context of practical instructions, it is made clear that the rules of international law must be respected when resorting to ruse. The basic principles of international law covering this subject are set forth in the Joint Service Regulation (ZDv) No. 15/10 ("General Provisions of Combatant Law and Law of Land Warfare"). It is pointed out that treachery and perfidious acts are prohibited because "they are incompatible with the military's sense of honour and the need to respect the enemy". In quoting examples of perfidious acts, reference is made not only to violations of Article 23 of the Hague Regulations; but also to "soldiers who pretend to surrender with the intent of resuming hostilities by way of surprise action". Finally, a brief survey of basic international principles of land warfare is contained in the annex attached to the Army Service Regulation (HDv) No. 100/1 ("Leadership and Command").

Particular attention should be devoted to the service manuals for the British and US forces which might serve as a basis for the development of more concrete rules on the prohibition of perfidy. Prohibited ruses of war quoted as examples in both the British and US manuals include the feigning of surrender so as to secure an advantage over the opposing belligerent; the dissemination — e.g. by wireless — of messages that an armistice has been agreed upon when such is not the case; or the demanding of a ceasefire agreement with the intention of violating such agreement in one's own interest. In accordance with the official views expressed in the US manual (73), a soldier feigning surrender is taking unlawful advantage of the rule that the enemy must give quarter and must not harm POWs. A false armistice agreement, it is pointed out, violates the recognized principle of international law that a true armistice suspends military operations.

The manuals also consider it to be prohibited to shoot behind the cover of a wounded man and feigning dead in order to attack the enemy when he is off guard. Referring to Article 28, 4th Geneva Convention and to Article 23, para 1, 3rd Geneva Convention, the manuals point out that it is prohibited to detain civilians or prisoners of war at places of strategic importance, such as factories or railway stations, or to rendering military units immune from military operations. Although such acts, in contrast with those prohibited in Article 23 (f) of the Hague Regulations, are not committed with the aim of deceiving the enemy, such abuse of protected persons is regarded as a form of (prohibited) ruse of war in accordance with the rationale and legislatory background of Article 23 (f).

IV. — RUSES OF WAR AND PERFIDY DE LEGE FERENDA

1. International Treaties

New provisions relative to ruses of War and the prohibition of perfidy are to be included in the envisioned Additional Protocols to the Geneva Conventions of 1949, where they will constitute an essential part of the rules governing the behaviour of combatants. Almost the entire amount of preparatory work accomplished to date was devoted to the First Additional Protocol on international armed conflicts.

The present study, therefore, proposes to deal primarily with this subject while giving special consideration to the applicability of the envisioned regulations in aerial and maritime warfare. Secondly, it is intended to discuss the problem of whether rules prohibiting perfidy may also be incorporated into the envisioned Second Additional Protocol, which deals with armed conflicts not of an international character.

The development of rules reaffirming the prohibition of perfidy was suggested by the ICRC as early as at the XXIst International Red Cross Conference held in Instanbul in 1969 (74). During its preparations for the Conference of Government Experts on the Reaffirmation and Development of International Humanitarian Law Applicable in Armed Conflicts, the ICRC set about the task of defining perfidy by way of a general clause, but it suggested at the same time that this general clause be complemented by a list of examples (75). The proposal submitted by experts of the Federal Republic of Germany at the first session of the conference of government experts comprises both a general clause and a list of examples of perfidy (76).

Finally, the ICRC, in its Basis Texts submitted to the second session of the conference of government experts, suggested that the provisions of the First Additional Protocol be worded as follows :

"Article 31 : *Prohibition of Perfidy.*

(1) It is forbidden to kill or injure by resort to perfidy. Unlawful acts betraying the enemy's confidence, such as the abuse of an international convention, truce or humanitarian negotiation, the misuse of internationally recognized protective signs, the feigning of surrender, the use of the enemy's distinctive emblems, are deemed to constitute perfidy.

285

(2) Ruses of war are not considered as perfidy. Ruses of war are those acts, such as camouflage, traps, mock operations, and misinformation, which, whilst infringing no recognized rule, are intended to mislead the enemy or to induce him to act recklessly.

Article 32 : *Recognized signs.*

It is forbidden to make improper use of the flag of truce, the protective signs of the red cross (red crescent, red lion and sun), the protective sign for cultural property and other protective signs specified in international conventions.

Article 33 : *Emblems of nationality.*

It is forbidden to make improper use of enemy and neutral flags, military insignia and uniforms. In combat their use is forbidden at all times."

The above articles reflect a cautious extension and development of the version set forth in the Hague Regulations. Efforts should, however, be made to eliminate some lacunae and imperfections that became apparent in the deliberations or government experts, even though it is recognized that discussions at the present stage are focused not so much on further development as on the reaffirmation of international custom and treaty law :

a) The ICRC draft states that it is forbidden to "kill or injure" by resort to perfidy. This could be misinterpreted as denoting that the draft affords a lesser degree of protection against perfidious acts than the Hague Regulations in their present form.
b) The draft gives only an incomplete general definition of perfidy; the examples enumerated are no sufficient substitute.
c) The catalogue of protective signs is incomplete; the term "misuse" is not defined.
d) The formulation used in Article 23 (f) of the Hague Regulations in connection with the use of enemy flags and uniforms, which was due to an editorial misunderstanding, appears again in the ICRC draft.
e) The draft offers no solutions to the topical problem of disguising combatants as civilians.
f) The list of prohibited acts of perfidy, while necessarily incomplete, could be arranged more clearly and might include examples of a more typical character.

Re a) :

It was pointed out on various occasions that the ICRC has shown some hesitation in dealing with the prohibition of perfidy when it drafted the

286

Ruses of War

relevant provision of its draft in the rather restrictive terms that "it is forbidden to kill or injure by resort to perfidy". As an alternative solution, Israeli government experts suggested a general clause to the effect that "Any act of perfidy towards the enemy is forbidden" (78) whereas other experts proposed that the first sentence in Article 31, para 1 should be worded : "It is forbidden to attack..." instead of "it is forbidden to kill or injure. .". As a minimum, the wording chosen for the ICRC draft could be so extended as to prohibit the taking of prisoners by resort to perfidy.

Many ruses of war, and perhaps even most of them, are not designed to kill or injure and have no direct relation to an attack. But it must be borne in mind that these ruses of war, too, may easily involve resort to perfidy.

However, it remains doubtful whether such ruses of war can be effectively dealt with in international treaties and whether they will fit in with the given legislative framework, that is to say with the envisioned Additional Protocols to the Geneva Conventions. The suggestions put forward by the ICRC have already gone very far beyond the traditional scope of the Law of Geneva which used to confine itself to the protection of war victims. Thus it was possible to surmount the traditional limits drawn between the "Law of Geneva" (i.e. humanitarian law in a restricted sense) and the "Law of The Hague" (i.e. the rules of international law governing the conduct of belligerents). All the same, the real substance of the rules embodied in the Hague Regulations cannot be replaced to the full extent by the envisioned Protocols. For the time being, legislative efforts will have to deal only with a limited sector of international law applicable to armed conflicts, and they will have to confine themselves to specific humanitarian aspects if they are to offer a reasonable chance of success. If it proves impossible to agree on a wider definition of the ban on perfidy than that contained in the ICRC draft, it should, therefore, be made clear that the Additional Protocols to the Geneva Conventions reflect only part of the norms embodied in generally acknowledged international customs.

On the other hand, it would appear possible to prohibit the misuse of international protective signs and of enemy or neutral flags, insignia and uniforms in more concrete terms. In this regard, a stronger basis of confidence among belligerents has evolved in the past, and the use of these signs and emblems — even that of flags and insignia used by the parties to a conflict — is nowadays more closely related to humanitarian aspects. Articles 32 and 33 of the ICRC draft therefore impose — and quite rightly so — an unqualified ban on the misuse of these objects, which is not restricted to cases of misuse with the intention to kill or injure.

Re b) :

The ICRC, in the early stages of current reformatory efforts, had considered it desirable to arrive at a better definition covering perfidy and ruses of war and to supplement this definition by a list of illustrative examples

287

D. FLECK

(75). Hence, the draft submitted by the ICRC must be considered all the more unsatisfactory. In the course of discussions on the definition of perfidy, the majority of government experts did not consider it advisable to include the word "unlawful" in the ICRC draft because this word might be misinterpreted as suggesting a restrictive definition. A large number of experts concurred, either orally or in writing, with a German proposal which defines perfidy as follows :

> ' Acts designed to mislead the adversary into the belief that protection under international law will be granted constitute perfidy."
> (80)

The essential criterion of perfidy, therefore, is the feigning of a situation where there is an entitlement to protection under the terms of international law. Those who resort to deception will in most cases pretend to be legally protected; yet such protection is also of direct importance for those betrayed because the latter take it for granted that protected persons are no longer entitled to commit belligerent acts. This was illustrated in this study (cf. section III, 2) by the example of the prisoner who has not made good his escape. The same situation obtains, for instance, in the case of wounded persons receiving humanitarian aid.

Other definitions of the term perfidy were not suggested at the Conference of Government Experts. Some experts who commented on this subject (81) adhered to the definition containes in the ICRC draft which gives only a few examples of perfidious acts which betray the adversary's confidence. However, an international convention which, apart from a few illustrative examples, provides no definition of that minimum basis of confidence which must be preserved even among belligerents will hardly be able to assure legal protection in cases not directly covered by these exemples.

Finally, it is still an unresolved problem whether only acts carried out with the intention of committing or resuming hostilities shall be deemed to constitute perfidy.

The ICRC draft, while making no express statement in this regard, assumed a rather unequivocal attitude when it confined the ban on perfidy to acts designed "to kill or injure". However, the examples quoted in the ICRC draft do not reflect this restriction with sufficient clarity. The German proposal referred to above makes it quite clear that the acts quoted as illustrative examples are carried out with the intention of committing or resuming hostilities.

Re c) :

Article 32 of the ICRC draft which affords special protection to internationally recognized signs will continue to be the subject of proposed amendments. It was already suggested in the past that various objects and organizations — such as police, schools, kindergartens, and civil defence organizations — be identified by additional protective signs. Although such protection is doubtless desirable, the introduction of additional signs for this purpose has also some serious disadvantages, which are aggravated by the need to frame detailed regulations aimed at preventing their abuse. Protective signs must be restricted to a very few exceptional cases if they are to be really effective in armed conflicts. A party to an armed conflict using protective signs which the adversary is not bound to respect pursuant to international conventions is likely to get into difficulties even if the items identified by these signs enjoy protection under international law. Both the introduction of additional protective signs — even if such signs are internationally recognized — and the more frequent use of recognized signs would be apt to reduce their practical effectiveness, increase the danger of misuse, and encourage the adversary to disregard the protection afforded by them.

Special consideration should be devoted to the suggestion that the United Nations flag should be a recognized protective sign, which was made by experts of various countries (82). The flag of the United Nations is in principle not a sign of neutrality affording protection. If UN forces become involved in an armed conflict, the UN flag is used in no other way than those of the belligerent parties. However, the significance of emblems of neutrality could be attributed to emblems of humanitarian UN activities, such as UNHCR, UNICEF, and UNESCO. For this purpose, such emblems should be defined in more precise terms. In so doing, the term "improper use" could be further specified by referring to the purposes of the lawful use of such emblems as laid down in international treaties or UN instruments.

Re d) :

Article 33 of the ICRC draft, which prohibits the improper use of enemy or neutral flags, military insignia and uniforms provides no answer to the question under what circumstances the use of such items may be considered as "proper". The addendum "In combat their use is forbidden at all times" does not resolve the problem. In conformity with the comments made earlier on Article 23 (f) of the Hague Regulations in the light of current international law, experts of the Federal Republic of Germany, with numerous other experts concurring, suggested that Article 33 be applied without qualifications, that is to say that it be so worded as to prohibit any use of enemy or neutral flags, distinctive emblems, military insignia and uniforms in a manner facilitating acts of combat.

Re e) :

According to the views held by a significant minority of experts, combatants do not commit an act of perfidy if they disguise themselves as civilians. Some experts have even suggested an express provision indicating that attacks from ambush, even if carried out in civilian clothes, are not prohibited (85). A rule to that effect, however, would run counter to traditional legal concepts governing the prerequisites of combatant status and would pose a serious threat to the legal protection of the civilian population in armed conflicts. The suggestion put forward by the aforementioned experts that a phrase " the creation, prior to attack, of an impression with the enemy of being a non-combatant" (86) be added to the examples of perfidy is not likely to avert these harmful effects. Such provisions would, on the contrary, encourage combatants to disguise themselves as civilians without incurring any risk of being held responsible. It is just as hard to say what combatants should do in these circumstances in order to convey the impression "of being a non-combatant" as it is to say what measures are expected of civilians who want to be clearly identified as such. In the interests of the protection of the civilian population, care should therefore be taken to ensure that attacks from ambush — which are of course permissible and whose success depends on the element of surprise — may only be carried out by combatants wearing uniforms or the distinctive emblems prescribed by international law.

The experts of the Federal Republic of Germany have therefore supported a proposal, which was put forward by numerous experts from other countries that the disguising of combatants as civilians be expressly mentioned among the prohibited acts of perfidy (87).

Re f) :

The examples of perfidious acts of war set forth in the ICRC draft are not meant to be exhaustive and can, therefore, be further supplemented and arranged more clearly. It is to be welcomed that the subject matter dealt with in Article 23 (f) of the Hague Regulations is covered by two separate provisions of the ICRC draft, viz. Articles 32 and 33. Yet it would also appear desirable to arrange Article 31 more logically by subdividing it into a general clause prohibiting perfidy on the one hand and a list of examples on the other. This would make it clear that the policy rules on ruses of war and perfidy enunciated in Article 31 apply equally to the examples enumerated in Articles 32 and 33. At the same time, it would become even more apparent that it is impossible to draw up an exhaustive catalogue of examples because any list of perfidious acts of war is bound to be incomplete.

Yet it should be accepted that Article 31 and 32 of the ICRC draft appear to cover in part the same subject matter : Article 31 prohibits the misuse of internationally recognized protective signs with the object of killing or injuring whereas Article 32 extends this prohibition to the use of such signs 'hors de combat'. Explicit cases of misuse have, therefore, rightly been dealt with separately in the context of Article 31 in order to prevent misunderstandings and to facilitate the enforcement of sanctions imposed against perfidious acts.

Ruses of War

Taking account of the proposals set forth above, the wording in the envisioned Additional Protocol to the Geneva Conventions of 1949 could be as follows :

"Article 31 : *Prohibition of perfidy.*

(1) [It is forbidden to (kill, injure or capture) (attack) by resort to perfidy.] [Any act of perfidy towards an adversary is forbidden.] Acts designed to mislead the adversary into the belief that there is an entitlement to protection under international law constitute perfidy.
(2) Ruses of war are not considered as perfidy, Ruses of war are acts such as camouflage, traps, mock operations and misinformation which, whilst infringing no recognized rule, are intended to mislead the enemy or to induce him to act recklessly.

Article 31a : *Specific acts of perfidy.*

In particular the following acts when carried out with the intention of committing or resuming hostilities are forbidden :

1) the feigning of a situation of distress, particularly through the misuse of internationally recognized protective signs;
b) the feigning of a cease-fire, of a humanitarian negotiation or of a surrender;
c) the disguising of combatants as civilians.

Article 32 : *Internationally recognized signs.*

It is forbidden to make use of the flag of truce, the distinctive emblem of the red cross (red crescent, red lion and sun), the distinctive emblem for cultural property or other internationally recognized protective signs for purposes other than those for which they are designed.

Article 33 : *Enemy and neutral emblems.*

It is forbidden to make use of enemy or neutral flags, distinctive emblems, military insignia or uniforms in such a way that it facilitates acts of combat."

For the present, the version suggested above relates only to land warfare; in order to attain a maximum degree of precision it is necessary to take account of the specific conditions obtaining in land, aerial,and maritime warfare. Thus, surprise attack from ambush in land warfare, which is considered permissible, finds its counterpart in maritime warfare in ships approaching the enemy under the protection of false flags. However, the

291

absence of any cover in aerial and maritime warfare may, along with the larger degree of mobility and vulnerability, necessitate the drafting of regulations different from those applying in land warfare. Some controversial statements on this subject were made at the conference of government experts, but no concrete opinions or suggestions were presented (88). Yet it should be borne in mind that the prohibition of perfidy in war is, by its very nature, indivisible. It cannot be enforced in land warfare unless it is to be applied just as well in maritime and air warfare. A serviceman who is called upon to act on his own initiative in ever-changing tactical situations without being able to refer to specific instruction is in need of a general yardstick whose reliability cannot be allowed to very depending on methods or theatres of war.

There are also many indications that the different legal criteria applied to ruses of war in land, maritime, and air warfare are gradually losing importance. Mobility has drastically increased in land warfare and air or maritime forces are no longer essentially more vulnerable to attack than land forces. The ruse of flying false flags, while sanctioned by international custom in maritime warfare, was at no time regarded as permissible in air warfare, not even as far as the use of false distinctive emblems or protective signs is concerned. This speaks in favour of the demand that this ruse of war be subjected to generally applicable restrictions. While in the first world war it was widely considered a permissible ruse of war for fighter pilots to feign a situation of distress to order to improve their position for attack or escape, a growing body of opinion is nowadays advocating stronger international protection for the crews of aircraft in distress. Such protection presupposes that its abuse is prohibited as a perfidious act. The time has, therefore, come to examine whether the application of different legal criteria to land, maritime and air warfare is still justified and to embark on the framing of new, convincing and — if possible — uniform regulations covering the prohibition of perfidy.

2. Rules Peculiar to the Law of Maritime Warfare.

Although privateering was solemnly abolished more than a hundred years ago (90), some characteristic traits of maritime warfare are still reminiscent of an earlier time.

Traditional methods of deception, such as the use of false superstructures and the unexpected opening of fire, are now as before of considerable importance in naval warfare.

Even the observance of internationally recognized customs and usages, while fundamentally distinguishing the conduct of regular combatants from the methods practised by privateers, has not led to a sufficient degree of mutual confidence among belligerents at sea. Efforts to ensure more effective protection under international law are bound to come in conflict with the conditions peculiar to the war at sea. It is difficult to reconcile greater mobility and, with it, greater vulnerability with the need to afford protection to an unsuspecting adversary. In addition, the fact that the law of naval war is only insufficiently covered by international treaties (91) poses a large number of complex problems, especially with regard to the many ways of using enemy or neutral flags. The use of such flags for the purpose of deception has been a controversial issue at all times since it puts the confidence among belligerents at sea to a severe test and runs counter to the interests of the states entitled to fly the flags involved.

All the same, rules prohibiting the use of enemy flags in naval war have found no recognition in international law.

Articles 6 of the Convention on the High Seas merely prohibits the use of false flags in peacetime. As for their use in wartime, different considerations will have to apply in the case of warships and of merchant vessels.

a. *Use of False National Flags by Warships.*

It was notably during the first world war that the use of enemy or neutral national flags by warships was increasingly recognized in international practice. Yet the general rule applying in peacetime, which forbids the use of deceptive flags, was never entirely abandoned in war. Hence, the London Declaration on Naval War of 1909 (92), while not expressly prohibiting the use of deceptive flags, provides that such use is void unless it is proved that it "was not made in order to evade the consequences to which an enemy vessel, as such is exposed" (Art. 56). The same principle is enunciated in Article 13 of the draft "Manual on the Laws of War" prepared by the Institut de Droit International in 1913 (93) which prohibits the use of false flags as "moyen perfide et barbare" The use of false flags is also regarded as illegitimate and prohibited in the draft report on "The Law of Naval War" which the British Maritime Law Committee submitted at the 29th conference of the International Law Association (ILA) held in Portsmouth in 1920 (94). However, the ILA draft which is based on a revision of the draft prepared by the Institut de Droit International and aimed at reconciling the rule of law with the conditions of warfare obtaining at the time, has found no response other than in academic studies.

Many problems pertaining the law of naval war are, therefore, only dealt with in national service manuals and regulations. The majority of these regulations permits the flying of false flags so long as recourse to this means of deception is made "hors de combat".

At all events, the commanders of warships have used false flags for the purpose of deception very frequently in recent times, and have thus succeeded in evading enemy attack, without being held responsible for perfidy (95). A well-known case in point is the "Seeadler", a German auxiliary cruiser which, when operating under the command of Count Luckner in 1916-1917, repeatedly flew the Norwegian or British flag but always disclosed her identity by hoisting the German war flag before

293

enemy craft were ordered to stop or were fired upon. When running the Allied blockade, the ship and her crew were so skilfully camouflaged as Norwegians that, on 12 December 1916, a prize crew of the British auxiliary cruiser "Avenger" mistook her for the Norwegian sailing ship "Irma" (96).

Cases involving the unlawful use of false flags are mainly reported from the more remote past. The best known example is that of the "Sybille", a French frigate which, in 1783, enticed the British warship "Hussar" to approach at close range by flying the British flag and giving herself the appearance of a British prize in distress (97). Although the "Sybille", while still flying the British flag, suddenly opened fire and tried to ram and sink the British ship, the commander of the "Hussar" evaded the attack by a quick manoeuvre and sank the "Sybille" with gun fire. He broke the sword of the French commander and accused him of perfidy. The French commander was later acquitted by a French courtmartial but was cashiered by his government. It is not quite clear whether his conduct was considered perfidious due to the "Sybille" 's having flown a false flag or to her having feigned distress. It is, however, certain that firing upon and attempting to sink the British warship were unlawful as long as the "Sybille" was flying a false flag.

Yet efforts have been made time and again, both in preparing the draft manuals on the laws of naval war published by the Institut de Droit International and the International Law Association and on various other occasions, to still further restrict the use of false flags by warships. This objective could not be attained by having recourse to flag law since it was found that claims based on the abuse of national flags, while acknowledged on principle, were logically not enforceable between parties to an armed conflict (98). More weight was, however, attached to another argument : the hitherto reported incidents involving the use of foreign flags were mainly cases in which a smaller vessel had resorted to ruse in order to escape from a superior enemy. By contrast, it was considered unlawful for a superior ship to fly a false flag with the object of enticing a smaller vessel to leave neutral territorial waters, or to approach at closer range, and then attacking it (99). If this argument were valid, flying false flags would be permissible only in self-defence and not with a view to fulfilling a specific military mission — a restriction which, although otherwise not applied to ruses of war in international law, would lead to equitable results and could be justified by the argument that the flying of false flags is much closer to perfidy than other ruses of war. The related problems have until now failed to attract much attention in international practice and legal theory. However, some noteworthy experts have held in recent times that the flying of false flags in naval war is only admissible in the case of ships which are either pursued by an enemy vessel or seeking to evade the enemy (100).

Ruses of War

b. *The Use of False Flags by Merchant Ships.*

Merchant ships using false flags are fundamentally in a position similar to that of warships which resort to that ruse. Yet the use of false flags by merchantmen poses no direct threat to an adversary and no protests were therefore normally lodged against the camouflage of merchantmen as long as that practice was confined to individual cases. International treaties have thus far not dealt with the problem whereas the flying of false flags by merchantmen was even sanctioned, either tacitly or expressly, under the terms of various national laws (101). When, however, large numbers of British merchant vessels resorted to the use of neutral flags during the first world war in order to prevent attacks by German submarines, Denmark, the Netherlands and the United States lodged repeated protests through diplomatic channels; they took the view that different legal standards must be applied to the occasional use of false flags on the one hand and to the general practice of using them in large geographic areas on the other because such a practice would render the protection granted to neutral ships practically useless. From then onward, many countries prohibited the use of their national flags by foreign merchant ships without any qualification, that is to say in peacetime as well as in war (102). Although the infringement of such national laws and regulations involves no violation of international law it would be desirable for international law to adopt the principle that merchant vessels are not entitled to use the flags of foreign countries if this would pose an additional danger to the ships of the countries concerned.

c. *Misuse of Protective Flags.*

No further comments are required to explain that the misuse of flags enjoying specific protection under international law, such as the red cross flag or the flag of truce, is also prohibited in naval war in all circumstances.

3. Ruses of War and Perfidy in Aerial Warfare.

The law of aerial warfare is in many respects based on conditions similar to those obtaining in naval war. It has to take account of the specific situation of the air forces which, like that of the maritime forces, is characterized by a greater measure of mobility and vulnerability as well as by closer international contacts established in peacetime. The criteria applied to perfidy in aerial warfare were also strongly influenced by the fact that air combat was regarded as one of the last domains of chivalrous combat in the 20th century — an opinion that was reconfirmed time and again notwithstanding the area bombardments of the second world war.

This greater emphasis on chivalrous combat methods may, for instance, account for the fact that the nationality of aircraft and warships must be clearly identified in combat whereas camouflage in land warfare has been sanctioned to such an extent that even no distinctive paint is required for land vehicles used by the parties to a conflict. It goes without saying that the use of false distinctive emblems in maritime and air warfare is no less strictly prohibited than in land warfare.

However, a cautious approach should be adopted in drafting rules prohibiting perfidy in air warfare. International treaties and conventions have not dealt with this subject until now, and international custom does not provide a sufficient basis for differentiated regulations. The only draft convention on aerial war drawn up to date, the Hague Warfare Rules (104), deal with ruses of war and perfidy only in the context of the prohibited use of distinctive emblems (Article 19) and of the prohibition of attacking the occupants of aircraft to distress who descend by parachute in order to save their lives (Article 20).

Traditional ruses, such as the dropping of dummies by parachute in order to deceive the enemy in respect of the strength of one's own forces, the setting up of decoy airfields (it may be noted here that some decoy airfields in Wurtemberg were occasionally attacked by the RAF with wooden dummy bombs during world war II) and notably the dissemination of false intelligence by using own or enemy radio frequencies must be regarded as permissible acts of war. Some of them, for instance deception through electronic means of warfare, are certainly likely to cause very serious harm to the enemy, but efforts to restrict their use in view of their dangerous character have apparently yielded no success. Prohibitive clauses to that effect would not even appear desirable since it would be as impossible to enforce them in practice as it is to impose a ban on the use of other dangerous means and methods of war.

Ruses of war in aerial warfare should, therefore, not be subjected to regulations different from those applying in land warfare. This principle is in conformity with the present legal situation. Some progress would, however, be achieved if the law of aerial warfare were to participate fully in the development of the rules covering the war on land and if detailed provisions to that effect were included in the envisioned international conventions.

4. Applicability to Non-International Armed Conflicts.

We have so far been dealing exclusively with the drafting of rules for conflicts of an international character. These rules cannot be applied unreservedly to non-international armed conflicts. No comparable rules covering non-international armed conflicts are contained in current international treaties and conventions. The common Article 3 of the Geneva Conventions restricts itself to granting minimum protection to defenceless victims of non-international armed conflicts without providing a basis for the drafting of rules governing the behaviour of combatants. Article 19 of the Convention on the Protection of Cultural Property affords a minimum degree of protection to cultural property in conflicts not of an international character. Additional

Ruses of War

protective clauses of international law can only be derived from the existing Conventions on Human Rights which, however, are not specifically designed to apply to armed conflicts and can be largely suspended in times of war.

Given this legal situation, it is somewhat surprising to note that, at the first session of the conference of government experts, it was held by many experts that the rules on the behaviour of combatants yet to be agreed upon should at the same time be deemed to constitute unwritten law governing internal conflicts (105). The ICRC concurred with this body of opinion at the second session of the conference when it suggested that identical prohibitions on perfidy should apply to international and non-international armed conflicts and has met with no policy objections in this regard (106).

Yet no conclusions of concrete significance can be drawn from these deliberations and suggestions. The conference of government experts, when dealing with the Additional Protocol to Article 3 of the Geneva Conventions which deals with non-international armed conflicts, confined itself to a preliminary exchange of views without prejudicing the version to be adopted in future. Significantly, one of the few points on which consensus was reached was that the need to extend the Protocol's scope of application as far as possible conflicts with the intention of drafting it in the most precise terms possible. It may be necessary to adopt a restricted version of the various provisions relating to non-international conflicts in order to ensure a wide scope of application.

In dealing with these problems it will be essential to take account of the differing standards of confidence obtaining between parties to an armed conflict. Newly agreed international regulations cannot be expected to have a significant impact on the behaviour of insurgents if the realities of modern conflict are disregarded. Important liberation movements in Africa and the Middle East have already declared in public that they will not recognize future international regulations as binding upon themselves unless they have taken part on equal terms in their preparation. Yet the governments concerned can hardly be expected to make such far-reaching concessions. Experience has shown that agreements likely to establish a minimum basis of confidence between a government and an insurgency movement cannot be entered into until the insurgents have been definitely successful. Equally, ad hoc arrangements — e.g. those between aircraft hijackers and the representatives of neutral countries involved — are largely regarded as legally irrelevant bacause they have been entered into under coercion. It is generally accepted that government authorities are free to disregard such arrangements if this is necessary to protect overriding interests and, specifically, to save the lives of innocent hostages. Ad hoc arrangements between guerillas and their adversaries in conflict are still unknown to date. Theorists of guerilla warfare have pointed out that arrangements between the parties to the conflict do not fit in with the pattern of that type of conflict to-day.

It. cannot be recommended that rash steps be taken to draft exhaustive legal rules which, given the realities of modern armed conflicts, would have only a microscopic chance of being complied with. The world-wide disregard of the ban on taking hostages, which is so clearly set forth in Article 3 of the Geneva Conventions, should prompt a reconsideration of their opinions by those who believe that new rules of international humanitarian law are likely to have an impact on the mutual confidence among belligerents.

V. – CONCLUSION

The above considerations have made it clear that new rules relative to ruses of war and the prohibition of perfidy are essential for the further development of humanitarian law applicable in armed conflicts. Efforts for a further development of international law in this field will have to concern themselves with the prohibition of perfidy if real progress is to be achieved. Yet it remains doubtful whether it will be possible to frame exhaustive legal rules covering this subject. Concrete provisions prohibiting specific acts of perfidy can, in most cases, be evaded by resorting to new ruses.
General clauses are subject to erosion by fresh feats of imaginatin. Any regulation framed in too. concrete terms is in danger of being invalidated by international custom.

Given this situation, all legislative efforts will have to proceed from the general rule that ruses of war are a permissible means of warfare. The prohibition of perfidious ruses must continue to be an exception. None the less, there is a need to arrive at a general definition of the term "perfidy"

The more unequivocally the ban on perfidy is stipulated in international law, the more effectively it will be possible to preserve an indispensable minimum of confidence among the parties to a conflict. The same applies to specific prohibitive clauses that may be required in addition to the general rule. Such clauses should be applicable in many situations of an armed conflict and could essentially contribute to enhancing the military's understanding of the practical value of international law of war.

The international armed conflict is the point of departure from which rules on the prohibition of perfidy should be developed. It cannot yet be foreseen whether this scope of application could be extended to non-international armed conflicts. Should it, however, be regarded as possible for international law to ensure more effective protection of human beings in such conflicts, then one should not lose sight of the fact that a legal ban on perfidy is an essential prerequisite.

Ruses of War

FOOTNOTES

(1) Art. 24 of the Hague Regulations merely provides, in general terms, that ruses of war are considered permissible. Specific rules on the prohibition of perfidy may be derived from Art. 23, 33, 34, 40, and 41 of the Hague Regulations and from other provisions affording protection under international law.

(2) V. CLAUSEWITZ, *Vom Kriege,* 16th. ed. Bonn 1952, IIIrd Book, 10th chapter, p. 285.

(3) Of the military literature covering this subject, the following works are of particular importance : Wojennaja chitrostj i smjotka, Moscow 1955, German edition : Kriegslist und Findigkeit, translated by H. Eder, Verlag des Ministeriums für Nationale Verteidigung, Berlin (GDR) 1956; MALCOLM W. BROWNE, *The new Face of War.* A report on a Communist Guerilla Campaign with a preface by Henry Cabot Lodge, London (Cassell) 1965; German edition : Das neue Gesicht des Krieges, with 17 illustrations, translated by H. Graf, M.L. Schuber and M. Schuber, Frauenfeld (Huber & Co. AG) 1966; B.R. DALLISH, *Battle Cunning,* in : Military Review, April 1954, p. 80; MALCHER-DUNDALSKI, *Taktische Täuschung,* in Wehrkunde vol. VI (1957) p. 405-10; SCHAEDLICH, *Das Trojanische Pferd.* Kriegslisten – gestern und heute, Bonn 1965; WEYDE, *Die Trojanische List.* Zur Theorie und Praxis der unkonventionellen Kriegführung, Köln (Markus-Verlag GmbH) 1965, 230 pages; WEYDE, *List und Tücke im Krieg,* in : Truppenpraxis 1965, p. 690-693.

(4) Cf. KRÜGER-SPRENGEL, *Kriegslist und Perfidieverbot – völkerrechtliche Regeln für das Verhalten zwischen Kombattanten,* Neue Zeitschrift für Wehrrecht 1971, p. 161 et seq.

(5) Cf. *U.S. Department of the Army Pamphlet* (DA PAM) 27-161-2, International Law, vol. II, Washington D.C. 1962, p. 57 : "the mind of man furnishing a fertile field for countless deceptions".

(6) Cf. 3rd Geneva Convention, Art. 23 para 1 and 4th Geneva Convention, Art. 28.

(7) Cf. PICTET, *Commentary,* vol. IV, Geneva Convention Relative to the Protection of Civilian Persons in Time of War, Geneva 1958, p. 208.

(8) GROTIUS, *De jure belli ac pacis libri tres,* Paris 1625, new German edition by Walter Schätzel, Tübingen 1950, 3rd book, 1st chapter, p. 427, concludes that it is justified to make lying an offence "whenever God's honour, charity, or the nature of the matter so demand." — See also KANT, *Zum Ewigen Frieden,* Ein philosophischer Entwurf, 1795, 1 : "Some degree of confidence in the enemy's way of thinking must be preserved even in wartime since, failing this, no peace could be concluded and hostilities would escalate into a war of extermination".

(9) Cf. SOPHOKLES, *Philoktet,* verse 107 : Neoptolemos : "Think you that lying is damnation ? " Odysseus : "No, by no means, if lying bring salvation ! ".

(10) ALBERT ZORN as quoted by v. Kirchenheim, *Kriegslist,* in : Hatschek-Strupp, Wörterbuch des Völkerrechts, Berlin-Leipzig 1924.

(11) SPAIGHT, *Air Power,* 3rd ed., p. 169-170; DA PAM 27-161-2 (see note 5 above) p. 52 : ("... ruses of war are permissible if they do not take advantage of the protection afforded by another law of warfare").

(12) This aspect, which is again of topical interest in modern guerilla war, was already mentioned by LUEDER, *Das Landkriegsrecht im Besonderen,* in : v. Holtzendorff, Handbuch des Völkerrechts, Vol. IV, Hamburg 1889, p. 459.

(13) Cf. HOMER, *Odyssey,* IV/272, VIII/492, XI/523.

(14) FRONTIN, *Kriegslisten,* Latin/German edition by Gerhard Bendz, Berlin (GDR) 1963.

(15) POLYAINOS, *Kriegslisten,* translated by Hermann Blume and Carl Fuchs, 4 volumes, Stuttgart 1833 – 1855.

D. FLECK

(16) Cf. FRONTIN, op. cit., 4th book, chapter 4. In his account of the feats of the Roman general Fabricius, Frontin relates that Fabricius was approached by King Pyrrhus' personal doctor who told him that he was prepared to poison his master if he were offered a reward commensurate with the importance of such a venture : "Fabricius, being convinced that he was able to vanquish his adversary without resorting to such a deed, revealed the doctor's infamy to the king, and his honesty prompted Pyrrhos to seek the friendship of the Romans".

(17) POLYAINOS, op. cit., 1st book, No. 45 : Lysander used to advise that "boys should be deceived with dice and the enemy with oaths," Frontin, op. cit., 1st book, 4th chapter, in giving examples on "how to pass with one's army through territory in enemy hands" relates that Aemilius Paulus, when his army was waylaid by the fleet of Tarent and attacked with missiles while on the move, protected his flanks with prisoners so that the enemy broke off his attack.

(18) VEIT WULFF VON SENFTENBERG, *Kriegsbrauch* in Mancherley Strategematibus und listigen Anschlägen (end of 16th century).

(19) Cf. DALLISH op. cit. (note 3 above).

(20) *Kriegslist und Findigkeit,* op. cit. (see note 3 above) p. 9.

(21) *Kriegslist und Findigkeit,* op. cit. p. 11.

(22) GROTIUS op. cit. (note 8 above), 3rd book, 1st chapter.

(23) GROTIUS op. cit. p. 424.

(24) See note 17 above.

(25) GROTIUS op. cit. p. 431.

(26) JOHANN CASPAR BLUNTSCHLI, *Das moderne Völkerrecht der zivilisierten Staaten als Rechtsbuch dargestellt,* 2nd ed., Nördlingen 1872.

(27) BLUNTSCHLI op. cit. paras 561, 315.

(28) BLUNTSCHLI op. cit. paras 565, 317.

(29) Instructions for the Government of Armies of the United States in the field (General order No. 100), reproduced by BLUNTSCHLI, op. cit., op 483-514.

(30) Art. 101 : "While deception in war is admitted as a just and necessary means of hostility and is consistent with honorable warfare, the common law of war allows even capital punishment for clandestine or treacherous attempts to injure an enemy, because they are so dangerous, and it is to difficult to guard against them".

(31) Article 148, 3rd sentence : "Civilized nations look with horror upon offers of rewards for the assassination of enemies as relapses into barbarism".

(32) ROUSSEAU, *Du contrat social,* 1762, chapter I 4.

(33) First President of the French Prize Court, 1801.

(34) *Kriegsbrauch im Landkriege,* published by the Supreme General Staff, Historical Research Department ("Kriegsgeschichtliche Einzelschriften", Vol. 31, Berlin 1902).

(35) Reichsgesetzblatt (RGB1) 1901 No. 49.

(36) Cf. *Völkerrecht im Weltkrieg 1914-1918,* Third Series of publications prepared by the study group set up by the German Reichstag and the German Constitutional National Assembly 1919-1928, Vol. 1, Berlin 1927, pp. 46 et seq.

(37) *Völkerrecht im Weltkrieg,* op. cit. pp. 33 et seq.

(38) *Kriegsbrauch im Landkriege,* op. cit. p. 23.

(39) *Kriegsbrauch im Landkriege,* op. cit. p. 24.

(40) *Actes de la Conférence de Bruxelles de 1874* sur le projet d'une convention internationale concernant la guerre, Paris 1874.

(41) *Institut de Droit International,* Les lois de la guerre, sur terre (Manuel d'Oxford), Brussels and Leipzig 1880.

(42) Cf. Report by Mr. Edouard ROLIN, adopted by the 2nd commission on July 5, 1899, in : *James Brown Scott* (editor), The Reports to the Hague Conferences of 1899 and 1907, Oxford 1917, p. 146 : "this provision... aims only to say that ruses of war... are not prohibited as such. They would cease to be "permissible" in case of infraction of a recognized imperative rule to the contrary".

Ruses of War

(43) Article 24 of the Hague Regulations : "Ruses of war and the employment of measures necessary for obtaining information about the enemy and the country are considered permissible".

(44) Article 22 of the Hague Regulations : "The right of belligerents to adopt means of injuring the enemy is not unlimited"

(45) WALTZOG, *Das Recht der Landkriegsführung,* Die wichtigsten Abkommen des Landkriegsrechts (commentary), Berlin 1942, p. 46.

(46) According to Article 23b, it is prohibited "to kill or wound treacherously individuals belonging to the hostile army or nation"

(47) Cf. PICTET, *Commentary,* Geneva Convention Relative to the Treatment of Prisoners of War, Geneva 1960, pp 453-454.

(48) Article 23 (f) provides that it is prohibited "to make improper use of a flag of truce, of the national flag, or of the military insignia and uniform of the enemy, as well as the distinctive badges of the Geneva Convention".

(49) TAKAHASI, *International Law Applied to the Russo-Japanese War,* London 1906, p. 161.

(50) SCHODENSACK, *Der Flaggenmissbrauch im Landkriege,* Berlin 1938, p. 26 and 28. The same conclusions were already drawn by GRABAU, *Der Gebrauch fremder Nationalflaggen im Landkrieg,* in : Zeitschrift für Völkerrecht Vol. 20 (1936) pp. 257-276 (269).

(51) VALENTINE JOBST III, *Is the Wearing of the Enemy's Uniform a Violation of the Laws of War ?* AJIL 35 (1941) pp. 435-442.

(52) *Trial of Otto Skorzeny and others,* General Military Government Court of the U.S. Zone of Germany, 18th August to 9th September, 1947 in : The United Nations War Crimes Commission, Law Reports of Trials of War Criminals, Vol. IX, London 1949, op. 90-94.

(53) *Department of the Army Field Manual (FM)* 27-10, Washington D.C. 1956, The Law of Land Warfare, No. 54.

(54) *The War Office,* Code No. 12333, London 1958, The Law of War on Land, being Part III of the Manual of Military Law, No. 320 : "... But there is no unanimity as to whether the uniform of the enemy may be worn and his flag displayed for the purpose of approach or withdrawal"

(55) *Bundesministerium der Verteidigung,* ZDv 3/11 Infanterie-Gefechtsausbildung aller Truppen, Bonn 1959, No. 303; ZDv 15/10 Kriegvölkerrecht, Leitfaden für den Unterricht (Teil 7), Allgemeine Bestimmungen des Kriegsführungrechts und Landkriegrecht, Bonn 1961, No. 101.

(56) Cf. Report by Mr. ROLIN, op. cit. (note 42 above) p. 146 which comments on recognized rules prohibiting perfidy as follows : "There are even some that are not expressly sanctioned in any article of the declaration".

(57) BLUNTSCHLI, op. cit. (note 26 above), p. 317.

(58) v. BOGUSLAWSKI, *Der kleine Krieg 1881,* pp. 26 et seq.; *Kriegsbrauch im Landkriege,* op. cit. (note 34 above), p. 24.

(59) *Actes de la Conférence de Bruxelles de 1874* (cf. note 40 above) p. 5 : Article 13 D of the Russian preliminary draft postulates the permissibility of "Toute espèce de ruses de guerre; mais celui qui emploie le pavillon national, les insignes militaires ou l'uniforme de l'ennemi dans le but de le tromper, se prive de la protection des lois de la guerre".

(60) *Actes de la Conférence de Bruxelles de 1874,* p. 9.

(61) *Actes de la Conférence de Bruxelles de 1874,* p. 41 : "parce que l'idée est suffisamment exprimée par le mot abus".

(62) *Manuel d'Oxford* (cf. note 41 above), Art. 8c and 8d.

(63) Cf. Report by Mr. ROLIN, op. cit. (note 42 above), p. 145 : "the new articles 22, 23 and 24 correspond exactly, aside from some changes or wording, to articles 12, 13 and 14 of the Declaration of Brussels".

(64) Cf. note 52 above.

D. FLECK

(65) Cf. PICTET Vol. III op. cit. (note 47 above), p. 454.

(66) BGBl 1967 II p. 1233, UNTS Vol. 249, p. 215.

(67) Abkommen, betreffend die Beschiessung durch Seestreitkräfte in Kriegszeiten (Convention concernant le bombardement par les forces navales en temps de guerre), RGBl 1910 p. 256.

(68) Treaty on the Protection of Artistic and Scientific Institutions and Historic Monuments (Roerich Pact) LNTS Vol. 167, p. 289; BERBER, Völkerrecht, Dokumentensammlung, Vol. II p.1948.

(69) RGBl p. 107.

(70) See also Art. 47, 1st Geneva Convention, Art. 48, 2nd Geneva Convention, Art. 127, 3rd Geneva Convention, and Art. 144, 4th Geneva Convention.

(71) Institut International de Droit Humanitaire, Seminaire sur l'enseignement du droit humanitaire dans les institutions militaires, Sanremo, Villa Nobel, 6-18 novembre 1972.

(72) Austria : Bundesministerium für Landesverteidigung, Grundsätze des Kriegs-völkerrechts, Anhang B der Truppenführung (TF), 1965 (p. 246-296);

France : Décret No 66-749 du 1er octobre 1966 portant règlement de discipline générale dans les armées (art. 34);

Federal Republic of Germany : Bundesministerium der Verteidigung, 20v 3/11, Infanteriegefechtsausbildung aller Truppen (Der Einzelschütze). Nov. 1959 (Nos 293-303, 375); ZDv 15/10, Kriegsvölkerrecht, Leitfaden für den Unterricht (Teil 7), Allgemeine Bestimmungen des Kriegführungsrechts und Landkriegsrecht, March 1961 (Nos 99-101); ZDv 15/11 (Draft), Kriegsvölkerrecht, Leitfaden für den Unterricht (Teil 8). Luftkriegsrecht, June 1958 (Nos 30-31); ZDv 15/12 (Draft) Kriegsvölkerrecht Leitfaden für den Unterricht (Teil 9) Seekriegsrecht, June 1967 (Nos 30-32b); HDv 100/1, Truppenführung, October 1962, Anhang Teil III, Völkerrechtliche Grundsätze der Landkriegführung;

Italy : Royal decree of 8 July 1938, No. 1415 (Gazetta ufficiale del Regno d'Italia, Supp. ord. No. 211 of 15 September 1938) (Art. 38 : Ruses of war in land warfare; Art. 83 : Abuse of armistice; Art. 138 : Ruses of war in naval warfare);

Sweden : Handbok i folkrätt under neutralitet och Krig, 1971, No. 106.

Switzerland : Eidgenössisches Militärdepartement, Handbuch über die Gesetze und Gebräuche des Krieges, Handbuch für die schweizerische Armee, 1963, Nos 35-37);

United States : Department of the Army Field Manual (FM) 27-10, 1956, The Law of Land Warfare, Nos 48-55;

United Kingdom : The War Office, Code No. 12 333, The Law on War on Land Being Part III of the Manual of Military Law, London 1958 (loose-leaf edition) (Chapter VIII).

(73) Op. cit. (note 5 above) pp 56-57.

(74) XXIe Conférence Internationale de la Croix Rouge, Réaffirmation et développement des lois et coutumes applicables dans les conflits armés, Rapport présenté par le CICR, Genève Mai 1969, p. 93.

(75) Conference of Government Experts on the Reaffirmation and Development of International Humanitarian Law Applicable in Armed Conflicts, Vol. IV, Rules Relative to Behaviour of Combatants, Submitted by the ICRC, Geneva, January 1971, pp 12-16.

(76) ICRC, Conference of Government Exports on the Reaffirmation and Development of International Humanitarian Law Applicable in Armed Conflicts (Geneva, — 24 May — 12 June 1971), Report on the Work of the Conference, Geneva August 1971, CE/Com III/C 1.

(77) CICR, Conférence d'experts gouvernementaux sur la réaffirmation et le développement du droit international humanitaire applicable dans les conflits armés, Genève, 3 mai — 3 juin 1972 (seconde session) I. Textes, Projet de protocole additionnel aux quatre Conventions de Genève du 12.8.1949.

(78) ICRC, Conference of Government Experts on the Reaffirmation and Development of International Humanitarian Law Applicable in Armed Conflicts, Second

Ruses of War

Session (3 May — 3 June 1972), Report on the Work of the Conference, Geneva, July 1972, Vol. II (annexes). CE/Com III/C 9. This proposal was later withdrawn.

(79) ICRC, op. cit. Vol. I, para 3.26.

(80) ICRC, op. cit. Vol. II, CE/Com III/C 1.70 : "Acts designed to mislead the adversary into the belief that protection under international law will be granted constitute perfidy".

(81) Cf. the Finnish proposal (CE/Com III/C 4) and the Norwegian proposal (CE/Com III/C 55).

(82) Cf. the proposal by experts of Norway, Rumania and the Sudan (CE/Com III/C 38).

(83) Cf. the proposal by experts of Australia, Belgium, Canada, the Federal Republic of Germany, the United Kingdom, and the United States (CE/Com III/C 60).

(84) Cf. CE/Com III/C 71.

(85) Cf. the Norwegian proposal (CE/Com III/C 55).

(86) Op. cit.

(87) Op. cit (note 80 above).

(88) ICRC, op. cit (note 78 above) Vol. I para 3.29.

(89) Cf. HAILBRONNER, *Die Notsituation im Luftkriegsrecht in : Fleck (ed.), Beiträge zur Weiterentwicklung des humanitären Völkerrechts für bewaffnete Konflikte,* Hamburg 1973.

(90) Point 1 of the Paris Declaration of 16 April 1856 regarding the application of certain rules of maritime law in times of war.

(91) Significantly, the Final Act of the Hague Peace Conference of 1907 considered it desirable that the Hague Regulations should, as far as possible, be also applied to the laws of maritime war : "The conference expresses the opinion that the preparation of regulations relative to the laws and customs of naval war should figure in the programme of the next conference, and that in any case the powers may apply, as far as possible, to war by sea the principles of the convention relative to the laws and customs of war on land".

(92) Art. 56 of the London Declaration Concerning the Laws of Maritime War.

(93) The Laws of Naval War governing the Relations between Belligerents (Manual adopted by the Institute of Interntional Law) dated 9 August 1913, published by Deltenre, Recueil général des Lois et Coutumes de la Guerre, Brussels 1943, pp. 666 et seq. :

"Art. 15. — *Treacherous and barbarous methods.*

Ruses of war are considered permissible. Methods, however, which involve treachery are forbidden.

Thus it is forbidden;

1. To kill or wound treacherously individuals belonging to the opposite side;
2. To make improper use of a flag of truce, to make use of false flags, uniforms, or insignia, of whatever kind, especially those of the enemy as well as of the distinctive badges of the medical corps indicated in Articles 41 and 42 (author's note : i.e. the red cross flag and the distinctive paint of government and private hospital ships)".

(94) *The Laws of Naval War* (Draft). published in : The International Law Association, Report of the 29th Conference, 1930, pp. 169 et seq. .

"Article 15, — *Treacherous and barbarous methods.*

Recognized ruses of war are legitimate. But any methods by war of an appeal to the observance of an agreement between the belligerents which results in a breach thereof is punishable as such.

Thus it is, *inter alia,* forbidden :

1. To make deceitful use of the laws and customs of war as laid down in international conventions ratified by the belligerents.
2. By treachery to kill or wound an opponent.
3. To make improper use of a flag of truce, to use false flags, false uniforms, or false badges whatever they may be, especially those of the enemy, as well as the

303

D. FLECK

distinctive marks of the hospital service mentioned in Arts. 41 and 42 (authors's note : that is of the red cross flag and the distinctive paint of hospital ships)"

(95) For examples see GRABAU, *Der Gebrauch fremder Nationalflaggen im Seekrieg,* Berlin 1936, p. 17 et seq.

(96) HURD, *The Merchant Navy,* in : History of the Great War, based on official documents, by direction of the Historical Section of the Committee of imperial Defence, New York, London etc., 1920 Vol. II pp 415 et seq.; GRAF LUCKNER, *Seeteufel,* Biberach/Riss 1921, pp. 134 et seq.

(97) CALVO, *Le Droit International Théorique et Pratique,* Paris 1896, Vol. IV, p. 185; HALLECK, *International Law,* London 1908, Vol. 1 p. 625; COLOMBOS, *The International Law of the Sea,* 4th edition, p. 432; WEHBERG, *Der "Hussar" -Fall,* in : Strupp — Schlochauer, Wörterbuch des Völkerrechts, Vol. I, 2nd ed. 1960, p. 800.

(98) GRABAU, op. cit., pp. 97 et seq.

(99) MÜLLER-MEININGEN, *Der Weltkrieg und der Zusammenbruch des Völkerrechts,* 3rd ed., Berlin 1915, p. 514.

(100) BERBER, *Lehrbuch des Völkerrechts,* Vol. II, 2nd ed 1969, p. 167.

(101) Cf. Section 69 of the British Merchant Shipping Act of 1894 :

"If a person uses the British flag and assumes the British national character on board a ship owned in whole or in part by any persons not qualified to own a British ship, for the purpose of making the ship appear to be a British ship, the ship shall be subject to forfeiture under this Act, unless the assumption has been made for the purpose of escaping capture by an enemy or by a foreign ship of war in the exercise of some belligerent right."

(102) Cf. Section 14 fo the US Neutrality Act of 4th November 1939 :

(a) It shall be unlawful for any vessel belonging to or operating under the jurisdiction of any foreign state to use the flag of the United States thereon, or to make use of any distictive signs or markings, indicating that the same is an American vessel.

(b) Any vessel violating the provisions of subsection (a) of this section shall be denied for a period of three months the right to enter the ports or territorial waters of the United States except in cases of force majeure.

According to Section 15, para 2 of the Flag Act of the Federal Republic of Germany of 8 February 1951 (BGB1 III No. 9514-1) as amended on 25 June 1969 (BGB1 I p. 645), the master of a seagoing vessel flying the flag of the Federal Republic without authorization shall be punished with imprisonment for a term not exceeding six months and/or a fine.

(103) Cf. MANFRED FREIHERR V. RICHTHOFEN, *Der rote Kampfflieger,* Berlin 1933; PETER TOWNSEND, *Un Duel d'Aigles,* Paris 1969, English edition : London 1970, German edition : Duell der Adler, Die RAF gegen die Luftwaffe, Stuttgart 1970.

(104) Rules for the Control of Radio in Times of War and Rules of Aerial Warfare, prepared by the Commission of Jurists convened at the Hague on II December 1922, on behalf of the Washington Disarmament Conference, to study and report on a revision of the laws of war, published in : AJIL Vol. 17 (1923) Suppl. pp 242 et seq. and : La documentation internationale, La Guerre Aérienne, The Hague 1922-1923, Paris 1930.

(105) ICRC, op. cit. (cf. note 76) para 522.

(106) ICRC, op. cit. (cf. note 78) Vol. I, para 2.415.

Name Index